IFIP Advances in Information and Communication Technology 384

IFIP – The International Federation for Information Processing

IFIP was founded in 1960 under the auspices of UNESCO, following the First World Computer Congress held in Paris the previous year. An umbrella organization for societies working in information processing, IFIP's aim is two-fold: to support information processing within its member countries and to encourage technology transfer to developing nations. As its mission statement clearly states,

> *IFIP's mission is to be the leading, truly international, apolitical organization which encourages and assists in the development, exploitation and application of information technology for the benefit of all people.*

IFIP is a non-profitmaking organization, run almost solely by 2500 volunteers. It operates through a number of technical committees, which organize events and publications. IFIP's events range from an international congress to local seminars, but the most important are:

- The IFIP World Computer Congress, held every second year;
- Open conferences;
- Working conferences.

The flagship event is the IFIP World Computer Congress, at which both invited and contributed papers are presented. Contributed papers are rigorously refereed and the rejection rate is high.

As with the Congress, participation in the open conferences is open to all and papers may be invited or submitted. Again, submitted papers are stringently refereed.

The working conferences are structured differently. They are usually run by a working group and attendance is small and by invitation only. Their purpose is to create an atmosphere conducive to innovation and development. Refereeing is also rigorous and papers are subjected to extensive group discussion.

Publications arising from IFIP events vary. The papers presented at the IFIP World Computer Congress and at open conferences are published as conference proceedings, while the results of the working conferences are often published as collections of selected and edited papers.

Any national society whose primary activity is about information processing may apply to become a full member of IFIP, although full membership is restricted to one society per country. Full members are entitled to vote at the annual General Assembly, National societies preferring a less committed involvement may apply for associate or corresponding membership. Associate members enjoy the same benefits as full members, but without voting rights. Corresponding members are not represented in IFIP bodies. Affiliated membership is open to non-national societies, and individual and honorary membership schemes are also offered.

Jan Frick   Bjørge Timenes Laugen (Eds.)

Advances in Production Management Systems

Value Networks: Innovation,
Technologies, and Management

IFIP WG 5.7 International Conference, APMS 2011
Stavanger, Norway, September 26-28, 2011
Revised Selected Papers

 Springer

Volume Editors

Jan Frick
Bjørge Timenes Laugen
University of Stavanger
UiS Business School
4036 Stavanger, Norway
E-mail: {jan.frick, bjorge.laugen}@uis.no

ISSN 1868-4238   e-ISSN 1868-422X
ISBN 978-3-642-33979-0   e-ISBN 978-3-642-33980-6
DOI 10.1007/978-3-642-33980-6
Springer Heidelberg Dordrecht London New York

Library of Congress Control Number: 2012948270

CR Subject Classification (1998): J.1, I.2.8-9, H.4.1, C.2, K.4.3

Typesetting: Camera-ready by author, data conversion by Scientific Publishing Services, Chennai, India

Printed on acid-free paper

Springer is part of Springer Science+Business Media (www.springer.com)

Preface

This proceedings book from the APMS 2011 conference consists of papers modified and reworked from those presented at the conference.

The Advances in Production Management Systems conferences are the main way for the working group 5.7 of IFIP, International Federation for Information Processing, to develop and promote knowledge to improve production management worldwide.

"The aim of WG 5.7 is to promote and encourage the advancement of knowledge and practice in the field of Integrated Production Management and to maximize global dissemination of this knowledge. This broad aim is achieved by a continuous development and refinement of an industry-based research agenda, focusing on industrial excellence for assessing best practices and stimulating young researchers seeking career in production management. WG 5.7 aims at developing a research culture that nurtures research that addresses industrial need whilst maintaining academic excellence and disseminating R&D results and best practices globally to both academics and practitioners through the group annual conference and the activities of its special interest groups" (http://www.ifipwg57.polimi.it/).

IFIP WG 5.7 believes that improved production management systems may improve industry worldwide to create and deliver for an improved future. As such the topics of the yearly APMS conferences develop according to the focus and work of researchers each year.

In 2011 the annual APMS conference was organized by the University of Stavanger in Norway. In total 124 participants contributed by presenting and discussing research on production management. In total, 124 papers were presented.

At the conference the authors presented a combination of careful investigations of topics that have been studied for a long time, and more explorative studies of recent topics and novel approaches to operations management. We saw contributions on business modeling, lean management, supply chain management, and production planning and control. Some of these topics have been of interest for the APMS network for many years, but papers were also presented on topics like cloud computing, gaming, etc., and the use and relevance of such phenomena on production management systems.

The emergence of new themes, topics, and phenomena demonstrates that operations management is a field that is constantly changing. Companies regularly need to investigate and adopt new products, technologies, and processes in order to keep up with the developments in the industry and markets. Likewise, academia needs to stay in the forefront of the developments taking place, to be able to describe and explain the new practices and priorities, and (aiming at) to predict future developments and trends. For decades, the trend for a large part of the manufacturing and assembly sector is outsourcing or off-shoring activities to companies located in emerging markets, either to get access to growing markets or to achieve cost reductions. For many companies, globalizing their value chain has proven more difficult than expected. Further, developments in technologies and processes have led to possibilities of replacing former labor-intensive operations with high technology. In particular, the interface between design and development and production is hard to manage when R&D and manufacturing are located far away from each other. The cost of labor is becoming less and less important for the total cost of many products, and further digitalization of manufacturing could lead to off-shored production being gradually moved back to developed countries. A recent article in the *Economist* labels such a development as "the third industrial revolution." However, acquiring novel technology is hardly enough to achieve a competitive edge over competitors. To achieve that, companies need to develop a system of technologies, processes, and people, over able to integrate, coordinate, and manage these dimensions effectively. This is very much in line with the aim of the APMS network, and also links nicely with the theme of the APMS 2011 conference: "Value Networks: Innovation, Technologies, and Management."

As organizers we were very pleased with the number and scientific content of the papers, and we believe that the APMS 2011 conference moved the knowledge on production management a step ahead.

The proceedings book is a selection of the papers submitted and presented at the APMS 2011 conference. Of the 124 papers presented at the conference, 66 were further developed and modified to be included in this book. The papers are significantly reworked and updated based on feedback from the editors and from comments and discussion at the conference.

The papers represent the breadth and complexity of topics in operations management, spanning from optimization and use of technology, management of organizations and networks, to sustainable production and globalization. In addition, the authors use a broad range of methodological approaches to study the topics of the papers, ranging from grounded theory and qualitative methods, via a broad set of statistical methods to modeling and simulation techniques. Thus, this book from the APMS 2011 conference gives a good overview and representation of the variety of the APMS network, both of topics and the way they are studied, as well as pin-pointing the challenges and difficulties managers need to cope with on a day-to-day basis. Operations management was never meant to be easy, but, hopefully, contributions in this book, and output from the APMS network, can make us all a bit wiser and, hence, better suited and prepared to take on and solve the challenges of the future.

We want to thank all who contributed to this book from the APMS 2011 conference. First and foremost, thanks go to the authors for their contributions and willingness to develop and share their ideas with the scientific community. Further, we are very thankful to the 33 reviewers and scientific committee for the efforts and engagement they invested to ensure the quality and relevance of the papers presented at the conference. Then we would like to thank the participants at the conference for providing important, valuable, and constructive comments and suggestions for improving the papers, and for stimulating scientific discussions during the conference. These events of presenting, sharing, and discussing findings and ideas are very important for the development of the APMS network and the scientific community in general. We sincerely hope that this proceedings book from the APMS 2011 conference will convey the spirit of all who contributed to it in Stavanger.

July 2012   Jan Frick
                                              Bjørge Timenes Laugen

Organization

Local Committee APMS 2011

Jan Frick	University of Stavanger
Ragnar Tveterås	University of Stavanger
Jayantha P. Liyanage	University of Stavanger
Bjørge Timenes Laugen	University of Stavanger
Jan R. Jonassen	University College of Haugesund Stord
Julie Ferrari	University of Stavanger
Atle Løkken	University of Stavanger
Erlend Kristensen	University of Stavanger
Arnljot Corneliussen	University of Stavanger
Per Morten Haarr	Stavanger Convention Bureau of the Municipality of Stavanger

Conference Chair

Jan Frick	University of Stavanger, Norway

International Advisory Board

Jan Frick	University of Stavanger, Norway
Dimitris Kiritsis	EPFL, Switzerland
Riitta Smeds	Aalto University, Finland
Volker Stich	FIR - RWTH Aachen, Germany
Marco Taisch	Politecnico di Milano, Italy
Bruno Vallespir	University of Bordeaux, France

Doctoral Workshop Chairs

Christopher Irgens	Strathclyde University, UK
Fredrik Persson	Linköping University, Sweden

Conference Secretariat

Julie Ferrari	University of Stavanger, Norway

APMS 2011 conference was organized by the University of Stavanger (UIS), with support by the:

- Foundation for Business Studies at the University of Stavanger
- Innovation Centre at the University of Stavanger

- Centre for industrial Asset Management (CIAM) at the University of Stavanger
- Stavanger Convention Bureau of the Municipality of Stavanger
- University of Stavanger

Keynote Speakers at APMS 2011

- Finn E. Kydland, Nobel Memorial Prize in Economics 2004, Professor at the University of California, Santa Barbara, USA: "Conditions for Industrial Development"
- Bjarte Bogsnes, VP Performance Management and Development at Statoil, Norway: "Beyond Budgeting — A New Management Model for New Business Realities"
- Tor-Morten Osmundsen, CEO at Laerdal Medical, Norway: "Operational Excellence"
- J.C. Wortmann, Professor at University of Groningen, The Netherlands: "The Effect of Software-as-a-Service on Our Economy and Society"

International Scientific Committee

Bjørn Andersen	Norwegian University of Science and Technology, Norway
Abdelaziz Bouras	University of Lyon, France
Luis M. Camarinha-Matos	New University of Lisbon, Portugal
Sergio Cavalieri	University of Bergamo, Italy
Stephen Childe	University of Exeter, UK
Alexandre Dolgui	Ecole des Mines de Saint-Etienne, France
Guy Doumeingts	University of Bordeaux, France
Heidi C. Dreyer	Norwegian University of Technology and Science, Norway
Christos Emmanouilidis	ATHENA Research & Innovation Centre, Greece
Peter Falster	Technical University of Denmark, Denmark
Rosanna Fornasiero	ITIA-CNR, Italy
Jan Frick	University of Stavanger, Norway
Susumu Fujii	Sophia University, Japan
Marco Garetti	Politecnico di Milano, Italy
Antonios Gasteratos	Democritus University of Thrace, Greece
Bernard Grabot	Ecole Nationale d'Ingénieurs de TARBES, France
Robert W. Grubbström	Linköping Institute of Technology, Sweden
Thomas Gulledge	George Mason University, USA
Hans-Henrik Hvolby	University of Aalborg, Denmark
Harinder Jagdev	National University of Ireland, Ireland
Athanassios Kalogeras	ATHENA Research & Innovation Centre, Greece
Dimitris Kiritsis	EPFL, Switzerland

Christos Koulamas	ATHENA Research & Innovation Centre, Greece
Andrew Kusiak	University of Iowa, USA
Lenka Landryova	VSB Technical University Ostrava, Czech Republic
Ming Lim	Aston University, UK
Hermann Lödding	Technical University of Hamburg, Germany
Vidoslav D. Majstorovic	University of Belgrade, Serbia
Kepa Mendibil	University of Stratchclyde, UK
Kai Mertins	Fraunhofer IPK, Germany
Hajime Mizuyama	Kyoto University, Japan
Irenilza, Nääs	Universidade Paulista, Brazil
Gilles Neubert	ESC Saint-Etienne, France
Jan Olhager	Linköping University, Sweden
Jens Ove Riis	University of Aalborg, Denmark
Henk Jan Pels	Eindhoven University of Technology, The Netherlands
Selwyn Piramuthu	University of Florida, USA
Alberto Portioli	Politecnico di Milano, Italy
Asbjorn Rolstadas	Norwegian University of Science and Technology, Norway
Paul Schoensleben	ETH Zurich, Switzerland
Dan L. Shunk	Arizona State University, USA
Riitta Smeds	Aalto University, Finland
Vijay Srinivasan	National Institute of Standards and Technology, USA
Kenn Steger-Jensen	Aalborg University, Denmark
Kathryn E. Stecke	University of Texas, USA
Volker Stich	FIR RWTH Aachen, Germany
Richard Lee Storch	University of Washington, USA
Jan Ola Strandhagen	SINTEF, Norway
Marco Taisch	Politecnico di Milano, Italy
Ilias Tatsiopoulos	National Technical University of Athens, Greece
Sergio Terzi	University of Bergamo, Italy
Klaus-Dieter Thoben	University of Bremen / BIBA, Germany
Mario Tucci	University of Florence, Italy
Bruno Vallespir	University of Bordeaux, France
Agostino Villa	Politecnico di Torino, Italy
Gregor Alexander von Cieminski	ZF Friedrichshafen AG, Germany
Dan Wang	Harbin Institute of Technology, China
J.C. Wortmann	University of Groningen, The Netherlands
Iveta Zolotová	Technical University of Košice, Slovakia

Reviewers and Technical Committee APMS 2011

Jan Frick	University of Stavanger
Ragnar Tveterås	University of Stavanger
Pieter Jozef Colen	KU Leuven
Peter Nielsen	Aalborg University
Ander Errasti	University of Navarra
Gokan May	Politecnico di Milano
Irenilza Naas	UNIP
Peter Falster	Technical University of Denmark
Wael Hafez	Enterprise Integration, Inc.
Fredrik Persson	Linköping University
Nobutada Fujii	Kobe University
Claudia Chackelson	Tecnun, University of Navarra
Gert Zülch	Karlsruhe Institute of Technology (KIT)
Thorsten Wuest	BIBA - Bremer Institut für Produktion und Logistik GmbH
Gregor von Cieminski	ZF Friedrichshafen AG
Patrick Sitek	BIBA- Bremer Institut für Produktion und Logistik GmbH
Takeshi Shimmura	National Institute of Advanced Industrial Science and Technology
Giovanni Davoli	University of Modena and Reggio Emilia
A.H.M. Shamsuzzoha	University of Vaasa
Frédérique Biennier	Université de Lyon - CNRS
Christina Thomas	WZL, Laboratory of Maschine Tools and Production Engineering
Eric Christian Brun	University of Stavanger
Martin Rudberg	Linköping University
Tatiana Iakovleva	University of Stavanger
Josefa Mula	Universitat Politècnica de València
Hirpa G. Lemu	University of Stavanger
Sergio Cavalieri	University of Bergamo
Jayantha P. Liyanage	University of Stavanger
Bjørge Timenes Laugen	University of Stavanger
Tore Markeset	University of Stavanger
Jan R. Jonassen	University College of Haugesund Stord
Hermann Lödding	Technische Universität Hamburg-Harburg

Table of Contents

Part I: Production Process

Part II: Supply Chain Management

Part III: Strategy

Part I

Production Process

Centralization or Decentralization of Remanufacturing Facilities in an After-Market Service Supply Chain

Kris T. Lieckens, Pieter J. Colen, and Marc R. Lambrecht

Faculty of Business and Economics, Research Center for Operations Management,
KU Leuven, Belgium

Abstract. Equipment manufacturers are increasingly selling complementary services such as remanufacturing services to their equipment customers. This servitization trend mandates that the remanufacturing supply chain network is optimized accordingly. In order to set up such network, investment decisions have to be made, not only regarding the number, locations and types of remanufacturing facilities, but also with respect to the appropriate capacity and inventory levels in order to guarantee a specific service level. These network decisions are influenced by the way remanufacturing services are offered. We consider here two service delivery strategies: either a quick exchange of the used part by an available refurbished one or re-installing the original part when all corresponding remanufacturing processes are finished. Given the high level of uncertainty in this context, we build a stochastic, profit maximizing model to simultaneously determine the optimal layout and the optimal service delivery strategy for a multi-level logistics network with single indenture repairable service parts. Model results for this case study are obtained by the differential evolution algorithm.

1 Introduction

In many mature markets, the large amount of machinery installed provides an opportunity to develop profitable maintenance service supported by significant remanufacturing activities [WB99, CL13]. Consequently, an increasing number of companies like Bosch and HP is intensifying their remanufacturing activities [GSWB06]. Our case-study company is an international original equipment manufacturer (OEM) of industrial equipment with a renewed focus on remanufacturing. Due to confidentiality reasons the company is referred to as AirCorp and financial specifications are omitted.

To set up a remanufacturing network, AirCorp has to decide upon the number, locations and types of remanufacturing facilities. Moreover, the appropriate capacity and inventory levels have to be set in order to satisfy the service levels set in the service contract. Furthermore, how the service will be delivered and other contractual arrangements like the part ownership will all have an impact on the optimal remanufacturing network. We develop a model that supports this complex decision making process.

J. Frick and B. Laugen (Eds.): APMS 2011, IFIP AICT 384, pp. 3–8, 2012.

2   Problem Description

AirCorp offers its customers a refurbishment service of the key component of the equipment it has sold: during refurbishment the part is cleaned, rebeared and restored to an as-good-as-new condition which will not only extend the life of the equipment, but also increase energy efficiency. The refurbishment itself takes place in a dedicated facility, i.e. a remanufacturing center. Because the machinery built by AirCorp is stationary, an AirCorp field technician has to travel to the customer to disconnect the worn-out part. There are two possible strategies to deliver the service: a refurbishment with an exchange and without an exchange. Under a refurbishment with exchange, further referred to as an "exchange strategy", the technician replaces the part by an already refurbished one. Contrary, if a refurbishment without the exchange option is selected, or shortly a "refurbishment strategy", the customer has to wait until its own part is refurbished and the field technician re-visits the site to install the part. With the exchange strategy, the company has to replace the worn-out part by a part taken from stock. This inventory of as-good-as-new parts is replenished either by refurbished parts from previous customers or by newly produced parts if the return volume is not sufficient to fulfill demand due to scrap or other sources of loss. The inventory can be held at the remanufacturing facilities or at a centralized distribution center (DC).

There are five potential locations to open a remanufacturing center, corresponding to five service regions. In each of these service regions hundreds of customers are located. In order to manage the data requirements and limit the model complexity, customers who are geographically dispersed can be clustered into five locations corresponding to the five service regions. Hence, for each region we have one customer location in which the demand is concentrated. Traveling times to these locations are set to the average travel times within the corresponding region. While the locations of the remanufacturing facilities are to be determined, the current locations of the production plant (for delivery of new parts) and the centralized distribution center are not to be altered. Customers of different regions differ in their preference for the two service delivery strategies. In some regions the exchange service can be sold with a premium, while in others customers value the exchange service equally to the refurbishment service. We include these regional difference by different demand and price levels between the customer regions. These data were obtained by contacting the regional Air-Corp offices. Clearly, the most profitable service delivery strategy might differ between the regions. Determining the optimal service delivery strategy within the separate regions is an important objective of our model.

Designing our remanufacturing network involves three related sub-problems: a facility location, a capacity and an inventory sub-problem. The first decision is where to open remanufacturing facilities. The second decision deals with the number of operators that should be employed at each facility. The third decision sets the appropriate inventory level subject to a given service level. How much inventory to carry will be greatly influenced by the chosen service delivery strategy. In the exchange strategy an inventory of already refurbished parts is required, while the refurbishment without exchange does not require such an investment. Apart from the inventory level, also the location of this inventory may be different.

Due to the interactions between the decisions with respect to facilities, capacities, inventories and the service delivery strategy, we take an integrated solution approach. Moreover, uncertainty in demand, processing and transportation times is taken into account by use of queuing theory. The resulting model is a mixed integer non-linear model that integrates queueing relationships and a profit maximization objective. We solve the model by a differential evolution search algorithm. Section 2.1 clarifies the model and presents the results of the case study. We conclude in Section 3.

2.1   Model and Results

The major contribution of this paper is its multi-disciplinary approach: we simultaneously solve a facility location, capacity and inventory problem. To the best of our knowledge, only [RVR09] and [vOBS06] have succeeded in simultaneously solving these problems, while taking into account uncertainty. Contrary to this earlier work, we consider two delivery strategies, i.e. exchange vs. refurbishment. We maximize profit because both costs and revenues depend on the selected delivery strategy. A profit maximizing objective is scarcely studied in reverse logistics networks [MNSdG09]. Consequently, the profit-orientation of our model can also be considered as a valuable contribution to the field of network design for remanufacturing activities. Lastly, the relevance and solvability of the problem is proven by the case-study. AirCorp uses the stochastic mixed integer non-linear model to support their network decisions. Next, we briefly present the integrated modeling approach for each of the three sub-problems mentioned above and explain the optimization procedure.

In the facility location sub-problem, we consider a multi-echelon network with multiple facility types that can be opened at locations chosen from a fixed, predetermined set of locations. We apply the model in a European context that consists of five service regions. In each service region, there is a potential location for opening a remanufacturing center. The stochastic nature of transportation times between nodes and demand that originates from the regions is modeled by assuming general and Poisson distributions, respectively. During the remanufacturing process, returned units from customer locations are restored to an as-good-as-new condition. Due to some level of scrap, demand for remanufactured parts is satisfied by new parts that are manufactured at the production plant. Both lead time calculations and routing decisions take into account the parts from both remanufacturing centers and the production plant. Facility location decisions determine the feasible flows of parts through the network: a part can only pass through a facility if it is opened. These flows are defined as routings, i.e. a sequence of facilities that each part will visit between the nodes where it enters and leaves the network.

In the capacity sub-problem, the optimal number of workers in each remanufacturing center is determined by considering the selected routings and the committed service levels. Queueing theory provides us with the relationships to link the demand volume and variability with the capacity requirements and lead times [HS00]. The reverse logistics network can be considered as a queuing system that consists of stochastic arrival and remanufacturing processes. $M/G/m$ queues are used at the first level in the network, while $G/G/m$ queues are used at other levels. Approximations that apply to a system under heavy traffic conditions with multiple parallel servers are used from [Whi93]. Hence, we take into account the trade-offs between capacity and lead time.

From an inventory perspective, there is a significant difference between the two service delivery strategies. In contrast to the refurbishment strategy, i.e. without exchanging parts from inventory, the exchange strategy requires an additional investment in inventory of parts that have finished the remanufacturing process. This additional investment can be justified by a higher selling price and/or savings in traveling for field technicians. Inventory of remanufactured parts is managed according to a continuous review one-for-one replenishment policy. Next to this inventory of remanufactured and finished parts, Little's Law is used to calculate the lead time dependent work-in-process inventory, which is obviously present in each network design regardless of the implemented service delivery strategy.

We solve the three sub-problems in an integrated way by evaluating the profit impact of the different decisions. The decision on the selected service delivery strategy affects revenue through different selling prices that apply. Total costs consist of facility costs, transportation costs, capacity (operator) costs, scrap costs, variable remanufacturing costs and field technician costs for traveling and wrenching. The resulting profit function is the objective of the mixed integer non-linear model. We opt for a differential evolution algorithm to solve this NP hard problem to optimality [BA02, LZ99, LV07, LV12].

In the case study, we optimize the network for different realistic scenarios of prices and volumes. Overall, the optimal network has always one echelon, i.e. parts are transported directly form the customer to an all-round facility and back to the customer. The possibility to use a dedicated centralized distribution center is not selected by the model. Next, we observe that demand volume is the key determinant for the level of centralization: whereas the number of remanufacturing facilities is limited with low demand, the number rises significantly with increasing demand levels. An important observation for AirCorp's management is that from a profit perspective, opening too many facilities is less detrimental than opening too few facilities (see Figure 1). Increasing demand levels also justify hiring more operators, while the optimal utilization rates of these operators increase.

As expected, the relative selling price of an exchange service plays a key role to determine the optimal service delivery strategy. Whereas the refurbishment strategy is preferred at low price levels for an exchange strategy, regions will switch towards an exchange strategy as its relative price increases. Interestingly, while switching to an exchange strategy, the optimal utilization rate of the operators goes down. Here the queueing dynamics are at play: lower utilization

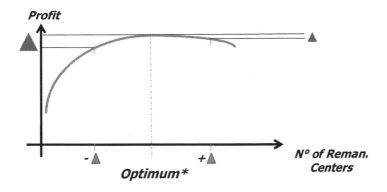

Fig. 1. Impact of the number of facilities on profits

rates equal shorter lead times. Due to the higher inventory requirements of an exchange policy, shorter lead times are especially advantageous because some expensive inventory holding costs can be avoided. In the exchange strategy, the potential savings in inventory are in favor of a higher investment in capacity and consequently target lower utilization levels in order to reduce the lead time of the remanufacturing process. Since the optimal network structure and the capacity level are influenced by the choice of the service delivery strategy, we emphasize the need to simultaneously analyze the network and service contract design.

3   Conclusions

In this paper we optimize the remanufacturing network design and the delivery strategy in order to maximize profits. Apart from the choice between two service delivery strategies and the profit perspective, our contribution lies in the simultaneous solution of three related network design problems, i.e. the facility location problem, the capacity and the inventory problem. In our case study we determine the optimal number, type and location of remanufacturing facilities for an international OEM. Variability in both demand and processing times is taken into account by integrating queuing relationships into the model. The mixed integer non-linear model is solved by a differential evolution search procedure. The case study results reveal that volume is key to determine the optimal number of facilities. Another observation is that the sales price determines the choice of the service delivery strategy. Furthermore, this choice also impacts the optimal capacity levels: exchange services require higher capacity investments in the remanufacturing centers. Hence, there is a clear need to simultaneously analyze the design of networks and the service delivery strategy. These results highlight the importance of taking an integrated approach by combining inventory, capacity, investment and service delivery decisions. Multiple extensions to our research are possible e.g. the impact of transportation batching. However, the model can be applied to many settings thanks to its general distributions for both transportation and remanufacturing times and the possibility to use multiple part classes, multiple resources and multiple network echelons.

References

[BA02]   Babu, B.V., Angira, R.: A differential evolution approach for global op-
           timization of MINLP problems. In: Proceedings of 4th Asia-Pacific Con-
           ference on Simulated Evolution And Learning, vol. 2, pp. 880–884 (2002)
[CL13]   Colen, P.J., Lambrecht, M.R.: Product service systems: Exploring
           operational practices. Service Industries Journal (2012),
           http://www.tandfonline.com/doi/abs/10.1080/
           02642069.2011.614344 , doi:10.1080/02642069.2011.614344
[GSWB06]   Guide, V.D., Souza, G.C., Van Wassenhove, L.N., Blackburn, J.D.: Time
           value of commercial product returns. Management Science 52(8), 1200–
           1214 (2006)
[HS00]   Hopp, W.J., Spearman, M.L.: Factory Physics. The McGraw-Hill Com-
           panies, New York (2000)
[LV07]   Lieckens, K., Vandaele, N.: Reverse logistics network design: The ex-
           tension towards uncertainty. Computers and Operations Research 34(2),
           395–416 (2007)
[LV12]   Lieckens, K., Vandaele, N.: Multi-level reverse logistics network design un-
           der uncertainty. In: International Journal of Production Research (forth-
           coming, 2012)
[LZ99]   Lampinen, J., Zelinka, I.: Mechanical Engineering Design Optimization
           by Differential Evolution. In: ch. 8, pp. 127–146. McGraw-Hill, London
           (1999)
[MNSdG09] Melo, M.T., Nickel, S., Saldanha-da Gama, F.: Facility location and sup-
           ply chain management - a review. European Journal of Operational Re-
           search 196(2), 401–412 (2009)
[RVR09]   Rappold, J.A., Van Roo, B.D.: Designing multi-echelon service parts net-
           works with finite repair capacity. European Journal of Operational Re-
           search 199(3), 781–792 (2009)
[vOBS06]   van Ommeren, J.C.W., Bumb, A.F., Sleptchenko, A.V.: Locating repair
           shops in a stochastic environment. Computers & Operations Research 33,
           1575–1594 (2006)
[WB99]   Wise, R., Baumgartner, P.: Go downstream: The new profit imperative
           in manufacturing. Harvard Business Review 77(1), 133–141 (1999)
[Whi93]   Whitt, W.: Approximations for the GI/G/m queue. Production and Op-
           erations Management 2(2), 114–161 (1993)

Energy Implications of Production Planning Decisions

Laura Bettoni and Simone Zanoni

Department of Mechanical and Industrial Engineering,
University of Brescia, Via Branze 38, 25123, Brescia, Italy
{laura.bettoni,zanoni}@ing.unibs.it

Abstract. The great attention toward environmental issues and especially on energy utilization, leads the European Union to implement the 2009/28/EC Directive, fixing three main goals to be achieved for 2020 by the EU member states: 20% reduction of the greenhouse gases emission, 20% increase of using renewable energy and 20% improving of energy efficiency. To achieve these objectives, new environmental and energy policies must be taken into account not only by governments but also by firms. This work focuses on the energy efficiency effects of production planning decisions in the die casting processes. We present a model based on related literature and on experimental data. The numerical model is based on the relationship between energy consumption of the machines and the production rate of the machines, with the aim to minimize the energy necessary to satisfy the demand of finished products. This model may support manager's decisions so as to minimize energy consumption and consequently environmental impact of die-casting operations.

Keywords: Lot sizing, Energy Savings, Die casting, Energy Efficiency.

1   Introduction

The increased level of environmental contamination, in particular air pollution, mainly caused by huge usage of non-renewable sources for energy production, the climate changing and the increasing of energy price, led all institutions (public government as well as private companies) all over the world to focus their attention on energy issues. The European Union recently adopted a directive with three main energy objectives: the reduction of 20% of the greenhouse gases emissions, the increase of 20% of using renewable energy and the improvement of energy efficiency of 20%, these objectives must be achieved by 2020. To achieve these objectives, given by European Union through 2009/28/EC Directive, the efforts of all companies with high energy intensive processes are necessary.

For this purpose, the firms firstly have to test their emissions level and their energy efficiency level, furthermore they have to increase the use of renewable energy. Once defined their actual state, they have to analyse the possible corrective actions to apply to improve energy efficiency so as to achieve the European Union's objectives. The energy efficiency, the minimization of energy consumption, the increase of using renewable energy, are now the main objectives for firms, guaranteeing them not only environmental benefits but also consistent economic savings.

J. Frick and B. Laugen (Eds.): APMS 2011, IFIP AICT 384, pp. 9–17, 2012.

The studies on the energy efficiency assessment are increasing and also the studies on corrective actions to minimize energy consumption. Different approaches are used to decrease energy consumption, the main are the technological and management approaches. There are some studies based on management actions to decrease energy consumption providing scheduling and management techniques and tools to improve energy efficiency in different manufacturing systems. Artigues et al. [1] analysed an industrial case and applied the Cumulative Scheduling Problem (CuSP) to energy issue, naming the specific approach as "Energy Scheduling Problem" (EnSP). Nolde and Morari [9] showed a different electrical energy scheduling in a steel plant: the problem is analysed in order to minimize peak and off-peak energy consumption, which are economically penalized. They used a continuous scheduling model to find a production schedule that achieves the objective of energy cost minimisation. Mouzon et al. [8] analysed the consumption of energy in manufacturing equipment: they observed that applying dispatching rules on the turn-on and turn-off of the machines allows reducing the energy consumption. They use a multi-objective mathematical programming model to decrease energy consumption and total completion time.

Eiamkanachanalai and Banerjee [3] developed a model that jointly determines the optimal run length and the rate of production for a single item; the output rate is the decision variable and the production cost per unit is defined as a quadratic function of the production rate; furthermore the desirability or undesirability of unused capacity, a linear function, is integrated in the model. Christoph H. Glock [4], analysed the total cost of a production system composed by single item worked by single facility and delivered to the subsequent stage in batch shipment, where the production rate is variable. He studied the case of equal- and unequal- sized batch shipments and proposed a solution procedure for the models. The numerical study shows that the variable production rate may reduce inventory carrying cost and thus the total cost of the system. Glock [5] analysed also the batch sizing with variable controllable production rates in a multi stage production system, reaching to the same conclusion.

The main aim of this research is to find possible actions to minimize energy consumption and costs looking at the energy consumption of the production machines in their different operative states. During the idle state the machine is on but it doesn't produces, however, all the auxiliary components are turned on and consume a lot of energy; while during the production state the machine is on and may produces at different production rates. Producing at different production rates implies that the consumption of energy depends on the production rate with which the machine is running. Therefore, to minimize energy consumption it is necessary to put the attention on the idle time of the process, where the machine consumes energy but doesn't produce anything, and on the production rate of the machine, that influences the specific energy consumption. We have proposed an analytical model based on the relationship among energy consumption, idle time, production rate and the demand rate, with the aim to find a trade-off among the variables that minimizes the energy and total costs. We also present a numerical analysis to show the applicability of the model in the field of die casting.

This paper is structured as follow: in section 2 the system studied, with reference to the die casting process, is described, in the section 3 the model developed is presented. The numerical results are offered in section 4 and in section 5 main conclusions with some further development are reported.

2   System Description

This study particularly looks at die casting process, with reference to the cold chamber configuration suitable for aluminium processing [2], where there is high energy consumption, both electric and thermal. In particular the use of furnace for melting metal and holding molten metal at a given temperature for a time period, coupled with the die casting machine, have made this area an important case study for the reduction of energy consumption using production management levers. The furnace uses both electrical (expressed in [kWh]) and thermal energy (expressed in m^3 of natural gas), while the die casting machine uses only electrical energy (expressed in [kWh]). So as to be able to compare the different energy sources we have used as main energy unit the [TOE] (tonne of oil equivalent).

The process consists of three main phases: the melting and the holding phases, belonging to the heating operation, and the press phase. In the melting phase the ingots are introduced in the furnace to be melted; the energy used in this phase is very high due to the high temperature needed to melt the metal, the energy supplied is electrical and thermal. The holding phase is needed to maintain the metal in molten state during the non-production time, i.e. the idle state. During the press phase, the molten metal is forced into a mould cavity under high pressure: the energy supplied is only electrical.

The system uses different levels of power in the different phases: during the melting the furnace to achieve high temperature to melt the metal consumes high thermal power, while during the holding the furnace consumes only the power to maintain the metal in molten state, i.e. the idle power. The die casting machine consumes only during production (processing and idle power), in fact it is turned-off at the end of the shift of production.

Our objective is to find the trade-off between the energy consumption of the production state and the energy consumption of the idle state, with the aim to increase energy efficiency and decrease energy cost.

3   Model

The model is based on the comparison between the consumption of energy during different states of the two machines of the system, assuming a variable production rate. The sum of Idle Energy Consumption (IEC) and Production Energy Consumption (PEC) is the Total Energy Consumption (TEC).

Once fixed the cycle time T of the process, varying the production rate, the idle time and the production time to satisfy the demand changes. In particular increasing the production rate the production time decreases and the idle time increases. The specific energy consumption (SEC) during production state decreases while increasing the production rate (Gutowski et al. [6]). The SEC is defined as the amount of energy required for processing a specific amount of product (i.e. in the die-casting expressed in kg of die-casted aluminium) and can be expressed in [TOE/kg].

Moreover the energy required for processing the material is inversely related to the production rate p, of the equipment adopted. This relationship is mainly due to the presence of the idle power required by the process, which is constant even if the production rate adopted may vary, as observed by Gutowski et al. [7].

Based on experimental data in the die casting process the relationship between energy required for processing one kilogram of aluminium (named e) and p can be expressed in the following way:

$$e_p = \alpha * p^{-\beta}. \tag{1}$$

where α and β are the coefficients that depends on the specific die casting equipment adopted, and p is the production rate implemented.

Let us introduce the following notations:

- E_{idle} energy required during idle time of the process, expressed in [TOE];
- W_0 the idle power of the processing equipment, expressed in [TOE/h];
- t_i the idle time varying with production rate, expressed in [h];
- t_p the production time, expressed in [h];
- T the cycle time, expressed in [h];
- e_p the specific energy consumption, expressed in [TOE/kg];
- E_{prod} energy required during production time, expressed in [TOE];
- D the demand, during the cycle time, expressed in [kg];

The Total Energy Consumption required for processing aluminium in both stages (furnaces and die casting machine), during idle time (i.e. E_{idle}, that is the energy required for holding the molten aluminium in the furnace) and during the production (energy required for melting the aluminium ingots and running the die casting machine) can be evaluated as following reported:

$$TEC\,(p) = E_{idle} + E_{prod} = W_0 \cdot t_i + e_p \cdot D = W_0 \cdot t_i + \alpha \cdot p^{-\beta} \cdot D. \tag{2}$$

It should be considered that the demand of products during the cycle time is considered as constant and must be satisfied with no stock out or backorder.

The TEC is a function of idle time and production time, the former one depends on the production rate, so as to completely satisfy the given demand according to the following relationship:

$$t_i = T - t_p = T - \frac{D}{p} \tag{3}$$

4   Case Study

So as to show the applicability of the model proposed, in this section we will present a numerical analysis based on real data collected from a die casting firm. Based on real data historically collected it has been possible to obtain the relationship between the specific energy consumption [expressed in TOE/kg] and the production rate, reported in Fig. 1.

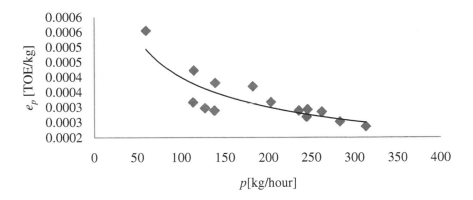

Fig. 1. Specific Energy Consumption for different production rate

In this case the relationship can be expressed with the following equation:

$$e_p = 0.0027 * p^{-0.412} \tag{4}$$

Moreover we have considered the following two assumptions:

1. the cycle time T consist of 24 hours.
2. the maximum production rate of the equipment is p= 500 [kg/hours].

We have analysed the trend of TEC varying the production time available for production and the corresponding idle time necessary for the holding phase. The production time was varied between 24 hours of production and the minimum hours necessary to satisfy the demand, i.e. if the demand is 2000 [kg/day] and the maximum production rate is 500 [kg/h] the minimum production time considered was 4 hours. Then, the corresponding idle time considered varied in the range between zero, i.e. 24 hours of production, and the maximum idle time given the constraint on the maximum production rate, i.e. 20 hours of idle time.

This analysis has been performed for two different value of demand: in the first case the demand value is set to 3500 [kg/day], in the second case is set to 7000 [kg/day].

The demand should be considered distributed throughout the week; therefore it is not considered the option of producing, without stops, during several days and then switch off the furnace for the rest of the days.

1   CASE 1: D=3500 [kg/day]

In Figure 2 we can see the trend of the Total Energy Consumption and its two components: the Idle and Production Energy Consumption. Varying the idle time between zero, i.e. all the cycle time is occupied by the production and the holding phase doesn't exist, and the maximum idle time possible, the PEC decrease, while the IEC increase. We have the minimum TEC when the idle time is zero, so it is better to work on a 3 shifts arrangement.

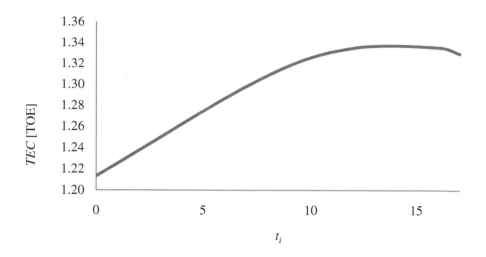

Fig. 2. Trend of TEC for D=3500 for different values of idle time

2   CASE 2: D=7000 [kg/day]

When the demand increase the trend of TEC changes and the minimum TEC occurs at the maximum idle time and minimum production time possible, which in this case are $[ti;tp]=[12.8;11.2]$. The analysis suggests that it is better, when the demand increases, to increase the production rate and to work only for two shifts, leaving the furnace in holding phase for the remaining time.

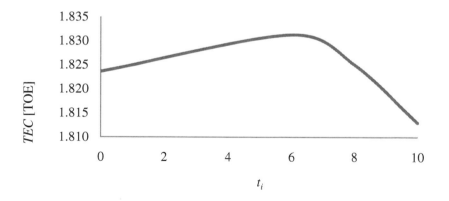

Fig. 3. Trend of TEC for D=7000 for different values of idle time

If we analyze the trend of the Specific Energy Consumption in [kWh/kg] while varying the demand rate, it is possible to determine the optimal production planning arrangement, in terms of idle time for each production day, in order to minimize the Total Energy Consumption.

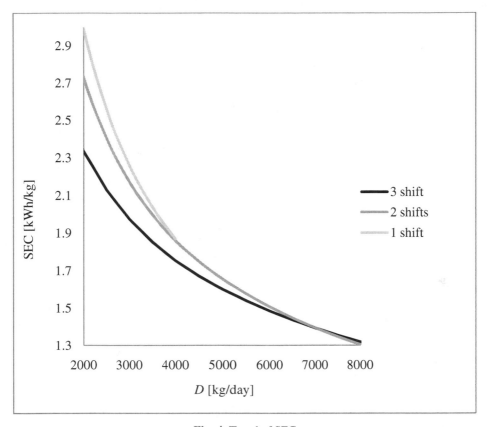

Fig. 4. Trend of SEC

Figure 4 shows the SEC increasing the demand between 2000 and 8000 [kg/day], for three different production planning arrangements: three shifts a day, two shifts a day and only one shift a day, considering 8 production hours for each available shift. As expected, the specific energy consumption decreases while increasing the demand, the minimum value (in our study about 1 kWh/kg), corresponds to the variable energy consumption, while for lower demand the SEC is greater due to energy fixed costs (Gutowski, 2006).

The graph can be divided in two areas, as shown in Figure 5, for demand rate less than 7000 kg/day it is better to plan the production on 3 shift basis, while increasing the demand it is better to plan the production on 2 shifts. This better explain what we have shown in figure 2 and 3.

This effect can be seen as an energy paradox: when the demand increases over a certain limit, instead of arranging a production plan according to 3 shifts, so as to minimize the TEC it is better to increase the production rate of the machines, in order to satisfy the demand using only two production shifts and then leave the machines in idle state for the other shift.

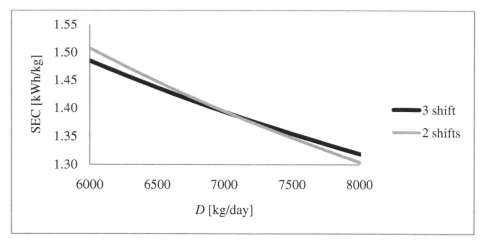

Fig. 5. Detail of the trend of SEC

This can be explained because increasing the production rate the specific energy consumption decreases significantly (e.g figure 1) and this decrease, over a certain limit of the daily demand, can compensate the increase of energy consumption caused by the holding phase during the idle time.

5   Conclusions

Aim of this study has been to look at production planning levers so as to reduce energy consumption and consequently energy costs in die casting processes. We have developed an analytical model to express the relationship between Production Energy Consumption, Idle Energy Consumption, and the production rates of the machines so as to find the minimum Energy Consumption and consequently the minimum Total Cost of the system satisfying the given demand in the time window considered.

The numerical analysis for different cases, based on the different demand rate settings, revealed the optimal planning policy to adopt (i.e. the optimal production rate and idle time, and consequently the shifts arrangement), so as to minimize energy consumption.

Further developments can be to extend the model and the numerical study to different production systems, such as metal forging or metal forging processes, where furnaces for warming and holding materials are key elements of the processes.

References

1. Artigues, C., Lopez, P., Hait, A.: The energy scheduling problem: Industrial case-study and constraint propagation techniques. International Journal Production Economics (2011), doi:10.1016/j.ijpe.2010.09.030
2. Boothroyd, G., Dewhurst, P., Knight, W.: Product design for manufacturing and assembly. Marcel Dekker, New York (2002)

3. Eiamkanchanalai, S., Banerjee, A.: Production lot sizing with variable production rate and explicit idle capacity cost. International Journal Production Economics 59, 251–259 (1999)
4. Glock, C.H.: Batch sizing with controllable production rates. International Journal of Production Research 48(20), 5925–5942 (2010)
5. Glock, C.H.: Batch sizing with controllable production rates in a multi – stage production system. International Journal of Production Research, 1–23, iFirst (2011)
6. Gutowski, T., Dalquist, S.: Life cycle analysis of conventional manufacturing techniques: die casting. Working draft (2004)
7. Gutowski, T., Dhamus, J., Thiriez, A.: Electrical energy requirements for manufacturing processes. In: 13th CIRP International Conference on Life Cycle Engineering (2006)
8. Mouzon, G., Yildirim, M.B., Twomey, J.: Operational methods for minimization of energy consumption of manufacturing equipment. International Journal of Production Research 45(18), 4247–4271 (2007)
9. Nolde, K., Morari, M.: Electrical load tracking scheduling of a steel plant. Computers and Chemical Engineering 34, 1899–1903 (2010)

Cyclic Steady State Refinement: Multimodal Processes Perspective

Grzegorz Bocewicz[1], Peter Nielsen[2], Zbigniew A. Banaszak[3], and Vinh Quang Dang[2]

[1] Koszalin University of Technology,
Dept. of Computer Science and Management, Koszalin, Poland
bocewicz@ie.tu.koszalin.pl
[2] Dept. of Mechanical and Manufacturing Engineering, Aalborg University, Denmark
peter@m-tech.aau.dk; vinhise@m-tech.aau.dk
[3] Warsaw University of Technology, Faculty of Management,
Dept. of Business Informatics, Warsaw, Poland
Z.Banaszak@wz.pw.edu.pl

Abstract. The cyclic scheduling problem modeled in terms of Cyclic Concurrent Process Systems is considered. The problem can be seen as a kind of Diophantine problem, hence its solvability, i.e. schedulability, plays a pivotal role in many supply-chain problems. In contradiction to the traditionally offered solutions the approach proposed allows one to take into account such behavioral features as transient periods and deadlocks occurrence. So, the contribution's aim is the modeling framework enabling an evaluation of cyclic scheduling problems solvability, i.e., the declarative approach to reachability problems regarding cyclic steady states determination as well as conditions guaranteeing assumed performance of multimodal processes executed within a concurrent cyclic processes environment.

Keywords: cyclic processes, multimodal process, state space, periodicity, dispatching rules.

1   Introduction

Operations in cyclic processes are executed along sequences that repeat an indefinite number of times. In everyday practice they arise in different application domains such as manufacturing as well as service domains (covering such areas as workforce scheduling, timetabling, and reservations [4], [6], [8]). Such systems belong to a class of systems of concurrently flowing cyclic processes (SCCP) [1], [2], [7], and relevant cyclic scheduling problems belong to a class of NP-hard ones [5]. Subway or train traffic can be considered as an example of such kind of systems.

Subway trains following particular metro lines can be treated as cyclic processes passing, the sequence of stations, allows one to state a question concerning a minimization of the total passenger travel time. So, if passengers travel between two distinguished locations in the transportation network for which no direct connection exists, i.e., transfers become inevitable, the relevant scheduling problem can be stated in the

J. Frick and B. Laugen (Eds.): APMS 2011, IFIP AICT 384, pp. 18–26, 2012.

following way. Given is a set of metro lines, i.e. the set of trains' routings. Some lines may share common stations. Given is also a headway time, i.e., the fixed interval between the trips of a line sometimes called the period time. The question considered is: Which transportation route between two designated terminal stations in the transportation network provides the shortest travel time subject to assumed constraints? So, the best transportation route of the multimodal process, i.e. sharing different lines, is sought. This type of system finds many analogies in manufacturing, in the form of routing between fixed manufacturing lines, e.g. routing and scheduling of AGVs within an Automated Storage and Retrieval System environment.

Many models and methods have been proposed to solve the cyclic scheduling problem. Among them, the mathematical programming approach (usually IP and MIP), max-plus algebra [7], constraint logic programming [2], [3], [9] evolutionary algorithms and Petri nets [1], [8] frameworks belong to the more frequently used. Most of these methods are oriented towards finding a minimal cycle or maximal throughput while assuming deadlock-free process flow. Approaches trying to estimate the SCCP cycle time from local cyclic processes structure and the synchronization mechanism used (i.e. rendezvous or mutual exclusion instances) are quite unique [1].

In that context our main contribution is to propose a new modeling framework enabling to evaluate the cyclic steady state of a given SCCP on the base of the assumed processes topology, dispatching rules employed, and an initial state. So, the objective of the presented research is to provide the observations useful in the course of multimodal processes routing and scheduling in systems composed of concurrently flowing cyclic processes interacting between oneself through mutual exclusion protocol. The goal is to provide the conditions useful for routing and scheduling of SCCP so as to be effective in the course of multimodal processes control.

In order to achieve it, the paper presents an introduction to the SCCP, and then to the concept of state space of considered systems. Consequently, the terms of a cyclic steady state and the corresponding space of cyclic steady states are introduced as well as conditions linking them with multimodal processes scheduling are presented.

2   Concept of Multimodal Processes System

2.1   Systems of Concurrent Cyclic Processes

Consider the digraph shown in Fig. 1. The distinguished are three cycles specifying routes of cyclic processes P_1, P_2 and P_3, respectively. Each process route, specified by the sequence of resources passed on among its execution, can interact with other processes through so-called system common resources. So, the process routes are specified as follows: $p_1 = (R_6, R_3, R_5)$, $p_2 = (R_2, R_3, R_4)$, $p_3 = (R_1, R_5, R_4)$, where the resources R_3, R_4, R_5, are shared resources, since each one is used by at least two processes, and the resources R_1, R_2, R_6, are non-shared because each one is exclusively used by only one process. Processes sharing common resources interact with each other on the base of a mutual exclusion protocol. Possible resources conflicts are resolved with the help of assumed priority rules determining the order in which processes make their access to common shared resources (for instance, in case of resource R_4, $\sigma_4 = (P_2, P_3)$ – the priority dispatching rule determines the order in which processes can access to the shared resource R_4, i.e. at first to the process P_2, then to the process P_3, next to P_2 and once again to P_3, and so on).

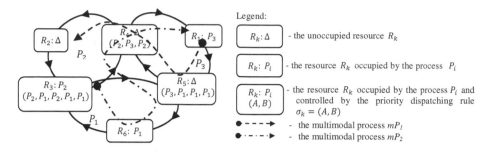

Fig. 1. Process routes structure of SCCP owning three processes

In general case, each process P_i (where: $P_i \in P = \{P_1, P_2, \ldots, P_n\}$, n – a number of processes) executes periodically a sequence of operations performed on resources creating the given process route $p_i = (R_{j_1}, R_{j_2}, \ldots, R_{j_{lr(i)}})$, $j_k \in \{1, 2, \ldots, m\}$, where $lr(i)$ – a length of cyclic process route, m -- the number of resources, and $R_{j_k} \in R = = \{R_1, R_2, \ldots, R_m\}$.

The time $t_{i,j} \in \mathbb{N}$, of operation executed on R_j along P_i, is defined in the domain of uniform time units ($\mathbb{N}$ – set of natural numbers). So, the sequence $T_i = (t_{i,j_1}, t_{i,j_2}, \ldots, t_{i,j_{l(i)}})$ describes the operation times required by P_i. To each common shared resource $R_i \in R$ the priority dispatching rule $\sigma_i = (P_{j_1}, P_{j_2}, \ldots, P_{j_{lp(i)}})$, $j_k \in \{1, 2, \ldots, n\}$, $P_{j_k} \in P$ is assigned, where $lp(i) > 1$, $lp(i)$ is a number of processes dispatched by σ_i. In that context a $SCCP$ can be defined as follows [3]:

$$SC_l = (R, P, \Pi, T, \Theta) , \tag{1}$$

where: $R = \{R_1, R_2, \ldots, R_m\}$ – the set of resources,
$P = \{P_1, P_2, \ldots, P_n\}$ – the set of local processes,
$\Pi = \{p_1, p_2, \ldots, p_n\}$ – the set of local process routes,
$T = \{T_1, T_2, \ldots, T_n\}$ – the set of local process routes operations times,
$\Theta = \{\sigma_1, \sigma_2, \ldots, \sigma_m\}$ – the set of dispatching priority rules.

Let us assume the all operation times are equal to a unit operation time (noted as: u.o.t.) , $\forall i \in \{1, \ldots, n\}$, $\forall j \in \{1, \ldots, lr(i)\}$, $(crd \, _jT_i = 1 \, u.t.)$. In the case of the SCCP considered the following constraints imposed on processes interaction are assumed:

- The new process operation may begin only if current operation has been completed and the resource designed to this operation is not occupied.
- The new process operation can be suspended only if designed resource is occupied.
- Processes suspended cannot be released and processes are non-preempted.

The main question concerns of a SCCP cyclic steady state behavior and a way this state depends on direction of local process routes as well as on priority rules, and an initial state, i.e. initial process allocation to the system resources. Assuming such a steady there exists the next question regarding of travel time along assumed multi-modal process route linking distinguished resources plays a primary role.

2.2   States Space

Consider the k-th state S^k (2) composed of the sequence of processes allocation A^k, the sequence of semaphores (encompassing the rights guaranteeing processes' access to a resource) Z^k, and the sequence of semaphore indices Q^k:

$$S^k = (A^k, Z^k, Q^k), \tag{2}$$

where: $A^k = (a_1{}^k, a_2{}^k, ..., a_m{}^k)$ – **the processes allocation** (m – a number of CCPS resources), $a_i{}^k \in P \cup \{\Delta\}$ (P – a set of processes: $P = \{P_1, P_2, ..., P_n\}$) means the process is allotted to the i-th resource R_i in the k-th state, $a_i{}^k = P_g$ means, the i-th resource R_i is occupied by the process P_g, and $a_i{}^k = \Delta$ - the i–th resource R_i is unoccupied.

$Z^k = (z_1{}^k, z_2{}^k, ..., z_m{}^k)$ – **the sequence of semaphores** corresponding to the k-th state, where $z_i{}^k \in P$ means the name of the process (specified in the i-th dispatching rule σ_i, allocated to the i-th resource) allowed to occupy the i-th resource R_i. $Q^k = (q_1{}^k, q_2{}^k, ..., q_m{}^k)$ – **the sequence of semaphore indices** corresponding to the k-th state, where $q_i{}^k$ means the position of the semaphore $z_i{}^k$ in the priority dispatching rule σ_i : $z_i{}^k = crd_{(q_i{}^k)}\sigma_i$, $q_i{}^k \in \mathbb{N}$ ($crd_i D = d_i$, for $D = (d_1, ..., d_i, ..., d_w)$.

The state $S^k = (A^k, Z^k, Q^k)$ **is feasible** only if for any of its $a_i{}^k$ co-ordinate in $A^k = (a_1{}^k, a_2{}^k, ..., a_m{}^k)$, the following conditions hold:

i) $$\forall_{i \in \{1,2,...,n\}} \exists!_{j \in \{1,2,...,m\}} (P_i = crd_j A^k), \tag{3}$$

ii) $$\forall_{i \in \{1,2,...,m\}} (crd_i A^k \in P \cup \{\Delta\}), \tag{4}$$

iii)   if the values of the semaphore Z^k and **the sequence of semaphore indices** Q^k result from allocation (3), (4) (i.e., semaphores determining busy resources show the processes allotted to them, while indexes show semaphore values).

The set of all feasible states is called **a state space** $\mathbb{S}$. The states $S^k \in \mathbb{S}$ and $S^l \in \mathbb{S}$ can be linked determining transitions among states, e.g. $S^k \rightarrow S^r$ means the state S^l follows the state S^k. In general case, the states can be linked via other states, e.g. S^r , S^w what leads to the following sequence of transitions: $S^k \rightarrow S^r \rightarrow S^w \rightarrow S^l$, $S^k \xrightarrow{i} S^l$ in short, where: i - means the number of states S^r, S^w linking S^k, S^l, e.g., in case consider $S^k \xrightarrow{2} S^l$, and $S^k \xrightarrow{0} S^r$. a transition $S^k \rightarrow S^l$, can be represented as the following function:

$$S^l = \delta(S^k) , \tag{5}$$

where: δ – is a transition function $\delta: \mathbb{S} \rightarrow \mathbb{S}$ [3].

The deadlock state S^k (denoted in the rest of the paper by S^*) is defined as the state such that does not exist any feasible state $S^l \in \mathbb{S}$, following the transition $S^k \rightarrow S^l$. So, the deadlock state means the all processes in the CCPS are suspended.

In a state space following from a given SCCP model (1), and the next state function (5) one can easily distinguish two kinds of reachability digraphs (see Fig. 2a). The properties specifying particular kinds of possible behaviors are as follows:

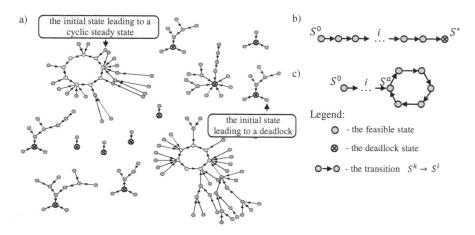

Fig. 2. Illustration of the state space $\mathbb{S}$ structure a), the string-like digraph ending with a deadlock state b), and the string-like digraph ending with a state belonging to a cyclic steady state c)

Property 1

Consider the SCCP model (2) and an initial state $S^0 \in \mathbb{S}$. The reachability digraph, generated from an initial state S^0, is either a string-like digraph ending with a deadlock state, i.e. (Fig. 2b): $S^0 \xrightarrow{i} S^*$, $i \geq 0$, or a string-like digraph ending with a state belonging to the cyclic steady state (Fig. 2c): $S^0 \xrightarrow{i} S^a \xrightarrow{Tc-1} S^a$, $i \geq 0$, where Tc – a number of states creating the cycle.

Property 2

Consider the sets of initial states ending with the same the k-th deadlock state $SD_k \subset \mathbb{S}$, and initial states ending with states belonging to the i-th cyclic steady state $SC_i \subset \mathbb{S}$, respectively. Assume a state space generated by the SCCP model (1) and the next-state function (5). The following conditions hold:

i) $\forall S^i, S^j \in \mathbb{S}^*, i \neq j \ \left[SD_i \cap SD_j = \varnothing\right]$, where: $\mathbb{S}^*$ – the set of deadlock states,

ii) $\forall S^l, S^k \in \mathbb{S}^t, l \neq k \ \left[SC_l \cap SC_k = \varnothing\right]$, where: $\mathbb{S}^t$ – the set of cyclic steady states.

That means the following questions can be considered:

- What are the sufficient conditions guaranteeing the state space is free of deadlock states and states leading to the deadlocks?
- What are the conditions guaranteeing transitions among assumed cyclic steady states?
- What is the period of the cyclic state of multimodal processes performed in the SCCP executed in a given cyclic steady state?

2.3   The Multimodal Processes

Let $\{P_i|\ i\in\{1,\dots,n\}\}$ be the set of cyclic processes determined by the set of process routes $\{p_i\ |\ i\in\{1,\dots,n\}\ \}$. Consider the set of multimodal processes $MP = \{mP_1, mP_2, \dots, mP_u\}$, where u- is a number of multimodal processes. Due to our informal definition, each multimodal process mP_i is specified by the transportation route mp_i which is a sequence of sections of local cyclic process routes:

$$mp_i = \left(mpr_j(a_j, b_j), mpr_k(a_k, b_k), \dots, mpr_h(a_h, b_h)\right), \tag{5}$$

where: $mpr_j(a, b) = \left(crd_a p_j, crd_{a+1}p_j, \dots, crd_b p_j\right), crd_i D = d_i,$ for $D = (d_1, d_2, \dots, d_i, \dots, d_w), \forall a \in \{1,2,\dots, lr(i)\ \}, \forall j \in \{1,2,\dots, n\}, crd_a p_j \in R.$

By   analogy   to   local   cyclic   processes   the   sequence $mT_i = \left(mt_{i,j_1}, mt_{i,j_2}, \dots, mt_{i,j_{lm(i)}}\right), mt_{i,j_k} \in \mathbb{N},$ describes operation times required by operations executed along mP_i (where: $lm(i)$ is the length of the i-th multimodal route mP_i). In that context a $SCCP$ can be defined as a pair [3]:

$$SC = (SC_l, SC_m), \tag{6}$$

where: $SC_l = (R, P, \Pi, T, \Theta)$ – is specified by the (1),
$SC_m = (MP, M\Pi, MT)$ – characterizes the SCCP behavior, i.e.
$MP = \{mP_1, mP_2, \dots, mP_u\}$ – the set of multimodal process, $M\Pi = \{mp_1, mp_2, \dots, mp_u\}$ – the set of multimodal process routes, $MT = \{mT_1, mT_2, \dots, mT_u\}$ – the set of multimodal process routes operations times.

Since, the multimodal processes execution depends on a steady state of the SCCP considered their periodicity depends on the current Tc of Sc (see Fig. 3). In turn that means that initial states and sets of dispatching rules can be seen as control variables allowing one to "adjust" multimodal processes schedule.

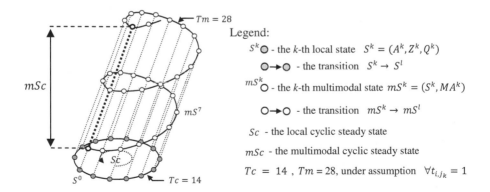

Fig. 3. Graphical illustration of the relationship between the cyclic steady state Sc of SCCP and the multimodal cyclic steady state mSc

3   Illustrative Example

The approach proposed is based on the system of concurrently flowing cyclic processes concept assuming its cyclic steady state behavior guaranteed by the given sets of dispatching rules and initial states. So, the multimodal processes scheduling, that can be seen as processes composed of parts of local cyclic processes, lead to the two fundamental questions. Does there exist a control procedure (i.e. a set of dispatching rules and an initial state) guaranteeing an assumed steady cyclic state subject to SCCP's structure constraints? Does there exist a SCCP's structure such that an assumed steady cyclic state (e.g. following requirements caused by multimodal processes at hand) can be achieved? In other words, an approach provides a framework enabling to take into account both the forward and backward way of cyclic scheduling problem formulation. Moreover, the question regarding possible switching among both the local and multimodal steady state states can be considered. The illustration of the local and multimodal cyclic state spaces prototyping is shown in the Table 1.

Table 1. The local and multimodal cyclic state spaces prototyping for SCCP from Fig. 1

Structure	Cyclic Steady State	Period of the Cyclic Steady State [u.o.t]	Period of the multimodal process [u.o.t]	Cyclic Steady State	Period of the Cyclic Steady State [u.o.t]	Period of the multimodal process [u.o.t]
SCCP (Fig. 1)	Sc_1	14	28	Sc_6	14	28
	Sc_2	14	28	Sc_7	12	24
	Sc_3	14	28	Sc_8	12	24
	Sc_4	14	28	Sc_9	12	24
	Sc_5	12	24	Sc_{10}	12	24

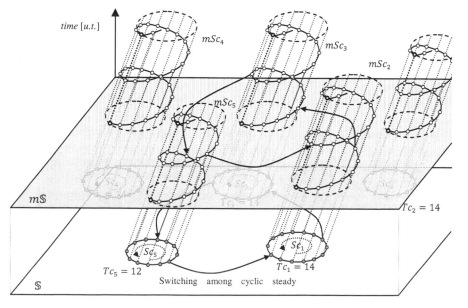

Fig. 4. Illustration of cyclic steady state spaces (Sc and mSc) for SCCP from Fig. 1

Because of the discrete structure of SCCP topology and dispatching rules as well as the discrete event nature of processes execution the considered problems of mSc and Sc scheduling (including switching among cyclic steady states) can be modeled in terms of Constraint Satisfaction Problem (CSP) [2], [3], and consequently implemented in declarative languages environment – OzMozart system. The illustration of possible cyclic schedules taking into account possible switching among cyclic steady states is shown in Fig. 4.

4   Concluding Remarks

In contradiction to the traditionally offered solutions the approach presented allows one to take into account such behavioral features as transient periods and deadlock occurrence. So, the novelty of the modeling framework offered lies in the declarative approach to reachability problems enabling multimodal cyclic process evaluation as well as in CSP-based evaluation of possible switching among cyclic steady states from both the local and multimodal cyclic state spaces.

The approach presented leads to solutions allowing the designer to compose elementary systems in such a way as to obtain the final SCCPSs' scheduling system with required quantitative and qualitative behavioral features while employing the sufficient conditions provided. So, we are looking for a method allowing one to replace the exhaustive search for the admissible control by a step-by-step structural design guaranteeing the required system behavior.

References

1. Alpan, G., Jafari, M.A.: Dynamic analysis of timed Petri nets: a case of two processes and a shared resource. IEEE Trans. on Robotics and Automation 13(3), 338–346 (1997)
2. Bocewicz, G., Wójcik, R., Banaszak, Z.: Design of Admissible Schedules for AGV Systems with Constraints: A Logic-Algebraic Approach. In: Nguyen, N.T., Grzech, A., Howlett, R.J., Jain, L.C. (eds.) KES-AMSTA 2007. LNCS (LNAI), vol. 4496, pp. 578–587. Springer, Heidelberg (2007)
3. Bocewicz, G., Wójcik, R., Banaszak, Z.A.: Cyclic Steady State Refinement. In: Abraham, A., Corchado, J.M., González, S.R., De Paz Santana, J.F. (eds.) International Symposium on DCAI. AISC, vol. 91, pp. 191–198. Springer, Heidelberg (2011)
4. Fournier, O., Lopez, P., Lan Sun Luk, J.-D.: Cyclic scheduling following the social behavior of ant colonies. In: Proceedings of the IEEE International Conference on Systems, Man and Cybernetics, pp. 450–454 (2002)
5. Levner, E., Kats, V., Alcaide, D., Pablo, L., Cheng, T.C.E.: Complexity of cyclic scheduling problems: A state-of-the-art survey. Computers and Industrial Engineering 59(2), 352–361 (2010)
6. Liebchen, C., Möhring, R.H.: A case study in periodic timetabling. Electronic Notes in Theoretical Computer Science 66(6), 21–34 (2002)
7. Polak, M., Majdzik, P., Banaszak, Z., Wójcik, R.: The performance evaluation tool for automated prototyping of concurrent cyclic processes. In: Skowron, A. (ed.) Fundamenta Informaticae, vol. 60(1-4), pp. 269–289. ISO Press (2004)

8. Song, J.-S., Lee, T.-E.: Petri net modeling and scheduling for cyclic job shops with block-ing. Computers & Industrial Engineering 34(2), 281–295 (1998)
9. Wójcik, R.: Constraint programming approach to designing conflict-free schedules for re-petitive manufacturing processes. In: Cunha, P.F., Maropoulos, P.G. (eds.) Digital Enter-prise Technology. Perspectives and Future Challenges, pp. 267–274. Springer (2007)

A World Class Order Picking Methodology:
An Empirical Validation

Claudia Chackelson[1,*], Ander Errasti[1], and Martín Tanco[2]

[1] Tecnun – University of Navarra, Manuel Lardizabal 13, 20018 San Sebastian, Spain
cchackelson@tecnun.es, aerrasti@tecnun.es
[2] University of Montevideo, Ponce 1307, 11300 Montevideo, Uruguay
mtanco@um.edu.uy

Abstract. Order picking is the process of retrieving products from storage in response to a specific customer order. Although this process' design has significant impact on warehouse global performance, a practical-oriented design procedure is still lacking in literature. This paper presents a novel order picking system design methodology based on Design for Six Sigma approach, that aims to assist designers making decisions by suggesting the most effective operational and organizational policies and the equipment needed in order to fulfill customer's orders. A case research in a home appliances manufacturer is presented in order to demonstrate the effectiveness of this approach.

Keywords: order picking process, design methodology, design for six sigma, case research.

1 Introduction

Picking is the process of retrieving products from storage in response to a specific customer order. It has been identified as a key warehouse activity due to its impact on operational costs and service level. An appropriate design can also directly improve global performance (De Koster et al. 2007). In addition, according to Rushton et al. (2006) and Errasti et al. (2010) the design of this process has become particularly important and complex due to recent trends in distribution centers: an increasing number of make to stock items in the warehouse, a reduction in delivery times to 24-48 hours, an increasing level of customization in orders, or a reduction in the number of minimum delivery units.

It has been pointed out that most of the research related to order picking focuses on a specific situation or design issue (De Koster et al. 2007, Manzini et al. 2007, Ekren et al. 2009). However, extrapolating methods developed for one particular situation to a different situation is not that simple. Even though some authors have identified the elements and alternatives (Goetschalckx and Ashayeri 1989) and other authors have identified the tasks (Yoon and Sharp 1996), a general design procedure for the order picking process is still lacking in the literature (De Koster et al. 2007).

---

* Corresponding author.

J. Frick and B. Laugen (Eds.): APMS 2011, IFIP AICT 384, pp. 27–36, 2012.
© IFIP International Federation for Information Processing 2012

Gu et al. (2010) state that it would be worthwhile to carry out research that characterizes order picking alternatives in such a way that they could support design process. Moreover, these authors conclude that both applied design models and practical cases that show the value of bringing academic research results to real situations are necessary. More case studies and computational tools for warehouse design and operation will help bridge the significant gap between academic research and practical application.

We propose a novel order picking system design methodology that aims to fill the following gaps: (1) the lack of a flexible order picking design framework, (2) the misuse of tools and techniques that allow the modeling and simulation of operative processes in the design or redesign phase of a operative process to be incorporated and (3) the scarcity of empirical investigations that allow the applicability of new procedures and technologies to be evaluated.

2   State of the Art

Yoon and Sharp (1996) outlined a procedure for analyzing and designing order picking systems with three steps: a) input stage, b) selection stage, and c) evaluation stage. After this last stage, different subsystems are compared, and overall performance is evaluated. These authors only suggested that these steps need to be taken; however they did not specify how these steps could be performed, nor how to select the most suitable picking configuration according to the complexity of the process. In this context, Baker and Canessa (2009) highlight that there is no consensus on the exact nature of the tools and techniques to be used for each design step. The same authors also state that great reliance is put on the knowledge of the designer in deducing which tools need to be used, and final design decisions are made based on intuition, experience and judgment.

Dallari et al. (2009) improved Yoon and Sharp (1996) design procedure with the development of a new taxonomy based on the analysis of 68 warehouses located in Italy. We believe that this has been an important step into bridging the existing gap, but a major degree of detail regarding to order picking alternatives is still needed in order to support effectively the design process.

We propose a novel order picking system design methodology for use in warehouses and distribution centers. This procedure assist designers making decisions, by suggesting the most effective operational and organizational policies, as well as the equipment needed in order to fulfill orders considering their typologies.

This procedure is based on the Design for Six Sigma (DFSS) approach (Yang and El-Haik 2003; Brue 2003). It has been developed for achieving Six Sigma process capabilities on the design side. In design, opportunities are virtually unlimited since most of the costs of a product are determined in the design stage (Montgomery 2005). We decided to adapt DFSS due to its focus on design or redesign products/processes right the first time, by integrating tools and methods that look for robustness. The DFSS approach with four stages ICOV (Identification of requirements, Characterization, Optimization and Verification) was followed, although there are varieties in literature such as DMADV, IDOV, etc.

Six Sigma is, by definition, analytical and profoundly rooted in statistical analysis. It was defined by Linderman et al (2003) as "an organized and systematic method for strategic process improvement and new product and service development that relies on statistical methods and the scientific method to make dramatic reductions in customer defined defect rates". A key difference between Six Sigma and other approaches is the integration of a highly disciplined process (such as IDOV) with one that is very quantitative and data oriented. This is a winning combination as evidenced by the results of the companies that have used it (Hahn 2005).

DFSS is one of the drivers of research and application of experimental design techniques. So is the expanding deployment of Six Sigma in general, where it is broadly recognized that Design of Experiments is the most powerful and important of the Six Sigma tools (Montgomery 2006). Therefore, the order picking system design methodology developed incorporates elements from the Design of Experiments (DoE) (Box et al. 2005) and the Discrete Event Simulation technique (Banks 2010) when selecting the most suitable design strategy from those suggested in a previous stage. A simulation model is developed, considering the external and internal factors that influence picking performance identified by Goetschalckx and Ashayeri (1989) and Frazelle (2002).

3   Order Picking Design Methodology

The proposed methodology takes the procedure proposed by Yoon and Sharp (1996) and fit its three steps (Input, Selection, and Evaluation) into a DFSS approach with four stages (Identification of requirements, Characterization, Optimization, and Verification). It also details how each stage is to be performed and what tools and techniques need to be used.

3.1   Identification of Requirements Step

According to Frazelle (2002), the factors that have to be considered when categorizing this process are:

- Order type (lines per order, items per line)
- Picking volume complexity (orders/t, lines/t, or items/t)
- Product characteristics (shape, volume, weight) and heterogeneity
- Storage unit vs. order unit
- Number of make to stock items.

The first stage of the proposed methodology takes these factors into account in order to establish the order picking complexity. The characterization is performed employing a priority matrix that assigns a discrete level of complexity: medium, high or extreme picking (Errasti 2011). This matrix has been gauged after a Delphi study carried out among 40 world class companies with different order picking complexities. Table 1 shows the valuation ranges and the weighing that have been given to the five factors previously mentioned.

Table 1. Priority matrix for determining order picking complexity level

FACTOR	Valuation Ranges			Weighing
Picking Volume (lines/t)	Lines<100	100<Lines<1000	1000<Lines	3
	1	2	3	
Storage unit vs. order unit	Ratio>75%	25%<Ratio<75%	25%>Ratio	3
	1	2	3	
Number of make to stock items	Number<100	100<Number<1000	1000<Number	2
	1	2	3	
Different order type	Number=1	Number=2	Number>3	1
	1	2	3	
Different Product characteristics	Number=1	Number=2	Number>3	1
	1	2	3	

The order picking complexity level is determined by calculating a value obtained after multiplying the valuation range and its corresponding weighing (see Table 2).

Table 2. Order picking complexity levels

Order Picking Complexity Level	Value
Extreme Picking	Value>=25
High Picking	20<=Value<25
Medium Picking	10<=Value<20

Once this characterization has been carried out, a group of possible designs are suggested in the following step.

3.2   Characterization of the Design Stage

This second step aims to delimit the large variety of solutions and parameters considered according to the process complexity, reducing the time required to find the most appropriate solution in the next phase. With this aim in mind, several charts of alternatives are proposed. Order picking processes design is highly complex owing to the high number of existing possibilities (Baker and Canessa 2009), thus this is an important contribution because it helps designers choose from among the most appropriate alternatives. The suggested designs are the result of a Delphi study carried out among 40 world class companies with different order picking complexities. In this phase, the designer needs to select the two or three designs they consider the most suitable according to their experience.

The alternatives suggested include the classic factors that influence picking performance identified by Goetschalckx and Ashayeri (1989): mechanization level (automated, semi-automated, mechanized or manual), order realize mode (wave-picking or continuous), zoning (one zone or multi-zone), batching (pick-by-order or pick-by-article, and pick-and-sort or sort-while-pick), storage (random, class-based, family grouping, or dedicated), and routing (heuristic or optimal), but also incorporate the new operational or technological options implemented by companies nowadays. Figure 1 shows the huge range of possibilities that warehouse managers face when designing order picking process.

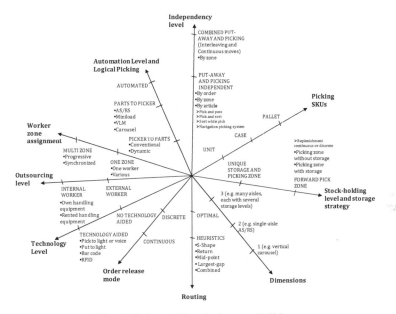

Fig. 1. Order picking design possibilities

Figure 2 exemplifies the alternatives proposed in view of the different order picking complexity levels.

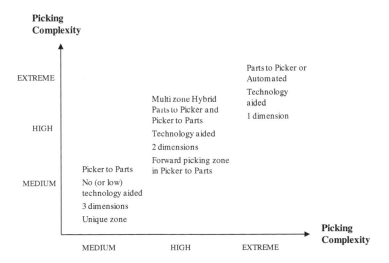

Fig. 2. General alternative chart

Three new charts with a higher degree of detailed of handling systems and equipments have been built in order to extend the information shown in Figure 2 (see Figure 3). Further information could be found in Errasti (2011).

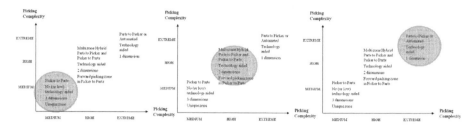

Fig. 3. Alternative charts according to order picking complexity level

3.3   Optimization of the Design Stage

In this step the most suitable alternative is selected. This selection is performed according to Frazelle's (2002) Key Performance Indicators KPIs (cost, utilization, productivity, quality and time), and a priority matrix is suggested in order to weight those metrics according to the business's characteristics.

The development of a Discrete Events Simulation model is suggested in order to compare the chosen alternatives during Characterization of the Design Stage. Chackelson et al. (2011) had verified the effectiveness of combining those techniques.

DoE is proposed with the aim of detecting interrelation between factors, and in order to be aware of how operational and organizational policies are affected by different demand characteristics. In other words, based on DoE approach, the methodology proposed in this paper involves a series of tests in which changes are made to the input variables of the process or system in order to observe and identify the impact of these changes on the output response(s) (Montgomery 2008).

The experiments are carried out in the simulation model, which allows for the comparison of the maximum number of input and output variables, identifying the most significant effects and discarding the variables with less influence on performance. This technique can be adapted to a variety of situations as well as to fluctuating business needs.

It important to highlight that warehouse processes design is highly complex and it may not be possible to identify what is the *optimum* solution, owing to the high number of existing possibilities (Baker and Canessa 2009).

3.4   Verification Stage

A Verification Stage is needed in order to corroborate that the simulation computer program performs as intended and that it is also an accurate representation of the system under study. The obtained results can be used to support decision making process only after the simulation model has been subjected to this verification and validation process (Law and Kelton 1991).

With this aim in mind, different techniques could be used such as Animation or the Comparison of Simulated and the Real data (Kleijnen 1995, Sargent 1996).

4   Case Research

In this study, we use a Case research carried out in the small appliances warehousing order picking process of a home appliances manufacturer in order to test the utility of the proposed methodology. The whole design procedure has been followed during the design of the order picking process, and at the moment the implementation is taking place successfully.

A description of the results obtained after the four steps of the order picking design methodology are described in this section.

Table 3. Case research priority matrix

FACTOR	Valuation Ranges			Weighing
Picking Volume (lines/t)	Lines<100	100<Lines<1000	1000<Lines	3
	1	2	3	
Storage unit vs. order unit	Ratio>75%	25%<Ratio<75%	25%>Ratio	3
	1	2	3	
Number of make to stock items	Number<100	100<Number<1000	1000<Number	2
	1	2	3	
Different order type	Number=1	Number=2	Number>3	1
	1	2	3	
Different Product characteristics	Number=1	Number=2	Number>3	1
	1	2	3	

According to Table 3, it is a Medium Picking situation because the value that determines the order picking complexity level is $19 = 2x3 + 2x3 + 2x2 + 2x1 + 1x1$. Figure 4 shows the chart of alternatives that corresponds to that complexity level.

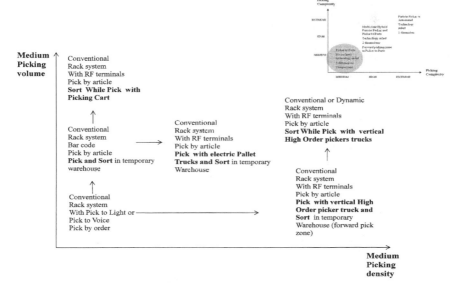

Fig. 4. Medium picking alternative chart

The warehouse designer selected a conventional rack system with electric pallet trucks. A discrete event simulation model using AnyLogic 6.6.0 University was built in order to analyze the following picking operational alternatives:

- Class-based storage strategy vs. family grouping
- Within-aisle vs. across-aisle storage implementation strategy
- Pick by-article vs. pick by-order.

The criteria selected in order to determine the most suitable alternative was the travel distance (m/day). The following table shows the comparison between the analyzed possibilities:

Table 4.

Storage strategy	Implementation policy	Batching	Travel distance	Improvement
Family grouping	-	By-order	46.191 m/day [2]	-
ABC class-based	Within-aisle storage	By-order	45.570 m/day [2]	1,4%
ABC class-based	Across-aisle storage	By-order	40.561 m/day [2]	14%
ABC class-based	Across-aisle storage	Combined [1]	39.724 m/day [2]	16%

[1] Combined: A-items by article and B and C items by order

The final design included an ABC class-based storage policy across-aisle, combined with a mix picking policy (A-items by article and B and C items by order) in a conventional rack system with electric pallet trucks.

5   Conclusion and Future Work

The present work is focused on order picking design. A novel methodology is proposed with the aim of filling: (1) the lack of a flexible order picking design framework, (2) the misuse of tools and techniques that allow the modeling and simulation of operative processes in the design or redesign phase of a operative process to be incorporated and (3) the scarcity of empirical investigations that allow the applicability of new procedures and technologies. Based on the Design for Six Sigma approach, this procedure assists the designer suggesting the most suitable picking alternatives according to the process complexity level (medium, high or extreme). The preferred alternatives are suggested to be compared according to according to Frazelle's (2002) Key Performance Indicators KPIs (cost, utilization, productivity, quality and time), and utilizing a discrete event simulation model. A Design of Experiments approach is also proposed with the aim of detecting interrelation between factors, and in order to be aware of how operational and organizational policies are affected by different demand characteristics.

A case research was carried out, where the warehouse designer admits to being satisfied with the support this methodology has provided him, and highlighted the power of visualizing the possible designs in a simulation model when selecting the final configuration.

Many authors state that *a comprehensive and science-based methodology for the overall design of warehouses does not appear to exist* (Baker and Canessa 2009,

Gu et al 2010). This important concept is being taken into account while improving the recommended order picking design approach, while looking at a modular point of view that allows it to be easily incorporated into a generic methodology.

In addition, the proposed methodology only addresses design aspects from a material flow point of view.   In future studies, sizing and dimensioning of order picking process from a stock perspective will be included.

References

1. Baker, P., Canessa, M.: Warehouse design: A structured approach. European Journal of Operational Research 193, 425–436 (2009)
2. Banks, J., Carson, J.S., Nelson, B.L.: Discrete-Event System Simulation. Prentice Hall, United States (2010)
3. Box, G.E.P., Hunter, J.S., Hunter, W.G.: Statistics for experimenters - Design, Innovation and Discover. John Wiley & Sons (2005)
4. Brue, G., Lausny, R.G.: Design for Six Sigma. McGraw Hill (2003)
5. Chackelson, C., Errasti, A., Cipres, D., Lahoz, F.: Design of a part to picker system. Design of experiments application aided by discrete event simulation. Dyna. 86, 515–522 (2011)
6. De Koster, R., Le-Duc, T., Roodbergen, J.: Design and control of warehouse order picking: A literature review. European Journal of Operational Research 102, 481–501 (2007)
7. Dallari, F., Marchet, G., Melacini, M.: Design of order picking system. International Journal of Advanced Manufacturing Technologies 42, 1–12 (2009)
8. Ekren, B., Heragu, S., Krishnamurthy, A., Malmborg, C.: Simulation based experimental design to identify factors affecting performance of AVS/RS. Computer and Industrial Engineering (2009) (article in press)
9. Errasti, A.: Logística de almacenaje. Diseño y gestión de almacenes y plataformas logísticas. World Class Warehousing. Ediciones Pirámide, España (2011)
10. Errasti, A., Chackelson, C., Arcelus, M.: Estado del arte y retos para la mejora de sistemas de preparación de pedidos en almacenes: Estudio Delphi. Dirección y Organización 40, 78–85 (2010)
11. Frazelle, E.: World-Class Warehousing and Material Handling. McGraw-Hill, New York (2002)
12. Goetschalckx, M., Ashayeri, J.: Classification and design of order picking systems. Logistics World, 99–106 (June 1989)
13. Gu, J., Goetschalckx, M., McGinnis, L.: Research on warehouse design and performance evaluation: A comprehensive review. European Journal of Operational Research 203, 539–549 (2010)
14. Hahn, G.J.: Six Sigma: 20 key lessons learned. Quality and Reliability Engineering International 21, 225–233 (2005)
15. Kleijnen, J.P.C.: Verification and validation of simulation models. European Journal of Operational Research 82, 145–162 (1995)
16. Law, A.M., Kelton, W.D.: Simulation Modeling and Analysis. McGraw-Hill, New York (1991)
17. Linderman, K., Schroeder, R., Zaheer, S., Choo, A.: Six Sigma: A goal-theoretic perspective. Journal of Operations Management 21, 193–203 (2003)
18. Manzini, R., Gamberi, M., Persona, A., et al.: Design of a class based storage picker to product order picking system. International Journal of Advanced Manufacturing Technologies 32, 811–821 (2007)

19. Montgomery, D.C.: Generation III Six Sigma. Quality and Reliability Engineering International 21, 3–4 (2005)
20. Montgomery, D.C.: Designed Experiments in Process improvement. Quality and Reliability Engineering International 22, 863–864 (2006)
21. Montgomery, D.C.: Design and Analysis of Experiments. John Wiley & Sons (2008)
22. Rushton, A., Croucher, P., Baker, P.: The handbook of logistics and distribution management. Kogan Page Publishers (2006)
23. Sargent, R.G.: Verifying and validating simulation model. In: Proc. of 1996. Winter Simulation Conf., pp. 55–64 (1996)
24. Yang, K., El-Haik, B.: Design for Six Sigma: A roadmap for product development. McGraw-Hill (2003)
25. Yoon, C.S., Sharp, G.P.: A structured procedure for analysis and design of order pick systems. IIE Transactions 28, 379–389 (1996)

Mathematical Formulation for Mobile Robot Scheduling Problem in a Manufacturing Cell

Quang-Vinh Dang, Izabela Nielsen, and Kenn Steger-Jensen

Department of Mechanical and Manufacturing Engineering, Aalborg University,
Fibigerstræde 16, 9220 Aalborg, Denmark
{vinhise,izabela,kenn}@m-tech.aau.dk

Abstract. This paper deals with the problem of finding optimal feeding sequence in a manufacturing cell with feeders fed by a mobile robot with manipulation arm. The performance criterion is to minimize total traveling time of the robot in a given planning horizon. Besides, the robot has to be scheduled in order to keep production lines within the cell working without any shortage of parts fed from feeders. A mixed-integer programming (MIP) model is developed to find the optimal solution for the problem. In the MIP formulation, a method based on the (s, Q) inventory system is applied to define time windows for multiple-part feeding tasks. A case study is implemented at an impeller production line in a factory to demonstrate the result of the proposed MIP model.

Keywords: Scheduling, Mobile Robot, MIP, Feeding Sequence.

1 Introduction

Production systems nowadays range from fully automated to strictly manual. While the former is very efficient in high volumes but less flexible, the latter is very flexible but less cost-efficient. Therefore, manufactures visualize the need for transformable production systems that combines the best of both worlds by using new assistive automation and mobile robots. With embedded batteries and manipulation arms, mobile robots are more flexible to perform certain tasks such as transporting and feeding materials, machine tending, pre-assembly or quality inspection at different workstations of production lines. These tasks have such relatively low level of complexity that mobile robots are able to take over. Besides, using mobile robots can lead to less energy usage or less tool-changing costs than commonly industrial robots attached to a fixed surface. These advantages pave the way for mobile robot to be implemented in the transformable production systems. Within the scope of this study, a given problem is particularly considered for a single mobile robot which will automate multiple-part feeding tasks by not only transporting but also collecting containers of parts and emptying them into the feeders needed. However, to utilize mobile robots in an efficient manner requires the ability to properly schedule these feeding tasks. Hence, it is important to plan in which sequence mobile robots process feeding operations so that they could effectively work while satisfying a number of technological constraints.

J. Frick and B. Laugen (Eds.): APMS 2011, IFIP AICT 384, pp. 37–44, 2012.

Robot scheduling problem which is NP-hard has attracted interest of researchers in recent decades. Dror and Stulman [4] dealt with the problem of optimizing one-dimensional robot's service movements. Crama and van de Klundert [1] considered the flow shop problem with one transporting robot and one type of product to find shortest cyclic schedule for the robot. Afterwards, they demonstrated that the sequence of activities whose execution produces one part yields optimal production rates for three-machine robotic flow shops [2]. Crame et al. [3] also presented a survey of cyclic robotic scheduling problem along with their existing solution approaches. Kats and Levner [5], [6] considered m-machine production line processing identical parts served by a mobile robot to find the minimum cycle time for 2-cyclic schedules. Maimon et al. [7] introduced a neural network method for a material-handling robot task-sequencing problem. Suárez and Rosell [8] dealt with the particular real case of feeding sequence selection in a manufacturing cell consisting of four parallel identical machines. Several feeding strategies and simulation model were built to select the best sequence. Most of the work and theory foundation considered scheduling robots which are usually inflexible, move on prescribed path and repeatedly perform a limited sequence of activities. There is still lack of scheduling a free-ranging mobile robot which is able to move around within a manufacturing cell to process multiple-part feeding tasks consisting of collecting, transporting, and delivering containers of parts to feeders. The scheduling problem becomes interesting as the robot has been coordinated to manufacturing so that robot's services maintain production in the lines. Therefore, in this paper we focus on scheduling a single mobile robot for multiple-part feeding tasks whose time windows could be determined based on the inventory system (s, Q) as well as predefined maximum and minimum levels of parts in feeders.

The remainder of this paper is organized as follows: in the next section, problem statement is described while the mathematical model is formulated in Section 3. A case study is investigated to demonstrate the result of the proposed model in Section 4. Finally, conclusions are drawn in Section 5.

2   Problem Description

Fig. 1 below shows a typical layout of the manufacturing cell. In particular, the work is developed for a real cell that produces parts for the pump manufacturing industry at a factory in Denmark. The cell consists of a central storage known as a part supermarket, a single mobile robot, and several production lines including multiple machines which are fed by multiple feeders. An operator is responsible to put parts into small load carriers (SLCs) which are placed in the storage. The robot will retrieve and carry several SLCs containing parts from the storage, move to feeder locations, feed all parts inside each SLC to each feeder, then return to the storage to unload all empty SLCs and take filled SLCs. Because of the limitation on capacity, the feeders have to be served a number of times in order maintain production without any shortage of parts. The mobile robot thus has a set of feeding tasks to carry out during a given planning horizon.

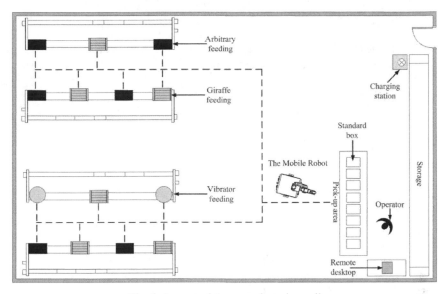

Fig. 1. Layout of the manufacturing cell

To enable the construction of a multiple-part feeding schedule of the mobile robot, the following assumptions are made: an autonomous mobile robot is considered in disturbance free environment; the robot is able to carry one or several SCLs at a time; all tasks are periodic, independent, and assigned to the same robot; working time and traveling time of the robot between any locations, and consuming rates of parts in feeders are known; all feeders of machines have to be fed up to maximum levels and the robots starts from the storage at the initial stage. In order to accomplish all the movements with a smallest consumed amount of battery energy, the total traveling time of the robot is an important objective to be considered. Hence, it is important to determine in which way the robot should feed the feeders of machines in order to minimize its total traveling time within the manufacturing cell while preventing the production lines from stopping working.

3   Mathematical Formulation

In this study, a mix-integer programming (MIP) model is developed to determine an optimal route of the mobile robot visiting a number of locations to process multiple-part feeding tasks. The model is inspired by well-known traveling salesman problem [9] and the (s, Q) inventory system [10]. The latter is applied to define time windows for the feeding tasks. In practice, the MIP model can be applied to small-scale problems with a few numbers of feeders and short planning horizon. Under these scenarios, the MIP model is reasonably fast to give exact optimal solutions, which can be used as reference points to quantify the scale of benefits achieved by a meta-heuristic method further developed. Notations, time windows, and a formulation for the MIP model are extensively described in the following subsections.

3.1   Notations

N : set of all tasks ($N = \{0, 1, 2, ..., n\}$ where 0: task at the storage)
n_i : number of times task i has to be executed
R : set of all possible routes ($R = \{1, 2, ..., R_{max}\}$ where $R_{max} = \Sigma\, n_i, \forall i \in N \setminus \{0\}$)
e_{ik} : k-th release time of task i
d_{ik} : k-th due time of task i
p_i : periodic time of task i
w_i : working time of robot at task i location
t_{ij} : traveling time of robot from task i location to task j location
c_i : consuming rate of parts in feeder at task i location
v_i : minimum level of parts in feeder at task i location
u_i : maximum level of parts in feeder at task i location
Q : maximum number of SLCs could be carried by robot
T : planning horizon

Decision variables:

$$x_{ik}^{jlr} = \begin{cases} 1 & \text{if robot travels from } k\text{-th task } i \text{ location to } l\text{-th task } j \text{ location in the route } r \\ 0 & \text{otherwise} \end{cases}$$

y_{ik} : route number to which k-th task i belongs
s_{ik} : k-th starting time of task i

3.2   Time Windows

Time windows of multiple-part feeding tasks of the mobile robot could be determined as shown in Equation (1), (2), and (3) below.

$$p_i = (u_i - v_i)c_i, \forall i \in N \setminus \{0\} \tag{1}$$

$$e_{ik+1} = e_{ik} + p_i, \forall i \in N \setminus \{0\}, k = 1 \div n_i \tag{2}$$

$$d_{ik} = e_{ik} + (v_i - 0)c_i, \forall i \in N \setminus \{0\}, k = 1 \div n_i \tag{3}$$

Task for feeder i whose periodic time is calculated as Equation (1) has a number of times/executions $n_i = \lfloor T / p_i \rfloor$ to be performed. The release time of an execution of task i is set when the number of parts inside feeder i falls to a certain level v_i (Equation (2)); while the due time of an execution of task i is defined when there are no parts in feeder i (Equation (3)).

3.3   Mixed-Integer Programming Model

Objective function:

$$\min \sum_{i \in N} \sum_{k=1}^{n_i} \sum_{j \in N} \sum_{l=1}^{n_j} \sum_{r \in R} t_{ij} x_{ik}^{jlr} \tag{4}$$

$$e_{ik} \le s_{ik} \le d_{ik} \qquad\qquad \forall i \in N \setminus \{0\}, k = 1 \div n_i \tag{5}$$

$$\sum_{j\in N\backslash\{0\}}\sum_{l=1}^{n_j} x_{01}^{jl1} = 1 \tag{6}$$

$$\sum_{j\in N\backslash\{0\}}\sum_{l=1}^{n_j}\sum_{r\in R} x_{01}^{jlr} \le 1 \tag{7}$$

$$\sum_{i\in N}\sum_{k=1}^{n_i} x_{ik}^{ikr} = 0 \qquad\qquad \forall r\in R \tag{8}$$

$$\sum_{r\in R} x_{ik}^{jlr} \le |Z|-1 \qquad\qquad \forall i,j\in N, k=1\div n_i, l=1\div n_j, i\ne j, Z\subseteq Z_T, Z\ne\Phi \tag{9}$$

$$\sum_{j\in N}\sum_{l=1}^{n_j}\sum_{r\in R} x_{ik}^{jlr} = 1 \qquad\qquad \forall i\in N\backslash\{0\}, k=1\div n_i \tag{10}$$

$$\sum_{i\in N}\sum_{k=1}^{n_i}\sum_{r\in R} x_{ik}^{jlr} = 1 \qquad\qquad \forall j\in N\backslash\{0\}, l=1\div n_j \tag{11}$$

$$\sum_{i\in N}\sum_{k=1}^{n_i}\sum_{j\in N\backslash\{0\}}\sum_{l=1}^{n_j} x_{ik}^{jlr} \le Q \qquad\qquad \forall r\in R \tag{12}$$

$$s_{ik} + \left(w_i + t_{ij}\sum_{r\in R}x_{ik}^{jlr}\right) - L\left(1-\sum_{r\in R}x_{ik}^{jlr}\right) + \left(y_{jl}-y_{ik}\right)\times\left(t_{i0}+w_0+t_{0j}-t_{ij}\right) \le s_{jl} \tag{13}$$

$$\forall i,j\in N, k=1\div n_i, l=1\div n_j$$

$$y_{jl} = \sum_{i\in N}\sum_{k=1}^{n_i}\sum_{r\in R} r\times x_{ik}^{jlr} \qquad\qquad \forall j\in N\backslash\{0\}, l=1\div n_j \tag{14}$$

$$y_{jl} \ge y_{ik}\sum_{r\in R} x_{ik}^{jlr} \qquad\qquad \forall i,j\in N, k=1\div n_i, l=1\div n_j \tag{15}$$

$$x_{ik}^{jlr} \in \{0,1\} \qquad\qquad \forall r\in R, \forall i,j\in N, k=1\div n_i, l-1\div n_j \tag{16}$$

$$y_{ik}: \text{positive integer variable} \qquad\qquad \forall i\in N, k=1\div n \tag{17}$$

The objective function (4) minimizes the total traveling time of the robot. Constraint (5) ensures that starting time of an execution of a task satisfies its time window. Constraints (6) and (7) indicate that the robot starts from the storage at the initial stage. Constraint (8) prevents the robot repeating an execution of a task. Constraint (9) eliminates the sub-tours among executions of tasks, where Z is a subset of Z_T, where Z_T is a set of all executions of tasks at feeders and the storage, and Φ denotes and empty set. Constraints (10) and (11) force an execution of a task in one route to be done exactly one. Constraint (12) forbids the robot to feed more SLCs than the maximum number of SLCs Q it allows to carry. Constraint (13) handles the traveling time requirements between any pair of executions of tasks, where L is a given sufficiently large constant. In case two executions of the same task or different tasks are connected but they are not in the same route, the robot should visit the storage to unload empty SLCs and load filled ones. Constraint (14) assigns an execution of a task to a route and constraint (15) guarantees the ascending sequence of route numbers for executions of tasks. Constraints (16) and (17) imply the types of variables.

4   Case Study

To examine performance of the MIP model, a case study is investigated at the CR factory at Grundfos A/S. The chosen area for this case study is the CR 1-2-3 impeller production line which produces impellers for industrial pumps. The CR line consists of four feeders that have to be served by the mobile robot. These feeders are indexed from 1 to 4 and named Back Plate, Van Feeder 1, Van Feeder 2, and Front Plate respectively. Besides, different feeders are filled by different kinds of parts, namely back plates for feeder 1, vanes for feeder 2 and 3, front plates for feeder 4. On the CR line, a number of vanes are welded together with back and front plates to produce an impeller. Fig. 2 below particularly illustrates the aforementioned production area where the proposed model has been implemented in the factory.

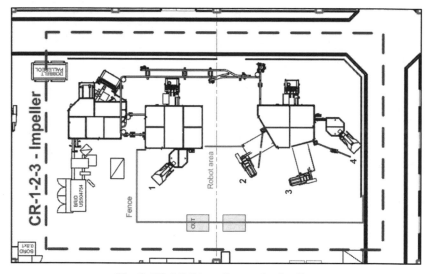

Fig. 2. CR 1-2-3 impeller production line

The maximum number of SLCs carried by the robot is 3. The average number of parts per SLC fed to feeder 1 or 4 is 125 (approximately 2 kg/SLC), while the average number of parts per SLC fed to feeder 2 or 3 is 1100 (approximately 1 kg/SLC). The maximum levels, minimum levels, consuming rates of parts, and working time of the robot are given in Table 1, while Table 2 shows traveling time of the robot from one location of a task to another (feeder 0 means the central storage).

Table 1. Maximum, minimum levels, consuming rates, and working time of robot at feeders

Feeder	0	1	2	3	4
Maximum level (part)	-	250	2000	2000	250
Minimum level (part)	-	125	900	900	125
Consuming rate (s/part)	-	4.5	1.5	1.5	4.5
Working time of robot (s)	90	42	42	42	42

Table 2. Traveling time of robot from one location to another

Traveling time (s)	0	1	2	3	4
0	0	43	33	27	48
1	46	0	29	30	53
2	32	34	0	36	42
3	29	26	35	0	40
4	47	60	46	39	0

The case study has been investigated during approximately 50 minutes because of the limitation on robot batteries. The MIP model has been coded in the mathematical modeling language ILOG OPL 3.6. The problem of case study has been run on a PC having an Intel® Core i5 2.3 GHz processor and 4 GB RAM. The optimal solution obtained is given as: $0 - 1 - 4 - 4 - 0 - 1 - 1 - 4 - 0 - 1 - 2 - 4 - 0 - 3 - 0$, with total traveling time being 503 seconds which makes up 16.4 % of the total time. With 4040 decision variables, the computational time for this case using the proposed model is 4305 seconds. The detailed solution is shown in Table 3 and Fig. 3 below.

Table 3. Detailed optimal solution of the case study

Task	Feeder	Index of execution	Starting time	Route
1	1	1	1030.0	1
2	4	1	1125.0	1
3	4	2	1375.5	1
4	1	2	1687.5	2
5	1	3	2155.0	2
6	4	3	2250.0	2
7	1	4	2549.0	3
8	2	1	2620.0	3
9	4	4	2704.0	3
10	3	1	3000.0	4

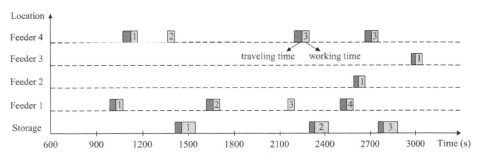

Fig. 3. Gantt chart for the optimal solution of the case study

The above optimal solution is an initial schedule for the robot. That schedule serves as an input to a program called Mission Planner and Control (MPC) which is implemented in VB.NET. The MPC program is accessed using XML-based TCP/IP communication to command and get feedbacks from the robot. During the practical feeding operations at CR 1-2-3 impeller production line, the initial schedule was executed in sequence and it prevented all of feeders running out of parts. Hence, the CR line can keep producing impellers without shortage of parts fed from feeders.

5   Conclusions

In this paper, a new problem of scheduling a single mobile robot for multiple-part feeding tasks in a manufacturing cell is studied. To accomplish all tasks within allowable limit of battery capacity, it is important for planners to determine optimal feeding sequence to minimize total traveling time of the mobile robot while considering specific features of the robot and a number of technological constraints. An MIP model is developed to find optimal solution for the problem. A particular real case of the impeller production line composing of four feeders is described to show result of the proposed model. The result was quite properly applied during practical feeding operations and it demonstrated that all feeders had no shortage of parts. For further research, the complexity of the problem will increase when considering a larger number of feeders and/or longer planning horizon. Hence, a meta-heuristic method will be taken into account for solving large-scale mobile robot scheduling problems. Besides, re-scheduling mechanisms based on obtained schedules and feedback from the shop floor will be developed to deal with real-time disturbances.

Acknowledgments. This work has partly been supported by the European Commission under grant agreement number FP7-260026-TAPAS.

References

1. Crama, Y., van de Klundert, J.: Cyclic Scheduling of Identical Parts in a Robotic Cell. Oper. Res. 45, 952–965 (1997)
2. Crama, Y., van de Klundert, J.: Cyclic Scheduling in 3-machine Robotic Flow Shops. J. Sched. 2, 35–54 (1999)
3. Crama, Y., Kats, V., van de Klundert, J., Levner, E.: Cyclic Scheduling in Robotic Flow-shops. Ann. Oper. Res. 96, 97–124 (2000)
4. Dror, M., Stulman, A.: Optimizing Robot's Service Movement: a One Dimensional Case. Comput. Ind. Eng. 12, 39–46 (1987)
5. Kats, V., Levner, E.: Parametric Algorithms for 2-cyclic Robot Scheduling with Interval Processing Times. J. Sched. 14, 267–279 (2011)
6. Kats, V., Levner, E.: A Faster Algorithm for 2-cyclic Robotic Scheduling with a Fixed Robot Route and Interval Processing Times. Eur. J. Oper. Res. 209, 51–56 (2011)
7. Maimon, O., Braha, D., Seth, V.: A Neural Network Approach for a Robot Task Sequencing Problem. Artif. Intell. Eng. 14, 175–189 (2000)
8. Suárez, R., Rosell, J.: Feeding Sequence Selection in a Manufacturing Cell with Four Parallel Machines. Robot Comput. Integrated Manuf. 21, 185–195 (2005)
9. Toth, P., Vigo, D.: The Vehicle Routing Problem. SIAM, Philadelphia (2002)
10. Silver, E.A., Pyke, D.F., Peterson, R.: Inventory Management and Production Planning and Scheduling. John Wiley & Sons, New York (1998)

A Proposed Approach to Extend the Economic Order Quantity (EOQ) Model Using Discrete Event Simulation

Giovanni Davoli and Riccardo Melloni

Department of Mechanical and Civil Engineering (DIMeC)
University of Modena and Reggio Emilia
via Vignolese 905, 41100, Modena, Italy
giovanni.davoli@unimore.it

Abstract. The economic order quantity (EOQ) and the economic production quantity (EPQ) are well-known and commonly used inventory control techniques. The standard results are easy to apply but are based on a number of unrealistic assumptions. One of the assumption is that the demand is normally distributed in any interval. In several practical cases the assumption about independence of successive demands, and consequently demand normal distribution in any interval, is not supported by real data. This paper investigates the effects on the expected service level (SL) after relaxing normal distribution assumption on the demand. The present work shows a possible strategy to use classic inventory model, such as EOQ/EPQ model, adopting discrete event simulation analysis to quantify model performances under relaxed assumptions.

Keywords: EOQ, inventory techniques, discrete event, simulation analysis.

1   Introduction

The economic order quantity (EOQ), first introduced by Harris [1], and developed by Brown [2] and Bather [3] with stochastic demand, is a well-known and commonly used inventory control techniques reported in a great variety of hand book, for example: Tersine [4] and Ghiani [5]. The standard EOQ and economic production quantity (EPQ) results are easy to apply but are based on a number of unrealistic assumptions [6]. One of the assumption is that the demand is normally distributed in any interval, it is assumed that successive demands are independent and, consequently, the accumulated demand over many time units is approximately normal. The realization that inventories operate under less than ideal situations gives rise to a subset of inventory modeling theory that performs sensitivity analysis on models operating under stochastic conditions [7]. Several extensions of the classic EOQ/EPQ model have been, Borgonovo [8] presents a good review of them across several fields of research. A branch comprises models where the assumption that all units are of perfect quality is removed, for a deep literature review you can see Chan [9]. Another field of EOQ extended models is focused on deteriorating inventory models for perishables management, for a good review you can see Goyal [10] and Ferguson [11]. Some papers mixed the two proposals to develop a model that better

J. Frick and B. Laugen (Eds.): APMS 2011, IFIP AICT 384, pp. 45–53, 2012.

fits real practice conditions, for example Inderfurth [12]. Other models modified demands assumptions, for example Chao [13] proposed an EOQ model in which the demand is characterized by a continuous-time Brownian motion process.

Limiting the literature review to nonzero lead time EOQ model, Lowe and Schwarz [14] performed research on the problem where parameters value are not known with certainty and they find that EOQ model is quite insensitive to errors in forecast of demand, their research was extended by Hojati [15] in recent years. Also Dobson [16] studied EOQ model sensitiveness and his results support the previous conclusions. On the other hand Mykytka and Ramberg [17] and later Mahmoud and Younis [18] examine the sensitivity of the EOQ model to errors in forecast of demand and they found that inaccurate estimation produces considerably different results, Higle [19] extends the previous works. There is a good quantity of works about inventory analysis through simulation: Meherez and Ben-Arieh [20] studied a model with stochastic demand and their simulation experiments reveal that the model is not sensitive to demand distribution and parameters accuracy; Naddor [21] states that model results depended on mean and standard deviation of demand, but not on the specific distribution, also Hebert and Deckro [22] results are quite insensitive to demand forecast errors. In contrast Benton [23] states that high measures of demand lumpiness resulted in high service level. Even Lau and Zaki [24] state that EOQ results depends on demand distribution. The various researchers not always agree with one other and the EOQ model sensitivity needs to be more evaluated under stochastic conditions [7]. EOQ model apathy for accurate parameter estimation may have contributed to low usage of the EOQ Ziegler [25]. While some case study reporting EOQ model application can be found, for example De Castro [26], EOQ model low usage and poor results in industrial practice are suggested by recent works in which corrections to the original model are proposed, for example Persona [27].

2   Purpose

The purpose of this paper is to investigate the possibility to use discrete event simulation to extend the EOQ model in order to relax some of the standard hypothesis. In several practical cases EOQ assumptions are not supported by real data. The hypothesis about independence of successive demands, and consequently demand normal distribution in any interval, is often not guarantee, for example, when the manufacture uses at the same time different channels selling goods to address the same customers: large scale distribution and traditional retail. In all these cases the total demand in a certain period could fluctuate according with a normal distribution but the successive daily demands are not independent. Moreover, in many practical cases the used time sample to analyze the historical demand is not related to the lead time, often a monthly time sample is used to determinate the standard deviation and the safety stocks (SS) are calculated consequently. In fact, many manufactures experiment that the achieved SL is significantly lower than the SL expected from the theoretical EOQ model. Discrete event simulation can be useful to extend classical model under more realistic hypothesis. An example of the proposed approach is given here where are presented the effects on the expected SL, after relaxing normal distribution and sampling assumptions on the demand.

Table 1. Symbol and definitions

Symbol	Unit	Definition
D_i	Unit/period	Mean demand per i-period in unit
σ_i	Unit/period	Standard deviation for demand per i-period in unit
d_k	Unit/day	Demand per k-day in unit
N	Day	Number of days for simulation
Np	Day	Number of days for period
C_l	Euro/batch	Set-up cost in euro per unit
C_s	Euro/ unit*year	Stock cost in euro per unit per year
Max_d	Unit	Maximum demand for a day in unit
Min_d	Unit	Minimum demand for a day in unit
Lt	Day	Lead time in day
σ_t	Day	Standard deviation for lead time in day
EOQ	Unit	Economic production quantity in unit
SS	Unit	Safety stocks in unit
SL_t	Rate	Service level, 1 minus the ratio between the number of "stock out" and the number of replenishment orders issued, while a "stock out" is considered when the total demand in a lead time exceeds the mean demand over the lead time.
SL	Rate	Service level, 1 minus the ratio between days of availability against total days, during the simulated period
SL_p	Rate	Service level, 1 minus the ratio between available units against demanded units, during the simulated period

3   Simulation Model

This paper is grounded on a discrete events simulation model reproducing a single-item fixed order quantity system acting under relaxed demand assumption. The model was used to quantify the effectiveness of SS, in term of SL, when SS are calculated according with the EOQ classic model. The notations used in this paper are illustrated in table 1. A set of stochastic functions, provided by SciLab, are used to generate the demand, the simulation model was tested performing normal distributed demand and then this hypothesis is relaxed.

3.1   Model Validation

The model validation represents a key aspect of the proposed approach especially because the considered discrete event simulation model is use under stochastic conditions. Simulation outputs are compared to the results provided by the theory, to validate the simulation model in a two steps process. First the behavior in term of stock during time is analyzed, second the achieved SL under stochastic conditions is compared. The first comparison, shown in Fig. 1, is performed for both: the deterministic EOQ model, where the demand is constant, and the stochastic EOQ model, where the demand is normally distributed. The figures shows that the simulation results fit with the standard EOQ theoretical model.

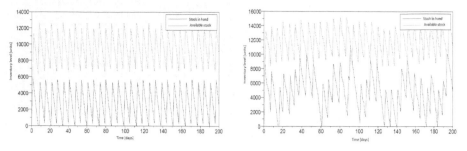

Fig. 1. Inventory level for deterministic (left) and normal distributed (right) demand

The second part of the validation process considers the achieved SL_t to compare simulation results to theoretical expected values. The SL used in the validation process is named SL_t defined according with the EOQ theoretical model as: 1 minus the ratio between the number of "stock out" and the number of replenishment orders issued, while a "stock out" is considered when the total demand in a lead time exceeds the mean demand over the lead time. This definition of SL_t is used only to validate the simulation model, while findings are presented in term of redefined SL and SL_p in order to have a more relevant definition for industrial practice. This second step of validation process involved only the stochastic model where the demand is normally distributed.

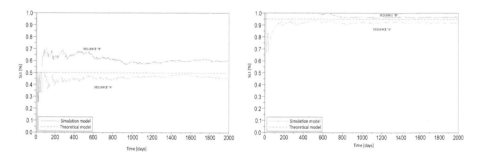

Fig. 2. SLt course for a SL target of 50% (left) and 95% (right)

The comparison of SL_t reveals a discretization problem when the model is implemented. In each day the model does these actions:

1. puts the incoming order to stock, increasing the inventory level;
2. fulfills the outgoing order, decreasing the inventory level;
3. checks the inventory level.

The theoretical EOQ model is a mathematical continuous model where all these actions occur at the same time and where an order to refurnish stock is placed when the inventory level reach the reorder point, whatever is the time instant. This continuous behavior could not be implemented in the developed simulation model where the check of the inventory level is done once in a day. The logical sequences used in the simulation model are two: sequence A (pre) and sequence B (post). In sequence A the simulation code performs, for each day, the actions in this order:

2-1-3 and this overestimates the inventory level. In sequence B the code performs: 2-3-1 and this underestimates the inventory level. The validation process considered the SL_t achieved with SS calculated according with the theoretical model, for a target of 50% SL_t (that means zero SS) and for a target of 95% SL_t. As shown in Fig. 2 the results are very different, in fact the gap between simulation outputs and theoretical expected values is relevant for a low SL_t target but this gap shrinks when the SL_t target grows. According with the fact that EOQ model is often used with high SL target, it is possible to validate the simulation model independently from the used sequences (A or B in this case). For the simulations the used sequence is B.

3.2   Model Implementation and Experiments Set

To prove the effectiveness of the proposed approach, the simulation experiments are developed to investigate the correlation between demand distribution and time sampling and expected SL. Demand is a normal distributed demand if the considered time sample is equal to a month and its shape is described by a minimum (Min_d) and a maximum (Max_d) value for the daily demand.

First the stochastic demand is generated, then the SS are calculated and the simulation model runs. Each simulation is performed with SS calculated but three different demand time sample are used to calculate σ_i. Time sample is set equal to:

1. a month;
2. a month, with SS calculated according with σ_i taken in the worst case;
3. the lead time, with SS calculated according with σ_i taken in the worst case.

In the first case demand time sample is set equal to the period of time used even for the stochastic generation of the demand, in other word, using this time sample the SS are calculated according with the imposed standard deviation used to generate the demand. In the second case the standard deviation σ_i of the generated demand is calculated N_p time and at each time the initial day of the period is translated by one. The SS are calculated according with the standard deviation σ_i of worst case, so the actual value of σ_i is considered. In the third case the time sample used is the lead time and the SS are calculated according with the worst possible case according with the procedure described above. The simulation results are given in terms of achieved SL and SL_p. The demand generation function is developed to be set with the parameters commonly available in practice. To characterize the stochastic demand the used parameters are: demand mean D_i and σ_i demand standard deviation, both referred to a monthly time sample, maximum demand Max_d experimented in a single day and minimum demand Mind experimented in a single day. The demand generation process acts as described below:

1. The demand D_i is randomly generated for the i-period, according with the assumption of normal distribution period by period;
2. The D_i period demand is divided into a defined number (N_p) of single daily demand (d_k) according with the following assumption:
    a. d_k must be higher than Min_d;
    b. d_k must be lower than Max_d;

c. the d_k daily demand are uniformly distributed between Min_d and Max_d;
d. the mean of the demand in the period is equal to D_i.

Table 2. Used parameters set

Parameter	Set value
D_i	100.000,00
N	10.000,00
Np	20,00
C_l	200,00
C_s	1,00
Lt	5,00
σ_t	0,00
Imposed SL	0,95

To investigate the influence of Min_d and Max_d at different level of σ_i all the other parameters of the model are set to specific values. The simulation model parameters are set in order to be representative for small-medium manufactures operating in the food sector. The used set is illustrated in table 2. The experiments investigate the various combination between Min_d and Max_d at different level of σ_i. The experiments were performed to investigate the range of Min_d between 0 to $D_i/2*N_p$ (in this case from 0 to 2.500 units, with a step of 500 units) and the range of Max_d from D_i/N_p to D_i (in this case from 5.000 to 100.000 units, with a step of 2.500 units). The demand monthly standard deviation σ_i varies from 0 up to the 20% of D_i (in this case from 0 to 20.000 units, with a step of 5.000 units), in order to simulate a scenario of long term demand stability and a scenario of long term demand fluctuation.

4   Findings

The presented experiment implies a number of 1.170 simulations, each of them is performed three times according with the choose time sample to evaluate σ_i and the consequent SS value, and each simulation provide two results: achieved SL and SL_p. The results can be represented with diagrams as shown in Fig. 3. The generated demands D_i were analyzed to check the assumptions described in chapter 3.2. The assumptions: a, b and c are always respected while the assumption d is not always guarantee. A level of 98% of D_i is undertaken to accept the results of the experiments. According with this threshold value, it is possible to observe that the assumption is not respected when the maximum value admitted for Max_d is small, lower than 12,5% of D_i. This area is not very interesting because under these conditions the model acts as the standard EOQ model. The imposed value of σ_i (considering the worst case using a time sample of a month) is respected only for the simulation with a low admitted Max_d. In all the other cases the variables Min_d and mostly Max_d drive the actual value of σ_i that became almost independent from the initial imposed value, see Fig 3. The results show how the achieved service level is significantly lower than the imposed value of 95% and the behavior of SL and SL_p is similar.

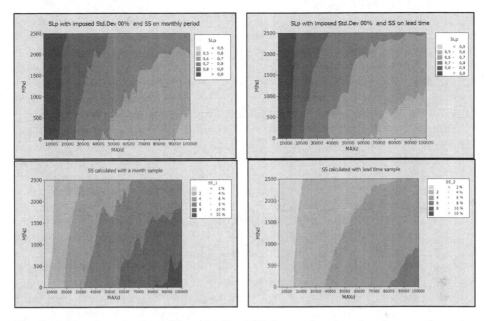

Fig. 3. Achieved service level SL_p and related SS for $\sigma_i = 0$ under relaxed assumption using different time sample (month on the left and lead time on the right)

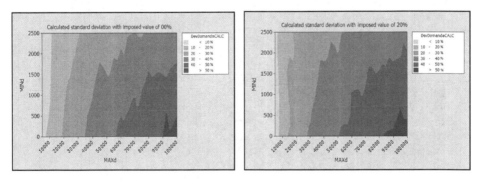

Fig. 4. Actual values of σ_i in simulations at different values of imposed for σ_i: 00% and 20%

5   Conclusions

The present work demonstrates that discrete event simulation approach can be useful to investigate EOQ model behavior under relaxed assumptions. Simulation technique can be useful to extend a mathematical continuous model even thought validation process has to be handled carefully because of discretization problems. In the presented example this approach is implemented to study the correlation between demand shape, sampling problems and achieved SL. The results show that when demand normal distributed hypothesis is removed the complexity of the EOQ model becomes very high and experimenters has to face different problems such as: how to describe demand shape and sampling problems. Moreover discrete event simulation model gives outputs for a specific parameters set and this prevents to enlarge automatically the results.

Although the previous considerations, the simulation experiments reveal that under relaxed demand assumptions the EOQ model performances are significantly different from theory. The achieved service level (SL) is significantly lower than the imposed value (in this case 95%). The expected SL depends on demand lumpiness that in these experiments is characterized by Max_d, Min_d and σ_i. The results shows that the expected SL is strongly related to the maximum demand Max_d admitted in a single day. High values of SL can be observed when Max_d is small, in these cases the model behavior is very similar to standard EOQ model. In general the achieved SL falls when Max_d grows and this effect is grater at small Min_d values, when the minimum demand admitted in a single day is close to zero. The periodic demand standard deviation σ_i seems to have a small influence on SL. Comparing a scenario with low σ_i with a scenario with high σ_i the results show a slight reduction for the achieved SL associated with an increase of the safety stocks SS. This SL reduction is appreciable for small values of Max_d and for high values of Min_d, when demand lumpiness is low. About the time sample used to calculate $\sigma_{i,\ and}$ SS, results show that, even with demand relaxed assumptions, a time sample equal to the lead time assures a good trade-off between SL and SS.

References

1. Harris, F.W.: Howmany parts to make at once. Factory, The Magazine of Management 10(2), 135–136, 152 (1913), reprinted in Operations Research 38(6) (November-December 1990)
2. Brown, R.G.: Smoothing, Forecasting and Prediction of Discrete Time Series. Prentice-Hall, Englewood Cliffs (1963)
3. Bather, J.A.: A continuous time inventory model. J. Appl. Prob. 3, 538–549 (1966)
4. Tersine, R.J.: Principles of inventory and materials management. North-Holland, Elsevier Science Publishing Co., Inc. (1988)
5. Ghiani, G., Laporte, G., Musmanno, R.: Introduction to logistics systems planning and control. John Wiley & Sons Ltd., West Sussex (2004)
6. Markland, R.E., Vickery, S.K., Davis, R.A.: Operation management, 2nd edn. South-Western, Ohio (1998)
7. Humphrey, A.S., Taylor, G.D.: Stock level determination and sensitivity analysis in repair/rework operations. Int. J. Op. & Prod. Man. 18(6), 612–630 (1998)
8. Borgonovo, E.: Sensitivity analysis with finite changes: An application to modified EOQ models. Eu. J. Op. Res. 200, 127–138 (2010)
9. Chan, W.M., Ibrahim, R.N., Lochert, P.B.: A new EPQ model: integrating lower pricing, rework and reject situations. Prod. Plan. & Cont. 14(7), 588–595 (2003)
10. Goyal, S.K., Giri, B.C.: Recent trends in modeling of deteriorating inventory. Eu. J. Opl. Res. 134, 1–16 (2001)
11. Ferguson, M., Jayaraman, V., Souza, G.C.: Note: Application of the EOQ model with nonlinear holding cost to inventory management of perishables. Eu. J. Opl. Res. 180, 485–490 (2007)

12. Inderfurth, K., Linder, G., Rachaniotis, N.P.: Lot sizing in a production system with rework and product deteriorating. Int. J. Prod. Res. 43(7), 1355–1374 (2005)
13. Chao, H.: The EOQ model with stochastic demand and discounting. Eu. J. Op. Res. 59, 434–443 (1992)
14. Lowe, T.J., Schwarz, L.B.: Parameter estimation for the EOQ lot-size model: minimax and expected value choices. Naval Res. Log. Quart. 30, 367–376 (1983)
15. Hojati, M.: Bridging the gap between probabilistic and fuzzy-parameter EOQ models. Int. J. Prod. Ec. 91, 215–221 (2004)
16. Dobson, G.: Sensitivity of the EOQ model to parameter estimates. Op. Res. 36(4), 570–574 (1988)
17. Mykytka, E.F., Ramberg, J.S.: On the sensitivity of the EOQ to errors in the forecast of demand. IIE Trans. 16(2), 144–151 (1984)
18. Mahmoud, M.S., Younis, M.A.: Sensitivity analysis of productive inventories under modeling errors. Mat. Comp. Mod. 13(7), 65–75 (1990)
19. Higle, J.L.: A note on the sensitivity of the EOQ. IIE Trans. 21(3), 294–297 (1989)
20. Mehrez, A., Ben-Arieh, D.: All-unit discounts, multi-item inventory model with stochastic demand, service level constraints and finite horizon. Int. J. of Prod. Res. 29(8), 1615–1628 (1991)
21. Naddor, E.: Sensitivity to distributions in inventory systems. Man. Sci. 24, 1769–1771 (1978)
22. Hebert, J.E., Deckro, F.: A simulation analysis of dynamic inventory policies in a generalized stochastic environment. In: Proc. of the W. Sim. Conf., Washington, DC, pp. 843–847 (December 1977)
23. Benton, W.C.: Safe stock and service levels in periodic review inventory system. J. Opl. Res. Soc. 42(12), 1087–1095 (1991)
24. Lau, H.S., Zaki, A.: The sensitivity of inventory decisions to the shape of lead time demand distribution. IIE Trans. 14, 265–271 (1982)
25. Ziegler, R.: Criteria for measurement of the cost parameters of an economic order quantity. Ph.D. dissertation, Univ. of North Carolina at Chapel Hill (1973)
26. De Castro, E., Tabucanon, M.T., Nagarur, N.N.: A production order quantity model with stochastic demand for a chocolate milk manufacturer. Int. J. Prod. Ec. 49, 145–156 (1997)
27. Persona, A., Battini, D., Manzini, R., Pareschi, A.: Optimal safety stock levels of subassemblies and manufacturing components. Int. J. Prod. Eco. 110, 147–159 (2007)

A Conceptual Model
for Integrating Transport Planning: MRP IV

Josefa Mula, Manuel Díaz-Madroñero, and David Peidro

Research Centre on Production Management and Engineering (CIGIP)
Universitat Politècnica de València, Escuela Politécnica Superior de Alcoy
Plaza Ferrándiz y Carbonell 2, 03801, Alcoy, Alicante, Spain
{fmula,fcodiama,dapeipa}@cigip.upv.es

Abstract. In this article, a conceptual model, called MRP IV, is proposed in order to serve as a reference to develop a new production technology that integrates material planning decisions, production resource capacities and supply chain transport for the purpose of avoiding the suboptimization of these plans which, today, are usually generated sequentially and independently. This article aim is twofold: (1) it identifies the advances and deficiencies in the MRP calculations, mainly based on the dynamic multi-level capacitated lot-sizing problem (MLCLSP); and (2) it proposes a conceptual model, defining the inputs, outputs, modeling and solution approaches, to overcome the deficiencies identified in current MRP systems and act as a baseline to propose resolution models and algorithms required to develop MRP IV as a decision-making system.

Keywords: MRP, integration, production planning, transport planning.

1 Introduction

Nowadays, the MRP (Material Requirement Planning) system, developed by Orlicky [1], continues to be the most widely used production planning system, despite the deficiencies identified in it. The evolutions of the MRP were reflected in the MRP II (Manufacturing Resource Planning) [2] system, which considers productive capacity constraints, MRP III (Money Resource Planning) [3], which introduces the financial function; and the MRP commercial evolution into the ERP (Enterprise Resource Planning) [4], which incorporates all the company functions into a unique decision system through modules whose central nucleus is the MRP. Later ERP systems developments have incorporated new information and communication technologies. Moreover, these have been adapted to the current economic context characterized by business globalization and the offshoring of suppliers by developing other functions such as supply chain management or transport, among others [5]. Original MRP systems were designed in the 70s as push systems in an environment where demand was greater than supply. Subsequently, and to adapt to new manufacturing environments where the supply was greater than demand pull systems appeared such as lean manufacturing and drum-buffer-rope. However, the inadequacy of push-based philosophy to today's environment characterized by high volatility and low demand, and the

J. Frick and B. Laugen (Eds.): APMS 2011, IFIP AICT 384, pp. 54–65, 2012.

limited set of tools for materials planning and inventory control in pull systems, has led to the emergence of a new MRP, called Demand-Driven MRP (DDMRP) [6].

Many works exist in the academic literature that have attempted to overcome some of the deficiencies of traditional MRP such as results optimization, considering uncertainty in certain parameters, inflated lead times, etc. However in both the commercial and academic environments, the MRP and its variants focus on material requirements and on production capacity planning, which are the main disadvantages in supply chains where there is considerable offshoring of raw materials and parts suppliers. In these contexts, transport planning plays a leading role since high costs and logistical constraints usually make the proposed production plans suboptimal, and even infeasible, and manual replanning is a common practice in companies. This work aims to develop a new conceptual model, the MRP IV, which integrates the material, production resource capacities and transport planning (type of transport, form of collection, etc.) decisions in the supply chain to avoid the suboptimization of these plans which, nowadays, are usually generated sequentially and independently.

The rest of the paper is arranged as follows: Section 2 offers a literature review about MRP and production planning problems. Section 3 presents the MRP IV conceptual model. Finally, the last section provides conclusions and directions for further research.

2   Literature Review

In today's competitive environment, organizations need MRP systems to optimize their production planning decisions. Thus according to Yenisey [6], although the earlier MRP formulations were not associated with any form of optimization, aspects such as profit maximization and constraints related to supply, demand or available resources were gradually incorporated to optimize MRP problems. In this sense, the seminal works of Karni [7] and Billington et al. [8] who model MRP problems with mixed integer linear programming can be highlighted. Later, Yenisey [9] presents a flow network with a side constraints approach to optimize material flows in MRP problems. Noori et al. [10] develop a fuzzy multi-objective linear programming model to extend the work proposed by Yenisey [9] which considers the minimization of total costs and time. However, the premise of a completely deterministic scenario does not match the reality of a manufacturing environment. The literature reports different approaches to consider uncertainty in MRP systems, such as simulation [11], [12], stochastic inventory control [13], fuzzy logic [14], fuzzy mathematical programming [15–18], fuzzy programming with resources based on the credibility theory [19] and MRP parameterization [20–22], among others. Other approaches to consider uncertainty in MRP systems can be found in several reviews [23–25].

On the other hand, the importance of the bill of materials (BOM) in MRP systems is reflected in several works that redefine the traditional BOM concept to adapt MRP systems to new manufacturing environments. Chen et al. [26] adjust the traditional MRP approach for the make-to-order environment to consider customization features by generating a BOM for each customized product. Ram et al. [27] propose a flexible BOM to deal with possible shortages when using MRP to plan the requirements of dependent demand items. The requirements stated in the MPS (Master Production Schedule) are met in a timely manner by substituting items for one another should shortages arise. A linear programming model is used to minimize deviation from the default BOM when shortage occurs. Lin et al. [28] develop a single-period, multi-period mathematical programming model to optimize the purchase quantity from suppliers, while they satisfy demand using specific characteristics from the TFT-LCD industry. These specific issues are based on the alternative bill of materials (ABOM), customer preference for ABOM and the purchase quantity ratio.

Standard MRP calculations are based on the dynamic multi-level capacitated lot-sizing problem (MLCLSP). Capacitated lot-sizing problems have attracted the scientific community's attention in recent decades and several literature reviews like [29–31], among others, have been published. Moreover, Buschkühl et al. [32] discuss both different modeling approaches to the optimization of MLCLSP problems and different algorithmic solution approaches by classifying them into five groups: mathematical programming-based, Lagrangian heuristics, decomposition and aggregation approaches, metaheuristics and problem-specific greedy heuristics. Armentano et al. [33] use a branch-and-bound procedure, with a linear programming relaxation based on a network flow formulation. The efficiency of the branch-and-bound method can be increased by reformulating the mathematical model, and by redefining the corresponding decision variables [34–37] and/or by introducing valid inequalities [38–40]. Other solution approaches can be found in the literature such as fix-and-relax heuristics [41], [42], rounding heuristics [43], column generation [44] and Lagrangian relaxation [45], among others. On the other hand, according to Jans and Degraeve [46], several metaheuristics have been developed for extensions of the standard lot sizing problems for which no good special purpose algorithm exists and which are too difficult to solve with commercial integer optimization. Metaheuristic algorithms range from simple local search procedures to complex learning processes which can handle large and complex problems. Chen and Chu [45] develop a heuristic method based on the combination of Lagragian relaxation and local search. At each iteration, a feasible solution of the original problem is constructed from the solution of the relaxed problem. This feasible solution is further improved by a local search that changes the values of two setup variables at each time. Barbarosoglu and Özdamar [47] analyze the performance of a general purpose simulated annealing procedure in solving the dynamic MLCLSP with general product structures. The proposed neighbourhood transition schemes are based on relaxing different types of constraints, each of which defines a different solution space. Moreover, Özdamar and Barbarosoglu [48] propose a solution method by combining the capability of the Lagrangean relaxation to decompose the hard-to-solve problems into smaller subproblems and the intensive search capability of the simulated annealing. Berretta et al. [49] develop a heuristic which integrates simulated annealing components and tabu search for solving MLCLSP with general product structures, setup costs, setup times, and lead times. Karimi et al. [50] propose a tabu search heuristic which starts from an initial feasible solution. The resulting feasible solution is improved by adopting the corresponding set-up and set-up carry-over schedule and re-optimizing variable costs, by solving a minimun-cost network flow problem. Besides, Hung and Chien [51] compare the performance of the tabu search, simulated annealing and genetic algorithms to solve MLCLSP. Xie and Dong [52] propose a heuristic genetic algorithm for these problems in which the presentation technique encodes only the binary variables for the setup patterns but derives other decision variables by making use of the problem-specific knowledge. Moreover, Jung et al. [53] present a genetic algorithm for the integrated production planning problem considering manufacturing partners (suppliers). The proposed genetic algorithm with a unique chromosome structure, chromosome generation method and genetic operators, generates quite good solutions when compared to commercial solvers.

However, despite the development of sophisticated solution methods, according to Lee et al. [54], the majority of lot-sizing models have not considered any production-inventory problem with incorporated transportation activities. Nowadays, the issue of transportation scheduling for shipping products (or delivering orders) by proper shipping modes at the right time becomes significantly important in production (or distribution) management, or for import and export activities. Thus, Lee et al. [54] analyze a dynamic lot-sizing problem which contemplates the order size of multiple products and a single container type simultaneously. The objective of this study is to determine the production lot sizes and the transportation policy that minimize total costs by means of a heuristic algorithm. Garcia-Sabater et al. [55] present an MRP model that successfully integrates delivery and production processes in an automotive supply chain with a just-in-time environment. Moreover, Hwang [56] provides efficient solution procedures to solve lot-sizing problems with integrated production and transportation operations. Concave production costs and stepwise transportation costs are assumed to model the economies of scale in production with the effect of shipment consolidation on transportation. In relation to inbound logistics, Ertogral [57] incorporates transportation costs into a multi-item, lot-sizing problem as a piecewise linear function of the amount transported. A Lagrangean decomposition-based solution procedure is suggested to compare the proposed model in different scenarios. Sancak and Salman [58] propose a multi-item, lot-sizing, mixed-integer mathematical programming approach to determine the number of items to order and how many trucks to use in a stochastic environment for the purpose of minimizing total inventory holding and transportation costs. However, neither case contemplates production planning.

3   MRP IV: A Conceptual Model

Today there is a large number of firms with offshore suppliers. The production planning systems they use do not simultaneously consider aspects relating to the transport of parts and raw materials to their installations. The most habitual procedure is MPS calculation and MRP, used to determine the quantities of each finished good to be produced in a given planning horizon, as well as the requirements of the associated parts and raw materials. Corresponding orders are firmly placed if the quantities to be ordered to suppliers can be transported via an existing transport network. Should the results obtained with MRP be infeasible as regards the transport network, the results obtained with MRP need to be manually amended until they are feasible, or it is necessary to increase the existing transport capacity and to rerun MRP. In this case, transport decisions are based on the commitment between covering demand, available occupation and the inventories of parts and raw materials. Generally in this context, transport planning is done manually with the help of spreadsheets, and is based on planners' experience and personal judgments; this situation generally implies obtaining suboptimum results.

This article proposes a conceptual model, called MRP IV, for production planning which integrates those aspects relating to provisioning transport. For this purpose, MRP IV contemplates various inputs (which could be considered in generic MRP and provisioning transport planning models) that generate different outputs to achieve one objective or several objectives. Figure 1 illustrates the proposed model. The left-hand side of Figure 1 includes the input parameters associated with production planning systems or MRP, while the right-hand side shows those relating to transport decision-making processes. Those parameters which can be used simultaneously for aspects relating to both production and transport planning are presented as elongated rectangles overlapping both areas. The MRP IV inputs, outputs, modelling and solution approaches are described below:

Inputs

1. Planning horizon with an equivalent extension to the suppliers' maximum lead time. The planning horizon is divided into equal periods, for instance, of a daily duration
2. Customer demand of the finished goods to be produced
3. BOM
4. Initial inventory and initial delayed demand of finished goods, parts and raw materials
5. Safety stocks of each finished good, part and raw material
6. The supply lead time of each part and raw material as it is considered null for finished goods. The lead time for parts and raw materials comprises the supplier production time, the transport time and the safety time.
7. Programmed receptions for each part and raw materials
8. Production system function costs. These are variable production costs, inventory holding costs, delayed demand costs, undertime hour costs of productive resources, overtime hour costs of productive resources and subcontracting costs
9. Production capacity of available productive resources
10. Production time. This is the time required to produce each product with the available productive resources
11. Setup time. It represents the capacity lost due to cleaning, machine adjustments, calibration, inspection, change in tooling, etc., when production for a new product starts
12. Production batch size
13. Parts and raw materials dimensions
14. Order lot size of each part and raw material. The quantities to order are multiple integers of this lot size. It may, or may not, coincide with the production lot size because, occasionally, the supplier can arbitrarily fix an order lot size in accordance with its preferences

15. Transport suppliers function costs. These are costs that are fixed per vehicle employed, variable costs according to occupied volume, discounts, costs for using extra transport capacity, costs incurred by urgent deliveries, waiting truck costs, etc.

16. Transport capacity. This corresponds to the capacity of the transport network between the suppliers of parts and raw materials and the manufacturer of finished goods. This transport network is generally stable and is regulated by contracts drawn up between the manufacturer receiving parts and raw materials and the logistics or transport suppliers

17. Shipment modes. Different shipment modes can be considered depending on the order size of parts and raw materials and the suppliers' geographic location. For instance, full-truckload (FTL) for those suppliers with whom large-sized orders are placed; less-than-truckload (LTL) for those suppliers with whom smaller-sized orders are placed; milk-run for those suppliers close by to whom small-sized orders are sent, which are delivered on a vehicle occupied by orders frequently received from several similar suppliers. Shipment modes can also be regulated by means of contracts drawn by with transport suppliers

18. Shipment frequency. This consists in the frequency of parts and raw materials arriving from different suppliers. Frequency of arrival can also be fixed by drawing contracts between the manufacturer of finished goods and its transport suppliers

19. Shipping units. They are required for transporting parts and raw materials; for example, special containers, racks, pallets, etc.

Modelling Approach

Different modelling approaches, such as linear programming, (mixed) integer programming, multiobjective programming, fuzzy programming, stochastic programming or simulation/hybrid models can be considered to develop an analytical model which would represent MRP IV. This model will be composed of several constraints and one or several objectives such as minimizing total production, inventory, delayed demand, overtime, undertime, subcontracting and transport costs.

Solution Approach

Buschkühl et al. [32] identify five groups of solution approaches to solve lot sizing problems:

1. Mathematical programming
2. Lagrangian heuristics
3. Decomposition and aggregation heuristics
4. Metaheuristics
5. Problem-specific greedy heuristics.

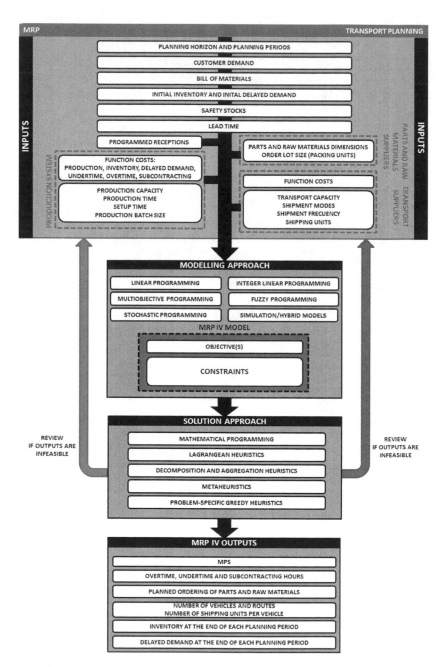

Fig. 1. MRP IV inputs, outputs, objectives, modeling and solution approaches

Outputs

1. MPS, which specifies the quantity to produce of each finished good
2. Overtime and undertime hours of productive resources and subcontracting hours
3. Planned ordering of raw materials and parts, which specifies the quantities to order of each part or raw material to each supplier
4. Number of vehicles and routes and number of shipping units per vehicle. The number of vehicles employed is obtained for each shipping mode, as is the number of shipping units that each vehicle transports. Likewise for the milk-run shipping mode, the route to be followed by each vehicle to reach the manufacturer of finished goods is also determined
5. Inventory at the end of each planning period
6. Delayed demand at the end of each planning period.

After obtaining the outputs for the MRP IV model, their feasibility has to be evaluated. If outputs are infeasible, this may be due to causes relating to the production or transport system design. Therefore when outputs are infeasible, it is necessary to especially examine production and transport capacities, and to adjust them suitably before rerunning the MRP IV. Moreover, if outputs are feasible, it is necessary to economically evaluate the solution obtained by bearing in mind the different costs associated with the model. Although this situation can lead to obtaining a feasible solution for the MRP IV model, truck occupation may diminish and some vehicles have available space, which might involve an inappropriate cost. Therefore, it is necessary to reach a compromise solution that enables better truck occupation and maintains acceptable inventory levels. Similarly, the MRP IV model should include a period that reviews the transport network and the production system so that it can adapt to the various changes taking place in the environment.

4   Conclusions

This paper has reviewed the main advances and deficiencies of MRP systems, one of which is sequential provisioning transport and production planning decision-making processes. In order to address this, we propose a conceptual model, the MRP IV, which acts as a reference to develop a new production technology which integrates transport planning and MRP systems in the same decision-making system. The main inputs, objectives and outputs of the MRP IV model have been identified. A forthcoming work is related to the modeling and solution approaches for the proposed conceptual model, MRP IV.

Acknowledgment. This work has been funded by the Spanish Ministry of Science and Innovation project: 'Production technology based on the feedback from production, transport and unload planning and the redesign of warehouses decisions in the supply chain' (REVOLUTION) (Ref. DPI2010-19977).

References

1. Orlicky, J.: Material Requirements Planning. McGraw-Hill, New York (1975)
2. White, O.W.: MRP II—Unlocking America's Productivity Potential. CBI Publishing, Boston (1981)
3. Schollaert, F.: Money resource planning, MRP-III: the ultimate marriage between business logistics and financial management information systems. Library Albert (1994)
4. Wylie, L.: ERP: A vision of the next-generation MRP II. Computer Integrated Manufacturing 300(339.2), 1–5 (1990)
5. Stadtler, H., Kilger, C.: Supply chain management and advanced planning: concepts, models, software and case studies. Springer, Berlin (2008)
6. Ptak, C., Smith, C.: Orlicky's Material Requirements Planning 3/E. McGraw-Hill Professional (2011)
7. Karni, R.: Integer linear programming formulation of the material requirements planning problem. Journal of Optimization Theory and Applications 35(2), 217–230 (1981)
8. Billington, P.J., McClain, J.O., Thomas, L.J.: Mathematical programming approaches to capacity-constrained MRP systems: review, formulation and problem reduction. Management Science, 1126–1141 (1983)
9. Yenisey, M.M.: A flow-network approach for equilibrium of material requirements planning. International Journal of Production Economics 102(2), 317–332 (2006)
10. Noori, S., Feylizadeh, M.R., Bagherpour, M., Zorriassatine, F., Parkin, R.M.: Optimization of material requirement planning by fuzzy multi-objective linear programming. Proceedings of the Institution of Mechanical Engineers, Part B: Journal of Engineering Manufacture 222(7), 887–900 (2008)
11. Tavakoli-Moghaddam, R., Bagherpour, M., Noora, A.A., Sassani, F.: Application of fuzzy lead time to a material requirement planning system. In: Proceedings of the 8th Conference on 8th WSEAS International Conference on Fuzzy Systems, vol. 8, pp. 208–213 (2007)
12. Sun, L., Heragu, S.S., Chen, L., Spearman, M.L.: Simulation analysis of a multi-item MRP system based on factorial design. In: Proceedings of the 2009 Winter Simulation Conference (WSC), pp. 2107–2114 (2009)
13. Inderfurth, K.: How to protect against demand and yield risks in MRP systems. International Journal of Production Economics 121(2), 474–481 (2009)
14. Barba-Gutiérrez, Y., Adenso-Díaz, B.: Reverse MRP under uncertain and imprecise demand. The International Journal of Advanced Manufacturing Technology 40(3), 413–424 (2009)
15. Mula, J., Poler, R., Garcia, J.P.: MRP with flexible constraints: A fuzzy mathematical programming approach. Fuzzy Sets and Systems 157(1), 74–97 (2006)
16. Mula, J., Poler, R., Garcia-Sabater, J.P.: Material Requirement Planning with fuzzy constraints and fuzzy coefficients. Fuzzy Sets and Systems 158(7), 783–793 (2007)
17. Mula, J., Poler, R., Garcia-Sabater, J.P.: Capacity and material requirement planning modelling by comparing deterministic and fuzzy models. International Journal of Production Research 46(20), 5589–5606 (2008)
18. Mula, J., Poler, R.: Fuzzy Material Requirement Planning. In: Kahraman, C., Yavuz, M. (eds.) Production Engineering and Management under Fuzziness. STUDFUZZ, vol. 252, pp. 39–57. Springer, Heidelberg (2010)

19. Li, T., Lin, P., Sun, G.J., Liu, H.H.: Application of Fuzzy Programming with Recourse in Material Requirement Planning Problem. In: International Conference on Measuring Technology and Mechatronics Automation, ICMTMA 2009, vol. 2, pp. 546–549 (2009)

20. Hnaien, F., Dolgui, A., Ould Louly, M.A.: Planned lead time optimization in material requirement planning environment for multilevel production systems. Journal of Systems Science and Systems Engineering 17(2), 132–155 (2008)

21. Louly, M.A., Dolgui, A., Hnaien, F.: Optimal supply planning in MRP environments for assembly systems with random component procurement times. International Journal of Production Research 46(19), 5441–5467 (2008)

22. Louly, M.A., Dolgui, A.: Optimal time phasing and periodicity for MRP with POQ policy. International Journal of Production Economics 131(1), 76–86 (2011)

23. Mula, J., Poler, R., Garcia-Sabater, J.P., Lario, F.C.: Models for production planning under uncertainty: A review. International Journal of Production Economics 103(1), 271–285 (2006)

24. Dolgui, A., Prodhon, C.: Supply planning under uncertainties in MRP environments: A state of the art. Annual Reviews in Control 31(2), 269–279 (2007)

25. Wazed, M., Ahmed, S., Nukman, Y.: A review of manufacturing resources planning models under different uncertainties: state-of-the-art and future directions (2010)

26. Chen, Y., Miao, W.M., Lin, Z.Q., Chen, G.L.: Adjusting MRP for dynamic differen-tiation of identical items for process customisation. Production Planning and Control 19(6), 616–626 (2008)

27. Ram, B., Naghshineh-Pour, M.R., Yu, X.: Material requirements planning with flexible bills-of-material. International Journal of Production Research 44(2), 399–415 (2006)

28. Lin, J.T., Chen, T.L., Lin, Y.T.: Critical material planning for TFT-LCD production industry. International Journal of Production Economics 122(2), 639–655 (2009)

29. Karimi, B., Fatemi Ghomi, S.M.T., Wilson, J.M.: The capacitated lot sizing problem: a review of models and algorithms. Omega 31(5), 365–378 (2003)

30. Jans, R., Degraeve, Z.: Modeling industrial lot sizing problems: a review. International Journal of Production Research 46(6), 1619–1643 (2008)

31. Quadt, D., Kuhn, H.: Capacitated lot-sizing with extensions: a review. 4OR: A Quarterly Journal of Operations Research 6(1), 61–83 (2008)

32. Buschkühl, L., Sahling, F., Helber, S., Tempelmeier, H.: Dynamic capacitated lot-sizing problems: a classification and review of solution approaches. OR Spectrum 32(2), 231–261 (2010)

33. Armentano, V.A., França, P.M., de Toledo, F.M.B.: A network flow model for the capacitated lot-sizing problem. Omega 27(2), 275–284 (1999)

34. Tempelmeier, H., Helber, S.: A heuristic for dynamic multi-item multi-level capacitated lotsizing for general product structures. European Journal of Operational Research 75(2), 296–311 (1994)

35. Stadtler, H.: Mixed integer programming model formulations for dynamic multi-item mul-ti-level capacitated lotsizing. European Journal of Operational Research 94(3), 561–581 (1996)

36. Stadtler, H.: Reformulations of the shortest route model for dynamic multi-item multi-level capacitated lotsizing. OR Spectrum 19(2), 87–96 (1997)

37. Denizel, M., Altekin, F.T., Süral, H., Stadtler, H.: Equivalence of the LP relaxations of two strong formulations for the capacitated lot-sizing problem with setup times. OR Spectrum 30(4), 773–785 (2008)

38. Belvaux, G., Wolsey, L.A.: Modelling practical lot-sizing problems as mixed-integer programs. Management Science, 993–1007 (2001)
39. Suerie, C.: Modeling of period overlapping setup times. European Journal of Operational Research 174(2), 874–886 (2006)
40. Absi, N., Kedad-Sidhoum, S.: The multi-item capacitated lot-sizing problem with setup times and shortage costs. European Journal of Operational Research 185(3), 1351–1374 (2008)
41. Suerie, C., Stadtler, H.: The capacitated lot-sizing problem with linked lot sizes. Management Science, 1039–1054 (2003)
42. Federgruen, A., Meissner, J., Tzur, M.: Progressive interval heuristics for multi-item capacitated lot sizing problems. Operations Research 55(3), 490 (2007)
43. Akartunalı, K., Miller, A.J.: A heuristic approach for big bucket multi-level production planning problems. European Journal of Operational Research 193(2), 396–411 (2009)
44. Degraeve, Z., Jans, R.: A new Dantzig-Wolfe reformulation and branch-and-price algorithm for the capacitated lot-sizing problem with setup times. Operations Research 55(5), 909–920 (2007)
45. Chen, H., Chu, C.: A Lagrangian relaxation approach for supply chain planning with order/setup costs and capacity constraints. Journal of Systems Science and Systems Engineering 12(1), 98–110 (2003)
46. Jans, R., Degraeve, Z.: Meta-heuristics for dynamic lot sizing: A review and comparison of solution approaches. European Journal of Operational Research 177(3), 1855–1875 (2007)
47. Barbarosoglu, G., Özdamar, L.: Analysis of solution space-dependent performance of simulated annealing: the case of the multi-level capacitated lot sizing problem. Computers & Operations Research 27(9), 895–903 (2000)
48. Özdamar, L., Barbarosoglu, G.: An integrated Lagrangean relaxation-simulated annealing approach to the multi-level multi-item capacitated lot sizing problem. International Journal of Production Economics 68(3), 319–331 (2000)
49. Berretta, R., Franca, P.M., Armentano, V.A.: Metaheuristic approaches for the multi-level resource-constrained lot-sizing problem with setup and lead times. Asia-Pacific Journal of Operational Research 22(2), 261–286 (2005)
50. Karimi, B., Ghomi, S.M.T.F., Wilson, J.M.: A tabu search heuristic for solving the CLSP with backlogging and set-up carry-over. Journal of the Operational Research Society (March 2005)
51. Hung, Y.-F., Chien, K.-L., et al.: A multi-class multi-level capacitated lot sizing model (November 2000)
52. Xie, J., Dong, J.: Heuristic genetic algorithms for general capacitated lot-sizing problems. Computers & Mathematics with Applications 44(1-2), 263–276 (2002)
53. Jung, H., Song, I., Jeong, B.: Genetic algorithm-based integrated production planning considering manufacturing partners. The International Journal of Advanced Manufacturing Technology 32(5), 547–556 (2007)
54. Lee, W.S., Han, J.H., Cho, S.J.: A heuristic algorithm for a multi-product dynamic lot-sizing and shipping problem. International Journal of Production Economics 98(2), 204–214 (2005)
55. Garcia-Sabater, J.P., Maheut, J., Garcia-Sabater, J.J.: A capacitated material require-ments planning model considering delivery constraints: A case study from the automotive industry. In: International Conference on Computers & Industrial Engineering, CIE 2009, pp. 378–383 (2009)

56. Hwang, H.C.: Economic lot-sizing for integrated production and transportation. Operations Research 58(2), 428–444 (2010)
57. Ertogral, K.: Multi-item single source ordering problem with transportation cost: A Lagrangian decomposition approach. European Journal of Operational Research 191(1), 156–165 (2008)
58. Sancak, E., Sibel Salman, F.: Multi-item dynamic lot-sizing with delayed transportation policy. International Journal of Production Economics (2011)

The Generic Materials and Operations Planning (GMOP) Problem Solved Iteratively: A Case Study in Multi-site Context

Julien Maheut[1], Jose P. Garcia-Sabater[2], and Josefa Mula[3]

[1,2] ROGLE – Departamento de Organización de Empresas, Universitat Politècnica de València,
Camino de Vera S/N, 46022 Valencia, Spain
[3] Research Center on Production Management and Engineering (CIGIP),
Universitat Politècnica de València, Plaza Ferràndiz y Carbonell 2, 03801 Alcoy, Spain
{Juma2,jpgarcia,fmula}@upv.es

Abstract. This paper addresses the Generic Materials and Operations Planning (GMOP) problem, a multi-site operations planning problem based on the "stroke" concept. The problem considers a multinational company subject to positive and negative backlogs imposed by using returnable racks that have to be filled by end products and transported to customers, alternative operations (purchase, transformation and transport), different BOM structures given the different operation types (injection operations, assembly operations) performed in the various factories of the supply chain, and capacitated production resources. This paper describes and defines the "stroke" construct that mathematically models the relationships between operations and materials. The mathematical modelling approach is provided, as is a brief description of an operations planning tool that has been implemented. Furthermore, some results obtained in a first-tier level supplier of the automotive industry have been introduced.

1 Introduction

One of the most well-accepted definitions in the literature of supply chain management (SCM) is that SCM is a task that involves integrating organisational units through the supply chain (SC) and coordinates the flow of material, information and financing for the purpose of fulfilling customer demands (Stadtler and Kilger 2002). Dudek (2004) states three SCM objectives: improve customer service; lower the amount of resources to serve customers; improve the SC's competitiveness. Improving competitiveness lies on two main pillars: integrating the SC and coordinating it (Stadtler 2005).

Many managers tend to think that Enterprise Requirement Planning (ERP) systems will solve their planning issues, but despite their name, ERP systems are usually transaction-based systems rather than planning systems. Traditional production planning methods, such as Material Requirements Planning (MRP), consider only availability of materials, and completely ignore factors such as capacity limits and SC configurations (Caridi and Sianesi 1999). In most software, alternative operations can be introduced as data, but the optimisation methods available do not consider them simultaneously.

J. Frick and B. Laugen (Eds.): APMS 2011, IFIP AICT 384, pp. 66–73, 2012.

Moreover, packaging and its planning is a special concern in some industries and, to the best of our knowledge, ERP cannot plan them in any detail. Furthermore, operations planning functions in large companies are usually executed by different organisational units at distinct locations. Generally, excess inventories, poor customer service and insufficient capacity utilisation are due to the lack of coordination between these operations planning functions. Broadly extended ERP systems have led to the emergence of the so-called Advanced Planning and Scheduling Systems (APS), which may be viewed as "add-ons" of the ERP system to plan and optimise the SC. For this support, APS uses optimisation techniques to model and determine the quantities to be produced, stored, transported, and procured by respecting the SC's real constraints (Garcia-Sabater et al. 2012; Günther and Meyr 2009).

The commonest name with which to consider the mathematical model that simultaneously solves the materials and operations planning problem is the Multi-level Capacitated Lot-Sizing Problem (MLCLSP). All in all, most works on the MLCLSP still assume that BOM is made up of assembly products. A series of problem variants based on amending the structure of BOMs may also be found in practice and in the literature. In (Garcia-Sabater et al. 2013), an extensive literature review about the MLCLSP and the need to use the stroke concept in the GMOP problem is introduced. In (Maheut and Garcia-Sabater 2011), a variant of the GMOP problem is introduced, which considers scheduled receptions and the initial stock level. Nevertheless, to the best of our knowledge, a case study about the multi-site, multi-level, capacitated operations planning problem with lead times that simultaneously considers alternative operations (purchasing, transport - replenishment, transshipments and distribution - and production) and returnable packaging has not yet been studied.

This paper proposes an alternative modelling technique that stresses what is known to be done rather than the result of the action (the product). The proposed modelling method is useful given its simplicity and generality. Furthermore, its proposal is feasible since the mathematical programming solving technology has considerably improved in the last 10 years. The model's objective is to minimise total costs by fulfilling lead times and by considering alternative operations and returnable racks. The model has been designed for a first-tier level company of the automotive sector and operations plans are performed daily.

2　The "Stroke" Concept

To consider this proposal, it is necessary to specify some concepts. Products must consider the site where they are stored at and also their packaging. This implies loss of generality, which is compensated by simplified data loading. For example:

- Part item "01" stored in factory A will be called P01@A,
- Rack "01" filled with 12 "02" part items stored in factory B will be called R01#12P02@A,
- Empty rack "01" in factory C will be considered R01#00@C.

Each stroke corresponds to a specific located operation (Maheut et al. 2012). It is characterised by the use of located resources. A set of products is assigned to each stroke, which is consumed when a stroke unit is executed. This set (known as "stroke input") can be null, unitary or multiple, while its coefficients (the Gozinto factor) can be above one unit. A set of SKUs is assigned to each stroke, which is produced when a stroke unit is carried out. This set (called "stroke output") can consist in several different items, a single item or none, and its coefficients (amount of each item produced) can be above one unit (Garcia-Sabater et al. 2013). Moreover, lead times, setup times and costs, time consummation and the costs of performing one stroke unit are assigned to the stroke and not to the result of the operation. Resources are associated with each stroke, but not with the product (or the series of products) obtained.

3   Mathematical Formulation of the GMOP Problem

Due to software limitations, the problem is solved on an iterative basis. Therefore, the GMOP problem was modelled by considering that each stroke level, or each stroke, was independent of the rest. The GMOP model presented herein has been, therefore, slightly modified to represent this new approach. To mathematically formulate the problem, it is necessary to define the nomenclature presented in Table 1. Table 2 contains the notations per parameter and Table 3 presents the notations per variable.

Table 1. Sets and indices

Symbol	Definition
$i \in P$	Index set of products (includes product, packaging and site)
$r \in R$	Index set of resources (includes product and site)
$k \in Z$	Index set of strokes (includes stroke and site)
$j \in J$	Index set of sites
$t = 1,...,T$	Index set of planning periods
Z_r	Set of strokes that are performed in resource $r \left(Z_r \subseteq Z \right)$
FP	Set of end-products $\left(FP \subseteq P \right)$

Table 2. Parameter notation

Symbol	Definition
D_{it}	Demand of product i in period t (due date)
$CA_{i,t}$	Acquired compromised in product i in period t (due date)
X_{it}^{rec}	Planned reception for products i in period t
H_i	Non-negative holding cost per period for storing one unit of product i
Y_i^0	Initial inventory of product i
P_i^F	Benefit of delivering product i
P_i^P	Cost of purchasing product i

Table 2. (*continued*)

Symbol	Definition
TO_{kr}	Capacity of resource r required for performing one stroke k unit (in time units)
TS_{kr}	Capacity required of resource r required for the setup of stroke k (in time units)
K_{rt}	Capacity available of resource r in period t (in space units)
M	A sufficiently large number
CO_k	Cost of performing one stroke k unit
CS_k	Cost of the setup of stroke k
SO_{ik}	Number of product i units produced by performing one stroke k unit (stroke output)
SI_{ik}	Number of product h units required for performing one stroke k unit (stroke input)
$LT(k)$	Lead time of stroke k
B_i	Initial backlog of product i
$C_{i,t}^{\beta+}/C_{i,t}^{\beta-}$	Cost of positive/negative backlogging for one unit of i in period t

Table 3. Variable notation

Symbol	Definition
z_{kt}	Quantity of strokes k to be performed in period t
$y_{it,}$	Inventory of product i at the end of period t
$o_{it,}$	Quantity of products i that it is to be delivered at the end of period t
$q_{it,}$	Quantity of demand of product i at the end of period t that it is not to be delivered
$w_{it,}$	Requirements of product i at the end of period t
δ_{kt}	Binary variable which indicates if stroke k is set up in period t
$\beta_{i,t}^+/\beta_{i,t}^-$	Positive/negative backlog of product i in period t

The GMOP problem adapted for an iterative resolution can be formulated as shown below:

$$Maximize\ F\left(o,z,y,\delta\right)=\sum_{i\in P}\sum_{t=1}^{T}\left(P_{it}^F\cdot o_{it}-P_{it}^C\cdot w_{it}\right)-\sum_{i\in P}\sum_{t=1}^{T}\left(\beta_{i,t}^+\cdot C_{i,t}^{\beta+}+\beta_{i,t}^-\cdot C_{i,t}^{\beta-}+H_{it}\cdot y_{it}\right)-\sum_{k\in Z}\sum_{t=1}^{T}\left(CO_k\cdot z_{kt}+CS_k\cdot\delta_{kt}\right) \quad (1)$$

Subject to

$$o_{it}+q_{i,t}=D_{i,t} \quad i\in P, i\in FP, t=1,...,T \quad (2)$$

$$y_{it}=y_{i,t-1}+X_{it}^{rec}+\sum_{k\in Z}\left(SO_{ik}\cdot z_{k,t-LT(k)}-SI_{ik}\cdot z_{kt}\right)-CA_{i,t}-o_{i,t} \quad i\in P, i\notin FP, t=2,...,T \quad (3)$$

$$\beta_{it}^+-\beta_{it}^-=\beta_{i,t-1}^+-\beta_{i,t-1}^-+X_{it}^{rec}+\sum_{k\in Z}\left(SO_{ik}\cdot z_{k,t-LT(k)}\right)+q_{i,t} \quad i\in FP, t=2,...,T \quad (4)$$

$$y_{i,1} = Y_i^0 + X_{i,1}^{rec} + \sum_{k \in L_0}\left(SO_{ik} \cdot z_{k,1} - SI_{ik} \cdot z_{k,3}\right) - CA_{i,1} - o_{i,1} \quad i \in P, i \notin FP \tag{5}$$

$$\beta_{i,1}^+ - \beta_{i,1}^- = B_i^0 + X_{i,1}^{rec} + \sum_{k \in L_0}\left(SO_{ik} \cdot z_{k,1}\right) + q_{i1} \quad i \in FP \tag{6}$$

$$w_{i,t} = \sum_k \left(SI_{ik} \cdot z_{k,1}\right) - X_{i,t} \quad i \notin FP, t \tag{7}$$

$$z_{kt} - M \cdot \delta_{kt} \le 0 \quad k \in Z, t = 1, \ldots, T \tag{8}$$

$$\sum_{k \in Z_r}\left(TO_k \cdot z_{kt} + TS_k \cdot \delta_{kt}\right) \le K_{rt} \quad r \in R, t = 1, \ldots, T \tag{9}$$

$$z_{kt} \in \mathbb{Z}_0 \quad k \in Z, t = 1, \ldots, T \tag{10}$$

$$o_{i,t}, q_{i,t}, w_{i,t}, y_{it}, \beta_{it}^+, \beta_{it}^- \ge 0 \quad i \in P, t = 1, \ldots, T \tag{11}$$

$$\delta_{kt} \in \{0,1\} \quad k \in Z, t = 1, \ldots, T \tag{12}$$

Objective (1) is to maximise the profit of delivering products minus the sum of the storage costs, the stroke execution costs, the stroke setup costs, and the positive (classical) and negative (serving in advance) backlogging costs. Equation (2) splits external demand into real sales and the demand that is to be delayed. Equations (3) and (5) provide the continuity equation of the inventory levels. The inventory level at the end of a period considers the inventory level at the end of the previous period, planned receptions, product demand, and the products generated and consumed after executing those strokes with their associated lead times. Equations (4) and (6) provide the continuity equation of the backlogging levels. Two types of backlogs exist: the traditional positive backlog (also called Delay at the shipment level or the underdelivery level) and the negative backlog (also called Serve in Advance or the overdelivery level). Given the difference with inventory levels, Backlogging levels are generally applied to the product in the inventory at customers' locations. Backlog levels are the determined inventory levels of products based on demand plans, but they do not have to be physical inventory levels in customer plans. This concept is regularly used in the automotive industry because products are sent in packaging (pallets or racks). In this case, if demand is regular and not proportional to the packaging capacity because of the cost of negative backlogging and the policy of optimising resources, packaging is fulfilled and a negative backlog level is generated. Constraint (9) evaluates the quantity of products i that should be acquired in order to fulfill requirements. Constraint (8) is introduced to know if stroke k is performed in t by, therefore, employing the capacity associated with the setup (setup forcing). Constraint (9) is a capacity constraint that limits the use of resource r in period t by considering both the setup and operations times. Constraints (10), (11) and (12) define the range of variables.

The model is solved iteratively for each product with internal or external demand. The value of o will be converted for the following iterations into a constant CA since it has been accepted. The value of w will be converted into new demand that will be fulfilled in subsequent iterations.

4   Case Study

This model is implemented to solve the problem faced by a company that manufactures plastic products from two factories located in Spain and which sells the product in this country. Production management develops a 3-month operations plan by considering the inventory level, resources capacity, routes and packaging availability to fulfill demand.

A specific operations planning tool has been deployed by the ROGLE research Group. The development process of the information system has been carried out completely. The system not only includes the model presented herein, but also other features related with SC activities, like Demand Planning or Scheduling tasks. The software runs beyond the official ERP system. To obtain data from it and to generate a parallel database that stores official company data and the rest of parameters that need to be used, specific connections were created using XML files. Users interact with the software by using standard browsers (to activate and input data) and spreadsheets (to analyse and use the results).

The operations plan consists in listing those operations with quantities to be performed with the different resources in the various factories for each time period of the horizon in order to serve customers in terms of time and quantity. Basically, operations are:

- Purchase operations, which determine the amount of raw material (plastic powder) to be purchased in each period by considering different lot sizes.
- The raw material is injected into a press injection machine and different products are obtained depending on the mould used.
- After injecting the obtained products, they are assembled on an assembly line to obtain the end products.
- End products must be stored in filled returnable racks and are transported to the customer's site.

Figure 1 displays a sharp drop in backlog levels. Throughout the horizon, a negative backlog is maintained because customers force the company to maintain a safety backlog level. Thanks to the operations planning tools, the company has been able to cut its overdelivery costs, while demand levels remain constant. In fact, this reduction might be considered the effect of simply applying the MRP concept.

With the software, we solved the GMOP problem by employing LP Solve IDE. We tested performance in a full-sized case study problem with seven different factories with approximately 500 end products, 30 resources and more than 700 different operations for distinct instances. The results show an average running time of 6 hours, for instance using a Pentium IV 1.22 GHz processor, 2 GB RAM and Windows XP as the OS.

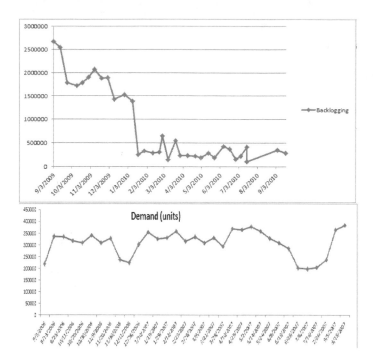

Fig. 1. Demand and Backlog levels

5   Conclusions

A form of modelling the relationship between operations and the materials required to manufacture a product has been considered. This way of defining the relationships between operations and materials suggests a compact mathematical programming model to plan operations in an SC. Apart from capacity constraints, this GMOP model also takes into account direct and reverse BOMs, multi-site, alternative operations by considering packaging, and briefly introduces one operations planning tool designed and used by one multinational company at the first-tier level of the automotive industry.

Two important research lines for the near future include the design of specific heuristics for the problem considered herein, and the incorporation of the central stroke concept for modelling and solving the distributed problems. The incorporation of variants such as uncertainty (if it is stochastic or uses fuzzy methods) is another future research line.

Acknowlegments. The work described in this paper has been supported by the "CORSARI MAGIC DPI2010-18243" project from the Spanish Ministry of Science and Innovation within the Programme entitled "Proyectos de Investigación Fundamental No Orientada". Julien Maheut holds a VALi+d grant funded by the Generalitad Valenciana (Regional Valencian Government), Spain (Ref. ACIF/2010/222).

References

Caridi, M., Sianesi, A.: Trends in planning and control systems: APS - ERP Integration. In: Mertins, K., Krause, O., Schallock, B. (eds.) Global Production Management. Kluwer Academic Publisher (1999)

Dudek, G.: Collaborative planning in supply chains. A negotiation-based approach. Springer, Berlin (2004)

Garcia-Sabater, J.P., Maheut, J., Garcia-Sabater, J.J.: A two-stage sequential planning scheme for integrated operations planning and scheduling system using MILP: the case of an engine assembler. Flexible Services and Manufacturing Journal 24, 171–209 (2012)

Garcia-Sabater, J.P., Maheut, J., Marin-Garcia, J.A.: A new formulation technique to model Materials and Operations Planning: the Generic Materials and Operations Planning (GMOP) Problem. European J. Industrial Engineering 7 (in press, 2013)

Günther, H.O., Meyr, H.: Supply chain planning and Advanced Planning Systems. OR Spectrum 31, 1–3 (2009)

Maheut, J., Garcia-Sabater, J.P.: La Matriz de Operaciones y Materiales y la Matriz de Operaciones y Recursos, un nuevo enfoque para resolver el problema GMOP basado en el concepto del Stroke. Dirección y Organización 45, 46–57 (2011)

Maheut, J., Garcia-Sabater, J.P., Mula, J.: A supply Chain Operations Lot-Sizing and Scheduling Model with Alternative Operations. In: Sethi, S.P., Bogataj, M., Ros-McDonnell, L. (eds.) Proceedings of Industrial Engineering: Innovative Networks, 5th International Conference on Industrial Engineering and Industrial Management, CIO 2011, Cartagena, Spain. ch. 35, Part 5, pp. 309–316. Springer, London (2011), doi:10.1007/978-1-4471-2321-73_5

Stadtler, H.: Supply chain management and advanced planning–basics, overview and challenges. European Journal of Operational Research 163, 575–588 (2005)

Stadtler, H., Kilger, C.: Supply Chain Management and Advanced Planning: Concepts, Models, Software and Case Studies. Springer (2002)

Two Distinct Theories of Production:
Lean and Toyota Management System

Rikke V. Matthiesen

Aalborg University, Center for Industrial Production,
Fibigerstræde 16, 9220 Aalborg, Denmark
rikkevm@production.aau.dk

Abstract. The paper analyses differences between "lean" and its sister concept "Toyota management system (TMS)" by drawing out deep-rooted theories of production within these two streams of literature. The paper argues that such deep-rooted beliefs should be the first target for organizational transformation as these beliefs provide an important contextual layer for any attempts to transfer organizational practices from one organization to another. Examples of implications in relation to translation are sketched out.

Keywords: Lean, TPS/TMS, translation theory, production philosophy.

1   Introduction

The literature on failed transition efforts inspired by Japanese concepts is abundant. Some writers have pointed to aspects of organizational environment, managerial behavior and beliefs, or leadership qualities in order to explain the performance and dynamic capabilities of Toyota. It appears from other analyses however, that lean evades precise definition and communication. Hines et al [1] find that the literature on lean is continuously expanding its focus in terms of scope of application in the supply chain. Liker et al [2] suggest that any core practices of Japanese management systems that is attempted transferred, will need to be integrated with systems and practices in a range of contextual layers in highly context specific ways. In line with this proposition, the expansion of the lean concept [1] may be interpreted as a matter of addressing ever more aspects of Toyota's managerial system in the lean literature.

Uncertainty regarding complicated interactions between various system aspects [2] has resulted in attempts to engage in perfect/complete practice adoption. The underlying assumption is that relevant contextual ties affecting core practices can be addressed if a wide set of peripheral practices are also implemented. This approach is supported by some research, see e.g. [3]. However, there are several risks involved in this approach, and conceptually, it may be neither feasible nor desirable. Several sources acknowledge that Toyota applies an integrated manufacturing and management system. In a sketch of a holistic model of such system, also product features may be included [4]. This illustrates the *span* of TPS. At the same time it has been suggested that TPS may establish a carefully designed *configuration* of job

J. Frick and B. Laugen (Eds.): APMS 2011, IFIP AICT 384, pp. 74–81, 2012.

characteristics that lead to worker motivation and positive employee outcomes required to operate other aspects of TPS [5]. In combination, these sources emphasize that TPS is not a discrete set of practices, a system perspective may be more appropriate. However, how to codify and transfer a system from one context to another?

2   Theoretical Background

The current approach found in lean literature tends to isolate sets of practices and present these as representative of the entire system. This approach falls in the category of analytical reduction; assuming the whole can be studied by studying the characteristics of the pieces. Such approach may be helpful in understanding how different practices work. But it is not helpful as the basis for organizational transformation. Any practice may in its implementation and use be distorted to reproduce former managerial assumptions [6] and they may be selected and/or enacted so that unfamiliar ideas are not adopted [7]. So while TPS *may* be conceptualized as a system of practices, organizational transformation on the other hand cannot be conceptualized as practice adoption. Selective practice adoption may not lead to the context specific configurations required to obtain the desired systems effects.

2.1   Concept Driven Change and Organizational Transformation

Gustavsen et al [8] describe the Japanese inspired change efforts as *"concept driven"* and characterize this type of change as widely communication driven. With communication as the change driver, translation theories show their relevance. Within translation theory, Røvik [9] describes the process of adopting managerial concepts as that of interpreting practices. In this process, practices may undergo considerable transformation either purposefully or unintended as referred to above. Therefore, as argued above, organizational transformation inspired by Toyota should not be seen as a matter of decontextualizing and transferring *practices* from one system to another. Instead, there is a need for re-conceptualizing *content and context*.

2.2   Design Principles as a Contextual Layer

Traditionally, contextual layers have been thought of as related to physical and institutional scope such as e.g. wider organizational practices [2], laws and regulations, or cultural traits [9]. Spear however, suggests that TPS practices should be considered *artefacts of a certain set of system design principles* applied within Toyota [10]. Within production and operations management, such system design principles could be seen as a more subject-relevant *contextual layer* influencing how production and operations practices are identified, captured, transferred, and managed across organizations. This implies that organizational transformation inspired by Toyota should be viewed as a matter of transferring concepts and design principles in use from one organization to another. At present, the literature on TPS production techniques (lean literature) function as one of two contexts for our understanding of Toyota.

Another context is the literature on organizational aspects within TMS and Japanese management systems. Unfortunately these two streams are poorly integrated. The aim of this paper is to identify the sets of deep-rooted beliefs that these streams of literature explicitly or implicitly represent in order to facilitate future integration.

2.3   Theories of Production as the Underlying Context

The objectives of the paper call for a framework that provides sufficient level of abstraction to handle the diverse perspectives or traditions. The paper proposes that such framework may be found in the work by Koskela [11] who proposes to address production theories at three levels:

1. A conceptualization of production.
2. Universal laws and causal relations that would apply under the specific conceptualization of production.
3. Design, control and improvement principles that follow from these causal relations.

Using this theoretical framework, Koskela identifies the deep-rooted beliefs held within three different production theories, among these the production theory that prevailed in the West before the strong orientation towards Japanese manufacturing as well as lean. This is detailed below. Using this framework, design principles as identified by Spear [10] are positioned as stemming from more fundamental beliefs about production. In order to identify the overarching conceptualization of production within TMS that matches these system design principles, a review of a narrow set of writings on TMS is conducted. First the application of the framework on lean literature will be detailed.

3   Theories of Lean Production

Koskela [11] describes the production theory that previously prevailed in the West as a *transformation perspective*. In this perspective, production is seen as a set of resource consuming transformation activities (cost centers) that should be optimized in terms of input/output. It is assumed within this perspective, that the entire transformation process can be subdivided into sub-processes which are also transformation processes and that the resources put into the set of individual transformation activities determine the overall cost of an item. I.e. sub-processes are considered to be independent.

Koskela characterizes Japanese manufacturing as embedding a *flow perspective*. In this perspective, time, not only as a dimension for coordination, but also as a valuable resource, is introduced into production theory. The notion of time as a resource allows us to see production as a coordinated flow of materials (level 1 in a production theory). This is a conceptualization of production distinct from the former Western conceptualization. It establishes queuing analysis as the set of governing laws (level 2 in a production theory). These laws establish the link between variability and deteriorated performance in terms of WIP levels, lead times, variable process times, and less than optimal capacity utilization [12]. Hopp & Spearman [12] suggest that lean production is aimed at minimizing the cost of buffering variability which can be achieved by a combination of intelligent buffer switching, use of flexible resources, and variability reduction (level 3 in a production theory). Understanding these fundamental design, control and improvement principles, a wide range of lean tools and techniques can be argued for theoretically instead of dogmatically.

4   Theories of Production within TMS

Koskela points out that he presents *"a 'pure' production theory [which] focuses just on the act of production. It does not deal with such issues as what is the nature of machines or humans as workers or how production should be divided among individuals (the problem of organizing)."* (p28)[11]. However, with a "pure production theory" as a starting point, the role of the wider organization including HR may easily be reduced to that of providing conditions favorable to smooth production. This includes the emphasis on HRM practices for ensuring employee motivation and worker flexibility found in previous lean literature. Broader issues of organizing are precisely the concern of literature on TMS. However, as indicated above, a theory of production within TMS is missing. In the following, work by de Treville and by Spear is reviewed in order to establish requirements for a theory of production within TMS.

In her PhD thesis [13], de Treville investigated JIT implementations and developed a typology of JIT systems as combinations of JIT flow control and either of the two elements: Flexible resources for improved line balance, and/or learning through disruptions occurring at less than optimal buffer levels. She argued that the application of JIT flow control alone would not lead to the ideal rate of learning (process improvement). She also argued that disruption as means for learning should primarily be applied in situations where production inefficiencies could not be found analytically. This implies situations in which queuing analyses may explain relationships between variability and deteriorated throughput rates but will not suffice to identify leverage points in the system. In her analysis of a set of JIT implementation cases, she found that learning through forced disruptions needs to be carefully managed. Otherwise this practice will lead to unnecessary productivity losses which will stress organizations that, in line with the transformation perspective, have been used to keeping all resources busy at all times and fail to see these disruptions as valuable sources of information. In [5] she furthermore position respect for people, the establishment of good job characteristics and motivation as an important *subsystem* of TPS in line with lean material flow. In regards to the establishment of a theory of production within TMS the key take aways from this work may be suggested to be:

- Proper operation of JIT requires a willingness to invest in learning by exchanging short term productivity for information in order to obtain long term productivity gains. *"All other aspects of JIT can be supported using traditional arguments"* (p1-16)[13].
- Idle workers may be seen as a resource rather than an issue. Cross training for improved line balance may also be considered a type of learning that can arise

from buffer removal. [13]. I.e. there are multiple ways of building up organizational resources associated with JIT practices.

- Using disruptions for learning requires careful management of improvement activities and buffers to avoid unnecessary productivity losses and organizational stress [13].
- JIT is constituted not of *one* system per plant or material flow but of one system between each two production groups. *"A separate decision as to the "best" type of JIT must be made for every intermediate buffer."* (p4-25)[13]. I.e. the application of JIT systems require significant amounts of context specific design choices.
- Employee motivation and respect are important subsystems of TPS. Worker motivation in a lean environment using job standards is especially dependent on the experience of skill variety and responsible autonomy [5]. I.e. application of lean production practices requires careful application of HR practices.

In the following, work by Spear [14, 10, 15] is reviewed. Spear & Bowen [14] describe Toyota as a community of scientists conducting scientific experiments. Spear [10] argues that constant application of rules-in-use (specify, build in tests and improve) to system design constitute meta routines that create *"highly situated learning that is both broadly distributed"* (p2) and where *"learning ... occurs through frequent practice that allows for repeated failure"* (p23) [10]. Spear [15] state that *"The point of process improvement is to improve the participants' process-improvement capabilities by coaching them as they try to improve the process."* (ibid p218). Toyota furthermore takes significant care to extract and disseminate learning from this process [15]. Engagement in Toyota style process improvement is thus a means for improving individual processes as well as a means for accumulating organizational resources in terms of individual skills for process improvement and in terms of widely distributed deep process and design knowledge. With these by-products of process improvement, Spear reverses the roles of organization and production: *"The factory was not only a place to produce physical products, it was also a place to learn how to produce those products and [...] keep learning how to produce those products."* (p15)[15]. In regards to the establishment of a theory of production within TMS, the following should be emphasized:

- System design rules that work to reduce variability combined with strict specification allows for detection of and learning about process inefficiencies. [14]
- Production may be thought of as repetitive activities that through permutations provide learning opportunities for the organization. [15]
- Learning opportunities should be exploited to create better process designs and build resources in terms of process improvement skills in the individual, and in terms of accumulated process knowledge. [15]
- The organization not only operates production but also continuously *redesigns* production. Highly situated learning [10] implies highly situated design which requires design knowledge and skills in even the smallest units: The work teams, team leaders etc.

5   Synthesis

Based on the above, three different theories of production can be sketched. A traditional Western *transformation perspective* offered by Koskela [11]. A lean production philosophy oriented towards *flow* offered by Koskela [11] and Hopp & Spearman [12] in line with industrial engineering reasoning. And a *theory of production within TMS*, which accommodates for a preference for learning and similar resource based concerns:

1. Production may be conceptualized as a stream of repetitive activities linked through material and information flows, which creates an arena for the organization's continued learning and design efforts.
2. The amount of information that can be extracted from the engagement in production activities depends on the extent to which activities are prespecified, production groups are linked in dedicated flows, relevant buffers are kept small enough for production inefficiencies to trigger disruptions and motivate improvement, as well as employee skills for designing and analyzing production.
3. Design, control and improvement principles should comply with the short term goal of optimizing individual processes in line with the lean production philosophy and with the long term goal of maximizing organizational capabilities for process design.

6   Implications

These three different theories of production may be regarded as different *contexts* for the design and management of various subsystems of production. This is exemplified in the following with a focus on HRM as a subsystem.

A transformation perspective may foster a view of labor as *cost* similar to other resources consumed in the transformation activities. In the extreme, the worker may be thought of as an acquired, temporary resource intended for certain production tasks. Training can extend the skills of the worker and may be a necessary investment required to make full use of the resource. However, there will be a balance between cost of training and process requirements. It follows that training is best invested in skills required for the operation of a limited number of production activities.

In a lean production philosophy, training may be more widely engaged in as multi skilling is a means for balancing production lines. The requirements for such multi skilling changes as the line is improved towards reduced variability. If the lean setup is established through the use of "lean tools", additional training may be required to equip the worker to operate these curious tools (kanbans, SOPs etc). The corresponding system specific knowledge in traditional operations may be tacit (who to contact in case of problems, in which cases is it considered appropriate to contact someone etc) and may not necessarily be accommodated for in the estimation of required training periods. In addition to undertaking work in a prespecified way to keep variability low, the lean production worker may also be engaged in the role as informant: He may be expected to signal process inefficiencies and share information on improvement opportunities. This additional role is not strictly necessary to the operation of a lean production setup but it may be applied as a means for reducing variability.

The TMS inspired theory of production accommodates for a quite different role for the worker. In this philosophy, the skills and knowledge of the worker is not only related to the role as producer and the worker's role in process improvement is not restricted to that of informant. Instead, she may be considered the *co-designer* of practices that simultaneously create lean processes and facilitate further experimentation and learning. In this process, she is also a learner as she improves her skills for undertaking this role and paradoxically also reduces the need for these skills in the specific production activity as it is gradually being stabilized and codified. Within Toyota, this paradox is resolved through the promise of a more transient role for the employee as indicated in several writings on TPS HRM practices. E.g. workers may be promised – if not life term employment then at least corporate commitment to long term employment [16], the most competent workers may be deliberately idled and eventually moved to other activities requiring improvement work [13] and team leader positions may be filled from within [17]. Such transient role also works to offset the larger investments in skill development as does the more general nature of these skills compared to the process specific skills emphasized under the transformation perspective.

This proposal for a TMS inspired theory of production may be applied in the attempt to discriminate between practices that are modeled over such theory-in-use versus practices that are modeled over alternative theories of production. Thereby research on TMS inspired organizational transformation may be improved. Presently this research suffer a severe limitation as only an isomorphic adoption of either lean practice or discourse are considered real exemplars of Toyota inspired transformation [18].

7   Conclusions

The paper suggests viewing managerial concepts as the content of organizational transformation, which then becomes a matter of adapting practices to match these concepts rather than that of adopting practices and discourse found in literature. Through the notion of "theories of production" a framework that encompasses and highlights differences between an industrial engineering perspective on Toyota (lean) and organizational theorists' perspectives on Toyota management system is developed. The paper contributes with a theory of production within TMS that is contrasted to both a traditional Western theory of production as well as an industrial engineering theory of Japanese production known as lean production. This proposed theory of production within TMS conceptualizes production as a unique arena for learning and thereby points out a bidirectional link between production and wider organization.

References

1. Hines, P., Holwe, M., Rich, N.: Learning to evolve - A review of contemporary lean thinking. International Journal of Operations & Production Management 24, 994–1011 (2004)
2. Liker, J.K., Fruin, W.M., Adler, P.S.: Bringing Japanese Management Systems to the United States. In: Liker, J.K., Fruin, W.M., Adler, P.S. (eds.) Remade in America; Transplanting and Transforming Japanese Management Systems, Oxford University Press, New York (1999)

3. Shah, R., Ward, P.T.: Lean manufacturing: context, practice bundles, and performance. Journal of Operations Management 21, 129–149 (2003)
4. Chan, J.S., Samson, D.A., Sohal, A.S.: An Integrative Model of Japanese Manufacturing Techniques. International Journal of Operations & Production Management 10, 37–56 (1990)
5. de Treville, S., Antonakis, J.: Could lean production job design be intrinsically motivating? Contextual, configurational, and levels-of-analysis issues. Journal of Operations Management 24, 99–123 (2006)
6. Lozeau, D., Langley, A., Denis, J.-L.: The corruption of managerial techniques by organizations. Human Relations 55, 537–564 (2002)
7. Spencer, B.: Models of organization and total quality management: A comparison and critical evaluation. The Academy of Management Review 19, 446–471 (1994)
8. Gustavsen, B., Hofmaier, B., Wikman, A., Philips, M.E.: Concept-driven Development and the Organization of the Process of Change: An Evaluation of the Swedish Work Life Fund. John Benjamins Publishing Company (1996)
9. Røvik, K.A.: Trender og translasjoner: ideer som former det 21. århundrets organisasjon. Universitetsforlaget, Oslo (2007)
10. Spear, S.J.: Just-in-Time in practice at Toyota: Rules-in-Use for building selfdiagnostic, adaptive work-systems. Working paper 02-043, Harvard Business School (2002)
11. Koskela, L.: An exploration towards a production theory and its application to construction. Doctoral dissertation, Helsinki University of Technology (2000)
12. Hopp, W.J., Spearman, M.L.: Factory Physics: Foundations of Manufacturing Management. McGraw-Hill, New York (2000)
13. de Treville, S.: Disruption, learning, and system improvement in just-in-time manufacturing. Doctoral dissertation, Harvard University (1987)
14. Spear, S., Bowen, H.K.: Decoding the DNA of the Toyota Production System. Harvard Business Review 77, 97–106 (1999)
15. Spear, S.J.: The High Velocity Edge, How market leaders leverage operational excellence to beat the competition. McGraw-Hill, New York (2009)
16. Pil, F.K., MacDuffie, J.P.: Transferring Competitive Advantage Across Borders. A Study of Japanese Auto Transplants in North America. In: Liker, J.K., Fruin, W.M., Adler, P.S. (eds.) Remade in America; Transplanting and Transforming Japanese Management Systems, Oxford University Press, New York (1999)
17. Adler, P.S.: Hybridization, Human Resource Management at Two Toyota Transplants. Ibid
18. Pettersen, J.: Translating Lean Production, From Managerial Discourse to Organizational Practice. Doctoral dissertantion, Linköping University (2009)

Order Quantity Distributions in Make-to-Order Manufacturing: At What Level of Aggregation Do They Respect Standard Assumptions?

Poul Svante Eriksen[1] and Peter Nielsen[2,*]

[1] Department of Mathematical Sciences, Aalborg University, Denmark
[2] Department of Mechanical and Manufacturing Engineering,
Aalborg University, Denmark,
Fibigerstraede 16, 9220 Aalborg Oest
peter@m-tech.aau.dk

Abstract. This paper presents both an analytical and a numerical investigation into the order quantities received by a company in the form of customer orders. A discussion of assumptions regarding the behavior of demand in the form of customer orders from various perspectives within manufacturing planning and control with a special emphasis on the make-to-order environment is presented. A methodological framework for analyzing the behavior of orders and investigate the validity of the assumptions is given. Furthermore, an analytical approach to identify the horizon needed for aggregating orders to achieve a stable demand is developed and tested on data from a real case.

Keywords: Poison process, aggregate demand, order sizes, planning horizon.

1 Introduction

Companies are in the business of satisfying customer demands in the form of customer orders. This paper focuses on the operational characteristics of ordering behavior in the form of demand and discusses the underlying assumptions within a number of fields. These characteristics include volume per planning period (demand rate – often disaggregated to several time horizons and described as a distribution of stochastic variables), accumulation of demand over the planning period, the number of orders per product per planning period and the standard order quantities for each product. The characteristics of the make-to-order manufacturing are depicted by Hendry and Kingsman [9] and Marucheck and McClelland [10]:

- resources are multi-task machinery and flexible workforce – a large number of possible end items within a product line,
- product lead time is vital for customer satisfaction and agreed with customer before production commences,

---

* Corresponding author.

J. Frick and B. Laugen (Eds.): APMS 2011, IFIP AICT 384, pp. 82–90, 2012.

- capacity planning is based on receipt of customer orders and cannot be planned for in advance,
- demand is volatile and can rarely be predicted – a small volume and high degree of demand variability both in quantity and product mix.

This paper focuses specifically on analyzing the distributions of customer orders, the transformation of these into demand rates and presents an analytical model to calculate the aggregation horizon necessary to ensure a stable planning environment. In this context a stable planning environment is defined as having a demand pattern approximately symmetrically distributed with a given (low) Coefficient of Variance (CV) (variance of distribution divided by mean). The presented model can be used to estimate the planning horizon (i.e. length of planning periods) necessary to ensure a stable demand rate in a given situation.

The remainder of the paper is structured as follows. First, a discussion of assumptions regarding demand in the form of customer orders and their behavior is presented. Second, a methodological framework for analyzing the behavior of orders is given. Third, an analytical approach to identify the horizon needed for aggregating orders to achieve a stable demand is developed. Fourth, a case study application of the presented framework. Finally conclusions and further research are presented.

2   Background, Implications and Approach to Analysis

Manufacturing Planning & Control involves coordinating any number of decisions [19]. Several of these are directly related to the customer orders and their characteristics. The demand experienced by companies comes in the form of customer orders that may consist of multiple order lines. Each order (line) will contain the following parameters relevant in this context: desired due date, product identification and quantity. These parameters are then transformed into various forms depending on the usage. Within line balancing customer orders are likewise transformed into demand rates (also termed release or launch rates [2]) for individual products and product mix [13] for a given line. Likewise within lot-sizing demand rates are typically considered deterministic or to stem from a stationary stochastic process [4], despite the fact that demand rates are composed of individual (in)dependent customer orders.

Regardless of application area, the general approach is to aggregate individual customer orders into demand rates for both individual products and product families and use e.g. MRP or MRPII to generate dependent demand and resource requirements [16], [19]. The aggregation can be conducted along a number of dimensions [22] (typically time and products [21]) until a stabilized customer ordering behavior is identified. To facilitate the aggregation and disaggregation of plans a number of assumptions are made regarding the orders handled by the system [1]. These assumptions can be abbreviated to assuming a one-to-one relationship in aggregation and disaggregation [7], [8]. As a result order quantities and the number of orders per period are assumed to be constant. This facilitates calculating time needed for changeovers and the number of changeovers needed per planning period (e.g. Silver et al. [16]). If this is not the case, the disaggregation of aggregate plans may result in suboptimal or even infeasible disaggregate plans. In reality this assumption can be relaxed if the order quantities come from i.i.d. symmetrical distributions (with a low CV; variance compared to the mean of the distribution). A chronological list of order lines for delivery can e.g. expect to exhibit non-stationary behavior. A typical manifestation of this will be if an order contains order lines for more than one product from the same product family. This becomes critical if the order lines are related in a manner so that their demand will be aggregated within the planning environment. On an individual product level assuming independently distributed order quantities is more reasonable, especially if many customers purchase the same products. For all areas a stabilized behavior is expected as demand is aggregated [6], [7], [17]. The critical aspect is here if the customer ordering behavior allows for a simple linear aggregation along product family or time dimensions? Furthermore, if linear relationships in aggregation are an oversimplification of the issue, what should be done instead? The research presented in this paper addresses the assumptions used to aggregate demand information for various planning purposes. The aim is first to design a method for robust estimation of the behavior of order quantities, i.e. determine whether they can be assumed to be independently distributed from a symmetrical distribution. The second step is to develop a mathematical model that describes the CV for the order quantities, under the assumption that the order quantities can stem from an arbitrary distribution and are dependently distributed. First tests of symmetrical distribution of order quantities are applied. If these are negative, they are considered to stem from a skewed distribution and are therefore also assumed to be non-constant. In order to investigate asymmetry of order quantity distributions, in this paper the following three different statistical tests will be applied:

— The MGG-test presented in Miao et al. [11]
— The CM-test described in Cabilio and Masaro [5]
— The Mira-test developed by Mira [12]

These tests are implemented in the R-package lawstat [15]. From the literature review it is known that the individual orders for each product can be considered to be independently distributed, while the aggregate behavior cannot necessarily be assumed to abide by the same behavior. To test for independence the autocorrelation function is used [3]. In the current work only one period lag is considered. Having first established whether the order quantities can be considered to stem from a symmetrical distribution, the next step is to investigate how to stabilize the demand behavior experienced in the form of customer orders. In practices this means determining the horizon needed (i.e. number of orders) to aggregate. The model should therefore be able to determine the number of consecutive orders to aggregate to achieve a distribution with a satisfactory behavior. In this case a symmetrical distribution, using the central limit theorem [20], with a low CV is considered satisfactory. The more aggregate the planning level, the lower CV is desired.

3   Analytical Modeling of the Aggregation Horizon

To formulate the models, the orders for the whole product family are assumed to come from an unbroken time series. We consider a time period of length T, where the number $N(T)$ of orders has mean λT and standard deviation $\tau\sqrt{T}$. In case of a Poisson process we have $\tau^2 = \lambda$. To describe the volatility of the order quantities the coefficient of variance (CV) is used (e.g. discussed in Nielsen and Eriksen [13] and used in Tsubone and Furuta [18]). The size Q of an order is assumed to have mean μ and standard deviation σ, i.e. Q has coefficient of variation $CV(Q) = \frac{\sigma}{\mu}$.

Furthermore, the autocorrelation function of successive order quantities is assumed to be zero except for lag one. The autocorrelation of lag one is denoted ρ. Let $Q_1, ..., Q_{N(T)}$ be the successive orders in the period. The aggregated order quantity is $= \sum_{i=1}^{N(T)} Q_i$, which has mean conditional on $N(T)$ given by $E\big(AQ|N(T)\big) = \mu N(T)$ and variance given by: $Var(AQ|N(T)) = \sigma^2(N(T) + 2\rho(N(T) - 1)) \approx \sigma^2(1 + 2\rho)N(T)$ under the assumption that N(T) is sufficiently large. For manufacturing environments with a low number of orders, other methods than aggregating orders are used to estimate demand. The mean of AQ is then given by $E(AQ) = \mu\lambda T$, whereas the variance is (approximated by):

$$Var(AQ) = E(Var(AQ|N(T)) + Var(E(AQ|N(T))) = \sigma^2(1 + 2\rho)\lambda T + \mu^2\tau^2 T$$

This leaves us with a coefficient of variation given by

$$CV(AQ) = \frac{\sqrt{\sigma^2(1 + 2\rho)\lambda + \mu^2\tau^2}}{\mu\lambda\sqrt{T}}$$

Aiming at a time horizon yielding a coefficient of variation given by CV_0, this is obtained when

$$T = \frac{\sigma^2(1 + 2\rho)\lambda + \mu^2\tau^2}{(\mu\lambda CV_0)^2} = \frac{CV(Q)^2(1 + 2\rho)\lambda + \tau^2}{(\lambda CV_0)^2}$$

Expressed in terms of the mean number of orders we obtain

$$E(N(T)) = \frac{CV(Q)^2(1 + 2\rho)\lambda + \tau^2}{\lambda(CV_0)^2}$$

and in case of a Poisson process this simplifies to:

$$E(N(T)) = \frac{CV(Q)^2(1 + 2\rho) + 1}{(CV_0)^2}$$

The conclusion is that for any given distribution of Q, for any given company and period it is (given sufficient observations) possible to estimate CV(Q) and ρ (only included if significant autocorrelation is present). From this it is then possible to decide upon a desired stability for the system in the form of CV_0 and calculate the number of order (E(N(T))) necessary to aggregate over to achieve this stability.

4   A Case Study Application

To illustrate the analysis a test using a set of orders for a product family with variables ItemID, Quantity and DeliveryDate covering a 6 year period was conducted in the statistical analysis tool R [15]. The total number of orders was 54,243 and 2,160 unique products. The data was arranged based on due date, and subsequently sequenced after creation time. This way order lines from the same order would be sequenced to facilitate an investigation of independence on the aggregate set.

First, the distribution of Quantity for the whole product family regardless of ItemID is considered. 99.1% of the order quantities were below 61 and the histogram of these is shown in fig. 1. The overall picture shows an exponential decay with isolated peaks at multiples of 10 and to some extend multiples of 5 and 12. All three tests of symmetry were highly significant with p-values below 10^{-15}. The estimated coefficient of variation was $CV(Q) = 1.2$, likewise indicating a very skew distribution.

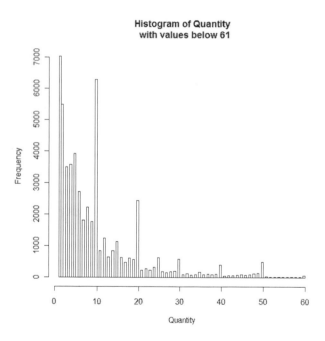

Fig. 1. Histogram of order quantities for the whole data set

The product specific analyses were limited to the 151 products that had more than 100 orders giving sufficient observations for applying the tests for symmetry. These products only represent 6% of the products, but cover 66% of the total quantity sold. Adopting a 5% significance level, the MGG-test showed that 77.5% of the products had a significant departure from symmetry of the Quantity distribution. The corresponding number for the CM-test was 76.9% and for the Mira-test 67.5%. The conclusion is that on an individual product level there is likewise a skewed distribution of order quantities. Another potential indicator of asymmetry is the CV. Figure 2 shows the histogram of the estimated CV's for the 151 products. Almost all the CV values are above 0.5 indicating significant skewness. For the Quantity time series for the whole product family we have an estimated mean of $\mu = 10.75$ and an estimated lag one correlation $\rho = 0.1105$. As we have no data on arrival times of orders, but rather delivery dates, we assume a Poisson arrival process, i.e. the aggregation level is determined by:

$$E(N(T)) = \frac{CV(Q)^2(1 + 2\rho) + 1}{(CV_0)^2}$$

Based on the data estimates, this yields the equation for determining aggregation level in terms of orders given by:

$$E(N(T)) = \frac{2.761}{(CV_0)^2}$$

If e.g. a $CV_0 = 0.2$ is used, we obtain the integer round up $E(N(T)) = 70$. Fig. 3 display the histograms of order quantities after aggregation over 70 orders. The distribution is clearly much closer to symmetry. The skewness is clearly much lower as reflected by the estimated coefficient of variation, which is 0.19.

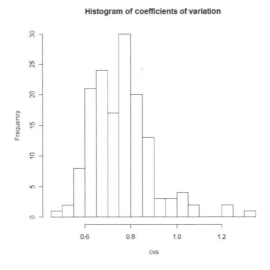

Fig. 2. Histogram of order quantity CV's for 151 products

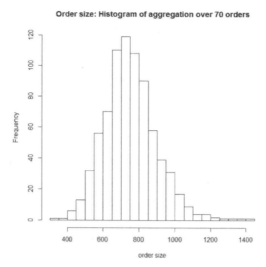

Fig. 3. Histogram of order quantities, when 31 orders are consecutively aggregated

The slightly skewed distribution, shown in figure 3, clearly indicates that if an aggregation horizon of 70 orders is used on the aggregate set, the order quantities tend to flow to a symmetrical distribution.

5   Conclusions and Further Research

The analysis and subsequent application of the analytical model gives a number of significant conclusions. First, the behavior of the particular case data set is as expected rather than as assumed in literature. The individual orders are, when the whole data set is considered, neither symmetrically nor independently distributed. Second, the order quantities for the products with sufficient orders are likewise to a large extend not symmetrically distributed. Third, the analytical models allows to calculate the number of orders needed to aggregate to achieve a given CV. Aggregating 70 orders to achieve a CV of approximately 0.2 on the aggregate set gives a distribution that is almost symmetrical. The conclusion is that although the individual customer orders are not behaving as expected, it is possible to aggregate over the order time series so that demand can be considered to stem from a symmetrical distribution. However, this indicates that demand can only be considered to stem from a symmetrical distribution with a sufficiently low CV if orders are aggregated. This is especially challenging in a make-to-order environment where the ability to buffer on time will be significantly influenced by market conditions. On a product family level this may not be a problem (in this example a desired CV of 0.1 on aggregate level would require aggregating 277 orders, 0.5% of the total number of orders, c. 2 weeks of orders). However, on an individual product level with high CV's aggregating even 10 orders indicates the need to aggregate over a very large time period indeed. This supports the assumptions in e.g. Fliedner [7] and Silver et al. [16]

regarding the stability of aggregate demand. Future work will focus on simulating the impact of different order quantity distributions on simple manufacturing systems and developing methods to translate the stability of order quantities into a planning horizon for a given manufacturing system.

References

1. Axäster, S.: Aggregation of Product Data for Hierarchical Production Planning. Operations Research 29, 744–756 (1981)
2. Becker, C., Scholl, A.: A survey on problems and methods in generalized assembly line balancing. European Journal of Operational Research 168, 694–715 (2006)
3. Box, G.E.P., Jenkins, G.: Time Series Analysis: Forecasting and Control. Holden-Day (1976)
4. Brander, P., Levén, E., Segerstedt, A.: Lot sizes in a capacity constrained facility-a simulation study of stationary stochastic demand. International Journal of Production Economics 93-94, 375–386 (2005)
5. Cabilio, P., Masaro, J.: A simple test of symmetry about an unknown median. The Canadian Journal of Statistics 24, 349–361 (1996)
6. Chen, A., Blue, J.: Performance analysis of demand planning approaches for aggregating, forecasting and disaggregating interrelated demands. International Journal of Production Economics 128, 586–602 (2010)
7. Fliedner, G.: Hierarchical forecasting: issues and use guidelines. Industrial Management & Data Systems 101, 5–12 (2001)
8. Hax, A.C., Meal, H.C.: Hierarchical Integration of Production Planning and Scheduling. In: Geisler, M.A. (ed.) Logistics. Studies in the Management Sciences, vol. 1. North-Holland/American Elsevier (1975)
9. Hendry, L.C., Kingsman, B.G.: Production planning systems and their applicability to make-to-order companies. European Journal of Operational Research 40, 1–15 (1989)
10. Marucheck, A.S., McClelland, M.K.: Strategic issues in make-to-order manufacturing. Production and Inventory Management 27, 82–96 (1986)
11. Miao, W., Gel, Y.R., Gastwirth, J.L.: A New Test of Symmetry about an Unknown Median. Random Walk. In: Hsiung, A., Zhang, C.-H., Ying, Z. (eds.) Sequential Analysis and Related Topics - A Festschrift in Honor of Yuan-Shih Chow. World Scientific Publisher, Singapore (2006)
12. Mira, A.: Distribution-free test for symmetry based on Bonferroni's measure. Journal of Applied Statistics 26, 959–972 (1999)
13. Nicholas, J.: Competitive Manufacturing Management: Continuous Improvement. Lean Production and Customer-focused Quality. McGrawHill, New York (1998)
14. Nielsen, P., Eriksen, T.: Towards an analysis methodology for identifying root causes of poor delivery performance. In: Conference Proceedings of IESM 2011, International Conference on Industrial Engineering and Systems Management (2011)
15. R-project (webpage) (2012), http://www.r-project.org
16. Silver, E.A., Pyke, D.F., Peterson, R.: Inventory Management and Production Planning and Scheduling, 3rd edn. John Wiley & Sons (1998)
17. Theil, H.: Linear Aggregation of Economic Relations, 1st edn. North-Holland Publishing Company (1955)

18. Tsubone, H., Furuta, H.: Replanning timing in hierarchical production planning. International Journal of Production Economics 44, 53–61 (1996)
19. Vollmann, W., Berry, D., Whybark, T.E., Jacobs, F.: Manufacturing Planning and Control for Supply Chain Management. McGraw-Hill, Singapore (2005)
20. Walpole, R.E., Myers, R.H., Myers, S.L., Ye, K.: Probability & Statistics for Engineers & Scientists. Prentice Hall, New York (2002)
21. Wijngaard, J.: On Aggregation in Production Planning. Engineering Costs and Production Economics 6, 259–266 (1982)
22. Zotteri, G., Kalchschmidt, M., Caniato, F.: The impact of aggregation level on forecasting performance. International Journal of Production Economics 93-94, 479–491 (2005)

Simulation Study of the Volatility
of Order Sizes and Their Impact on the Stability
# of a Simple Manufacturing Environment

Peter Nielsen[1,*] and Grzegorz Bocewicz[2]

[1] Department of Mechanical and Manufacturing Engineering,
Aalborg University, Fibigerstraede 16, DK 9220 Aalborg Oest, Denmark
`peter@m-tech.aau.dk`
[2] Koszalin University of Technology,
Dept. of Computer Science and Management, Koszalin, Poland
`bocewicz@ie.tu.koszalin.pl`

Abstract. Customer ordering behaviorin the form of size and timing of orders are critical for manufacturing systems such as make-to-order or assemble-to-order systems. To be competitive a Make-to-order manufacture must be flexible, both with regards to volume and product mix. A particularly critical parameter in determining the flexibility needs in the case of responsive manufacturing environments is the distribution of order sizes. In this paper several methods for describing the volatility of order sizes are presented. A discrete event simulation of a single server batch manufacturing system is subsequently conducted using various distributions of order sizes. The aim is to investigate 1) which measures for order size volatility best relates to the volatility of the output rate from the manufacturing system 2) how does the output stability from the system deteriorate as order sizes become more volatile.

Keywords: Simulation study, order sizes, discrete event.

1   Introduction

The performance of planning approaches within Manufacturing Planning and Control to a large extend depends on the planning foundation [6]. This foundation is for the purpose of this paper be limited to a simple model consisting of external demand / supply conditions, internal structure (planning approach and customer order decoupling points, Bill-of-Material/Bill-of-Resources structure and Product family structure). The internal structure should match the external conditions and enable an effective and efficient transformation of input from suppliers (materials and resources) to matching customer requirements [11]. For simplicity's sake this paper will focus on the orders arriving to the systems and more specifically to the size of orders rather than the timing of their arrival. The timing of orders rightfully falls in

---

* Corresponding author.

J. Frick and B. Laugen (Eds.): APMS 2011, IFIP AICT 384, pp. 91–98, 2012.

the domain of demand forecasting modeling, where this paper focuses on the response to the order sizes themselves. The considered system will be a simple single server system responding directly to customer orders. This system could correspond to a simple make-to-order manufacturing system. This paper has three main contributions. First, a method for evaluating the variation of order sizes is discussed. Second, a discrete event simulation study of a single server system is conducted to investigate the impact of order size volatility on a make-to-order system. Third, various measures for describing order size volatility are compared to the stability of the output from the manufacturing system to identify which order size volatility measure best predicts the volatility of the output. The remainder of the paper is structured as follows. First, a brief literature review is presented. Second, a new method for evaluating order size volatility is presented. Following this a simulation study of the impact of order size volatility on the output is presented. This is followed by a section discussing the experimental results before finally conclusions and further research is presented.

2   Literature Review

Orders form the foundation for demand. However, they typically act in an unpredictable manner [6], and are as a consequence typically aggregated to give stability and to serve as a planning input [10]. Wijngaard [12] identify four normal dimensions for aggregation: Types of products, production stages, capacities and time. Of these the types of products and time are the two typical used dimensions when aggregating demand information, as seen in e.g. Vollmann et al. [11]. Especially the time dimension is often used so that orders are aggregated over time in a way that ensures that the aggregated demand information can be translated into allocations in the internal manufacturing system structure [11]. The further up-stream the customer order decoupling point is placed, the more a company will be reacting directly to the customer ordering information as structured in the customer order [1], [7]. This also means that the planning approach is adapted according to the customer ordering decoupling point [8] and that impact of variation in order sizes will depend on the context. The consequence is that while it may be possible to allocate resources, materials and balance manufacturing lines pre-ante based on aggregate forecasts of demand translated into demand rates for individual products, the system it-self will in fact be reacting to a customer ordering behavior that may differ significantly from the assumptions. So while aggregate demand may be stable [13] and comply with standard assumptions such as stationary demand rates [3] the output may in fact be unstable or dependent. Because of this, it is relevant to investigate the behavior of customer demand in the form of the order sizes and the impact on a simple manufacturing system. This also has a number of further implications for e.g. line balancing that is highly sensitive to the distribution of orders [4]. In the case of line balancing it will be of significant value to have not just a clear picture of overall volumes and mix of orders, but also have a clear idea of the size of orders per product received. The more volatile the order sizes, the more difficult line balancing becomes [4]. For these reasons it is critical to have a clear picture of the volatility of order sizes faced by the company and how the manufacturing system reacts to these. This paper focuses on the second point.

3   Method for Evaluating Order Size Volatility

An often used term to describe the volatility of a given distribution is the Coefficient of Variance (CV), the standard deviation of the observed values, divided by the mean of the observed values. CV can be adapted to describe the volatility of order sizes by $CV_Q = \frac{\sigma_Q}{\mu_Q}$, where σ_Q is the standard deviation of order sizes and μ_Q is the mean order size. This term is particular suitable if the observations are i.i.d. from e.g. the normal distribution. However, since the likelihood of normality is limited we use another term to establish the volatility of order sizes [5]. The measure of variation is established as the following. First, sort the orders for the period by size. Second, calculate the accumulated demand for the sorted set of orders, i.e. the increase to total demand by adding the next order. Third, calculate the relative amount of total demand for all percentiles of orders. In the ideal situation of constant order sizes one order will proportionally increase the accumulated demand as much as any other orders. This means that e.g. 25% of the orders should amount to precisely 25% of the total demand. The higher the CV, the more one would expect the percentiles to deviate. Figure 1 illustrates the proposed measure of order size stability, with the three percentiles 90%, 95% and 98% illustrated on the bottom graph with respectively a green, blue and red line.

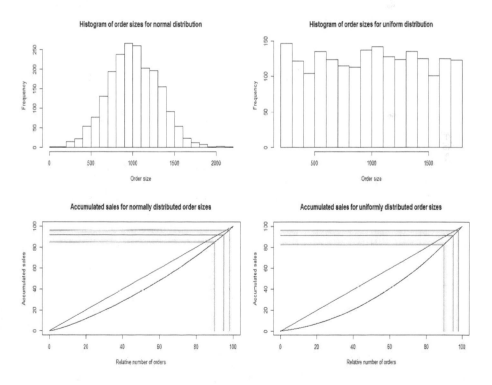

Fig. 1. Top: Histogram of order sizes from a normal (left) and uniform (right) distribution. Bottom: The corresponding accumulated demand profiles.

The order size distributions shown in figure 1 are 2,000 observations from a normal distribution, with a mean of 1000 and standard deviation of 300 (CV=0.3) and a uniform distribution with minimum 200 and a maximum of 1800 (approx. CV=0.46). The bottom graphs in figure 2 illustrate the concept of variation of order size, while the histograms illustrate the distributions. The curved graphs are the accumulated demand with orders sorted by order size. The lower the corresponding value is for a given percentile, the further from the assumption of constant order size is from actual distribution and the higher the CV will be. As such the percentiles become substitute measures describing the relative skewness of a given distribution. The more the distribution deviates from symmetry the lower values will be achieved for a given percentile.

4   Simulation of Impact of Volatility on Planning Environment Stability

The experimental setup has three aspects, the various data sets of order sizes used, the simulated manufacturing system and the measures used to describe the input and output. The considered manufacturing system consists of a single server processing orders from an infinite queue taking orders FIFO. The server processes the orders as batches and the orders exit the system as a batch when all the order has been processed. The server has the following properties:

- Process times dependent on order size, and stem from a i.i.d. normal distribution, with a situational mean of $Q_j * PrT$ and standard deviation $\sqrt{Q_j} * \sigma_{PrT}$, where Q_j is the order size of order j, and PrT is the average processing time per unit, and σ_{PrT} is the standard deviation per processed unit. Processing times are i.i.d.
- Setup time is constant and independent of order size and set to $\frac{\mu_{Q*PrT}}{2}$.
- Orders are batch processed and no units of the order are released until the whole order is completed.
- PrT is in the simulation set to 1 min. /unit and σ_{PrT} is set to 0.3*PrT.

Order sizes are drawn from the following distributions (and rounded to integers):

- sets from normal distributions with CV's 0.05, 0.10, 0.15, 0.20, 0.25, 0.30, (labeled respectively norm_set_1:6)
- sets from uniform distributions with limits 18:22, 15:25, 12:28, 9:31, 6:34 and 3:37 (labeled respectively uni_set_1:6)
- 1 set from a an exponential distribution (exp_set)
- 1 set with constant order size (cst_set)

All 14 order size distributions have a mean (μ_Q) of 20 units.
To evaluate the stability of the order sizes for the various distributions the order size distribution scheme proposed in the previous section is used in combination with

the CV_Q. The order distribution scheme allows for the calculation of any number of percentiles of order sizes and their contribution to the total processed demand. In this case the 30%, 40%, 50%, 60%, 70%, 80%, 90%, 95%, 98% and 99%-percentiles were chosen. To evaluate the stability of the manufacturing system under investigation the following measures are proposed:

$$CV_{V,i} = \frac{\sigma_{V,i}}{\mu_{V,i}}$$, where $\sigma_{V,i}$ is the standard deviation of total demand processed (i.e. volume in units outputted) in a time interval of i and $\mu_{V,i}$ is the mean demand processed in time interval i.

$$CV_{N,i} = \frac{\sigma_{N,i}}{\mu_{N,i}},$$ where $\sigma_{N,i}$ is the standard deviation of the number of orders processed in a time interval of length i and $\mu_{N,i}$ is the mean number of orders processed in a time interval of length i.

5   Experimental Results

For data analysis and data generation the statistical software package R [9] is used, while Enterprise Dynamics© is used for the discrete event simulation. A simulated manufacturing run was conducted for 200 hours of manufacturing time. The results of the output variation and order size characteristics are shown below in table 1 and figure 3 and the order size distributions' variation are shown in figure 2.

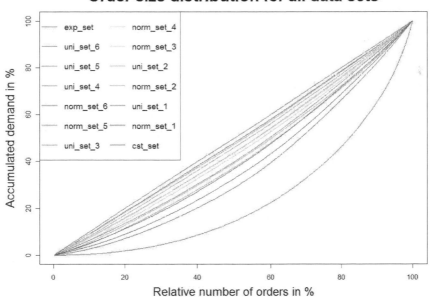

Fig. 2. The accumulation of demand graph for all 14 data sets used in the simulation study. Each line represents a different set of order size distributions.

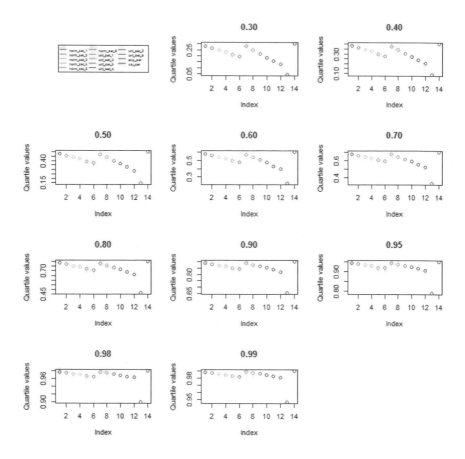

Fig. 3. The quartiles from the 14 data sets used in the simulation study. Top left graph indicates color of each experiment.

Table 1. The descriptive statistics for both the order size distributions and the output stability of the manufacturing system per 1 hour

	norm_set_1	norm_set_2	norm_set_3	norm_set_4	norm_set_5	norm_set_6	uni_set_1
CV_Q	0.05	0.10	0.15	0.19	0.27	0.31	0.06
$CV_{V,1}$	0.12	0.16	0.17	0.21	0.21	0.24	0.13
$CV_{N,1}$	0.12	0.16	0.17	0.20	0.21	0.25	0.13
	uni_set_2	uni_set_3	uni_set_4	uni_set_5	uni_set_6	exp_set	cst_set
CV_Q	0.14	0.23	0.31	0.40	0.48	1.04	0.00
$CV_{V,1}$	0.14	0.20	0.23	0.26	0.33	0.53	0.10
$CV_{N,1}$	0.15	0.20	0.21	0.26	0.31	0.67	0.10

The processing and setup time should on average allow for 2 orders per interval (i.e. 2 orders per hour) and an output of 40 units per hour. As can be seen the output is quite naturally more unstable for the more unstable order size distributions. While $CV_{N,1}$ and $CV_{V,1}$ seem to be more or less perfectly correlated, there seems to be a marked difference when the exponentially distributed order sizes are considered. This is clearly seen from table 1. This seems to indicate that the manufacturing system is more sensitive to asymmetrically distributed order sizes.

Table 2. Correlation values between order size volatility measures and output volatility

	Percentiles					
	0.30	**0.40**	**0.50**	**0.60**	**0.70**	**CV_Q**
$CV_{N,1}$	-0.972	-0.980	-0.987	-0.991	-0.993	0.992
$CV_{V,1}$	-0.927	-0.943	-0.957	-0.972	-0.985	0.987
	0.80	**0.90**	**0.95**	**0.98**	**0.99**	
$CV_{N,1}$	-0.987	-0.97	-0.951	-0.936	-0.93	
$CV_{V,1}$	-0.995	-0.997	-0.991	-0.984	-0.981	

As can be seen from table 2 strong correlation is found between all the order size stability measures. The strongest relations are for $CV_{N,1}$ found in CV_Q and the values for 50%-80% percentiles. This means that the $CV_{N,1}$ is equally well described by the simple measure of CV_Q and the percentiles. For $CV_{V,1}$ the higher values (80%-95%) of the percentiles of order size distribution, better describe the variation of the output in form of total volume. So while CV_Q is a an adequate predictor for the $CV_{N,1}$ behavior, the order size volatility measures better describe the $CV_{V,1}$.

Another interesting aspect that merits investigation is whether the output is in fact also independently distributed. To investigate whether the output is in fact independently distributed the autocorrelation function is used [2]. The conclusion is that both output measures are in fact highly dependent for almost all distributions. This could have big implications if e.g. the aim is to balance a production line [4], as dependently distributed output could indicate poor balance and difficulties in achieving a proper performance. Using Pearson correlation measures it is clear that there is a significant correlation (better than 0.01) between the input volatility and the lag 1 autocorrelation. This strongly indicates that while the input order sizes may independently distributed (as is the case for all but the constant order sizes), the volatility of order sizes actually has a strong impact on the output stability of the manufacturing system. So if a particular output rate is desired the volatility of order sizes must be taken into account. This is critical for any system reacting directly to customer orders as the dependencies of output directly influences the need to buffer as the need for buffering to achieve the same performance (e..g delivery time) increases as distributions go from independent to dependent. This can explain deviations in real life systems between expected and actual output, while having a relatively constant demand rate. Another observation is that the dependencies of output are quickly reduced after only a few periods (almost no lags greater than 1 are significant). This would seem to indicate that the disturbances tend to be absorbed by the system over time. The time horizon needed for the dependencies to disappear could be a valid measure for a reasonable delivery time for the system.

6 Conclusions and Further Research

A number of significant conclusions can be reached based on the results presented in this paper. First, the new measures for order size volatility are robust estimators of volatility. Second, as order size volatility increases, the output volatility naturally increases also. Third, the need to aggregate in time to achieve a given stability of output is increasing disproportionally to the increases in order size volatility. Fourth, while the order sizes are i.i.d. the output is actually dependently distributed. The conclusion must by necessity be that the volatility of order sizes must be taken into account. Future research will focus on finding the aggregation of time (planning period length) needed to ensure that a given order size volatility can be used as input to a manufacturing system and give an output that can be considered stable.

References

1. Berry, W.L., Hill, T.: Linking Systems to Strategy. International Journal of Operations & Production Management 12, 3–15 (1992)
2. Box, G.E.P., Jenkins, G.: Time Series Analysis: Forecasting and Control. Holden-Day (1976)
3. Brander, P., Levén, E., Segerstedt, A.: Lot sizes in a capacity constrained facility-a simulation study of stationary stochastic demand. International Journal of Production Economics 93-94, 375–386 (2005)
4. Nicholas, J.: Competitive Manufacturing Management: Continuous Improvement. Lean Production and Customer-focused Quality. McGraw-Hill, New York (1998)
5. Nielsen, P., Eriksen, T.: Towards an analysis methodology for identifying root causes of poor delivery performance. In: Conference Proceedings of IESM 2011, International Conference on Industrial Engineering and Systems Management (2011)
6. Nielsen, P., Nielsen, I., Steger-Jensen, K.: Analyzing and evaluating product demand interdependencies. Computers in Industry 61, 869–876 (2010)
7. Olhager, J.O.: Strategic positioning of the order penetration point. International Journal of Production Economics 85, 319–329 (2003)
8. Olhager, J., Wikner, J.: Master Production Scheduling. In: Beyond Manufacturing Resource Planning (MRPII): Advanced Models and Methods for Production Planning, pp. 3–20. Springer (1998)
9. R-project.org (webpage) (2012)
10. Silver, E.A., Pyke, D.F., Peterson, R.: Inventory Management and Production Planning and Scheduling, 3rd edn. John Wiley & Sons (1998)
11. Vollmann, W., Berry, D., Whybark, T.E., Jacobs, F.: Manufacturing Planning and Control for Supply Chain Management. McGraw-Hill, Singapore (2005)
12. Wijngaard, J.: On Aggregation in Production Planning. Engineering Costs and Production Economics 6, 259–266 (1982)
13. Zotteri, G., Kalchschmidt, M., Caniato, F.: The impact of aggregation level on forecasting performance. International Journal of Production Economics 93-94, 479–491 (2005)

Game Theoretic Analysis of Production Structures in the Japanese Animation Industry: Comparison of Conventional and Production Committee Systems

Nariaki Nishino and Satoshi Kawabe

Department of Technology Management for Innovation,
School of Engineering, The University of Tokyo
7-3-1 Hongo, Bunkyo-ku, Tokyo 113-8656, Japan
nishino@tmi.t.u-tokyo.ac.jp

Abstract. This paper presents a game theoretic analysis of production structures including several stakeholders in the Japanese animation market and its related goods markets. We construct a decision-making model of the industry including players of four kinds: an animation studio, a broadcasting company, a related products manufacturer, and consumers. Additionally, we model two production structures: the conventional system and the production committee system. By analyzing the equilibrium states of this model, we conclude theoretically that the animation studio raises the effort level with decreasing marginal costs of related products and/or with increasing network externality effect and increasing royalties the studio receives. For the total profit and the effort level, we found that the production committee system is better than the conventional system.

Keywords: Japanese animation industry, Game theory, Decision-making, Production committee system.

1 Introduction

In Japan, the content industry market size, including that for Animation, is estimated at more than 100 billion dollars. Particularly, Japanese animation is so popular throughout the world that the role of the Japanese animation industry is expected to become increasingly important in the future[1]. Furthermore, although the animation industry is a service industry, it is closely related to tangible manufacturing products because related goods such as DVDs, character figures, and TV games are produced and provided in parallel.

According to a report released by the Digital Content Association of Japan[2], however, some problems exist in the content industry. Although the content industry in America, exemplified by that in Hollywood, earns profits worldwide, the Japanese content industry cannot make big gains abroad in spite of its

J. Frick and B. Laugen (Eds.): APMS 2011, IFIP AICT 384, pp. 99–106, 2012.

popularity. Some reasons underlie the current situation. One problem is piracy, which is an important issue in the content industry[1][2]. Many researchers have conducted studies of piracy. Tanaka[3] studied the effect of file-sharing software on music CD sales in Japan. Smith et al.[4] pointed out that increased broadband internet penetration has led to a significant increase in DVD sales in the US.

Another problem is the "production structure" of the Japanese animation industry. This industry has many stakeholders: for example, animation companies to which animation creators belong, broadcasting companies, manufacturers of DVDs and other anime-related goods, advertising agencies, trading companies, consumers, and so on. The most important issue in this structure is that animation studios, most of which are small, cannot obtain sufficient profits to maintain the quality of their content because large companies such as broadcasting companies dominate negotiations. Animation studios will be disadvantaged if these circumstances continue. Concern persists about the decline of this industry in the future. Nevertheless, few studies have used a mathematical analysis approach to examine these problems related to the Japanese animation industry.

This study examines production structures of the Japanese animation industry, especially addressing two kinds of production structures: the conventional and the production committee systems. Based on a game theoretic approach, we formulate stakeholders' decision-making and production structures. Then, we analyze them theoretically and compare the two structures.

2   Modeling of Animation Production Structures in Japan

2.1   Formulating Each Player

We construct a game theoretic model of Japanese animation industry composed of players of four kinds: an animation studio, a broadcasting company, a related products manufacturer, and consumers.

Animation Studio. The animation studio receives a budget from the broadcasting company. Then the studio makes a decision about the effort level, which dictates the amount of its production expenditure. In addition, the studio receives as royalties some revenues from sales of the products that the related product manufacturer produces. The profit function is therefore defined as $\Pi_s = B - F(x) + \alpha \sum_{k=1}^{s} p_k q_k$, where B signifies the budget from the broadcasting company, p_k and q_k respectively denote the price and the sales quantity of product k, α is the rate of royalties which the studio receives, s is the number of types of anime-related goods that the manufacturer produces, x stands for the effort level of the studio, and $F(x)$ is the cost of producing the anime, which is the function of the effort level x. The studio decides the effort level x to maximize its profit.

Broadcasting Company. The broadcasting company pays some revenues from sponsors to the animation studio for its production. The company also receives a part of the sales of anime-related products as royalties. The profit is $\Pi_b =$

$A - B + \beta \sum_{k=1}^{s} p_k q_k + L$, where A signifies the budget from sponsors, β denotes the rate of royalties which the company receives, and L is defined as the license fee from a related products manufacturer. Herein, A, β, and L are exogenous variables. Then the company decides how much of budget B is paid to the studio.

Manufacturer. The related products manufacturer produces anime-related goods and pays a part of its sales to the studio and company as royalties. The profit is described as $\Pi_m = (1 - \alpha - \beta) \sum_{k=1}^{s} p_k q_k - \sum_{k=1}^{s} (c_k(q_k) + f_k) - L$, where $c_k(q_k)$ and f_k respectively stand for the variable cost and fixed cost of production for product k.

Consumers. The utility function of consumer i who purchases product k is $U_{i,k} = v_{i,k} + a_k(m) - p_k$. In that equation, $v_{i,k}$ denotes consumer i's own utility of product k. In addition, $a_k(m)$ signifies the increment of utility by increasing m. Here, m is defined as the number of consumers who have watched the anime. Consequently, $a_k(m)$ denotes the effect of indirect network externalities.

2.2   Production Structures

Conventional Production System. A conventional production system can be depicted as Figure 1. There are interdependent relationships among the players. Their decisions are fundamentally made with the sequence of a broadcasting company, an animation studio, and related products manufacturers. Therefore, the game structure in our model can be described simply as a sequential game with perfect information: first, the company chooses budget B; then the studio makes a decision about the effort level x; finally, the manufacturer decides the price p_k of product k.

Production Committee System. This type of system has been emerging recently in anime production in Japan. In the production committee system, stakeholders form a committee by agreeing to finance the project. Therein, a chain of decision process from animation production to selling related products is conducted collaboratively. Thereby, their decisions are made by working together. The structure is depicted in Figure 2. It can be represented by replacing each profit with the total profit that is the sum of each player's profit. The decision sequence is the same as the previous one.

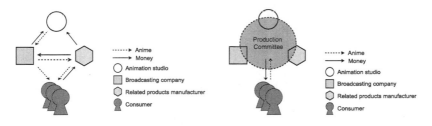

Fig. 1. Conventional production   **Fig. 2.** Production committee system

3 Theoretical Analysis

3.1 Condition Setup

For simplicity, we assume that the related products manufacturer produces only one type of product. Accordingly, we can omit k from the formulas. The variable cost and indirect network externalities are defined as $c(q) = cq$ and $a(m) = a(m(x)) = rx$, respectively. Herein, c stands for the marginal cost. $a(m)$ is assumed as a linear function of m and m as a linear function of x; r is a constant and signifies the effect of indirect network externalities related to the anime. Moreover, we simplify the anime production cost as $F(x) = x^2 + d$, where d is the fixed cost to produce the anime. By such an arrangement, consumer i's utility function can be represented as $U_i = v_i + rx - p$. Then, we assume that the value of v_i is distributed with uniformity from 0 to 1 and that consumers purchase the product only if consumer i's utility U_i is positive. Consequently, the sales quality q is calculated as $q = \int_{U_i \geq 0} dv = \int_{p-a(m)}^{1} dv = rx - p + 1$, which signifies the demand function. Constraint $rx \leq p \leq rx + 1$ can be derived by the assumption of a uniform distribution of v_i in $[0, 1]$.

3.2 Deriving Equilibrium

Subgame perfect Nash equilibrium in the conventional production system can be derived using backward induction. First, we calculate the price p for which the manufacturer makes a decision to maximize the profit Π_m. The price p^* in equilibrium is calculated as $p^* = \underset{p}{\mathrm{argmax}}\, \Pi_m$. Second, we derive the effort level x of the animation studio. The studio makes a decision in anticipation of the manufacturer's decision. Therefore x is calculated as $x^* = \underset{x}{\mathrm{argmax}}\, \Pi_s$ s.t. $p = p^*$. If the studio's profit Π_s is a negative value, we assume that the studio produces no cartoon film and that each decision-maker's profits are zero. Finally, we calculate budget B. The broadcasting company makes a decision in anticipation of the decision of the animation studio. Here, B is calculated as $B^* = \underset{B}{\mathrm{argmax}}\, \Pi_b$ s.t. $x = x^*$ and $p = p^*$.

In the production committee system the decisions can be made cooperatively. They make decisions to maximize the total profits of $\Pi_{total} = \Pi_s + \Pi_b + \Pi_m$. Subgame perfect Nash equilibrium is similarly derived as follows: first, p^* is calculated using $p^* = \underset{p}{\mathrm{argmax}}\, \Pi_{total}$ and then x^* is determined by $x^* = \underset{x}{\mathrm{argmax}}\, \Pi_{total}$ under the condition of $p = p^*$. Here, B^* cannot be determined because variable B disappears from the formula of Π_{total}.

3.3 Subgame Perfect Nash Equilibrium in The Two Structures

Equilibrium states are presented in Tables 1 – 3. Tables 1 and 2 present the theoretical equilibrium in case of the conventional production system. The equilibrium values of p^* and x^* are classified according to the values of α, r, and c.

The company decides budget B^* on the condition that the value of studio's profit Π_s is positive. Therefore B^* depends on x^* as well as some exogenous variables such as d, A, and L. Therein, l is defined as $l = 1 - \alpha - \beta$.

Table 3 presents the theoretical equilibrium for the production committee system. As in the previous case, the equilibrium values of x^* and p^* are classified according to the values of r and c.

4   Discussion

4.1   Implications from Theoretical Analysis

We discuss the structures of the animation industry. Figure 3 depicts the reaction function of the manufacturer (3-(a), 3-(b)) and the profit function of the studio (3-(c), 3-(d)) in the conventional production, which are derived as an theoretical output especially in case of $0 < \alpha r^2 < 2$. First, see 3-(a) and 3-(c) in Figure 3. As shown in 3-(c), the effort level, $x^* = \frac{\alpha r}{4 - \alpha r^2}$, brings about the largest studio's profit and the manufacturer's best response p^* is determined by selecting the corresponding point from the reaction function in 3-(a). In this case, the studio's effort level x^* is positive, derived as an inner point. In addition, the value of $x^* = \frac{\alpha r}{4 - \alpha r^2}$ at equilibrium means that the studio's effort level is increasing by a large α or r, implying that the increment of royalties to the studio or large effect of network externalities makes the studio's effort level enlarge. For example, to increase r, social networking services might be useful to promote communication among anime fans, thereby producing word-of-mouth effects[5][6].

Meantime, in case of $c \geq \frac{2l}{\sqrt{4 - \alpha r^2}}$ (3-(b), 3-(d)), the effort level at equilibrium is $x^* = 0$. Therefore, as the manufacturer's marginal cost c increases, it decreases the studio's effort level. Therefore, for high-quality anime, it is necessary to reduce the marginal cost of the related products manufacturer. For instance, it can be considered that the manufacturer should provide an online distribution service instead of DVD packages because the marginal cost to copy digital data is almost zero.

The same effects are basically present in cases of the production committee system as well. Such indirect effects imply that the relationship among stakeholders is intricately interwinced, demanding careful strategies to foster high-quality anime production.

4.2   Problems in Conventional Production Structure

Table 2 presents many cases in which the animation studio's profit Π_s is zero even if the production is conducted and makes other players profitable because the broadcasting company provides a very small budget to the studio, meaning the decision is best for the company at theoretical equilibrium. The situation indicates that the studio cannot obtain profits because the broadcasting company has a clear advantage over the animation studio in the production structure. The studio will suffer financially and creators associated with the studio will be

Table 1. Theoretical equilibrium in conventional production: x^* and p^*

Condition of α and r	Condition of marginal cost	x^*	p^*
$0 < \alpha r^2 < 2$	$0 < c < \frac{2l}{\sqrt{4-\alpha r^2}}$	$\frac{\alpha r}{4-\alpha r^2}$	$\frac{1}{2}(\frac{\alpha r^2}{4-\alpha r^2} + \frac{c}{l} + 1)$
	$c \geq \frac{2l}{\sqrt{4-\alpha r^2}}$	0	1
$2 \leq \alpha r^2 \leq 3$	$0 < c < \frac{(\alpha r^2 - 2)l}{2}$	$\frac{\alpha r}{2}$	$\frac{\alpha r^2}{2}$
	$\frac{1}{2}(\alpha r^2 - 2)l \leq c < \frac{2(\alpha r^2 - 2)l}{4-\alpha r^2}$	$\frac{l+c}{rl}$	$\frac{l+c}{l}$
	$\frac{2(\alpha r^2 - 2)l}{4-\alpha r^2} \leq c < \frac{2l}{\sqrt{4-\alpha r^2}}$	$\frac{\alpha r}{4-\alpha r^2}$	$\frac{1}{2}(\frac{\alpha r^2}{4-\alpha r^2} + \frac{c}{l} + 1)$
	$c \geq \frac{2l}{\sqrt{4-\alpha r^2}}$	0	1
$\alpha r^2 > 3$	$0 < c < \frac{(\alpha r^2 - 2)l}{2}$	$\frac{\alpha r}{2}$	$\frac{\alpha r^2}{2}$
	$\frac{1}{2}(\alpha r^2 - 2)l \leq c < (\alpha r^2 - 1)l$	$\frac{l+c}{rl}$	$\frac{l+c}{l}$
	$c \geq (\alpha r^2 - 1)l$	0	1

Table 2. Equilibrium in conventional production: B^* and profits

x^*	Condition	B^*	Π_b^*	Π_s^*	Π_g^*
$\frac{\alpha r}{2}$	$d < \frac{\alpha^2 r^2}{4}$	0	$A + \beta\frac{\alpha r^2}{2} + L$	$-d + \frac{\alpha^2 r^2}{4}$	$\frac{l\alpha r^2}{2} - c - f - L$
	$\frac{\alpha^2 r^2}{4} \leq d < A + L$ $+\beta\frac{\alpha r^2}{2} + \frac{\alpha^2 r^2}{4}$	$d - \frac{\alpha^2 r^2}{4}$	$A - d + L + \frac{\alpha + 2\beta}{4}\alpha r^2$	0	$\frac{l\alpha r^2}{2} - c - f - L$
	$d \geq A + L$ $+\beta\frac{\alpha r^2}{2} + \frac{\alpha^2 r^2}{4}$	0	0	0	0
$\frac{l+c}{rl}$	$d < \alpha\frac{l+c}{l} - (\frac{l+c}{l})^2$	0	$A + \beta\frac{l+c}{l} + L$	$-d + \alpha\frac{l+c}{l} - (\frac{l+c}{l})^2$	$l - f - L$
	$\alpha\frac{l+c}{l} - (\frac{l+c}{l})^2 \leq d < A + L$ $+(\alpha + \beta)\frac{l+c}{l} - (\frac{l+c}{l})^2$	$d - \alpha\frac{l+c}{l}$ $+(\frac{l+c}{l})^2$	$A - d + L$ $+(\alpha + \beta)\frac{l+c}{l} - (\frac{l+c}{l})^2$	0	$l - f - L$
	$d \geq A + L + (\alpha + \beta)\frac{l+c}{l} - (\frac{l+c}{l})^2$	0	0	0	0
$\frac{\alpha r}{4-\alpha r^2}$	$d < \frac{\alpha}{4l}(l^2 - c^2) + \frac{\alpha^2 r^2}{4(4-\alpha r^2)}$	0	$A + \frac{\beta}{4l^2}\{(\frac{4l}{4-\alpha r^2})^2 - c^2\} + L$	$\frac{\alpha}{4l}(l^2 - c^2)$ $+\frac{\alpha^2 r^2}{4(4-\alpha r^2)} - d$	$\frac{1}{4}(\frac{\alpha r^2}{4-\alpha r^2} + \frac{c}{l} + 1)^2 - \frac{4c}{4-\alpha r^2} - f - L$
	$\frac{\alpha}{4l}(l^2 - c^2) + \frac{\alpha^2 r^2}{4(4-\alpha r^2)} \leq d <$ $\frac{\alpha}{4l}(l^2 - c^2) + \frac{\alpha^2 r^2}{4(4-\alpha r^2)} + A + L$ $+\frac{\beta}{4l^2}\{(\frac{4l}{4-\alpha r^2})^2 - c^2\}$	d $-\frac{\alpha}{4l}(l^2 - c^2)$ $-\frac{\alpha^2 r^2}{4(4-\alpha r^2)}$	$A - d + \frac{\alpha}{4l}(l^2 - c^2)$ $+\frac{\alpha^2 r^2}{4(4-\alpha r^2)}$ $+\frac{\beta}{4l^2}\{(\frac{4l}{4-\alpha r^2})^2 - c^2\} + L$	0	$\frac{1}{4}(\frac{\alpha r^2}{4-\alpha r^2} + \frac{c}{l} + 1)^2$ $-\frac{4c}{4-\alpha r^2} - f - L$
	$d \geq \frac{\alpha}{4l}(l^2 - c^2) + \frac{\alpha^2 r^2}{4(4-\alpha r^2)} +$ $A + L + \frac{\beta}{4l^2}\{(\frac{4l}{4-\alpha r^2})^2 - c^2\}$	0	0	0	0
0	$d < A + L$	d	$A - d + L$	0	$-f - L$
	$d \geq A + L$	0	0	0	0

Table 3. Equilibrium in production committee system

Condition of r	Condition of c	x^*	p^*	Π_{total}^*
$0 < r^2 < 2$	$0 < c \leq 1$	$\frac{(1-c)r}{4-r^2}$	$\frac{-r^2 c + 2c + 2}{4 - r^2}$	$A - f - d + \frac{(1-c)^2}{4 - r^2}$
	$c > 1$	0	1	$A - f - d$
$2 \leq r^2 < 4$	$0 < c \leq \frac{1}{2}(r^2 - 2)$	$\frac{r}{2}$	$\frac{r^2}{2}$	$A - f - d + \frac{r^2}{4} - c$
	$\frac{1}{2}(r^2 - 2) < c \leq 1$	$\frac{(1-c)r}{4-r^2}$	$\frac{-r^2 c + 2c + 2}{4 - r^2}$	$A - f - d + \frac{(1-c)^2}{4 - r^2}$
	$c > 1$	0	1	$A - f - d$
$r^2 \geq 4$	$0 < c \leq \frac{r^2}{4}$	$\frac{r}{2}$	$\frac{r^2}{2}$	$A - f - d + \frac{r^2}{4} - c$
	$c > \frac{r^2}{4}$	0	1	$A - f - d$

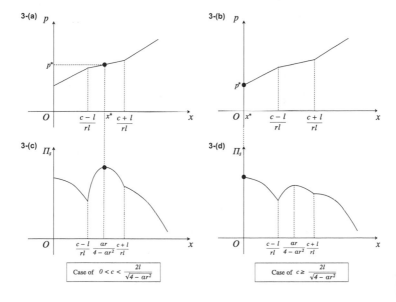

Fig. 3. Manufacturer's reaction and studio's profit functions in case of $0 < \alpha r^2 < 2$

forced to work in harsh conditions at low pay. If such a situation were to continue, talented creators in the next generation would decrease and they would shun the industry. Eventually, the Japanese animation industry might lose competitiveness in international markets, as reported by the Digital Content Association of Japan[2].

4.3   Comparison of Two Production Structures

In terms of profits and the effort level, we can compare the two production structures. Because there are many theoretical equilibrium states by a combination of some parameters, it is difficult to compare the two structures analytically. We therefore compare them with numerical calculations as follows:

- r is set, varying in $[0.1, \; 3.0]$ with an increment of 0.1
- c is set, varying in $[0.1, \; 2.0]$ with an increment of 0.1
- α and β are set, respectively varying in $[0.01, \; 1.00]$ with an increment of 0.01 to satisfy the condition of $0 < \alpha + \beta < 1$

Accordingly, combinations of values of those parameters are 3,090,600. Figure 4 presents the comparison of the two production systems with numerical calculation. The circle graphs represent the ratio, counting the frequency of outputs of the numerical comparison with respect to the total profit and the effort level. Herein, the total profit stands for the sum of the studio's profit, the broadcasting company's profit and the manufacturer's profit. The result means that the total profit of the production committee system is greater than or equal to that

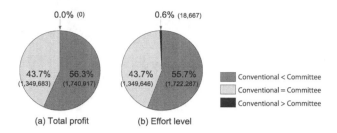

Fig. 4. Comparison between the conventional and the production committee systems

of the conventional system in all parameter combinations. Regarding the effort level, the cases that the conventional system is greater are very few. Therefore, the production committee system can be regarded as a good structure in anime production.

5   Concluding Remarks

In Japan, the animation industry will become increasingly important in the future. However, it confronts severe problems in its production structure. To elucidate the mechanism, we constructed and analyzed a game theoretic model comprised of decision-makers of four kinds. Results show that the studio reduces the effort level with increasing marginal cost of related products. For example, an online distribution service might be a more valid method than DVD packages to increase the studio's effort level. In addition, the effort level of the studio becomes high with increasing royalties from the manufacturer and with the effect of externalities. Comparison between two production structures shows that the production committee system is better than the conventional one in terms of the total profit and the effort level. Approaches like those in our study are important to assess the future development of competitiveness in this industry.

References

1. Ministry of Economy, Trade and Industry: Current Status and Issues Facing Japanese Industries (2010)
2. Digital Content Association of Japan: Digital Content White Paper 2010 (2010)
3. Tanaka, T.: Does file sharing reduce music CD sales?: The case of Japan. IIR Working Paper 05-08, Institute of Innovation Research, Hitotsubashi University (2004)
4. Smith, M.D., Telang, R.: Piracy or promotion? The impact of broadband Internet penetration on DVD sales. Information Economics and Policy 22, 289–298 (2010)
5. Duan, W., Gu, B., Whinston, A.B.: The dynamics of online word-of-mouth and product sales – An empirical investigation of the movie industry. Journal of Retailing 84, 233–242 (2008)
6. Reynolds, K.E., Beatty, S.E.: Customer Benefits and Company Consequences of Customer–Salesperson Relationships in Retailing. Journal of Retailing 75, 11–32 (1999)

An Efficient Heuristic Algorithm for Capacitated Lot Sizing Problem with Overtime Decisions

Cagatay Iris and Mehmet Mutlu Yenisey

Department of Industrial Engineering,
Istanbul Technical University, 34367, Macka, Istanbul, Turkey
{ciris,yenisey}@itu.edu.tr

Abstract. Capacitated Lot Sizing Problem is a very important tactical level decision making problem that answers the questions of producing when and how many in dynamic demand environment. Solving Capacitated Lot Sizing Problem with Overtime decisions (CLSPO) and extensions derived from the fundamental structure optimally suffer from combinatorial nature of the problem. The aim of the study is to form a two-stage heuristic algorithm to solve related problem in polynomial time. In first part, characteristics of problem structure are presented. Dominance properties are presented to help algorithm obtain a bounded search area. Proposed algorithm directly utilizes such shortcoming. Performance of approach is tested by using different criteria. And finally, robustness test are applied to check how well algorithm performs against fluctuations in its data. Simulated annealing as improvement heuristic performs well for related problem. It is also observed that fluctuations of data directly affects performance outcome. Obtained results also reveal that performance of improvement heuristic highly depends on constructive heuristic. Algorithm is also applied to an industry case study to plan master production schedule with minimum costs.

Keywords: Production Planning, Lot Sizing with Overtime Decisions, Global Search, Simulated Annealing.

1 Introduction

As the increase in competition, the importance of efficient planning has rapidly increased. Companies in this sense focus on how to reduce production cost by efficiently planning production systems. The difficulty in optimizing planning of production relies on two different tight constraints. Solutions found should be feasible with capacity of period and inventory balance between consecutive periods [1]. CLSP may be enlarged with different types of product structures, setup time, overtime, backlogging, lead times, time windows, planning horizon etc. The resulting combination of alternatives becomes more complicated. It is shown that finding a feasible solution becomes NP-complete whenever setup times are incorporated into model [2]. In most of studies, objective function of problem is formulated as a minimization of production, holding, setup, overtime and backlogging costs [3].

J. Frick and B. Laugen (Eds.): APMS 2011, IFIP AICT 384, pp. 107–114, 2012.

Traditional CLSP and extensions derived from main structure have attracted the attention of researchers over the last fifty years. Reference [4] clusters lot sizing problems regarding demand type and resource constraint. The fundamental aspects covered in this survey. However, it isn't sufficient to reflect problem characteristics by only focusing on problem structure. Reference [5] gives detailed information on solution strategies for CLSP problem. Heuristics and Metaheuristics are most common solution strategies. Simulated Annealing, Genetic Algorithms and Lagrangean Relaxation are apparently most popular techniques for related problem type. It is deduced that neighborhood structures proposed for CLSP apparently performs well for such heuristics. One of the most familiar researches in literature to ours was published in 2000. In the paper, an integrated lagrangean relaxation-simulated annealing approach was presented. However, related study lacks efficient search strategies and real-life implementation [2].

Our study aims at combine a very "easy to implement algorithm" which is lot-for-lot (LFL) and global search procedures to solve CLSPO. Lot-for-Lot heuristic which neglects capacity constraint while maintaining inventory balance equations is employed to find an initial solution. The results derived from this phase have been given as an input for improvement heuristic. Global search procedure is capable to improve given initial solution within the feasible solution. The philosophy maintained in improvement heuristic is transferring some amounts of lots from one period to another. Simulated annealing (SA) has been utilized not get stuck in local optimum.

2   Problem Structure and Dominance Properties

The paper focuses on CLSP in two further aspects. It assumes that two sources of capacity exist as regular time and overtime. Since, overtime and regular time has different costs, basic model should be extended. The related mathematical model is:

$$z = Min \ \Sigma t \Sigma i \ (c_{i,t} X_{i,t} + h_{i,t} I_{i,t} + os_t C_t + ov_t O_t) \tag{1}$$

$$s.t. \ I_{i,-1} + X_{i,t} - I_{i,t} = D_{i,t} \qquad \forall i, \forall t \tag{2}$$

$$\Sigma i \ cp_i X_{i,t} \leq C_t + O_t \qquad \forall t \tag{3}$$

$$C_t \leq MaxC_t \qquad \forall t \tag{4}$$

$$O_t \leq MaxO_t \qquad \forall t \tag{5}$$

$$X_{i,} \geq 0, \ I_{i,t} \geq 0, \ O_t \geq 0, \ C_t \geq 0 \qquad \forall i,t \tag{6}$$

The model covers multiple-items with single-level product structure to be planned over T periods. The objective (1) aims to minimize total cost of production, holding, regular and overtime. Constraint (2) is inventory balance equation for each product and period. Due to the fact that, there are two different resources, capacity limitations formulated by constraint (3) consist of production time with an upper bound of threshold of regular and overtime. Constraint (4) and (5) are control parameters to limit maximum available regular time and overtime. Constraint set (6) reflects non-negativity conditions.

It should be emphasized that lot sizing problem for single-level product structures doesn't require setup time as an individual parameter because most commonly, setup times do not change between periods. Hence, setup times are included in unit processing time of each product.

A tradeoff between cost of working with overtime and holding a unit of inventory in stock occurs in periods where demand result in idle capacity. It may be logical to produce more and hold inventory rather than using overtime in such peak periods [3]. Hence, proposed neighborhood strategy is based on transferring lots from one period to another regarding such tradeoffs. SA controls the amount tradeoff before taking a move, thus it is considered to be a proper metaheuristic for such neighborhood structures. More precisely, hierarchy of decisions to shift a lot to another period is determined by considering cost parameters of predecessor and successor period in SA [2]. In improvement heuristic, a move is generated by transferring a lot between periods in order to restore feasibility of capacity constraint or improve objective function. It depends totally on the constructive heuristic solution whether to improve objective function or attaining capacity feasibility. Since, LFL heuristic may produce capacity infeasible solution, a control mechanism is adopted.

There are three fundamental decisions that should be made: period to shift a lot from/to, item that will be shifted and amount of transfer. After determining the period and item that will be shifted, amount of lot that will be transferred may be determined. Transferring a lot between periods will result in a cost fluctuation by changing the indices of related cost parameter. Forming a dominance property on one-at-a-time lot transferring may be useful for problem structure. These properties help to limit search space, and results in high efficiency in search procedures.

Dominance Properties: $Z = f(c_1, c_2, ..., c_n)$ is the value of measure (objective function in our case) that characterizes iteration S and that $Z' = f(c_1', c_2', ..., c_n')$ represents the value of the same measure under some different iterations S'. Then, dominance set is applied as long as condition $Z' \geq Z$ implies that $c_j' \geq c_j$ for some parameters j [6].

Property-1: Transferring an amount of Δ *(Delta)* from t_2 to t_1 is dominance property-1 as: Property-1.1: *(where $t_1 \leq t_2$ and t_2 is most overloaded period in respect to $C_{t2} + O_{t2}$)*; Property-1.2:

$$proper \ for \ S = \{min \ \{c_{i,1} + h_{i,t1} - c_{i,t2} - h_{i,t2}\} \} \qquad (7)$$

$$otherwise \ \{max \ X_{i,2} * cp_i \ otherwise \ rnd_i\} \qquad (8)$$

Starting from the period with highest load and item with highest gap in total holding and production cost with previous period will form a dominance set for backward scheduling procedure. Here function of otherwise reflects whether the related production quantity is adequate. If $X_{i,t2}$ equals to zero, then there is no proper lot to be shifted from t_2 to t_1. Product with highest capacity consumption is selected to be shifted in such cases. If $X_{i,t2}$ still doesn't change, a random product may be selected for shifting procedure. Those factors that don't belong to dominant set will be clarified in algorithm explanations.

After determining the periods to transfer the lot in between and item to be transferred, amount that may be shifted may be calculated. There are two alternatives on transferring a lot. Direction of transfer may be forward or backward. Amounts that may be transferred purely depend upon forward or backward procedure. As mentioned above, constructive heuristic is lot-for-lot, so there will be no inventory on hand at the start of each period in initial solution. Therefore, backward transferring of production lots will be sensible by accumulating on hand inventory for improvement heuristic.

Property-2: If decision is to transfer the lot in backward (which means transferring a lot from $t+1$ *(t2)* to t *(t1)*) direction, the maximum quantity that may be shifted depends upon the feasibility of the solution where the search is initiated and in all feasible solutions, the idea is to improve objective function. The maximum quantity of item i to be transferred is [7];

$$Delta\_max=max\{0,min\ \{X_{i,t2},Q_{t1}\}\} \qquad (9)$$

The maximum quantity that may be shifted from $t2$ to $t1$ is limited to the amount of product that is produced in $t2$ and the available production capacity in $t1$. The related Q_{t1} is calculated by dividing available time in $(C_{t1}+O_{t1})$ to unit processing time of determined item i which is cp_i.

However, if decision is to transfer the lot in forward (which means transferring a lot from t *(t1)* to $t+1$ *(t2)*) direction, the maximum quantity that may be shifted depends upon the performance of backward shifting and inventory on-hand in analyzed period $t1$. The maximum quantity of item i to be transferred is [7];

$$Delta\_max=max\{0,min\ \{I_{i,t1},Q_{t2}\}\} \qquad (10)$$

The maximum quantity that may be shifted from $t1$ to $t2$ is limited to the amount of product that is on hand in $t1$ and the available production capacity in $t2$. The limitation here is directly related to the initial performance of lot-for-lot schedule. The quantity that will be shifted is determined by using random integer generators between 0 and *Delta_max* values [7].

3   Heuristic Algorithm

As mentioned above, algorithm consists of two consecutive stages. In the first, there is an "easy to implement" constructive heuristic which is lot-for-lot technique. Solution set obtained in first phase (Step 0) are inputs for improvement heuristic. Lot-for-lot technique results in zero on-hand inventories as initial solution, so related improvement algorithm starts with an accumulation strategy with backward shifting. The following pseudo code gives information about the flow of algorithm:

Step 0: Obtain an initial solution regarding demand by using LFL heuristic, and calculate all of parameters.

Step 1: Find periods where lot transfer take place by dominance property-1.1

Step 2: After determining periods, identify product that will be backward shifted by using holding and production cost savings via dominance property-1.2

Step 3: Calculate maximum possible amount of lot transfer by dominance property-2, determine lot size to be shifted randomly

Step 4: Transfer required production lot between periods, control overall cost change in objective function. If the change in cost is negative, then apply move. Otherwise, calculate simulated annealing parameters

Step 5: If move is rejected, initialize forward shifting procedure, apply step 2 and 3 iteratively, and transfer an amount of production lot to forward periods

The parameters which are underlined will be changed systematically to understand robustness of proposed algorithm. These variations should give information about how well algorithm performs under different circumstances.

Once algorithm obtains an initial solution, improvement heuristic is applied for n times. The number of n is determined as a function of actual stopping criteria. Improvement heuristic initiates backward shifting of lots with aforementioned dominance properties. Some nervousnesses may reveal in this phase. First nervousness of Dominance property-1 considers whether most loaded period (regular and overtime) $t2$ is 1. If $t2$ is equal to one, there will be no convenient period prior to $t2$. Therefore, a random t should be assigned to update $t1$ and $t2$. The step taken by this command may not yield a better solution, but this will help to search for global optimum without getting stuck in local optimum. After that, available capacity for period $t1$ is calculated, and then maximum quantity of item i which can be shifted without violating feasibility of available capacity is calculated.

Exact amount of transfer is determined by using dominance property-2. Whenever a step is taken, the value of objective function is updated. If there is an improvement in the objective function, new values are set as solution. Otherwise, ($\Phi_{cost} \geq 0$), PA, tSA values are calculated according to geometric cooling schedule formulated in [2]-[8]. If the related parameter is greater than threshold value, the move is accepted. Otherwise, lots are transferred from period t to $t+m$ (where m is a random integer between 1 and T-1) to overwhelm problems derived from backward shifting. The adjustments made by forward shifting are directly applied without assessment.

4   Computational Tests

Computational tests are executed on a personal computer with Intelcore i5, 2.53 GHz, 64 byte. Performance of algorithm is checked with two classes of problem sets. Class A problems are used to control optimality, while Class B is intended to reflect characteristics of algorithm for bigger problem instances [1]. The related problem type is not studied in pervious literature. Hence, data are produced with special pre-determined characteristics.

The tests of optimality (Class A) consist of 4 items, 4 periods. These set of data are used to understand how well the proposed algorithm approaches to optimal solution. Class A consists of 20 different data sets. Demands of items are normally distributed with a mean of 140 units and a standard deviation of 60. The factor h/ov is held in two levels as 1.1 and 0.9. To reflect different types of products in the data set, 4 different levels of c/h are imposed in each period. Item1 has a c/h with a mean of 12 and a standard deviation of 8. Item1 represents products with higher production cost respect to holding cost. Item2 has a c/h ratio with mean 14 and a standard deviation of 12. These types of products have huge deviations in each period in c/h level. That means for item2, there is a great fluctuation in its data for each period. For item3, the ratio is normally distributed with a mean of 7 and standard deviation of 3. Item4 has a c/h with a mean of 2 and standard deviation of 1. These types of products represent the items with high holding costs. The performance of algorithm is evaluated by using 5 different performance measures in Table 1. (Z is the objective function value of given alternative (H: Heuristic, O: Optimal, C: Lot-for-Lot))

Table 1. Results for Class A problems and deviation from optimality

	Mean	Std. Dev.	Parameters
GAP_1	3,58	2,85	$[(Z_H-Z_O)/Z_O]*100$ (distance of heuristic from optimal)
GAP_2	18,09	17,16	$[(Z_C-Z_O)/Z_O]*100$ (distance of constructive from optimal)
GAP_3	47,43	26,3	$[(Z_C-Z_H)/Z_C]*100$ (distance taken from constructive to heuristic solution)
GAP_4	54,80	44,44	$[(Z_H-Z_O)/(Z_C-Z_O)]*100$ (distance by heuristic solution to constructive solution)
GAP_5	4494 \$	3707	$[Z_H - Z_O]$ (cost gap of heuristic from optimal solution)

The related data set is analyzed in detail and it is found out that algorithm performs quite well in CLSPO. It is also understood that solution set cannot be improved if constructive heuristic yields a GAP_2 value lower than 8 percent. Due to the fact that, lot-for-lot doesn't guarantee a capacity feasible initial solution, performance criteria based on constructive heuristic may yield some misunderstandings. Overall heuristic performance highly depends on characteristics of initial solution. Starting with a good initial solution may not yield a proper ending result. The algorithm approximately takes 1 CPU second to solve the problem. For Class A type problems total numbers of iterations have not exceeded 50 in each run. The number of optimal solution obtained by using algorithm is one for this data set.

Larger instance data is collected from a propeller shaft production company, and two different sub-classes are formed. In Class B1, 20 periods (5 months in company's MRP system) are planned for 7 different basic products. In Class B2, 35 different items have been scheduled in 6 production periods. Results obtained are evaluated with two different characteristics. One of them is actual stopping criterion and other is CPU seconds. For Class B1, algorithm mostly stopped by maximum number of iteration criterion which is fixed at 5000 for each run to facilitate a fair comparison. Approximate time to obtain a result is 8-15 CPU seconds for Class B1. Company plans to schedule its production based on %70 of its product mix. Hence, other class contains more products. Most of runs in Class B2 stopped by losing forward move capability because of high number of products within short planning horizon. For this set of problem, approximate solution time is 10-20 CPU seconds. These results show that algorithm performs quite well in big problem sets as well. Another critical performance criterion is parametric robustness of algorithm. Given high fluctuations in data with item2, results obtained have low standard deviations in optimal solutions. Further analysis will be made regarding parameter dependent tests about robustness in next phase.

5   Robustness Tests

The performance of heuristic also depends on robustness of structure. In proposed CLSP heuristic, there are three sources of variability. One of most influential variability is demand pattern of products. Standard deviation of demand (STD) is widely used to test this aspect. Hence, we set three levels of demand deviation (Scenario 1-2-3). The ratio of average production cost to average holding cost is another source (c/h, Scenario 4-7). There are also some other sources of volatility which depends on metaheuristic used by algorithm. Determining the amount of lot to transfer backward or forward between periods is key source of algorithmic variability. The one which is uniform(both), right triangular to Delta_max (forward-backward), right triangular to zero (both shifting direction), and lastly right skewed right triangular for forward shifting and left skewed right triangular for backward shifting (Scenario 8-11). Algorithm simulation of different levels for these characteristics is listed in Table.2.

Table 2. Robustness Results for Class A problems

Sce. (S)	Deman. Mean (STD)	C/H Mean (STD)	Min COST	S	Delta Pattern	Dem. STD	C/H Mean (STD	Min COST
1	140(70)	7(3)	114628	8	delta_unif_unif	70	7(3)	114628
2	140(140)	7(3)	122992	9	delta_triatria_max	210	7(3)	140774
3	140(210)	7(3)	140390	10	delta_tria_tria_min	70	7(3)	116956
4	140(70)	1(2)	42486	11	tria_min_tria_max	210	7(3)	140771
5	140(70)	7(7)	84513					
6	140(70)	7(4)	99732					
7	140(70)	7(1)	155347					

It can be understood that increasing values of coefficient of variation (CV) in demand pattern results in higher overall costs. The first three scenarios also give information about computational efficiency of algorithm. Whenever standard deviation of demand is increased time required to obtain a solution also increases.

Scenario 1,5,6,7 have "c/h ratio" fixed at seven while standard deviation is changed. It can be interpreted as; decreasing values of standard deviation in c/h, results in higher overall cost. This result is quite interesting, although given fluctuation in parameters is increased while cost associated is decreased. The underlying reason is capability of algorithm which is a function of dominance properties decreases with lower values of standard deviation.

Scenarios 8-11 show us that there is not any specific best performing conditions for Delta pattern. It is also deduced that for scenarios 8 and 10, algorithm performs better. It is found out that fluctuation of input-algorithmic variables directly affect obtained results. These validations help us to understand characteristics of problem better.

6   Conclusion

In this chapter, a two-stage heuristic algorithm is presented to solve capacitated lot sizing problem with overtime decisions. Results obtained indicate that algorithm is quite satisfactory in respect to optimality tests and computational time. Further robustness test shows that algorithm is very stable against fluctuations in its parameters.

As long as the production planning department has an access to real-time inventory data, the production plan generated by algorithm may be frequently updated or the study may be used as an MPS tool to execute in weekly basis (planning horizon) for such kinds of facilities that mostly have single-level items with continuous production flow. Hence, proposed heuristic procedure may be used as a part of MRP planning tool of facilities where continuous production take place. Future studies will focus on applicability of algorithm to multi-level product structures and optimization of simulated annealing parameters for this problem type.

References

1. Tempelmeier, H., Derstroff, M.: A Lagrangean-based Heuristic for Dynamic Multilevel Multiitem Constrained Lotsizing with Setup Times. Management Science 42(5), 738–757 (1996)
2. Ozdamar, L., Barbarosoglu, G.: An integrated Lagrangean relaxation-simulated annealing approach to the multi-level multi-item capacitated lot sizing problem. International Journal of Production Economics 68(3), 319–331 (2000)
3. Ozdamar, L., Bozyel, M.A.: The capacitated lot sizing problem with overtime decisions and setup times. IIE Transactions 32(11), 1043–1057 (2000)
4. Bahl, H.C., Ritzman, L.P., Gupta, J.N.D.: Determining lot sizes and resource requirements: A review. Operations Research 35(3), 329–345 (1987)
5. Jans, R., Degraeve, Z.: Modelling Industrial Lot Sizing Problems: a Review. International Journal of Production Research 46(6), 1619–1643 (2008)
6. Baker, K.R.: Introduction to Sequencing and Scheduling. John Wiley and Sons, USA (1974)
7. Barbarosoglu, G., Ozdamar, L.: Analysis of solution space-dependent performance of simulated annealing: the case of the multi-level capacitated lot sizing problem. Computers & Operations Research 27(9), 895–903 (2000)
8. Tang, O.: Simulated annealing in lot sizing problems. International Journal of Production Economics 88(2), 173–181 (2004)

ERP Support for Lean Production

Daryl Powell[*], Erlend Alfnes,
Jan Ola Strandhagen, and Heidi Dreyer

Department of Production and Quality Engineering,
Norwegian University of Science and Technology,
Trondheim, Norway,
SINTEF Technology and Society, Trondheim, Norway
daryl.j.powell@ntnu.no

Abstract. In the traditional sense, IT has often been viewed as a contributor to waste within lean production. However, as the business world changes and competition from low-cost countries increases, new models must be developed which deliver competitive advantage by combining contemporary technological advances with the lean paradigm. By applying an action research approach, this paper evaluates the support functionality of ERP systems for lean production. We address the fundamental principles of lean production in comparison with the functionality and modules of a contemporary ERP system.

Keywords: Lean production, Enterprise resource planning, Action research.

Introduction

Though the theory of lean production is nowadays well understood, the relationship between information technology (IT) and lean production remains a controversial and far less explored topic. While lean is often characterized by decentralized coordination and control, ITs such as enterprise resource planning (ERP) systems are typically best suited to support centralized production planning. However, Powell and Strandhagen (2011) identify and explore the lean-ERP paradox, and suggest that there is a synergistic impact to be realised in combining ERP systems within the lean paradigm. Riezebos et al. (2009) also argue that modern IT can indeed be tailored to support lean, but state that further research is required to evaluate the combination of lean production principles and ERP. Therefore, the purpose of this paper is to evaluate the support functionality of a contemporary ERP system for lean production by addressing the following research question:

How can a contemporary ERP system be used to support lean production principles?

---

[*] Corresponding author.

J. Frick and B. Laugen (Eds.): APMS 2011, IFIP AICT 384, pp. 115–122, 2012.

Theoretical Background

The term lean production was popularized by Womack et al. (1990) when they compared the mass production principles of the Western world to the very simple production principles of Toyota. However, this philosophy was primarily directed at the organization and less on information technologies (Zuehlke, 2010). As such, IT has since been viewed as a contributor to the waste to be eliminated, rather than as a tool to help achieve and sustain positive change (Bell, 2006). The increasing rate of development of IT today is constantly increasing manufacturing companies' ability to react quickly and reliably to demand through increased transparency, visualization and processing capabilities. Moody (2006) suggests that, although profitability can be enhanced in any number of ways, one of the most rewarding and direct avenues is through the use of technology. Riezebos et al. (2009) suggest that modern IT (such as contemporary ERP systems) can be tailored to support lean production.

ERP is one of the most widely accepted choices to obtain competitive advantage for manufacturing companies (Zhang et al., 2005). ERP systems are designed to provide seamless integration of processes across functional areas with improved workflow, standardization of various business practices, and access to real-time data (Mabert et al., 2003). The fundamental benefits of ERP systems do not in fact come from their inherent "planning" capabilities but rather from their abilities to process transactions efficiently and to provide organized record keeping structures for such transactions (Jacobs and Bendoly, 2003).

In order to evaluate the support functionality offered by ERP systems for lean production, we use the fundamental principles of lean manufacturing identified by Womack and Jones (1996): *"precisely specify **value** by specific product; identify the **value stream** for each product; make value **flow** without interruptions; let the customer **pull** value from the producer; and pursue **perfection**"* (Hines, 2010).

By conducting a study of the extant literature in the form of academic journals, trade journals, textbooks, and white papers; we identify 15 fundamental areas in which an ERP system could be configured to support lean production principles. The 15 areas, which we call the 15 keys to ERP support for lean, are summarized in Table 1:

Table 1. 15 keys to ERP support for lean production

No	Principle	An ERP system for lean production should:	Reference:
1	Value	Support customer relationship management	(Chen and Popovich, 2003)
2		Automate necessary non-value adding activities (e.g. backflushing)	(Hamilton, 2009)
3	Value stream	Enable process-modelling to support standard work processes	(IFS, 2008, Prediktor, 2010)
4		Provide a source for easy-to-find product drawings and standard work instructions	(Houy, 2005, Tjahjono, 2009)
5		Support information sharing across the supply chain	(Bjorklund, 2009, Koh et al., 2008)

Table 1. (*continued*)

6	Flow	Create synchronized and streamlined data flow (internal & external)	(Hamilton, 2003)
7		Support line balancing	(Steger-Jensen and Hvolby, 2008)
8		Support demand levelling	(Hamilton, 2009)
9		Support orderless rate-based planning (e.g. takt-time)	(IFS, 2010)
10		Provide decision support for shop floor decision making	(Hamilton, 2009)
11	Pull	Support kanban control	(Hamilton, 2009, Masson and Jacobson, 2007)
12		Support production levelling (Heijunka)	(Masson and Jacobson, 2007)
13		Support JIT procurement	(Masson and Jacobson, 2007)
14	Perfection	Provide a system to support root-cause analysis and for the logging and follow-up of quality problems	(Bjorklund, 2009)
15		Provide highly visual and transparent operational measures (e.g. real time status against plan)	(Prediktor, 2010)

Research Methodology

In this study we adopt an action research approach by following an ERP implementation project at a case company in Trondheim, Norway. One of the authors has been actively involved at the case company during the introduction of lean practices since 2009, and has also been present during the design and analysis phase of the ERP implementation process since January 2011.

Action Research

Philips (2004) suggests that there is a broad Scandinavian tradition for action research. Action research can be defined as a participatory, democratic process concerned with developing practical knowing in the pursuit of worthwhile human purposes, grounded in a participatory worldview (Reason and Bradbury, 2006). Essentially, it focuses on bringing about change (action) and contributing to knowledge (research). McNiff and Whitehead (2009) suggest that doing action research involves the following:

1. Taking action (changing something);
2. Doing research (analyzing and evaluating both the change and change process);
3. Telling the story and sharing your findings (disseminating the results).

Action research is considered as an appropriate methodology for this study as both lean production and ERP systems are very much applied in industry, thus a "learning by doing" approach is very suitable.

Client System: Noca AS

Noca is a manufacturing and service supplier within electronics and electronics development. Established in 1986, Noca delivers development, prototypes, batch production, and assembly for customers within innovation and entrepreneurs in high-tech industries. Noca has 50 employees and an annual turnover of €11.5m (2010). The company is currently actively applying lean practices to their operations, having started with value stream mapping (VSM) in 2009, followed by 5S in 2010. Noca has also identified a need to enhance their supporting processes, such as production planning and control, and have therefore chosen to implement a new ERP system, Jeeves Universal (Figure 1). Recognised as "Sweden's most popular ERP system – 2009", Jeeves Universal is claimed to be a flexible (customized) standard ERP system (ERPResearch.org, 2010). The ERP implementation process at Noca will consist of three phases – a design and analyse phase (phase zero); an implementation phase (phase one); and an improvement phase (phase two). This paper considers phase zero only.

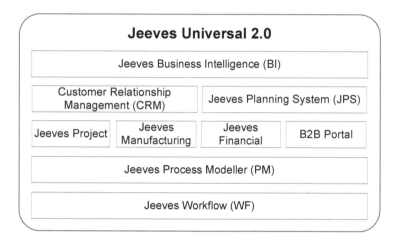

Fig. 1. The "Jeeves Universal" ERP system and selected modules

Results

This paper presents preliminary findings following phase zero of the ERP implementation project, which we call the design and analysis phase. By evaluating the functionality of the chosen ERP system and selected modules (Figure 1) against the lean principles identified by Womack and Jones (1996), we are able to propose a theoretical framework for ERP support for lean production (Figure 2). This framework can be used by researchers and practitioners when combining lean and ERP.

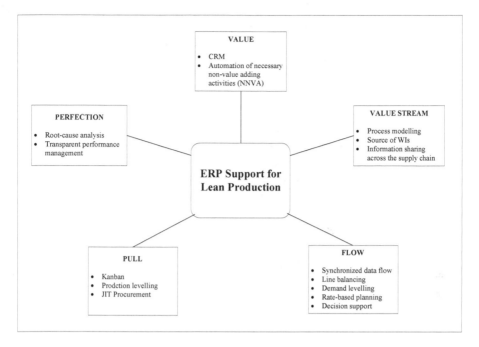

Fig. 2. ERP Support for Lean Production – a Conceptual Framework

Value
It was identified that a significant element of the ERP system that helps contribute to value creation from the point of view of the customer was the application of a customer relationship management (CRM) module. The ERP system also offered select functionality to automate the necessary, non-value adding activities, such as back-flushing (e.g. Hamilton, 2003).

Value Stream
In terms of supporting the value stream, it was shown that the ERP system offered process modelling functionality to support the creation of standard work processes, as well as providing a source for easy-to-find product drawings and work instructions. Functionality that enables the sharing of information across the supply chain is also offered with the B2B Portal. The ERP system also supports a number of different levels within the factory, ranging from the individual operation (process level), through production group (work cell level), to flow group (value stream level).

Flow
The main module of the ERP system supporting flow manufacturing was identified as the Workflow (WF) module, which integrated all functions of the enterprise and aided the creation of a "paperless" paper-trail for continuous flow of information supporting the production processes. Functionality is also offered to support line balancing; demand levelling; and orderless rate-based planning through the use of Jeeves planning

system (JPS). Finally, and particularly through the use of business intelligence (BI), decision support for shopfloor decision making allows shopfloor workers to become even more empowered in the lean environment.

Pull

Even though the client system is too early in its lean journey to implement a pull system, ERP support for pull production was still taken into consideration. It was noted in particular that the JPS is a very useful visual tool that can be used to support production levelling (heijunka). It is also anticipated that the WF module can be used to support pull production through enabling and supporting material and information flow. JIT procurement can be supported through integrating a product's BOM within both Jeeves Project (for prototyping and ramp-up) and Jeeves manufacturing (for volume production).

Perfection

Finally, in terms of perfection and continuous improvement, it was highlighted how the ERP system can make use of both BI and JPS (as a visual tool) to provide a system for logging and follow-up of quality problems, and to provide a system for highly visual and transparent operational measures.

Conclusion

By considering the functionality of the Jeeves Universal ERP system against the five lean principles, we conceptualized a framework for ERP support for lean production, which we call *"the 15 keys to ERP support for lean production"*. The framework (shown in Table 1) highlights the theoretical support functionality of the Jeeves Universal ERP system for lean production. This can be used by researchers and practitioners for the future integration of ERP systems within the lean paradigm.

Though measures have been taken to increase the validity of this research, a number of limitations do however exist. For example, a commonly cited limitation of the action research approach is the focus upon only one company. Though it is often not the main goal of action research to generalise results, the results herein can be used as a template for reflecting on new experience (Friedman, 2010). We also only considered an ERP system of one single vendor, Jeeves. We suggest that further investigation with other case companies and/or other ERP system vendors would help to make our framework more generalizable.

A particularly interesting subject that arose as a result of the work was ERP support for pull production. Therefore, the authors suggest that a greater focus should be taken on the role of ERP systems in helping manufacturers to realise JIT production, one of the most important dimensions of lean. Further work should therefore investigate ERP support for pull production, helping to strengthen the validity and contribution of this work.

References

Bell, S.: Lean Enterprise Systems: Using IT for Continuous Improvement. Wiley and Sons, Hoboken (2006)

Bjorklund, J.: 10 Ways to Use ERP to Lean the Manufacturing Supply Chain. Managing Automation (2009), http://www.managingautomation.com/uploadedimages/downloads/10_Ways_ERP_Lean_Manuf.pdf (accessed September 2010)

Chen, I.J., Popovich, K.: Understanding customer relationship management (CRM). People, process and technology. Business Process Management Journal 9, 672–688 (2003)

Erpresearch.org. What is Jeeves Universal ERP? (2010), http://octavesolutions.com/erpresearch/?p=5 (accessed June 2011)

Friedman, V.J.: Action Science: Creating Communities of Inquiry in Communities of Practice. In: Reason, P., Bradbury, H. (eds.) The Handbook of Action Research. Sage, London (2010)

Glenday, I., Sather, R.: Breaking Through to Flow (2005), http://www.leanuk.org/downloads/LFL_2005/Day2_Plenary_Glenday_Sather.pdf (accessed May 2009)

Hamilton, S.: Maximizing your ERP system: a practical guide for managers. McGraw Hill, New York (2003)

Hamilton, S.: Managing Lean Manufacturing using Microsoft Dynamics. McGraw Hill, New York (2009)

Hines, P.: The Principles of the Lean Business System. S A Partners (2010), http://www.sapartners.com/images/pdfs/the%20principles%20of%20the%20lean%20business%20system.pdf (accessed February 2011)

Houy, T.: ICT and Lean Management: Will They Ever Get Along (2005), http://mpra.ub.uni-muenchen.de/2502/ (accessed September 2010)

IFS. Going Lean, Step by Step, with IFS Applications (2008), http://www.manmonthly.com.au/Article/Going-Lean-Step-by-Step-with-IFS-Applications (accessed September 2009)

IFS. IFS Applications for Lean manufacturing. IFS AB (2010)

Jacobs, F.R., Bendoly, E.: Enterprise resource planning: Developments and directions for operations management research. European Journal of Operational Research 146, 233–240 (2003)

Koh, S.C.L., Gunasekaran, A., Rajkumar, D.: ERP II: The involvement, benefits and impediments of collaborative information sharing. International Journal of Production Economics 113, 245–268 (2008)

Mabert, V.A., Soni, A., Venkataramanan, M.A.: Enterprise resource planning: Managing the implementation process. European Journal of Operational Research 146, 302–314 (2003)

Masson, C., Jacobson, S.: Lean Planning and Execution Software: Extending Lean Thinking Across the Enterprise (2007), http://www.oracle.com/corporate/analyst/reports/industries/aim/amr-20378.pdf (accessed September 2010)

Mcniff, J., Whitehead, J.: Doing and Writing Action Research. Sage, Los Angeles (2009)

Moody, P.E.: With Supply Management, Technology Rules! Supply Chain Management Review (May/June 2006)

Philips, M.E.: Action research and development coalitions in health care. Action Research 2, 349–370 (2004)

Powell, D., Strandhagen, J.O.: Lean Production Vs. ERP Systems: An ICT Paradox? Operations Management 37, 31–36 (2011)

Prediktor. Lean (2010), http://www.prediktor.no/business_solutions/lean/Pages/default.aspx (accessed February 2011)

Reason, P., Bradbury, H. (eds.): Handbook of Action Research. Sage Publications, London (2006)

Riezebos, J., Klingenberg, W., Hicks, C.: Lean Production and information technology: Connection or contradiction? Computers in Industry 60, 237–247 (2009)

Steger-Jensen, K., Hvolby, H.-H.: Review of an ERP System Supporting Lean Manufacturing. In: Koch, T. (ed.) Lean Business Systems and Beyond. IFIP AICT, vol. 257, pp. 67–74. Springer, Boston (2008)

Tjahjono, B.: Supporting shop floor workers with a multimedia task-oriented information system. Computers in Industry 60, 257–265 (2009)

Womack, J.P., Jones, D.T.: Lean Thinking: Banish Waste and Create Wealth in Your Corporation. Simon and Schuster, New York (1996)

Womack, J.P., Jones, D.T., Roos, D.: The Machine that Changed the World. Harper Perennial, New York (1990)

Zhang, Z., Lee, M.K.O., Huang, P., Zhang, L., Huang, X.: A framework of ERP systems implementation success in China: An empirical study. International Journal of Production Economics 98, 56–80 (2005)

Zuehlke, D.: SmartFactory - Towards a factory-of-things. Annual Reviews in Control 34, 129–138 (2010)

High Resolution Supply Chain Management –
A Structural Model for Optimized Planning
Processes Based on Real-Time Data

Volker Stich, Tobias Brosze, Fabian Bauhoff, Florian Gläsner,
Simone Runge, and Marcel Groten

Institute for Industrial Management at RWTH Aachen University,
Pontdriesch 14/16, 52062 Aachen, Germany
{Volker.Stich,Tobias.Brosze,
Fabian.Bauhoff,Florian.Glaesner,Simone.Runge,
Marcel.Groten}@fir.rwth-aachen.de

Abstract. The following paper presents an approach for enabling manufacturing companies to cope with dynamic environment conditions and the increasing planning complexity of present supply chains. High Resolution Supply Chain Management (HRSCM) strives to meet these challenges by applying cybernetic principles to the Production Planning and Control (PPC). Therefore, standardized information channels and coordination mechanisms are defined to be able to react even faster and more flexible. The presented structure of the HRSCM is derived from principles of the Viable System Model. Based on this the different system elements of the HRSCM, their functions and their interactions are described. Finally it is outlined how the developed model will be experimentally evaluated and gradually enhanced in future to enable improved decisions on all levels of production under volatile environmental conditions.

Keywords: production management system, high resolution supply chain management, system engineering, cybernetic, adaptability.

1 Introduction

Today, the production industry is increasingly confronted with the influences of a dynamic environment and the ensuing continuously increasing planning complexity [1], [2]. Therefore, a successful Supply Chain Management depends beside the process efficiency on high information availability for being able to handle this challenge. In contrast, the lack of standardized interfaces and channels of information combined with complex processes and a low automation level characterizes the current status in many companies. The consequences are wrong decisions in the planning processes, caused by poor communication, data based on experience and the application of average values, as well as uncertain values of demand, costs and inventory. Current solution approaches try to tackle these problems by using highly sophisticated and centralized planning methods [3]. These centralized planning approaches constrain the ability of companies to react quickly and flexibly on internal

J. Frick and B. Laugen (Eds.): APMS 2011, IFIP AICT 384, pp. 123–131, 2012.

and external disturbances. This leads to an increasing gap between plans and reality and a decreasing effectiveness of companies [4].

High Resolution Supply Chain Management aims to reduce the planning complexity by applying decentralized, self-optimizing control loops to the Production Planning and Control (PPC). Changable organizational structures and processes, a high information transparency, increased capacity flexibility, as well as the continuously synchronization of the concerned planning elements are necessary preconditions for ensuring the achievement of the above mentioned aims [1], [2].

2   Methodological Approach and Preconditions for HRSCM

Conditioned by technological innovations like RFID and the informational integration of companies, operational information are recently available in a new level of granularity and time offset [5]. The HRSCM approach uses such information in the context of production management and combines the functional principle of control loop based planning with an appropriate organizational structure for production management.

In this context the term "High Resolution" stands for the new quality of information referring to granularity and time offset. To fulfill the challenge of a higher changeability, it is necessary to remove the static planning processes of central-controlled approaches [4], [6]. The object in focus is specified by the term "Supply Chain Management" (SCM). HRSCM offers a framework for allocating all intra- and inter-company SCM activities within the focus of a company's order processing.

Conditioned by the interdisciplinary character of HRSCM, the approach has to meet technological and organizational requirements. The technological preconditions for the HRSCM are given by the necessity for realistic and achievable values for planning, which depend on the generation of information in the required quality by e.g. sensors and their availability through IT systems. The organizational preconditions are determined by the complexity of organizational entities and their dynamic environment. The organizational structure of HRSCM must be able to handle this complexity with due regard to maintain the internal stability and the fit to the external environment.

3   Findings: Structure of HRSCM

The structure of the HRSCM reference model is determined by the above-mentioned preconditions. The ability for handling the company complexity and the influences of a dynamic environment of production industry, as well as the reduction of efforts for coordination, can only be achieved by using structural decentralization and high reactivity [7].

Different models have been tested for their eligibility for fulfilling the mentioned requirements: Architecture of Integrated Information Systems (ARIS), Dortmund Process Chain Model and the Stuttgart Business Model. These models describe companies in a steady-state status and disregard the issues of changeability, decentralization, self-optimizing and the adaption to a dynamic environment.

An established management cybernetic reference model, which meets the requirements, is the Viable System Model (VSM) [8], [9], [10]. Therefore it is appropriate to use the VSM as a structural framework for HRSCM.

3.1   Viable System Model

The VSM was evolved by BEER in the 1960s as a management model to support managers dealing with complex management processes. BEER underlines, that viability in the context of business management does not mean the bare survival of a firm. Rather it is to be understood as a continuous maintenance of the system identity within a steadily changing environment [11].

Three fundamental cybernetic principles are the basis of the VSM. Viability implies that a company must react to internal and external disturbances in an appropriate way, in order to sustain its existence. Recursiveness is a principle to structure organizational systems in a self-similar way. Hence, a viable system is a composition of nested systems, which are viable systems, too [6], [12]. In this context, autonomy means that a system can act independently as long as it is in accordance with its meta-systems' rules [11], [13].

BEER introduces for realizing these three principles a specific structure for systems, which is a necessary condition for their viability. According to that every viable system consists of five subsystems, which have to fulfill specific functions (see Figure 1).

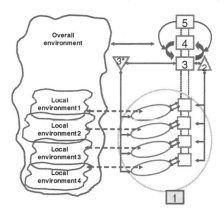

Fig. 1. Structure of the VSM, following [11], [12], [13], [14]

System 1 contains the operative units, which are responsible for the fulfillment of the essential purpose of the organization. The elements of System 1 come with relative autonomy, which means that they plan, execute and control the assigned task with consideration of their given target system and boundaries. They are embedded in a multi-level managerial structure (Systems 2-5). The coordination system (System 2) ensures that the operative units cooperate for a common purpose. The target systems and boundaries of autonomy of the operative units are defined by the operative management (System 3). System 3 obtains information on the internal stability from the managerial units of System 1, the coordination system and the monitoring system

(System 3*). From above it gets information and instructions from the hierarchically superior Systems 4 and 5. The assignments of System 4 and 5 include the observation and analysis of the relevant environment (System 4), as well as the definition of the system identity and the overall target system [15].

3.2   Application of Viable System Model to Supply Chain Management

The VSM-based reference model of SCM is characterized by an explicit process orientation and includes the whole order processing from the processing of an offer, to the production and delivery of the finished product [16]. In contrast to a conventional order processing, the cybernetic approach increases the ability of dealing with internal or external disturbances and ensures a continuous checking for necessary system adaptions. As already mentioned in chapter 2 the focus is on the inter-factory order processing. Consequently the selected operational units are the processes of the order processing: quotation processing, projecting, construction, ordering, purchasing, manufacturing, assembling, shipping and after sales.

These processes of order processing are embedded in meta-systemic managerial structure, consisting of the operative Process Management and Control, the Process Coordination Center and the Tactical, Strategic and Normative Production Management (see Figure 2). The aim is to provide the operative units with the greatest possible autonomy, which is only limited by the necessity for coherency of the overall system. The extent of autonomy depends on the situational environmental disturbances, thus it is variable over the time. In general case all tasks of order processing are handled decentralized by the operational units. The meta-systemic management units are only in charge for sustaining the synchronization of the overall system [15]. For handling these disturbances and dynamic environment conditions it is necessary to specify dynamic reference value corridors, reference values with high granularity and accuracy, as well as to take care for short response-times for every system level.

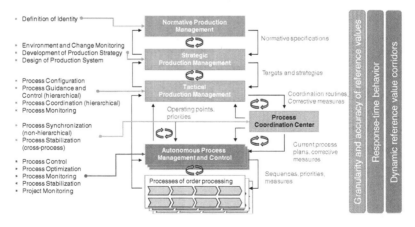

Fig. 2. Assignment of the order processing to the structure of the VSM

The functions and interactions of the elements of a changeable Production Management System are briefly specified below [15].

The Autonomous Process Management and Control consists of the local management and control units of the above mentioned operational processes. The tasks of the local Process Management units consist in the controlling and monitoring of the operative processes. It is responsible for determining the local target systems of the processes in coordination with the Tactical Production Management. The instruction of the higher managerial levels are interpreted and passed as concrete measures to the different processes. Furthermore the Process Management units are competent to define rules of conduct, routines, sequences and priorities for the processes, as well as developing and optimizing methods and tools to eliminate local disturbances. The local process control units gather and observe defined process indices and share status messages of orders and resources with the control units of the other processes. Beside this they are in charge for the planning and execution of routines to react on known disturbances, as well as implementing measures of the managerial units.

The stabilization, synchronization and the project controlling of the operative processes is ensured by the Process Coordination Center. In the context of stabilization of the processes it is responsible for controlling the observance of the operating points, the damping of oscillations between the processes by using standardized measures and the implementing of formal and informal communication channels. Additionally tasks are the controlling of defined priority rules and the usage of routines for synchronizing the different measures of and between the processes. Tasks of project controlling consist in the monitoring of the order progress and basic dates and the implementing of measures to ensure the order fulfillment, if there is a deviation compared with the plan.

The overall internal stabilization of the operative processes is the guiding principle of the Tactical Production Management. It defines guidelines and scopes of action for the Process Management and Control and the Process Coordination Center. The four primary duties are the process configuration, the process controlling of the internal operative processes at a higher level, the superior process coordination and the monitoring of the operative processes. For accomplishing these duties, it is exemplarily competent to define operating points for the overall system, to specify superior targets, priorities and rules of conduct, to arrange adaptations of the system structure and to optimize the used measures and tools for ensuring the striving for the common target system.

The long-term maintenance and improvement of the companies' competitive advantages by anticipating possible future prospects, adapting the organizational structure to dynamic environmental changes and the consequent alignment of the production system are the key aspects of activity of the Strategic Production Management. Consequent subtasks encompass the monitoring of the environment, the strategic production development and configuration of the production system. The continuous matching between the market-driven requirements and the internal capability to fulfill these is a prerequisite for deriving strategic factors of success and defining priorities and challenges for the production logistics. Within the framework of the production configuration for example logistical targets and defaults of location planning are defined.

The highest level of the production management system is represented by the Normative Production Management. It accounts for aligning the overall target system with due regard to the companies' identity, values and norms. That leads to the desired condition of the overall production system.

Concluding it is important to straighten out that the introduced reference model is not constructed in a classically hierarchical way. The authority results from the different logical capacity of the management units.

4   Application and Enhancement of the Reference Model

In the following a description of how the developed model will be applied and enhanced in future is given. First, the general approach of concretion based on experiments is described and afterwards it is outlined what has to be considered when performing experiments.

Based on the developed cybernetic reference model, test-beds of a self-optimizing production will be build and studied in different use cases and the results will be evaluated. Different disciplinaries will be incorporated and the influence of human decision making is an important factor to examine. In this way a holistic view on a socio-technical production system under consideration of the factors human, technology and organization will be reached.

To assure analysis on all levels of production systems, three use cases have been defined. These use cases will address the comprehensive application of self-optimizing control. The control loops on cell-level, Production Planning and Control (PPC) as well as on Supply Chain level will be integrated.

One use case addresses the supply chain level. The use of high-resolution data in the supply chain level for local planning will be investigated. Questions regarding the granularity of information are considered as well as the visualization of information for the planner. Another use case will focus on the interface between human and machine as well as the design and coordination of autonomous sub-systems on production level to converge a global optimum under consideration of all of these aspects. The third use case will lay its focus on the integration of human decision making in complex situations in the context of production control.

The test-beds of these use cases will be linked gradually and will be integrated afterwards in a real-production environment. Results will be reflected against the developed model to identify weaknesses and improve the model based on scientific results. The model integrates control loops on different levels and thus enables improved decisions on all levels of production under volatile environmental conditions. This leads to adaption of an optimal operating point and integrates the deterministic and the cybernetic perspective.

As the test-beds will be linked and integrated in a real production environment, the resulting potential of integrated research means a paradigm shift in research of production systems. Such research environments establish new ways of analyzing the connections in production systems.

Test-beds enable experimental research in real production environments. When performing experiments in real-life the complexity of the experiments increases significantly [17]. Thus, the considered system shows a high complexity. In order to control the systems complexity it is necessary to manage the experimental real production environment in a pre-defined manner. In this way it is possible to obtain out of the high amount of factors in a complex system a well-structured analysis that delivers the required results.

For that reason, a statistical design of experiments is a possible approach to decrease the complexity while maintaining high information content of the experimental results [18].

When applying the method of statistical design of experiments, in first place an experimental design has to be developed. One has to take into account the information that is required to choose the correct factors. For that reason, it is necessary to identify all possible factors in a screening of the experimental environment. This enables to differentiate significant factors from non-significant factors. Due to this reduction of factors, first experiments can be done with an acceptable amount of time and money.

It is recommended to choose a high distance between the factors in a first set of experiments, so that it is possible to identify first influences of the chosen factors on the system behavior [17]. Where significant factors on the system behavior can be identified, these can be studied in further experiments with an increasing amount of factors. In this way a good ratio between input resources and significant results can be achieved.

In the following figure 3 the context between the factors (Input), the system and the results is shown. There are factors which can be modified by the design of experiments and those who are given by the experimental environment. Depending on the behavior of the system results can be obtained for certain factors [17], [18].

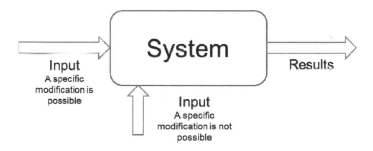

Fig. 3. Schematic representation of a System with different types of input and system-dependent results

By the application of statistical design of experiments, it is also possible to identify not only the main effects, but also interactions between factors. Using a computer, statistical analysis can be obtained with low effort and in this way the significance of certain factors can be proved easily.

5   Conclusion

Within the paper a changeable Production Management System has been presented, for decreasing the planning complexity in Supply Chains and improving the handling of dynamic environment conditions within PPC. After introducing the preconditions of the model, we have derived the structural framework of the HRSCM from the Viable System Model and specified the functions of the system elements and their interactions. Further research is needed to verify and validate the model. To that purpose use-cases on different levels of production have been defined and the results of these experiments will we contribute to further enhancement of the model. Thereby a specific focus should be dedicated to the determination of the granularity and accuracy of the individual reference values, the specific response-time behavior and the corresponding dynamic reference value corridor. As shown before an adequate way for the investigation could be the statistical design of experiments as this method allows generating statistically proofed results in an acceptable amount of time.

References

[1] Brosze, T., Bauhoff, F., Stich, V., Fuchs, S.: High Resolution Supply Chain Management – Resolution of the Polylemma of Production by Information Transparency and Organizational Integration. In: Vallespir, B., Alix, T. (eds.) APMS 2009. IFIP AICT, vol. 338, pp. 325–332. Springer, Heidelberg (2010)

[2] Schuh, G., Stich, V., Brosze, T., Fuchs, S., Pulz, C., Quick, J., Schürmeyer, M., Bauhoff, F.: High resolution supply chain management: optimized processes based on self-optimizing control loops and real time data. In: Production Engineering, pp. 433–442. Springer, Heidelberg (2011)

[3] Meyer, J., Wienholdt, H.: Wirtschaftliche Produktion in Hochlohnländern durch High Resolution Supply Chain Management. In: Supply Chain Management III, vol. 7, pp. 23–27 (2007)

[4] Fleisch, E., Fuchs, S., Gottschalk, S., Güthenke, G., Höhne, T., Jacobs, G., Junker, F., Millarg, K., Narr, C., Nyhuis, P., Schuh, G.: High Resolution Production Management. Auftragsplanung und Steuerung in der individualisierten Produktion. In: Brecher, C., Klocke, F., Schmitt, R., Schuh, G. (eds.) Wettbewerbsfaktor Produktionstechnik. Aachener Perspektiven, pp. 451–472. Shaker, Aachen (2008)

[5] Fleisch, E., Müller-Stewens, G.: High Resolution Management: Konsequenzen der 3. IT-Revolution auf die Unternehmensführung. Schäffer-Poeschel, Stuttgart (2008)

[6] Beer, S.: Brain of the firm: the managerial cybernetics of organization. The Penguin Press, London (1972)

[7] Frank, U., Giese, H., Klein, F., Oberschelp, O., Schmidt, A., Schulz, B., Vöcking, H., Witting, K.: Selbstoptimierende Systeme des Maschinenbaus. Definitionen und Konzepte. Bonifatius GmbH, Paderborn (2004)

[8] Rüegg-Stürm, J.: Das neue St. Galler Management-Modell. Grundkategorien einer integrierten Managementlehre: Der HSG-Ansatz. Haupt, Bern (2003)

[9] Schwaninger, M.: Intelligent organizations. Powerful models for systemic management. Springer, Berlin (2009)

[10] Westkämper, E., Zahn, E.: Wandlungsfähige Produktionsunternehmen. Das Stuttgarter Unternehmensmodell. Springer, Berlin (2009)

[11] Beer, S.: The heart of enterprise. Wiley, Chichester (1979)

[12] Malik, F.: Strategie des Managements komplexer Systeme. Ein Beitrag zur Management-Kybernetik evolutionärer Systeme. Haupt, Bern (2006)

[13] Gomez, P.: Die kybernetische Gestaltung des Operations Managements. Eine Systemmethodik zur Entwicklung anpassungsfähiger Organisationsstrukturen. Haupt, Bern (1978)

[14] Espejo, R., Harnden, R.: The viable system model. Interpretations and applications of Stafford Beer's VSM. Wiley, Chichester (1989)

[15] Brosze, T.: Kybernetisches Management wandlungsfähiger Produktionssysteme. Dissertation RWTH Aachen, Aachen (2011)

[16] Balve, P., Wiendahl, H., Westkämper, E.: Order management in transformable business structures – basics and concepts. In: Robotics and Computer Integrated Manufacturing, vol. 17, pp. 461–468 (2001)

[17] Siebertz, K., van Bebber, D., Hochkirchen, T.: Statistische Versuchsplanung – Design of Experiments. Springer, Heidelberg (2010)

[18] Kleppmann, W.: Taschenbuch Versuchsplanung – Produkte und Prozesse optimieren. Carl Hanser Verlag, München (2008)

A Framework Based on OEE and Wireless Technology for Improving Overall Manufacturing Operations

Martha-Patricia Garcia[1], Javier Santos[2], Mikel Arcelus[2], and Elisabeth Viles[2]

[1] Instituto Tecnológico de Chihuahua II, Chihuahua, México
patytec2@yahoo.com
[2] TECNUN - School of Engineering, University of Navarra, San Sebastian, Spain
{jsantos,marcelus,eviles}@tecnun.es

Abstract. Manufacturers have the challenge to increase productivity given complex manufacturing environments. A source that provides substantial levels of productivity is the overall equipment effectiveness (OEE) metric, which is an indicator to improve not only equipment utilization; but also the overall manufacturing operations, because of the valuable information that comes from the availability, performance and quality rates. Although information technologies have been introduced, companies use manually recorder data and have complicated measurement procedures. As a consequence, inaccurate information is generated and opportunities to improve productivity are missed. This paper presents a continuous improvement framework based on Lean manufacturing philosophy, operated by a system of wireless devices to support the real time equipment performance metrics. In order to validate the framework, results of a case study are exposed.

Keywords: Continuous improvement, Total productive maintenance, overall equipment effectiveness, lean manufacturing, operations management.

1 Introduction

Manufacturers usually consider the overall equipment effectiveness (OEE) as a metric that is only related to maintenance activity, and they do not take into account other valuable OEE-information for improving their entire manufacturing operations; this valuable information comes only if companies have a set of precise elements such as: an accurate data, proper calculation of rates, and adequate analysis of information in order to identify and locate the six main losses proposed by Nakajima and other hidden production losses.

In this manufacturing edge the manufacturing environment is complex, there are many electronic systems, intelligent systems and software tools supported by information technologies (IT) available for equipment monitoring and control, which includes automatic data collection, OEE calculations and a variety of key performance indicators (KPI). However, many manufacturing companies are using as a traditional way, manually recorder data. Additionally, the use of sophisticated systems does not guarantee optimum improvements, particularly because of the lack of a proper continuous

J. Frick and B. Laugen (Eds.): APMS 2011, IFIP AICT 384, pp. 132–139, 2012.
© IFIP International Federation for Information Processing 2012

improvement methodology [8]. Thus, collecting accurate data, understanding manufacturing losses and adopting a suitable continuous improvement methodology are significant factors that this study is concerned with.

This paper presents a study for developing a continuous improvement framework, whose purposes are the accurate calculation of the OEE indicators and the systematic integration of improvement methodology based on lean manufacturing tools. This framework has the advantage of using a portable wireless system called Plug&Lean (which is composed of a set of wireless devices) [12] to support the real time automated collection, calculation, and graphic presentation of data. The research methodology utilized is a case study.

2   Literature Review

Three theoretical concepts are relevant to our study: Lean manufacturing, Continuous Improvement and a combination of TPM and OEE:

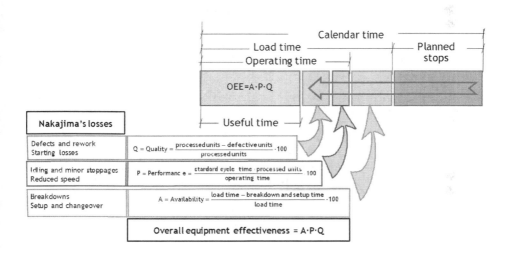

Fig. 1. The OEE and the six main losses [13]

- Lean manufacturing considered as an operational management philosophy focused on reducing waste in a manufacturing system. The literature defines waste as everything that increases cost without adding value for the customer [16]. This philosophy is composed of principles, methodologies and tools, and it functions on the basis of continuous improvement and worker involvement.
- Continuous improvement (CI) can be literally defined as continuous incremental improvement of the standard way of working [7]. The existing literature shows that there is no theoretical base for CI as a concept for what is considered into the quality terms given its attributes [2].

- TPM methodology [11] has been expanding significantly within manufacturing companies, because of the tangible results it provides. This is an improvement methodology developed by Nakajima, who proposes OEE as a measure that attempts to reveal hidden losses. The OEE calculation is split into three components: availability, performance and quality, which identify the six big losses (Figure 1).

3   Related Work

Bhuiyan and Baghel [3] state that although the continuous improvement (CI) methodology has evolved over the years, little research has been directed towards developing a model that allows organizations to structure a CI methodology that suits in a better shape to their needs and motivate an authentic participation of workers.

There are several studies on the Lean and OEE that result in different opinions about its potential. Grishnik and Winkler [6] state that companies avoid understanding all the component of an entire Lean implantation, missing gold opportunities to grow a better competitive position. Abdulmalek and Rajgopal [1] use a case study to demonstrate how lean manufacturing tools, when used appropriately, can help the process industry improve product quality and increases overall operational effectiveness.

Other authors [4] explored the use of the OEE not only as an operational measure but also as an indicator of process activities, and they concluded that the OEE should be balanced by other traditional measures. Jonsson and Lesshammar [8] proposed that planned downtime be taken into account as an important measure, and that it should be added to the OEE in order to have the whole picture of manufacturing performance. Ljungberg [9] discussed the importance of the personnel's understanding of the magnitude of and reason for machinery losses in order to provide an appropriate base for planning improvement activities; Dilorio and Pomorsky [5] proposed a TPM loss analysis model for generating accurate and non-theoretical OEE metrics; Wang and Pan [15] concluded that the process of collecting data in an automatically way provides high levels of accuracy in the OEE calculations and it makes it easier to see hidden losses.

4   Research Methodology

The methodology utilized in this study is the case study, which has been recognized as being particularly suitable for theory refinement [14]. According to Yin [17], a case study is a linear but iterative process where the experimental study shows primary results. Miles and Huberman [10] established that, in case study research, it is necessary to have very well defined key factors that lead to the expected results. The present study focuses on the development of continuous improvement activities as a systematic way of improving equipment efficiency, thus our key factors are equipment efficiency and continuous improvement, and the link between them conceptualizes our proposed framework.

5   The Framework

The framework was developed as a functional framework based on the lean manufacturing philosophy and the operation is supported by the wireless Plug&Lean-system. Figure 2 shows the frameworks's design. There are four specific objectives of the framework, which are described as follows:

- To automate the collection of equipment performance data in real time
- To display graphical information and charts related to the production performance indicators
- To determine the root cause of losses
- To drive towards to implement a structured methodology to improve manufacturing operations by using OEE information

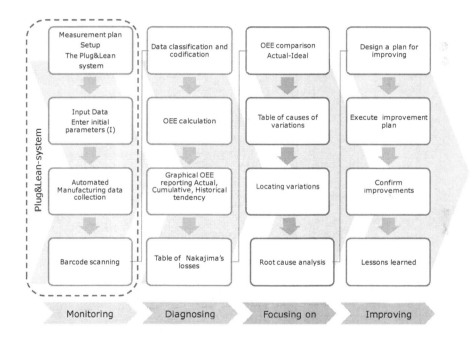

Fig. 2. The Plug&Lean-CiMo framework's design

The operation of the overall framework depends on the processes, procedures and activities and their interrelation. This means that each process is represented by a procedure and a series of activities linked to the resources required for operating. The focus of this framework is: make bottom-line improvements with less effort in an easily structured way.

5.1   Plug&Lean System

The framework proposes the utilization of a new device to facilitate the gathering of data. The Plug to Lean wireless tool is a handle set of compact wireless components: sensors and a laptop computer, that seamlessly work together. It simply needs to be plugged into a designated area to sense the performance of equipment during a selected production time.

The device is not only for collecting data, it also contains software for displaying a series of events to conduct improvement actions in a focus area (Figure 3).

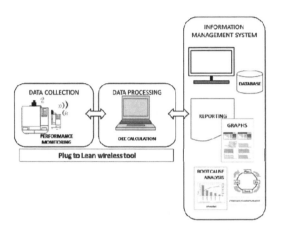

Fig. 3. The Plug&Lean system schema

5.2   Framework Operation

This section describes the procedures, activities and resources required for each process whose descriptions are given in the following paragraph:

5.1.1   Monitoring

This stage encompasses the procedure for collecting the manufacturing data by monitoring the performance of equipment or production process during a period of time. This stage is composed of 2 processes: (1) setting up the Plug&Lean system, and inputting the initial parameters, and (2) measuring the performance through the automated collection of data from machinery; a barcode system is utilized in order to scanner the codes of both the losses and the causes of performance variations presented. The gathered information is stored in a data-base.

5.1.2   Diagnosing

The Diagnosing stage is a procedure for processing the collected data and reporting real levels of OEE through graphics and charts in order to allow the examination of availability (A), performance (P), quality (Q), utilization (U) and OEE indicators. It uses software based on a conventional Microsoft application and Nakajima's theory of losses, taking information from the data-base. This stage comprises three processes: (1) conformation of the table of manufacturing data collected in order to make a classification; (2) determine the Nakajima's losses based on grouping and codifying the collected data; (3) Calculation of metrics and the graphical report. The graphical report consists on the presentation of current OEE indicators, the presentation of cumulative and historical OEE charts and the economic impact of losses.

5.1.3   Focusing On

The Focusing On stage is a procedure to analyze the information that comes from the diagnosis stage, for localizing and analyzing causes of performance variation in equipment. It is composed of three processes: (1) the analysis of losses by a comparison between actual and ideal OEE rates; (2) the localization of the losses through the 5M's; (3) the root-cause-analysis (RCA) which is supported by the seven quality tools, RCA methodology and other lean tools, in order to determine the source of losses.

5.1.4   Improving

The Improving stage is where a structured continuous improvement plan is developed in order to implement actions to eliminate or mitigate losses. This stage takes the information from the Focusing On stage, and then suggests for each kind of losses the suitable Lean manufacturing tools that should be implemented as a countermeasure. In addition, this stage is for confirming the improvements undertaken in terms of quality, cost and time. After confirmation of improvements, the lessons learned process is suggested.

6   Case Study

The manufacturing company we selected, as a case study, is located in the Basque region of Spain and operates three semi-automated and one automated continuous production lines. The continuous improvement framework was tested from May to December 2009, on the one automated line.

The first task carried out in the case study was to choose a multidisciplinary team member to plan the overall testing activities for the device. Meanwhile, another important task was conducted: an analysis to determine the procedure that the company was following at the time to collect data and how it calculated its efficiency or performance state. Next, OEE calculations were introduced to four automated production lines, a new classification of downtime was proposed, and a new way of teamworking to achieve improvement was suggested. One of the study reports is presented in Figure 4, which content a graphic which allows comparing indicator levels after implementing our framework.

Three important contributions was achieving during the study: (1) the company understood the importance of the identification of planned and non planned downtime as well as to count the re-work activity as a quality loss; (2) The company's management created its first multidisciplinary team formed by personnel from the quality, the maintenance and the production areas, they were involved in order to participate, and make suggestions and decisions during the implementation of the framework; and (3) the company's acceptance of the OEE metrics and the adoption of the framework.

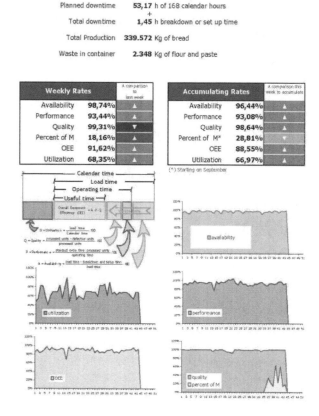

Fig. 4. Case study reporting graph

7   Conclusions

The proposed framework is driven by two key factors: the OEE indicators and the continuous improvement methodology. The advantage of the framework is that it operates with a structured CI methodology and accurate information thanks to the integration of the Lean manufacturing tools and the Plug&Lean system. The framework was tested on a continuous manufacturing production line, and future work related to this study will be to test the framework in a discrete manufacturing system. The study's contributions are: the integration of a cutting edge wireless device in the field of operations management, not only for maintenance but also for continuous improvements activities and a valuable affordable procedure for businesses, especially small ones, that increases efficiency in the entire manufacturing operation.

References

1. Abdulmalek, F.A., Rajgopal, J.: Analyzing the benefits of lean manufacturing and value stream mapping via simulation: a process sector case study. IJPE 107(1), 223–236 (2007)
2. Besant, J., Calfyn, S., Gallagher, M.: An evolutionary model of continuous improvement behavior. Technovation (21), 67–71 (2001)
3. Bhuiyan, N., Baghel, A.: An overview of continuous improvement: from the past to the present. Management Decision 43(5), 761–771 (2005)
4. Dal, B., Tugwell, P., Greatbanks, R.: Overall equipment effectiveness as a measure of operational improvement. A practical analysis. IJOPM 20(12), 1488–1502 (2000)
5. Dilorio, S., Pomorski, T.: SEMI Equipment Performance and Productivity Measurement – Methods, Algorithms, and Standards. In: Brooks-PRI Automation, Asia User Conference, Shanghai (2003)
6. Grishnik, K., Winkler, C.: Make or break. How manufacturers can leap from decline to revitalization. McGraw-Hill, Company, USA (2008)
7. Imai, M.: Kaizen. The key to Japan's competitive success. Random House, Inc., Canada (1986)
8. Jonsson, P., Lesshammar, M.: Evaluation and improvement of manufacturing performance measurement systems – the role of OEE. IJOPM 19(1), 55–78 (1999)
9. Ljungberg, O.: Measurement of overall equipment effectiveness as a basis for TPM activities. IJOPM 18(5), 495–507 (1998)
10. Miles, H., Huberman, M.: Qualitative data analysis: A sourcebook. Sage Publications, Beverly Hills (1994)
11. Nakajima, S.: Introduction to TPM. Productivity Press, Cambridge (1988)
12. Santos, J., Garcia, M.P., Arcelus, M., Viles, E., Uranga, J.: Development of a wireless Plug&Lean system for improving manufacturing equipment diagnosis. IJCIM 24(4), 338–351 (2011)
13. Santos, J., Wysk, R.A., Torres, J.M.: Improving production with Lean thinking. John Wiley& Sons, Hobokcn (2006)
14. Voss, C., Tsikriktsis, N., Frohlich, M.: Case research in operations management. IJOM 22(2), 195–219 (2002)
15. Wang, T.Y., Pan, H.C.: Improving the OEE and UPH data quality by automated data collection for the semiconductor assembly industry. Expert System with Applications 38, 5764–5773 (2010)
16. Womack, J., Jones, D.: Lean Thinking. Simon and Schuster, New York (1996)
17. Yin, R.: Case Study Research Methods. Sage Publishing, Newbury Park (1994)

Consideration of Changing Impact Factors
for Optimization of Post-series Supply

Uwe Dombrowski, Sebastian Weckenborg, and Christian Engel

Technische Universität Braunschweig,
Institute for Production Management and Enterprise Research,
Langer Kamp 19, 38106 Braunschweig, Germany

Abstract. The increased use of electric and electronic components is a trend in several branches of industry. The short life cycles of these innovative components compared with the life cycles of the primary products lead to challenges regarding an effective spare parts management. To guarantee an availability of spare parts during the whole period of the post-series supply, a period of up to 15 years in the automobile industry, a structured planning process is needed. The current approaches for the planning of the post-series supply concentrate on static impact factors to evaluate a supply scenario for the post-series supply, but for a detailed assessment of possible supply strategies changing impact factors have to be considered. A methodical approach for this will be described in this paper.

Keywords: Spare Parts Management, Post-Series Supply, Changing Impact Factors, Product Development.

1   Life-Cycle-Oriented Spare Parts Management

The efficient supply of spare parts during the whole product life cycle is a quality aspect of manufacturing companies, which can lead to a better customer loyalty and thus to a stronger market position [1]. However, the increasing product complexity and shorter product life cycles cause a higher effort in the spare parts management. Especially the increased use of innovative components like electric and electronic components is a challenge for many companies because of the short innovation cycles of these components and the fact, that these components are often assembled in primary products, which have a life cycle that is much longer.

1.1   Supply Strategies and Supply Scenarios

The model of the life-cycle-oriented spare parts management focuses on this specific problem and contains several supply strategies to realize an efficient post-series supply. Common supply strategies are the development of a compatible successive product generation, storing a final lot, the periodical internal or external production, the reuse of used components and the repair of used components. [2], [3] These six strategies are explained in the following part.

J. Frick and B. Laugen (Eds.): APMS 2011, IFIP AICT 384, pp. 140–147, 2012.

Compatible Parts: In this strategy parts from the current series production are used for the spare parts supply of the previous product generation. A requirement for this strategy is the backward compatibility of the new product generation. It has to be sure that the functionality, the interfaces and installation space of the new part generation are matching the specifications of the older product.

Storing a Final Lot: This strategy is based on a forecast of the all-time demand of the spare parts. The all-time demand is manufactured in a final lot and stored in a warehouse. The spare part demand during the supply period is satisfied from this existing stock. Due to the long supply period, the lack of historical data and the random failure behavior of many electric and electronic parts, the forecasts are afflicted with a high uncertainty. So the risk of under- or overstocking is given. In addition, a long storage time of the spare parts might lead to technical problems and high storage costs.

Internal Production: A periodical internal production over the entire supply period avoids the difficult forecast and technical problems due to a long storing period. However, a production could become impossible because of a discontinuation notice of required components. In addition, the internal production may be inefficient as a result of poor capacity utilization of testing and production facilities.

External Production: Using the strategy external production companies try to minimize the inefficiencies of the periodical internal production by outsourcing the production process to a third company. The external manufacturer has adjusted its production to the requirements of the post-series supply (e.g. high flexibility, small quantities) and can produce more efficient.

Reuse of Used Components: According to new laws more and more products are taken back by the manufacturers at the end of the primary products life cycle. Well functioning components (e.g. electronic control units) can be reused as an overhaul spare part after the reliability was checked. [4]

Repair of Used Components: This strategy includes the repair and overhaul of used defective parts. Mainly due to increased legal framework in the field of environmental protection, this strategy is gaining more and more importance.

In many cases it is not possible for the manufacturers to use only one of these strategies for the entire period of the post-series supply. Therefore supply strategies are combined to a supply scenario as shown in figure 1. In this example after the end of production of the primary product, the demand of spare parts is first covered with the strategy of internal production. At a certain point it becomes cheaper for the company to store a final lot. To compensate missing parts due to a wrong forecast of the all-time demand, it can be necessary to change the strategy again at the end of the supply period. In this phase it is appropriate to use the strategy repair of used components. Because the original production and testing equipment probably is not available any more, in most cases this strategy is the only way to satisfy the customers' needs. A detailed planning process under consideration of the specific circumstances of the company is necessary.

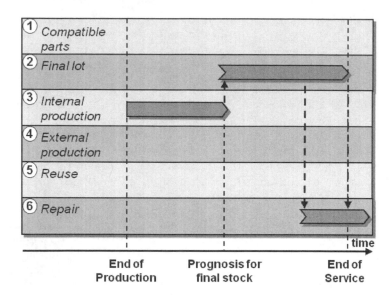

Fig. 1. Supply strategies and supply scenarios

Support for the selection of a supply scenario may be given by a decision matrix which is a result of a joint research project. Figure 2 shows a decision matrix for the pre-selection of possible supply scenarios by using three different impact factors. The first impact factor is the possibility of using compatible parts. The storability of a specific spare part and the ability of an uncomplicated reconditioning are further impact factors in this decision matrix. The impact factors compatible parts and the storability are subdivided into two categories, whether compatible parts exist or not and if the shelf life is high or low. The impact factor reconditioning is subdivided into three categories. These describe if it is generally possible and if it is reasonable from an economical point of view or not. If a recondition might generally be possible but uneconomic the strategy recondition can merely be used as a contingency strategy. However, if it is technical and economical feasible, the strategy of recondition can be used as main strategy.

In comparison with the described supply strategies the matrix contains five modified strategies. The internal and external production are combined to the strategy periodical production and the strategy recondition integrates the repair and the reuse of used components. Figure 2 shows an example for a chosen strategy by using the decision matrix. The selection of a supply scenario is shown for a spare part with no compatible parts. However there is no problem by storing the spare part for a longer period. From the technical point of view the spare part has the ability to be reconditioned but using this strategy is uneconomic. This leads to the supply scenario PFA. The spare parts supply is ensured by the internal production in the first phase. If the production is no longer economically possible, for example because the quantity of demanded products is too low, it will be switched to the strategy of storing a final lot. Because it is technically possible to recondition used parts it is not necessary to have a high safety stock. Thus the risk of overstocking is minimized; a shortfall can be intercepted by reconditioning. The matrix can vary depending on the products and the approved supply strategies (e.g. no reconditioning for security-related components). Therefore, the matrix has to be adapted company specific. [1]

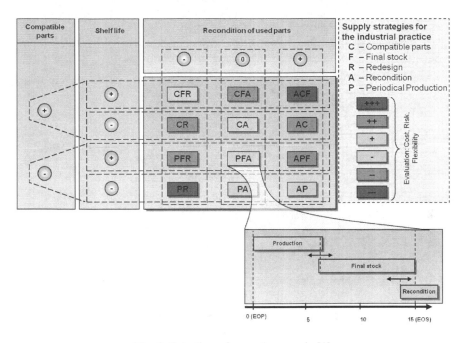

Fig. 2. Selection of a supply scenario [1]

1.2   Deficits of the Current Planning Process of the Post-series Supply

In the field of electronics for the automobile industry the period of post-series supply is about 15 years. In this period the availability of the products has to be ensured. The previously mentioned impact factors are only a small selection of factors which have an impact on the choice of a supply scenario. To ensure that the post-series supply is assured it is necessary that all relevant impact factors are considered in a structured process. In the current planning process only static impact factors are considered even though the development over time of each impact factor is important and has an influence on the suitability of a supply strategy. Furthermore, the current process only supports planning the post-series supply of existing product structures and does not provide a feedback to product development. This feedback is necessary in order to develop products according to the requirements of the post-series supply. In the following part an approach to avoid the identified deficits will be described.

2   Approach for Consideration of Changing Impact Factors

The approach for consideration of changing impact factors contains four main steps. These are the identification of relevant impact factors (1), the rating of the identified impact factors (2), the evaluation of impact factors in regard to each supply strategy (3) and the analysis of conflictive impacts and feedback to the product development (4). Each step contains different tasks. A structured overview is given in figure 3.

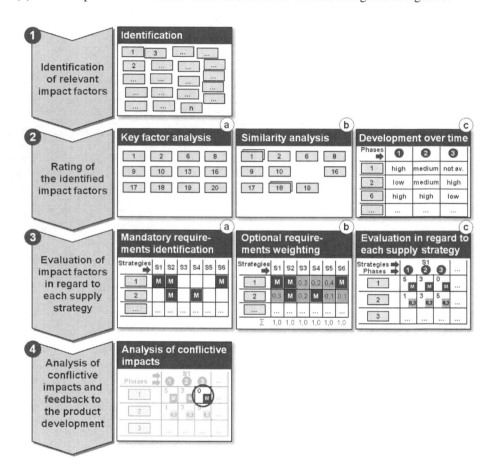

Fig. 3. Consideration of changing impact factors

2.1   Identification of Relevant Impact Factors

In the first step the relevant impact factors have to be identified. This identification has to take place in an early stage of product development process and requires experts from different divisions of the company, e.g. sales, research, development or production. In addition to the previously mentioned factors, further factors with respect to the post-series supply of electronic devices can be named, e.g. legal terms, changes of customer requirements, prices of components, quantity of suppliers, and changes in business competition influence the post-series supply. The identification and assessment of the impact factors has to be based on experience of specialists and can be supported by the use of structuring methods, such as mind maps or the Delphi-method [5], [6]. This identification should be done for each product. However, most of the impact factors are general or depend on the branch of industry. If new relevant impact factors are identified in the course of time these can be integrated in the method.

2.2   Rating of the Identified Impact Factors

The rating of the identified impact factors is the second step of the method. First the most relevant impact factors, the key factors, have to be identified (see figure 3, 2a). The key factor analysis can be supported by an impact matrix, which is also used in the scenario technique. By this analysis the number of impact factors can be reduced and the following steps of the methods will be less time-consuming. In addition to the impact analysis an impact factors similarity analysis can be used to combine similar factors (see figure 3, 2b). [7] This is important because these impact factors would be double-weighted in the next steps of the method otherwise.

The evaluation of the expected development over time is the following task. This is necessary because the relevance of the different impact factors varies depending on the phase of the post-series supply. For this assessment the rating scales for the impact factors and the length of the phases have to be defined (see figure 3, 2c). The literal description of the development is useful in this step because this will prevent misunderstandings. The rating scales are to be chosen according to the products, the supply periods and the required level of detail. There are also industry-specific differences which have to be taken into account. E.g. in the first phase of post-series supply the quantity of required products is higher than in the second or third phase but the predictability of the demands is best in the third phase. The availability of the components is highest in the first phase of the post-series supply. The method should not be understood as a tool for a single use but as a tool for a continuous improvement process. Initially, a low level of detail is helpful to understand the system. Later on the method can completed with additional details. The use of classic time series analysis methods, lifetime analysis methods and causal analysis methods are suitable for the evaluation of the rate curves. Also comparisons with previous series based on analogy methods can be used to identify the development over time. [8]

2.3   Evaluation of Impact Factors in Regard to Each Supply Strategy

The identified development over time allows evaluating the impact factors in regard to the different supply strategies. Therefore a classification of the impact factors in mandatory requirements, that have to be fulfilled to realize a strategy, and optional requirements is necessary. For this purpose a matrix can be used (see figure 3, 3a). For example, the availability of components is a mandatory requirement for the strategy internal reproduction. For the strategy of storing a final lot on the other hand the storability of parts is mandatory. The optional requirements of each strategy are weighted (see figure 3, 3b). This can be done using the pairwise comparison, a cost-benefit analysis or the analytic hierarchy process [9], [10]. The change in customer requirements can be described as an example. Customer requirements will probably decrease over the time and the customer will be satisfied with a used spare part after 15 years. Thus, this impact factor has a different relevance on the strategy production as on the strategy repair. As another example, the influences of increasing prices for purchased parts during the supply can be described. The increased costs of purchased parts are not important for the strategy storing a final lot in contrast to the strategy internal production.

To evaluate the suitability of each strategy, the identified development over time has to be quantified. E.g. the demand of spare parts has an influence on the strategy of internal production. If the demand decreases over time the suitability of the strategy will deteriorate continuously due to small lot sizes which are unsuitable for certain types of manufacturing because of long machine setup times. Furthermore the predictability of the demands can only be determined inaccurately in the first phase of the supply period. The accuracy of the forecast will increase in the following phases, so that the suitability of the strategy internal production will rise. The quantified values have to be analyzed for each strategy and each phase of the post-series supply (see figure 3, 3c). Finally the mandatory requirements and the different weighted values lead to a value of benefit for each phase of each strategy. This allows deriving adequate strategies for each phase, which are suitable for the impacts. The combination of the most suitable phases of the supply strategies finally leads to one or more preferred supply scenarios.

2.4   Analysis of Conflictive Impacts and Feedback to the Product Development

In the fourth step the preferred supply scenarios are analyzed in detail. The impact factors are sometimes conflictive so that a specific supply scenario cannot be implemented. Conflicting impact factors are identified and their impacts are rated. For each of this impact factors the alternatives can be described systematically, e.g. the use of another component which has a better availability. If it would be recognized that the availability of the components are critical for a certain strategy, the availability can be increased by early negotiations with the supplier. By the adaption of the impact factors in the product development the feasibility of the supply scenarios and thereby the post-series supply can be optimized [3].

3   Summary

Due to the increased use of innovative components and the life cycles between these components and the primary products it is necessary to establish an effective spare parts management. This can lead to a better customer loyalty and thus to a stronger market position. The current approaches for the planning of the post-series supply generate an efficient supply scenario. These approaches concentrate on static impact factors to evaluate a supply scenario for the post-series supply, but for a detailed assessment of the possible supply strategies the dynamic of the impact factors has to be considered.

In this approach changing impact factors are considered in a structured process. Relevant impact factors are identified and rated and transferred to each supply strategy. Conflictive impacts are analyzed and a feedback to the product development is given. By this adaption of the impact factors in the product development the feasibility of the supply scenarios and thereby the post-series supply can be optimized.

References

1. Dombrowski, U., Schulze, S., Wrehde, J.: Efficient Spare Part Management to Satisfy Customers Need. In: Proceedings of the International Conference on Service Operations and Logistics and Informatics, Philadelphia, pp. 304–309 (2007)
2. Hesselbach, J., Dombrowski, U., Bothe, T., Graf, R., Wrehde, J., Mansour, M.: Planning Process for the Spare Part Management of Automotive Electronics. In: WGP Production Engineering, vol. XI/1, pp. 113–118 (2004)
3. Dombrowski, U., Weckenborg, S., Schulze, S.: Method-supported Product Development for Post-series Supply. In: Bernard, A. (Hrsg.) Global Product Development. Proceedings of the 20th CIRP Design Conference, Ecole Centrale de Nantes, Nantes, France, April 19-21. Springer, Heidelberg (2010)
4. Hesselbach, J., Mansour, M., Graf, R.: Reuse of components for the spare part management in the automotive electronics industry after end-of-production. In: Proceedings of the 9th CIRP LCS, Erlangen, pp. 191–197 (2002)
5. Gracht von der, H.A., Darkow, I.-L.: Scenarios for the Logistics Service Industry: A Delphi-based analysis for 2025. International Journal of Production Economics 127(1), 46–59 (2010)
6. Buzan, T., Buzan, B.: The mind map book: Unlock your creativity, boost your memory, change your life. Pearson/BBC Active, Harlow (2010)
7. Gausemeier, J., Fink, A., Schlake, O.: Szenario-Management: Planen und Führen mit Szenarien. 2. bearbeitete Auflage. Hanser, München (1996)
8. Loukmidis, G., Luczak, H.: Lebenszyklusorientierte Planungsstrategien für den Ersatzteilbedarf. In: Barkawi, K., Baader, A., Mantanus, S. (Hrsg.) Erfolgreich mit After Sales Service: Geschäftsstrategien für Servicemanagement und Ersatzteillogistik. Springer, Berlin (2006)
9. Saaty, T.L.: Decision Making for Leaders: The Analytic Hierarchy Process for Decisions in a Complex World, 3rd edn. RWS Publishing, Pittburgh (2001)
10. Bullinger, H.-J.: Einführung in das Technologicmanagement: Modelle, Methoden, Praxisbeispiele. Teubner, Stuttgart (1994)

Loss Prevention in Transportation to Ensure Product Quality: Insights from the Cargo Insurance Sector

Alexander C.H. Skorna[1] and Elgar Fleisch[1,2]

[1] University of St.Gallen, Institute of Technology Management
[2] ETH Zurich, Chair of Information Management
{Alexander.Skorna,Elgar.Fleisch}@unisg.ch,
efleisch@ethz.ch

Abstract. Transport operations are vulnerable to many types of risks due to an increasing dynamic and structural complexity of today's supply chain networks. Globally distributed sourcing and production lead to more transported goods in general but also to more high-value cargoes being shipped around the world. However, detailed information about the transport condition and integrity are not available in the end-to-end chain as transportation operations lack in full transparency. Therefore, this paper identifies causes and risks of cargo-related losses by an analysis of cargo insurance claims. Based on these results, appropriate preventive measures to improve the product quality during transportation are derived.

Keywords: Cargo insurance, claims analysis, loss prevention, quality improvement, supply chain risk management, transportation.

1   Introduction

Production and retail companies as shippers focus today on global distribution and local buying strategies to achieve comparatives advantages as well as to realize persistent growth. Shippers redesigned their transportation concepts to make themselves more flexible to customer needs and less vulnerable to market fluctuations as well as supply chain disruptions. Companies demand high levels of transport flexibility, customized transportation solutions, information systems integration, and short transit times at low costs. Therefore, today's transportation networks are highly complex and tightly-coupled systems that are vulnerable to many types of disturbances [1,2]. Transportation is thus mainly outsourced to logistics companies. On the one hand, this redesign results in a decreasing size of shipping units and higher transportation frequency to make the supply chains more agile. On the other hand, it leads to reduced dispensable safety stocks to follow state-of-the-art lean production programs [3].

Transportation is vulnerable to numerous types of risks such as loss or damages through temperature, humidity, tilt, and shock. Damages and losses mean problems for all supply chain actors, for instance due to business interruptions, lack of product availability and in consequence lost sales. Lately, new approaches of cargo insurance practices can be observed offering support and know-how to shippers for safeguarding their

J. Frick and B. Laugen (Eds.): APMS 2011, IFIP AICT 384, pp. 148–156, 2012.
© IFIP International Federation for Information Processing 2012

supply chains from these risks. These measures are preventive and aim at the improvement of transport processes as well as product quality, for instance, by fostering risk awareness among personnel employed in transportation and by the implementation of new devices to monitor and control transport conditions. Obviously, cargo insurance companies recognized claims prevention as an instrument to handle challenges and risks proactively [4]. A cargo insurance contract covers usually goods in-transit from the point of production to distribution and retail with all temporary storages in between. Thereby, the terms of contract (Incoterms) determine the liable actor in case a claim occurs in a transportation network.

2   Related Work on Loss Prevention and Transportation

To gain a deeper understanding of the potentially conflicting topics of insurance and prevention we review insurance research and insurance theory literature considering the prevention concept in general. Smith [5] has investigated the optimal insurance coverage due to the basic mechanisms of insurance. He distinguishes between 'over insurance', when the insurer overcompensates the insurance holder in terms of the occurred loss, and 'insurance selling', when the insurer pays not the full compensation but a proportion of it. We focus on the latter case, in which the insurance holder is taking a short position in its own loss. This is sensible because in this case risk prevention leads to balance the 'short position' [6,7].

In terms of cargo insurance the insurer usually compensates the shipper with the insured value of the affected goods when the claim is proven. But consequential losses due to e.g., business interruptions or out-of-stock situations (OOS) are not insured, which constitute the main motivation to implement prevention ensuring product quality in transportation from the shipper side, too.

Ehrlich and Becker [8] were the first to distinguish traditional 'market insurance' from two types of protection against damages and in particular loss. These are today typically referred to as 'loss reduction' and 'loss prevention' in insurance literature. Both represent engineering-types of traditional insurance alternatives which Ehrlich and Becker consider as 'self-insurance' and 'self-protection' respectively. Particularly, self-insurance lowers the financial severity of any occurred loss, while self-protection reduces the likelihood of loss [8,9]. An example of self-insurance is the installation of a sprinkler system to protect buildings or warehouses against fire damages. Accordingly, an example of self-protection is the equipment of doors with high security locks to hinder potential thieves from entering.

Impulses related to risk mitigation and prevention in transportation can be assigned to the supply chain risk management literature. It summarizes all strategies, measures, processes, and technologies to reduce supply chain risks [10-11]. As the authors explain, this is mainly achieved by (1) the avoidance of risks through proactive elimination of claims causes, (2) transferring risks to external parties through outsourcing or cargo insurance contracts, and (3) handling risks through setting intervention plans.

Identifying and assessing likely risks and their possible impact on operations across the supply chain is a complex challenge [12]. However, to properly assess vulnerabilities in a supply chain, firms should not only identify direct risks to their operations, but also the risks to all other entities as well as those risks caused by the transportation linkages between organizations [11]. Risk itself is an elusive construct that has a variety of different meanings, measurements and interpretations depending on the academic research field. Following the theoretical prevention concepts in insurance research outlined above, we use a hazard-focused interpretation common in risk management. Risk is defined as the probability of a given event multiplied by the severity of a negative business impact [13]. Sources of risk are losses e.g., theft, damage due to shock or tilt, spoilage of goods due to temperature or humidity as well as in-transit or customs delays [14]. Usually, this goes in line with quality drops affecting the transportation operations as well as the shippers' commitment to supply their customers. The causes of these risk sources can occur from inside and outside of a transportation network and vary greatly in their magnitude, attributes, and effects. Their consequences can be very heterogeneous, especially considering the often global scales of logistics operations [15,16] and networks [17] in which transportation is conducted.

Risk management related to the transportation chain includes processes which reduce the probability of occurrence and/or impact that detrimental supply chain events have on the specific company. Typical risk management strategies rely on closer partnerships among the transportation actors and risk sharing, e.g., outsourcing or consignment stocks [18]. Christopher and Lee [19] suggest improved end-to-end visibility as one key element in any strategy designed to mitigate supply chain risk. The authors argue that supply chain confidence increases with the quality of supply chain information.

The literature analysis reveals that first insights on quality improvements due to managing risks in supply chains exist. But, which particular impact a quality drop has on a transportation network remains still unclear. Moreover, the exact causes of claims and their impact on transportation processes are so far under researched. The following section provides first insights from the insurance sector.

3   Empirical Analysis of Cargo Insurance Claims

In order to impose proactive loss prevention measures, it is essential to have reliable information on the major problem areas in transportation. Therefore, we investigate original cargo claims reported to one of the largest cargo insurance companies in the Swiss insurance market over a time period of four years (2005 - 2008). The sample consisted in total of 7.284 claims. As claims reporting within cargo insurance usually is delayed by several months, insurance data have been generated out of the insurer's claims system in late 2009 and the analysis was conducted during 2010.

The average loss per incident was US$ 19.265 indicating the great potential of possible quality improvement and loss prevention activities. The five largest incidents involved trucks as transportation mode and pharmaceuticals as affected goods. At this point it is important to note that the sample is not fully representative for the entire cargo insurance industry, as the customer portfolio is focused on the typical Swiss industries as pharmaceutical, chemical, and machinery as well as banks. Still, it provides some valuable insights for the identification of the current problem areas in transportation.

The analysis follows two different perspectives. (1) The *insurance view* focuses on the effective claims handling costs per incident. This reveals areas for possible reductions in payments and resources as well as premium adjustments. (2) The *client view* focuses on the claims frequencies in order to identify possible areas to optimize transportation processes and product quality with cargo related loss prevention measures. The following two figures demonstrate these two perspectives and the related differences by analyzing causes and transportation mode relevant for claims incidents. As shown, frequent losses are not always simultaneously expensive ones.

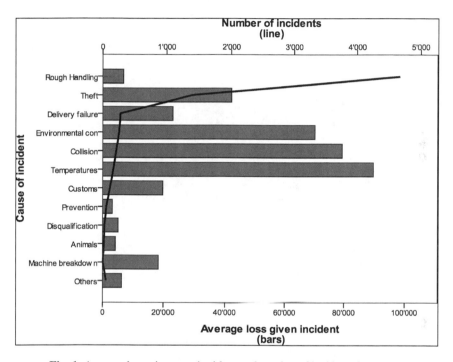

Fig. 1. Average loss given per incident and number of incidents by causes

We investigated the claims causes in detail and compared the average loss given incident and number of incidents shown in Figure 1. Overall more than 90 percent of the claims can be allocated to the following six causes: rough handling, theft (includes pilferage), delivery failures, environmental impact (includes condensation, moisture, fire, and oxidation), collisions, and temperature. More precisely, about 60 percent of the claims incidents are related to rough handling, but only 20 percent of the claims costs involve rough handling. Thus, the average loss given in terms of rough handling with US$ 6.237 is relatively low.

Theft in particular of high value cargo is a serious threat to the profitability of companies. According to the claims statistic a third is spent on theft incidents, which account in terms of loss incidents for 20 percent of all claims. In this case we identified that especially high value air cargo shipments and full truck loads in Eastern Europe and the Russian Federation are a special target for organized crime.

Moreover, and in comparison to Western Europe, the claims data sample indicates that cargo theft is also a major concern in North America.

The impact of temperature as the cause with the highest average loss given per incident involved primarily food, special chemicals, and pharmaceuticals. The restrictive handling advices and close temperature corridors, in which the shipments have to be distributed, makes cool chain transportations a complex task. Besides the main causes of loss rough handling and theft, the analysis also demonstrates a need for action for environmental and temperature related impacts.

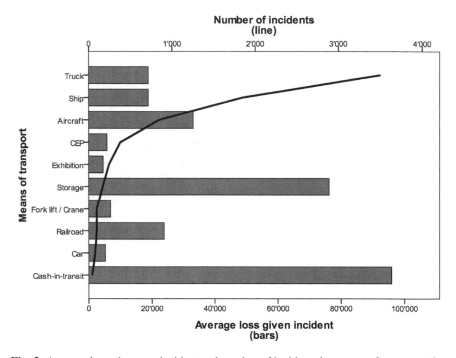

Fig. 2. Average loss given per incident and number of incidents by means of transportation

Extending the view of claims causes with the detailed analysis of the transportation mode Figure 2 shows that the main incidents occur in road transportation, sea as well as air freight. Hereby, it is remarkable that the average loss given incidents for truck and ship are about identical, while it is distinctly higher in case of air cargo. Imports and exports due to trade volumes in Europe are dominated by sea (72%/ 73%), but according to the trade value we see an increase of air cargo shipments which account for 23% (import) and 29% (export) [20]. Air cargo shipments focus on high value cargo such as consumer electronics, spare parts, pharmaceutical, and chemical products which also explains this shift in terms of average loss given.

The high average loss at storage is particularly tightened by the impact of environmental conditions, while changes in temperatures pose a significant threat to transportation, too. Remarkable is the extreme average loss related to cash-in-transit. These rare events are related to secure transportation and theft cases and a particular problem for the cargo insurance industry in general. Insurance companies have to hold funds available when insuring these 'big loss' risks in the form of financial reserves which are not eligible for investment purposes. This has a comparably high impact on the investment strategy of an insurance company and makes cargo insurance a complex niche market due to the ever possible big loss threat.

According to the above considerations, we derive suitable areas for quality improvement and claims prevention measures. In terms of claims frequency these are related to rough handling and theft as well as to the main transportation modes truck, sea, air, and its related transportation concepts. Due to the high average loss given we particularly focus on theft and high value shipments which are often also affected by environmental and temperature conditions.

In the following section we provide useful loss preventive measures to improve product quality and avoiding losses during transportation.

4   Measures to Improve Product Quality and Prevent Cargo Losses

In general, the installation of a supply chain wide risk management is sophisticated. The more supply chain actors need to be integrated into risk management and the more risk situation, risk bearing ability, and risk management approaches differ from each other, the higher the implementation complexity. We distinguish *technology-oriented* and *organizational measures*, which both are suitable to prevent cargo losses and in parallel retain product quality as well as the retail shelf live.

Supply chains with lesser turnovers and direct deliveries have advantages in terms of successful operational process improvements. Thus, the choice of transportation routes so that the smallest possible amount of turnovers is necessary is a first obvious step. Henceforth, the choice or change in the transportation company because of their higher transportation quality or better damages and losses record in comparison to the existing one may be considered. The reduction of the transportation time e.g., by express deliveries or air freight reduces the exposure of the goods to loss risks. The implementation of special packaging concepts e.g., air cushions or foam pads increases the goods resilience to shock and drop events. Logistics companies so far only rely on mandatory trainings for their personal related to freight securing as well as handling dangerous and sensitive goods. Several authors mention the poor training level in these operations [11,21,22].

The problem of above mentioned organizational measures is their poor transparency. Shippers can hardly control if the requested and paid special handling of goods complies with the actual operating procedures. Due to standardization efforts and decreasing prices for electronic parts, localization and condition monitoring has become a widely common service proceeding to even make risk monitoring and controlling autonomously possible. The assessment of changes in environmental conditions, e.g., temperature, humidity, and shock is a most important task for risk monitoring and controlling in transportation. This is also closely linked to detect quality losses by taking the changes in environmental conditions into account. According to Jedermann and Lang [23] only few sensor types are suitable for integration into transportation because of cost and energy consumption constraints. Temperature and humidity sensors consume the least energy as measures have to be taken only in intervals of several minutes. But shock and acceleration sensors have to operate permanently; otherwise they might miss a shock event.

However, cargo insurance companies begin to integrate prevention measures into their business and try to motivate clients implementing these accordingly. We developed together with a Swiss cargo insurance company a new technology-based prevention approach to be implemented at the insurance clients. The suggestions range from the implementation of very basic but inexpensive and easy to use prevention measures as indicators and data-loggers to compound sensor-telematic devices. All trigger the relevant risks derived in the previous section but achieve different levels of transparency and monitoring capabilities. Thus, basic indicators are in general more appropriate for frequent losses, telematic devices in turn are suitable for expensive losses with high loss amounts per incident. Shipping and handling monitors such as impact, tilt or temperature indicators are effective, highly regarded devices which can be considered as "low-tech" sensors. Once the goods are subjected to an impact exceeding a specified range, the indicator changes its color creating a permanent and immediate indication of mishandling. In contrast, telematic devices can be equipped with various sensors measuring i.e., temperature, humidity, and acceleration. The devices are capable for GPS localization and real-time data transmission through mobile and/or satellite networks. The devices are usually linked to web portals, which summarize the actual cargoes' status of integrity and transport conditions. Thus, damage and theft locations can be exactly pinpointed enabling fast corrective actions to be taken at any time. In between of indicators and telematic devices, data-loggers record the conditions during transportation which can be analyzed after the final delivery.

5   Conclusion

Integrated risk management in the insurance industry focuses so far on claims management and risk transfer through underwriting. Addressing risks in the supply chain requires the identification of risky events and vulnerabilities. The results shown in the claims analysis proofs the potential of risk preventive measures in transportation. These measures and related operative risk management principles expand the traditional risk management approach regarding loss prevention, consulting, implementation of risk controlling, and cooperation in the field of technology-supported early intervention to avoid or at least minimize losses. Risk prevention should consequently be based on continuous monitoring of the transport and warehousing conditions aiming to confine claims amounts. Implementing such technologies creates transparency and supports to identify and control cargo claims as well as vulnerabilities in transportation operations. In parallel, shippers, distributors, and retailers can improve packaging as well as adjusting the transportation processes according to their respective conditions and supply chain risks. This eventually leads to quality improvements of shipments as fewer claims in terms of cargo damage and losses occur.

References

1. Wagner, S.M., Bode, C.: An empirical investigation into supply chain vulnerability. Journal of Purchasing and Supply Management 12(6), 301–312 (2007)
2. Blackhurst, J., Craighead, C., Elkins, D., Handfield, R.: An empirically derived agenda of critical research issues for managing supply-chain disruptions. International Journal of Production Research 43(19), 4067–4081 (2005)
3. Christopher, M., Towill, D.R.: Developing Market Specific Supply Chain Strategies. International Journal of Logistics Management 13(1), 1–14 (2002)
4. Skorna, A.C., Bode, C., Wagner, S.M.: Technology-Enabled Risk Management along the Transport Logistics Chain. In: Wagner, S.M., Bode, C. (eds.) Managing Risk and Security, pp. 197–220. Haupt, Berne (2009)
5. Smith, V.: Optimal Insurance Coverage. Journal of Political Economic 68, 68–77 (1968)
6. Gollier, C.: The Comparative Statistics of Changes in Risk Revisited. Journal of Economic Theory 66, 522–536 (2004)
7. Schlesinger, H., Venezian, E.: Insurance markets with loss-prevention activity: profits, market structure, and consumer welfare. Rand Journal of Economics 17(2), 227–238 (1986)
8. Ehrlich, I., Becker, G.S.: Market Insurance, Self-Insurance, and Self-Protection. Journal of Political Economy 80(4), 623–648 (1979)
9. Schlesinger, H.: The Theory of Insurance Demand. In: Dionne, G. (ed.) Handbook of Insurance. Springer, Berlin (2000)
10. Christopher, M., Peck, H.: Building the resilient supply chain. International Journal of Logistics Management 15(2), 1–13 (2004)
11. Jüttner, U.: Supply chain risk management - Understanding the business requirements from a practitioner perspective. International Journal of Logistics Management 16(1), 120–141 (2005)
12. Pfohl, H. C., Köhler, H., Thomas, D.: State of the art in supply chain risk management research: empirical and conceptual findings and a roadmap for the implementation. Logistics Research 2, 33–44 (2010)
13. March, J.G., Shapira, Z.: Managerial perspectives on risk and risk taking. Management Science 33(11), 1404–1418 (1987)
14. Peleg-Gillai, B., Bhat, G., Sept, L.: Innovators in Supply Chain Security: Better Security Drives Business Value. Manufacturing Institute, Washington, DC (2006)
15. Manuj, I., Mentzer, J.T.: Global Supply Chain Risk Management. Journal of Business Logistics 29(1), 133–155 (2008)
16. Manuj, I., Mentzer, J.T.: Global supply chain risk management strategies. International Journal of Physical Distribution & Logistics Management 33(3), 192–223 (2008)
17. Harland, C., Brenchley, R., Walker, H.: Risk in supply networks. Journal of Purchasing & Supply Management 9, 51–62 (2003)
18. Zsidisin, G.A., Ellram, L.: An agency theory investigation of supply chain risk management. Journal of Supply Chain Management 39(3), 15–27 (2003)
19. Christopher, M., Lee, H.: Mitigating supply chain risk through improved confidence. International Journal of Physical Distribution & Logistics Management 34(5), 388–396 (2003)
20. Pongas, E.: Extra EU-25 trade in goods by mode of transport. Statistics in focus 2/2006. European Communities, Luxembourg (2006)

21. Finch, P.: Supply chain risk management. Supply Chain Management: An International Journal 9(2), 183–196 (2004)
22. Ritchie, B., Brindley, C.: Supply chain risk management and performance: A guiding framework for future development. International Journal of Operations & Production Management 27(3), 303–322 (2007)
23. Jedermann, R., Lang, W.: The Benefits of Embedded Intelligence – Tasks and Applications for Ubiquitous Computing in Logistics. In: Floerkemeier, C., Langheinrich, M., Fleisch, E., Mattern, F., Sarma, S.E. (eds.) IOT 2008. LNCS, vol. 4952, pp. 105–122. Springer, Heidelberg (2008)

The Staff Assignment Graph –
Planning, Evaluating and Improving Personnel
Deployment in Assembly Systems

Gert Zülch, Michael Leupold, and Thilo Gamber

ifab-Institute of Human and Industrial Engineering,
Karlsruhe Institute of Technology (formerly University of Karlsruhe),
Karlsruhe, Germany
{gert.zuelch,michael.leupold,thilo.gamber}@kit.edu

Abstract. With regards to methods of assembly systems planning we are familiar with the depiction of the technical structure using capacity fields and graphs in addition to the modelling of assembly activities as a precedence diagram. However, no form of presentation has yet been defined that describes the assignment of staff within an assembly system. This paper discusses the concept of the staff assignment graph used to balance a hybrid assembly system, and in doing so marks a first attempt to close this gap and develop a more comprehensive planning method. The paper also explains how to evaluate staff assignment graphs and presents an algorithm for automatically generating them based on existing capacity graphs and taking a multi-criteria goal function into account.

Keywords: Assembly planning, Line balancing, Precedence diagram, Staff assignment graph.

1 The Challenges for Assembly Planning

Assembly systems are traditionally characterized by a high proportion of manual activity and correspondingly high labour costs. The prevailing competitive pressure results in the increased use of automation [1]. However, because complete automation is usually either impractical or intricate to implement for technical or economic reasons, hybrid assembly systems are often established consisting of both manual workstations and at least partially automated stations [2, 3].

This presents new challenges for the planning of such assembly systems due to the fact that an alternating sequence of manual and (partially) automated processes makes it difficult to balance them. According to Müller [4], the requirements of the assembly task as well as the employees and equipment involved in the assembly process must be looked at differentiated, paying particular attention to the distribution of personnel and machinery capacities.

J. Frick and B. Laugen (Eds.): APMS 2011, IFIP AICT 384, pp. 157–164, 2012.
© IFIP International Federation for Information Processing 2012

2   Formal Gap in the Planning of Assembly Systems

Concerning the state of the art of assembly system balancing, the precedence diagram is still an important tool although it was introduced by Prenting and Battaglin as early as 1964 [5]. In this diagram, the individual assembly activities are depicted as nodes in a network that are linked both logically and timely (Fig. 1). In this presentation format, the time required for each activity is depicted as a supplementary attribute of each node.

In addition, Dittmayer introduced the capacity field in 1981, which helps divide up capacity in structured assembly systems that operate according to the division of labour [6, 7]. To this end, the cycle times per activity are recorded on the abscissa and the daily volume to be produced on the ordinate. Because the capacity required for an assembly task is generally greater than the capacity available at an individual assembly workstation, the required capacity must be broken down into individual subsections in such a way that each of the sections can be covered by the available capacity of a single workstation. Horizontally partitioning the required capacity divides it by volume, while vertical division is by type.

In 1995, Braun proposed the so-called complex diagram in order to support the planning of model mix assembly systems. This diagram combines the different precedence diagrams for each of the product variants in order to give an overall representation of all of the activities to be carried out in an assembly system [8, pp. 56].

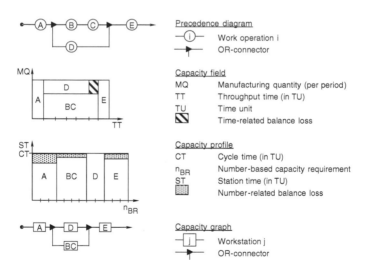

Fig. 1. Methods for assembly systems planning

Braun then refined the idea of the capacity field to develop the capacity graph [8, pp. 69]. This gives an equivalent diagrammatic representation of the capacity field. The areas of the capacity field are incorporated into the capacity graph as nodes, with arcs always inserted at the points where the respective areas within the capacity field touch along their vertical partitioning lines. Taking the cycle time per unit into account, the capacity profile can be used in conjunction with the complex diagram to balance the model mix assembly system.

The planning of hybrid assembly systems throws up further challenges due to the fact that the capacity required by the activities in terms of workers, equipment and the work object differs. Nevertheless, traditional concepts for planning hybrid assembly systems often only take the perspective of one of these process elements, typically that of the bottleneck resource [9]. Müller goes one step further and develops a multi-stage precedence diagram concept that allows differentiation between assembly activities from the perspective of the workers, equipment and the work object. He is also the first to propose a staff assignment model for assembly systems in which groups of workers are assigned to several workstations within the assembly system in order to iron out differences in utilisation.

3   The Staff Assignment Graph

However, no satisfactory solution has yet been found for the problem of distributing capacity within hybrid assembly systems with regards to the equal utilisation of both equipment and staff. A suitable method of representation and planning should above all take into account the assignment of staff in a model mix assembly line, for example multi-station assignments, group work and the use of stand-in workers. The idea of the staff assignment graph aims to close this gap in assembly planning. One first example of this can already be found in the above diagram following Müller [4, p. 101]. In the simple example given in Figure 2, an individual workstation is followed by an assembly step that is operated by two workers in a group.

Figure 3 shows a staff assignment graph using the example of a structured hybrid assembly system. The staff assignment graph is based on the capacity graph and its assignment of assembly activities from the precedence diagram to assembly workplaces. One node on the capacity graph is considered to be one assembly workplace. Parallel paths through the diagram represent parallel workplaces, each of which belongs to one workstation.

Similarly to Müller [4, pp. 99], workers can be assigned to multiple assembly workstations as a work group. This assumes that any such work group consists of workers with the same level of qualification who are therefore able to perform all assembly activities required. The number of workers within a work group is recorded in its upper left corner in the staff assignment graph.

In the case of multiple workstation operation, it can be assumed that the time required by the worker to cover the distance between the individual workstations accounts for a not-unsubstantial fraction of his/her total available capacity. For this reason, these times should also be recorded when planning the assembly system. This is done here by introducing a new kind of directed arc, the pathway arc, which defines the start, the end and the direction of movement. To store the time needed, the arc can either be annotated, or all of the time values can be recorded separately in a travel time matrix in order to avoid making the staff assignment graph unnecessarily complicated. In this matrix, the assembly stations make up the rows and columns. An individual value within the matrix represents the time required by the worker to move from the assembly station given by the row to the one given by the column.

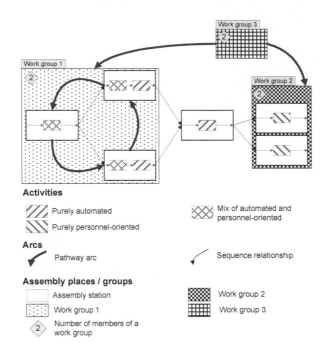

Activities

▨ Purely automated   ⧆ Mix of automated and personnel-oriented

◨ Purely personnel-oriented

Arcs

✔ Pathway arc   ✓ Sequence relationship

Assembly places / groups

☐ Assembly station   ▨ Work group 2

▤ Work group 1   ▦ Work group 3

⬨2 Number of members of a work group

Fig. 2. Concept for a staff assignment graph using the example of a hybrid assembly line

Semi-autonomous work groups can be modelled using the work group concept already described for the staff assignment graph. Pathway arcs between the assembly stations assigned to the work group are not used. This indicates that the decision regarding the processing sequence is made by the semi-autonomous work group themselves, e.g. work group 2 in Figure 2.

The operation of multiple workstations by one or more workers can be indicated by first grouping the individual workstations within a local work group. The worker is then assigned to this group as one single group member. Optimised pathways between the individual assembly stations can be depicted using path arcs. One example for multiple machine operation is work group 1 in Figure 2.

One or more stand-in workers can be indicated by assigning them to a separate stand-in group which is annotated with the number of stand-in workers it contains and then linked to the workstations or assembly subsections it supports using pathway arcs. One example for the representation of a stand-in worker is work group 3 in Figure 2.

4   Evaluating Staff Assignment Graphs

Both static, graph-theoretical key figures and dynamic key figures derived from simulation can be used to evaluate staff assignment graphs in terms of their implications on the assembly system. Our previous contribution [13] focused on the static evaluation taking the ratio of the number of work groups to the number of assembly workstations and the cluster coefficient of the staff assignment graph into account.

In order to dynamically evaluate a staff assignment graph a personnel-based simulation procedure can be used to analyse their dynamic impact on production logistics performance indicators. To this end, the OSim [12] simulation tool developed by the ifab-Institute has been expanded in order to support the depiction and simulation of staff assignment graphs. This also includes the ability to input a travel time matrix and model pathway arcs in order to depict the pathways covered by workers operating more than one workstation.

Using these new features it is possible to simulate and evaluate the effects of various staff assignment graphs in combination with existing precedence diagrams and capacity graphs. Relevant key figures which are output by the simulation tool typically include goal achievement degrees for lead times, resource utilization and process costs [13]. Additionally the key figure travel time for recording the time spent on the workers' movement in the assembly system was introduced.

5   Deriving Staff Assignment Graphs

In a next step, a basic algorithm for deriving a good staff assignment graph for an existing capacity graph according to a multi-criteria goal function was designed and implemented. One of the problems for such an algorithm is that out of the huge number of staff assignment graphs only a small fraction is valid. This is due to the fact that automatically generated staff assignment graphs may be acyclic or that assembly stations are kept idle for too long so that buffers overflow.

Thus, the algorithm is divided into two steps. The first step determines all valid staff assignment graphs while the second and compares those graphs using simulation and evaluates them with the pre-defined set of criteria.

5.1   The Backtracking Algorithm

The design of the algorithm follows the backtracking technique. Backtracking is a meta-algorithm for algorithmically enumerating all possible solutions to a problem [14, p. 105]. Using a depth-first search a tree of partial solutions to the problem – each represented by a node of the rooted backtracking tree – is built. Possible continuations of a partial parent solution are represented by the node's children. If the evaluation of a partial solution leads to the conclusion that no feasible solution can be derived from it, its node is rejected and the search is continued with the next node. The tree's leaves represent final solutions to the whole problem. If the search reaches a leaf, the algorithm could either stop if only a single feasible solution is searched, or track back to the leaf's parent node to search and enumerate more solutions [14, p. 106 ff.]. Figure 4 depicts the order in which the tree of solutions is built during the search process. Partial solutions without a feasible continuation and final solutions are marked accordingly.

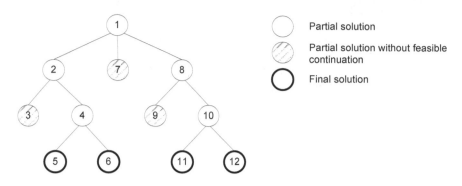

Fig. 3. Tree representation of the backtracking algorithm

5.2   Backtracking for Deriving Staff Assignment Graphs

The implementation of the backtracking algorithm for deriving staff assignment graphs constructs sequences of staff movements similar to how a discrete event simulation procedure works. One possible "simulation run" is represented by a path in the tree starting from the root node and ending at a leaf node. Each node of the tree marks an intermediate point in time. Each child node depicts a possible continuation of the simulation run which is created by adding one or more pathway arcs to the staff assignment graph.

Building and searching the tree is handled by the function nextEvent which operates in several steps:

1. Handle current events like the arrival of an assembly order, the end of a worker's movement or the completion of an assembly activity as part of the order.
2. Check if the current node represents a feasible partial solution to the problem, if it is not, mark the node unfeasible and track back to the parent node.
3. If the node is a possible final solution, evaluate it with the defined criteria (see 5.3).
4. Determine possible continuations by adding a child node for each combination of pathway arcs that could be added to the staff assignment graph. When adding a pathway arc, start the corresponding assembly worker's movement.

Input parameters to the algorithm are the assembly system to be planned, the available number of assembly workers as well as the cycle length. A multi-criteria goal function in order to evaluate and compare feasible solutions is also a needed input of the algorithm.

5.3   Multi-criteria Evaluation

When a feasible final solution is found by the backtracking algorithm (see 5.2), it is evaluated using the simulation procedure described earlier (see 4). All performance indicators supported by the simulation procedure can be used as goal criteria. These performance indicators are computed as results of the simulation run and are stored for each of the feasible solutions. After all alternative solutions have been evaluated a lexicographic, an additive or a maximin preference order [15, pp. 184 ff.] is used to combine the goal criteria and to determine the optimal solution.

5.4   Pilot Study

In order to verify the algorithm and to check its runtime behaviour a pilot study was conducted using a synthetic assembly line with seven assembly activities. The assembly line initially consisted of five assembly stations arranged in U-shape and was operated by five assembly workers. Due to the automation of two of the assembly activities, utilisation at two of the stations dropped below 30 %. Thus it was assumed that four assembly workers could suffice for operating the line.

The backtracking algorithm found the apparent optimal solution in which one of the workers operated both of the assembly workstations containing automated activities. During the backtracking procedure, 18,960 nodes of the solution tree were handled and 648 solutions in leaf nodes were found. Runtime was 19 s on a desktop PC, 14.5 s of which was spent on the multi-criteria evaluation of the feasible solutions.

The conclusion is that while the optimal solution was found by the algorithm - verifying that it works – the runtime behaviour might not yet be suitable for more complex problems. Therefore, further investigations and improvements will have to be carried out.

6   Targeted Planning of Assembly Systems

Braun [8, pp. 129] was able to quantify relationships between the precedence resp. complex diagrams and the capacity graphs. Regression equations could be derived for certain influential parameters with regards to selected target values. This made it possible to create meaningful capacity graphs using the parameters for the precedence or the complex diagram.

Expectations are that it will also be possible to derive quantifiable relationships between the planning parameters for staff assignment and individual target criteria using the structural parameters of the capacity graph and staff assignment graph. It is also necessary to verify whether staff assignment graphs with different parameters show different results even when their corresponding precedence diagram and capacity graph are the same. To this end, factorial experiments should be used to determine the influence of each parameter on the target criteria. The interaction of parameters identified as being significant should then be investigated using statistical design of experiments.

7   Conclusions and Further Research

This paper presents the concept of the staff assignment graph and an algorithm which can be used to derive a staff assignment graph for an existing capacity graph. Further research should evaluate the algorithm using examples from literature and practice. Moreover, the algorithm should be improved regarding runtime behaviour.

To draw conclusions suitable for practitioners, it will be necessary to perform studies using examples from existing work systems in order to verify the usefulness of the algorithm for its use in industry. Also, further investigations should try to compare staff assignment graphs and the corresponding capacity graphs. Based on an appropriate design of experiments, influential factors should be determined and if possible, rules should be derived describing which kinds of staff assignment graphs best suit various forms of capacity graphs.

References

1. Lotter, B.: Sicherung der Montage am Standort Deutschland. In: Lotter, B., Enderle, W., Rosskopf, M., Olbrich, W., David, V., Oldenburg, S. (eds.) HYMOS - Hybride Montagesysteme, Schlussbericht zum BMBF-Verbundprojekt, pp. 11–18. Verlag der Gesellschaft für Arbeitsschutz- und Humanisierungsforschung, Dortmund (1999)
2. Seliger, G., Neu, S.: Montagesysteme. In: Eversheim, W., Schuh, G. (eds.) Produktion und Management "Betriebshütte", Teil 2, pp. 10–35. Springer, Heidelberg (1996)
3. Spath, D., Baumeister, M.: Synchronisation of material flow and assembly in hybrid and modular systems. Assembly Automation 21, 152–157 (2001)
4. Müller, R.: Planung hybrider Montagesysteme auf Basis mehrschichtiger Vorranggraphen. Shaker, Aachen (2002)
5. Prenting, T., Battaglin, R.M.: The Precedence Diagram: A Tool for Analysis in Assembly Line Balancing. Journal of Industrial Engineering 15, 209–213 (1964)
6. Dittmayer, S.: Arbeits- und Kapazitätsteilung in der Montage. Springer, Heidelberg (1981)
7. Warnecke, H.-J., Dittmayer, S.: Planning of Division of Labor in the Assembly Environment. CIRP Annals - Manufacturing Technology 30, 395–400 (1981)
8. Braun, W.J.: Beitrag zur Festlegung der Arbeitsteilung in manuellen Montagesystemen. Universität Karlsruhe, Karlsruhe (1995)
9. Müller, R., Schneck, M.: Dynamische Bewertung von Planungen für hybride Montagesysteme. In: Heel, J., Krüger, J. (eds.) Personalorientierte Simulation - Praxis und Entwicklungspotential, pp. 73–88. Shaker, Aachen (1999)
10. Watts, D.J., Strogatz, S.H.: Collective dynamics of "small-world" networks. Nature 393, 440–442 (1998)
11. Lewis, T.G.: Network Science: Theory and Applications. John Wiley and Sons, Hoboken (2009)
12. Jonsson, U.: Ein integriertes Objektmodell zur durchlaufplanorientierten Simulation von Produktionssystemen. Shaker, Aachen (2000)
13. Zülch, G., Leupold, M., Gamber, T.: The Staff Assignment Graph – A New Approach to Assembly Systems Planning. In: Frick, J., Laugen, B. (eds.) APMS 2011. IFIP AICT, vol. 384, pp. 157–164. Springer, Heidelberg (2012)
14. Kreher, D.L., Stinson, D.: Combinatorial Algorithms. CRC, London (1999)
15. Körth, H.: Zur Berücksichtigung mehrerer Zielfunktionen bei der Optimierung von Produktionsplänen. Mathematik und Wirtschaft, 184–201 (1969)
16. Zülch, G., Fischer, J.: An Integrated Object Model as a World of Model Components for an Activity Network Based Simulation Approach. In: Verbraeck, A., Krug, W. (eds.) Simulation in Industry, pp. 74–79. SCS-Europe, Delft (2002)

Remanufacturing/Refurbishment with RFID-Generated Item-Level Information

Wei Zhou[1,3] and Selwyn Piramuthu[2,3]

[1] Information & Operations Management, ESCP Europe, Paris, France
[2] Information Systems and Operations Management, University of Florida
Gainesville, Florida 32611-7169, USA
[3] RFID European Lab., Paris, France
wzhou@escpeurope.eu, selwyn@ufl.edu

Abstract. As an integral component of sustainable manufacturing, recycling and remanufacturing have been gaining popularity in line with
Green initiatives. While the importance of item-level information their
success has been stressed, the potential of RFID technology in recy-
cling/remanufacturing has not received much attention in the research
literature. We attempt to address this gap by considering RFID tags
and their applications from a recycling/remanufacturing perspective and
propose a knowledge-based framework to assist such process based on
RFID-generated item-level information. Specifically, we consider quality improvement issues related to repair and refurbishment as well as
end-of-life recycling issues from the perspective of item-level information
generated through RFID tags.

1 Introduction

The increase in recent initiatives associated with green supply chains have
spawned a plethora of related initiatives in the manufacturing sector. Specifically, recycling and remanufacturing have been identified as means to address
some of the issues related to material wastage (e.g., Aras et al. 2006; Darnall et
al. 2008). The process of remanufacturing include the collection of defective (due
to manufacturing) and end-of-life products as well as manufacturing byproducts
and re-engineering or reassembling of products back to new, as-new, or refurbished condition. While it is generally accepted that RFID tags provide cost-
effective means to facilitate recycling and remanufacturing, existing published
literature provide very little guidance in this regard.

Motivated by RFID's unprecedented characteristics of item-level auto-
identification (e.g., Kohn et al. 2005; Zhou 2009), we propose an adaptive
knowledge-based framework to utilize RFID-generated item-level information
for product remanufacturing/refurbishment and illustrate its usefulness in this
domain. We consider product remanufacturing process from a heuristic perspective with the goal of (1) reducing both environmental and economical waste, (2)
improving manufacturing quality to decrease the rate of defects, (3) improving

J. Frick and B. Laugen (Eds.): APMS 2011, IFIP AICT 384, pp. 165–170, 2012.

the efficiency of remanufacturing process, (4) facilitating product design and (5) enhancing Customer Relationship Management (CRM).

Specifically, we consider products that have manufacturing defects with missing or defective components, end-of-life used products that have some salvageable component parts in them and manufacturing byproduct into consideration. Most manufacturers treat remanufactured items that are put together using unused components from defective products as new and those that were used for a short period of time as refurbished. We restrict ourselves to considering only issues related to quality improvement from repair and refurbishment as well as end-of-life recycling process from the perspective of item-level information generated through RFID tags.

The remainder of this paper is organized as follows: we consider quality improvement of repair and refurbishment in Section 2 and develop a model to analyze the dynamic in this scenario. We then consider the end-of-life recycling process scenario in Section 3 with an example. We conclude the paper with a brief discussion in Section 4.

2   Quality Improvement of Repair and Refurbishment

Generally speaking, the process of repair and refurbishment in remanufacturing scenarios identify and replace parts from tested products that are found to be defective. By incorporating RFID-generated item-level information and its tracking/tracing capability for repair and refurbishment processes, it is possible to improve the overall quality of the resulting products. This is primarily due to the lower granularity of information that is generated through item-level RFID tags that enable the process to uniquely identify the specific characteristics of each of the product and tailor the best possible means to address any issues that are present.

Remanufacturing facilities generally keep inventory of both new parts and working parts that are taken from defective products. Consider a dysfunctional product, for example, with a defective component that needs to be replaced with a working component of the same specifications that is taken from another dysfunctional product. Traditionally, during the remanufacturing process, parts are randomly chosen to replace the defective ones. This process introduces variance in the remanufactured product quality due to uncertainties in quality of replacement component parts as well as in compatibility match. This variance is due to mismatch introduced by the randomness present in the process.

For illustration purposes, assume that we have five parts to fit the dysfunctional product mentioned above and that the key specification of these parts is represented by $\{10, 9.8, 10.2, 8, 12\}$. As a result of compatibility issues, the normalized quality of the possible resulting product is $\{5, 4.3, 4, 2, 1\}$. Without the use of RFID-generated item-level information, the average quality of this remanufactured product is 3.26 with a standard deviation of 1.68. However, with the use of RFID-generated item-level information, the quality of this product is 5 with certainty due to specifically tailoring the processes to address identified deficiencies that are specific to each product.

The beneficial properties present in this scenario is multiplied when there are multiple products are simultaneously processed. If we have two dysfunctional products with similar defective components, the normalized resulting quality from replacing the five available parts for these two products (say) are $\{5, 4.3, 4, 2, 1\}$ and $\{3.2, 5, 4.5, 3.2, 2.9\}$. The average quality for the second product is 3.76 with a standard deviation of 0.93. The overall average quality of these products is invariably low. However, with the use of RFID-generated item-level information, the quality of both remanufactured products reach their maximum possible value of 5 simply because of the targeted focus in identifying issues and addressing those with the most appropriate response.

2.1   Model and Analysis

In general, factory restored products are usually characterized by a high degree of uncertainty with respect to their quality primarily due to variances in quality control and unobservable history of the components within. With RFID-generated item-level visibility, it is possible to identify the components uniquely as well as their specifications at the item level. Moreover, traditionally, components are labeled as qualified if they pass certain quality tests. Consider a repair task with a need to replace $m - 1$ components when there are m components in total $\{\Gamma | \Gamma_1, \Gamma_2 \cdots \Gamma_m\}$ including the primary component. Each component Γ_i has n_i items $\{\Gamma_i | \gamma_{i1}, \gamma_{i2}, \gamma_{i3} \cdots \gamma_{in_i}\}$ that have all passed the quality test. $\{\Gamma | \Gamma_1, \Gamma_2 \cdots \Gamma_m\}$ follow joint distribution $f_{\Gamma_1, \Gamma_2 \cdots \Gamma_m}$. Then with production function $g(\cdot)$, we can characterize the output $Y = g(\Gamma_1, \Gamma_2 \cdots \Gamma_m)$ in its cumulative density function as:

$$F_y(y) = \int \int \cdots \int_{g(\Gamma_1, \Gamma_2 \cdots \Gamma_m) \leq y} f_{\Gamma_1, \Gamma_2 \cdots \Gamma_m}(\Gamma_1, \Gamma_2 \cdots \Gamma_m) d\Gamma_1, d\Gamma_2 \cdots d\Gamma_m$$

In the ideal scenario where RFID-generated item-level information can be effectively used to address issues, the quality improvement of refurbished products is given by:

$$\Delta_Q = max\{Y\} - E[Y] \tag{1}$$

Since Y takes $N : \{N = n_1 \cdot n_2 \cdots n_m\}$ different possible values, the distribution of $max\{Y\}$ follows: $f_N^y(y) = Nf(y)F(y)^{N-1}$. Therefore Δ_Q becomes:

$$\Delta_Q = \int_y (Nu^{N-1} - 1)yu'dy \tag{2}$$

where

$$u = F_y(y) \tag{3}$$

If there are k products with multiple defects that need to go through the same repair procedure, the distribution of $max\{Y\}_k$ is

$$f_{k:N}^y(y) = \frac{N!}{(k-1)!(N-k)!} u^{k-1}(1-u)^{N-k} f_y(y)$$

And the total quality improvement for all these k refurbished products becomes:

$$\Delta_Q = \sum_{i=1}^{k} (E[y_{i:n}] - E[y]) \tag{4}$$

$$= \int_y (NF_{binomial(N-1,u)}(k) - k) \cdot y f_y(y) dy \tag{5}$$

If the production itself is stable, the quality improvement Δ_Q therefore would depend mostly on the uncertainty from the input $\delta(\Gamma)$. Since we have more control over the process when low granularity information at the item-level is used, we can clearly see that this leads to improvement in the quality of the resulting products.

3   EOL Recycling Process Optimization

A relatively large portion of end-of-life (EOL) products go into their last mile of recycling before they are decomposed into simple formats such as simple chemical compounds. This stage of recycling usually involves using very brutal forces such as grinding, burning, chemical eroding which produce a large amount of waste and pollution. The ultimate goal of close-loop or green supply chain is to minimize the size of this recycling process that nevertheless seems unavoidable in any industry.

Traditionally, EOL products at this stage are pre-sorted in order to go through several different recycling processes. The sorting preparation is normally not very accurate because of the size of operation as well as the cost. As a result, more pollution is generated when the EOL products go through a wrong recycling process (Figure 1). For example, any material made up of potentially harmful chemicals when burned (even if by mistake) releases harmful particulate matter into the environment.

With RFID tagging, the sorting process and the following recycling processes can be operated more accurately. As a result, the unnecessary pollution caused by mis-operation can be minimized. The actual effects of using RFID in recycling process however depend on several major factors, including the degree of randomness during the sorting process and the severity of consequences due to mis-operation.

For example, consider n different recycling processes in a recycling plant that map the transformational operations of the n different categories of EOL inputs X. In a typical scenario, each input item goes through its corresponding process and produces an amount of valuable output Y as raw material for remanufacturing as well as a certain amount of pollution Z, such that

$$\{Y, Z\}_i = f_i(X) \tag{6}$$

However, if the input is produced by a wrong process, an additional amount of pollution is generated resulting in the loss of valuable output.

$$Z_{ij} = g_{ij}(X_i) \tag{7}$$

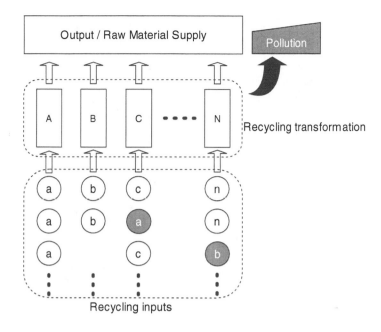

Fig. 1. Recycling process with mis-matched products

where i indicates the input category and j indicates the recycling procedure. The set of G forms a recycling transformation matrix that represents all possible outcomes. For an example scenario with two kinds of input, the transformation function matrix can be represented as:

$$G_{2\times 2} = \begin{bmatrix} f_1 & g_{12} \\ g_{21} & f_2 \end{bmatrix}$$

With item-level RFID-tagging, the system generates perfectly transparent information and in a perfect operational scenario, and the output is given by

$$\{Y, Z\}_{RFID} = \sum_{\forall X_i \in X} \sum_{i=1}^{n} f_i(X_i) \qquad (8)$$

Without sufficient tracking and monitoring tools, the output becomes

$$\{Y, Z\}_{NON} = \sum_{\forall X_i \in X} \sum_{i=1}^{n} \sum_{j=1}^{n} [f_i(X_i)\delta(i,j) + g_{ij}(X_i)(1 - \delta(i,j))] \qquad (9)$$

where the incidence function $\delta(i, j) = 1$ if $i = j$ and $\delta(i, j) = 0$ otherwise.

The difference between equation 8 and equation 9 represents the benefit, which is indeed the effect when the item and recycling process don't match ($i \neq j$). It can be written as

$$\Delta_R = \sum_{\forall X_i \in X} \sum_{i=1}^{n} \sum_{j=1}^{n} [f_i(X_i) + g_{ij}(X_i)] \, (1 - \delta(i,j)) \qquad (10)$$

Equation 10 indicates that the potential benefits of utilizing RFID at the recycling stage of remanufacturing depends on three factors: the value transformation $f_i(\cdot)$, the pollution factors $g_{ij}(\cdot)$, and the dynamics of input $\delta(\cdot)$. These expressions provide us an estimate and guideline on the benefit to expect with item-level information generated through RFID tags.

4   Discussion

As green initiatives expand to more domains, it is important to critically examine processes that could be improved to those that result in less wastage. This is especially true in manufacturing where remanufacturing and recycling can be used to reduce wastage as well as improve the effectiveness of usage of constrained resources. We considered a practical problem with respect to dynamically adjusting manufacturing/remanufacturing process through use of RFID-generated item-level information. This process can be automated and operationalized in a seamless fashion through RFID-embedded component tags on individual parts. These RFID-tagged manufacturing parts also enable the quality manager to continually adjust manufacturing parameters at the item-level as is deemed necessary to improve the overall quality of the finished products.

In general, in a closed-loop supply chain (e.g., Fleischmann et al. 2003), RFID could possibly be beneficial for: (1) Improved manufacturing quality and reduced waste; (2) More efficient remanufacturing process (optimized diagnosis and reduced cost); (3) Improved quality of remanufactured products; (4) Reduced pollution in recycling / decomposition. The level of operational uncertainty plays a critically important role to evaluate an RFID project for remanufacturing. We modeled two scenarios and developed expressions that illustrate the benefits that could be obtained through item-level RFID-tagging and the appropriate use of the information generated in the process.

References

1. Aras, N., Verter, V., Boyaci, T.: Coordination and priority decisions in hybrid manufacturing/remanufacturing systems. Production Operations Management 15, 528–543 (2006)
2. Darnall, N., Jolley, G.J., Handfield, R.: Environmental management systems & green supply chain management: Complements for sustainability? Business Strategy & Environment 17(1), 30–45 (2008)
3. Fleischmann, M., van Nunen, J., Gre, B.: Integrating closed-loop supply chains and spare-parts management at IBM. Interfaces 33, 44–56 (2003)
4. Kohn, W., Brayman, V., Littleton, J.: Repair-control of enterprise systems using RFID sensory data. IIE Transactions 37(4), 281–290 (2005)
5. Zhou, W.: RFID and item-level information visibility. European Journal of Operational Research 198(1), 252–258 (2009)

Manufacturing Cell Simulation Environment for Automated Visual Inspection Using Robot First Report: Fundamental System

Hironori Hibino[1,2], Toshihiro Inukai[3], and Yukishige Yoshida[3]

[1] Technical Research Institute of JSPMI
(Japan Society for the Promotion of Machine Industry),
1-1-12 Hachiman-cho, Higashikurume, Tokyo, Japan
hibino@tri.jspmi.or.jp
[2] Tokyo University of Agriculture and Technology, Tokyo, Japan
[3] DENSO Wave Inc., Aichi, Japan

Abstract. Recently the industries provide visual inspection processes in the plants for keeping and guaranteeing product quality. Many visual inspection processes are normally operated by the manual visual inspection. The results of the manual visual inspection are often unstable because the results are depended on the inspection worker skill. Currently the automated visual inspection technologies are getting more important to stably keep and guarantee product quality. Specially, the automated visual inspection technologies using robots attract the industries. The robot usually has several industrial cameras and LED lights on its hand. However based on our analysis for the typical implementation procedure of the automated visual inspection technologies using robots, the period to implement the inspection processes are usually very long. The reasons are that there are many adjustment activities in the real plant concurrently concerning the imaging conditions, the robot motion conditions, and the visual inspection conditions. In order to reduce the period to implement the automated visual inspection processes, it is very important to reduce the adjustment activates in the real plant. Therefore it is necessary to develop the simulation technologies to support the adjustment activates on the virtual beforehand. We focus on the manufacturing cell simulation environment for the automated visual inspection using robots. The manufacturing cell simulation environment which provides to support the above adjustments on the virtual even if the robot and the target product are not existed, is proposed and developed. In this paper, the manufacturing cell simulation environment to solve the problems is proposed. Seven requirements for the simulation environment are defined. The fundamental system with five functions to implement the simulation environment is proposed and implemented. Hypothetic fundamental case studies are carried out to confirm effective of our proposed manufacturing cell simulation environment.

Keywords: Automated visual inspection, robot, virtual camera, Manufacturing system, simulation.

J. Frick and B. Laugen (Eds.): APMS 2011, IFIP AICT 384, pp. 171–180, 2012.
© IFIP International Federation for Information Processing 2012

1   Introduction

Recently Japanese industries are becoming more important to keep and guarantee product quality even if low skilled workers make the product because the highly skilled workers in Japan are decreasing in the workshop by increasing the highly skilled workers who are close to the retirement age, and the workers who need more education and skill to product are increasing in the globally localization plants [1]. In order to solve the problem, the industries provide visual inspection processes in the plants. Many visual inspection processes are normally operated by the manual visual inspection. The results of the manual visual inspection are often unstable because the results are depended on the inspection worker skill. Currently the automated visual inspection technologies are getting more important to stably keep and guarantee product quality. Specially, the automated visual inspection technologies using robots attract the industries. The robot usually has several industrial cameras and LED lights on its hand. The robot precisely inspects the target product while inspecting many inspection points by moving the cameras and lights. The inspection process using the robot is usually implemented as one type of the manufacturing cells. Figure 1 shows the typical automated visual inspection technologies using robots.

However based on our analysis for the typical implementation procedure of the automated visual inspection technologies using robots, the period to implement the inspection processes are usually very long. The reasons are that there are many adjustment activities in the real plant concurrently concerning the imaging conditions, the robot motion conditions, and the visual inspection conditions as follows. Firstly there are many inspection items and points for each product in an inspection process, although there are many kinds of products to inspect in the inspection process. Secondly there are many numbers of adjustments for taking images by the industrial cameras while deciding the efficient robot motions. In order to accurately take the images, it is very important to adjust the focal length for the industrial cameras, to adjust suitable timing to take the images, and to adjust suitable lighting conditions. Thirdly there are many numbers of adjustments for making and evaluating the visual inspection programs while taking the images. Fourthly in the cases to additionally inspect new products, the above adjustments are needed to consider on the workshop while the inspection processes are interrupted during the adjustment activities period.

In order to reduce the period to implement the automated visual inspection processes, it is very important to reduce the adjustment activates in the real plant. Therefore it is necessary to develop the simulation technologies to support the adjustment activates on the virtual beforehand [2][3][4][5][6][7][8]. We focus on the manufacturing cell simulation environment for the automated visual inspection using robots. The manufacturing cell simulation environment which provides to support the above adjustments on the virtual even if the robot and the target product are not existed, is proposed and developed. In this paper, the manufacturing cell simulation environment to solve the problems is proposed. Seven requirements for the simulation environment are defined. The fundamental system with five functions to implement the simulation environment is proposed and implemented. Hypothetic fundamental case studies are carried out to confirm effective of our proposed manufacturing cell simulation environment.

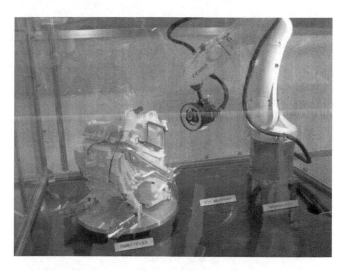

Fig. 1. The typical automated visual inspection technologies using robots

2   Our Proposed Simulation for Automated Visual Inspection Using Robot

Based on our analysis for the typical engineering procedure to construct the automated visual inspection using robot, the current engineering procedure to construct the automated visual inspection using robot can be shown as follows. Figure 2 shows the current engineering procedure.

1. The use company engineer gets the target products and defines the inspection items.
2. The engineer for the automated visual inspection makes the visual inspection specification on the desk.
3. The engineer for robot makes the robot program specification and the parts of motion program on the desk.
4. The engineer for robot makes robot motion program in the real plant.
5. The engineer for robot and the engineer for the automated visual inspection are working together and defining the imaging conditions in the real plant by considering the focal length for the industrial cameras, suitable timing to take the images, and suitable lighting conditions while deciding the efficient robot motions.
6. The engineer for the automated visual inspection makes the visual inspection program in the real plant while taking the images.

80% of the total lead-time to construct the automated visual inspection is time for the adjustment activities as No.4, 5, and 6 in the real plant repeatedly and concurrently. In the cases to additionally inspect new products, the above adjustments are needed to consider on the real plant while the inspection processes are interrupted during the adjustment activities period.

In order to reduce the period to construct the automated visual inspection using robot, it is very important to reduce the period for the adjustment activates in the real plant. Our research focuses on the simulation technologies to solve the problems. We develop the simulation technologies for the automated visual inspection using robots, which support the adjustment activities on the virtual concerning the imaging condition adjustment, the robot motion condition adjustment, and the visual inspection condition adjustment even if the robot and the target product do not exist. Figure 2 shows our proposed engineering procedure using the simulation technologies. The final goal for the manufacturing cell simulation environment is to reduce 80% of the adjustment activities in the real plant.

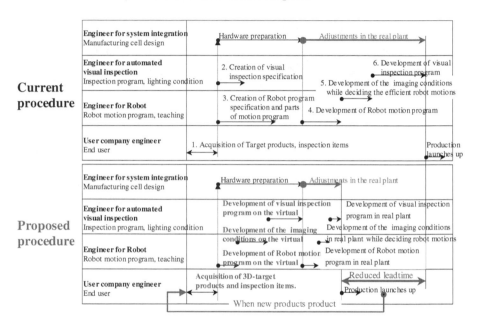

Fig. 2. Engineering procedure to construct automated visual inspection using robot

3   Requirements for Manufacturing Cell Simulation Environment for Automated Visual Inspection Using Robot

On the situations that the robot and the target product do not exist, our proposed simulation supports firstly deciding conditions for taking images on the virtual while arranging the industrial cameras, the lightings and so on, secondly developing the robot motions programs and the control programs for programmable logic controller (PLC), and thirdly developing the visual inspection programs. Figure 3 shows an outline of our proposed simulation. In order to realize the simulation, the necessary requirements are defined as follows.

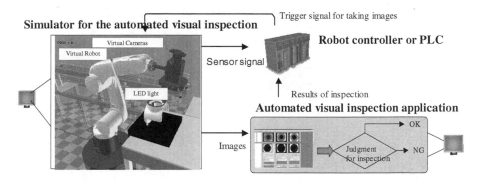

Fig. 3. An outline of our proposed simulation

For deciding conditions for taking images on the virtual while arranging the industrial cameras, the lightings and so on, two requirements are proposed.

1. Inspection condition design support to design suitable inspection conditions for taking images on the virtual while arranging the industrial cameras, the lightings, the robots, and the product.
2. Inspection point design support to design suitable inspection points on the virtual while considering the industrial cameras condition such as the focal length and the wide angle, the robot motion conditions such as the reachable space, and the inspection specifications such as the inspection items.

For developing the robot motions programs and the control programs for programmable logic controller (PLC), three requirements are proposed.

3. Image creation support to take images on the virtual which include grayscale image information by the influence of the lighting conditions, and include the images with the inspection target field and outside of the inspection target field such as background by considering the focal length and the wide angle.
4. Device control program creation support to make automated control programs for devices such as ladder programs for PLC.
5. Robot control program creation support to make robot control programs while considering suitable robot trajectories without interferences and with high productivity.

For developing the visual inspection programs, two requirements are proposed.

6. Visual inspection program creation support to make visual inspection programs using the images by the image creation support.
7. Visual inspection program improvement support to improve visual inspection programs while using failure images which are taken on the virtual such as images with scratches, lack of holes, and so on.

4   Fundamental System for Manufacturing Cell Simulation Environment for Automated Visual Inspection Using Robot

In order to realize seven requirements for the simulation environment, the fundamental system with five functions is proposed. Five functions are defined as follows.

1. Manufacturing cell simulation function (Visual inspection imaging function) to take images with an inspection target field by virtual industrial cameras on a virtual robot in the computer graphic space while synchronizing the virtual robot motion. Then the virtual camera images a virtual product model created by three-dimensional CAD.
2. Image transfer function to transfer the created image to visual inspection application.
3. Real time synchronization function to synchronize among the manufacturing cell simulation and real controller equipment such as PLC.
4. Distributed simulation function to synchronize among the manufacturing cell simulation and the robot simulation.
5. Failure image creation function to make necessary kinds of failure images using a virtual product model created by three-dimensional CAD such as images with scratches, lack of holes, and so on.

In order to implement the manufacturing cell simulation function, the manufacturing cell simulator (EMU) is developed. EMU mainly provides six functions.

In order to implement the image transfer function, the soft-wiring system is developed. The soft-wiring system provides to wire image information such as bitmap information between EMU and the visual inspection applications with real time. The semi-standard industrial middleware ORIN [9] is used for the soft wiring system.

In order to implement the real time synchronization function, the soft-wiring system is also developed. The soft-wiring system provides to wire control information such as I/O, BCD parameter between EMU and real controller equipment such as PLC with real time.

In order to implement the distributed simulation function, the conservative type of synchronization mechanisms [10] is used and implemented.

In order to implement the failure image creation function, the failure image creation methods are proposed and implemented on EMU.

Figure 4 shows an outline of the proposed fundamental system with five functions. Figure 5 shows the system structure of the proposed fundamental system.

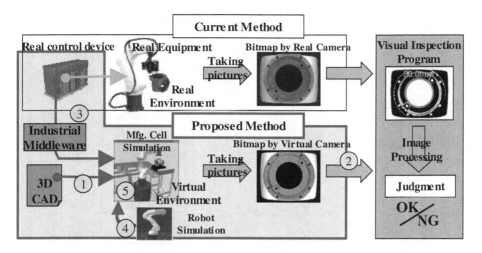

Fig. 4. An outline of the proposed fundamental system with five functions

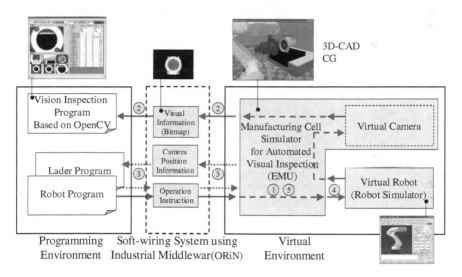

Fig. 5. The system structure of the proposed fundamental system

5   A Case Study

A case study was carried out using a manufacturing cell which consists of a robot, three industrial cameras, three LED lights, a visual inspection application. The inspection target product is an aluminum housing which is one of the parts for the industrial robots. The main inspection items are six which are the inspection for product numbers on the housing, scratches, burrs, dimensions, arrangements of things such as holes, layouts, lack of things such as holes. The real aluminum housing and the virtual aluminum housing which is three-dimensional model with 65481 polygons, are provided.

Through this case study, it was confirmed that our proposed fundamental system could be used to support implementation procedure on the virtual even if the robot and the target product are not existed. The implementation procedure on the virtual includes deciding conditions for taking images, deciding the robot motions and to develop control programs for the robot, and developing the visual inspection programs.

Figure 6 shows our developed EMU. Figure 7 shows the created images by EMU and the real industrial camera for the same inspection point. Figure 8 shows the GUI of the visual inspection program.

The future work is to be continued confirming our proposed fundamental system through other cases.

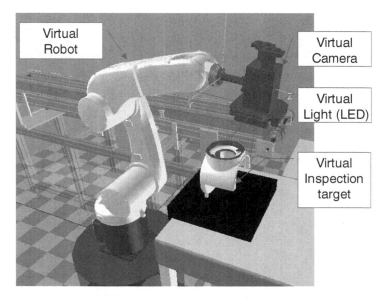

Fig. 6. Our developed EMU

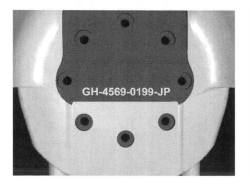

Fig. 7. The created images by EMU and the real industrial camera for the same inspection point

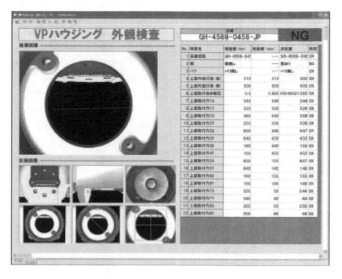

Fig. 8. GUI of the visual inspection program

6   Conclusion

In this paper, the manufacturing cell simulation environment for the automated visual inspection using robot is proposed and developed. The manufacturing cell simulation environment provides to support the engineering procedure to implement the automated visual inspection using robot on the virtual even if the robot and the target product are not existed.

The results were:

1.   To summarize problems to implement the automated visual inspection using robot.
2.   To propose the manufacturing cell simulation environment for the automated visual inspection using robot.
3.   To define and clarify necessary seven requirements for the manufacturing cell simulation environment for the automated visual inspection using robot.
4.   To define and propose the fundamental system with five functions to implement the simulation environment.
5.   To confirm through a case study that the proposed fundamental system could be used to support implementation procedure on the virtual even if the robot and the target product are not existed.

References

1.   Tanaka, K., Hibino, H., Fukuda, Y.: Module Structured Production System. In: 41st CIRP Conference on Manufacturing Systems, pp. 303–308. Springer, Heidelberg (2008)
2.   Hibino, H., Fukuda, Y.: Emulation in Manufacturing Engineering Processes. In: 2008 Winter Simulation Conference, pp. 1785–1793 (2008) ISBN: 978-1-4244-2708-6

3. Hibino, H., Fukuda, Y., Fujii, S., Kojima, F., Mitsuyuki, K., Yura, Y.: The Development of an Object-oriented Simulation System based on the Thought Process of the Manufacturing System Design. I. J. Production Economics 60, 343–351 (1999)

4. Hibino, H., Fukuda, Y.: A User Support System for Manufacturing System Design Using Distributed Simulation. Production Planning and Control 17, 128–142 (2006)

5. Hibino, H., Fukuda, Y., Yura, Y., Mitsuyuki, K., Kaneda, K.: Manufacturing Adapter of Distributed Simulation Systems Using HLA. In: 2002 Winter Simulation Conference, pp. 1099–1109. Institute of Electrical and Electronics Engineers, Inc., New Jersey (2002)

6. Hibino, H., Fukuda, Y.: A Synchronization Mechanism without Rollback Function for Distributed Manufacturing Simulation Systems. J. Japan Society of Mechanical Engineers 68, 2472–2478 (2002) (in Japanese)

7. Hibino, H., Inukai, T., Fukuda, Y.: Efficient Manufacturing System Implementation based on Combination between Real and Virtual Factory. I. J. Production Research 44, 3897–3915 (2006)

8. Hibino, H.: Simulation Environment for Efficient Manufacturing System Design and Implementation Using Network Middleware ORiN and HLA. J. Society of Instrument and Control Engineers 46, 545–560 (2007) (in Japanese)

9. ORiN (2011), http://www.orin.jp/

10. Kuhl, F., Weatherly, R., Dahmann, J.: Creating Computer Simulation Systems. Prentice-Hall (2000) ISBN 0-13-022511-8

Application of the Advanced Quality Improvement Techniques: Case Study

Vidosav Majstorovic[1] and Tatjana Sibalija[2]

[1] Faculty of Mechanical Engineering, University of Belgrade,
Kraljice Marije 16, 11 000 Belgrade, Serbia
[2] Faculty of Engineering International Management,
European University, Carigradska 28, 11 000 Belgrade, Serbia
vidosav.majstorovic@sbb.rs, tsibalija@gmail.com

Abstract. Implementation of the advanced cost-effective methodologies for product and/or process quality improvement is an effective mean to fulfil or exceeds customer's expectations. This paper presents the analysis of a performance of automatic enamelling process for a non-normal data distribution, conducted within the six sigma project implemented in a production system. Drawing on the process analysis results, process optimisation was performed using location and dispersion modelling. It proved its effectiveness in determining the significant effects of process factors on the response mean and variation, and in obtaining the optimal factors setting of the observed single-response process.

Keywords: process performance analysis, non-normal distribution, process parameters optimisation, location and dispersion modelling.

1   Introduction

The challenge in today's competitive markets is to be on the leading edge of producing high quality products at minimum costs. The implementation of the advanced quality improvement programs, such as six sigma, could help in improving company's competitiveness which is a key issue in a fast-moving global industry. Six sigma is a disciplined approach for process and/or product quality improvement, based on customer quality requirements. It takes users away from 'intuition-based decisions' to 'fact-based decisions'. For the existing system, six sigma is deployed according to DMAIC (Define-Measure-Analyse-Improve-Control) procedure. This paper deals with a case study performed in a Serbian cookware production system with the aim to reduce waste and cost of poor quality (COPQ) and improve the process sigma level, using six sigma methodology. In section 2, steps of define and measure stages were presented in brief, followed by detailed presentation of the process performance analysis for non-normally distributed data. In the improvement phase, the usage of location and dispersion modelling for the process parameters optimisation was shown. The discussion regarding the significance and effectiveness of the used techniques was also presented. Section 3 provides the concluding remarks on the applied techniques.

J. Frick and B. Laugen (Eds.): APMS 2011, IFIP AICT 384, pp. 181–189, 2012.

2   Six Sigma Application

This study illustrates parts of a six sigma project conducted according to DMAIC. In the define stage, IDEF0 method was used to map the system, showing detailed presentation of main processes, sub-processes and activities. Pareto analysis was developed to rank the defect types detected in the automatic enamelling process. The major defects were mainly related to the product characteristic - pot enamel thickness. Then, Ishikawa diagrams were used to analyse main causes of major defects, showing that the most problematic sub-process is base enamelling [1]. In order to verify the measuring system, the detailed measuring system analysis (MSA) was performed in the measure stage (Figure 1). The gage R&R study was conducted to calculate the equipment variation (repeatability), operator variability (reproducibility) and variation of pot enamel thickness (part-to-part variation). Since operators and equipment caused less than 20% of the total variation and the gage bias was statistically insignificant, the measuring system was accepted for the measurement and process analysis [2].

2.1   Process Performance Analysis for Non-normally Distributed Data

Capability studies are used to predict the overall ability of a continuous distribution process to make products within the required specifications. Process capability analysis entails comparing the performance of a process against its specifications, thus enabling analysis of previous and current performance, and benchmarking. Process capability and performance indices were widely investigated as means of summarizing process performance [3], [4]. Several recent studies were dedicated to capability and performance indices [5], [6]. The simplest capability index Cp presents the ratio of the specification width to the natural tolerance spread of a process. To incorporate the measure of process location, Cpk index was created [3], [4], considering how well the process spread is located about the target and the specification limits. The interpretation of the capability indices implies the following assumptions [3]: process stability; representative samples; normality; independences of observations. Capability indices show what is achievable rather than what is currently being achieved. As a response to this, the process performance indices Pp and Ppk were developed. Performance indices are calculated using the same formulae as for capability indices. However, performances indices do not assume that the process is in-control or is normally distributed and they use all of the data collected (both points in- and out-of-control). The process performance indices make used of the within sample standard deviation including both common and special cause of variation. Therefore, they provide a more realistic assessment of what is actually being produced [3]. It is more realistic to use Pp and Ppk than Cp and Cpk as the process variation cannot be tempered with by inappropriate subgrouping. The essential assumptions for the capability indices use are that the process is stable and the output is normally distributed.

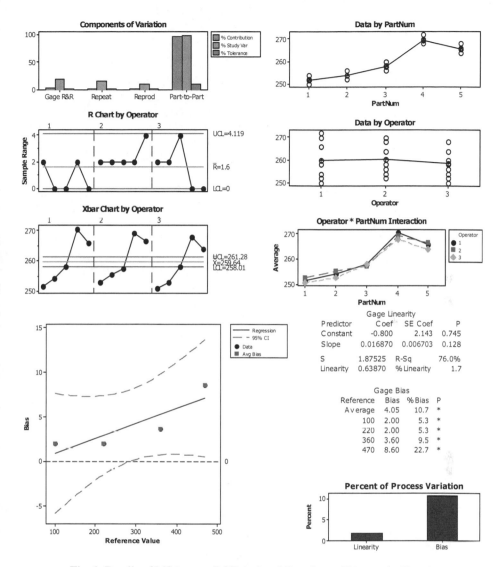

Fig. 1. Details of MSA: gage R&R (up) and linearity and bias study (down)

When the distribution is non-normal, capability indices calculated using conventional methods could often lead to erroneous conclusions. If the capability indices based on the normal assumption are used to deal with non-normal observations, the values of the capability indices may be incorrect and quite likely misrepresent the actual process and product quality [4]. For non-normal distributions, by replacing the unknown 6σ distance by $Up - Lp$ calculated based on the available sample data using the estimates of the mean, standard deviation, skewness and kurtosis, a natural tolerance is [4], [5]:

$$Tolerance_{natural} = Up - Lp = X_{0.99865} - X_{0.00135} \qquad (1)$$

where: Up and Lp estimate the 99.865 and the 0.135 percentile, respectively, to imitate the normal distribution property that the tail probability that the process is outside $\pm 3\sigma$ limits from the average equals 0.27%; $X_{0.00135}$ and $X_{0.99865}$ are values that meet the conditions: $P(X<X_{0.00135})=0.00135$, and $P(X<X_{0.99865})=0.99865$, respectively. Values $X_{0.99865}$ and $X_{0.00135}$ are the z-values of the non-normal cumulative distribution curve at the 99.865 % point and the 0.135 % point, respectively. The distance between the 99.865th and 0.135th percentiles is equivalent to 6σ spread in the normal case. The process median is presented by the 50th percentile for the non-normal distribution, which is equivalent to the average value for normal distribution. The relations above were concluded from Clements' method of determining percentiles based on Pearson family of distribution. Clements developed a method for capability indices calculation for non-normal distributions, utilising Pearson curves to provide accurate estimates of $X_{0.0013}$, $X_{0.50}$ and $X_{0.99865}$, and based on the skewness and kurtosis assessment [4].

Since the process performances calculation does not require the assumption that the data are normally distributed, it makes sense to evaluate process performance indices in discussing the actual process for non-normal data. Based on the relation (1), the process performance indices for non-normal distribution could be formulated as:

$$Pp = \frac{USL - LSL}{X_{0.99865} - X_{0.00135}}, \quad Ppk = \min\left\{ \frac{USL - X_{0.50}}{X_{0.99865} - X_{0.50}} ; \frac{X_{0.50} - LSL}{X_{0.50} - X_{0.00135}} \right\} \quad (2)$$

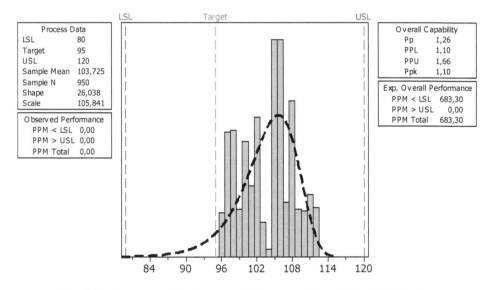

Fig. 2. Performance of the base enamelling process for a Weibull distribution

In the observed six sigma project, as a part of Statistical Process Control (SPC) implementation, the analysis of the base enamelling process was performed using $\overline{X}$, R control chart and process capability and performance analysis. Specification limits for base enamel thickness are: LSL÷USL=80÷120μm; the specified target value is 95 μm.

After concluding that the process is statistically stable, process probability plot showed that the process data are not normally distributed. Several probability plots for different non-normal distributions were tested, and the Weibull distribution is found the best one to fit the actual process data. The Anderson-Darling goodness-of-fit test and p-value test were used to evaluate the hypothesis that the Weibull distribution provides the best fit. Capability plot for Weibull distribution showed that the actual overall process tolerance interval is contained within the specification interval. Figure 2 presents the base enamelling process performance for a Weibull distribution. The process capability estimation was performed using the overall process performance indices calculated using relation (2). Pp value of 1.26 shows that the process is capable of producing at least 99.74 % of conforming parts. Since Pp is greater than Ppk and PPU is greater that PPL, the process median is off the target and closer to USL. This clearly indicates the location problem. The non-conformance rate is estimated as 683 parts per million.

2.2   Process Parameters Optimisation Using Location and Dispersion Modelling

If the process is not capable of producing virtually all conforming products, it is necessary to improve process performance using advanced experimentation methods, such as Taguchi robust parameter design. Taguchi's orthogonal experimentation is frequently adopted to reduce the trials number but still obtain reasonably rich information with certain statistical level of confidence. Robust parameter design was successfully used in optimising many single-response processes, optimising both the mean and the variance of a response, making a process immune to noise sources, and ultimately improving process and/or product quality. In a modern industry, demands for short life cycles and high-quality products require efficient and objective use of experimentation. With the limited amount of data provided in an unreplicated experiment based on orthogonal array, it is very demanding to study both location and dispersion effects. The identification of the control factor effects on location (mean) and dispersion (variation) of the observed quality characteristic (response) has been proven effective in many single-response process optimisations [7], [8], [9]. The location and dispersion modelling approach gives models for measures of location and dispersion separately, in term of control factors and interactions main effects on a response. At each control factors setting, the sample mean y_i and sample variance σ_i (where n_i is number of replicates at for the ith control factors setting), are used to present the location and dispersion [7]:

$$\gamma_i = \frac{1}{n_i} \sum_j y_{ij} \, , \; \sigma_i^2 = \frac{1}{n_i - 1} \sum_j (y_{ij} - \overline{y_i})^2 \tag{3}$$

The half-normal probability plot is a graphical tool that uses ordered estimated effects to help assess which factors are important. A half-normal distribution is the distribution of the $|Y|$ with Y having a normal distribution. Quantitatively, the estimated effect of a given main effect or interaction and its rank relative to other main effects and interactions is given via least squares estimation. Unimportant factors are those that have near-zero effects and important factors are those whose effects are considerably removed from zero. Hence, unimportant effects tend to have a normal distribution centred near zero while important effects tend to have a normal distribution centred at their respective true large (but unknown) effect values [9].

From the analysis presented in section 2.1 it was concluded that the process needs optimisation in order to solve the location problem (achieve the target base enamelling thickness) and improve process performance. An experiment was performed to identify the optimal setting of critical-to-quality (CTQ) control factors. The parameters adopted as control factors and their values used in the experiment (Table 1) are: enamel parameters: SW, DW, and SW DW interaction; process parameters: PS, AS, and PS AS interaction. In order to accommodate four control factors and two interactions studied at two levels, orthogonal array L16 was used to design the experimental plan [10].

Table 1. Control factors and levels used in the experiment

Control factor	Symbol	Unit	Level '-1'	Level '+1'
Specific weight	SW	gram cm^{-3}	8	11
Deposit weight	DW	gram cm^{-3}	1,68	1,70
Pouring speed	PS	turns min^{-1}	0	3
Automat speed	AS	parts min^{-1}	5	9

Half-normal plots were developed to show the significance of the effects of control factors and their interactions on the response (base enamelling thickness) location and dispersion. Half-normal plot for the response location (MEAN) is shown at Figure 3 up. From the location plot it is visible that effects of factors SW, DW, PS and interaction AS·SW·DW are significant. Then, the regression analysis for the response location (MEAN) was conducted, showing regression equation as follows:

$$MEAN = 87.8 + 6.51 \cdot SW + 5.74 \cdot DW + 3.02 \cdot SW \cdot DW \cdot AS + 2.79 \cdot PS \tag{4}$$

Table 2 shows statistical parameters for the regression equitation (4). The above significant control factors and interaction for the response location are used as predictors. Each predictor in a regression equation has a coefficient associated with it. In multiple regressions the estimated coefficient (*Coef.*) indicates the change in the mean response per unit increase in the responding predictor when all other predictors are held constant. If the *p*-value of a coefficient is less than the α-level (α=0.05), there is evidence of a significant relationship between the predictor and the response. Value *T* is used for comparison with the *t*-distribution to determine if a predictor is significant.

Figure 3 down shows the half-normal plot for the response dispersion, presented over *Ln Sigma*^{2}. The reason to use the natural logarithm is that it maps positive values to real (both positive and negative) values, and by taking its inverse transformation, any predicted value on the *ln* scale will be transformed back to a positive value on the original scale. Also, *ln* transformation converts a possible multiplicative relationship into an additive relationship, which is easier to model statistically [7]. The dispersion plot shows significant effects of PS, PS·AS, DW and PS·DW for the response dispersion. Statistical parameters for the dispersion regression equitation are given in Table 2. The obtained regression equation for the response dispersion (*Ln Sigma*^{2}) is:

$$LnSigma^2 = 3.22 + 0.25 \cdot PS + 0.2 \cdot PS \cdot AS + 0.19 \cdot DW + 1.6 \cdot DW \cdot PS \tag{5}$$

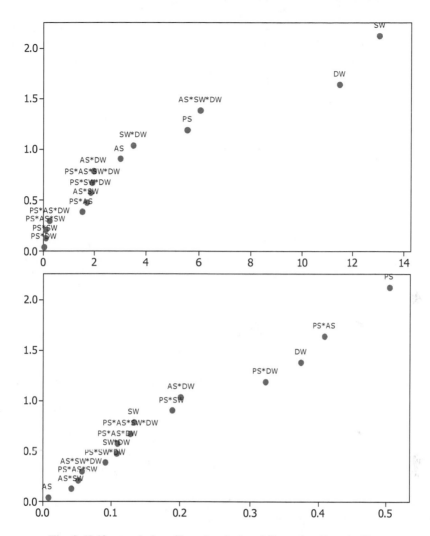

Fig. 3. Half-normal plot of location (up) and dispersion (down) effects

Since the objective of the experiment is to achieve the nominal (target) response mean value, and following the two-step procedure for Nominal-the-Best (NTB) problems [7], the first step is to select the levels of dispersion factors to minimise dispersion. From the dispersion effects relation (5), in order to minimise dispersion the following levels of dispersion factors are selected: PS level '-1', AS level '+1'. The factor SW could be used to bring the mean on the target (value 95 μm), depending on DW level. This is presented in the equitation (6), obtained from the location effects relation (4):

$$95 = 87.8 + 6.51 \cdot SW + 5.74 \cdot DW + 3.02 \cdot SW \cdot DW \cdot (+1) + 2{,}79 \cdot (-1) \quad (6)$$

There are two possible solutions of the equitation (6): (a.) if DW is set to level '-1' then calculated SW is 16.2; (b.) if DW is set to level '+1' calculated SW value is 10.5. Since due to machine limitation it is impossible in practice to set the SW value to 16.2, the second solution is adopted resulting in the final optimal control factors setting: DW=1.70; SW=11; PS=0; AS=9.

Table 2. Statistical parameters of regression equitation for location and dispersion modelling

Location modelling				Dispersion modelling			
Predictor	Coef.	T	P	Predictor	Coef.	T	P
Constant	87.80	95.79	0.000	Constant	3.22	55.33	0.000
SW	6.51	7.10	0.000	PS	0.25	4.33	0.001
DW	5.74	6.26	0.000	PS·AS	0.20	3.51	0.005
SW·DW·AS	3.02	3.30	0.007	DW	0.19	3.20	0.008
PS	2.79	3.04	0.011	DW·PS	0.16	2.76	0.018

2.3   Discussion

Process analysis performed under the assumption of normally distributed data provided highly misleading results, showing that process performance indices are higher than capability indices, which is practically impossible. This highlights the importance of the accurate process performance calculation, providing correct data for the customer and for the process improvement. Based on the conclusions drawn from the process analysis for a non-normal distribution, the experiment was performed to optimise the process with respect to the target value for the product's characteristic mean (location) and to reduce variation (dispersion). The experimental analysis was performed using ANOVA and using location and dispersion modelling. Although both methods displayed the same optimal factors setting, the later showed significant interaction effects on mean (AS·SW·DW) and variation (PS·DW), that ANOVA did not detect [10]. Verification run was performed using optimised factors setting, confirming the experimental results. The obtained results present significant improvement in comparison to the previous performance. According to Taguchi's quality loss function, loss caused by previous performance was Lp(Y) = K·70.06 units [1], and loss encountered after optimisation is Lo(Y) = K·2.99 units. The achieved improvements are monitored in a practice and documented to ensure the sustainability. Significant reduction of a waste, COPQ and non-added-value activities rework and inspection, and improvement of process performance are expected to be sustained.

3   Concluding Remarks

Important issues regarding process analysis and improvement have been highlighted in this study. The significance of the accurate estimation of process performance indices for non-normal distribution was shown. The use of the location and dispersion modelling clarified a total contribution to the process variation, and it was shown as a successful method to optimise the observed single-response process.

However, it would be difficult to apply the presented method for the multi-response process optimisation. Therefore, the authors developed the method consisted of two stages. In the first stage, a statistical factor effects approach was developed, based on Taguchi's quality loss function, principal component analysis and grey relational analysis, to uncorrelated and synthesis responses into a single measure. Since this approach could not provide the overall global optimum, in the second stage the intelligent approach was developed using neural networks (to model the process behaviour) and a genetic algorithm (GA) (to perform search in a continual space), to ensure that the actual global optimum is found [11]. The method was further improved using simulated annealing (SA) as the optimisation tool, instead of GA [12].

Implementation of six sigma presented first steps in introducing the advanced quality improvement programs in Serbian industry. While six sigma is widespread adopted as a primary quality improvement program among a variety of industries, authors stressed on the importance of a business culture changes and a theoretical underpinning, in order to bridge the gap between the theory and practice of six sigma methodology.

References

1. Majstorovic, V., Sibalija, T.: An Application of DMAIC Approach to Process Quality Improvement – Case Study. In: Proceedings of IFAC Workshop on Manufacturing, Modelling, Management and Control - MIM 2007, pp. 102–108 (2007)
2. Cagnazzo, L., Sibalija, T., Majstorovic, V.: The Measurement System Analysis as a Performance Improvement Catalyst: a Case Study. In: Taticchi, P. (ed.) Business Performance Measurement and Management, New Contents, Themes and Challenges, pp. 269–292. Springer, Heidelberg (2010)
3. Keats, J.B., Montgomery, D.C.: Statistical Applications in Process Control. Marcel Dekker, Inc., New York (1996)
4. Pearn, W.L., Kotz, S.: Encyclopaedia and Handbook of Process Capability Indices. World Scientific Publishing Co. Ltd., Singapore (2006)
5. Rezaie, K., Ostadi, B., Taghizadeh, M.R.: Applications of Process Capability and Process Performance Indices. Journal of Applied Sciences 6, 1186–1191 (2006)
6. Chen, J.-P., Ding, C.G.: A new process capability index for non-normal distributions. Int. J. Qual. Reliab. Manag. 18, 762–770 (2001)
7. Wu, C.F.J., Hamada, M.: Experiments – Planning, Analysis and Parameter Design Optimisation. John Willey & Sons Inc., New York (2000)
8. Wang, P.C., Lin, D.F.: Dispersion effects in signal-response data from fractional factorial experiments. Computational Statistics & Data Analysis 38, 95–111 (2001)
9. McGrath, R.N., Lin, D.K.J.: Analyzing location and dispersion in unreplicated fractional factorial experiments. Statistics & Probability Letters 65, 369–377 (2003)
10. Sibalija, T., Majstorovic, V., Rosu, S.M.: Location and dispersion effects in single-response system data from Taguchi orthogonal experimentation. In: Proceedings in Manufacturing Systems, vol. 4, pp. 383–388. Romanian Academy Publishing House, Bucharest (2009)
11. Sibalija, T., Majstorovic, V.: An integrated approach to optimise parameter design of multi-response processes based on Taguchi method and artificial intelligence. J. Intell. Manuf. (2010), doi:10.1007/s10845-010-0451-y
12. Sibalija, T., Majstorovic, V.: An integrated simulated annealing-based method for robust multiresponse process optimisation. Int. J. Adv. Manuf. Technol. 59(9), 1227–1244 (2012)

Analyzing the Effects of Production Control on Logistic Targets with Web-Based Simulation Model

Guenther Schuh, Till Potente, Sascha Fuchs, and Christina Thomas

Laboratory for Machine Tools and Production Engineering,
Steinbachstrasse 19, 52074 Aachen, Germany
{g.schuh,t.potente,s.fuchs,c.thomas}@wzl.rwth-aachen.de

Abstract. Manufacturing companies are facing the challenge to cope with individualized process chains in spite of high market dynamics. In order to achieve high process efficiency by realizing logistic targets, two main leverages can be identified: adjustment of production structure and configuration of production control. The production structure represents the layout and arrangement of machines, the organization of production processes as well as the information and material flow. Once installed, it is often set for a long period of time and therefore represents the basis for further elements in a production environment such as production control. The dilemma of production planning and control is to achieve high process efficiency, low throughput times and good planning confidence while customers demand short product-lifecycles, an increasing product variety and a growing individualization of products. Within this paper, a simulation-based study about the effects of production structure and production control to logistical targets is introduced.

Keywords: production control, production structure, simulation model, manufacturing control principles.

1 Introduction

Manufacturing companies are facing the challenge to cope with individualized process chains in spite of high market dynamics. In order to achieve high process efficiency by meeting logistic targets, two leverages exist: adjustment of production structure and configuration of production control. The production structure represents the foundation of production processes. It determines the layout and arrangement of machines, the organization of production processes as well as the information and material flow. Once installed, it is often set for a long period of time and therefore represents the basis for further elements in a production environment such as production control. The dilemma of production planning and control is to achieve high process efficiency, low throughput times and good planning confidence while customers demand short product-lifecycles, an increasing product variety and a growing individualization of products. In order to realize robust processes within a turbulent environment, the challenge of production control is determined by an

J. Frick and B. Laugen (Eds.): APMS 2011, IFIP AICT 384, pp. 190–199, 2012.

adequate adaption of control mechanisms according to production's conditions. Within this paper, a simulation-based study about the effects of production structure and production control to logistical targets is introduced and an approach to standardize simulating processes is given.

1.1   Challenges in Production Structure

Following Ulrich, a company can be understood as a complex structure with an interdisciplinary character. Financial, material and information flows connect a company to its environment [1]. The internal structure of a company resembles a system. The elements of this system are people and machines. Furthermore, materials can be interpreted as objects to be transformed, money as an instrument of payment and information as a condition for goal-oriented activities of each production element. In order to make the system a functional one, the mentioned elements have to be arranged in an appropriate way. This arrangement can be defined as the system structure in which elements have a certain relationship to each other [2]. The definition of a production structure can be derived from the system definition by Ropohl. He describes every system with a working and an information system [3]. Therefore, the production structure determines the layout and arrangement of machines, the organization of production processes as well as the information and material flow. I.e. both, visual elements in the physical production process such as machines and their capacity as well as organizational elements like the lot size or work in process, are included. Finally, production structure can be defined as the foundation of production processes.

The challenge of production structure is to enhance robust processes on the one hand and on the other hand to enable adaptive and versatile structures which can be changed according to market dynamic. Once installed, a production structure is often set for a long period of time and therefore represents the basis for further actions in a production environment such as production control.

1.2   Challenges in Production Planning and Control

The challenge of production control is to achieve high process efficiency, low throughput times and good planning confidence despite of a turbulent, customer-oriented environment with short product-lifecycles, an increasing product variety and a growing individualization of demands [4]. To overcome this problem of transparency, a multitude of IT-tools were developed: Supply Chain Management (SCM), Enterprise Resource Planning (ERP) and Manufacturing Execution Systems (MES) are examples of software tools to deal with growing complexity [5]. Thereby, the main challenge in production control is on the one hand to fulfil the classic logistic targets defined by Wiendahl [6] such as low stocks, short throughput times and a high adherence to delivery dates, but following Goldratt [7] also to maximize the throughput at a minimum of operating costs despite any turbulence. In order to react to economic crises or booms, production has to be flexible. This urges companies to react to these circumstances in a faster and more efficient way than their competitors [8]. Consequently, the configuration of control task is a main challenge for operators involved in production control.

1.3   The Tasks of Production Control

The configuration of control tasks follows the four functions of production control defined by Lödding: Order generation, order release, sequencing and capacity utilization control [9].

Order generation generates production orders and determines plan figures for accesses and exits. Trigger for an order generation may be customer orders, material removals from the finished goods warehouse or the production program. As psychological effects and intransparent parameters can lead to major bullwhip effects in the value stream, methods of forecasting need to be carefully applied. Order release determines the date of the start of production. In fact it influences work in process and capacity utilization and therefore determines the average throughput time of orders. The sequencing of waiting queues has the main influence on the distribution of throughput times and thus the adherence of delivery dates. The sequence is defined by certain rules, which assigns priorities to orders. More detailed methods of sequencing become necessary if the structure of the production process becomes more complex, the variety of processes increases or if the volatility of the market demand is very high. Finally, capacity utilization control has a major influence on productivity and production costs. It pre-determines necessary capacities for production while taking disturbances and planning errors into consideration. Beyond, flexible capacities in form of additional machines or resources help to ensure on-time delivery.

An expansion of these four tasks of production control described by Lödding is the value stream oriented concept described by Schuh [10]. It integrates the logic of the production control by Lödding. In contrast to most other approaches which mainly consist of control strategies for job release and sequencing at machines, the concept of value stream oriented production control also includes job creation.

The basic framework for the configuration of production control is a three layer model that starts with the value stream on the shop floor (see Fig. 1). The value stream represents the production process. The intention is to display segments of equal production control configuration along the production process. The production control layer describes the configuration of the production control and the information needed both from the master data, order data and from the shop floor. Manufacturing master data and order data are the input for all planning and control activities. They consist of work plans, bill of material and customer demands represented in a master production schedule. The third layer allows the link between changes of the configuration of production control or on the shop floor and changes within master data, as data inconsistencies are often the origin of many problems in production control [11].

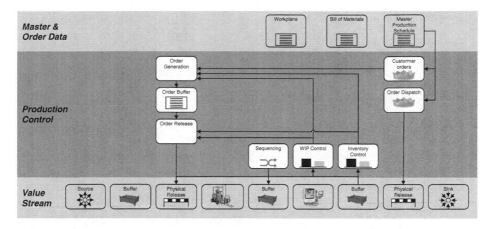

Fig. 1. The three layers model of production control

Only by including all parameters of the production control, it is possible to find a customized and optimized configuration for a company. That is the reason why the value stream oriented production control approach determines the influence of the configuration of the production control on logistic performance factors (inventory, delivery accuracy, throughput time, capacity utilization) as a whole.

2   Right Adjustment and Understanding of Production Control

In the wake of the rapid development of information technology and information management in production systems, Advanced Planning and Scheduling (APS) systems are used more and more often to plan and to control production processes. The basic idea of these systems is to make use of real-time feedback from production to adapt the production schedule continuously to any kind of disturbances [12]. Due to continuously changing conditions, the program may possibly reject several scheduling proposals made within one day as they lead to chaos within the production and distrust in the planning system. Often, the result is a redundant reschedule of the employees.

It is questionable whether a high-frequent intervention in the production process is beneficial. The funnel-experiment by Deming shows that there is a maximum amount of reasonable interventions within process operations. Within this experiment, balls are dropped through a funnel on a calibrated surface [13]. Thereby, the scattering of points of impact is measured in relation to the target impact. The results of this experiment show the influence of interventions on the scattering: the more interventions were undertaken by the operator, the higher was the scattering of points of impact. These findings can be transferred to production control: in order to avoid a turbulent production, the optimal amount of interventions and the improvement of the production system are crucial to be found. Systemic process variations or rather the scattering of the points of impact within the experiment cannot be reduced by permanent correction of the funnel-position. A reduction of the scattering can only be achieved by a dedicated improvement of the system.

In addition to the right adjustment of production control, employees have to be involved within decision process. Since the options of different configurations in production control are enormous, a number of predictably irrational decisions are made [14]. For instance, qualitative or quantitative models do, up to now, not universally analyse the effectiveness of priority rules for order sequencing [15]. Despite numerous studies there is a need for a stronger generalization for industrial environments. Furthermore, many employees do not understand the influence of work in process on throughput times. This lack of knowledge leads to an on-going, controversial debate about the effects of different control methods among practitioners. The insufficient achievement of logistic targets is therefore caused by a lack of knowledge of the operators [16]. Consequently, counterproductive decisions lead to a poor performance of logistic targets in production. The most common pitfalls leading to such behaviour are for example the wrong understanding of pull or push principles, especially regarding to the impact of work in process [17]. The results of several industry cases of the Laboratory for Machine Tools and Production Engineering (WZL) have shown, that simple structural solutions like first-in-first-out production is often more successful regarding the achievement of logistic targets than is a complicated APS system which is not understood and supported by its operators.

Therefore, the interaction of production structure and production control has an important bearing on the efficiency of production. This interaction is not sufficiently described in literature so far. Often, different adjustments cannot be tested in operation and results of simulation cannot be used because of the non-comparability of existing models [18]. In existing simulation studies, different models are exclusively designed. Hence, the results of these studies are not comparable and cannot be used to derive adequate statements about production control. The usage of a low amount of working systems and product variants is followed by a characteristic and low complexity of these systems [19]. Therefore, an analysis of a universal production system model is needed in order to analyse the effects of production structure and production control on logistic targets sufficiently.

3   State of the Art: Analyzing the Effects of Production Structure and Production Control on Logistical Targets Using Simulation

The aim of this paper is to design a model which ensures an analysis of the effects of production structure and production control on logistical targets in a general way. According to Rabe, the following steps have to be defined in order to generate the simulation model [20]:

At first, the definition of the target system determines command variables to be analysed within the simulation. To obtain meaningful results, these command variables can be determined as averages or standard deviation. In this context, logistic targets like utilization, work in process, cycle time, adherence to delivery times and compliance of sequence shall be analyzed. In addition, the focus should be on changing the sequence, which can be seen as a performance indicator for the deviation of sequencing.

In a second step, system boundaries, system variables, subsystems and elements of the simulation model have to be defined. The definition of system boundaries includes the material and information interfaces to its environment. In order to analyze single tasks of production control, it is necessary to narrow the system with a dedicated control task to focus on. The result of such a system analysis is a clarification of the system, the organizational structure and the flow structure (see Fig. 2). In this example, the focus is on analyzing the influence of sequencing rules.

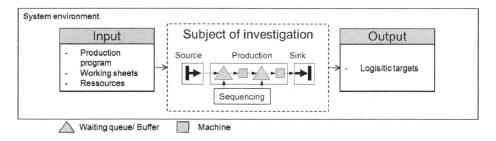

Fig. 2. System environment of simulation model

Then, the collection and preparation of data and information like manufacturing principle, material flow, production type, amount of variants and complexity of material flow as well as system load is needed. Important information for the analysis of effects of a changing production structure is lot sizes. Since there is a trend to more product variants and smaller production volume, levelling of lot sizes supports decoupling of production and customer demand in order to achieve a harmonized production [21].

Based on the system analysis and collection of the database, a simulation model with the purpose to analyse the defined task can be designed. Here again, this is shown using the example of different sequencing rules. The simulation evaluates the achievement of logistic targets regarding different settings of the production structure und production control. Concerning throughput time (see Fig. 3) for instance, the result of the simulation provides a ranking of the sequencing rules, used in this simulation model. The result of the simulation also underlines the success of a sequencing rule which prioritizes orders with the shortest operating time (SOT). For this sequencing rule, the average throughput times are the lowest. The second best rule within the simulation is a sequencing rule which combines orders with the aim of reducing setup times. Finally, this one is followed by the sequencing rule of slippage, which indicates the amount of time until planned delivery date that is not required for further production or transport.

In this case, the first three steps of lot size levelling deteriorate average throughput times. Only the ideal scenario represents an improvement of throughput times. This effect is due to bottlenecks. Therefore, the results of the simulation have to be evaluated with consideration to these bottlenecks. With respect to the simulation model, further scenarios have to be simulated in order to analyse the effects of changing bottlenecks.

As shown, the simulation-based approach, in this case done with the simulation tool "PlantSimulation" (by Siemens), facilitates an evaluation of production control principles with regard to a certain production structure. The results of the presented simulation model show a ranking of sequencing rules regarding different levels of lot size levelling. Thus, it represents an important analysis of interaction of production structure and production control. The benefits are on the one hand the possibility to compare certain production control methods and on the other hand the evidence of the impact of production structure in order to maximize the production systems' targets.

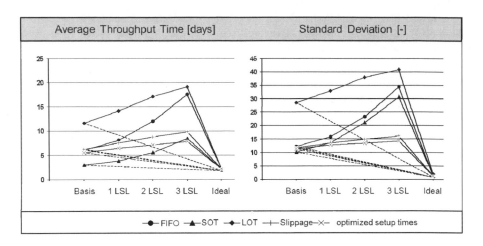

Fig. 3. Example of simulation results regarding throughput times

Despite the benefits of simulation-based approaches for production control, the modelling process of high quality models is still time consuming and in addition requires expert knowledge in different areas. Consequently, carrying out simulation projects is linked with high costs, which makes it an issue especially for smaller and middle sized companies. Once set up, the models have to be verified. This is an iterative process as, referring to chapter 2, adjustments cannot be made in operation. Even in case the models turn out to be accurate, a broader understanding of their mode of functioning has to be installed amongst employees. A lack of transparency and understanding often deteriorates acceptance. Also the fact that simulating results often turn out not to be comparable, as the underlying model has been designed for a special environment, does not contribute to acceptance.

Consequently there is the challenge of finding a certain degree of standardization in the simulation process and therefore of allowing also non-experts to make use of simulating tools.

4   Approach of a Web Based Simulation Model

In order to face the challenge described above, a web-based framework has been developed which takes the idea of simulating to another level. The main idea of this web-based simulation model is a modular structure with a user-friendly interface. Ths user is able to upload input data easily and to configure production control by just pressing buttons. Thereby, no simulation knowledge is needed because the simulation takes place in the background of this model. The web-based surface is structured by a field for input data, a field for the configuration of production control and a field for the results of the simulation (see Figure 4).

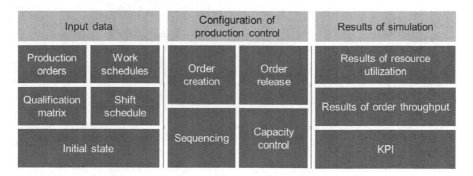

Fig. 4. Mock-up of web-interface of simulation

Simulation input data are in general work schedules, production orders and shift schedules for example. These data are provided by Enterprise Resource Planning-system (ERP). Based on these input data, the resources and orders for simulation can be generated automatically within the simulation model. Based on shift schedule and qualification matrix, availability of employees is covered. This is important in order to model flexible employment in case operators get sick for instance. The initial state of simulation is given by the production data from ERP-system. Since input data are in general historical feedback data from production for a certain time period, the initial state can be exemplary derived by the order mixture at a certain date.

After uploading input data, configuration of production control strategies is done by defining the four tasks of production control. This procedure follows the concept of value stream oriented production control (see chapter 1.3). While the production structure is represented by the value stream and production program, the production control can be selected manually by using the web-based surface of simulation model. Thereby, the control strategies can be allocated to the machines. This allocation is done by drag and drop, so there is no simulation knowledge necessary. The operator just interacts with the web-based user interface while the simulation is running in the background of the system.

Then, the simulation can be started. The results of simulation represent logistic targets of production like the resource utilization and the throughput of orders etc. The results are also presented on web-surface which enables the user to interactively analyze the results.

5   Conclusion and Outlook

The simulation-based approach facilitates an evaluation of production control principles in regard to a certain production structure. By using the web-based simulation model, no simulation expert knowledge is required. The advantage of this web-based value stream oriented simulation model is its modular structure and its simple adaptability. Thus, the impact of different control methods for a certain production structure can by analyzed. By deriving arrangements, production system's targets can be maximized. By integration of employees within the simulation generation process, the acceptance in simulation and in simulation results increases.

The next step is to develop a optimization of production control automatically by exchanging the described control modules for job creation, job release, sequencing and operational capacity control. The user will be able to automatically receive the optimized controlling and sequencing parameters as well as their optimization potential. This will be done with the help of genetic algorithms. Therefore, the user has to describe its optimization goal like e.g. delivery accuracy or throughput time.

Acknowledgements. The concept of manufacturing control with consideration of production structure is one part of the framework developed within the excellence initiative "Integrative production technology for high wage countries" at Aachen University as a part of the "High Resolution Supply Chain Management" cluster. The main research objective is to develop decentralized production planning and controlling concepts and to develop new solutions for existing PPS concepts.

References

1. Ulrich, H.: Der systemorientierte Ansatz in der Betriebswirtschaftslehre. In: Kortzfleisch, G. (ed.) Wissenschaftsprogramm und Ausbildungsziele der Betriebswirtschaftslehre, 1st edn., pp. 45–49. Duncker und Humblot, Berlin (1971)
2. Ulrich, H., Schwaninger, M.: Systemorientiertes Management. Das Werk von Hans Ulrich, p. 14. Paul Haupt Verlag, Bern (2001)
3. Ropohl, G.: Allgemeine Technologie: Eine Systemtheorie der Technik, 3rd edn. Universitätsverlag Karlsruhe, Karlsruhe (2009)
4. Jones, D.: Creating Lean Solutions, 2. Lean Management Summit, Aachen, Germany, pp. 17–28 (2005)
5. Milberg, J., Neise, P.: Organizational Design of Supply Chains. WGP, Production Engineering XIII/2, 181–186 (2006)
6. Wiendahl, H.-P.: Betriebsorganisation für Ingenieure, 4th edn. Hanser (1997)
7. Goldratt, E., Cox, J.: The Goal: Excellence in Manufacturing. North River Press, Croton-on-Hudson (1984)
8. Petermann, D.: Modellbasierte Produktionsregelung. Fortschittsberichte VDI, Reihe 20, Nr. 193, Düsseldorf, p. 1 (1996)
9. Lödding, H.: Verfahren der Fertigungssteuerung, 2nd edn. Grundlagen, Beschreibung, Konfiguration. Springer, Berlin (2008)
10. Schuh, G., Franzkoch, B., Potente, T., Fuchs, S.: Simulation based configuration of value stream oriented production control. In: Conference Proceedings, POM 21st Annual Conference, POM 2010 Conference Program Bulletin, Vancouver (2010)
11. Schuh, G., Kampker, A., Potente, T., Stollwerk, A., Müller, C.: Wertstromorientierte Konfiguration der Produktionssteuerung mit Enterprise Dynamics (Value stream oriented configuration of the production control with Enterprise Dynamics. In: Zülch, G., Stock, P. (eds.) Integrationsaspekte der Simulation: Technik, Organisation und Personal, pp. 413–420. KIT Scientific Publishing, Karlsruhe (2010b)
12. Zijm, W.H.M.: Towards Intelligent Manufacturing Planning and Control Systems. Journal OR Spectrum 22(3), 313–345 (2000)
13. Deming, W.E.: The New Economics: for industry, government, education, 2nd edn., p. 190. Center of Advanced Educational Services, Cambridge (1994)

14. Schuh, G., Lenders, M., Nussbaum, C., Kupke, D.: Design for Changeability. In: ElMaraghy, H. (ed.) Changeable and Reconfigurable Manufacturing Systems. Springer, London (2008)
15. Nyhuis, P., Hartmann, W., et al.: Der Einfluss von Prioritätsregeln auf logistische Zielgrößen. Productivity Management 14(3), 17–20 (2009)
16. Nyhuis, P.: Beiträge zu einer Theorie der Logistik. Springer (2008)
17. Schuh, G., Franzkoch, B., Potente, T., Fuchs, S.: Simulation based configuration of value stream oriented production control. In: Conference Proceedings, POM 21st Annual Conference, POM 2010 Conference Program Bulletin, Vancouver (2010)
18. Framinan, J.M., et al.: Input control and dispatching rules in a dynamic CONWIP flowshop. International Journal of Production Research 38(18) (2000)
19. Day, J.E., Hottenstein, M.P.: Review of sequencing research. Naval Research Logistics Quarterly 17, 11–39 (1970)
20. Rabe, M., Spieckermann, S., Wenzel, S.: Verifikation und Validierung für die Simulation in Produktion und Logistik. Springer, Heidelberg (2008)
21. Deuse, J.: Entwicklung einer systematischen Vorgehensweise zur Produktionsnivellierung der variantenreichen Kleinserienfertigung. AiF-Schlussbericht 15865 N/1 (2010)

Management of Tags and Tag-Related Technical Information in Small and Large Scale Modifications: An Application for a Drilling Rig

Jawad Raza[1] and R.M. Chandima Ratnayake[2]

[1] Apply Sørco, Sandnes, Norway
[2] University of Stavanger, Stavanger, Norway
Jawad.raza@applysorco.no, chandima.ratnayake@uis.no

Abstract. Considerable amount of Oil and Gas (O&G) production and process installations operating in the North Sea are getting aged and requiring continuous modifications. Nature of such contractual jobs is relatively short term with demanding deliverables. Hence, the engineering contractors require excellent coordination and seamless communication during all phases of a project. For any contractor/supplier, it is of utmost importance to ensure that equipment related technical information is made available at the right time to avoid any unexpected project delays. Experience shows that poor coordination among project participants can result in failing to comply with regulatory and governing requirements. Also, there are other challenges to managing tags, databases and tag history as well as keeping technical information integrity. This manuscript illustrates role of a tag management system developed by an engineering contractor company which provides services to operators in NCS. The particular system is developed and customized to meet a drilling rig client's specification.

Keywords: Tag Manager, Technical information management, Maintenance and Modification, Life Cycle Information (LCI), Project Execution Model (PEM), Norwegian rig market.

1 Introduction

Recent findings reveal that the Maintenance and Modification (M&M) of the assets used within the Oil and Gas (O&G) drilling discipline are facing numerous unique challenges [CCR, 2011; Staff, 2012]. It is undoubtedly quite significant to have a system to manage tags and their corresponding Life Cycle Information (LCI) in order to meet the project targets. The offshore drilling industry (i.e. rig market) is considered as chronically cyclical and extremely capital intensive. For instance, once a rig is built, the owner is strongly motivated to secure work at any reasonable cost, as the expenses related to maintain an idle rig is extremely high. This creates a very competitive pricing environment for even modest amount of rig shut down to carry out M&M [Simmons, 2002] whilst compensating interests between continuation of drilling operations and shutting down for maintenance. For instance, "BP was not obliged to pay for time in excess of 24 hours each month spent on certain repairs on

J. Frick and B. Laugen (Eds.): APMS 2011, IFIP AICT 384, pp. 200–212, 2012.
© IFIP International Federation for Information Processing 2012

"Deepwater Horizon". As a result, drilling priorities took precedence over planned maintenance. For instance, "the Deepwater Horizon had never been to dry dock for shore-based repairs in the nine years since it had been built" [CCR, 2011]. Consequently, a leading O&G operator company, BP, was almost brought to bankruptcy due to Macondo well blowout in the Gulf of Mexico [Ratnayake *et al.*, 2011]. Therefore, it is vital to have an approach to enhance and optimize small and large scale M&M projects on rigs. Hence, this manuscript elaborates a system developed for management of tags and tag-related technical information in modifications that supposed to be carried out on a drilling rig.

2 Background

A recent survey by Norwegian Petroleum Authority (PSA) reveals that about 50 percent of all existing installations in the North Sea are approaching their design life [MPE, 2010]. Hence, M&M plays a significant role for continue operation on these installations in a safe manner. This resulted to award giant M&M (Maintenance & Modification) and EPCIC (Engineering, Procurement, Construction, Installation & Commissioning) contracts in past few years to the contractor companies from the operator companies [ON, 2012]. Successful execution and completion of small and large scale projects relies on factors such as technical information, competencies, teamwork, tag management, communication and quality assurance, etc. It is also important that all the vital elements of a project to be coordinated for meeting the deliverables and milestones. Figure 1 shows key elements in M&M and EPCIC project execution.

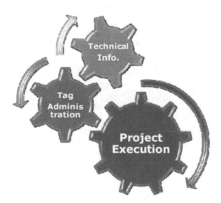

Fig. 1. Project execution in M&M and EPCIC

Based on the scale of a modification project, there may be several parties, tools and complex work processes involved in planning and execution. This demand for tools to communicate and manage project deliverables as well as retain the integrity of technical information through all the phases of the project. Failing to establish a seamless communication may result in failing to comply with the Norwegian and company specific regulatory requirements.

In any M&M project, administration of equipment and equipment-related information provides basis for design, installation, maintenance planning, scheduling and spare parts evaluation, etc. All the equipments and components in a M&M project are designated as particular code which is named as a 'tag number' or simply a 'tag'. Basically the 'tag' or 'tag number' is a unique code that defines the functional location and function of a physical component or equipment in the main facility [NORSOK Z-DP-002, 1996]. The 'tag number' assigned to each equipment is based on Company's Engineering Numbering System (ENS) guidelines in compliance with applicable equipment coding standards.

Managing documentation integrity in small and large-scale modification projects has always been a challenge for many Oil and Gas (O&G) organizations and rig market. This can be even more challenging for those organizations that are lacking necessary resources and appropriate tools. A basis study conducted by Norwegian Oil Directorate [OD, 1998] revealed that many organizations struggle with dynamic updating and validating of the technical documentation. Flow of equipment related technical information and coordination among all involved parties is a must for successful execution of any modification project.

Figure 2 shows the role of technical information in managing technical information integrity in modification projects.

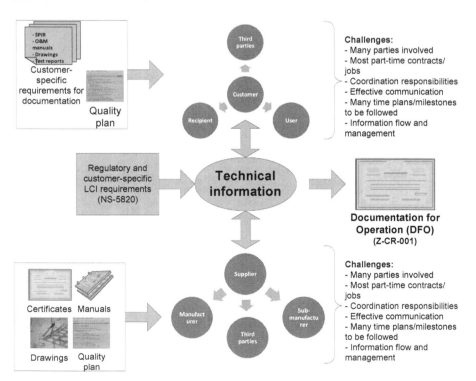

Fig. 2. Flow of technical information in M&M projects

Equipment/tag related technical information may include Data for HSE, Piping & Identification Diagrams (P&IDs), data sheets, drawings, O&M manuals, single line diagrams, EX-certifications, System control diagrams etc. Customers define criteria for the requirements in accordance with applicable LCI regulations and standards.

The Life Cycle Information (LCI) can be defined as:

"Information required by Company for engineering, preparation for operation, start-up, operation, maintenance, repair, modification and decommissioning of a plant/installation" [NORSOK NS5820, 1994].

LCI include both information submitted to the Company and/or retained by the Supplier on behalf of the Company. LCI includes what has previously been termed as Documentation For Operation (DFO). Updates of LCI information may be required with any modifications.

Such information is usually in manuals or datasheets provided by the supplier (usually in pdf or Excel format). The required information is delivered from supplier together with a quality plan that is mutually agreed upon with the customer's requirements. Once all the requirements are fulfilled, the information is released for a DFO.

In general, all such information is to be made available well before the project reaches its completion phase. The flow of this information should be ensured based on the Company-specific PEM. Failing to fulfill such requirements in-time may affect the overall project progress leading to inadequate equipment-/tag-information in the tag database (Referred to as master register in this context). Master register keeps information of all tags with a reference to the relevant technical information. This database must be accurate and updated at all times as this usually forms the basis for Computerized Maintenance Management System (CMMS). Any incomplete or wrong information in the master register can affect maintenance management of the asset. Such nonconformities in the master register can further affect quality in terms of double registration of tags, poor administration, lack of historical track of new and existing tags and inadequate technical information. Experience within Norwegian O&G industry reveals that most projects, both large and small scale, suffer due to inadequacy and lack of technical documentation, therefore many companies fail to comply with corporate LCI requirements and NORSOK requirements.

In order to comply with applicable regulatory and standard requirements to manage all tags and tag-related technical information and to keep the information integrity intact in an M&M project, Apply Sørco developed a web-based tag management system, named as TAG Manager. TAG Manager is developed in a dynamic web-based environment (i.e. ASP.Net) and provides easy access to all users to manage tags for modification and to follow up tag-related technical information. The System also maintains a log database for any operations being performed in the System. It keeps interactive tag status, manages technical information and provides flexible audit trail.

Offshore O&G industry involves high risk and therefore Norwegian Petroleum Authorities have large focus on safe and effective maintenance of the asset. An overview of relevant legislation and standards for NCS are summarized in the next section.

3   Norwegian Legislation and Standardization

Norwegian PSA has defined set of central regulations for offshore and onshore activities. These include regulations for framework HSE, management, facilities, activities and technical & operational regulations [PSA, 2011]. All petroleum related activities conducted onshore and offshore on the North Sea are obliged to follow governing regulations and other applicable standard requirements.

In M&M and EPCIC projects, both contractor/supplier and operator must align their activities within defined premises of the Norwegian regulations. Some of the applicable regulations and significant standard requirements related to M&M projects are summarized here:

3.1   Management Regulations

Ref. § 13 Work processes: [PSA, 2011]

- *The responsible party shall ensure that the work processes and the resulting products fulfil the requirements related to health, safety and the environment.*

- *Work processes and associated interfaces of significance to health, safety and the environment shall be described. The level of detail in the description shall be adapted to the importance of the process for health, safety and the environment.*

Ref. § 15 Information: [PSA, 2011]

- *The responsible party shall identify the information necessary to plan and carry out the activities and improve health, safety and the environment.*

- *It shall be ensured that the necessary information is acquired, processed and communicated to relevant users at the right time.*

- *Information and communication systems shall be established that safeguard the need for acquiring, processing and communicating data and information.*

3.2   The Framework Regulations

Ref. §17 Management system: [PSA, 2011]

- *The responsible party shall establish, follow up and further develop a management system designed to ensure compliance with requirements in the health, safety and environment legislation.*

- *The licensee and owner of an onshore facility shall establish, follow up and further develop a management system to ensure compliance with requirements in the health, safety and environment legislation directed toward licensees and owners of onshore facilities.*

3.3 NORSOK Standard Requirements

The purpose of NORSOK standards is to reduce implementation time and costs for construction and operation of petroleum installations on the NCS. These provide guidelines and best practices that ensures a safe and cost-efficient environment for activities related to offshore and onshore. For instance NORSOK NS5820 (1994) provides a framework for the extent and presentation of suitable documentation for equipment deliveries. The standard is used for all types of equipments, from standard products to package equipment. NORSOK Z-001(1996), defines the extent of technical information which shall be available for use in the operational phase. It emphasizes that:

- *All information <u>shall</u> have As-built status and be available on electronic media.*

NORSOK Z-003 (1996) provides requirements for electronic storage and interchange of technical information and data between all parties and during all phases of an offshore installation's life cycle. Among other requirements, it includes:

- *Enabling cost-effective electronic information interchange between all parties. Electronic information <u>shall</u> be accepted as an original*

- *Ensuring that electronic information at any time has only one source and responsible owner.*

- *Contributing to the production and use of correct data of a known quality throughout the total life cycle.*

- *Ensuing that information structures, data bases and systems that enable concurrent engineering <u>shall</u> be used (i.e. maximize information sharing).*

4   Gaps and Practical Challenges

Independent of the scale of M&M projects, all involved parties need to perform the job in a safe and cost efficient manner under the applicable regulatory and company-specific requirements. This requires seamless communication and deliverables as defined in the Company's PEM. Based on vast experience from M&M and EPCIC project execution, extensive manual efforts are required to track and follow up technical documents, to track any missing or inadequate information, coordinating other disciplines (LCI, maintenance etc.). Figure 3 indicates structure of LCI requirements that are defined by the customer in line with applicable regulatory and governing standard requirements.

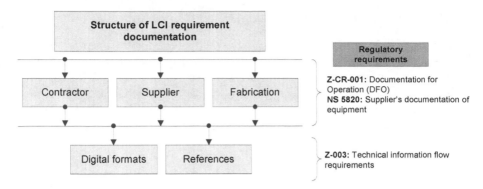

Fig. 3. Structure of LCI requirement documentation

Based on experience from large-scale modification projects identified gaps and challenges are summarized here with respect to applicable regulatory requirements and standard practices.

Practical challenges associated with M&M project execution include:

1. To establish a common platform for effective communication and coordination as many parties involved in a PEM.

2. To effectively manage tags and related technical information during a PEM

3. Local and global standardization of tag management process

4. To fulfill LCI requirement

5. To define a quality plan between customer and supplier to ensure high quality of project deliverables

6. To receive all necessary technical documentation on the right time during a PEM

7. To actively follow-up with the supplier in different phases of a PEM execution

8. To maintain a tidy-up master register with up-to-date status of tags highlighting modified/demolished/obsolete tags etc.

9. To maintain information of non-maintainable tags such as cables and pipeline information

10. To manage and administer dynamic records and history of all tag(s) in the data-base

11. To manage updated tag-related technical information in the database

In order to comply with applicable regulatory requirements and standards, robust technological solutions are needed.

In order to meet these challenges, TAG Manager offers an opportunity to manage tags and flow of technical information in PEM thereby ensuring safe and cost-effective process. Main features and capabilities of the Apply Sørco's TAG Manager are summarized in the next section.

5 TAG Manager

TAG Manager is developed by Apply Sørco in line with applicable regulatory requirements and norms. It offers great flexibility in managing tags and tag-related technical information in modification projects. It is developed to meet the requirements for large- and small-scale modification projects.

Main features of TAG Manager System are:

- Setting up a work process for safe and efficient management of tags and tag-related technical information in compliance to client's PEM *(In compliance with § 13 Work processes)*

- Automated flow of information of tags and dynamic reference of tag-related technical information, according to applicable LCI and standard requirements, to and from the vendor in-line with PEM phases *(In compliance with § 15 Information)*

- Dynamic update of tag-related technical information *(In compliance with NORSOK standard requirements)*

- Minimum human efforts required to reserve new tags for modifications *(In compliance with gaps and challenges item 2)*

- Update of tag status in compliance to client's PEM defined milestones *(In compliance with NORSOK standard requirements)*

- Automatic update of master tag-register with relevant technical information according to applicable LCI requirements *(In compliance with NORSOK standard requirements)*

- Automatic deletion of any "reserved" tags so that these are available for re-use *(In compliance with gaps and challenges item 10)*

- Keep history of all tags in a manner that there are minimum possible unused tags left in the master tag-register. *(In compliance with gaps and challenges item 8)*

- Helps standardizing (both local and global) of tag management process on many installations

- Helps keeping database clean, updated and free from unused/obsolete tags *(In compliance with NORSOK standard requirements)*

- Multiple levels of user access including read-only, write and administrator level, ensuring the integrity of the tag database *(In compliance with § 15 Information)*.

- Flexible report generator feature, keeping logs of users and the work history etc.

- User friendly interface with extensive database search capabilities

- Easy customization to any special requirements of the client

- Flexible to communicate and integrate with other management systems

- A common mail box for keeping all communication to-and-from the customer and supplier(s)

- Integrated module capabilities including tag and functional hierarchy and criticality evaluation

Figure 4 shows role of TAG Manager with respect to a standard PEM.

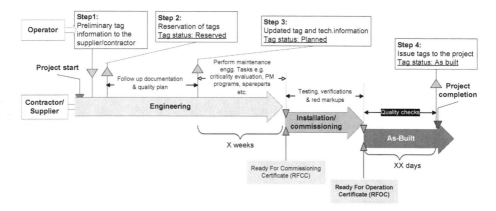

Fig. 4. TAG Manager System integrated with modification project execution model

TAG Manager is Apply Sørco's product which is customized to meet the customer-specific. Customization is performed in three steps as shown in figure 5.

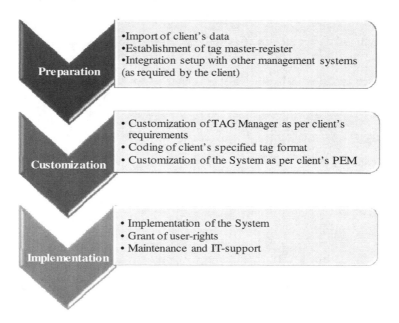

Fig. 5. Customization of TAG Manager for the client

All databases and relevant existing tags and tag-related technical information need to be imported in form of a large tag database. In this phase, the opportunities to integrate TAG Manager with other management system with the client are discussed. Excel spreadsheets for different tag categories are also prepared as a part of the process. This is further customized to integrate with client's PEM. All tag formats are coded and programmed in the System.

To align TAG Manager with PEM, it is recommended to start using TAG Manager System immediately with start of modification project. Figure 6 shows screen shot of start screen that includes configuring project, establishing project number and Purchase Order (PO) as well as distributing user-permissions to those involved in the project. Project responsible/manager is responsible for establishing necessary project information and distributing necessary accesses to project team members.

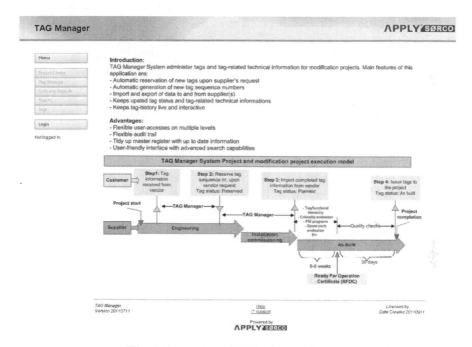

Fig. 6. Screen shot of TAG Manager System

TAG Manager specifies role of company (customer) and the vendor (supplier) in successful execution of modification project.

In operation, TAG Manager is based on 5 simple functional steps. During each step an effective coordination is required from all involved parties (e.g. project/contract responsible, discipline lead, LCI coordinator and any involved 3rd parties).

Step 1: Sending request to supplier/contractor

TAG Manager has capabilities to send necessary documentations directly to the supplier. The requested information from supplier is according to regulatory LCI requirements and customer's governing documents. The documentation is part of the delivery from supplier and the extent of documentation is limited to that strictly required by the customer.

Step 2: Reservation of tags

Upon supplier's request, the number of required tag(s) are reserved with assigned sequence numbers based on availability in the master tag-register. This is performed automatic with minimum human intervention. TAG Manager has the capabilities to search for available sequence number and reserving tags for the project. Once these sequence numbers are generated these are issued back to supplier to provide required information for each type of equipment.

Step 3: Updating tag status during PEM execution

As the project approaches completion of the engineering phase, all tags received from the supplier with "planned" status. Supplier can leave any unused tags with "reserved" status. The updated information is automatically imported in TAG Manager and is kept in the TAG Manager database. Relevant discipline has the responsibility to ensure that all the right information is being supplied by the supplier prior to proceeding ahead with project.

Step 4: Revised and demolished tags

TAG Manager has the ability to handle different status of tags, such as those have been re-used by the project. Upon supplier request, these are flagged as "demolished", "deleted" or "revised" tags. TAG Manager flags each tag with relevant status offering historical overview of any such tags. No tag is physically deleted from the System, all such tags are kept in the database for historical purposes.

Step 5: Completion of a project

All planned tags, including those with "revised" and "demolished" tags are to be evaluated for criticality, spare parts and preventive maintenance activities. All of these updates should be completed in a given time frame that starts prior to mechanical completion. Upon successful completion, all planned tags are flagged as "As-built" and ready to be issued for the project.

A quality control of all tags with respect to tag description and necessary information is performed prior to handing over to the project. Immediately when these tags are handed-over, any tags with "reserved" status are deleted and removed from the tag database. This is performed automatically so that their sequence number is ready for re-use for other projects. This minimizes any unnecessary loop-holes in numbering of the tags.

Reports and User-Logs

TAG Manager System keeps predefined reporting features for ease of generating reports for review/audit purposes. User logs are automatically generated and available as per needs lists all major actions performed by different users.

6 Discussions and Conclusions

In order to ensure successful M&M project execution, the TAG Manager offers great flexibility and interactivity to align with regulatory requirements. Effective integration of the System with PEM can significantly enhance the efficiency and profitability of the whole process of managing tags and tag-related technical information. Based on scale and complexity of modification projects, one of the key challenges is to manage and track modified equipments (tags) and relevant technical information as the project progresses. TAG Manager provides a systematic solution to manage tags and tag-related information integrity in M&M project execution. Some of the recommended good practices in using TAG Manager are summarized as follows:

- Start of communication of project requirements and milestones as early in project startup phase among involved project team(s)/member(s) and TAG Manager users/administrators.

- Integration of TAG Manager System with project plan/milestones in the earliest engineering phase to assist ensure seamless communication between customer and supplier(s) as early in start of a modification project

- Use of TAG Manager for tag and tag-related technical information management forming a robust network for communication in a project

- Perform necessary quality control of deliverables from supplier according to mutually agreed quality plan among customer and supplier(s)

- Ensure necessary training for all participants including for customer and contractor/supplier and mutual understanding and agreement of deliverables and deadlines as defined in PEM

- It is necessary to define an interface/work process to coordinate with other disciplines via TAG Manager to meet LCI and project specific requirements

- Involvement of all parties through TAG Manager in all PEM phases, starting from project start-up to project handover

Acknowledgements. Authors would like to thank the specialist from Apply Sørco for technical input and fruitful discussions in writing the paper.

References

CCR, Chief Counsels Report: Chapter 4.10: Maintenance, pp. 221–224 (2011), http://www.oilspillcommission.gov/chief-counsels-report (accessed on July 18, 2011)

Ministry of Petroleum and Energy (2010), http://www.regjeringen.no (accessed May 24, 2012)

NORSOK Z-003, Technical information flow requirements (1996), http://www.standard.no (accessed on May 05, 2011)

NORSOK Z-001, Document For Operation (DFO) (1996), http://www.standard.no (accessed on July 03, 2011)

NORSOK NS5820, Supplier's documentation of equipment (1994), http://www.standard.no (accessed on July 05, 2011)

NORSOK Z-DP-002, Design principles; coding system (1996), http://www.standard.no (accessed on June 12, 2011)

OD, Basisstudie vedlikeholdsstyring Metode for egenvurdering av vedlikeholdsstyring. Olje Directorat (1998)

ON, Offshore News (2012), http://offshore.no/nyheter/Nyhetskategori.aspx?qcat=9 (accessed May 17, 2012)

PSA, Petroleum Safety Authority regulations (2011), http://www.ptil.no/regulations (accessed on July 17, 2011)

Ratnayake, R.M.C., Samarakoon, S.M.S.M.K., Gudmestad, O.T.: Integrity Management for Sustainable Asset Operations: The Role of Qualification Process. In: Proceedings of the 24th International Congress on Condition Monitoring and Diagnostics Engineering Management (2011) ISBN 0-9541307-2-3

Simmons, M.R.: Offshore rig market could be on verge of recovery. Drilling Contractor (May/June 2002)

Staff, C.: Petroleum Safety Authority Flags Transocean Citing "Serious Breaches" (2012), http://gcaptain.com/petroleum-safety-authority-flags/?45641 (accessed on May 25, 2012)

Extending the Service Life Span
of Ageing Oil and Gas Offshore Production Facilities

Sushil Palkar[1] and Tore Markeset[2]

[1] Aker Solutions, Bergen, Norway
sushil.palkar@gmail.com
[2] University of Stavanger, N-4036 Stavanger, Norway
tore.markeset@uis.no

Abstract. A large number of facilities and parts of the infrastructure of offshore oil and gas reservoirs worldwide are approaching or have exceeded their original design life. The petroleum fields are still producing substantial levels of hydrocarbons which are recoverable and profitable if the field's lifetime is extended. Thus, parts of this infrastructure are being considered for use beyond their planned design life. However, focusing on safety considerations, the condition of systems, structures and components (SSC) may not be acceptable for extended operation. The purpose of this paper is to discuss guidelines for assessing life extension in order to ensure the technical and operational integrity of these ageing facilities. The objective is to highlight those mechanisms by which the installation is degraded physically and functionally including the human factors and organizational issues. This documentation on ageing mechanisms will provide the foundation for a service lifetime extension process.

Keywords: Ageing oil and gas production facilities, Maintenance, Extension of petroleum production facility service life span.

1   Introduction

1.1   Background

Many offshore oil & gas installations are in the life extension stage, as they have passed their original design life. There will be a time when an installed facility has to be closed down permanently as per the original design life. However, with certain processes and criteria, the life of this facility can be extended without compromising the safe working limits. This concept of increasing the life of a facility without increasing the risk is termed as *Lifetime Extension* [1].

1.2   Problems Description

There are many factors that influence the decision to extend the operation of a producing facility. Some of these include:

- The oil reservoir produces more oil than estimated.
- The advancement in techniques related to extraction of oil allows greater extraction.

J. Frick and B. Laugen (Eds.): APMS 2011, IFIP AICT 384, pp. 213–221, 2012.

- Improved techniques to access seismic data provide more details about the reservoirs.
- The provision of processing capability at a nearby subsea or minimum facility platform.

When planning for life extensions of old platforms, it is beneficial to review the integrity management systems and the manpower required to manage an ageing installation. There are a number of threats to integrity from physical degradation mechanisms that are time-dependent and therefore increase with the age of an installation.

1.3   Main Objective

The main objective of this paper is to provide some guidelines for assessing life extension in order to ensure the technical and operational integrity of these ageing facilities. Furthermore, the paper will identify aspects of ageing management (material degradation, obsolescence, human & organizational concerns/issues), the main tasks of the life extension process, and some of the knowledge gaps. Suggestions and recommendations will be made for the lifetime extension process.

1.4   Research Method

The report is based on a broad literature study together with discussions and interviews with oil and gas industry specialists. Industry standards and guidelines are used to develop the report.

2   Identify Aspects of Ageing Management

The management of ageing offshore facilities is an important issue for companies that intend to extend the lifetime. To extend the life span of offshore facilities, installations must be sufficiently safe and economical to remain in operation. This can be achieved by identifying aspects of the management of ageing and implementing them to control and mitigate the degradation of the facilities. Material degradation, obsolescence, and organizational issues are the three aspects of ageing. These will be discussed in the following.

2.1   Material Degradation

This is a broad term encompassing some of the major reasons for ageing and therefore the reason for the life extension process. The degradation can be associated with physical, operational and environmental factors. Also, major unfavorable maintenance practices can lead to material degradation.

- Corrosion – Loss of material due to electro-chemical reaction with the environment.
    - Internal – Most of the internal corrosion problem are due to the corrosive contents of the produced well fluids, such as dissolved gases e.g. – CO_2 and H_2S. The constitution of the well fluids changes with time and old fields tend to be sourer, leading to an increasing rate of corrosion.
    - External – This can be due to offshore environments, with sea water in the air. Corrosion under cladding or coating (e.g. PFP, insulation) is a significant issue

and difficult to detect. Corrosion of exposed steel work is an increasing problem of ageing installations, particularly if maintenance (repainting) is poor.

- Ageing of topside equipment includes the whole range of equipment placed on the topsides of any installations include wearing out of moving or rotating equipment due to friction, and erosion due to the removal of material from the fluid flow. This effect of degradation includes:
  - Wearing out of moving or rotating equipment due to friction particularly.
  - Erosion due to removal of material from fluid flow, particularly if the fluid contains solid particles, prior to separation on valve seats and other high velocity areas in the process.
- Environmentally assisted cracking: This is cracking due to electrochemical reaction of material with the environment, which includes stress corrosion cracking (SCC) and hydrogen embrittlement. The extent and rate of these processes are age related.
- General fatigue failures of welds and material: The structure is the primary mechanism of any installation whether fixed or floating, above or below water, which provides a supporting framework within a band of tolerance of movements that ensures the equipment and personnel continue to function properly & safely. Structures are subjected to changing loads and susceptibilities (e.g. – Increasing loads due to the marine growth) causing fatigue (it is caused due to the development of cracks under cyclical stresses). There will be general fatigue due to failure of welds and materials due to repeated cyclic stresses and vibration fatigue caused due to high cycle low amplitude cyclic stresses due to poor fixing, resonance such as in small bore piping attachments.
- Accumulated damage: There may be substantial accumulated damages such as dents and gouges primarily due to the impact from objects dropped from the platform or attendant vessels or as a result of maintenance.
- Scour: Scour is the erosion of loose seabed material directly around offshore structures. This can increase the height of the structure subjected to hydrodynamic loading.
- Increased structural load: Changes in effective water depth can increase both hydrodynamic loading on the structure and the probability of the deck being inundated during extreme weather conditions; effective water depth can be increase due to – settlement, subsidence, vertical movements of the tectonic plates.
- Blockages: Blockages of pipe work, valves, heat exchanger tubes, pressure relief systems, etc., due to build-up of corrosion products, fouling and scaling, etc.

2.2   Obsolescence

Due to prolonged use, the equipment gradually becomes out-of-date and this signifies ageing. Equipment becomes out of date or back logged and this represents a form of ageing. For example – the corrosion management system may no longer be suitable for current product chemistry, backlogs can develop in planned maintenance & inspection and the plans themselves may need to review or revise to reflect the state ageing equipment. In addition to outdated technology, obsolescence includes new needs, where one need gives rise to another. For example, to extract oil from reservoirs located further away from the facility and existing wells, new tie-ins and new types of wells are needed. This in turn results in a need for a new technology. An assessment of the extent and accuracy of available knowledge, and the adequacy of that knowledge to make sound judgments, is an essential part of the life extension process.

2.3   Organizational Issues

Usually both the work force and the installation platform are ageing simultaneously and therefore the transfer of information may not function properly. The workforce, the team dedicated or allotted for particular installation, age and change, therefore level of knowledge and preparedness particularly in the event of emergency or crisis, have to be regularly tested and refreshed especially for their influence on or participation in any proposed management system. Arrangements for maintaining a trained and competent workforce with an awareness of equipment ageing and its effects is an issue to be addressed. Much of the current workforce is acknowledged to be approaching retirement and the succession needs to be part of life extension planning. Loss of corporate knowledge with retiring staff is also an issue.

The teams that are ageing are more than just operational teams or design teams that support as well as undertake new builds. On account of very limited new people entering in teams, succession of knowledge is hindered. Also the teams represent a significant proportion of organisational memory. Usually both the work force and the installation platform are ageing simultaneously and therefore the transfer of information mechanism may not function properly.

Any degradation or problem on the installation if not managed in a good way, may pass on a message of corporate negligence to the staff working offshore which will in some way affect their acceptance of any new integrity management scheme. Thus extension planning can help to ensure that the organizational issues and knowledge are up to date and hence they are not hampering any progress. Also the success of management scheme developed to manage life extension should be in accordance with abilities, skills and aptitude of the workforce who are intended to implement them.

3   Identify the Main Tasks of Life Extension

To maintain the structural and functional integrity of the equipment in order to carry out life extension, good knowledge of past and present condition of the equipment is of utmost importance. The main task is to check whether the equipment is functional and fit for purpose. It is suggested that the lifetime extension process should include the following activities, which will be discussed thereafter:

1.   Strategic collection of data and information
2.   System breakdown, criticality screening, monitoring and testing
3.   Secondary screening and detailed analysis
4.   Risk factors and assessment with respect to ageing
5.   Screening of factors regarding obsolescence and organizational challenges
6.   Possible challenges in the lifetime extension process with respect to degradation
7.   Outline of the challenges identified
8.   Estimation and evaluation of risk
9.   Lifetime extension management plan
10.   Uncertainties related to the lifetime extension

3.1   Strategic Collection of Data and Information

This is the basic and most important step of the lifetime extension process. Various data and information from the initial phase to the time of installation and its working life should be collected and accessed to analyze the risk-producing and -reducing factors, including the (risk) acceptance criteria, without compromising on safety.

The Design of the Equipment and Its Operating Life

Typically 20-25 years from the time of its construction have been considered as the safe working life of an installation. The estimation of the design life of equipment is a useful measure to maintain the integrity of SSC (structure, system and components). Design life represents the limit of foresight and experience of the original designers. Moreover, it is necessary that we collect data about the design, fabrication and installation (DFI) which provides information about the different phases of installation [2].

During the process when more data is collected, gathered and shared, the following issues are highlighted:

- The local conditions and environment stresses
- What the installation demands in order to give satisfactory performance
- The organizational practices and safety regulations
- The type of work force working offshore, their cultures and attitudes.

Important Checkpoints to Be Addressed
There may be many checkpoints to deal with, of which a few basic points are:

- To check whether the equipment still satisfies the functional requirements and safety limits of its original specification, design and construction standards.
- To check whether equipment meets the latest standards. To check these, standard norms have been incorporated or applied on equipment.
- To check the quality of original fabrication.
- To check whether the equipment meets its current functional requirements, so that it is suitable for the purpose.

An assessment for good fabrication standards should be made, identifying the pros and cons. Signs of poor fabrication can be:

- Misalignment welds, partial penetration, weld repairs, welding spatter and defects.
- Poor finishing such as incomplete or thin paintings or coatings.
- Poor fitting joints, or overloaded seals, glands and gaskets, leak weeps.
- Vibrating and out-of-balance rotating equipment.
- Stiffness or looseness in moving parts and mechanisms.
- Insufficient fixtures and supports.
- Damage or excessive force applied during installation.

3.2   System Breakdown, Criticality Screening, Monitoring and Testing

The screening activity is based on the classification of critical failures and the consequences of the failures of structures, systems and components (SSC). This is a risk-based approach inspired by NORSOK Z-008 [3]. Risk depends on both probability of failure (PoF) and the consequence of failure (CoF). The consequences can be categorized as 'high', 'medium' or 'low'. If the consequence for a function/system or SSC falls within the category 'high', further analysis (reliability centered maintenance actions) is required or the system needs to be redesigned or modified to reduce the risk with respect to cost and production loss, without compromising on safety. If the consequence falls in the category 'medium', it is not mandatory to carry out a detailed analysis (focusing on risk of major hazards); it should be sufficient to follow safety management/maintenance management systems. If the consequence falls in the category 'low', it is generally recommended to carry out planned corrective maintenance activities or to follow the maintenance activities recommended by the original equipment manufacturer [4].

3.3   Secondary Screening and Detailed Analysis

This criticality screening is based on the primary investigation for material degradation, obsolescence, and organizational issues. Now, for those SSC that have a high risk factor based on the primary screening, there should be a secondary screening, based on the aspects of ageing and acceptability for the lifetime extension process. This should be especially done for those SSC which are inaccessible for continuous and detailed inspection. In order to assess their state, they should be analyzed in detail with respect to material degradation. The critical SSC can be classified according to:

- Their availability for monitoring/inspection.
- Their accessibility for modification and maintenance.

3.4   Risk Factors and Assessment with Respect to Ageing

In reviewing the equipment for life extension, the effect of various risk-reducing measures should be analyzed – increased testing, replacement, etc. The workforce needs to be aware of any factors that could increase the risk and rate of ageing and their effects during the life of the equipment.

3.5   Screening of Obsolescence and Organizational Challenges

The following are the challenges, gaps and measures related to obsolescence and organizational issues [5]:

- Requirements – are they satisfactory?
- New operational conditions need to be anticipated for the lifetime extension period.
- Equipment being or becoming 'out-of-date', possibly causing challenges, e.g. related to availability of spare parts.
- Introduction of new technology foreseen for the lifetime extension period.

- Possible reorganizations (e.g. introduction of integrated operations[1] [6] or company merging).
- Maintaining personnel competence (e.g. ageing of personnel).
- Transfer of knowledge during the lifetime extension period.

It should be kept in mind that these two factors, i.e. new technology - new competence of maintenance operators, are closely intertwined.

3.6   Possible Challenges in the Lifetime Extension Process with Respect to Material Degradation

The possible challenges identified with respect to material degradation are as follows:

- Understanding the ageing mechanisms, failure causes, and modes of failure of the SSC. This is not possible unless and until a complete set of quality data is available.
- Understanding the good models to describe the degradation in terms of a specific parameter to have a clear picture of the damage.
- The choice of correct parameters to describe the current state of damage is also an important issue.
- Having sufficient knowledge and models for the effect of maintenance on the degradation process to be understood.
- Having sufficient competence and knowledge among the workforce to carry out the lifetime extension plan.

These challenges are only relevant depending upon the actual systems and how accessible they are in their current state of degradation.

3.7   Outline of the Challenges Identified

This section deals with the level of risk of the facility, within the acceptable limits during the execution process. Also, systems and components are checked and followed up for updating and maintenance in terms of risk related to major hazards (e.g. fire/explosion, dropped objects, structure collapse).

3.8   Estimation and Evaluation of Risk

Many system failures are consequential and not the result of one break or malfunction but of a sequence of many failures. As a result, reliability and risk analysis must not be conceived as a static exercise. Risk and reliability analysis is a dynamic process which must be updated and upgraded as additional information is available. In other words, the estimation of risk may be quite uncertain; this can be due to the difficulty of predicting the future state of some equipment [7]. If the probability of failure (PoF) and/or consequence of failure (CoF) are considered to be very uncertain, one should not use 'best estimate' of these, but rather apply more conservative values. Usually those with uncertain estimated values result in higher risk.

---

[1] Integrated Operations is about ensuring people, new work processes and technology work much more efficiently together, in order to reach safe and better decisions faster.

3.9   Lifetime Extension Management Plan

After risk assessment is carried out and resulting measures are implemented, a management plan for the lifetime extension should be prepared. Now we have a final 'action plan' consisting of risk-reducing measures (maintenance, modifications, other compensating measures and defenses) that should be implemented before the lifetime extension assessment plan and during the lifetime extension period.

3.10   Uncertainties Related to the Lifetime Extension

There are two types of uncertainties that exist related to probabilities of failure. They are Type (I) & Type (II):

- Type (I) - Referred to as natural, physical, inherent, this incorporates natural randomness.
- Type (II) - Referred to as unnatural, modeling, cognitive, this incorporates the imprecise nature of theoretical models and our knowledge. These types of uncertainties are seen in the lifetime extension process.

Analysis capabilities may have improved, but often there is insufficient data to support the analyses and thus to predict a future state of an SSC.

4   Conclusion and Suggestions

The life extension process should be carried out for future economic consideration without compromising on safety standards. Life extension of fixed offshore installations can actually help to maintain their integrity (for example topsides equipment, pipelines, flexible risers, etc.), and therefore they can perform adequately giving good results.

It is always said that "Prevention is better than cure". Therefore periodic inspections of SSC can help operators to be informed about the current status of the installation. These inspections should be based on proper documentation with clear ideas and understanding so that dissemination of the knowledge is feasible. For example, information should be stored in the form of response measurement. Also response data can be used to calibrate and improve the design process of future systems.

An informed team/workforce is the first step toward the success of the lifetime extension assessment. Proper communication within the various departments such as process, piping, maintenance, mechanical, electrical, instrument, structural, project & planning, safety, etc. is very important. Also, it is equally important to learn lessons during the operation which can be implemented in the next project. It is also important to share the knowledge because information and knowledge remain in a system and not just within an individual. This guarantees a more secure handover or changeover in staff.

The software system also plays an important role. It helps in intelligently analyzing the data, assessing the changes in integrity status and visually reporting back to the end user both strategic and detailed information. This is beneficial to help manage some of the problems associated with data management and data sharing.

References

1. Palkar, S.: Lifetime Extension of Ageing Oil and Gas Platforms. Master Thesis University of Stavanger, Stavanger, Norway (June 2010)
2. Wintle, J., Sharp, J.: TWI REPORT 17554/1/08 – Requirements for Life Extension of Ageing Offshore Production Installations. For Petroleum Safety Authority (2008)
3. NORSOK STANDARD – Z-008: Criticality Analysis for maintenance purposes. Rev. 2 (2001)
4. Panesar, S.S., Kumar, R., Markeset, T.: Development of Maintenance Strategies for Offshore Production Facilities. In: The Proceedings of the 3rd World Congress on Engineering Asset Management and Intelligent Maintenance Systems (WCEAM-IMS 2008), October 28-30, pp. 1227–1232. Beijing International Convention Center, Beijing (2008) ISBN 978-1-84882-216-0
5. Hokstad, P., Håbrekke, S., Johnsen, R., Sangesland, S.: Ageing and life extension for offshore facilities in general and for specific systems. SINTEF Report for the Petroleum Safety Authority Norway (2010)
6. Jansen, B., Høydalsvik, H., Nordtvedt, J.E., Håvard, M.: Potential Value of Integrated Operations on the Norwegian Shelf. Study by Epsis and ABB commissioned by OLF - Norwegian Oil Industry Association (2006)
7. Kumar, U.: Risk based maintenance strategies for mechanised and automated systems. University of Stavanger, Norway

Assessing Maintenance Time, Cost and Uncertainty for Offshore Production Facilities in Arctic Environment

Eirik Homlong[1], Dina Kayrbekova[3], Sukhvir Singh Panesar[2], and Tore Markeset[3]

[1] Bergen, Norway
eirikhomlong@netcom.no
[2] Apply Sørco, Stavanger, Norway
sukhvir.singh.panesar@applysorco.no
[3] University of Stavanger, N-4036 Stavanger, Norway
{dina.kayrbekova,tore.markeset}@uis.no

Abstract. Many of the oil and gas fields on the Norwegian Continental Shelf are entering their tail-end phase of the production life cycle, and the production in temperate areas is slowly declining. Thus, the oil and gas industry looks northwards, and this trend can be seen in all countries bordering the Arctic. Arctic conditions in the form of climate, darkness, ice, remoteness from infrastructure, etc. will cause different and bigger strains on the human factor of the working personnel and machinery than can be seen in more temperate areas. Furthermore, the fact that less data exists – in the form of both statistics and experience of the operation and maintenance strategies to be executed in the Arctic areas – poses additional challenges for the design of offshore production facilities to be used in the less familiar environment of the Arctic. This paper introduces and discusses a method for maintenance cost and time assessments and their uncertainty, using the Monte Carlo simulation method. The method is to be employed when designing for operation and maintenance in Arctic conditions of offshore production facilities. The proposed method can enable a decision maker to assess and adjust maintenance time and cost data more realistically.

Keywords: Operation, Maintenance, Offshore production facility, Arctic conditions, Cost assessment, Monte Carlo Simulation method.

1 Introduction

With oil and gas production reaching its tail end on many fields on the Norwegian Continental Shelf (NCS), the industry is looking towards the Arctic to start exploration and production. It is estimated that as much as 14% of the world's remaining oil and gas reserves are found in Arctic areas, most of these offshore [1]. The harsh Arctic conditions concerning climate, lack of infrastructure and the long distances to shore generates challenges concerning the operation and maintenance of offshore production installations in Arctic areas. Maintenance expenses contribute to a large percentage of the operating cost for an offshore production installation. Continuous preventive and corrective maintenance, together with inspections etc., is important to keep the regularity high and the risks low for the installation. An increasing need for energy, a decreasing amount of resources in temperate areas, new technology, large

J. Frick and B. Laugen (Eds.): APMS 2011, IFIP AICT 384, pp. 222–232, 2012.
© IFIP International Federation for Information Processing 2012

amounts of offshore resources in Arctic areas and melting ice caps in the Arctic Ocean make this an important location for future developments.

The challenges for offshore oil and gas production in the Arctic can be greater than for oilfields in more temperate areas. In the Arctic areas the climate is hard with strong winds, low temperatures and long periods of darkness, resulting in greater and different strains on machinery, structure and personnel, and this complicates resupplying and maintenance [2], [3]. Due to the remote location and long distances, the infrastructure is less developed; large areas are scarcely populated and it is far from the suppliers of spare parts and competence [4], [5]. All of these factors are further complicating the operation and maintenance of an installation operating in the Arctic.

Another important factor for the Arctic offshore areas is the lack of statistical data. Large areas lack statistical data on metocean factors, sea ice, icing, currents and on equipment failure rates and failure modes. Experience from the Norwegian Continental Shelf together with data gathered in the OREDA database [6] can give us a good basis for much equipment performance and failure data, but the information is not good enough to use directly when moving production into the Arctic because it does not take into account the differences in operating conditions. In general, quantitative data from the Arctic is hard to obtain due to the small amount of industry and experience in the area. For assessing the impact Arctic conditions will have on the time spent on maintenance tasks and the increased costs this implies based on the scarce statistical and experience data, Monte Carlo simulation can be a valuable tool.

Because of the lack of statistical data on environment factors and data on repair times for weather-exposed equipment in the Arctic, the case study in this paper will be based on assumptions, which will also be necessary in the early phases of production in Arctic areas. The factors presented will vary based on the geographical area and plant-specific variables. The consequences of longer repair and maintenance duration will be very different from equipment to equipment, from process equipment where the downtime can be very expensive to routine maintenance operations where the only cost will be the increased man-hours spent on the task.

This paper indentifies and discusses some influencing factors of the Arctic environment on the operation and maintenance of an offshore production facility. Moreover, this paper proposes a method for maintenance cost and time assessment by using Monte Carlo simulation method for uncertainty analysis which is to be used by a decision maker when designing for an offshore production facility to be used in the less familiar environment of the Arctic.

2   Operation and Maintenance of an Offshore Production Facility under the Influencing Factors of Arctic Conditions

Some of the factors influencing the operations in the Arctic include [7], [8], [9], [10], [11], [12], [13], [2] and will be further described in the following chapter.

2.1   Arctic Climate

The arctic operative environment is an extremely inhospitable environment that is characterized by extremely cold temperatures, high intensity and shifting winds, fog, darkness, icing, etc. These characteristics are further discussed below:

- **Low Temperatures:** The Arctic areas are characterized by very low temperatures in most parts of the year. The average winter temperatures range from 0C° to -40C° and the average summer temperatures range from -10C° to +10C° [14]. In addition, there can be large temperature variations throughout the year.
- **High Intensity Winds:** The winds in Arctic areas can be very strong and can change direction quickly. The polar low pressure storms caused by hot southern air meeting cold Arctic air streams can cause sudden changes in wind direction and increase in wind intensity that is hard to model for meteorologists, and may result in unforeseen strong wind conditions.
- **Foggy Conditions:** The Arctic area is very susceptible to fog throughout the year. Burt (2007) [15] states that the Grand Banks off the shore of Newfoundland are considered to be the foggiest place on the earth with over 200 foggy days annually.
- **Darkness:** The Arctic regions experience extremes of solar radiation, with a total absence of sunlight in winter and sun the whole day in summer. Especially the absence of sunlight in the winter season can create bad working conditions.
- **Icing:** A challenge when the combined effects of low temperatures and high air humidity or low temperatures (T<10 C°) and strong wind cause spray blowing of the sea and freezing on the platform or ship superstructure. This has a potential of causing loss of stability and ice covering the hull and equipment.
- **Ocean Temperature:** Studies done by the Norwegian Polar Institute [16] show that the ocean temperatures in large parts of the Arctic and Sub-Arctic areas reach sub-zero temperatures in the winter time. This potentially increases strain on saltwater pumps, firewater systems and subsea equipment.
- **Waves:** The wave fetch are long in many Arctic areas - meaning the waves can gain more energy due to longer stretches of ocean [17]. In addition, the strong winds in the Arctic can further energize the waves that could result in high waves.
- **Icebergs:** Icebergs of varying size and shapes are found in different parts of the Arctic Ocean (see Kvitsrud, 1991 for details of icebergs [18]). These icebergs have a potential of creating large collision loads on the platforms as well as scouring of sea bottom structures in the shallow areas.
- **Sea Ice:** The Arctic Ocean is covered by ice cover in most of the seasons, the extent of ice cover varies from year to year. The ice cover poses a challenge to the vessel transportation to and fro from the offshore facilities in the Arctic Ocean. However, the damage potential from sea ice depends on the thickness of the ice cover, velocity of the ice and the size of the ice fields [18].

2.2   Underdeveloped Infrastructure

The Arctic areas are sparsely populated and generally the infrastructure is underdeveloped. This poses its own challenges for installation, operation and maintenance of facilities located in offshore areas.

- **Long Distances from Markets and Few Supply Bases:** The distance to the suppliers and the market can be long resulting in long delivery times of supplies and spare parts.
- **Shortage of Competence:** Due to the sparse population, harsh conditions and the early phase of offshore production it can be a challenge to find and employ competent as well as experienced personnel in the arctic areas. Moreover, effort will be required to generate willingness amongst the competent and experienced personnel to work in the arctic conditions.
- **Lack of Emergency Infrastructure:** In the Arctic there is a shortage emergency infrastructure to contain the consequences of major accidents.
- **Lack of Robust Weather Predictions:** In the Arctic areas there are few weather stations and a limited statistical data to predict and make precise weather forecasts. Braset (2007) [19] states that statistical data from wind and wave measurements have their limitations due to the rapid changes in the climate experienced in the arctic areas.
- **Political Issues:** Preservation of environment in the arctic areas is a focus area in the government because of its vulnerability and pristine nature. The government regulations are stringent and the ambition is zero discharges and zero damage to environment. Wildlife protection and social cooperation with the groups of indigenous people are important. Failure in maintaining cordial relations has a potential of creating large impacts on the company's reputation.

Most of these factors will influence the design and the safe operations of the facilities. In the subsequent part of the paper, we will consider describe how these influencing factors will be modeled in the case study.

2.3   Modeling the Influencing Factors

To model the effect of the Arctic factors described in the previous chapter six parameters are identified, they are:

- **Weather:** Cold weather, strong winds, rain and snow slow down the work.
- **Darkness:** Darkness complicates the work and resupplying. This can be mitigated by the use of artificial light, but can still be a challenge.
- **Sea Ice:** Sea ice features delay operations and logistics, especially for operations where ROVs and divers are needed.
- **Equipment Failure:** Failures in tools, cranes, etc. can occur due to increased strains on hydraulic fluids, lower battery capacities and larger risk of human failures due to harsh conditions.
- **Delays in Parts/Personnel Delivery due to Weather and Infrastructure:** Delivery of parts/crew needed for the operations that are not stored/stationed on the platform can be delayed due to poor infrastructure and bad weather.
- **Delays in Parts/Personnel Delivery due to Sea Ice:** Delivery of parts/crew not stored/stationed on the platform can be delayed due to sea ice features.

However, for the equipment which is sheltered or placed indoors, the weather will not have any effect on the task itself, and the same conditions as on the Norwegian

Continental Shelf can be expected, but delivery of parts and competent personnel can still be a problem. Sea ice will only be a problem in certain geographical areas; climatic conditions will vary a lot based on the season and geographical location of the installation. Even though industries such as mining, shipbuilding and onshore oil and gas production are well known and important in the Arctic region, and offshore exploration started several decades ago, only a few offshore production facilities have been built and put into production.

There is less experience from operations in these areas, and statistical data obtained from the Norwegian Continental Shelf may not be directly applicable for the Arctic [20], [21], [22], [23], and [24]. Also, based on the findings in a study by Homlong, an increase in failure rates and man-hours can be expected in the Arctic compared to more temperate areas [7], [9]. The model presented in this paper gives a tool that can help engineers, decision makers and planners make more realistic estimates of the man-hours used on operations and maintenance in Arctic areas through playing with different scenarios and equipment.

Gao presented a model in which production performance under Arctic conditions is predicted [20], [21], and [22]. The model presented in this paper is an alternative approach, where values are assigned directly to failure rates and climatic conditions to make it easier to implement and update data as more experience and statistical data is obtained. In the following chapter, a case for a specific seawater lift pump will be presented.

3   A Seawater Lift Pump to Be Operated on a Floating Production Facility in the Southern Part of the Barents Sea: An Example

Based on the research conducted on Arctic conditions a case study and model is developed to estimate the increases in man-hours and costs that can be expected in Arctic areas due to the differences in conditions from the NCS. The Monte Carlo simulation method will be used to give time and cost assessments for operations and maintenance. This method is useful in modeling phenomena with significant uncertainties in the input. The method relies on random sampling to compute the results. A series of discrete random events is established to generate a probability distribution [25]. This method is a more certain tool than many other alternative methods or human intuition and can give valuable information for both the design of the platform, maintenance planning, spare part logistics and for general operation because it gives probability distributions based on the identified parameters. The assigned parameters in the simulation can easily be updated as more statistical and experience data are obtained to give stronger results. The software Crystal Ball is used in the case study. Oracle Crystal Ball is a spreadsheet-based application for Monte Carlo simulations, risk measurement and reporting and time-series forecasting and optimization [26].

An annual flow test of the seawater lift pumps conducted in early spring show that one of the pumps has been damaged during the winter season and has lost much of its capacity, causing the need for a corrective repair of the pump. The pulling of the pump is expected to be an extensive operation on this platform where external experts have to be present. The time estimate for a similar setup on the Norwegian Continental Shelf is 168 hours for pulling the pump and 168 hours for placing a spare. Based on these experience data from the task on the NCS and data on Arctic factors a set of assumptions is made. These assumptions are assigned different probability distributions to give an estimate on the delays and increased man-hours that can be expected for the replacement or repair of the pump.

Table 1. Assumed increase in man-hours due to Arctic conditions

	Increase in manhours (%)	Mean (%)	Median (%)	Correlated to	Correlation (%)	Min (hrs)	Mean (hrs)	Median (hrs)	Max (hrs)
Task: Pulling of seawater lift pump									
Estimated manhours NCS							336		
Weather	0-30%	18 %	20 %			0	61	67	101
Darkness	0-5%	3 %	3,5 %	Weather	50 %	0	10	12	17
Machine failures	0-10%	5 %	5 %	Weather	80 %	0	17	17	34
Delivery of supplies, weather	0-300%	11 %	7,5 %	Weather	80 %	0	37	25	1008
Sea ice	0 %	0 %	0 %			0	0	0	0
Delivery of supplies, sea ice	0 %	0 %	0 %	Sea ice	90 %	0	0	0	0
Forecast, additional manhours						0	125	121	1160

The table shows the minimum, mean and maximum addition to man-hours assumed for the task in Arctic conditions. The mean values are set for all the factors except for the "delivery of supplies, weather" where the median value is set. The minimum values are calculated with the formula below; the max values are calculated by changing the minimum percentage values for increase in man-hours with the maximum percentage value.

FCA min(hrs) = $\Sigma((W(min\%) \times ENCS) + (D(min\%) \times ENCS) + (MF(min\%) \times ENCS) + (DSW(min\%) \times ENCS) + (SI(min\%) \times ENCS) + (DSI(min\%) \times ENCS))$ (1)

Where FCA min(%) is the smallest increase in forecasted additional man-hours (%) defined in the assumption and ENCS is estimated man-hours for the NCS. The other abbreviations are: W is weather, D is darkness, MF is machine failures, DSW is delivery of supplies, weather, SI is sea ice and DSI is delivery of supplies, sea ice. The input distributions for the case study are:

- Weather
- Darkness
- Equipment failure
- Delayed delivery of spare parts and specialists due to bad weather and infrastructure
- Delay on delivery of spare parts/personnel due to sea ice

Sea ice is not considered in this scenario because it is not considered a problem for the Southern Barents Sea in this season.

Weather: The transition between winter and spring is a period where harsh weather can be experienced in the Barents Sea with low temperatures, storms and blizzards. The operation considered in the case study is weather-sensitive. The weather delays are modeled as a triangular distribution with assigned values from 0-101 (0-30%) for increase in man-hours, with the likeliest value of 61 hours (18%) as shown in Fig. 1.

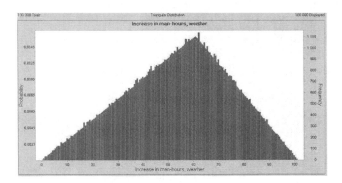

Fig. 1. Triangular distribution of increase in man-hours due to weather

Darkness: Early spring in the Barents Sea means that there is little daylight. It is modeled as a triangular distribution, assigned with the value 0-17 hours (0-5%) with the likeliest value of a 10-hour (3%) increase because of strain on personnel, areas without proper lighting, etc. as shown in Fig. 2. This value is correlated by 50% to the weather values because the darkness increases with cloud coverage etc.

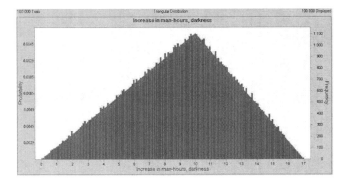

Fig. 2. Triangular distribution of increase in man-hours due to darkness

Equipment Failure: Failures in tools and equipment are modeled as a triangular distribution with the values 0-34 (0-10%) increase in work-hours with the likeliest value of 17 hours (5%) as shown in Fig. 3. This factor will be 80% correlated to the weather factor because in good weather the strains on equipment and personnel will be similar to the NCS and the same failure modes and frequencies can be expected.

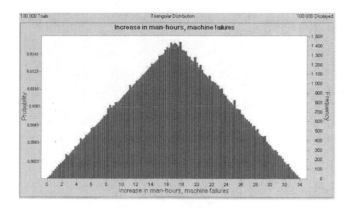

Fig. 3. Triangular distribution of increase in man-hours due to equipment failure

Delivery of Spare Parts and Specialists due to Bad Weather and Infrastructure: This factor is gamma distributed and assigned values from 0-1,008 hours (0-300%) with a median value of 25 hours as shown in Fig. 4. It is assumed that a spare pump is stored on the platform, but other necessary parts, tools and experts might be delayed. This factor is considered weather-sensitive and 80% correlated with the weather factor. The 300% delay will be very rare, caused by long storm periods, equipment deliveries over long distances by truck, etc. The largest uncertainty in the simulation is found in this distribution; it has a variance of 1,488 hours due to the uncertainty in data. The Gamma distribution for the supply delays from weather gives very low chances for delays over 200 hours; this is due to difficulties in making distributions with the likeliest value much lower than the maximum value. If statistical data on weather can be obtained, this problem can be mitigated by making discrete probability distributions based on the weather observations.

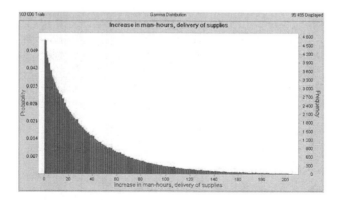

Fig. 4. Gamma distribution of increase in man-hours due to delays caused by weather and poor infrastructure

Delay on Delivery of Spare Parts/Personnel due to Sea Ice: This factor is assigned the value 0% in this case because ice features are not expected in the Southern Barents Sea in this season.

Based on the probability distributions described, a Monte Carlo simulation with 100,000 trials is run, giving the gamma distribution shown in Fig. 5. The distribution has a mean increase in man-hours of 117 hours with a variance of 4,005 hours. The large variance illustrates that there are large uncertainties in the estimate. However, this will get better when more data on the input distributions are gained from experience and analyses. In spite of the large uncertainties, the model gives reason to believe that for this operation there will be an increase in man-hours due to Arctic conditions.

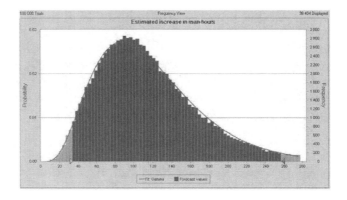

Fig. 5. Estimated increase in man-hours

By using Fig. 5, a probability of 50% of delays between 75 and 140 hours is identified. To find the economic consequence of this delay, the price pr. man-hour is analyzed; for this case, where there is no production downtime, this will be solely the price pr. hour pr. worker. In this case, it is assumed that the price pr. man-hour pr. external specialist is 650 NOK. This assumption gives a 50% chance that the increase in costs for this task is between 48,750 NOK and 91,000 NOK (22-41% increase in costs). The mean time increase identified in the model will be 117 hours (34%) meaning a cost increase of 76,050 NOK. If the worst-case scenario defined in the assumption happens, the delay will be 1160 hours, meaning a cost increase of 754,000 (345%). Based on this model, the chance of this is negligible.

4   Concluding Remarks

Based on the example and results presented and discussed in this paper, we can conclude that the Arctic climate can have a significant influence on the time and cost of the maintenance of offshore production facilities in the less familiar environment of the Arctic. Furthermore, lack of experience and statistical data might give large uncertainties in estimates and result in higher operational expenditures. The method presented in this paper can be used in maintenance time and cost assessment or when designing for operation and maintenance in order to provide more realistic cost and time estimates. As more experience and statistical data can be obtained, the method can be adjusted and optimized.

References

1. U.S. Geological Survey: Fact sheet; USGS Arctic Oil and Gas Report: Estimates of Undiscovered Oil and Gas North of the Arctic Circle (2008),
   http://geology.com/usgs/arctic-oil-and-gas-report.shtml
2. Freitag, D.R., McFadden, T.: Introduction to Cold Region Engineering. ASCE Press, Reston (1997)
3. Holmer, I., Granber, P., Dahlstrom, G.: Cold environments and cold work (2010),
   http://www.ilo.org/safework_bookshelf/english?content&nd=857 170522
4. Gudmestad, O.T., Løset, S., Alhimenko, A.L., Shkinek, K.N., Tørum, A., Jensen, A.: Engineering aspects related to arctic offshore developments. LAN Publishing House, ST. Petersburg (2007)
5. Markeset, T.: Design for Production Performance in Arctic Locations Considering Maintenance and Support Services. In: The Proceedings of the Mine Planning and Equipment Conference (MPE 2008), Beijing, China (October 2008)
6. OREDA: Offshore Reliability Data, 5th edn. Topside Equipment, vol. 1. SINTEF Technology and Society, Trondheim (2009)
7. Homlong, E., Panesar, S.S., Markeset, T., Kumar, R.: Influence of Arctic Environment on Reliability, Availability, Maintainability and Supportability. In: The Proceedings of the COMADEM 2011 Conference, Stavanger, Norway (May 2011)
8. Linnè, A., Juntti, U.: Improving Conditions for Personnel Performing Condition Based Maintenance on Infrastructure by Measuring/Monitoring Their Winter Performance Ability. In: The Proceedings of the COMADEM 2011 Conference, Stavanger, Norway (May 2011)
9. Homlong, E.: Reliability, Availability, Maintainability and Supportability factors in an Arctic offshore operating environment: Issues and challenges. Master thesis, University of Stavanger, Stavanger, Norway (2010)
10. Larsen, A.C., Markeset, T.: Mapping of Operations, Maintenance and Support Design Factors in Arctic Environments. In: The Proceedings of the European Safety and Reliability Conference (ESREL 2007), Stavanger, Norway (June 2007) ISBN 978-0-415-44786-7
11. Markeset, T.: Design for High Performance Assurance for Offshore Production Facilities in Remote Harsh and Sensitive Environment. Quarterly Journal of the Operational Research Society of India, OPSEARCH 45(3), 275–290 (2008)
12. Markeset, T.: Design for Petroleum Production Performance in Arctic Locations Considering Maintenance and Support Services. In: The Proceedings of the Mine Planning and Equipment Selection Conference (MPES 2008), Beijing, China (October 2008)
13. Gudmestad, O.T., Zolothukhin, A.B., Ermakov, A.I., Jacobsen, R.A., Michtchenko, I.T., Vovk, V.S., Løset, S., Shkinek, K.N.: Basic of offshore petroleum engineering and development of marine facilities with emphasis on the Arctic offshore (1999) ISBN 5-7246-0100-1
14. Serreze, M., Roger, B.: The Arctic Climate System, 385 p. Cambridge University Press, New York (2005)
15. Burt, C.: Extreme Weather a guide & record book. Norton, NY (2007)

16. Søreide, E.J., Hop, H., Falk-Petersen, S., Gulliksen, B., Hansen, E.: Macrozooplankton communities and environmental variables in the Barents Sea marginal ice zone in late winter and spring. Norwegian Polar Institute, Tromsø, Norway (2003)
17. Norwegian Centre of Expertise Instrumentation (NCEI), http://Barentssea.no (accessed February 15, 2010)
18. Kvitsrud, A.: Environmental Conditions in the Southern Barents Sea (1991), http://home.c2i.net/kvitrud/Arne/Environmental-condtions-Barents-Sea.htm (accessed February 20, 2011)
19. Braset, E.:: Evaluering av de fysiske forhold på boredekk og I boretårn ved operasjoner I arktiske Atlanterhavet med spesiell oppmerksomhet mot effektene vind og lave temperaturer skaper. MSc thesis, University of Stavanger, Norway (2007)
20. Gudmestad, O.T., Løset, S., Alhimenko, A.L., Shkinek, K.N., Tørum, A., Jensen, A.: Engineering aspects related to arctic offshore developments. LAN Publishing House, ST. Petersburg (2007)
21. Gao, X., Barabady, J., Tore Markeset, T.: Criticality Analysis of a Production Facility using Cost Importance Measures. International Journal of Systems Assurance Engineering and Management 1(1), 17–23 (2010)
22. Gao, X., Markeset, T., Barabady, J.: Design and Operational Maintainability Importance Measure - A Case Study. Quarterly Journal of the Operational Research Society of India, OPSEARCH 45(3), 189–208 (2008)
23. Barabadi, A., Markeset, T.: Reliability and Maintainability Performance under Arctic Conditions. International Journal of System Assurance Engineering and Management 2(2) (2011)
24. Barabadi, A., Barabady, J., Markeset, T.: Maintainability Analysis Considering Time-Dependent and Time-Independent Covariates. Reliability Engineering & System Safety 96(1), 210–217 (2011)
25. CSEP (Computational Science Education Project): Introduction to Monte Carlo Methods (1995), http://www.phy.ornl.gov/csep/CSEP/MC/MC.html
26. Oracle: Oracle Crystal Ball overview (2011), http://www.oracle.com/technetwork/middleware/crystalball/overview/index.html

Identifying the Drivers of Economic Globalization and the Effects on Companies' Competitive Situation

Knut Erik Bang and Tore Markeset

University of Stavanger, N-4036 Stavanger, Norway
{knut.e.bang,tore.markeset}@uis.no

Abstract. Globalization has changed the world. This paper aims to contribute to the understanding of how companies' competitive situation is affected by globalization. The paper identifies the main drivers of economic globalization and categorizes the effects into size effects, location effects and pressure effects. Size relates to the magnitude of the potential competition. Location relates to the potential impact on a company's activities in terms of what to do where and by whom. Pressure effects are the ones that are related to competitive pressure.

Keywords: Economic globalization, outsourcing, offshoring, value chain fragmentation, company competition.

1 Introduction: Globalization, Effects and Company Competition

Globalization has changed the world and the competitive situation of companies, and has affected us as individuals. The objective of this study is to contribute to the understanding of how globalization affects the competitive environment of companies. The drivers and effects from globalization are identified and defined, and their impact on the forces of competition evaluated.

A review of existing literature was carried out to identify a list of the main drivers of the economic globalization, and to establish the main effects from these drivers that are relevant in terms of affecting the competitive situation for companies. The approach focused on the impact on Michael Porter's [1] model of the competitive situation and on the value chain.

1.1 Globalization as a Process

The term 'globalization' is used in literature in a variety of settings and contexts to account for a number of different things. According to Stiglitz [2], the phenomenon of globalization encompasses the international flow of ideas and knowledge, the sharing of cultures, global civil society and the global environmental movement. Steger [3] separates globalization into four dimensions, namely economic, political, cultural and ecological. However, he stresses that the dimensions are overlapping and interconnected. For the objective of investigating the effects of globalization on companies' competitive situation, we will limit our use of the term to economic globalization,

J. Frick and B. Laugen (Eds.): APMS 2011, IFIP AICT 384, pp. 233–241, 2012.

which according to Stiglitz [2] entails the closer economic integration of the countries of the world through the increased flow of goods and services, capital and labor.

Another necessary limitation and clarification arises from the fact that, according to Steger [3], the term 'globalization' is used to describe a process, a condition, a force, a system and an age. We choose here to use the term 'globalization', in accordance with Ellwood [4], to be the process of accelerating integration of the global economy. The process is characterized by movement toward greater interdependence and integration [3].

By defining globalization as a process, we have defined it to be something that brings us from one state to another [3]. Globalization is ongoing, indicating that the process will continue and that we have not reached the end state yet, though our economies and markets have come to be marked by the process and are molded toward the end state. We therefore define globalized markets as markets that have become significantly marked by the integration of the global economy, not ones that have come to an end state of globalization. Similarly, we define globalized economies as economies that have become significantly marked by the integration of the global economy. Defining globalization as an accelerating process signals an expected intensified movement in this direction.

1.2   Porter's Model of Competition

Harvard professor Michael Porter's model of the five forces on competition [1] (see Figure 1) has become one of the most established approaches to view competition. It can be used for industry competition or for a company's place within an industry competition. With the introduction of the model of the five forces of competition, Porter lifted the view on competition from being focused on the rivalry between competitors in an industry to include a number of other potential competitors: the suppliers through their bargaining power, the buyers of the industry's products through their bargaining power, the potential threat from new entrants to the industry competition, and finally the threat of substitutes through their potential to take market shares from the industry. The model thus introduced a new dynamic situation where players from all these forces over time are potential competitors, instead of a previously more static picture focused on the existing rivals.

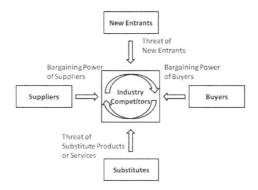

Fig. 1. The five forces of competition [1] as represented in [5]

However, to be able to assess the impact of globalization on the competitive situation, we will also need to address another of Porter's concepts, namely the value chain [5]. The value chain offers a view of a company as a set of interlinked activities. Porter argues for the necessity of addressing the strategic choices for the individual activities to gain competitive advantage. The activities in the model are shown either as sequential, as part of the production process, or as support activities. The model is shown in Figure 2.

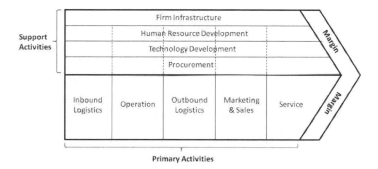

Fig. 2. The value chain from Porter (1985)

The question formed here is: What are the drivers and effects of globalization that affect the model of the five forces of competition? To evaluate this, we start by investigating what the literature on the subject has to say on what are the different drivers and the effects of these.

2   Drivers of Globalization

It is emphasized that in the evaluation of drivers of globalization the focus is on the ones that are considered to have a significant effect on the competitive situation of companies. Politics and social factors are major forces behind globalization (e.g. [2], [6], [7], [8], [9]) and have led to the reduction of trade barriers and economic reforms, paving the way for economic integration. Stiglitz [2] claimed that politics shaped globalization. In this evaluation it is considered a predecessor event and omitted.

In evaluating the effects of globalization, it can be useful to separate drivers and effects, though both can affect the competitive situation of a company. The drivers of globalization are the forces that lead towards closer economic integration. Rather than setting up a comprehensive list, the paper focuses on the factors mentioned most in the literature. These can be summarized as:

- Lower trade barriers
- Lower transportation costs
- Lower communication costs
- Information and communication technology (ICT) development
- Spread of technology

2.1 Lower Trade Barriers

Lower trade barriers are recognized as one of the main drivers. The International Monetary Fund (IMF) [10] states that the expansion of world trade through the elimination or reduction of trade barriers, such as import tariffs, is a core element of globalization. Lowering trade barriers involves more than just reducing import tariffs; the IMF further mentions openness to foreign technology, investments (especially foreign direct investments), and a participation in – and integration with – the global economy. Defined this way, the lowering of trade barriers includes the attaching of national economies to global trade, as has gradually happened with India and China. (See e.g. [6] and [8]).

2.2 Lower Transportation Costs

Lower transportation costs and lower communication costs are described by Stiglitz [2] as the main parts of economics that are driving globalization. Lower transportation costs enable products manufactured far from the market to become more competitive. Rubin [11] demonstrates how changes in fuel and transportation costs act the same way as changes in import tariffs on products manufactured far from the market. Reduced transport costs have enabled the world markets and economies to become more linked together and integrated.

2.3 Lower Communication Costs

The same applies to communication costs. The costs of international or overseas phone calls have been reduced significantly over the last two decades. According to Friedman [6], the massive investment in IT-infrastructure, especially fiber optic cables, up to the dot.com bust in 2001 and the subsequent lowering of data transfer cost to practically zero was one of the main drivers of globalization.

2.4 Information and Communication Technology Development

It is not just the cost of communication that has improved; it is the whole way we communicate and interact. Over the last two decades we have seen the internet evolve and spread as a source of information as well as a tool for communication. The latter is shown in terms of e-mails taking over from normal post, cheaper solutions for phoning, video conferencing, massive amount of data transfer and so on. Friedman [6] further points to the evolution of shared work platforms that enable people from different locations to work together on the same project as one of the things that have a significant effect on how we work and share work between locations. Milberg and Winkler [12] note that the progress in electronic communication has enabled the massive expansion of international supply chains, that again lead to more foreign investments and aligning with foreign suppliers, creating the potential for cost reductions.

2.5 The Spreading of Technology

The potential from the developments in information and communication technology could not be achieved if not for the widespread use of the technology. Former HP

CEO, Carly Fiorina (cited in [6]), described how everything from photography, word processing, architectural drawings to home appliances are being digitized and can be transmitted, shaped and manipulated from other locations wirelessly on a computer or by handheld devices like PDAs or cell phones. The digitization thus plays its part in globalizing the world, but without the spread of the technology to link to this information (PCs, PDAs, smartphones, iPads and so on), the digitization would not help much. James [13] argues that much of the difference in growth patterns in the developing world comes from exactly this: the difference in the spread of information technology. Manufacturing and production technologies are other enabling technologies that are spreading [14], and access to technological progress gathers speed. The spread of technology, whether in the form of information technology or for manufacturing or agriculture, is as important as its development in the first place and is considered a driver of globalization.

3   Effects of Globalization

The literature study further identified numerous effects of globalization in various areas. These effects were evaluated in terms of which could influence the competitive situation of companies. The ones that had an influence were grouped according to how they could influence the situation. The effects of globalization on companies' competitive situation have therefore been grouped under three headings: size, location and pressure. Size covers the factors of larger market potential, larger numbers of potential clients, larger numbers of potential competitors, and larger numbers of potential suppliers and co-operating partners. Location covers disaggregation of value chains, offshoring, outsourcing, and complex supply chains. Pressure covers cost and price pressure, higher rates of change, more diverse markets, lower start-up barriers, and lower visibility.

3.1   Size Effects

The market in which a company is competing is no longer one or a group of regional geographically isolated markets. According to a study by Harvard University ([15] cited in [6]), "the global economic world" in 1985 consisted of North America, Western Europe, Japan and parts of Latin America, Africa and the countries of East Asia, and the total population of this area participating in international trade was about 2.5 billion people. By 2000 the former Soviet Union, India and China had joined the global economy and its population had expanded to 6 billion people. As the trade barriers have come down, most of the globe acts more like one single market. That does not imply that it is one homogenous market place, but that the markets are being linked together, hurdles that prevented foreign competition have gradually been reduced and that it is possible for others to enter. The national markets may be diverse, but the market potential for products and services is to a large extent now global not local. This means that for an individual company's or an industry's products and services, the market potential is larger where previously there was segmentation through limitations in the geographical reach of the industry boundary. As a natural consequence of the increasing total market, so the number of potential clients, number of potential competitors, and the number of potential suppliers and co-operating partners also increase. The literature has focused more on the increased competition (e.g. [16], [7] and [17]) than on increased markets and the potential and challenges related to suppliers and co-operating partners.

3.2   Location Effects

Location addresses the globalization effects that have a potential impact on a company's activities: what activities to do where and by whom. Fragmentation of the production process has become a major theme in international economics research (e.g. [18], [19], [20], [21]). Krugman [22] referred to this phenomenon as "slicing up the value chain" and argued 16 years ago that this is one of the major trends in international trade, resulting in higher growth in trade than in the underlying growth in value-adding or the gross domestic product (GDP) of countries. This higher trade growth comes from the increased options of locations across borders for the value-adding of the different slices of the value chain resulting from lower barriers for the flow of goods, capital and technology. Exploiting these options is normally termed 'offshoring' and has become another major theme in research (e.g. [23], [12]). Offshoring may be defined as transnational relocation or dispersion of activities in line with Doh et al. [24]. Some of these relocations of activities across borders happen within the firm by setting up their own facilities, normally termed Foreign Direct Investment (FDI), and some of the relocations happen in the form of outsourcing to other companies.

For the last 20 years there has been a general trend in corporate restructuring to concentrate on the core activities and outsourcing of a range of business functions [25]. For firms that they studied, Mudambi and Venzin [23] noted that "the magnitude of offshoring appears to be increasing for all firms. However, the magnitude of outsourcing is not uniform." This implies that while companies continue to relocate activities to low-cost countries, the setting of firm boundaries varies. Lau and Zhang [26] find that the main economic factors of outsourcing are cost reduction, cost savings and reduction in capital investment. Levy [27] argues that what has enabled these latest forms of offshoring and outsourcing is "the increased organizational and technological capacity of companies, particularly multinational companies, to separate and coordinate a network of contractors performing an intricate set of activities." These increasingly more complex supply chains "are playing an increasingly crucial role in the competitiveness of companies and national economies" [28].

3.3   Pressure Effects

The last grouping of factors is related to competitive pressure. Liemt [29] states that "economic globalization has intensified competitive pressures." The increased pressure comes along several axes at the same time. Cost and price pressure has increased (e.g. [30], [20]) as a result of the new openness of economies. The pressure to cut costs in order to stay competitive acts in a loop so as to put increased pressure on further offshoring and outsourcing of activities, and also on further specialization or fragmentation of the value chain. There is also a higher rate of change in a company's competitive environment (e.g. [7], [6]). The higher rate of change relates to product cycles, production technology, competitors and customer preferences. Another factor that adds to the pressure is the added diversity of the market (e.g. [16]). With industry boundaries changing to becoming global, added complexity comes from the diversity within this new larger market. Competitors can have a larger global potential, but to achieve it this added diversity must be addressed, and companies that are better at it will gain a competitive advantage. The spread of technology and information has also led to lower start-up barriers for setting up companies (e.g. [6]). Another factor that relates to the model is lower visibility. In a regional geographic market prior to globalization, a medium-sized company could have a relatively good overview of its competitive situation. We can visualize this by a pie chart where white represents the known part, black the unknown, and gray the 'hinted' part which is suspected or on which some partial knowledge exists. The expansion from regional to global then can be represented as in Figure 3. In the new markets it is generally more difficult to get an overview, and it might be impossible to get the full picture. This representation can be used on all the different parts of the competition model, to represent the direct competition, potential buyers and suppliers alike.

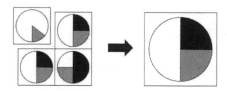

Fig. 3. Reduced visibility in the integrated market (white representing known, gray representing partly known, and black representing the unknown part of the competitive situation)

4   Concluding Remarks

Based on a literature study, the main drivers of economic globalization that affect the competitive situation have been identified to be lower trade barriers, lower transportation costs, lower communication costs, ICT development and the spread of technology. These have a number of effects that have been grouped into the areas of size, location and pressure according to how they influence the competitive situation as shown in Figure 4.

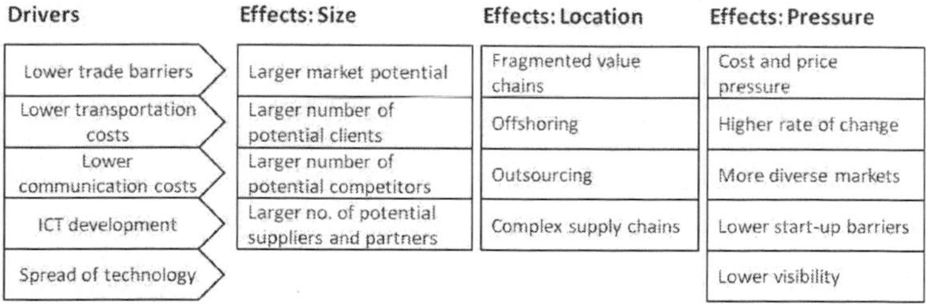

Drivers	Effects: Size	Effects: Location	Effects: Pressure
Lower trade barriers	Larger market potential	Fragmented value chains	Cost and price pressure
Lower transportation costs	Larger number of potential clients	Offshoring	Higher rate of change
Lower communication costs	Larger number of potential competitors	Outsourcing	More diverse markets
ICT development	Larger no. of potential suppliers and partners	Complex supply chains	Lower start-up barriers
Spread of technology			Lower visibility

Fig. 4. The drivers and effects from globalization affecting the competitive situation

The size effects relate to the fact that as the markets of the world comes closer together, the market potential for individual companies increase several-fold, but the number of potential competitors increases too. Larger number of potential customers increases the potential, but also the complexity.

Location effects relate to the increased fragmentation of value chain into smaller and more standardized activities, and to the increased use of outsourcing and/or offshoring to relocate activities to the outside of the company or to other low cost countries.

Pressure effects relate to the factors that increase the pressure on the competitive situation. These include a higher cost and price pressure, higher rate of change, more diverse markets, lower start-up barriers and lower visibility. Higher rate of change can include rate of change for products (shorter product cycles) changes to production technology or changes in competitors. The competitive situations of companies are changing at an unprecedented rate.

References

1. Porter, M.E.: How Competitive Forces Shape Strategy. Harvard Business Review, 137–145 (March/April 1979)
2. Stiglitz, J.E.: Making Globalization Work. Norton & Company, Inc., New York (2006)
3. Steger, M.B.: Globalization: A very short introduction. Univ. Press, Oxford (2009)
4. Ellwood, W.: The No-Nonsense Guide to Globalization, 2nd edn. New Internationalist, Oxford (2006)
5. Porter, M.E.: Competitive Advantage: Creating and Sustaining Superior Performance. The Free Press, New York (1985)
6. Friedman, T.L.: The World is Flat: A Brief History of the Twenty-First Century. Farrar, Straus and Giroux, New York (2005)
7. Sirkin, H.L., Hemerling, J.W., Bhattacharya, A.K.: Globality: Competing with Everyone from Everywhere for Everything. Business Plus, New York (2008)
8. Meredith, R.: The Elephant and the Dragon: The Rise of India and China and What It Means for All of Us. W.W. Norton & Company, Inc., New York (2007)
9. Goldin, I.: Globalization and Risks for Business: Implications of an Increasingly Interconnected World. Lloyd's 360^0 Risk Insight (2010), http://www.lloyds.com/360 (acc. December 19, 2010)
10. IMF: Globalization: A Brief Overview. IMF Issue Brief, No. 02/08 (2008), http://www.imf.org (acc. December 19, 2010)
11. Rubin, J.: Why Your World Is About to Get a Whole Lot Smaller: Oil and the End of Globalization. Random House, Toronto (2009)
12. Milberg, W., Winkler, D.: Globalization, Offshoring and Economic Insecurity in Industrialized Countries. DESA Working Paper, No. 87 (2009)
13. James, J.: Information Technology, Cumulative Causation and Patterns of Globalization in the Third World. Review of International Political Economy 8(1), 147–162 (2001)
14. Easterbrook, G.: Sonic Boom: Globalization at Mach Speed. Random House, NY (2009)
15. Freeman, R.B.: Doubling the Global Work Force: The Challenge of Integrating China, India, and the Former Soviet Bloc into the World Economy. Peterson Institute of International Economics (2004), http://www.iie.com/publications/papers/freeman1104.pdf (acc. July 18, 2011)

16. Agtmael, A.: The Emerging Markets Century: How a New Breed of World-Class Companies is Overtaking the World. Simon & Schuster UK Ltd., London (2007)
17. Teagarden, M.B., Cai, D.H.: Learning from Dragons who are Learning from us: Developmental Lessons from China's Global Companies. Organizational Dynamics 38(1) (2009)
18. Defever, F.: Functional Fragmentation and the Location of Multinational Firms in the Enlarged Europe. Regional Science and Urban Economics 36, 658–677 (2006)
19. Hummels, D., Ishii, J., Yi, K.M.: The Nature and Growth of Vertical Specialization in World Trade. Journal of International Economics 54, 75–99 (2001)
20. Burda, M.C., Dluhosch, B.: Cost Competition, Fragmentation, and Globalization. Review of International Economics 10(3), 424–441 (2002)
21. Macher, J.T., Mowery, D.C.: Vertical Specialization and Industry Structure in High Technology Industries. Advances in Strategic Management 21, 317–355 (2004)
22. Krugman, P.: Growing World Trade: Causes and Consequences. Brookings Papers on Economic Activity (1), 327–377 (1995)
23. Mudambi, R., Venzin, M.: The Strategic Nexus of Offshoring and Outsourcing Decisions. Journal of Management Studies 47(8), 1510–1533 (2010)
24. Doh, J.P., Bunyaratavej, K., Hahn, E.: Separable But Not Equal: the Location Determinants of Discrete Services Offshoring Activities. Journal of International Business Studies 40, 926–943 (2009)
25. Flecker, J.: Outsourcing, Spatial Relocation and the Fragmentation of Employment. Competition and Change 13(3), 251–266 (2009)
26. Lau, K.H., Zhang, J.: Drivers and Obstacles of Outsourcing Practices in China. Int. Journ. of Physical Distribution & Logistics Management 36(10), 776–792 (2006)
27. Levy, D.L.: Offshoring in the New Global Political Economy. Journal of Management Studies 42(3), 685–693 (2005)
28. Hameri, A.P., Hintsa, J.: Assessing the Drivers of Change for Cross-Border Supply Chains. Int. J. of Physical Distr. and Logistics Management 39(9), 741–761 (2009)
29. Liemt, G.: Economic Globalization: Labour options and Business Strategies in High Labour Cost Countries. International Labour Review 131, 453–470 (1992)
30. Ross, A.: Fast Boat to China: High-Tech Outsourcing and the Consequences of Free Trade – Lessons from Shanghai. Pantheon Books, New York (2006)

Mapping Factors Influencing
the Selection of Subsea Petroleum Production Systems

Jorge Moreno-Trejo[1,2] and Tore Markeset[1]

[1] University of Stavanger, N-4036 Stavanger, Norway
{jorge.m.trejo,tore.markeset}@uis.no
[2] PEMEX Exploración y Producción, Ciudad Del Carmen, Campeche, México

Abstract. The development, design and selection of subsea petroleum production equipment and facilities are critical activities, as the decisions made will
impact the success and profitability of the project. Technical, economic and
government regulations are some of the factors that need to be evaluated in order to contract subsea services and procurement activities. Pre-studies need to
be conducted to design the best subsea concept and to assess the development
costs in order to succeed in the project execution and to keep the production
rate and profits as expected. There are many factors that should be addressed
before selecting the concept. By identifying and studying these aspects, the
project management will be able to develop an optimum production system and
select the best equipment to cover the functions needed, as well as identify
health, safety, environmental and quality requirements and spare parts' availability for maintenance interventions. This will help to achieve the integrity of
the installation and to reduce risks. In this paper we identify various aspects,
factors and design criteria that need to be addressed in the design phase.

Keywords: Petroleum industry, Subsea installations, Production facilities,
Influencing factors.

1   Introduction

The oil and gas industry worldwide is changing due to the introduction of new technology as well as exploitation in deeper water. The industry is striving to exploit reservoirs in the best way – both technically and economically – and to reduce operational and capital expenses in new developments. Subsea technology is increasingly
being developed and used instead of building traditional platforms. Smaller fields can
be exploited and interconnected to make them economically profitable, and standard
technology can be used to conduct fast-track projects. However, new challenges that
did not exist required in earlier projects arise during the selection of subsea production system solutions and have to be analyzed and developed.

Front-end engineering design (FEED) studies are carried out to identify possible
solutions based on requirements in the various life cycle phases. Specialists from
various fields are gathered to enrich the project. Reservoir characteristics, infrastructure, installation, transportation, environmental issues and subsea processing are

J. Frick and B. Laugen (Eds.): APMS 2011, IFIP AICT 384, pp. 242–250, 2012.

analyzed in the first stage. Selecting the best production system will lessen the risk of cost overruns and delays. Analyzing and defining the health, safety, environmental and quality (HSEQ) requirements, as well as maintenance and spare parts' availability at an early stage, will increase the possibility for achieving the installation's integrity and reduce the risk of failure [1].

There are also external and non-technical factors that may impact the production concept, such as the political environment, local interests and regulations. These factors influence the decision-making process and need to be mapped. Country-specific agencies regulate international companies working in their territory, and these regulations may influence decisions and reduce the risks. Hence, the process of taking decisions on the selection of production facility solutions is not only economic and technical; local factors and laws concerning health, safety and environmental issues are also involved.

The development and exploitation of oil and gas reservoirs entails huge investment and long-term commitment. It involves establishing contracts and agreements with many service and manufacturing companies to supply the material, equipment, services and specialists required. Personnel chosen to work in the project need the experience and correct specialist knowledge to be able to analyze the reservoir characteristics, processes, technology, etc. Furthermore, the selection of equipment has to comply with technical and HSEQ requirements as well as international standards and guidelines. In cases where the technology does not exist, companies have to investigate and carry out more studies to figure out possible solutions. Hence, most often proven technology used in similar projects will be preferred over new, costly and unproven technology.

After geologists and geophysicists have analyzed the reservoir information and identified the reservoir production profile and where to place the production wells, the subsea production facilities need to be decided. Various options should be identified and assessed based on available information, and the best one selected to justify further investment.

The field development project not only has to focus on technical challenges, but also challenges related to budgeting, planning, management, statutory regulations, project documentation, contracts, etc. need to be taken care of before the project's execution. Since different points of view and experience contribute to making better decisions, a multidisciplinary team is needed with personnel who have work experience from similar projects.

Risk and costs analysis are fundamental in such development projects, as initially there is not much detailed information. During the design phase all possible risks should be assessed in order to identify and mitigate risk. Therefore, it is of utmost importance to identify and map possible factors that may affect the project and the integrity and performance of the installed subsea solution.

Definition of the development strategy in the initial stage is a key factor in system selection. The optimum production system will determine the success of the project. This phase is critical, as wrong decisions will have greater economic impact. The costs of making changes are higher after the project has moved into the execution phase.

Based on a case study, this paper maps factors for selecting the subsea production facility from a business perspective.

2   Mapping Factors Influencing the System Selection Process

There are many technical components to assess in detail during the system design. However, there are three typical business drivers to analyze; namely regulatory, commercial and technical drivers. The regulatory drivers represent the authorities, legislation and standards regulating the oil and gas industry. Governmental authorities are responsible for the field exploitation in their respective countries. They set the rules for exploring and exploiting the oil and gas fields in their territory and prioritize the factors for granting permissions before petroleum activities begin.

The commercial drivers are related to the viability of the project, taking into account the oil and gas price fluctuations and the long-term economic profits, etc. The technical drivers are related to the possibility to extract hydrocarbons using the best technical solutions and following the international standards. Technical challenges are focused on how to bring the hydrocarbons from the reservoir to the customers. Developments could vary, but the principles tend to become standardized. In this paper, only some of the technical and regulatory issues and their impact from a business perspective are discussed.

2.1   The Influence of the Regulatory Drivers

The oil and gas industry is governed by the laws established by the state where the fields are located. Regulations are primarily focused on maintaining national sovereignty, the safety of the communities and workers, natural resources, as well as state profits in order to improve the national economy.

These drivers are at the top of the pyramid as they were written to safeguard public interests and regulate the petroleum sector. Countries manage their natural assets as they decide, and the form of carrying out some activities may vary from one government to another. Various political or local interests may therefore influence the decision process. Some countries have created separate regulatory functions and the policies, regulatory and commercial models work in autonomous entities, while others have kept a monopoly for administering their national resources [2]. These differences are related to individual countries, history, external relations and the importance they place on some factors.

For example, some countries may use their own standards for regulating technical issues in foreign oil companies but also may choose to use international standards such as ISO13628, ANSI/API 17A in order to regulate some technical activities for the operation of subsea production systems [3], [4]. In some cases, international companies have elaborated higher requirements in their processes, overwhelming local specifications in order to assure their high quality and reputation worldwide.

2.2   Issues Affecting the Selection of the Technical Drivers

The exploitation of a field is driven by the feasibility of technical options in order to assess the risks in the initial development phase. According to earlier experiences, there may be two, three or more technical alternatives to analyze during the concept selection, but solutions may impact more in one region than another. For example, FPSO (floating, production storage and offloading) facilities are designed to operate in remote locations, and for some projects this could be a viable option. However, in the USA this is not an accepted economical solution. In the USA, FPSOs are regulated by the Jones Act which states that crews must be citizens of the USA, the tankers must have at least 75% American ownership, and tankers for transporting hydrocarbons must be built in the USA [5]. This becomes a very expensive solution with high CAPEX and OPEX. However, the use of FPSOs is becoming increasingly accepted in other regions such as Brazil.

2.3   Advantages in Using Subsea Processing Technology

Bai and Bai [6] define subsea processing as *"any handling and treatment of the produced fluids for mitigating flow assurance issues prior to reaching the platform or onshore"*. The processing requirements should be designed to fit with other interfaces such as drilling and flow lines. The main benefits of carrying out production with subsea technology are (Saipem CITEPH report cited in [6]):

- Reduce CAPEX and OPEX. Subsea technology could avoid the topside processing plant
- Optimize production. Small and close satellite fields could be connected to existing infrastructure
- Extend the life of mature fields by connecting to existing infrastructure
- Optimize production on the seabed
- Improve the flow assurance
- Reduce the impact on the environment

Computer-aided design programs (CAD) are used during the modeling and evaluation of production systems. However, specific and detailed information is required to be able to design the overall concept which is sometimes not complete and precise in the preliminary studies [7]. In most cases, the subsea concept is designed using the experience of similar projects. The subsea industry would like to standardize solutions worldwide to get the equipment faster from the manufacturers. However, there are special cases with extreme reservoir conditions, as well as environmental forces, where the technology could still not be available in the market.

2.4   Identification of Factors That Influence the Selection of Subsea System

Fields have different characteristics and vary according to the geographic location and reservoir complexity; hence, field development may involve several challenges for each case [8]. Exploitation can be carried out with several solutions, and earlier analysis will determine the best technical and economic option. The use of subsea technology for exploiting reservoirs could be an advantage.

According to NORSOK U-001 [9], a typical subsea system includes: 1) wellhead, tubing hanger, X-mas tree; 2) production control system; 3) umbilical; 4) intervention system; 5) subsea structures and piping systems; 6) flowlines, and 7) subsea processing, boosting, separation, etc.

The type of equipment selected will mainly depend on the reservoir characteristics and the environmental conditions. Facilities available close to the field could influence the decision-making. It is easier and faster to connect the stream production in an existing infrastructure rather than in a new one which can take more time to build and which also could have an impact on the environment. The effect of building a new facility may increase the cost per barrel by up to 50% [10].

Initially the influencing factors should be identified and assessed. Table 1 shows some of the factors to take into account to select the most feasible option.

Table 1. Factors influencing the field development strategy

Area	*Influencing factors*
Financial	CAPEX, OPEX, interest rates, exchange rates, etc.
Reservoir and environment	Reservoir characteristics, seabed characteristics, weather, etc.
Manufacturing, installation and testing	Quality assurance, supplier selection, commissioning, testing and test criteria, hand-over acceptance criteria, etc.
Procurement	Technology qualification, selection of suppliers, contractors, service providers, etc.
Operation and maintenance	Flow assurance, operational performance assurance, technical integrity, intervention services

The goal of obtaining the first production is usually one of the most important factors to evaluate, as it means the field could begin to generate profits. Stakeholders expect income and cash flow from the project to re-invest in the following stages or to begin other projects. Moreover, the coordination of multiple activities during the field life cycle is a challenge due its complexity. The project has several processing periods called "windows", during which many companies interact to achieve a certain goal. The window for each service company and the interfaces between each process should be carried out according to the plan; otherwise one should adjust the next activities in order to keep the project on time. During the planning phase, some delays for uncertainties should be taken into account, such as reservoir changes or the weather. On the other hand, classification and selection of the best providers is also a key factor in the success of the project.

To be able to economically assess the project, all major costs should be addressed. Around 40% of expenses are related to the cost of facilities and 60% of expenses concern the well and surface [11].

Identification of risks is essential to maintain the integrity of people and facilities. The risk analysis and the health, safety, environment and quality (HSEQ) strategy are fundamental in subsea processes.

2.5   Selecting Facilities Suited to the Reservoir Characteristics

Selection of subsea facilities entails several factors, and the analysis begins with the reservoir characteristics. These have a major influence on the system selection and will determine the technical characteristics of equipment.

Information about the reservoir's rock characteristics, fluid densities, pressure and flow rates allow potential areas to be identified and provide assistance for building the production profile [12]. In addition to oil and gas, the well-stream may also contain water and sand. Processing oil and gas on the seabed has several advantages as discussed above. By separating out as water and sand and other unwanted components on the seabed, the hydrocarbon extraction will be improved, and one may avoid the use of a topside oil or gas production facility. This may result in increased recovery and efficiency, as well as faster reservoir exploitation as compared with other solutions [13]. It also will reduce costs and increase profits.

2.6   The Influence of the Geographical Location

Exploitation of oil and gas reserves will be influenced by the geographic location of the reservoir. The environment and local conditions will influence the design of the subsea production facility [14]. Some of the forces affecting the equipment include the soil support capacity, seabed pockmarks and terrain characteristics, as well as equipment weight, size, shape, etc. From the soil characteristics and topography surveys one will solve some of the challenges of laying down the flowlines and pipelines. One also would be able to identify some of the factors affecting the deployment of the equipment on the seabed. The soil needs to be stable to ensure that it is able to withstand heavy equipment during the equipment deployment and later settlements.

Detailed topography and bathymetry surveys and studies are needed to map the seabed terrain. This will identify steep slopes, ravines, depressions and boulders that may restrict routes to onshore. The goal is to identify the optimum pipeline routes and to avoid obstacles and steep slopes, as well as reduce trenching activities. However, sometimes specially designed mattresses will need to be installed to stabilize the seabed. This could result in extra costs and time.

During the concept selection, one must make some assumptions in order to make preliminary subsea equipment designs, pipeline and umbilical routes for calculating the costs and to identify potential limitations such as high slopes or free span areas. On the other hand, pockmarks might not be detected in bathymetric surveys, and they could represent further potential problems (e.g. the equipment's inclination) [14].

2.7   Waves, Currents and Weather Affecting the Subsea Installation

Waves, currents and weather create dynamic loads that affect the subsea facilities during the whole life cycle. Therefore, facilities should be designed and prepared to support the worst conditions. Statistical data should be taken into account to predict the oceanographic behavior in the area where the equipment is going to be installed.

However, information about the environmental conditions might not be available from historical data. Therefore, surveys should be carried out and analyzed with meteorology, oceanography and hydrodynamics specialists [15]. Estimations for more extreme waves, currents and weather are generally performed by probabilistic as well as experience records in the region. In order to maintain the integrity of people and installations, the subsea system should be designed to resist stronger currents, soil movements and sliding to be able to guarantee production regularity.

2.8   Optimizing the Reservoir Flow

Flow assurance relates to the process of transporting the hydrocarbons from the reservoir to the processing facilities located onshore. By analyzing the hydrocarbons and reservoir characteristics, pipelines and production facilities can be designed which will enable the unrestricted flow of hydrocarbons from the reservoir to the onshore facilities. Flow assurance is a critical issue in system selection due to hydrate block formations in the streamlines. Injections of various chemicals and hydrate inhibitors also increase OPEX.

The low temperature on the seabed can cause conditions that affect production flow, such as slugging, scale and hydrate formations. Wellheads, jumpers and flow lines are in risk of plug formations due to the flow is through narrow spaces. Therefore, the subsea system design should be able to mitigate the flow restrictions or blockages by injecting inhibitors in the system. Other issues that should be taken into account are the possibility of hydrate formations in shut-in periods, upset conditions as result of pigging or as result of re-start operations in the well [16].

The flow assurance department makes estimations based on fluids and reservoir properties samples from logging tools or production tests, but initially there is not much information available. Otherwise, the fluid's values are taken from neighboring fields. The reservoir's analysis may include hydrate stability curves, cloud and pour point measurements, wax deposition patterns, asphaltene stability testing and a scale analysis of the water [17]. The information obtained help to select the best overall subsea solution that will fit with the flow assurance strategy, and to plan the system operation and the equipment including the chemical process needed.

One strategy has been to maintain the temperature and pressure from the well under certain levels to avoid formations. The tubing head can use a vacuum insulated tubing to improve the thermal performance in the well. The benefices are a more turndown ratio, as the flowing temperature is higher at low rates, and a faster warm-up, as the tubing head is insulated and the stream fluids do not face directly low temperatures [18]. Moreover, if the subsea system receives production in better processing conditions from the well, the production can be optimized to transport it.

Assessing the flow assurance risks in the system selection phase will contribute to success the field development. Previous tests of the fluids will help to take better decisions to mitigate the flow risks, as compounds in the pipeline can cause severe operational stoppages. The analysis of aquifer areas around the reservoir is essential, as it may be contaminated by drilling mud [19]. Water injection (i.e. produce water mixed with seawater) is often used to maintain the pressure in the field, causing souring, scaling or corrosion in the subsea equipment.

Another importance issue for optimizing the reservoir flow is to avoid further interventions in the subsea system. Repairing a blockage is expensive, as it requires specialize vessels equipped with ROVs or ROTs. In extreme situations, the substitution of the blocked area may be the best economic and viable solution [17].

2.9   Infrastructure Available

The use of existing platforms, processing facilities and pipelines could significantly reduce the CAPEX. Exploitation of new fields tied to existent facilities using subsea technology enables the developing of projects with marginal reserves or the increasing of production in mature reserves, making them economically viable. Infrastructure available close to the site may have a high impact on the project and system selection.

3   Conclusions

In this paper various factors influencing the selection of subsea petroleum production facilities have been discussed and are summarized in Figure 1. The influencing factors vary according to the strategy adopted by each oil company. In the process of selecting subsea systems, the companies focus on achieving the schedule, reducing risks or reducing costs. The business philosophy may be different, but the oil companies tend to reduce risks to maintain the integrity of people and installations.

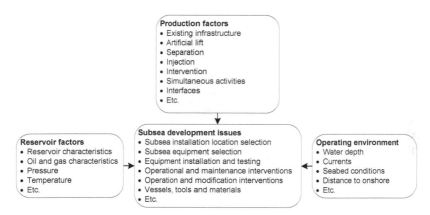

Fig. 1. Factors influencing the selection of subsea production facilities

The selection of reliable contractors is a key factor in the project's success due to their product quality and schedule goals. Oil companies may take the decision to split the processes across several service companies or to select just a few contractors to carry out the project. Having fewer contractors could entail spreading out more responsibilities and risks across fewer service companies. These decisions could increase or reduce the business risks. However, the options should be analyzed from the technical, commercial and HSEQ points of view.

The system selection entails choosing the option which fits, in the best way, with the other activities during exploitation. The schedule to obtain the first oil production could be impacted by delays in drilling activities or pipeline installation. Optimization of the field layout could improve scheduling and avoid vessels' traffic in the area. Subsea, drilling and pipeline activities could cause some interference around the wells; therefore, it is necessary to build a strategy for merging them.

The "window" for each activity may change as a result of unexpected issues such as the weather, reservoir uncertainties and, in some cases, vessels' availability. New processes are being developed to improve the current systems, taking into account stronger HSEQ practices. The selection of the optimum production system will improve business performance and stakeholder profits.

References

1. Moreno-Trejo, J., Markeset, T.: Identifying Challenges in the Maintenance of Subsea Petroleum Production Systems. In: Frick, J., Laugen, B. (eds.) APMS 2011. IFIP AICT, vol. 384, pp. 251–259. Springer, Heidelberg (2012)
2. Thurber, M.C., Hults, D.R., Heller, P.R.P.: Exporting the Norwegian model: the effect of administrative design on oil sector performance. Energy Policy (2011), doi: 10.1016/j.enpol.2011.05.027
3. ANSI/API RP 17A. Design and Operation of Subsea Production Systems. Recommended Practice 17A, 3rd edn. American Petroleum Institute (September 2002)
4. ISO 13628. Petroleum and natural gas industries - Design and operation of subsea production systems - Part 1: General requirements and recommendations, 2nd edn. (2005)
5. Lovie, P.: FPSOs enter the Gulf of Mexico operator tool box. Journal of Petroleum Technology 62(5), 32–35 (2010)
6. Bai, Y., Bai, Q.: Subsea engineering handbook, p. 49. Gulf, Burlington (2010)
7. Woldemichael, D.E., Hashim, F.M.: Development of conceptual design support tool for subsea process equipment design. International Journal of Mechanical & Mechatronics Engineering 9(10), 12–17 (2010)
8. Moreno-Trejo, J., Markeset, T.: Identifying Challenges in the Maintenance of Subsea Petroleum Production Systems. In: Frick, J., Laugen, B. (eds.) APMS 2011. IFIP AICT, vol. 384, pp. 251–259. Springer, Heidelberg (2012)
9. NORSOK U-001. Subsea production systems, Rev. 2 (1998) (accessed January 3, 2011)
10. Jenner, G.P., Ford, J.T., Tweedle, J.A.: Economic evaluation of subsea development options in the North Sea. Journal of Petroleum Technology, 1484–1489 (December 1991)
11. Vardeman, D., McGee, K., Kubota, R.K., Heijermans, B., Huff, J., McCurley, M., Khurana, S.: Panel: Collaboration among operators and contractors in deepwater and ultradeepwater fields. In: The Proceeding of the Offshore Technology Conference (OTC 2005), Houston, Texas, May 2-5 (2005)
12. Shell: The Petroleum Handbook. Elsevier, Amsterdam (1983)
13. Lyons, W.C., Plisga, G.J.: Standard handbook of petroleum & natural gas engineering, 2nd edn., p. 107. Gulf, Burlington (2005)
14. Guidance Notes. Guidance notes on geotechnical investigations for subsea structures. Prepared by the Subsea Working Group of the Offshore Soil Investigation Forum, p. 8 (2000), http://sig.sut.org.uk/pdf/subseaguidancenotes.pdf, (accessed July 8, 2011)
15. ABS Guide. Guide for building and classing subsea riser systems, pp. 37–39. American Bureau of Shipping, Houston (2006)
16. Gudimetla, R., Carroll, A., Havre, K., Christiansen, C., Canon, J.: Gulf of Mexico Field of the future: subsea flow assurance. In: The Proceedings of the Offshore Technology Conference (OTC 2006), Houston, Texas, May 1-4 (2006)
17. Kaczmarski, A.A., Lorimer, S.E.: Emergence of flow assurance as a technical discipline specific to deepwater technical challenges and integration into subsea systems engineering. In: The Proceedings of the Offshore Technology Conference (OTC 2001), Houston, Texas, April 30-May 3 (2001)
18. Hudson, J.D., Dykhno, L.A., Lorimer, S.E., Shoppa, W., Wilkens, R.J.: Flow assurance for subsea wells. In: The Proceedings of the Offshore Technology Conference (OTC 2000), Houston, Texas, May 1-4 (2000)
19. Song, S.: Managing flow assurance and operation risks in subsea tie-back system. In: The Proceedings of the Offshore Technology Conference (OTC 2008), Houston, Texas, May 5-8 (2008)

Identifying Challenges in the Maintenance of Subsea Petroleum Production Systems

Jorge Moreno-Trejo[1,2] and Tore Markeset[1]

[1] University of Stavanger, N-4036 Stavanger, Norway
[2] PEMEX Exploración y Producción, Ciudad Del Carmen, Campeche, México
{Jorge.m.trejo,tore.markeset}@uis.no

Abstract. Maintenance strategies for subsea oil and gas production installations entail the use of specialized equipment and vessels to carry out subsea interventions. The costs for carrying out preventive maintenance are significantly lower compared to the costs of unpredicted failures where in some cases it is necessary to reduce or stop the oil production. Based on a literature review and inputs from industrial experts, this paper discusses maintenance challenges for subsea oil and gas facilities.

Keywords: Subsea petroleum production facilities, Maintenance challenges.

1 Introduction

Oil companies are trying to improve their performance to carry out more effective strategies in order to reduce interventions due to failures. Identifying some of the factors impacting the subsea production systems during the exposure on the seabed will allow them to maintain the integrity of facilities according to safety regulations as well as environmental and quality requirements.

Maintenance strategies for the infrastructure of platforms in earlier projects were produced as an afterthought [1]; however, subsea facilities entail identifying alternatives to carry out preventive and corrective maintenance before the exploitation begins in order to plan individual maintenance activities and establish frame agreements with qualified service providers. Moreover, challenges are focused on reducing the possibility of failures in subsea production systems during the field life cycle.

Subsea components are affected by the stress, environmental issues and individual conditions resulting from the geographic location where the production system has been installed. Environmental and reservoir factors are always impacting the equipment's performance, even though equipment is designed to work under extreme conditions. The deterioration of subsea equipment will be faster after it is deployed on the seabed and begins to work. Therefore, maintenance strategies should analyze the factors which could further affect the performance of subsea installations in order to identify possible solutions.

The inspection of installations without the use of divers in fields located in deeper water has made for more complex interventions. Hence, the strategy to carry out integrity programs using ROVs (remotely operated vehicle), AUVs (autonomous underwater

J. Frick and B. Laugen (Eds.): APMS 2011, IFIP AICT 384, pp. 251–259, 2012.

vehicle) or ROTs (remotely operated tool) to verify the state of equipment has become increasingly important in the field development strategy.

However, failures still happen and, due to the deep-sea location, the maintenance is challenging and expensive. Subsea development failures may happen in the first stages of production, and often the causes are found in the design, construction or installation's activities [2]. Harsh conditions on the seabed, sand, salt, low temperatures easily affect the installed equipment. Corrosion is often one of the main elements, causing failures over time, and has to be prevented. Equipment and tools have to be maintained, and preventive activities have to be carried out as well as operations when is necessary to repair equipment in deep-water environments.

Hence, corrective maintenance on subsea equipment is needed less frequently, allowing money to be saved, and increasing the opportunities for developing other fields.

Based on a literature review and information from industrial experts, this paper explores and identifies typical failures as well as maintenance challenges of subsea petroleum production facilities.

2   Subsea System Failures

Subsea developments are exposed to stress and corrosive environments which can affect their performance after a term settled on the seabed. Flanges or fasteners can be corroded, even with the use of anodes installed on the equipment; subsea control systems having electronic components which could be uncalibrated and also hydraulic components such as valves could be affected by environmental issues as they are in frequent movement. Fasteners can usually fail for these causes (see e.g. [3]):

- Overload
- Corrosion
- Fatigue
- Corrosion fatigue
- Environmentally assisted cracking

To monitor the equipment, there are several types of sensors providing constant information from the well, such as acoustic control systems, multiphase flowmeters, and sand and leak detection systems; these enable the detection of any abnormal function and measure the state of hydrocarbons, for example, pressure, temperature, leaks and sometimes include a detector for dropped objects [4].

When the failure occurs, the signal is sent to the control module and interpreted by the operators who have the responsibility to verify it. The damage type and the significance of the failure will determine how fast the activities for resolving the problem are carried out by the operator. Often these types of failures are unexpected and appear suddenly without any warning.

All subsea activities entail the use of vessels or barges, and in some operations a crane is required [5]. If such as vessel or equipment is needed the costs may increase. If the vessel is not on a chartered contract with fixed prices, the time before the vessel is available will be longer [6]. In order to get vessels fast, tools and spare parts need to be ready to use in the field. The contract's specifications may vary according to the strategy of each operator. However, operators tend to sign frame agreements with selected contractors to assure quality and schedule, as well as to reduce risks related to the subsea interventions.

During the design phase of the equipment, one may identify and analyze potential subsea components' failures and identify critical processes that may represent a great benefit to the project [2]. The objective is to identify components that will need to be inspected and monitored, and allocate spare parts and the tools and type of vessels needed for maintenance interventions. This will enable the management to react faster in the case of a sudden maintenance intervention.

Each component in the subsea system has a mean time between/to failure (MTBF/MTTF). Subsea well control systems, for example, have a MTBF of more than 30 years [7]. Based on this, the operators expect the system to work reliably without failure for five years, and plan to carry out preventive maintenance at least every five years.

Infant mortality is related to failures during the first period after the installation. When the system is installed and working according to its design, some random failures may occur or unexpected performance problems may be detected during the testing or normal work conditions. The installation on the seabed is complex due to transportation, water depth and environmental elements; underwater flow can cause a hit or shock during deployment on the seafloor. Extreme conditions such as depth, temperature, salt, sea current or accidents during operations can increase the risk of failures.

Some components are subjected to wear processes or corrosion and need to be replaced. A replacement program for such components and the resources needed for carrying out the replacement activities should be planned and prepared. In the worst case, spare parts may be obsolete resulting in entire systems needing to be replaced to assure the integrity of the subsea production facility.

Failures are prevented by identifying and categorizing the risks in the project using tools such as HAZOP (Hazard Operation) studies and HAZID (Hazard Identification) studies. The purpose is to measure the risks based on experience in five common change factors: reliability, technology, architecture and organizational complexity [8]. Specialists from different areas meet to give input to the process, classifying operations in risks from the scale D (low impact) to A (very high impact). The results of accidents may result in loss or damage to offshore O&G installations. The causes vary but they can be grouped by: human errors, inadequate maintenance, equipment failure, simultaneous operations, collision, etc. Human errors are often the major cause of accidents [9].

The risks are not the same for a subsea production system, as they require different operations in each phase. Some phases entail higher risks than others .The geography, weight, geometry or shape of the equipment, as well as the production fluids leaving from the reservoir could represent higher temperatures near to the well, and may influence on how to handle the equipment to reduce risks.

Since the installation phase entails several service providers interacting, the risks in this phase may increase [10].

3   Maintenance Challenges for Subsea Installations

The maintenance philosophy should be decided during the design phase in order to plan the strategy to procure and contract the vessels, tools and equipment in the operational phase [11]. The first responsibility for operators is to keep the integrity of people and installations. It has become the main objective for international companies nowadays to maintain a good image and reputation worldwide.

Maintenance is carried out during the exploitation phase of the subsea life cycle and involves both preventive and corrective activities. Unplanned corrective maintenance may be very expensive, and one therefore prefers that all maintenance and modification activities should be planned well ahead of time. In order to plan the maintenance activities, the subsea equipment condition performance has to be monitored from the surface. Such monitoring and maintenance activities often involve special purpose-built ships and equipment and may be expensive. The integrity process includes inspection activities using remotely operated vehicles (ROVs) and remotely operated tools (ROTs) to respond to the damage caused by, for example, pipeline and flow line vibration, or corrosion and internal erosion.

Subsea maintenance entails the use of specialized equipment to carry out the subsea activities underwater and is more expensive than shallow-water interventions. It also involves high capital investments as activities in deep-water environments entail working in extreme conditions, as well as the waiting time needed in operations with vessels. However, after subsea systems are installed, they have low operational expenditures [12].

New technology in the subsea field has improved significantly, and the equipment has been designed for resisting severe conditions. The use of new technology need to be qualified as it may represent high risk [8]. Modern technology also has high maintainability, which makes it easier to perform easy maintenance. Analysis of historical data can help to determine servicing, condition monitoring and repair. The use of new and more reliable components allows steady uninterrupted subsea production activities. Maintenance of subsea systems should allow the system to work without interruptions due to failures. However, Markeset [13] asserts that "it is almost impossible to design a system that is maintenance-free".

Components in subsea facilities are designed to work for many years, even without maintenance. However, over time the system still will often degrade and maybe fail. When equipment condition is based on maintenance, the result is higher availability rates and moderate costs compared with costs related to production loss or breakdown [14]. Mostly failures in subsea facilities are due to design during the installation process. Electronic devices for measuring have to be treated carefully; if, for example, the ROV controller hit the equipment during operations, it may need to be re-calibrated.

Hence, decisions about the maintenance strategy should be based on recommendations and planned costs for future activities. As discussed above, one will know the equipment type needed based on the oil characteristics of the reservoir, well-stream, sea depth, etc. Furthermore, by analyzing the seabed characteristics, water temperature, seasonal weather, underwater currents, etc., one can make estimations about future maintenance required for the subsea installation.

Usually the operator prepares the subsea activities, scheduling them one year ahead, taking into account the season, the probability for bad weather, high waves and swells, as well as programming and discussing with the involved service companies (see e.g. [5]). The operators check the recommendations given by the original equipment manufacturers. The influence of the weather varies according to the geographic location. In the North Sea, maintenance is carried out during the summer due to the harsh climatic conditions during the winter. In the Gulf of Mexico, the maintenance could be carried out during the whole year, but most often the subsea work program is modified in the hurricane season from June to November in collaboration with the operator, service companies, weather forecasting authorities, etc. Some years more hurricanes are expected, resulting in a need for modifying the maintenance programs.

The subsea activities planned by the operator will determine the maintenance strategy carried out by the service companies. The common strategies for maintenance in subsea facilities are: planned modifications, unplanned corrective maintenance and planned maintenance [6]. Subsea production systems sometimes need to be modified to improve for example, the capacity performance, the control system, to replace existing components such as valves with more reliable components, etc. (see e.g. [5]). Often such modifications are integrated with planned maintenance activities.

With planned maintenance, one often refers to predetermined periodic preventive maintenance based on operational use or calendar time, or condition-based maintenance based on observations through condition monitoring or regular inspection activities [see. e.g. 13]. Planned corrective maintenance is also used for failures of low risk, but is more seldom used for subsea petroleum installations due to the high cost of maintenance and downtime.

3.1   Preventive and Corrective Maintenance

One of the main subsea operational challenges is to avoid failures. Roberts and Laing [15] assert that: "experiences of failures in subsea technology have had a significant impact on both costs and schedule". Maintenance costs are included in the field exploitation costs, and managers have designed and executed a maintenance strategy that reduces the need as much as possible for maintenance in deep water.

Subsea installations that are in contact with water, salt and currents continually over longer periods corrode, beginning with a small corrosion in any area of the equipment. If not appropriately maintained, the corroded area may grow and result in function failure, leakage, or even production losses. However, usually blocks of zinc anodes are used for cathodic protection. The anodes corrode instead of the material and need to be replaced after some time, depending on corrosion speed. Therefore, inspection is performed to identify early signs of failure [16]. With proper preventive maintenance, companies can reduce the probabilities of failures in the production system, saving money in the long term and avoiding further problems.

Equipment and components are designed for working under certain conditions. When they are forced to work outside of the design parameters they usually fail, causing partial or complete loss of functions, reducing the process capacity, etc. However, a failure can be managed more easily if the functions' losses are kept at the unit level [17]. Moreover, the costs due to deep-water maintenance and modification interventions result in increased focus on stakeholders' expectations about production levels.

Subsea interventions are very expensive due to the use of vessels and specialized equipment such as ROV and ROT.

According to the failure type, companies can take different decisions about what to do in case that they have to maintain degraded components, or to repair or replace faulty components. Most often it is an advantage to perform maintenance on the component before a failure occurs, if the spare parts are available or can be brought fast, and if there is also the proper vessel available for carrying out the work. When equipment is designed, engineers usually test the equipment and do statistical studies of the main components that are more likely to break down as a result of the environment and working conditions.

During the procurement, the manufacturers usually offer operators a "package" of subsea spare parts which, according to their analysis, are more likely to fail due to the environmental issues and constant use. It is up to the operators and their maintenance strategy to buy this additional "package" because it also represents storage and inventory costs. However, components which are more likely to break down often need to be kept in stock. Some companies have special agreements with suppliers for holding the main spare parts in their stock. Operators usually have frame agreements with the vessels' contractors in the case of something unexpected occurring in their subsea facilities. The communication between them has been essential to carry out successful maintenance interventions. If the intervention is going to take a long time, the equipment may have to be taken to the manufacturer's onshore facilities for maintenance.

Due to the high costs associated with deep-water equipment interventions, it is quite common to evaluate the failure processes before carrying out compensating maintenance actions. Sometimes it is necessary to shut down part of the production system due to the associated failures costs being too high. Mainly there are two costs: the cost of maintaining the component including the vessel costs and the cost of spare parts and personnel, and the loss of production from one or more wells [18].

Monitoring the production processes with sensors helps to control the systems and identify failures so that decisions can be taken opportunely. Often failures may be detected by using active condition monitoring systems and by analysis of signals from the subsea control system. Some of the common subsea inspection methods include [16]:

- Visual Inspections. The purpose is to verify the physical state of the equipment and welds and to look for abnormal conditions around the subsea system.
- Corrosion Assessing. The zinc anodes are inspected and replaced when necessary.
- Full Survey of Risers, Conductors, and Caissons. A general evaluation of the equipment with cameras and sensors. Verifying the proper function of the equipment or detecting any physical damage.
- A Survey of the Seabed. Accumulation of fragments and rocks in the seabed due to subsea works or environmental conditions that could cause accidents or delays.

Inspections in subsea environments are carried out with special equipment such as remotely operated vehicles designed for the high pressures and low temperatures. New vessels often use two ROVs, one for remote inspection and observation and the other for executing maintenance works. ROVs are deployed from a platform or a vessel and are controlled remotely. ROVs facilitate subsea interventions as they can move and be controlled easily though subsea systems. Generally the team members comprise an operation controller, a submersible engineer, a submersible pilot, an observer, a winch operator and a deployment system operator; personnel are required with knowledge in electronics, hydraulics and driving the ROVs under certain conditions [16].

Access to the Internet has improved the subsea condition monitoring as it allows the equipment to be monitored 24 hours per day in real time if needed, producing condition data that can be analyzed and assessed using, for example, statistical tools. By the use of condition monitoring techniques, the cost can be reduced, the availability improved, and maintenance planned. This allows the operators to be better informed about the situation at the seabed, to know how the equipment is working, to detect possible failures and to be prepared to overcome unplanned events. Hence, the use of condition monitoring has helped to reduce failures and accidents.

Furthermore, the use of e-maintenance (see e.g. [19]; [20]) for subsea systems has supported the activities executed in the field. The installation of sensors to capture the performance and condition data, as well as the communication equipment to transmit the information faster, has developed new techniques for a better understanding of the process. It allows the managers to get an understanding of the real conditions underwater. They even have the possibility of watching the production system from any part of the world.

Corrective maintenance can be divided into planned and unplanned. Planned corrective maintenance is used for non-critical equipment where the consequences of failure are low. Unplanned corrective maintenance is used when it is necessary to repair equipment after an unexpected failure. Sudden system failures are the consequence when a system without an apparent reason is beginning to work outside of the expected performance. It could be caused by a component such as a valve, a component of the control system, an electronic component, etc., or by software errors.

4   Intervention Vessels and Equipment for Maintenance

Intervention vessels and equipment are needed to perform preventive and corrective maintenance activities. Operators most often sign agreements and contracts with service companies specializing in subsea intervention to have vessels, equipment and spare parts ready for preventive maintenance activities [21]. Also, unexpected failures should be included in the strategy and agreements. Unplanned subsea maintenance requiring intervention vessels and tools may prove costly unless it is already in the contract. If the operator has to wait for available intervention vessels, the cost of shortening the waiting time may be very high. Price negotiations should be carried out before beginning the offshore activities.

Specifications given by the fabricator and statistics about failures are useful for deciding the maintenance strategies and for selecting spare parts. Critical spare parts should be kept in stock since storage may be cheaper than the cost of long downtime due to lack of spare parts.

To reduce the cost of the intervention vessels, companies generate simulation models to quantify mobilizations, interventions, preventive and corrective maintenance and even the stopping activities caused by weather disruptions. This helps in reducing costs when contracts are made and ensuring the availability of vessels during operations.

5   Concluding Remarks

Challenges related to the maintenance of subsea facilities have been discussed based on a literature review and information from experts. Many of these challenges may be avoided by proper design as well as by planning and structured maintenance strategies in the design phase. However, it is a challenge for the petroleum companies to define maintenance strategies for reducing maintenance cost. Most of the subsea production facilities are customized designs requiring customized tools and equipment for maintenance interventions. The recent disasters in the Gulf of Mexico [22] have made companies think further about installation integrity, security and ecology, as laws and regulations will be implemented focusing on avoiding such events in the future. The companies are trying to prevent failures, focusing their strategies on preventive maintenance with the purpose of maintaining the integrity of the installation. The maintenance strategy should be addressed in the design phase to be able to take the best economic decisions. The front-end engineering design (FEED) study is a good tool to evaluate costs and activities in the early phase of the interventions, using divers, ROVs, AUVs or ROTs, as well as to identify critical stages in the field life cycle as a result of corrosion or load fatigue. By using condition monitoring and analysis of real-time data, failures may be predicted in advance. This enables the companies to plan the maintenance interventions in advance and to reduce the costly unplanned downtime. By optimizing the subsea maintenance interventions, the use of specialized and costly vessels is reduced.

References

1. Webb, G.D.: Inspection and repair of oil and gas production installations in deep water. Journal of Ocean Management 7, 313–326 (1980)
2. Roberts-Haritonov, C., Robertson, N., Strutt, J.: The design of subsea production systems for reliability and availability. In: The Proceedings of the Offshore Technology Conference (OTC 2009), Houston, Texas, May 4-7 (2009)
3. Esaklul, K.A., Ahmed, T.M.: Prevention of failures of high strength fasteners in use in offshore and subsea applications. Journal of Engineering Failure Analysis 16, 1195–1202 (2008)
4. ISO 13628. Petroleum and natural gas industries - Design and operation of subsea production systems - Part 1: General requirements and recommendations, 2nd edn. (2005)
5. Uyiomendo, E.E., Markeset, T.: Subsea maintenance service delivery: Mapping factors influencing scheduled service duration. Special Section on Maintenance and Safety Management in Process Plants, International Journal of Automation and Computing (IJAC) 7(2), 167–172 (2010)
6. Eriksen, R., Gustavsson, F., Anthonsen, H.: Developing an intervention, maintenance, and repair strategy for Ormen Lange", Society of Petroleum Engineers, SPE96751. In: The Proceedings of the Offshore Europe Conference, Aberdeen, Scotland, September 6-9 (2005)
7. Byrne, S.: Subsea well control systems the specification of reliability, availability and maintainability. In: The Proceedings of the International Underwater Technology Conference (UTC 1994), London, UK, April 20-21 (1994)

8. API RP (Recommended Practice) 17N, Recommended Practice for Subsea Production System Reliability and Technical Risk Management. American Petroleum Institute, Washington, D.C. (2009)
9. Visser, R.C.: Offshore accidents, regulations and industry standards. In: The Proceedings of the Society Petroleum Engineers (SPE 2011), Anchorage, Alaska, May 7-11 (2011)
10. Energy Institute and Lloyd's Register, Guidelines for the management of integrity of subsea facilities, England, p. 4 (2009)
11. Moreno-Trejo, J., Markeset, T.: Mapping Factors Influencing the Selection of Subsea Petroleum Production Systems. In: Frick, J., Laugen, B. (eds.) APMS 2011. IFIP AICT, vol. 384, pp. 242–250. Springer, Heidelberg (2012)
12. Brandt, H., Eriksen, R.: RAM analysis for deepwater subsea developments. In: The Proceedings of the Offshore Technology Conference (OTC 2001), Houston, Texas, April 30-May 3 (2001)
13. Markeset, T.: Design for performance: Review of current research in Norway. In: The Proceedings of Condition Monitoring and Diagnostic Engineering Management (COMADEM 2010), Nara, Japan, June 28-July 2 (2010)
14. Schneider, J., Gaul, A., Neumann, C., Hogräfer, J., WellBow, W., Schwan, M., Schnettler, A.: Asset management techniques. International Journal of Electrical Power & Energy Systems 28(9), 643–654 (2006)
15. Roberts, C., Laing, T.: Achieving reliability improvement for subsea challenges. In: The Proceedings of the Subsea Controls and Data Acquisition Conference (SCADA 2002), Paris, France, June 13-14, pp. 101–110 (2002)
16. Last, G., Williams, P.: An introduction to ROV operations, p. 107. Oilfield Publications, Ledbury (1991)
17. Kelly, A.: Strategic maintenance planning, p. 91. Elsevier, Amsterdam (2006)
18. Goldsmith, R., Eriksen, R., Childs, M., Saucier, B., Deegan, F.: Lifecycle cost of deepwater production systems. In: The Proceedings of the Offshore Technology Conference, OTC 2001, Houston, Texas, April 30-May 3 (2001)
19. Holmberg, K., Adgar, A., Arnaiz, A., Jantunen, E., Mascolo, J., Mekid, S. (eds.): E-maintenance, 1st edn. Springer, London (2010) ISBN 978-1-84996-204-9
20. Phillips, R., Holley, S.: Creating value and enhancing operational efficiency with the subsea e-field. In: SPE128705, The Proceedings of the SPE Intelligent Energy Conference, Utrecht, The Netherlands, March 23-24 (2010)
21. Moreno-Trejo, J., Markeset, T.: Identifying Challenges in the Development of Subsea Petroleum Production Systems. In: Frick, J., Laugen, B. (eds.) APMS 2011. IFIP AICT, vol. 384, pp. 251–259. Springer, Heidelberg (2012)
22. McAndrews, K.L.: Consequences of Macondo: a summary of recently proposed and enacted changes to US offshore drilling safety and environmental regulation. In: SPE143718, The Proceedings of the SPE Americas E&P Health, Safety, Security and Environmental Conference, Houston, Texas, USA, March 21-23 (2011)

Improving Periodic Preventive Maintenance Strategies Using Condition Monitoring Data

Guro Ravnestad[1], Sukhvir Singh Panesar[2], Dina Kayrbekova[2], and Tore Markeset[2]

[1] Apply Sørco, P.O. Box 8040, 4068 Stavanger, Norway
{guro.ravnestad,sukhvir.singh.panesar}@applysørco.no
[2] University of Stavanger, N-4036 Stavanger, Norway
{dina.kayrbekova,tore.markeset}@uis.no

Abstract. Due to reduction in petroleum production and aging production facilities, the Norwegian oil and gas industry is interested in optimization maintenance strategies and reducing costs. Currently the maintenance strategies are based on predetermined periodic (calendar or use time) preventive maintenance strategies that are developed based on statistical data and/or recommendation from the manufacturers. One possibility currently being explored is to use condition monitoring data available in the process monitoring system, to update and improve the predetermined periodic preventive maintenance strategies. Furthermore, we discuss some issues and challenges of the integration of available condition monitoring data in the planning and optimization of predetermined preventive maintenance strategies.

Keywords: Predetermined periodic preventive maintenance, Condition based predictive maintenance, Maintenance strategy.

1 Introduction

Globalization, high customer needs and tough competition force companies to reduce the production downtime and increase the reliability and performance of their equipment [1]. This is also the case in the oil and gas industry on the Norwegian Continental Shelf (NCS) where there is an increasing focus on the development of maintenance strategies that are cost-effective and efficient as well as reducing risks to health, safety and environment (HSE). Generally, the maintenance routines are developed based on the generic maintenance strategies, best practices, manufacturers' recommendations, etc., and are tailor-made for each installation. Currently, on many of the older offshore installations, the preventive maintenance programs are mainly predetermined periodic based (calendar time or operational use). However, many researchers recommend maintenance strategies based on the real asset condition [2], [3] where condition monitoring data enables proactive planning and optimization of maintenance activities based on the real equipment degradation.

In recent decades there has been a change in how the industry handles maintenance partly due to the development in information and communication technology (ICT)

J. Frick and B. Laugen (Eds.): APMS 2011, IFIP AICT 384, pp. 260–267, 2012.
© IFIP International Federation for Information Processing 2012

[4]. Furthermore, recent advances in sensor- and inter-communication technology have enabled the collection and interpretation of useful information concerning the equipment health. It is possible to generate data that gives valuable information about the asset condition [5]. The inherent advantage with this kind of strategy is that some of the redundant maintenance activities can be avoided, thus optimizing maintenance strategies.

However, the limitation is often the lack of appropriate sensor technology designed for petroleum production facilities which have set requirements with respect to explosion-proof technology. Also, the sensor technology is mainly developed on rotary equipment, but static equipment still lacks robust sensors and remote control technology [6]. The condition of such assets can mainly be assessed by inspections which are expensive and prone to risks as well as subject to individual judgments [7], [8]. However, on oil and gas facilities there is a large amount of instrumentation. This may possibly provide a large source of information concerning the condition and state of the equipment if efforts are taken to explore the possibilities of using the information for the purpose of equipment condition and health assessment.

Much research has been performed with respect to the development of preventive maintenance programs [9-11]. There also exists abundant literature on condition monitoring at equipment level as well as for single systems [12], [13]. However, the literature is scarce for the development of CBM on multi-systems as well as for the development of dynamic preventive maintenance strategies.

Based on a study in the Norwegian oil and gas industry and on a literature review, this paper identifies and discusses some of the issues, opportunities and challenges concerning the integration of condition monitoring data to improve the effectiveness and efficiency of predetermined periodic preventive maintenance strategies.

2   Maintenance Practices on the NCS

The Norwegian oil and gas industry has a high focus on maintenance strategies, both in planning and performance. In addition to the stringent regulations being set for new installations, installations that outlive their initial design life as a result of improved drilling technologies are placed under strict safety demands through national and international standards. The use of integrated operations in the maintenance activities is increasing, and more and more maintenance activities can be performed and/or planned from onshore communication and control posts [14]. The integration of operation and maintenance activities is constantly revised.

Developing effective and efficient maintenance strategies is essential to a company operating in the oil and gas industry wishing to ensure safe, effective and efficient production processes and profitability. Through defining maintenance goals and objectives and formulating maintenance strategies, the company can reach the overall aim of creating value by ensuring the highest possible HSE levels, increasing the reliability of the production, ensuring cost effectiveness, and increasing the competitive ability of the company [15]. Offshore maintenance activities are based on the company's overall maintenance strategy and in some cases on specific maintenance strategies for certain types of equipment.

Safe operations and prevention of accidents is a regulatory requirement. The safety of the installation, systems and the equipment is a responsibility of the operator companies. No comprises can be made on the safety related issues. Furthermore, the equipment connected to the safety functions and/or barrier system become part of the critical equipment. In addition to the equipment failure modes, the availability and performance requirements influence the maintenance requirements of such equipment. The safety requirements influence the facility, system and equipment performance and thus the maintenance needs. The important step in the optimization process is to identify the maintenance needs based on the performance requirements and on the needs to maintaining the technical condition of the equipment. Once the maintenance needs are identified then "just sufficient" maintenance activities are planned and executed at "just in time" to minimize or reduce the unexpected equipment failures. Maintenance strategies developed and implemented with this philosophy can help in optimization of maintenance on a facility.

2.1   Predetermined Periodic (Time or Use Based) Preventive Maintenance

Preventive maintenance is planned maintenance that aims to mitigate wear by maintaining the equipment from the start, and throughout all, of its operating lifetime [10]. Studies have shown that this fashion of operation costs about $13 per horsepower per year [16]. Preventive maintenance activities can be either calendar time based or operational use based, meaning that the maintenance activities planned are based on either fixed time intervals or on accumulated operational/running time. The key objective in this strategy is to perform improvement and restorative maintenance before the equipment breaks down or no longer performs to the originally set standards. The preventive maintenance strategy allows maintenance activities to be planned and executed at times when the impact of downtime will be the least.

Different types of equipment acquire different maintenance intervals based on frequency of failure and failure criticality. One of the challenges in preventive maintenance is to set the right interval. It is essential to ensure that: 1) Costly and unnecessary maintenance activities are not performed long before maintenance is actually needed; 2) Costly corrective failures do not occur due to too long intervals between planned preventive maintenance activities [17].

Companies delivering maintenance or condition monitoring services often also offer analyses to find such best time intervals. These intervals are normally based on manufacturers' recommendations, general industry recommendations, governing rules and regulations, statistical data and experience.

2.2   Condition Based (Predictive) Preventive Maintenance

Condition based predictive maintenance is a systemized maintenance strategy that aims to forestall failure based on tracking the performance or state of a piece of equipment. Predictive maintenance aims to run equipment for as long as possible before maintenance is performed through planning and executing maintenance activities based on condition monitoring data and estimates of wear development based on historical data and experience as well as statistical information.

Condition monitoring is defined in [18] as "*the continuous or* periodic *measurement and interpretation of data to indicate the degraded condition (potential failure) of an item and the need for maintenance*". Beebe [13] explains that "*condition monitoring, on- or offline, is a type of maintenance inspection where an operational asset is monitored and the obtained data analyzed to detect signs of degradation, diagnose cause of faults, and predict how long it can be safely or economically run*". The aim of condition monitoring is to be able to provide condition based maintenance, increasing the functional lifetime of the asset and decreasing the life cycle costs [19].

Condition monitoring of equipment can be performed manually, automatically or as a mix of the two, and concerns all processes of gaining, transforming and interpreting data concerning the state of equipment or processes. Physical features of the equipment are monitored using different types of sensors and instrumentation. Such features can be process variables like pressure, flow and temperature, or equipment variables such as vibration.

Offline condition monitoring refers to such measurements being taken repeatedly in set time intervals, often performed by specialists physically going out in the field to take the measurements or by process workers familiar with the technology and equipment. Online condition monitoring refers to the sampling of measurements in a continuous manner, with sensors and transponders connected to the equipment sending the signal in real time.

The choice of utilizing on- or offline condition monitoring is based on several factors, the most important of them being:

• The rate of change in the feature that is to be measured
• The criticality of the equipment with respect to HSE factors
• The criticality of the equipment with respect to production
• The expected mean time before failure (MTBF)

The idea is to monitor and log machinery and equipment performance through key performance indicators in order to predict maintenance demands early. One can thus estimate how the degradation evolves and the performance decreases over time. Through using such performance indicators one can measure the performance of the equipment and compare the results with initial performance levels. Thus the output is found, and analysis can determine the equipment condition. When performance degradation is observed the organization can start planning appropriate compensative maintenance activities and execute them at a time convenient for the management and projection plans before the actual failure event, as shown in Figure 1a [20].

By utilizing predictive maintenance one can schedule maintenance activities when the potential production losses are minimal, thus decreasing the total cost of the maintenance activity. Figure 1b illustrates that the speed of performance degradation is important. If the failure is instantaneous, as in curve A, the failure is difficult if not impossible to predict using condition monitoring. If the performance degradation is as shown in curves B and C, one may choose continuous or periodic condition monitoring respectively, also dependent on the criticality of the equipment.

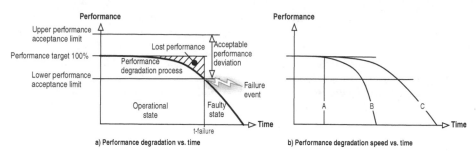

Fig. 1. System performance degradation: a) Performance degradation and failure vs. time; b) Performance degradation speed vs. time [20]

3   Potential of Using Condition Monitoring to Improve Periodic Preventive Maintenance

An integrated maintenance scheme is being developed with and alongside condition monitoring and is believed to have great potential. The advantage of this method is that downtime due to maintenance is reduced as activities are not performed when they are not needed, and an increase in uptime can be achieved, as shown in Figure 2. If properly implemented, this strategy would yield longer time for planning activities and purchasing spare parts, decreasing the need for large and/or expensive spare parts inventories. As maintenance work can be planned for in advance, activities can be planned at the opportune moment with respect to production and availability of personnel, as shown in Figure 2.

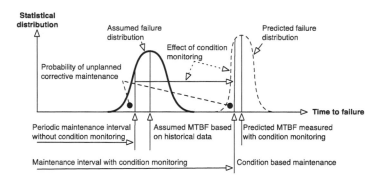

Fig. 2. Periodic maintenance based on assumed failure distribution and maintenance based on monitoring of real performance degradation and condition [20]

The disadvantages of this method are that unnecessary maintenance work might be performed if the degradation of the equipment is not correctly assessed. A need for post-maintenance maintenance might occur due to the break-in of new components, improper assembly or failures induced during maintenance [17]. Furthermore, the probability of detecting the failure is never 100%, and failures requiring expensive correction may occur [20]. In addition, by introducing more sensors and instrumentation, one also increases the complexity of the system, and one may experience sensor or instrumentation failures as well. Predictive maintenance also requires that the maintenance workers have skills and competence in condition monitoring practices, techniques and analysis to be able to take full advantage of the methods. Thus, either an adequate training program needs to be started or the work can be outsourced to a service company that is capable of providing the necessary skills and techniques.

The frequency of conduct of maintenance activities has to be linked to realistic mean time between failures. Moreover, functionality and performance degradation of the equipment has to be monitored in a manner that sufficient time is available for the maintenance managers to plan and organize selected maintenance activity execution. The subsystems and components will have different deterioration processes depending on their construction, materials, usage, and exposure to external conditions. Deterioration may be modelled based on failure characteristics and operating environmental characteristics; i.e., modeling deterioration in terms of a time-dependent stochastic process [21]. Relevant models are, for example, the P-F interval, proportional hazard modeling (PHM) - a multivariate regression analysis and Markov-processes [22].

The other method to estimate equipment degradation is by use of condition monitoring techniques such as vibration monitoring (e.g. belt, gear drive, or surfaces with components with relative motion), temperature (e.g. electrical components, bearing houses, hydraulic pumps, etc.), lubricant monitoring (transmission components like gears, cams, bearings). The operating context is an important factor, which influences degradation and can be classified into three operating regimes, namely, normal, marginal and hostile operating contexts [23]. Under the influence of operating context, condition levels are modulated, thereby true level of degradation cannot be inferred by mere trending of condition indicator's level. Hence, operating context needs to be considered while using condition indicator level to infer state of equipment.

4   Discussion and Concluding Remarks

Basing preventive maintenance on time and usage intervals alone may no longer be the best practice and an optimized way of developing maintenance programs. In general, the preventive maintenance programs are developed in the pre-operation stages, and the information from the condition monitoring is received in the operation stages.

Condition based maintenance (CBM) can in principle help in improving the effectiveness and efficiency of predetermined periodic maintenance strategies, but the industry faces challenges in effectively implementing the CBM. Moreover, the challenge is to integrate the information available from the condition monitoring sources as well as from the preventive maintenance plans to improve the effectiveness and efficiency of the maintenance programs [24].

The process of integrating the condition monitoring should be planned in the pre-operation stages. The maintenance engineers responsible for the development of maintenance programs should be able to foresee and plan the integration of likely condition monitoring information available in the operations stage. By identifying opportunities to include real-time condition data, the preventive maintenance routines based on fixed schedules should become more dynamic, and equipment health should improve.

However, today the information from sensor technology is mainly utilized for better and safe control of operations. Measurements such as flow, pressure and temperature assist in control of the processes, and most of the process shutdowns, emergency shutdowns and equipment shutdowns are conducted through the control rooms by use of the sensor technology. The same sensors may be used to gain information of the health of the equipment and the performance degradation processes, but, as mentioned, the integration of such vital process information in maintenance management is still a challenge.

The main focus of any production company is to strive towards minimizing their failure rate and downtime in order to maximize production – without production no income is generated, but expenses are still running for the company. The actual cost of equipment downtime may be more than that of the repair and maintenance work, spare parts and the maintenance logistics and administration.

If failure occurs at a time where the market value of the product or the production itself is high, the financial disadvantages will be larger than if one can plan and executed a maintenance task at times with reduced production. In order to minimize the cost of downtime and failures, maintenance management is important, and activities must be carefully planned and executed to occur at a specific time, when the cost of production downtime is the least.

Thus arises the classic dilemma within maintenance: as the operation crew craves maximum uptime in order to produce as much as possible, the maintenance crew craves more downtime in order to provide better care for the equipment. To balance the internal differences, maintenance strategies are based on the company's goals and objectives, and activities are planned and scheduled based on the available technology and nature of the equipment.

The industrial maintenance practices can be considered a result of the mixture of the industrial and academic research and development. The maintenance strategies must encompass the financial demands for effectiveness and the overall safety standards, and are subject to change as the technology progresses. By combining the benefits from predictive and preventive maintenance, a more knowledge-based approach to maintenance can be achieved. However, this is rarely seen in the industry, where the two strategies often coexist without merging.

References

1. Tsang, A.H.C.: Condition-based maintenance: tools and decision making. Journal of Quality in Maintenance Engineering 1, 3–18 (1995)
2. Tsang, A.H.C., Yeung, W.K., Jardine, A.K.S., Leung, B.P.K.: Data management for CBM optimization. Journal of Quality in Maintenance Engineering 12, 37–51 (2006)
3. Dhillon, B.S.: Reliability-centered maintenance - engineering maintainability. Gulf, Houston (1999)
4. Kans, M.: The advancement of maintenance information technology - a literature review. Journal of Quality in Maintenance Engineering 15, 5–16 (2009)
5. Campos, J.: Development in the application of ICT in condition monitoring and maintenance. Computers in Industry 60, 1–20 (2009)
6. Ravnestad, G.: Integration of condition monitoring data to preventive maintenance activities: Issues, opportunities and challenges. Master thesis, University of Stavanger, Norway (2010)

7. Levitt, J.: Complete guide to preventive and predictive maintenance. Industrial Press, New York (2003)
8. Wireman, T.: Preventive maintenance. Industrial Press, New York (2008)
9. Löfsten, H.: Management of industrial maintenance ± economic evaluation of maintenance policies. Int. Journal of Operations & Production Management 19, 716–737 (1999)
10. Mobley, R.K.: Designing a preventive maintenance program - maintenance fundamentals, 2nd edn. Butterworth Heinemann, Burlington (2004)
11. Eti, M.C., Ogaji, S.O.T., Probert, S.D.: Reducing the cost of preventive maintenance (PM) through adopting a proactive reliability-focused culture. Applied Energy 83, 1235–1248 (2006)
12. Rao, B.K.N.: Condition monitoring - The way forward - handbook of condition monitoring. Elsevier, Oxford (1996)
13. Beebe, R.S.: Predictive maintenance of pumps using condition monitoring. Elsevier, Oxford (2004)
14. Stacey, A., Sharp, J.V.: Safety factor requirements for the offshore industry. Engineering Failure Analysis 14, 442–458 (2007)
15. Panesar, S.S., Kumar, R., Markeset, T.: Development of maintenance strategies for offshore production facilities. In: The Proceedings of the 3rd World Congress on Engineering Asset Management and Intelligent Maintenance Systems (WCEAM-IMS 2008), Beijing, China, October 28-30, pp. 1227–1232 (2008) ISBN 978-1-84882-216-0
16. Piotrowski, J.: Effective predictive and pro-active maintenance for pumps. Maintenance World (2007)
17. Markeset, T.: Design for production performance in Arctic locations considering maintenance and support services. In: The Proceedings of the Mine Planning and Equipment Selection Conference (MPES 2008), Beijing, China, October 20-22 (2008)
18. NORSOK Z008 Criticality analysis for maintenance purposes. Norwegian Technology Centre (2001), http://www.standard.no/PageFiles/961/Z-008.pdf (accessed June 2)
19. Conachey, R.M., Montgomery, R.L.: Application of reliability-centered maintenance techniques to the marine industry. SNAME, Texas Section (2003)
20. Markeset, T., Kayrbekova, D.: Capacity-driven, activity-based life-cycle costing in strategic maintenance decision-making: modeling the cost of performance. To appear in Journal of Quality in Maintenance Engineering (2012)
21. Moubray, J.: Reliability-centered maintenance. Butterworth-Heinemann, Oxford (1997)
22. van Noortwijk, J.M.: A survey of the application of gamma processes in maintenance. Reliability Engineering and System Safety 94(1), 2–21 (2009)
23. Edwin, V.K., Chaturvedi, S.K.: Application of predictive maintenance techniques for failure rate modelling of electric motors in process industry. In: The Proceedings of the International Conference on Reliability and Safety Engineering, INCRESE 2006 (2006)
24. Saranga, H.: Relevant condition-parameter strategy for an effective condition-based maintenance. Journal of Quality in Maintenance Engineering 8, 92–105 (2002)

Identification of Factors Causing Time and Cost Overruns in Offshore Petroleum Modification Projects

Dina Kayrbekova[1], Tore Markeset[1], and Sukhvir Singh Panesar[2]

[1] University of Stavanger, N-4036 Stavanger, Norway
{dina.kayrbekova,tore.markeset}@uis.no
[2] ApplySørco, P.O. Box 8040, N-4068 Stavanger, Norway
sukhvir.singh.panesar@applysorco.no

Abstract. Many of the production facilities and technologies operated on the Norwegian Continental Shelf are getting older and need to be modified to maintain the production performance at the desirable level. Each modification project is unique, and therefore needs to be evaluated and verified with consideration to all specifications. However, the oil and gas industry experience shows that the execution of modification projects within predefined time and cost are rather an exception, than a rule. In this paper we identify and discuss some of the factors that cause time and cost overruns in offshore facility modification projects. Furthermore, we discuss alternative cost methods to improve the quality and the accuracy of costs and time assessments.

Keywords: Modification project, Time and cost overruns factors, Cost evaluation, Activity-based life-cycle cost method.

1   Introduction

The development of offshore oil and gas is technologically complex and capital-intensive and utilizing increasingly advanced and complex products. In Norway many offshore production facilities have been developed in the North Sea in the south of Norway and in the Norwegian Sea. However, many of the oil and gas production facilities operated on the Norwegian Continental Shelf are getting older and require more investment, upgrades, modifications and more maintenance to achieve the maximum economic potential from the petroleum production operations. A large percentage of the projected cost can be allocated to maintenance and support activities associated with keeping the production facility at a desirable operational state. The cost of system maintenance and support can often be substantial, depending on industry and type of systems. Moreover, more reliable, cost-effective and environmentally friendly technical solutions are required to keep production performance and Health, Safety and Environment (HSE) issues at an acceptable and desirable level. Each modification project is unique and can vary in size, character and complexity. Modification project design assumptions are subject to creative solutions, as the fast speed of technology development and equipment degradation makes equipment/systems which are already in use, obsolete.

J. Frick and B. Laugen (Eds.): APMS 2011, IFIP AICT 384, pp. 268–275, 2012.

Furthermore, modification work (e.g. material cost and installation methods), depends on the modifications' purposes related to a specific function, or facility or location. The purpose of the modification project is to utilize the existing infrastructure for a new bulk of modified functions. New duties and functions can lead to disruption of the orderly progress of work on ongoing production and a growth trend in more material needs. Also, an increase in the complexity of work will strain project resources and time frames. Poor quality concept development in the modification projects can increase the risk of overrun from the pre-defined time and cost and of exposure to a change in the nature and quantity of work to be performed (e.g. resources and man-hours). A change in the quantity of resources and man-hours can result in cost growth and time overruns. Thus, modification project development phases need to be evaluated and verified with special consideration [see e.g. 1, 2] as it is still a challenge to execute modification projects effectively and within pre-defined, expected and predicted costs and time frames.

In the European standard prEN 13306, modification is defined as: "*a combination of all technical, administrative and managerial actions intended to change an item*" [3]. A modification project is a temporary multi-discipline alliance of work with defined tasks, goals, framework and budget. Furthermore, different installations' locations, work and installation technologies, climate conditions, authorities' recommendations and regulations need to be considered during the concept development of a modification project. It is important to identify all related cost elements. The direct and overhead costs are often not visible at the beginning of the modification project development. The oil & gas industry experience shows that modification projects always tend to rise above pre-defined and predicted costs and time, "*and large cost and time overruns has been the rule rather than the exception*" [4].

In this paper, we identify and discuss some of the factors that result in time and cost overruns in the development and execution of a modification project. Furthermore, we propose and discuss alternative cost assessment methods to be used in modification project development to reduce time and cost overruns.

2   Identification of Factors Causing Time and Cost Overruns in Modification Projects

Based on discussions with industrial experts from the Norwegian oil and gas industry as well as a literature review, the following factors are identified as causing time and cost overruns in the development and execution of an offshore production facility modification project:

1. Project control and integrated project team competence (management quality, human factors, work environment)
2. Data availability and uncertainty (information sources, knowledge, quality assurance, experience)
3. Reports and documentation (quality control, document formats and standards)
4. Indeterminate interface between the existing facility and the new installation – integration (depth of the technical understanding, micro/macro thinking, strategy and tactics)
5. Evaluation methods of technical solution alternatives (credible decision making, suitable decision-making support tool, suitable cost-assessment method)

2.1   Project Control and Integrated Project Team Competence

A multi-discipline organization such as that used in modification projects needs high quality supervision, coordination and control. The key responsibilities of modification project management are to keep an accurate overview and precise control during all phases of the project's concept development and execution to ensure that all required and reasonable decisions are taken, and all associated work and support activities are planned and will be followed up circumspectly. It is important to have an environment of good cooperation between involved project divisions, and to ensure that all goals and requirements for the project's development and its execution are met and clearly understood in the early stages of the modification project development. Later changes in the project can be costly and/or result in delays.

During the review process, the following issues need to be assessed: resources, available technical solution alternatives, HSE issues, vendor market and cost. Moreover, in order to develop a selected concept, relevant uncertainties need to be assessed and a plan for uncertainty reduction needs to be established. It is essential to have control processes in place; these aim to approve the selected concept for further detailed development, to verify that the concept is likely to be profitable and technically feasible in accordance with the pre-defined time plan and costs, and to provide the best management prospects possible, this will ensure the opportunity to take corrective actions in time to avoid growth in the volume of resources and significant deviations from the original assumptions regarding costs and time. It is critical to perform a systematic review and control of the modification project's baselines, such as scope verifications and updating costs' estimates; this should take place as an interactive process between the project controllers and estimators [5], [1].

The management work processes may be optimized for more efficiency and better quality by employing a highly qualified integrated project team; by application of suitable project decision-making support tools, resourceful databases and first-class organized execution procedures; and by skilled usage of existing experience. For example, individual understanding of the equipment and the long experience of the specialist can affect and increase the quality and reliability of the engineering decision making during the project's concept development. The more skilled specialists are involved in the modification project team, the better track records and more accurate time and costs' assessment can be expected during the project's development and execution phases. It is important to emphasize that it is advantageous for the team members responsible for economic evaluation to have a competence in the technical environment as well [6], [7].

2.2   Data Availability and Uncertainty

Each modification project is unique. Thus it is difficult to use a previous project's budget estimates without adjustments to evaluate the project costs at hand. The uniqueness of some modification projects can make for restricted availability of data. The quality of the available data may be hard to assess and the uncertainties need to be taken into account and analyzed separately. Nevertheless, the data and costs' estimates from similar modification projects can be accessible and obtainable if the information is open to use and not sensitive. Existing experience, knowledge and data from similar modification projects can be used as the basis for costs' and time assessments, as well as being helpful for gaining better knowledge of how to increase the quality of control and the total overview of the modification project at hand. Data and information which may be used for the evaluation of alternative technical solutions may be obtained from multiple sources and need to be meaningful and comparable. Reliable and meaningful data is one of the key factors in the early stages of the modification project's development, as poorly conducted early phases and poor quality data used in the development of the modification project can in turn lead to costs' and time overruns.

This can be exemplified in obviously different data packages which can be provided by different suppliers or vendors. In addition, the vendor/supplier can lack relevant equipment reliability and maintenance data and have a low capability to optimize a product or fail to provide the right technical solution. The consequence of this misinterpretation of data collected during concept evaluation may also result in costs' and time overruns from the pre-defined budget of the modification project during the execution phases. As poor quality data will be used in the development phases of the modification project, so the actual cost will overtake the budgeted cost. Moreover, the high uncertainty and incorrectness in costs and time assessments can be revealed due to the lack of suitable decision-making support tools and cost assessment methods. Uncertainty analysis must be performed in order to identify uncertainty elements that may affect cost and time; analysis of the uncertainties can be performed using variable statistical methods such as stochastic variable or probability distribution, etc. [8].

2.3   Reports and Documentation

The outcome from the early phases of the modification project's development is typically reports and documentation which the basis for approving the project according to economic and technical criteria. These reports and documentations normally need to be sent to the management, partners and authorities. The level of detail given in the various documentations needs to be sufficient to satisfy the requirements. The requirements for the level of detail will vary among management, partners and authorities. The consequence of an unsatisfactory level of provided details can result in delays; for example, one of the parties will require more information and data reports which will take time to produce.

However, reports which are too detailed can result in delays as well, as it can take time to decipher relevant information and data which are of importance. Thus, it is critical for involved parties to agree about the level of detailed information, data and specifications that they may require during the development and execution phases of the modification project. Many modification projects have been delayed or terminated in the early development phases due to disagreement between parties concerning the execution plans and the lack of required information in time [5].

2.4   Indeterminate Interface between Existing Facility and the Modification

The integration of the modification solution with the existing industrial facility is one of the core activities of the modification project. Lack of details on systems surrounding structure, bulk of the existing infrastructure, specifics and parameters of installations, as well as lack of detailed identification of modification activities and their detailed descriptions (e.g. type and volume of work, duration, scheduling of activities' performance, man-hours and competence of workers needed) may significantly impact on the modification project's development, costs and execution time. An indeterminate interface between the existing facility and the modification can challenge the execution of the project within the expected time and budget. It is a challenge to perform an accurate and adequate assessment of the time, costs and resources (e.g. material, man-hours) needed for the integration of the modification solutions and existing installations. Due to this uncertainty, it is hard to execute it within predefined costs and time frames. The industrial facility's function can be affected by integration activities, but these effects are hard to assess in the early phase of project development; often it can be evaluated more precisely only when project development proceeds to its detailed engineering phase.

The integration and installation processes require an extensive quantity of temporary work, demolitions, and relocations, etc. All concerns which are specific to a modification project need to be considered with respect to HSE requirements, reliability issues and from an economic perspective. Moreover, it is important to identify general complexities and specific conditions related to modification work as early as possible. The tendency of the work's complexity and need for extra resources to expand can interrupt ongoing work processes and can result in cost and time overruns [1]. For example, the modification changes (e.g. new equipment) to be implemented in one system can affect the function of other systems and produce the need for extra activities, which can be costly and time-consuming processes as well as creating contractual, administrative or organizational challenges for the project team. Furthermore, mitigating actions to reduce the possible cost and time overruns need to be considered.

2.5   Evaluation Methods of Technical Solution Alternatives

The evaluation of the technical solution alternatives' profitability and their business opportunities' feasibility needs to be performed in accordance with corporate requirements and business plans. Examining, comparing and selecting reliable and cost-effective technical, managerial and organizational solutions still constitute one of the bottlenecks when designing or modifying oil and gas production facilities. The economic evaluation of the comparable alternative technical solutions usually starts in the feasibility phase of the modification project development. The goal of this economic assessment is to select the most technologically acceptable and cost-effective alternative and eliminate uneconomic solutions. The cost assessment and estimation performance can continue through all the project's development phases, normally to the end point of concept development. However, it is still a challenge to make credible engineering decisions from an economic perspective and to provide reliable and well predicted end results. Moreover, it is still a challenge to predict from all related and possible perspectives, the consequences and changes of the selected technical solution alternative (modification) on the function of the modifying facility.

A suitable decision-support tool in a modification project cost assessment can be one of the key elements that can increase the cost and time assessment quality and provide support for the engineering decisions which need to be made during the selection and assessment processes. However, there are no standard decision-support tools which are suitable for cost and time assessments and capable of taking into account all the different modification project specifications. A tool that would help to inform a decision maker about future expenditure, and how to manage the existing budget and how to make decisions which lead to the lowest costs. A tool is needed that will assist a decision maker in obtaining more reliable and accurate cost and time assessments, in harnessing detailed information of the project control activities (typically estimates, collected data with metrics), and in eliminating data duplication processes in project administration [9], [1].

3   Discussion: Activity-Based Life-Cycle Costing as an Alternative Decision-Making Tool

In spite of long experience with offshore modification projects, we often find that they result in time and cost overruns. We identified some of the factors that cause time and cost overruns and found they are multifaceted, intertwined and complex. In the European standard definition it is noted that a modification is not a "replacement by an equivalent item" and that it has to do with "changing the required function to a new required function" [3]. This means that new or at least newer technology needs to be integrated with old or existing technology. Not only does the project team need to understand the existing technology used on the offshore production facility, but it needs to select the best option from the alternative technical solutions and integrate it with the existing installed technology.

Often one finds that information and data are missing about the existing installation, the new technology, and how the existing and new technology should be integrated. This may result in the team not being able to estimate what kind of activities are needed, how long they will take, what kind of material and tools are needed, how they should be tested, and so on. In addition, the project team lacks a tool that is better suited for the difficult task of planning the time and estimating the costs in modification projects. The goal of such a tool should be to define, evaluate and select the most cost-effective, reliable and suitable solution and to accurately predict the time the project will take [see e.g. 10-16].

Different engineering and economic techniques exist with the main goal of identifying and choosing the technical alternative that generates the highest revenue over the expected lifetime (e.g. life-cycle cost (LCC) analysis, cost-benefit analysis, activity-based life-cycle costing (AB-LCC), capacity-driven or time-driven activity-based life-cycle cost analysis) (see [10-19]). The goal is to justify alternative technical solutions with financial perspectives using net present value concepts and providing net present value calculations for discrete or probabilistic decisions [10], [15]. Moreover, the tools should help the decision maker to screen and eliminate costs before they can be incurred by taking mitigating actions and managing some economic risks related to cost and cash flows.

However, experience shows that often the standard LCC and cost benefit methods cannot handle uncertainty credibly enough, and this leads to wrong cost estimates. Thus, an alternative costs' evaluation method is needed [12]. Turney [17], in discussing activity-based costing, suggests that knowledge of activity costs may help a decision maker to focus attention on activities' performance processes, structure and flow, and be helpful in identifying activity drivers with the greatest potential for costs' reduction, as well as to model the impact of cost-reduction actions. We know that a traditional cost method such as LCC will fail to provide information about activities that are needed to ensure modification project execution is continuously within the predicted and expected time and budgeted cost limits. A modification project is a complex blend of multi-discipline work and activities.

Emblemsvåg [14] suggests that the identification of the underlying drivers of business performance and critical success factors' processes can be performed and managed more efficiently using activity-based life-cycle costing (AB-LCC). Kaplan & Anderson [18] also suggest a simplified activity-based costing technique, named time-driven activity-based costing method, in which one identifies activities and then uses estimates of activity times to predict costs. We believe that by using a time-driven AB-LCC analysis method, a decision maker should be able to establish cause-and-effect relationships between the activities, time duration and the costs [see also 19]. Thus, one should be able to increase the long-term profitability by identifying improvement opportunities and by making appropriate and proactive adjustments during the project phases. In addition, it will be easier to keep track of what efforts are needed to achieve the desired performance and to avoid non-value-adding activities with respect to quality, time and efficiency.

4   Concluding Remarks

In this paper we have identified some of the main factors that cause time and cost overruns in offshore petroleum production facility modification projects. The use of better and more suitable cost and time evaluation methods are needed to improve the accuracy and quality of costs' evaluation and time predictions as well as support engineering decision-making during the design phases. It may be easier to avoid non-value-adding activities with respect to quality, time and efficiency, as well as to establish cause-and-effect relationships between the modification activities and the cost and to show what activities take place and to keep track of what efforts are needed to achieve the desired performance during modification project development and execution. Due to the need of identifying detail activities and equipment and technology in interfacing the modification with the existing production facility structure and equipment, we found that the activity based costing, time-driven activity-based costing, as well as time-driven activity-based life-cycle costing may be alternative assessment and decision-making tools in modification projects to reduce time and cost overruns. These methods are based on the identification and pricing of detail project activities, resources, material and overhead costs.

References

1. Fouche, D.P.: Performance Measurement, Estimating and Control of Offshore Modification Projects. Doctoral thesis. NTNU, Trondheim, Norway (2006) ISBN 82-471-7853-4, ISSN 1503-8181
2. Løkling, Ø.: Cost and Schedule Overruns in Modification Projects: Reasons and Measures to Avoid. Master thesis, University of Stavanger, Stavanger, Norway (2010)

3. PrEN, 13306: Draft European Standard, Maintenance Terminology. European Committee for Standardization (1998)
4. Lunde, H., Tjaland, K.: Cost Effective Strategy for Modification Projects. In: The Proceeding of International Conference of Offshore Europe, Aberdeen, United Kingdom, September 5-8 (1995)
5. Coker, J., Gudmestad, O.: Introduction to Development of a Petroleum Installation (2003), http://www.norad.no/en/Thematic+areas/Energy/Oil+for+Developme nt/OfD+Information+Package/Resource+Management/_attachment/ 132962?_download=true&_ts=12375ce725a
6. NORSOK O-CR-002: Life Cycle Cost for Production Facility (1996), http://www.standard.no/en/Sectors/Petroleum/NORSOK-Standard-Categories/O-Operation/O-CR-002/
7. ISO: Petroleum and Natural Gas Industries-Life Cycle Costing - Part 3: Implementation guidelines. International standard (2001)
8. Aven, T.: Foundation of Risk Analysis: A Knowledge and Decision-Oriented Perspective. Wiley, Chichester (2003)
9. Kueng, P.: Process Performance Measurement System (PPMS): a Tool to Support Process Based Organizations. Journal of Total Quality Management 11(1), 67–85 (2000)
10. Fabrycky, W., Blanchard, B.S.: Life Cycle Cost and Economic Analysis. Prentice Hall, Englewood (1991)
11. Barringer, P., Weber, D.: Life-Cycle-Cost Tutorial. In: The Proceedings of the Fifth International Conference on Process Plant Reliability, Texas, Houston, USA, October 2-4 (1996)
12. Kaplan, R., Cooper, R.: Cost and Effect: Using Integrated Cost Systems to Drive Profitability and Performance. Harvard Business School Press, Boston (1998)
13. Kawauchi, Y., Rausand, M.: Life Cycle Cost (LCC) Analysis on Oil and Chemical Process Industries, Report, Norwegian University of Science and Technology, Trondheim, Norway (June 1999)
14. Emblemsvåg, J.: Life Cycle Costing Using Activity Based Costing and Monte Carlo Methods to Manage Future Costs and Risks. Wiley, New Jersey (2003)
15. Barringer, P.: Life-Cycle-Cost Summary. In: ICOMS 2003, Perth, Australia (2003)
16. Kayrbekova, D., Markeset, T.: Activity-based Life-cycle Costing Analysis for Design of Arctic Petroleum Facilities. In: The Proceedings of the 20th International Conference on Port and Ocean Engineering Under Arctic Conditions, Luleå, Sweden, June 9-12 (2009)
17. Turney, P.B.B.: Common Cents: How to Succeed with Activity-Based Costing and Activity-Based Management. McGraw-Hill, New York (2005)
18. Kaplan, R.S., Anderson, S.R.: Time-driven Activity-based Costing: A Simpler and More Powerful Path to Higher Profits. Harvard Business School Press, Boston (2007)
19. Markeset, T., Kayrbekova, D.: Capacity-driven, Activity-based Life-cycle Costing in Strategic Maintenance Decision Making: Modeling the Cost of Performance. Accepted for publication in Journal of Quality in Maintenance Engineering (2012)

Impact of Globalization on Model of Competition and Companies' Competitive Situation

Knut Erik Bang and Tore Markeset

University of Stavanger, N-4036 Stavanger, Norway
{knut.e.bang,tore.markeset}@uis.no

Abstract. Globalization has changed the competitive environment of companies. This paper aims to contribute to understanding the changes a company can face through analyzing the impact of drivers and effects of globalization on the models of industry competition and the company value chain. The boundaries between the forces of competition are fading as economic globalization has led to a new dynamic in the competitive situation where companies and activities of the value chains change places between forces and impact and interact with each other in new ways. The boundaries of companies and their core can and are being redefined. As this potential evolves through offshoring, outsourcing and value chain fragmentation, the pressure of competition forces a continuing and increasing move in this direction.

Keywords: Economic globalization, outsourcing, offshoring, value chain fragmentation, company competition.

1   Introduction

Economic globalization has changed the world over the last couple of decades. The objective of this study is to contribute to the understanding of how globalization affects the competitive environment of companies. The hypothesis put forward is that the increased competition from globalization has a significant impact on all the five forces of competition [1], creating a new dynamic where the boundaries between the forces and the boundaries of the company fade away. The impact of the drivers and effects of globalization on the forces of competition is evaluated.

In a literature study by Bang and Markeset [2], the main drivers of economic globalization that affect the competitive situation are identified to be 1) lower trade barriers; 2) lower transportation costs; 3) lower communication costs; 4) ICT development; and 5) the spread of technology, as shown in Figure 1.

These have a number of effects that are grouped into the areas of size, location and pressure. The size effects are larger market potential, larger number of potential clients, larger number of potential competitors and larger number of potential suppliers and partners. The location effects are fragmented value chains, offshoring, outsourcing and complex supply chains. The pressure effects are cost and price pressure, higher rate of change, more diverse markets, lower start-up barriers and lower visibility.

J. Frick and B. Laugen (Eds.): APMS 2011, IFIP AICT 384, pp. 276–286, 2012.

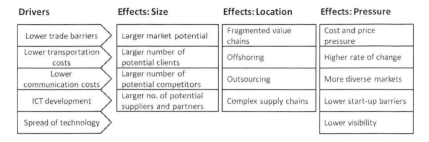

Fig. 1. Summary of the drivers and effects from globalization that affect the competitive situation [2]

When investigating how companies' competitive situations are affected by globalization, it is important to have a clear representation of what we mean by the competitive situation. Michael Porter's model of the five forces on competition [1] has become one of the most established approaches for viewing industry competition, and it is also applicable at the company level. The five forces consist of the industry rivalry between competitors, the bargaining power of buyers, the bargaining power of suppliers, the threat of new entrants and the threat of substitute products or services. To be able to assess the impact of globalization on a company's competitive situation, it will also be necessary to use the representation of a company as a value chain [3]. The company value chain shows the company as a set of value-adding activities linked together.

2   Effects on the Forces of Porter's Model of Competition

The drivers and effects of globalization are here evaluated in terms of their impact on the model of the five forces of competition.

2.1   Drivers

The drivers of globalization influence the five forces' model, as shown in Figure 2. Lower trade barriers affect the geographic barriers, both in opening up toward similar market segments and their internal competition, but also toward the other potential threats those markets might have. For a multi national company (MNC) that already has a worldwide presence, this can represent more potential competition within the different regions. For smaller and medium-sized companies that are present in a limited number of regions and often have been able to develop under protection from foreign competition, this can have a much more significant effect when their markets are opened up to foreign competition. In terms of the model, the boundaries around the industry competition start to fade away.

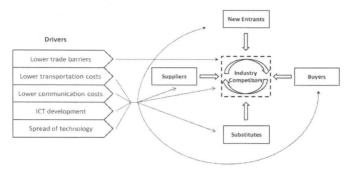

Fig. 2. The drivers of economic globalization and their effects on the forces of competition

Lower transportation costs and lower communication costs affect all the five forces of the model. Lower transportation cost increases sourcing opportunities within the industry, and, for the buyers, and the suppliers, supply options increase. Lower communication costs knit parties of the different forces together and reduce the benefits of previously limited knowledge. The developments within information and communication technology further level the playing field [4] and reduce the benefits of being an established player in the industry. It becomes more difficult to have unique knowledge of market potential, production techniques, methods and industry profitability. It then becomes easier for suppliers to make the step down the value chain or for buyers to decide to take a step up the chain. New entrants will likewise be better informed on the decision of entry. With regard to substitutes, the buyers will be more informed of their potential and they can access market channels more easily. The spread of technology, not only of ICT but also of manufacturing technology, further enables all of the parties to enter the competition. Access to the manufacturing technology may no longer be limited to existing industry players.

The impact of these changes is not only limited to the static picture of the model. The products and services of the competitive situation also change. The developments in ICT have led to digitization of most areas and the inclusion of a new technology in existing areas, or to a replacement of these. Porter [5] demonstrates how the forces of competition are affected by the internet and how the barriers are reduced and differences between competitors and between potential competitors are reduced. He argues that the fundamentals of competition have not changed, though new means of conducting business have become available and the possibilities the internet opens are included in the businesses and the products. In summary, the drivers are tearing down the barriers to industry competition and enable parties of the potential external forces to join in with the competition more easily.

2.2   Size Effects

The size of a company's competitive arena is arguably the biggest change caused by globalization. As the barriers of the competitive arena are reduced, the potential rivalry of competition includes all the players of previously separate markets now merged into one, as shown in Figure 3.

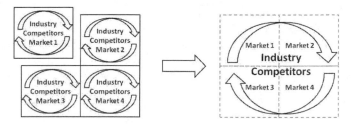

Fig. 3. Merging of separate markets into one large market

This theoretical model does not reflect the diversity and differences in preferences between the segments. However, it does show something more important: the increased number of potential direct competitors. For an individual company, the competitiveness in the integrated market depends on the competitiveness of the industry segment in which it is competing. Highly competitive segments that have been formed in a strong competitive cluster [6] should then in theory be successful also in the integrated market. However, the comparative differences [7] of locations, like wage differences, can change the relative competitiveness. In becoming part of a larger market, the market potential becomes larger, and the number of potential customers increases. While increased market and revenue potential is positive, the increase in number of clients at many locations increases the business complexity and places new requirements on the operation and management of a company. Moreover, all the forces affecting the competitive market increase as well, as shown in Figure 4. There are more potential suppliers to choose from, and more options in terms of how to set up your own value chain. Potential threats from new entries and from substitutes increase in the same fashion.

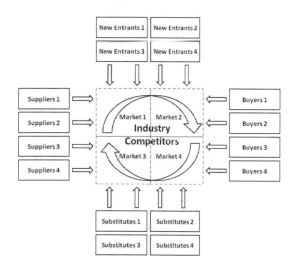

Fig. 4. Expanding the competition model

The model of the five forces of competition changes in the form of size and of diversity through markets coming together. Questions that then arise are whether the growth of the model is followed by integration, and whether the only change is the size. Porter [8] emphasize that the definition of boundaries for the industry is dependent on the five forces and how and where they interact. When the opportunities for a company have increased and allow them to sell products and services worldwide, the definition of the industry boundaries should possibly also be extended to include this geographical expansion. As we shall see from the other effects of globalization, the answer is more complicated than a simple yes.

2.3   Location Effects

Porter's value chain is a visualization of the activities in a company. A company's value chain is often shown as a sequence of value chains with the down-stream supplier's value chain preceding it, and the upstream buyer's value chain following it, as shown in Figure 5. Shown this way it is a simplification of a more complex reality with a company having multiple products and services, each having multiple suppliers and customers at different levels. It does however provide a useful model for analysis.

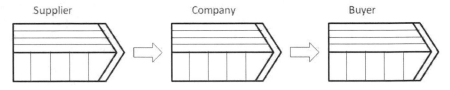

Fig. 5. The company value chain in a sequence of value chains

   In order to look into the effects of fragmentation of value chains, offshoring, outsourcing and complex supply chains, it is useful to put this sequence of value chains that is representative of a company's situation into the model of the five forces of competition representing the industry's competition. This is visualized in Fig. 6 and shows one company's situation in the competition and its relationships with other players.

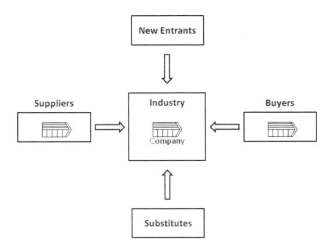

Fig. 6. A sequence of value chains represented in the model for industry competition

Fragmentation of value chains, or vertical disintegration, leads to more specializa-tion on individual tasks. For a traditional manufacturing company that has been li-mited in its geographical reach and has the production process located within that geographical reach, the fragmentation of the value chain can be seen as selection of which activities to keep within that area and within company boundaries. Figure 7 shows how the activities of a company's value chain through outsourcing can be spread out to be performed by several other companies.

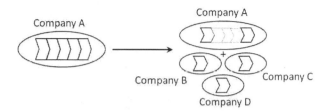

Fig. 7. Fragmentation of a simplified value chain

As the opportunities for offshoring and outsourcing have opened up through the ongoing process of globalization, the individual companies have to face these choices. The questions take the following form: for which activities is the company best able to add a higher value than competitors, and what kind of control should it have over the different activities? Mudambi and Venzin [9] state that:

"Offshoring and outsourcing are best analyzed as aspects of the global disaggrega-tion of the value chain and as attempts by firms to combine the comparative advantages of geographic locations with their own resources and competencies to maximize their competitive advantage. The interplay of comparative and competitive advantages deter-mines the optimal location of value chain components (offshoring decisions) as well as the boundaries of the firm and the control strategy (outsourcing decisions)."

A company can choose to keep the R&D activities and to offshore the different produc-tion activities and assembly to locations with lower wage costs, but keep the branding and sales and marketing functions. Putting this fragmented value chain into a static picture of the model of the five forces, it might look like Figure 8. Here different geo-graphical locations and parties of the different forces have come together in one com-bined market, but with regional differences of the forces. The R&D function (1) is kept in the original location. The first part of production (2) is offshored to a second location and outsourced to a supplier that represented a potential threat. He is then included in the value chain and in the industry competition somehow, but the idea here is to look at the static picture before implementation. The second part of production (3) is outsourced to a company at a different location; again, that will be a new player in the industry and thus represents a potential new entry in the model. Assembly of the parts into a final product (4) is also carried out at a different location, but is set up as a facility owned by the com-pany, hence being offshored but not outsourced. Another option that would be represented in the same way in the model would be to outsource assembly to a competi-tor or to establish a joint venture at that offshored location. The branding and marketing (5) is shown as being kept at the company's original location.

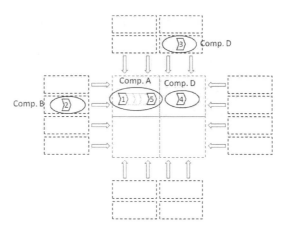

Fig. 8. Example of fragmentation and spread out of a value chain

The expanded model of the five forces can thus illustrate some of the new dynamics from these factors. In a competitive situation where offshoring and outsourcing have become viable options that reduce costs, a company may not gain competitiveness from these options if the competitors do the same, but may lose competitiveness and market position from the lack of exploiting these options. Mudambi and Venzin [9] assert that *"the distribution of value creation among individual value chain activities is not static. Value creation 'travels' in terms of location and control"*. This implies that the dynamics of the model will also change. Potential threats to competition become part of the industry whilst other threats vanish. The changes speed up, and the categorization of the different forces blurs as players from these categories enter or leave the competition and the interdependencies between parties increase.

2.4   Pressure Effects

The increased competitive pressure adds another dimension to the model. There is not only a sequential relationship between the drivers, the factors of size, the factors of location and the factors of pressure. The increased pressure on costs and prices adds to the drive for further offshoring and splitting-up activities between existing competitors and outsourcing to new ones that perform an even more specialized part of the value chain. The boundaries of the industry can then be hard to define. It may have expanded geographically, but should it still include the whole value chain as it was prior to globalization, or should the performance of the specialized tasks of the disintegrated value chain be defined as separate industries. The specialized tasks can be both an industry in itself before the interfaces between tasks change again, and they can be part of a higher-level industry. In a globalized world, the geographical boundaries can be easier to define than the industry itself. However, the increased diversity of the global market may add to the confusion of where the geographical boundaries should be placed. Lower barriers to start-up affect all the different forces. It adds to the ease with which a new player can enter the industry, as well as to how easy a substitute can be set up as a rival, or the suppliers and customers can enter the competitive arena.

The sum is that the competition speeds up; all the forces are much more closely interrelated and affect each other. The model of the five forces of competition can be argued to have become more a model of a whirlpool, as shown in Figure 9. The industry competition is getting tougher and the changes are more frequent in terms of product development and changes to companies' roles in the model. Many players change from being part of one force to being part of several forces. Players of the different forces have the potential to impact each others as well as partaking in the speeding-up of the internal industry competition. When so many players have the potential to influence each other and induce changes, the natural further evolution of the model of competition is to continue to pick up speed of changes.

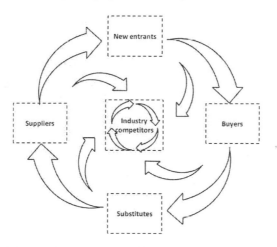

Fig. 9. The interrelations and connectedness of the forces can be represented as a whirlpool

3   Discussion

The general hypothesis of this paper was that the drivers and effects of economic globalization are distorting Porter's model of company competition, making it less clear and maybe less relevant. The model of the five forces of competition is affected by the drivers like lower trade barriers, lower transportation and communication costs, and technology development by the enabling of the different parties to enter the industry competition. Differences between the parties of the different forces in terms of information and technical capabilities are broken down and the effects grouped together as size expands the model in terms of bringing together previously geographically separated markets into one big global market. This, of course, is a simplification, and not a step change but something that happens gradually through the process of globalization. The gradual inclusion of India and China in the world economy can be seen this way. It is still not a complete all-encompassing free market place where everybody participates at the same level. But with the gradual inclusion of these countries, and by the evolvement of a middle class and competitive companies therein, we can see how the model of competition is gradually expanded. All the forces are affected in numbers of potential participants, and it is a gradual and continuous expansion. The effects grouped as location related, namely fragmentation of value chains, offshoring, outsourcing and complex supply chains, add another dynamic to the model by the dispersion of value-adding activities in the value chain to different locations inside or outside the boundaries of the company. This dispersion happens toward parties that could previously have been part of any or none of the forces of competition. The fact that the new dispersed value chain does not remain static but continues to change, and that competitors can set it up in different ways, adds to the complexity and the problem of defining the boundaries and relevant competition for an industry model. With the added effects categorized as pressure- namely cost and price pressure, higher rate of change, more diverse markets and lower start-up barriers - are included with its feedback loop to the location effects, the image of the competition model starts to resemble a whirlpool. The impact of the different drivers and effects on the competition model is shown in Figure 10.

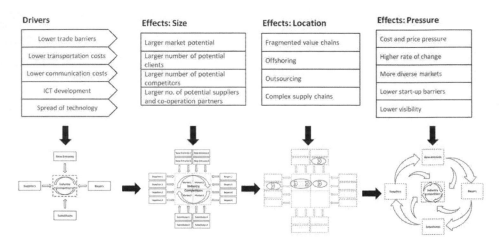

Fig. 10. The drivers and effects of globalization and how they affect the competitive situation

The whirlpool image can be used to symbolize the new interdependencies between the forces of the model and how they all have the potential to affect each other. It can be argued that the drivers and effects from globalization affect several aspects of the model at the same time, creating a different dynamic where the model might be obsolete or at least the boundaries might fade. On the other hand, it can be argued that the model enables evaluations like the one done here and therefore has become more important in a rapidly changing competitive environment as a model for understanding and analyzing our surroundings.

The model of competition and the model of the company as a value chain help explain the changes happening to companies. Disintegrating value chains, offshoring and outsourcing, and the tendency to set out production to others and focus on R&D and the branding and marketing part of the value chain change both what the company is, its focus of operations, and the management requirements. What the company is in terms of its assets, boundaries, competence requirements and relations changes. Innovations and intellectual property rights (IPR) have become increasingly more important. The nature of the company's assets changes from physically based, to knowledge-based intellectual properties [10]. The boundaries change as the level of outsourcing and offshoring changes over time. The competence requirements change when the focus changes from production to innovation and IPR and the handling of a complex supply chain network. Relations to co-operation partners, suppliers in your network and competitors change over time and become more important. The company operations, or the main activities in a company, change to innovation and IPR management and to supply-chain management as the new core. The company's management requirement thus also changes to incorporate innovation and IPR focus and strategy, value chain re-engineering and network management. Put another way, globalization can totally redefine what a company is and its core.

With a larger market potential and tougher competition, the market potentials and the cost reduction potential must both be explored to keep up with industry competition. Then it is not about Porter's competitive advantages versus Ricardo's comparative advantages. On the contrary, as argued by Mudambi and Venzin [9], these should be considered together. For the individual activities of a company's value chain, both the comparative advantages of locations, and thereby possible offshoring, should be considered in combination with the company's competitive advantages for the decision to outsource or not. Since the resulting choices do not reflect a new static situation, but an interim stage on a continuous journey, it is important to include in such a consideration how today's choices will affect and limit tomorrow's choices. Another important factor is the company's ability to handle multi-location and multi-national networks of its value chain, whether or not parts of it are outsourced and thereby inside or outside the boundary of the company. Handling these types of questions and of this magnitude and importance for the company is a relatively new management responsibility and requirement that has evolved over the last few decades, during which the pace of globalization has accelerated. As globalization continues to gain speed and strength, it is likely that more and more companies and managers will be affected.

4   Conclusions

It is observed that some of the characteristics of the competition model have changed. Firstly, the boundaries of the forces of the model are fading. The drivers of competition affect all the five forces and make their opportunities more equal, and the entry barriers to the industry's internal competition are lowered. Secondly, the model has become less static, with the value-adding activities of the value chain of companies shifting around both locations and within and outside the company's boundaries. Further, the forces and the market are more diverse than before. Even though products and services can have a global potential, the market segment can have very different preferences, and the players can have different business practices. Defining the boundaries of the industry has, in itself, become more difficult.

The competitive situation a company operates in has become more uncertain with lower visibility and higher uncertainty: a new dynamic with a higher speed of change and potential new interaction and relationship between the players. Fragmentation of value chains and complex supply chains make the picture more complex and the individual company's position more uncertain, both on relative strength in the overall competition and on the future direction. Globalization opens up opportunities of offshoring and outsourcing, and through these options being available to industry competitors, forces decisions on these areas of company value activities, their locations and company boundaries. In utilizing these options, companies tend to shift the focus to innovation and intellectual property rights, and to branding. This shift has the potential to redefine what a company is and its core from products or production to innovation and IPR.

As areas for further study, the authors point to the changes in assets and the resulting necessary changes to the area of asset management, and to the changes in management requirements in general.

References

1. Porter, M.E.: How Competitive Forces Shape Strategy. Harvard Business Review, 137–145 (March/April 1979)
2. Bang, K.E., Markeset, T.: Identifying the Drivers of Economic Globalization and the Effects on Companies' Competitive Situation. In: Frick, J., Laugen, B. (eds.) APMS 2011. IFIP AICT, vol. 384, pp. 233–241. Springer, Heidelberg (2012)
3. Porter, M.E.: Competitive Advantage: Creating and Sustaining Superior Performance. The Free Press, New York (1985)
4. Friedman, T.L.: The World is Flat: A Brief History of the Twenty-First Century. Farrar, Straus and Giroux, New York (2005)
5. Porter, M.E.: Strategy and the Internet. Harvard Business Review, 63–78 (March 2001)
6. Porter, M.E.: The Competitive Advantage of Nations. The Free Press, New York (1990)
7. Ricardo, D.: On the Principles of Political Economy and Taxation, 3rd edn. (e-book). John Murray, London (1821), available through: Library of Economics and Liberty http://www.econlib.org/index.html (accessed February 3, 2011)
8. Porter, M.E.: The Five Competitive Forces that Shape Strategy. Harvard Business Review, 79–93 (January 2008)
9. Mudambi, R., Venzin, M.: The Strategic Nexus of Offshoring and Outsourcing Decisions. Journal of Management Studies 47(8), 1510–1533 (2010)
10. Fatehi, K., Veliyath, R., Derakhshan, F.: Emergent Realities of Global Competition: The Changing Demands on Managers and Governments. International Journal of Commerce and Management 18(1), 77–92 (2008)

Identifying Challenges in the Development of Subsea Petroleum Production Systems

Jorge Moreno-Trejo[1,2] and Tore Markeset[1]

[1] University of Stavanger, N-4036 Stavanger, Norway
[2] PEMEX Exploración y Producción, Ciudad Del Carmen, Campeche, México
{Jorge.m.trejo,tore.markeset}@uis.no

Abstract. There are many challenges associated with development of offshore petroleum fields. Subsea production facilities are increasingly used in the petroleum industry as the technology has matured and quality increased. The use of subsea technology has advantages as well as challenges. Based on a literature review this paper identifies some if the development challenges related to the design and operation of subsea petroleum production facilities.

Keywords: Subsea petroleum production facilities, Development challenges.

1   Introduction

Oil companies are tending to use subsea technology in new field developments because it has several advantages over traditional exploitation. The type of technology used for reservoir exploitation and challenges should be determined before operations are started. Identifying activities associated with the development of subsea systems entails knowing and designing for the oil and gas (O&G) production process, reservoir flow and seabed conditions, environmental risks, costs and performance requirements. Each subsea installation design case may be different since the equipment needs to be designed for the reservoir fluid composition, oil and/or gas quality, pressure and flow, as well as sea depth, seabed conditions and topography, distance to shore, etc. Furthermore, from a management perspective, in each petroleum production development phase there are many companies involved which need to be coordinated and managed with respect to work activities, contractual issues, scheduling, supply logistics and quality assurance, etc.

For example, in Norway the Ormen Lange gas field located in the Norwegian Sea, at 800-1100 m depth approximately 140 km from the coast, was developed as subsea production for a new onshore gas processing plant [1]; [2]. The field was discovered in 1997, and production started in 2007. The field is located far from shore and even farther from the market and presented many unprecedented challenges including the fact that Norwegian industry lacked experience with such deep-water gas production. The operator performed high-resolution seismic surveys, seabed mapping, shallow coring and deep geotechnical drilling. The gas, condensate and water are transported from subsea installations using pipelines to an onshore process terminal where they are processed before a further 1200 km transportation through a pipeline to the UK

J. Frick and B. Laugen (Eds.): APMS 2011, IFIP AICT 384, pp. 287–295, 2012.
© IFIP International Federation for Information Processing 2012

via the Sleipner production platform in the North Sea. This is the largest pipeline in the world, and it required one million tonnes of steel and 25,000 tonnes of reinforced iron to build it. The subsea installations were designed to take into account the currents and sub-zero temperatures on the seabed, as well as extreme wind and wave conditions creating problems during installation and maintenance work. The field is expected to continue to produce gas for 30-40 years and delivers up to 20% of the UK´s gas requirements. The total costs are reported to be 66 billion Norwegian Crowns (NOK) (approximately 12 billion USD, June 2010 exchange rate) [3].

Preview studies of the reservoirs will decide the necessary subsea infrastructure, the number of production years expected and the total O&G assets' value. Often long and expensive engineering studies are needed to decide the production installation type, size and location. However, sea floor production installations are increasingly used as an alternative to topside facilities. Thus, the use of new and more reliable technology in deep-water environments has helped to bring about faster production, reducing risks and equipment failures.

Operators often choose to work with proven technology that is used in projects with the same or similar environmental characteristics and technical requirements. Waiting time costs money, and managers usually have economic pressures to complete the production facilities. Competition forces companies to work in the same technological conditions, getting new processes and technology as soon as they are in the market [4]. The experience gained in earlier projects, and the acquisition of assets needed in those projects, allows companies to develop new projects faster, getting data for statistical analysis and, moreover, valuable experience in subsea environments. However, in each exploration area there are uncertainties and new challenges that will need new or improved technological solutions. With new technology and prototype equipment, the uncertainty increases and unforeseen events may occur due to the fact that the equipment has not been totally proven [5].

Based on a literature review and interviews of industrial experts this paper identifies and discusses some of the challenges related to development of subsea petroleum production facilities.

2   Field Development

The oil and gas production can broadly be defined in two phases, namely the oil and gas exploration and the oil and gas exploitation phase. There are direct and indirect costs as well as taxes and insurances which all have to be taken into account in both phases.

2.1   Exploration Phase

There are high investment costs related to the exploration phase, and the use of advanced technology does not always result in finding a viable O&G field. Exploration and development activities are long-term investments and quite important to companies which can learn from the information that they acquire [6]. Operators lease a geographical area based on geological analysis, geophysical data, etc., and invest in equipment and knowledge to obtain additional data about the potential for finding hydrocarbons in the ground [7]. Often drilling and exploration efforts result in no

O&G found in the reservoir. The reasons are many, but are often due to imprecision in the pre-exploratory studies of geophysical data. This results in a loss for the operator. Furthermore, if O&G is found, the question remains of what technical solution should be used to produce the O&G.

Exploration is the first activity that oil companies have to carry out, mapping the area for further analysis. When a rock formation containing potential oil and gas is found, it is necessary to drill wells to obtain data and information about the geology, and then the type of equipment needed in the production systems will be decided. The drilling of wells generates information about hydrocarbon reserves, quantity and type, as well as information about reservoir characteristics and other factors which will later determine the possible oil exploitation. Results and data obtained from this phase provide valuable information for use in the production system's design and the strategy for developing the oil field.

However, the probabilities of a commercial discovery are low, often less than 10% [6]. Furthermore, reservoirs have to be capable of producing oil and/or gas at a minimum flow rate to be economically profitable. Large companies develop their studies and decisions for drilling in a new field based on the production expected and the size of the organization. Hence, a lot of smaller reservoirs are not economically attractive to the large companies.

2.2   Exploitation Phase

The raw oil and gas comes from reservoirs containing "pollutants" or organic compounds which need to be separated before it is sent to the customers. Depending on the oil, gas and water composition of the well-stream, one makes decisions about the design of the process plant. One has to decide whether to use a topside process facility or a subsea facility. One also has to consider risks related to costs, HSE (Health, Safety and Environment), flow assurance, asset integrity, and operational and maintenance strategies. The conditions in each well will influence the chosen concept; low flow rates and the composition fluids are going to make the well behave differently at the beginning of the operations [8].

Some decisions are influenced by the reservoir depth. For instance, the separation process may have to be carried out on the seabed if the crude has high viscosity. In some cases it may be cheaper to install separation equipment on the seabed instead of pumping it to the surface. Processing decisions depend on the seabed soil type, reservoir characteristics, environmental conditions, company policies and technical feasibility. However, the final decision will be based on economics and technical solutions [9].

Many activities, equipment and people with different expertise areas are needed to move the oil and gas from the reservoir to the surface. There are many companies involved in getting the oil to the surface, and the costs may be tremendous. People and companies working on the project and service activities have to align their activities with the operator's strategy [10]; [11], according to their role in the subsea installation life cycle. Companies with different expertise and culture join in the project and should be coordinated and managed. This is not an easy task, as one has to be able to maximize the resources of the company during the total life cycle cost [12]. The purpose is to plan and ensure the resources are available before they are needed to keep expenses as low as possible.

Subsea systems involve separators, valves, compressors, pumps and associated piping [13]. Nowadays 3D design and modeling software tools are used to design the hardware and to implement complex technical requirements and operating strategies. This reduces costs as it enables operational subsea activities to be simulated before the expensive resources are used in the project implementation and execution phase [14]. When a subsea production system is shown in a computer simulator, it is easier to recognize the critical points and the challenges that will face the project. One can figure out the equipment needed such as the type of Christmas tree, manifolds, control systems, vessels, as well as decisions related to the pipelines routes [12]. Also, the costs in drilling operations have been reduced with the 3D technology.

Installation of subsea production systems entails the use of vessels capable of moving equipment and tools with cranes to the seabed. Oil and gas produced are transported through flow lines and risers to platforms, using production systems. In some cases, companies send the oil to land facilities for further processing [15]. Occasionally, new equipment failures occur in the design, fabrication or installation phases [16].

The installation of subsea systems involves many vessel movements; the equipment also has to be set in accordance to the specifications provided by the fabricator. Different types of vessels are used such as drilling, derrick barge, and tugs. Before starting operations the equipment is usually tested by the fabricator, checking that all is working before sending it offshore to be installed on the seabed. In this phase it is important that the management coordinates the activities and services provided by external companies, verifying that the system quality is working. Changes that have to be made offshore represent high costs. Hence, coordination, scheduling and prediction of activity duration are factors that should be considered [17].

3   Factors Influencing the Subsea Design

By surveying and analyzing the subsea petroleum resource, the operator may decide what types of production systems are needed. Furthermore, they have to make sure they are selecting the suppliers and service providers that are able and best suited for the tasks considering their products, quality, experience and after-sales support. Challenges in subsea operations include environmental factors such as temperature, salinity, depth and sea currents. In the design of equipment for reservoir exploitation, one has to consider factors such as structure types, vessels and the people needed for operating and controlling them [18].

Harsh climate and environmental conditions may affect the subsea installations or the interventions performed with vessels as they can contribute to damages and failures, add loads to marine structures or recalibration of subsea instruments and components [19]. Historical environmental data of the area is used in the design of the equipment and to establish the strategy to transport and install it, as well as to plan maintenance requirements.

The pressure and temperature of the O&G arriving from the well may vary from field to field. The pressure required to lift production to the host facility in shallow water is typically between 6.89 to 13.78 bars, and from reservoirs located in deep water between 68.9 to 138 bars [20]. The characteristics of hydrocarbons and the mixture between temperature and flow rate can cause solid deposits forming hydrates, waxes or asphaltenes inside the flowlines or pipelines.

3.1   Environment and Location Factors

The strategy will be different for each field due to the geographical locations. For example, subsea designs in the Gulf of Mexico are focused on the metocean conditions caused by hurricanes [15]. However, in all cases, drilling and producing oil and gas in deep water mean high pressure as well as rock formations and disruptions on the seafloor. The main environmental factors that have to be taken into account are temperature, salt, and geographical location.

3.2   Temperature

Cold and warm environments change the properties in metal and steel. Therefore, the structures and pipelines have to be fabricated and coated in accordance with the temperature on the seabed. When the oil comes to the seabed it is warm due to the temperature in the reservoir, and the oil produced tends to behave differently when temperature and pressure change. Hence, the oil will be cold in the flow lines, and need to be insulated to stabilize the temperature for maintaining the oil properties and transporting production to onshore [21]. Designers have to take into account the materials and equipment for resisting local temperatures, and measure and test the performance in each case. Using equipment and materials that can resist different temperatures without losing their properties will allow for better performance and durability, and there will be less need for corrective maintenance.

3.3   Salinity

The exposure to salt in the sea environment causes the equipment to deteriorate. Oxygen in the water reacts with salt and causes pipelines, risers and any equipment underwater to corrode. Corrosion is the transfer of electrons from one substance to another and is an electrochemical reaction that oxidizes metals very quickly [22]. Hence, the preventive maintenance should be focused on preparing the equipment and tools for working under these conditions. More research is needed to design materials for resisting the salt effects for longer periods, thus resulting in lower maintenance costs.

3.4   Geographical Location

Maintenance strategies also need to be designed according to the field location. There are zones with soil disruptions or pockmarks where it is sometimes necessary to level the land to install and stabilize the equipment. It also may be necessary to install additional equipment or concrete mattresses, special support structures or ramps for withstanding the weight or to balance structures or pipelines.

If the seabed is uneven, debris could accumulate over time. As a result, it may become necessary to remove debris brought by currents from the area where the pipelines and umbilicals are placed. The production system and the pipeline route selection is one of the more critical activities. If it is done poorly without taking care of the geotechnical and marine conditions, it may be costly and result in operational delays [23].

4   Intervention Vessels and Equipment

Since deep-water interventions represent high costs, companies need to optimize the use of vessels, equipment, subsea services and intervention activities in general. It is common for operators to sign agreements and contracts with service companies to have equipment ready for installation, testing, preventive maintenance activities, as well as corrective maintenance.

Specialized vessels are also contracted to carry out the offshore subsea intervention activities and to transport the equipment and tools. The vessels stop approximately four hours every two weeks for maintenance and supply, and stay in motion around 20 to 30 percent of the time [24].

The oil prices worldwide have increased, and oil-producing countries have changed companies' policies to explore and exploit new reservoirs. The demand for vessels is higher, and the competition for getting new vessels is harder as equipment is busy and the market prices are higher. In 2007, the time needed for the construction and delivery of a new vessel was close to two and a half to three years [24]. It has also become more difficult to find and employ qualified and experienced personnel to work on vessels.

New smaller vessel companies have identified the trend and, in pursuit of profits, they are now getting involved in subsea operations. However, they focus on providing integrated and complete services, taking into account all the subsea areas. They design new vessels that can carry out packages of activities to install, inspect, maintain, store and transport materials as well as repair eventual failures.

The use of support vessels is planned one or two years ahead by the operator. To select the type of vessel needed, the type of activities to be performed is analyzed. One of the primary activities before installing any subsea equipment is to inspect the seafloor area. The vessel provider should ensure that the area is free of debris by the use of ROVs. However, the sea conditions in the area may influence the launching of the ROVs from the vessel. To launch the ROVs the wave height should be maximum 3m Hs. However, modern vessels with a wave heave compensating system can handle from 4.5 to 5m Hs. Specialized vessels with moonpool systems can deploy ROVs and equipment with a wave height up to 6m Hs [25]. Table 1 shows some of examples of average wave heights for various offshore regions.

Table 1. Wave heights conditions for offshore locations

Location	Hs (m)
Gulf of Mexico (offshore Mexico)	2.45
Kikeh (offshore Malaysia)	3.5
Girassol (west coast of Africa)	3.4
Campos Basin (offshore Brazil)	5.7
Shtockman (eastern Barents Sea)	9.4
Snøhvit (southern Barents Sea)	10.0
White Rose (Grand Banks)	10.5
Oseberg (northern North Sea)	10.8
Ormen Lange (Norwegian Sea)	11.7

The analysis of contracting multi-tasks vessels to develop subsea operations should be considered. It is cheaper to use the same vessel for surveying, installing and tie-in of subsea components instead of contracting individually [26]. This analysis should be performed in the initial stage to plan the subsea development in the life cycle. To be able to execute actions fast in case of unexpected happenings, it is important to establish frame agreements for contracting vessels early. The mobilization of equipment and vessels to carry out subsea operations takes around two or three days, and demobilization between 12 to 24 hours. In addition, the traveling to the field might take from 12 hours to several days, considering the distance to the field site [27].

5   Concluding Remarks

Based on a literature review this paper has identified some of the development challenges related to subsea petroleum production facilities. The subsea life cycle through the exploration and exploitation was briefly reviewed and also some of the factors influencing the design were discussed. Even though there has been a tremendous development in subsea technology there still are many challenges to overcome. Each subsea field is different with its unique characteristics. Therefore, each field requires a customized design and this makes it difficult to standardize the technological solutions.

References

1. Ormen Lange. "Ormen Lange". North Sea Northern, Norway (2010),
   http://www.offshore-technology.com/projects/ormen/
   (accessed: July 14, 2010)
2. Statoil. Facts about Ormen Lange (2010),
   http://www.statoil.com/en/OurOperations/ExplorationProd/partne
   roperatedfields/OrmenLange/Pages/default.aspx (accessed: July 15, 2010)
3. Ormen Lange (October 2006), http://www.touchoilandgas.com/ormen-lange-a6444-1.html (accessed: July 14, 2010), Originally printed in Exploration & Production: The Oil And Gas Review (2006)
4. Brandt, H., Eriksen, R.: RAM analysis for deepwater subsea developments. In: The Proceedings of the Offshore Technology Conference (OTC 2001), Houston, Texas, April 30-May 3 (2001)
5. Eriksen, R., Saucier, B.: Selecting cost-effective and safe deepwater completion tieback alternatives. In: The Proceedings of the Offshore Technology Conference (OTC 2000), Houston, Texas, May 1-4 (2000)
6. Kaiser, M.: Hydrocarbon production cost functions in the gulf of Mexico. Energy 31, 1726–1747 (2005)
7. Kaiser, M.: Modeling the time and cost to drill an offshore well. Energy 34, 1097–1112 (2009)
8. Duhon, J., Garduno, J., Robinson, N.: Planning and procedures for the initial startup of subsea production systems. In: The Proceedings of the Society of Petroleum Engineers (SPE 2009), New Orleans, Louisiana, October 4-7 (2009)

9. Moreno-Trejo, J., Markeset, T.: Mapping factors influencing the selection of subsea petroleum production systems. In: The Proceedings of the international Conference of Advances in Production Management System (APMS 2011), Stavanger, Norway, September 26-28 (2011)

10. Markeset, T., Kumar, U.: Dimensioning of Product Support – Issues, Challenges, and Opportunities. In: The Proceedings of The Annual Reliability and Maintainability Symposium (RAMS 2004), Los An-geles, California, USA, January 26-29 (2004) ISBN 0-7803-8215-3, ISSN 0149-144X

11. Kumar, R., Markeset, T.: Development of performance-based service strategies for the O&G industry: A case study. Journal of Business and Industrial Marketing 22(4) (2007)

12. Foster, L., Hebert, P., Nisbet, W., Sabatini, D., Bellegem, B., Faucheux, D.: Life cycle management for Gulf of Mexico subsea portfolio. In: The Proceedings of the Offshore Technology Conference (OTC 2001), Houston, Texas, April 30-May 3 (2001)

13. OCS Report MMS 2000-015. Deepwater development: A reference document for the deepwater environmental assessment, Gulf of Mexico OCS (1998 through 2007), U.S. Department of the Interior Minerals Management Service, Gulf of Mexico OCS Regional office, New Orleans (2000), http://www.gomr.mms.gov/PDFs/2000/2000-015.pdf (accessed: June 7, 2010)

14. McKinnon, C., Kenny, J.: Design, material and installation considerations for ultra deepwater pipelines. In: The Proceedings of the Society of Petroleum Engineers (SPE 1999), Aberdeen, Scotland, September 7-9 (1999)

15. Heideman, J., Finn, L., Hansen, R., Santala, M., Vyas, Y., Wong, P.: Deepwater production systems for the bay of Campeche. In: The Proceedings of the Society of Petroleum Engineers (SPE 1994), Veracruz, Mexico, October 10-13 (1994)

16. Moreno-Trejo, J., Markeset, T.: Identifying challenges the maintenance of subsea petroleum production systems. In: The Proceedings of the international Conference of Advances in Production Management System (APMS 2011), Stavanger, Norway, September 26-28 (2011)

17. Uyiomendo, E.E., Markeset, T.: Subsea maintenance service delivery: Mapping factors influencing scheduled service duration. Special Section on Maintenance and Safety Management in Process Plants, International Journal of Automation and Computing (IJAC) 7(2), 167–172 (2010)

18. Dixon, M., David, E.: Installation-driver field developments for deepwater subsea projects. In: The Proceedings of the Offshore Technology Conference (OTC 2008), Houston, Texas, May 5-8 (2008)

19. DNV-RP-C205, Environmental conditions and environmental loads. Recommended practice. Det Norske Veritas, Norway (2010)

20. Devegowda, D., Scott, S.L.: An assessment of subsea production systems. In: The Proceedings of the 2003 SPE Annual Technical Conference, Denver, CO, October 5-8 (2003)

21. Laing, N., Graham, G., Dyer, S.: Barium sulphate inhibition in subsea systems – the impact of cold seabed temperatures on the performance of generically different scale inhibitor species. In: The Proceedings of the Society of Petroleum Engineers (SPE 2003), Houston, Texas, February 5-7 (2003)

22. Last, G., Williams, P.: An introduction to ROV operations, p. 107. Oilfield Publications, Ledbury (1991)

23. Palmer, A., King, R.: Subsea pipeline engineering, 2nd edn. Pennwell, Tulsa (2008)

24. Hovland, E.: Evaluation of vessel concepts for subsea operations in northern seas. PhD Thesis no. 43, University of Stavanger, Stavanger, Norway (2007) ISBN: 978-82-7644-335-6, ISSN: 1890-1387

25. Hovland, E., Gudmestad, O.T.: Selection of support vessels for offshore operations harsh environments. Exploration & Production – Oil & Gas Review 6(2) (2008)

26. ISO 13628-1, Petroleum and natural gas industries - Design and operation of subsea production systems - Part 1: General requirements and recommendations, 2nd edn. (2005), http://www.iso.org/iso/iso_catalogue/catalogue_tc/catalogue_detail.htm?csnumber=36458 (accessed January 26, 2011)

27. Energy Institute and Lloyd's Register, Guidelines for the management of integrity of subsea facilities, England, p. 35 (2009)

Part II

Supply Chain Management

A Multi-agent Based Negotiation
for Supply Chain Network Using Game Theory

Fang Yu, Toshiya Kaihara, and Nobutada Fujii

Graduate School of System Informatics, Kobe University, 1-1 Rokkodai,
Nada, Kobe, Hyogo, 657-8501, Japan
yufang@kaede.cs.kobe-u.ac.jp, kaihara@kobe-u.ac.jp,
nfujii@phoenix.kobe-u.ac.jp

Abstract. This paper focuses on the single-issue negotiation between Manufacture Agent (MA) and Material Supplier Agent (MSA) of the supply chain. MSA resorts to find partners to cooperate when it cannot finish the order independently. A two stage negotiation protocol is proposed. The cooperative game is combined with MA-Stackelberg game to resolve the negotiation problem. It is used to establish the coalitions. Then, the final determined coalition negotiates with MA to reach an agreement using the Stackelberg game. Protocols without concession and with concession are respectively discussed. Simulations and comparisons are provided to verify the effectiveness and superiority of the proposed protocol.

Keywords: Multi-agent, supply chain, negotiation, game theory.

1 Introduction

Negotiation is the process of arriving at a state that is mutually agreeable to a set of agents, that ranges from situations where resources must be allocated to agents to situations involving agent-to-agent bargaining. There are many negotiations among MAs, MSAs and CAs (Customer Agent) in Supply Chain Network (SCN) model. Game theory has become a primary methodology used in SCN-related problems. Primary methodological tools for dealing with these problems are Nash game and Stackelberg game, which focus on the simultaneous and sequential decision-making of multiple players, respectively [2]. The applications of game theory in Supply Chain Management (SCM) were surveyed by [1] and [2]. The reviews consist respectively of game theoretical techniques and SCM topics.

This paper focuses on the resource allocation of the negotiation using game theory. The negotiations between one MA and multiple MSAs are discussed. It is assumed that MSAs only accept the order which is in their abilities. They are compelled to reject the order against their will when the materials MA orders are too large to be provided by themselves. In general, MA decomposes the order into pieces and allocates them to multiple MSAs to resolve this problem. This research tries to find another way to resolve this problem which can maintain the integrity of the order. We focus on the side of MSAs and devote our efforts to let MSAs find partners to build

J. Frick and B. Laugen (Eds.): APMS 2011, IFIP AICT 384, pp. 299–308, 2012.
© IFIP International Federation for Information Processing 2012

coalitions when the order is out of their abilities. A two stage negotiation protocol is proposed. The coalition formation problem of the MSAs is modeled as a cooperative game in the first stage. Theories of coalition formation were presented in [3-5]. In the second stage, the final determined coalition negotiates with MA to reach an agreement using Stackelberg game ([6-7]). MA announces his strategy to the MSAs at first, and then MSA chooses his best response to MA's decision. Thus, the problem can be modeled as finding the Stackelberg equilibrium ([8-9]). A two-stage protocol is proposed, which resolves the problem when the supplier cannot complete the order independently. It maintains the integrity of the order, and reduces the cost and workload of MA.

This paper is organized as following. Section 2 describes the SCN model used in this paper and gives a two-stage negotiation protocol. Each stage of negotiations is discussed in detail in section 3 and in section 4. Simulations and analysis are discussed in section 5 to verify the effectiveness and feasibility of the proposed protocol. In conclusion, we have commented on contributions and the direction of future work research.

2   Two-Stage Negotiation Protocol

All organizations of the SCN in this study are divided into three groups based on the multi-agent methodology: MSA, MA and CA. The model of the SCN is shown in Fig. 1. Discussion is provided only on the negotiations between one MA and multiple MSAs are discussed.

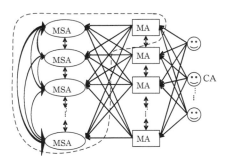

Fig. 1. The model of SCN

The negotiations between one MA and multiple MSAs, where the quantity of the order required by MA is too large for MSA to complete independently, are discussed in this study. MA broadcasts an order $(M_k, Q_k, PA_k(0), TD)$ when inventory material is requested, where M_k is the material MA wants to order, Q_k is the quantity of M_k, $PA_k(0)$ is the initial price of M_k of MA, TD is the due time. It wants to find the optimal MSA with the lowest price. It is assumed in the proposed model that MSAs accept only orders which are able to fulfill. In the real market, the order frequently happens out of the abilities of MSAs. They will be compelled to reject the order against their will in that case. In order to resolve this problem, researchers tend to decompose the order and then allocate it to multiple MSAs. This study tries to find another way to resolve this problem which can maintain the integrity of the order. Efforts are devoted to let MSAs combine with each other as a coalition and then negotiate with MA to acquire the order. A two-stage negotiation protocol is proposed as follows:

Stage1: Negotiation among MSAs (Sect. 4). MSAs evaluate the order and check whether it can be finished by themselves. If they can do it, they can go to the second stage of negotiation directly; if they cannot, then they can negotiate with the other MSAs to build a coalition. A cooperative game is used for the coalition formation. At the end, the final determined coalitions or MSA enter(s) into the second stage.

Stage2: Negotiation between MA and MSA or final coalition (Sect. 5). MA negotiates with the final coalition to find the Stackelberg equilibrium.

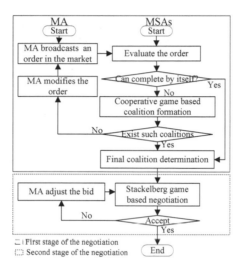

Fig. 2. Flow chart of the two-stage negotiation protocol

The flowchart is shown in Fig. 2. The first stage is used for preparation. There are MSAs which cannot complete the order by themselves. Thus, they should find partners to build a coalition. The final negotiation about the price is started at the second stage.

3   Negotiations among MSAs

MSA starts to negotiate with other MSAs in the SCN to establish a coalition if it cannot complete the order by itself. The way to establish coalitions, determination of the final coalition, and profit allocation are discussed in the following sections, respectively. The n-person cooperative game is introduced to build the coalitions.

3.1   Coalition Formation

A cooperative n-person game ([4]) is a pair (N, v) where $N= \{1,...,n\}$ denotes the set of players (MSAs), v is the characteristic function and $v(S)$ defines the amounts of profit of players in set S which they could win if they form a coalition. $S = (S_1,..., S_N)$ denotes all partitions (coalition structure), $S_i=(s_{i1},..., s_{im})$ is the coalition structure of MSA i $(m=2^n-1)$, and s_{ij} is one of the possible coalition of MSA i. Let $S_i^*=\{ s_{ij} =\mathrm{argmax}\{v(s_{ij})|\ s_{ij} \in S_i,\ i \in N\}$ be the optimal coalition set of the game (N, v). A feasible payoff profile is defined as a vector of u_i such that $\sum_{i\in S_i} u_i =v(S_i)$.

Each player $i \in N$ seeks to maximize its utility function u_i by belonging to a coalition. Therefore, the search for optimal coalition can be converted into the calculation of the core of the game. A cooperative game is applied into the SCN negotiation as in the following. Firstly, some useful definitions are given:

$$PR_{ik}=(1+\alpha_i)*C_{ik} \tag{1}$$

$$IV_{ik}(TD)= IV_{ik}(TC)+\gamma_{ik}*(TD\text{-}TC) \tag{2}$$

$$PC_{ijk}= \frac{1}{|S_{ij}|}(1-\sigma_j)\sum_{i\in s_{ij}} PR_{ik} \tag{3}$$

$$u(s_{ij})= \sum_{i\in s_{ij}} (PC_{ijk} - C_{ik})Q_{ik} \tag{4}$$

where PR_{ik} is the price of M_k of MSA i, α_i is the percentage of profit of MSA i want to gain, C_{ik} is the production cost of MSA i for M_k, $IV_{ik}(TD)$ is the inventory level of M_k of i, γ_{ik} is the productivity of M_k of i, TC is the current time, $|s_{ij}|$ is the number of members in s_{ij}, PC_{ijk} is the price of M_k of coalition s_{ij}, σ_j is the discount of coalition s_{ij}, Q_k is the quantity of M_k that MA ordered, Q_{ik} is the quantity of M_k of i acquired in coalition s_{ij}.

3.2   Coalition Determination

Each MSA i expects to maximize its profit. Thus, the determination of the final coalition of each MSA i is transformed into finding the optimal coalition set $S*$. We have discussed before that the search for optimal coalition can be converted into the calculation of the core of the game. Therefore, the determination of the final coalition is equivalent to calculating the core of the game. It can be resolved by finding a solution to the following problem:

$$\arg\max_{s_{ij}\in S_i} u(s_{ij}) = \arg\max_{s_{ij}\in S_i} \sum_{i'\in s_{ij}} (PC_{ijk} - C_{i'k})*Q_{i'k} \tag{5}$$

$$\text{s.t.} \qquad \sum_{i'\in s_{ij}} IV_{i'k}(TD) \geq Q_k \tag{6}$$

$$\sum_{i'\in s_{ij}} Q_{i'k} = Q_k \tag{7}$$

The optimal coalition S_i^* of each MSA i can be reached, but the coalition is determined only if all MSAs in s_{ij} reach an agreement. An agreement is reached between MSA i and j only if MSA i asks j to be a partner and vice-versa at the same time. All MSAs in coalition S_i^* must have maximal profits because they are all selfish. The coalition S_i^* with the maximal value of u is determined as the final coalition SF_i of MSA i after the agreement is reached.

3.3   Profit Allocation

The profit allocation among the members after the coalition gets the order is discussed in this section. It is easy to do it when the order just meets the demands of all members. However, what should be done when the order is not enough to fulfill the total supply of the coalition? In other words, if $\sum_{i \in SF_i} IV_{ik}(TD)$ is greater than Q_k, what can be done? As we know, each player in the coalition has main interests in its individual benefit and tries to maximize its own profit. Thus, we should assign the profit impartially. For this purpose, we present the following allocation rule:

Rule: The MSA who contributes more to the coalition, gains more.

   Therefore, we allocate the profit among the members according to their contributions to the coalition. Let π_i be the profit of player i, and $\pi_{sij} = (\pi_1, ..., \pi_m)$ denotes a profit allocation of the coalition s_{ij}. To be efficient, one must have $\sum_{i \in s_{ij}} \pi_i = u(s_{ij})$.

We can get that $\pi_i = u(s_{ij}) * \dfrac{Q_{ik}}{Q_k}$ according to the rule. It means that the profit allocation depends on the allocation of the order quantity among the players in the coalition. The order is allocated according to the ability (productivity) to be fair:

$$Q_{ik} = \frac{IV_{ik}(TD)}{\sum\limits_{i \in s_{ij}} IV_{ik}(TD)} * Q_k \tag{8}$$

4   Negotiation between MA and the Final Coalition

4.1   Protocol without Concession

The negotiation between MA and SF_i starts to reach an agreement on the price of M_k after SF_i is determined. However, the target of SF_i is contrary to MA's. Each individual wishes to maximize the utility of himself. On one hand, SF_i aims to maximize its payoff by increasing the price; on the other hand, MA tries to maximize its profit by reducing the price in order to lower the production cost and therefore to minimize the total payment. We have:

$$PF_{ik}[t]=PF_{ik}[t-1]-\frac{PF_{ik}[t-1]-PFI_{ik}}{(TN-t)/TS} \qquad (9)$$

$$PM_k[t]=PM_k[t-1]+\frac{PMA_k-PM_k[t-1]}{(TN-t)/TS} \qquad (10)$$

where $PF_{ik}[t]$ is the price of M_k of SF_i at t and $PF_{ik}[0]=PC_{ijk}$ where j=argmax$\{u(s_{ij})| s_{ij} \in s_i\}$; PFI_{ik} is the minimal price of M_k of SF_i and $PFI_{ik}=\{ PC_{ijk} | a_i=a_i^{min}\}$; $PM_k[t]$ is the price of M_k of MA at t; the maximal price PMA_k and initial price $PM_k[0]$ of M_k from MA are given by the order; TN is the deadline of negotiation, TS is the negotiation step.

Stackelberg equilibrium applies when one of the players move before the other player and the player who moves firstly is assumed as the leader [2]. In the proposed model, MA first announces its strategy to the MSAs. Thus, the negotiation between MA and SF_i can be seen as MA-Stackelberg game and the determination of the final strategy is transformed into finding the Stackelberg equilibrium of the game. The determination of the Stackelberg equilibrium can be transformed into finding the optimal proposal and so to maximize the profits of MA (u_{MA}) and SF^* (u_{SFi}). In other word, the purpose is to maximize the total profit of the whole SCN (u_{SCN}). Thus, the problem of finding the Stackelberg equilibrium can be transformed into solving the following problem:

$$\arg\max_i u_{SCN} = u_{MA}+u_{SF_i}$$

$$= (PS_k-FS_{ik})*Q_k+\sum_{i'\in s_{ij}}(FS_{ik}-C_{i'k})*Q_{i'k} \qquad (11)$$

$$\textbf{s.t.} \qquad FS_{ik} = \arg\max_{PM_k[t]} u_{MA}+u_{SF_i} \qquad (12)$$

$$FS_{ik} \geq PF_{ik}[t+1] \qquad (13)$$

where PS_k is the selling price of M_k of MA. The equilibriums can be reached by resolving (12), which means that the agreement between MA and SF_i on the price of M_k is FS_{ik}. The final supplier is determined by solving (11)-(13) and the negotiation terminates.

4.2   Protocol with Concession

Sim et al. ([10-11]) proposed a MDA model for designing negotiation agents that make adjustable rates of concession for a given market situation by considering factors such as trading opportunity, competition, remaining trading time and eagerness. The effect of the remaining trading time is considered in this research. The concession strategies are given as follows based on Sim's:

1. For MA:

$$\delta_k^M[r] = T_k^M(t_r, \tau, \varepsilon)(k_{max}^M - k^M[r-1]) \tag{14}$$

$$T_k^M(t_r, \tau, \varepsilon) = (\frac{r}{\tau})^{\frac{1}{\varepsilon}} \tag{15}$$

where k^M is the value of attribute k of MA, k_{max}^M is the maximum value of attribute k of MA, $\delta_k^M[r]$ is the spread of MA of attribute k at round r, τ is the negotiation deadline. Different strategies in making concession related to the remaining trading time are classified as follows ([12]):

— $\varepsilon=0$: means agent is totally not interested in negotiating.
— $\varepsilon=1$: makes a constant rate of concession;
— $0<\varepsilon<1$: makes a smaller concession in early rounds and larger concession in later rounds;

2. For MSA i:

$$\delta_{ik}^S[r] = T_{ik}^S(t_r, \tau, \varepsilon)(k_i^M[r-1] - k_{i,min}^S) \tag{16}$$

$$T_{ik}^S(t_r, \tau, \varepsilon) = (\frac{r}{\tau})^{\frac{1}{\varepsilon}} \tag{17}$$

where k_i^S is the value of attribute k of MSA i, $k_{i,min}^S$ is the minimum value of attribute k of MSA i, $\delta_{ik}^S[r]$ is the spread of MSA i of attribute k at round r.

Equations (9) and (10) are reduced to:

$$PM'[t] = PM'[t-1] + (\frac{t * TSTEP}{TN})^{\frac{1}{\varepsilon}}(PMA_k' - PM'[t-1]) \tag{18}$$

$$PF_{ik}'[t] = PF_{ik}'[t-1] - (\frac{t * TSTEP}{TN})^{\frac{1}{\varepsilon}}(PF_{ik}'[t-1] - PFI_{ik}') \tag{19}$$

Then, the equilibriums and final supplier(s) are determined by solving (11) - (13) where $PM_k[t]$ and $PF_{ik}[t]$ are respectively equal to $PM'_k[t]$ and $PF'_{ik}[t]$,.

5   Simulations and Analysis

It is supposed that there are 5 MSAs and one MA distribute in the SCN (the initial values of MSAs are shown in Table 1) and the MA is price prior. The parameters settings are: $\underline{a}_i$=0.3, α_i^{min} =0.2, σ_j=0.2, TN=60s, TS=2s, PMA_k=11, PMI_k=8.5, PS_k=15, TD=10.

Table 1. Initial information of MSAs

Supplier	γ_{ik}	C_{ik}	PR_{ik}	Supplier	γ_{ik}	C_{ik}	PR_{ik}
MSA1	125	7.116241	10.283	MSA4	104	7.040015	9.971
MSA2	224	7.603996	10.660	MSA5	201	7.545082	10.166
MSA3	220	7.216251	10.140				

Firstly, the proposed protocol is compared with the greedy algorithm under three cases to verify the feasibility and superiority, where:

— *Greedy algorithm:* MA selects the MSA with the lowest price as the supplier. If the selected MSA cannot complete the order by itself, then MA splits the order and allocate the remaining quantity to other MSAs with the lowest price and so on;
— *Case1:* Q=1000, which means that in this case all the MSAs can complete the order by themselves;
— *Case2:* Q=2000, which means that some MSAs cannot complete the order by themselves, thus, they need to find partners;
— *Case3:* Q=3000, which means that no MSA can complete the order by itself.

The comparisons are shown in Table 2. All the MSAs in both protocols can complete the order by themselves in *Case1*, they choose the same supplier with the lowest price. Thus, the profits of both protocols are the same. The order is out of the abilities of some MSAs in *Case2*. The final suppliers of the greedy algorithm and the proposed protocol are {4, 3} and {4, 5}, respectively. The profit of the MA in the proposed protocol is higher than in the greedy algorithm. All MSAs in SCN cannot finish the order by themselves in *Case3*. The final suppliers of both protocols are the same, but the profit in the proposed protocol is still higher than in the greedy algorithm.

Table 2. Comparisons of greedy algorithm and proposed protocol under three cases

	Case1		*Case2*		*Case3*	
	Greedy	Proposed	Greedy	Proposed	Greedy	Proposed
Suppliers	{4}	{4}	{4,3}	{4,5}	{4,3}	{4,3}
Profit of MA	4997.5	4997.5	9446.25	11044.25	14846.25	16586.63

Analysis: The greedy algorithm adopts the method of splitting the order and allocating it to multiple MSAs. It increases the workload of MA. The proposed protocol solves this problem from the side of the MSA. It tries to build coalitions and MA just announces the order and waits for the responses. The proposed protocol is much more superior to the greedy algorithm. It doesn't only maintain the integrity of the order, and reduces the workload of MA, but also increases the profit of MA. We can see from Table 2 that the proposed protocol improves the profit margins from 0 to 1598, and 1740.38 in three cases, respectively.

Secondly, the comparisons between the protocol without concession and with concession are provided where $\varepsilon=0.3$. The results are shown in Fig. 3.

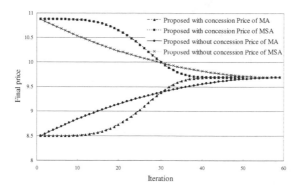

Fig. 3. Comparisons of the protocol without concession and with concession

Analysis: It indicates that the protocol with concession reaches the same agreement with the protocol without concession, but it is faster than the protocol without concession. Furthermore, the concession rate is related to ε.

6   Conclusion

In this paper, a multi-agent based negotiation protocol for supply chain network using game theory was discussed. A two stage negotiation protocol is proposed. Cooperative game was adopted in the first stage of negotiation for the coalition formation. The negotiation among the MSAs was transformed into the calculation of the core of the game. A MA-Stackelberg game was introduced for the negotiation between MA and the final coalition. Thus, the negotiation problem can be resolved by finding the Stackelberg equilibrium. Then, concession strategies were taken into account based on the proposed protocol. The main contributions of the proposed protocols are that the resolution of the problem when the supplier cannot fulfill the order independently and the maintenance of the integrity of the order. Comparisons verified that the proposed protocol had a better performance than the greedy algorithm and the protocol with concession is faster than the protocol without concession.

This paper only considered the single-attribute negotiation between one MA and multiple MSAs, we will study the multi-attribute negotiation between one MA and multiple MSAs in a future work. Furthermore, we will extend our negotiation protocol to the negotiations between multi-MA and multi-MSA which are much more complex. In this paper it was assumed that MA has price priority, but in real SCN, when the order is urgent, the time must be taken into account, thus, we will discuss the price and lead time dimensions, respectively.

References

1. Cachon, G.P., Netsssine, S.: Game theory in supply chain analysis. In: Simchilevi, D., Wu, S.D., Shen, Z. (eds.) Handbook of Quantitative Supply Chain Analysis: Modeling in the E-Business Eram, pp. 13–66. Kluwer (2004)
2. Leng, M.M., Parlar, M.: Game theoretic applications in supply chain management: a review. INFOR 43(3), 187–220 (2005)
3. Willam, A.G.: A theory of coalition formation. American Sociological Review 26(3), 373–382 (1961)
4. Shenoy, P.P., Lawrence: On coalition formation: a game-theoretical approach. International Journal of Game theory 8(3), 133–164 (1979)
5. Nagarajan, M., Sosic, G.: Game-theoretic analysis of cooperation among supply chain agents: review and extensions. Eur. J. Oper. Res. 187, 719–745 (2008)
6. Hennet, J.C., Mahjoub, S.: Toward the fair sharing of profit in a supply chain network formation. Internatioanl Journal Production Economics 127, 112–120 (2010)
7. Fiestras-Janeiro, M.G., Garcia-Jurado, I., Meca, A., Mosquera, M.A.: Cooperative game theory and inventory management. Eur. J. Oper. Res. 210, 459–466 (2011)
8. Rezapour, S., et al.: Strategic design of competing supply chain networks with foresight. Adv. Eng. Softw. 42, 130–141 (2011)
9. Lu, J.C., Tsao, Y.C., Charoensiriwath, C.: Competition under manufacturer service and reatil price. Economic Modelling 28, 1256–1264 (2011)
10. Sim, K.M., Wong, E.: Toward market-driven agents for electronic auction. IEEE T. Syst. Man Cy. A 31(6), 474–484 (2001)
11. Sim, K.M.: Negotiation agents that make prudent compromises and are slightly fiexible in reaching consensus. Computational Intelligence 20(4), 643–662 (2004)
12. Ren, F.H., Zhang, M.J., Sim, K.M.: Adaptive conceding strategies for automated trading agents in dynamic, open markets. Decis. Support Syst. 46, 704–716 (2009)

Integration Alternatives
for Ship Designers and Shipyards

Dag E. Gotteberg Haartveit[1], Marco Semini[1], and Erlend Alfnes[2]

[1] SINTEF Technology and Society, Department of Industrial Management
Trondheim, Norway
[2] Department of Production and Quality Engineering,
Norwegian University of Science and Technology, Trondheim, Norway
{dag.haartveit,marco.semini}@sintef.no,
erlend.alfnes@ntnu.no

Abstract. The offshore oil industry in Norway has for decades required advanced special purpose equipment for its operations. Norwegian shipbuilders have supplied the offshore industry and specialized in producing customized and technologically advanced ships. Shipbuilding is a typical Engineer-to-Order (ETO) industry. While the ship concept and design continues to be developed in Norway, ship production is increasingly performed at foreign yards. This characteristic makes the industry an interesting case for studying integration between actors. This paper presents a typology of different integration alternatives for ship designers and shipyards. The three alternatives presented are ownership, partner yard and market yard. The paper also identifies and discusses industry-relevant business factors that are affected by the choice of integration level.

Keywords: Supply Chain Management, Vertical Integration, Engineer-to-Order, Shipbuilding.

1 Introduction

Despite the fact that Engineer-to-order (ETO) manufacturing is widespread in many industries, and customization has been promoted as a source of competitive advantage [1], operations and supply chain management have mainly focused on high-volume manufacturing. In contrast to high-volume manufacturing, ETO manufacturing is characterized by low-volumes, high degrees of customization and project-based processes. Research addressing the design and management of supply chains with those characteristics is scarce [2]. This paper addresses collaboration and integration between supply chain actors in the archetypical ETO industry: shipbuilding. The shipbuilding industry is by definition concerned with the production of vessels above 100 gross tones. The industry is characterized by site production, temporary work organization, high degrees of customization and project organizations. The shipbuilding process is usually an endeavor lasting several years. During the process customer specifications, technological advances and other factors change the design

J. Frick and B. Laugen (Eds.): APMS 2011, IFIP AICT 384, pp. 309–316, 2012.
© IFIP International Federation for Information Processing 2012

of the ship. These changes demand collaboration between, and integration of, actors in order to be successful. Different levels and types of integration affect crucial business factors which imply different advantages and drawbacks. Choosing the right integration alternative should therefore be made in a systematic, informed way. There is however a lack of research addressing this issue.

The purpose of this paper is to develop a typology of different integration alternatives between two key actors in shipbuilding, the ship designer and the shipyard, and to identify the effects of different integration choices. The outcome should support managers in their effort to align supply chain strategy with overall business strategy and priorities.

The stated purpose is achieved by performing a literature review and several exploratory case studies at a Norwegian shipbuilder. The specific advantage of case studies is that great insight can be achieved by means of direct contact with key informants.

The case company produces customized and technologically advanced ships. The ships are tailor made to customer needs and especially attractive to customers providing services for the offshore oil industry. While the ship concept and design still are developed by the case company in Norway, ship production is increasingly performed globally; in countries and regions such as China, Brazil and the Middle East. This characteristic makes the case company an interesting case for studying integration between ship designer and shipyards. The topic of this paper is relevant to the case company and the study was conducted through frequent interviews and discussions with key personnel.

The remainder of this paper is structured as follows: First, the shipbuilding industry is briefly introduced. This introduction focuses on aspects relevant for the purpose of the present paper. Next, existing literature on vertical integration and supplier relations is reviewed. Chapter four contains this paper's main contribution; three different integration alternatives between designers and yards are introduced and their effect on industry-relevant factors highlighted. The paper is finalized by a conclusion and suggestions for further research.

2   Shipbuilding

This chapter will introduce shipbuilding characteristics relevant to the topic at hand. The characteristics are based on the case study. Ships for other market segments are often built differently.

2.1   Main Processes

Ships are complex engineered systems, and building ships is similar to building heavy machinery, capital goods or buildings. Such undertakings are usually organized as projects, and shipbuilding can therefore be considered as a project-based industry. A typical shipbuilding project includes the following main processes:

- Concept design
- Contract design
- Basic and functional design

- Purchasing
- Engineering
- Production

- Assembly
- Commissioning
- After-sale

The different processes often overlap and their borders are blurred. Even the order and amount of effort put into each process can vary. Note that contract signing happens after Concept -, Contract -, and Basic and functional design. These non-physical processes are considered core capabilities for ETO companies [3].

2.2   Main Actors

The processes presented in the previous section are often not carried out by a single company, but a network of geographically dispersed actors. The processes carried out by each actor vary and so does the level of integration and coordination between them. This is an important characteristic of shipbuilding. At an aggregated level our case study revealed the following main roles, which may or may not belong to the same company:

- The ship designer
- The shipyard

- Main equipment suppliers
- The ship owner

There is a need for actors holding these roles to communicate and collaborate. This paper focuses on the ship designer and the shipyard which are presented in more detail below. Collaboration between them is needed to ensure effective, high quality production according to specifications.

The Ship Designer. The ship designer has the overall responsibility of concept design and basic and functional design. These two processes are the ones that determine the physical shape, performance and capabilities of the ship. These are ultimately the most important factors to the customer, thus the ship designer usually also carries out the marketing and communication efforts towards customers.

The Shipyard. The shipyard's main responsibility is production and assembly. In addition, it carries out purchasing and engineering, which are typically split between the ship designer and the yard to varying degrees. The shipyard is either chosen by the customer or in collaboration with the ship designer.

3   Literature Review

The literature review conducted for the paper covers design and management of supply chains with a focus on vertical integration and supplier relations, as this is relevant theory when discussing different levels of integration between companies. Special attention is given to literature concerning ETO companies and supply chains. Research in this field is not nearly as comprehensive as that of the high volume industry, but there is some relevant literature addressing the engineering and construction industry [4, 5].

3.1   Vertical Integration Decisions

Vertical integration decisions are of strategic importance. These decisions determine how much of the supply chain the company will own and which activities it will perform. Companies usually vertically integrate to achieve one of two goals: To increase profit margins or to improve control over their business environment [6].

The result of vertical integration decisions affects companies on many levels. Porter [7] and Hayes and Wheelwright [6] explained the advantages and disadvantages of vertical integration. More recently, Beckman and Rosenfield [8] gathered the current body of knowledge and found four main sets of factors to be considered when making vertical integration decisions. The factors and their effects are summarized in Table 1.

Table 1. Factors For and Against Vertical Integration [8]

Factors	Vertically Integrate to:	Vertically Disintegrate to:
Strategic Factors	- Develop and retain core and essential competences.	- Access a core or essential capability externally while working on its development internally.
Market Factors	- Control cost, quality, availability, features/innovativeness and environmental performance in unreliable markets. - Shift power relationships in the industry. - Reduce dependency on suppliers.	- Leverage competition among suppliers to access best-in-class performance. - Aggregate demand at suppliers thus generating economies of scale and improved responsiveness to variability in demand.
Product and Technology Factors	- Control integral or critical technologies. - Integrate design and production or service delivery under certain conditions.	- Access current technologies not available internally. - Obtain leverage available from modular product architectures.
Economic Factors	- Minimize transportation and logistics costs. - Minimize transaction costs.	- Access lower production or service delivery cost. - Minimize investment costs.

Hicks et al. [3] found that levels of vertical integration varied considerably between ETO companies and that these variations were consequences of the varying factors they were subjected to. At the same time they saw a trend towards vertical disintegration driven by financial pressure and cost reduction efforts.

3.2   Enterprise Collaborations

A company not completely vertically integrated must necessarily interact with other actors in a supply chain. This interaction varies depending on the relationship between the actors. According to Jagdev and Thoben [9] the collaboration between actors ranges from Market transactions to Integrated company. Table 2 illustrates the spectrum of relationships between two supply chain actors in which one acts as the supplier to the other. The level of formalization, commitment and duration of relationship increases downwards in the table.

Table 2. Spectrum of Relationships with Supply Chain Actors (Adapted from Jagdev and Thoben [9])

Type of Collaboration	Description
Market Transaction	Relationship strictly transaction based.
Non-Contractual Agreements	Long lasting market transactions based on trust.
Contractual Agreements	Long-term supply contracts or agreements between companies providing complementary products.
License Agreements	License provided to supplier in technology that host firm develops. Example: franchising.
Joint Venture	Companies supplying complimentary products or services join forces for mutual benefit.
Integrated Company	A single company owns the activity.

Deciding what kind of relationship the company should have to other actors is a decision of strategic importance and should differ according to the role of the actor [10, 11]. That role depends upon a number of factors including supply risk and impact on profit. These were identified by Kraljic [12] as the main determinants for a suitable sourcing strategy.

When considering supplier relations Hicks et al. [3] found that an ETO company could have the whole spectrum of relationships to its suppliers due to differing integration levels, the supply risk and impact on profit of the sourced product, and levels of desired concurrent engineering, to name a few. They also caution about the lack of transferability of supply chain management practices from the high volume sector. In the next chapter, the reviewed theory will be applied to shipbuilding with this warning in mind.

4   Integration Alternatives

Different forms and levels of integration exist between actors in shipbuilding. Despite the importance of selecting appropriate integration alternatives between different actors, the literature lacks frameworks addressing this issue. The purpose of this chapter is to develop a typology of integration alternatives for the ship designer and the shipyard, and to discuss consequences of different integration choices. The results are presented in table 3.

Table 3. Industry-Relevant Business Factors and How Integration Alternatives Affect Them

	Ownership	Partner Yard	Market Yard
Strategic Factors			
Capacity. Access to the right production capabilities and capacity is essential and can be scarce in high demand market situations.	Full access to capacity.	Access to capacity depends on contractual agreements.	Access to capacity depends on yard availability and can lead to lost sales.
Core Capability – Project Execution. Ships are customized and adapted to customer requirements throughout the project period. Being able to comply with changes customers require in an efficient manner is considered a capability for shipbuilders, like the case company.	Integration between functions creates flexibility through collaboration and coordination.	Long-term relationships facilitate collaboration and coordination.	Project changes require collaboration between functions with no experience collaborating and coordinating.
Core Capability - Knowledge. Designs are to a large degree sold by referring to previously built ships and the designers' ability to develop solutions which exactly fits customer needs. Designing technologically advanced ships requires being able to integrate complex sub-systems and state-of-the-art technologies. This requires knowledge and experience acquired by building ships.	Integration between functions secures knowledge sharing.	Long-term collaboration facilitates knowledge sharing.	Knowledge sharing on a project-to-project basis.
Market Factors			
Market Access. Ship production contracts are won on cost and political considerations. The yard industry is highly competitive and governments have been setting up tax schemes and local content regulations to promote production in their country. In order to benefit from those incentives customers will in many cases require a specific location/yard. (Quality and perceived risk also influence choice of yard)	Production constrained to one or a small number of yards reduce market access.	Production, limited to a number of yards reduces market access.	Production can be at any yard and does not reduce market access.
Product and Technology Factors			
Intellectual Property. A shipyard with full access to detailed design drawings and the experience gained by building an offshore vessel is a potential competitor.	Full control of integral or critical technologies. Low risk of intellectual property theft.	Reduced risk of intellectual property theft due to long-term partnership.	A market yard lacks long-term commitment and can easily become a competitor.
Economic Factors			
Investment Costs. Shipyards are capital intensive and the market they compete in is volatile. This implies that the integration level has different capital investment requirements and risks associated with it.	High investment requirements: Facilities, equipment, IT-systems and organizational changes.	Low investment requirements: IT-systems and organizational changes.	No investment requirements.
Transaction Costs. Shipbuilding characteristics drives costs and integration between functions is identified to facilitate cost control [4].	Coordination costs and contract negotiations should be low or not existing.	Long-term relationships facilitate collaboration and ease of coordination.	High transaction costs due to contract negotiations and complex coordination

By taking the perspective of the ship designer, the integration alternative with the yard can be classified as ownership, partner yard, or market yard. This division is inspired by the work performed in the MODNET-project [13]. A similar division was mentioned but not further elaborated.

Ownership. Ownership implies that the designer and shipyard are part of the same company. The functions are thereby vertically integrated. This integration alternative also includes functions that are integrated through joint ventures. Ownership usually implies the highest level of collaboration.

Partner Yard. The partner yard alternative implies that long-term, contractual agreements or strategic alliances between the ship designer and the shipyard are in place. The ownership and partner yard alternatives imply that the ship designer will collaborate with specific yards several times. This creates incentives for improving collaboration.

Market Yard. The market yard alternative implies no long-term relationship. Contrary to the two other alternatives, this category implies a one-project-at-the-time focus for the collaboration between the actors. A ship designer will in practice have a limited number of vertically integrated yards or partner yards. For market yards, there are basically no restrictions.

Each pair of designer and yard can be characterized by its integration alternative. In practice, different shipbuilders adapt different strategies. Some build ships mainly through the ownership model, others pursue a more diversified strategy. The case company has for example evolved from being a shipbuilder in the ownership category to being in all three categories.

The three integration alternatives can be further characterized by how they affect various industry-relevant business factors. Such factors were identified in collaboration with the case company. They were structured into strategic, market, product and technology, and economic factors, as Beckman and Rosenfield [8] do in the context of vertical integration decisions (Table 1). Even though the division between partner yard and market yard is not a matter of vertical integration, the factors have been found relevant for comparing all the three integration alternatives.

5   Conclusion and Further Research

In this paper we have identified three different levels of integration between ship designers and shipyards. Industry-relevant business factors are identified and combined with the three integration alternatives in table 3. The table exemplifies consequences of the three integration choices. The theoretical contribution of this paper is thus a typology of different integration alternatives for ship designers and shipyards and the industry-relevant factors identified. The paper will hopefully contribute to managers' ability to take structured and informed decisions. The results should support efforts to align supply chain strategy with overall business strategy and priorities by presenting implications of each integration alternative.

The results presented in this paper rest mainly on case studies of several ship projects undertaken by a shipbuilder producing ships for the offshore industry. The proposed typology and industry-relevant factors should be validated by means of additional case studies from other shipbuilders, as well as surveys covering a larger number of shipbuilders. After validation the results could be generalized for all ETO industries. An additional opportunity for further research is to create a framework for deciding on integration levels between ship designers and main equipment suppliers.

References

1. Amaro, G., Kingsman, L.: Competitive advantage, customization and a new taxonomy for non-make-to-stock companies. International Journal of Operations & Production Management 19(4), 349–371 (1999)
2. Gosling, J., Naim, M.M.: Engineer-to-order supply chain management: A literature review and research agenda. International Journal of Production Economics 122, 741–754 (2009)
3. Hicks, C., McGovern, T., Earl, C.: Supply chain management: A strategic issue in engineer to order manufacturing. International Journal of Production Economics 65(2), 179–190 (2000)
4. Venkataraman, R.: Project Supply Chain Management: Optimizing Value. The Way We Manage the Total Supply Chain (2007)
5. Yeo, K., Ning, J.: Integrating supply chain and critical chain concepts in engineer-procure-construct (EPC) projects. International Journal of Project Management 20(4), 253–262 (2002)
6. Hayes, R.H., Wheelwright, S.C.: Restoring our competitive edge. John Wiley & Sons, New York (1984)
7. Porter, M.E.: Competitive Strategy: Techniques for Analyzing Industries and Competitors. Free Press, New York (1980)
8. Beckman, S.L., Rosenfield, D.B.: Operations Strategy, Competing in the 21st Century, International ed. McGraw-Hill, New York (2008)
9. Jagdev, H.S., Thoben, K.D.: Anatomy of enterprise collaborations. Production Planning & Control 12(5), 437–451 (2001)
10. Persson, G., Håkansson, H.: Supplier segmentation–when supplier relationships matter. IMP Journal 1(3), 26–41 (2007)
11. Bensaou, M.: Portfolios of buyer-supplier relationships. Sloan Management Review 40(4), 35–44 (1999)
12. Kraljic, P.: Purchasing must become supply management. Harvard Business Review 61(5), 109–117 (1983)
13. Longva, T., Horgen, R., Brett, P.O.: Teknisk rapport, DP1 - Konkurransekraftutvikling, verdiskaping og usikkerhet ved samvirkende forretningskonsepter i norskkontrollert skibsbygging. Det Norske Veritas (2007)

Two Multi-criteria Approaches
to Supplier Segmentation

Jafar Rezaei and J. Roland Ortt

Section Technology, Strategy and Entrepreneurship,
Faculty of Technology, Policy and Management, Delft University of Technology
Jaffalaan 5, 2628 BX Delft, The Netherlands
{j.rezaei,j.r.ortt}@tudelft.nl

Abstract. Supplier segmentation is a strategic business activity whereby suppliers of a firm are categorized on the basis of their similarities. Instead of handling all suppliers separately, segmentation yields a manageable number of segments, each of which requires a similar strategy. Standard methods of supplier segmentation have serious shortcomings: they often use a limited number of criteria and do not capture the complicated interaction between different supplier aspects. There is often little by way of data that can be used to apply more advanced statistical segmentation approaches. In this paper, we use two overarching dimensions to capture all available segmentation criteria: supplier capabilities and supplier willingness. We propose two multi-criteria approaches to assess the position of suppliers with regard to these dimensions and subsequently that outcome to identify segments. These multi-criteria approaches, a fuzzy rule-based system and a DEA-like linear programming model are applied to a real-world case to demonstrate how the results can be used in practice. The results of the two approaches are compared and some strategies are suggested to handle different segments.

Keywords: supplier segmentation, supplier relationship management, buyer-supplier relationship, fuzzy rule-based system, linear programming, DEA.

1   Introduction and Review of Literature

Supplier relationship management (SRM) provides a structure for firms to develop and maintain relationships with their suppliers [1]. SRM does not refer to managing individual relationships with suppliers, but means that different groups of suppliers, each of which with different characteristics, can be handled in different ways [2]. A close relationship should be developed and maintained with key suppliers, whereas the traditional procurement strategies may be adopted for other suppliers. Supplier segmentation is a prerequisite for SRM, it provides a framework to identify different groups of suppliers.

Compared to customer segmentation [3], supplier segmentation has received relatively little attention. Customer segmentation is aimed at dealing with heterogeneity on the demand side of the market, while supplier segmentation focuses on the supply side of the market [4].

J. Frick and B. Laugen (Eds.): APMS 2011, IFIP AICT 384, pp. 317–325, 2012.
© IFIP International Federation for Information Processing 2012

The term supplier segmentation originated in early 1980s, when Parasuraman [5] and Kraljic [6] proposed two different approaches to supplier segmentation. Parasuraman [5] proposed a four-step process for supplier segmentation: (1) Key features of customer segments are identified; (2) Key characteristics of suppliers are identified; (3) Relevant variables for supplier segmentation are selected; and (4) Suppliers are segmented based on these variables. Parasuraman [5] did not specify the variables to segment the suppliers. By contrast, Kraljic [6] pre-specified the segmentation variables when he proposed two dimensions, profit impact and supply risk, for segmenting suppliers, which are measured for different products supplied to a firm. Considering two levels (low and high) for each dimension a 2×2 matrix distinguishes four segments: (1) Non-critical items (supply risk: low; profit impact: low); (2) Leverage items (supply risk: low; profit impact: high); (3) Bottleneck items (supply risk: high; profit impact: low); and (4) Strategic items (supply risk: high; profit impact: high). Kraljic [6] then suggested different strategies for handling these supplier segments. Kraljic's approach [6] is extended by several researchers. For example, Olsen and Ellram [7] proposed a supplier segmentation based on two dimensions: difficulty of managing the purchase situation, and strategic importance of the purchase. Bensaou [8] considered two other dimensions: the supplier's specific investments and the buyer's specific investments. Kaufman et al.' segmentation [9] was based on two dimensions: technology, and collaboration. Supplier commitment and commodity importance are the two dimensions of Svensson' approach [10]. Hallikas et al. [11] used supplier dependency risk and buyer dependency risk as the two dimensions of their proposed approach. For a discussion of supplier segmentation approaches, see Rezaei and Ortt [12].

Several two-dimensional approaches have been proposed for supplier segmentation, each of which includes some important segmentation variables, while neglecting some other important ones. The shortcoming of the approaches can lead to a lack of homogeneity within segments and a lack of heterogeneity between supplier segments. Recently, Rezaei and Ortt [12] have proposed a supplier segmentation framework that consists of two overarching dimensions: supplier capabilities and supplier willingness. They define supplier capabilities and supplier willingness as follows:

"Supplier's capabilities are complex bundles of skills and accumulated knowledge, exercised through organisational processes that enable firms to co-ordinate activities and make use of their assets in different business functions that are important for a buyer."

"Supplier's willingness is confidence, commitment and motivation to engage in a (long-term) relationship with a buyer".

These two dimensions encompass almost all of the variables previously proposed for supplier segmentation. Methods to measure and combine the variables in each of the dimensions are proposed to satisfy another general requirement of a segmentation approach: measurability. This approach also creates a connection between different supplier-related activities such as supplier relationship management and supplier development, in the supply chain management framework. Finally, this approach enables a buying firm to explicitly assess the combination of segmentation variables that best fit its specific company, supplier and market conditions.

In this paper, we adopt the supplier segmentation framework proposed by Rezaei and Ortt [12]. To measure and integrate the variables of the different dimensions, we apply a fuzzy rule-based system and a DEA-like linear programming model, which are briefly discussed in section 2 and 3 respectively. In section 4, the two approaches are illustrated for the suppliers of a broiler company. The managerial implications of the outcomes are discussed and future work is described in section 5.

2   Fuzzy Rule-Based System

A fuzzy rule-based system [13] is a system that is used to govern the relationship between input and output variables. Here, supplier capabilities and willingness are considered as the output of two fuzzy rule-based systems, while the criteria used to evaluate the different dimensions serve as input. First of all, based on expert knowledge, these variables are fuzzified, which means that linguistic values (fuzzy subsets) are used (like low, medium and high) and fuzzy numbers are formed for each linguistic value. Secondly, a fuzzy rule base is provided based on the expert knowledge. These rules make a logic connection between different linguistic values that have been defined for input and output variables. A typical fuzzy rule has the form: IF antecedent THEN consequent. The number of rules is a function of the number of input variables and the number of linguistic values defined for inputs. If we have n inputs and k linguistic values for each input, then the total number of rules is k^n. Next, a fuzzy inference engine should be designed. The evaluation of a rule is based on computing the truth value of its premise part and applying it to its conclusion part. This results in assigning one fuzzy subset to each output variable of the rule. This inference engine performs mathematical computations based on the fuzzy numbers. As the final operation of a fuzzy inference system, the fuzzy output produced by the system is converted to a crisp number. More information about fuzzy rule-based systems can be found in [13, 14].

3   Data Envelopment Analysis (DEA)-Like

Here, we describe a simple DEA-like linear programming model introduced by Rezaei et al. [15].

Suppose we have N suppliers. The level of willingness of supplier i (Ei) is seen as the sum product of its item measures $d_{ij}, j = 1, ..., J$ by their weights $w_{ij}, j = 1, ..., J, \left(\sum_{j=1}^{J} w_{ij} d_{ij}\right)$. We can measure the level of capabilities of the supplier in the same formulation. Now, if supplier i is allowed to maximize its level of willingness/capabilities, providing the level of willingness/capabilities of other suppliers do not exceed 1, then the calculated maximum level of willingness/capabilities of this supplier denotes its relative willingness/capabilities. The mathematical programming model for supplier i is as follows.

$$\max(E_i) = \sum_{j=1}^{J} w_{ij} d_{ij} \tag{1}$$

s.t.
$$\sum_{j=1}^{J} w_{ij} d_{nj} \leq 1, n = 1, ..., i, ..., N \quad \text{(N is the number of suppliers)}$$
$$w_{ij} \geq 0, j = 1, ..., J. \quad \text{(J is the number of items)}$$

Solving N models for supplier willingness, and N models for supplier capabilities, the relative level of willingness and capabilities for each supplier are determined in the range of [0,1]. The results can then be used as a base to segment suppliers. For example if we consider the middle of the range of supplier willingness and supplier capabilities scores as two cut-off points, then we can form two levels for willingness and capability scores and combine them to segment the suppliers into four segments.

4   Implementation of the Approaches, and Discussion

In this section, we describe the implementation of the supplier segmentation using the two approaches discussed above: (1) A fuzzy rule-based system, and (2) a DEA-like linear programming model for a broiler company.

The broiler company receives newly hatched chicks, feed, medications and other equipment and materials from 43 suppliers. The company raises the chicks to market weight in about six weeks and the chickens are then delivered to a processing plant to be stunned and undergo further processing. To manage the relationship with a large number of suppliers, the broiler company needs to segment them. Interviewing the managers of the company yielded six criteria (price, delivery, quality, reserve capacity, geographical location and financial position) for measuring the supplier's capabilities, and another six criteria (commitment to quality, communication openness, reciprocal arrangement, willingness to share information, supplier's effort in promoting JIT principles, and long term relationship) for measuring the supplier's willingness (to see a comprehensive list of the relevant criteria and their selection procedure, see [12]). We then asked the manager to evaluate all the suppliers using scores between 1 (very low) to 5 (very high) for all criteria.

4.1   The Rule-Based Systems

To measure the aggregated degree of supplier's capabilities and supplier's willingness, we designed two fuzzy rule-based systems each of which consists of six input variables and a single output. To fuzzify the variables we considered two fuzzy subsets (e.g., Low and High, or Bad and Good) and their equivalent triangular membership function based on the knowledge of the company manager and two experts. The intended fuzzy rule-based systems are shown in Fig. 1.

Considering the number of criteria and the number of fuzzy subsets, we had to make $2^6 = 64$ rules for each system. Below, an example rule of the second system is presented that is designed to measure a supplier's willingness.

"IF 'supplier's commitment to quality' is Low AND 'communication openness' is Low AND 'reciprocal arrangement' is Low AND 'willingness to share information' is Low AND 'supplier's effort in promoting JIT principles' is High AND 'length of relationship is Short, THEN supplier's willingness is Low"

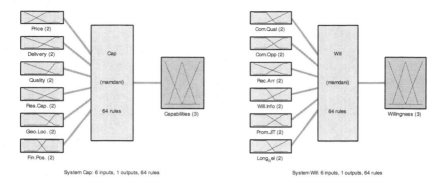

Fig. 1. Fuzzy rule-based systems (FS). Left: FS1 (capabilities); Right: FS2 (willingness).

This rule shows how particular values (i.e., high or low) of the criteria are combined into an overall value for supplier willingness. We then use the inference engine developed by Mamdani and Assilian [16] by applying a compositional minimum operator, which represents a conservative attitude towards measuring the supplier's capabilities and willingness. At a minimum inferencing, the entire strength of the rule is considered as the minimum membership value of the input variables' membership values.

$$\mu_{output} = \min\{\mu_{input1}, \mu_{input2}, \dots, \mu_{inputN}\}$$

The output of the fuzzy inference engine is a fuzzy number that needs to be defuzzified. We applied the Center of Gravity (COG) defuzzification method, one of the most commonly used defuzzification methods, as follows:

$$y_c = \frac{\int_i \mu_F(y_i) y_i dy_i}{\int_i \mu_F(y_i) dy_i} \tag{2}$$

where y_i is the representative value of the fuzzy subset member i of the output, and $\mu_F(y_i)$ is the confidence in that member (membership value) and y_c is the crisp value of the output.

To calculate the final aggregated scores, we used MATLAB's Fuzzy Logic Toolbox. Based on the two final scores for each supplier, the suppliers are assigned to four segments (see the left side of Fig. 2) (it is, however, clear that more segments can be formed). Of the 43 suppliers, three are segmented as Type 1 (low capabilities and low willingness), nine as Type 2 (low capabilities and high willingness), three as Type 3 (high capabilities, and low willingness) and, finally, 28 as Type 4 (high capabilities, and high willingness).

4.2   DEA-Like Linear Programming Model

To measure the aggregated degree of a supplier's willingness and capabilities, we formulate 86 linear programming problems of type (1). That is to say, two linear programming problems for each supplier are formulated and solved: one to determine the relative willingness and one to determine the relative capabilities of the supplier. As such, two aggregated scores are obtained for each supplier in the range of [0, 1]. Considering the actual minimum and maximum aggregated scores for supplier willingness and capabilities, two cut-off points are determined to divide the suppliers into four segments. In our case, the minimum and maximum aggregated scores for supplier willingness are 0.6 and 1.0 respectively. The minimum and maximum aggregated scores for supplier capabilities are 0.8 and 1.0 respectively. Therefore, we determined 0.8 and 0.9 as the cut-off points for supplier willingness and supplier capabilities, respectively, as a base to segment the suppliers to four segments (see Fig. 2). Of the 43 suppliers, four are identified as being Type 1 (low capabilities and low willingness), nine as Type 2 (low capabilities and high willingness), two as Type 3 (high capabilities and low willingness) and, finally, 28 as Type 4 (high capabilities and high willingness).

As can be seen from the right side of Fig. 2, the number of suppliers assigned to each segment is almost the same in the two approaches, but there are some differences. For example, both approaches assign 28 suppliers to segment Type 4. However, only 22 of these 28 suppliers are assigned to this segment in both cases, which has to with weight of the various criteria.

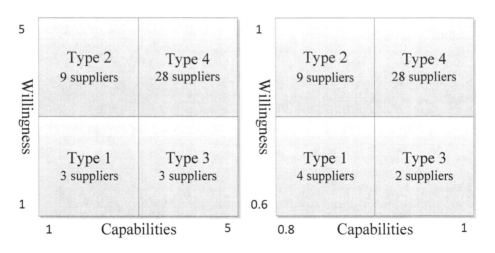

Fig. 2. The final supplier segmentation results; Left: fuzzy rule-based, Right: DEA-like

4.3   Managerial Implications

Generally speaking, firms can use our approach to formulate different strategies for handling different segments. Our approach condenses a comprehensive set of segmentation criteria into two overarching dimensions: supplier willingness and supplier capabilities. The values that specific suppliers assign to on these dimensions are subsequently used to segment the suppliers. In this article, we created 2×2 = 4 segments. Each of these segments requires a different strategy from the buying company. Type 4 suppliers, for example, are the most capable suppliers who are also highly willing to cooperate with the buying firm. However, because of their capabilities, they are likely to be attractive to other firms as well. Therefore, the firm in question should try to maintain strong relationships with those suppliers. Type 3 suppliers are also highly capable, but they are less willing to cooperate with the firm. The firm should try and become more attractive to these suppliers and show greater loyalty, for example by increasing communication and purchase volume. Type 2 suppliers are very willing to cooperate, but less able to meet the buyer's requirements. A general suggestion is to help these suppliers improve their capabilities and performance. Finally, Type 1 suppliers are less capable and less willing to cooperate with the firm. In all likelihood, it is best to maintain an arm's length relationship to manage the relationship with these suppliers.

In addition, strategies can be formulated to improve the (capabilities or willingness of) suppliers and thereby upgrade them to other segments. The main supplier development strategies mentioned by Krause et al. [17] are: supplier assessment, providing suppliers with incentives for improved performance, instigating competition among suppliers, and direct involvement of the buying firm's personnel with suppliers. These strategies to a large extent focus on improving capabilities. Although, as a result of these strategies, supplier willingness may also increase; specific strategies can be used that focus specifically on this aspect. We believe that the key concept here is trust. Trust is a crucial component in the dimension of supplier willingness. As has been argued in various studies (e.g. [18]), a buyer's trust in a supplier can enhance that supplier's willingness to share information, make investments specifically with regard to the buying firm and maintain a long-term relationship.

These strategies can be implemented to promote suppliers in segment Type 1 to segment Type 3, for example. Type 4 suppliers are key suppliers with whom a firm should try to maintain a close long-term relationship.

Specifically, the analysis yielded interesting insights into some of the broiler company's suppliers. Some suppliers with low scores on both dimensions were nevertheless allowed to continue as suppliers to meet seasonal peaks in demand. The company has already started implementing strategies to manage the relationship with its suppliers, and to develop those who are segmented as Type 1 to 3, especially Type 2 and 3.

5   Conclusion

In this paper, we proposed two multi-criteria methodologies to measure supplier capabilities and willingness: A fuzzy rule-based system and a DEA-like linear programming model. The final scores of these two dimensions are used to divide suppliers into four segments. Supplier segmentation allows firms to maximize its efforts to formulate suitable strategies for handling different suppliers. The approaches to assess the suppliers' positions on the dimensions of capability and willingness help connect the related activities of supplier selection, supplier relationship management and supplier development. The rule-based approach proved a very flexible approach that can be designed by interviewing a limited number of knowledgeable managers or experts within the company. It has some advantages over other methods, such as the ability to handle the inherent interdependencies, vagueness and contingencies of segmentation variables. The DEA-like methodology, on the other hand, is a data-based methodology that requires a minimum number of data [15]. However, it is more flexible in terms of weighting the criteria. Both approaches are suitable when a high data volume is not available and advanced statistical methodologies are not possible.

As pointed out by several researchers (e.g. [19]), matching certain characteristics between buyers and suppliers is an important factor in the success of their partnerships. Therefore, as a future research direction, we suggest studying the relationship between symmetry in capabilities and willingness between various buyer and supplier segments and partnership success. It is interesting to compare the proportion of different segments for different industries and situations. We also suggest integrating supplier segmentation into other supplier-related activities, such as 'lot-sizing with supplier selection' [20]. Finally, we suggest studying the relationship between partnership with suppliers from different segments and firm performance.

References

1. Lambert, D.M. (ed.): Supply chain management: Process, partnership, performance, 3rd edn. Supply Chain Management Institute, Sarasota (2008)
2. Wagner, S.M., Johnson, J.L.: Configuring and managing strategic supplier portfolios. Industrial Marketing Management 33(8), 717–730 (2004)
3. Smith, W.R.: Product differentiation and market segmentation as alternative marketing strategies. The Journal of Marketing 21(1), 3–8 (1956)
4. Erevelles, S., Stevenson, T.H.: Enhancing the business-to-business supply chain: Insights from partitioning the supply-side. Industrial Marketing Management 35(4), 481–492 (2006)
5. Parasuraman, A.: Vendor segmentation: An additional level of market segmentation. Industrial Marketing Management 9(1), 59–62 (1980)
6. Kraljic, P.: Purchasing must become supply management. Harvard Business Review, 109–117 (September/October 1983)
7. Olsen, R.F., Ellram, L.M.: A portfolio approach to supplier relationships. Industrial Marketing Management 26(2), 101–113 (1997)
8. Bensaou, B.M.: Portfolios of buyer-supplier relationships. Sloan Management Review 40(4), 35–44 (1999)
9. Kaufman, A., Wood, C.H., Theyel, G.: Collaboration and technology linkages: a strategic supplier typology. Strategic Management Journal 21(6), 649–663 (2000)
10. Svensson, G.: Supplier segmentation in the automotive industry: A dyadic approach of a managerial model. International Journal of Physical Distribution & Logistics Management 34(1), 12–38 (2004)
11. Hallikas, J., Puumalainen, K., Vesterinen, T., Virolainen, V.M.: Risk-based classification of supplier relationships. Journal of Purchasing & Supply Management 11(2-3), 72–82 (2005)
12. Rezaei, J., Ortt, R.: A multi-variable approach to supplier segmentation. International Journal of Production Research (forthcoming), doi:10.1080/00207543.2011.615352
13. Jang, J.S.R.: ANFIS: Adaptive-Network-Based Fuzzy Inference System. IEEE Transactions on Systems, Man and Cybernetics 23(3), 665–685 (1993)
14. Ross, T.J.: Fuzzy logic with engineering applications, 2nd edn. Wiley & Sons (2004)
15. Rezaei, J., Ortt, R., Scholten, V.: Measuring entrepreneurship: Expert-based vs. data-based methodologies. Expert Systems with Applications 39(4), 4063–4074 (2012)

16. Mamdani, E.H., Assilian, S.: An experiment in linguistic synthesis with a fuzzy logic controller. International Journal of Man–Machine Studies 7(1), 1–13 (1975)
17. Krause, D.R., Scannell, T.V., Calantone, R.J.: A Structural Analysis of the Effectiveness of Buying Firms' Strategies to Improve Supplier Performance. Decision Sciences 31(1), 33–55 (2000)
18. Doney, P.M., Cannon, J.P.: An Examination of the Nature of Trust in Buyer-Seller Relationships. The Journal of Marketing 61(2), 35–51 (1997)
19. Wilkinson, I., Young, L., Freytag, P.V.: Business mating: Who chooses and who gets chosen? Industrial Marketing Management 34(7), 669–680 (2005)
20. Rezaei, J., Davoodi, M.: Multi-objective models for lot-sizing with supplier selection. International Journal of Production Economics 130(1), 77–86 (2011)

Review on Collaborative Decision Making in Supply Chain: The Relationship between E-Collaboration Technology and Development of Inter-organizational Trust

Nora Azima Noordin[1], Umit S. Bititci[1], and Robert Van Der Meer[2]

[1] Department of Design, Manufacture and Engineering Management
{nora.noordin,u.s.bititci}@strath.ac.uk
[2] Department of Management Science
University of Strathclyde, Glasgow, UK
{robert-van.der.meer}@strath.ac.uk

Abstract. In successful supply chain collaborations, effective communication and the development of inter-organizational trust are a key factor. The purpose of these literature review paper is to initially review the previous literature on the relationship between the adoption of e-collaboration technology and factors influencing the development of trust in supply chain collaborations. This study is important to answer the questions whether the adoption of e-collaboration technology may help or hinder inter-organizational trust in collaborative decision-making in supply chain area.

Keywords: Supply Chain Management, Supply Chain Collaboration, Collaborative Decision-Making, E-Collaboration Technology, Inter-Organizational Trust.

1   Introduction

The literature review found that there are key elements to create successful supply chain collaboration; cross-functional activities, process alignment, joint decision-making and supply chain metrics (Barratt, 2004). Nowadays, the collaborations have expanded globally. It is important to open and develop clear and broad lines of communication (Frankel et al, 2002), to foster information sharing and to create a shared understanding (Ireland and Bruce, 2000). Rapid changes in information and communication technology (ICT) have eased the way to collaborate. Partners in collaborative companies can communicate and exchange information easily and of course cheaply using advanced technology in ICT such as e-collaboration technology. Evidently, the number of companies working together for a mutual objective is accelerating and has almost doubled in the past ten years. It is also predicted this will further increase in the future (Zineldin and Bredenlow, 2003).

Successful partner relationships involve the existence of several characteristic traits and it is widely acknowledged that trust is one of them (Wehmeyer and Riemer, 2007).

J. Frick and B. Laugen (Eds.): APMS 2011, IFIP AICT 384, pp. 326–341, 2012.
© IFIP International Federation for Information Processing 2012

Trust that will be discussed in this research is 'inter-organizational trust' in the context of collaborative supply chain. Scholars from a number of disciplines have agreed conceptually and empirically that inter-organizational trust, as well as trust in general, plays vital roles in firm behavior and performance. Issues associated with organizational trust have generated deal of broad scholarly interest. There are significant amounts of literature discussing trust in organizational context as well as some other interesting fields such as interpersonal trust and social networks. However, there are lacks of scholarly work on relationship between e-collaboration technology and inter-organizational trust in supply chain area. Thus, the goal of this paper is to investigate and initially review the previous works on the relationship of e-collaboration adoption and factors influencing the development of inter-organizational trust, specifically in the context of collaborative decision-making in supply chain.

The following sections will be organized as follow: Section 2 describes the methodology and process used to carry out the literature review. Section 3 addresses the definition of the terms discussed in this paper based on the previous literature. Section 4 presents the results of this review, we survey the literature on the relationship of e-collaboration adoption and inter-organizational trust in collaborative supply chain, identify and integrate the key themes that emerge from the empirical contribution on the subject. Then, several factors that influence the development of inter-organizational trust are described. Finally section 5 concludes the findings of the paper and directions for future research.

2   Methodology

The information used in this study was gathered using a systematic literature review approach as described in Figure 1. The three research questions taken into consideration were as below.

Table 1. Literature Review Process

Research Questions	1. What are the types of collaborative decisions in supply chain? 2. What kind of E-Collaboration technology adopted in decision-making process? 3. What are the factors influencing inter-organizational trust development?
Boundary Setting	Search engines: Science Direct, ISI Web of Knowledge, Emerald, SAGE Journal, Elsevier. Keyword entered: Supply Chain Management, Supply Chain Collaboration, Collaborative Decision-Making, E-Collaboration Technology, E-Business Technology, Inter-Organizational Trust Search field: Abstract, Title Typology: Journal Paper, Conference Paper Research Methodology: Empirical Research, Literature Review

The study initially reviews four types of literature; the literature on collaborative supply chain, collaborative decision-making, e-collaboration technology and inter-organizational trust. However, not all type of research issues were selected, only papers that made contribution to the research objectives was selected during the review process.

It started with exploring random literature review in order to get the view on earlier and current researches done in the topics until the research gap was found. Then the systematic literature review approach was adopted during the process of selecting relevant literatures. The researcher applied the concept of systematic literature review to identify high quality literature. A systematic literature review involves two processes (Easterby-Smith et al, 2008):

Defining reviews protocols and mapping the field by accessing, retrieving, and judging the quality and relevance of studies in your research areas and reporting the findings to identify where gaps in the current research exist and so indicate where your research might make a useful contribution.

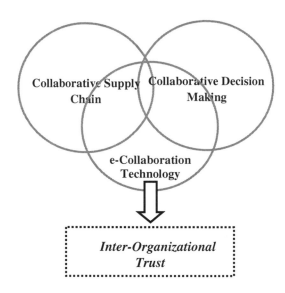

Fig. 1. This figure shows the research gap between three types of research areas. Inter-organizational trust is a result from the integration between collaborative processes in supply chain activities that become a research gap for this study.

3   Definition and Terms

There are several terms that need to be defined clearly in this paper. The study consists of four types of broad research areas; supply chain collaboration, collaborative decision-making, collaborative technology and inter-organizational trust. Each area has its own definition and meaning. This paper identifies definitions of each area from the previous literatures that contain a number of different definitions to refer to the same object.

3.1   What Is Collaboration?

Collaboration, in the context of supply chain is still relatively embryonic. Collaboration is a very broad and encompassing term and when it is put in the context of the supply chain, it needs yet further clarification (Barratt, 2004). Bititci, 2007, Jordan Jr. and Michel, (2000) defined collaboration literally as 'working together'. The term is often used when individuals or organizations work together towards some common aim. Huxam (1996) suggested collaboration as a positive form of working in association with others for some form of mutual benefits. Cropper (1996) defined it as a distinctive mode of organizing with a positive and purposive relationship between organizations that retain autonomy, integrity and distinct identity, but at the same time, the possibility to withdraw from the relationship is exist.

All of the above definitions are similar and complementary each other. For the purpose of this review, authors attempt to combine them into single comprehensive definition that cover all of dimensions on existing literature as follow:

"Collaboration is a number of autonomous organizations in the supply chain that are actively working together towards common objectives, and is characterized by sharing information, knowledge and risk for mutual benefits. Collaborative organizations make decisions together and it is mutual goal setting that goes far beyond a written contract."

3.2   Collaborative Decision-Making

Essentially, collaborative decision-making is a process of doing decisions together and achieving same agreement from collaborated parties. It involves process of identifying and choosing alternative courses of action in a manner appropriate to the demand of the situations. In management decisions, terms that most often used suggested by Ofstad (1961). Management decision has been defined in many ways. As suggested by Ofstad: "...to say that a (manager) has made a decision may mean: (1) that he (or she) has started a series of (actions) in favor of something, or it may mean (2) that he (or she) has made up his (or her) mind to do a certain (thing)... But perhaps the most common use of the term is: "to make a decision" means (3) to make a judgment regarding what one ought to do in a certain situation after having deliberated on some alternative courses of action (Ofstad, 1961).

In this research, the authors apply decision's definition suggested by Harrison (2000); a decision is defined as:

"A moment in an ongoing process of evaluating alternatives for meeting an objective, at which expectations about a particular course of action impel the decision maker to select that course of action most likely to result in attaining the objective".

3.3   E-Collaboration Technology

Electronic collaboration technology (e-Collaboration) is operationally defined as collaboration using electronic technologies among different individuals to accomplish a common task (Kock and D'Arcy, 2002, 2001). McDonell (2001) considers e-collaboration as internet-based collaborations, which integrates people and processes giving flexibility to supply and service chain. There are other streams in defining e-collaboration as virtual teaming of structured communication activities by using electronic tools. IBM defined e-collaboration as anything that allows people to collaborate or work together more easily using electronic tools.

In this paper, e-collaboration technology in the context of supply chain is referred to the Internet-based communication platforms used by collaborative organizations to communicate and sharing information and a platform that can be used to assist deci-sion-making process during online meeting. The authors agree with e-collaboration definition in the context of supply chain suggested by Johnson and Whang (2002):

"E-collaboration is business-to-business interactions facilitated by the Internet. These interactions go beyond simple buy/sell transactions and may be better described as relationships. These include such activities as information sharing and integration, decision sharing, process sharing and resources sharing".

3.4   Definition of Trust and Inter-organizational Trust

For the last two decades researchers from various disciplines have interpreted trust in different ways and given different dimensions by focusing on specific aspect of trust. Studies from Laeequddin et al. (2010) identify trust in different context and in each context trust can be bestowed upon a person, place, event or object (Giffin, 1967), between individuals (George and Swap, 1982; Mayer et al., 1995), organizations (Gu-lati, 1995), individuals and organizations (Zaheer et al., 1998), partner's competence (Barber, 1983), process, characteristics and institutions (Zucker, 1986), system (Gid-dens, 1990), calculations (Anderson and Narus, 1990), economics (Larson, 1992), intentional relations (Nooteboom et al., 1997) and between a user and an IT system (Lippert, 2001), technology (Jones et al., 2000), or financial services (Wang, 2008). Trust may function as glues n a relationship (Jarillo, 1988) and trust may function as a lubricant (Arrow, 1974).

Different concepts of trust have been provided by various studies. Basically, trust relations involve participation of at least two parties: the trustor, the party who places him or herself in a vulnerable situation under uncertainty; and the trustee, the party on whom the trust is placed, who has the opportunity to take advantage of the trustor's vulnerability (Laeequddin et al., 2010). Most common used definition of trust is as suggested by some researchers such as by Mayer et al. (1995). He defined trust as "the willingness of a party based on the expectations that the other party will perform a particular action important to the trustor, irrespective of the ability to monitor or control the party". Kim et al. (2009) defined trust as a complex and multifaceted construct.

This study focuses on inter-organizational trust concept. The definition of inter-organizational trust that agreed to be used in this research is as suggested by Zaheer, McEvily and Perrone (1998).

"Inter-organizational trust is the extent to which members of one organization hold a collective trust orientation toward another organization".

4   Analysis

4.1   Decision-Making Concept

A decision is choice out of several alternatives or options made by the decision maker to achieve some objectives in a given situation. Business decisions are those, which are made in the process of conducting business to achieve its objective and a given environment. Managerial decision-making is a control point for every managerial activity may be planning, staffing, directing, organizing, controlling and communicating. Decision-making is the art of reasoned and judicious choice of many alternatives. Once decision is taken, it implies commitment of resources.

The business managers have to take variety of decisions, some are routine and others are long-term implementation decisions. The managerial decisions are grouped as strategic, tactical and operational decision. Strategic decisions are known as major decision influence whole or major part of the organization. Such decision contributes directly to the achievement of common goals of the organizations, have long-range effect upon the organization. These types of decision are basically based on partial knowledge of the environment factors which are uncertain and dynamic, therefore such decision are taken at the higher level of management. Tactical decision relate to the implementation of strategic decisions, directed towards developing divisional plans, structuring workflows and establishing distribution channels. These decisions are taken at the middle level of management. While operational decision relate to daily operations of the enterprise having a short-term horizon and are always repeated. These decisions are based on facts regarding the events and do not require much business judgments. Operational decisions are taken at lower level of management.

4.2   Types of Collaborative Decisions in Supply Chain

The development of an integrated supply chains means the management should take a look of material flow from three perspectives. As suggested by Stevens (1993) the management have to consider three level of management that are strategic, tactical and operational level where each levels have its own task, the use of facilities, people, finance and systems must be coordinated and harmonized as a whole. The focus at strategic level should be to develop are (Stevens, 1993):

- Objectives and policies for the supply chain. These should be expressed in terms of what supply chain has to do well to support the needs of the business for example be responsive to change, operate at lowest cost, ensure a high level of product availability;
- The shape of the supply chain in terms of key facilities and their locations;
- The company's competitive package, planned by product and market availability, service level, lead time, technical support and after-sales support;
- An outline organizational structure able to bridge functional barriers and operate an integrated supply chain effectively.

From the tactical perspective, the management should focus on the means by which the strategic objectives can be realized. It involves translating the strategic objectives into goals for each function, enabling the functions to provide complementary balance as parts of the supply chain. The functional goals provide the focus for achieving the balance, and inventory, capacity and service are the levers by which balance is achieved. The operational perspective should be concerned with the efficient operation of the supply chain. It focuses on the detailed systems and procedures, and ensures that appropriate controls and performance measures are in place. Typically, a company should measure the performance of the supply chain in terms of five areas as suggested by (Stevens, 1993):

- Inventory investment;
- Service level;
- Throughput efficiency;
- Supplier performance;
- Cost.

Using literature review, this section describes types of collaborative decisions involved in supply chain process. These decisions are made in various levels of supply chain management; strategic, tactical and operational level. Each level has its own activities and processes that need decision-making integration between collaborated supply chain organizations. Generally, Table 2 describes type of processes and decisions involve in supply chain activity in each level.

Table 2. Types of Decisions in Supply Chain Process

Strategic Level	
Muckstad *et al.* (2001)	Strategic decisions typically deal with market entry and mobilizing resources needed to meet market requirements over time.
Van Goor *et al.* (1996)	Strategic logistics decisions concern major capital commitments and long time horizon, including the location choices between a distribution networks or more basic make or buy decisions
Tactical Level	
Huin *et al.* (2002)	Medium level decisions are made, such as weekly demand forecasting, distribution and transportation planning, and materials requirement planning.
Operational Level	
Huin *et al.* (2002)	Operational level is concerned with the very short-term decisions made from day-to-day.

Table 2. (*continued*)

Van Goor *et al.* (1996)	Operational logistics decision-making relates to day-to-day operations and usually involves low capital investment. Examples include the order control policy (frequency, replenishment time, back order procedures), order picking (order picking strategy procedure, warehouse routing) and route planning (scheduling, assignment of vehicles).

The Supply Chain Planning Matrix by Fleischmann et al. (2002) classifies the planning tasks in two dimensions "planning horizon" and "supply chain process". Figure 2 below shows typical supply chain tasks but with various contents in the particular supply chain levels.

However, some scholars agreed that it remains disputable at what level of decision-making a particular decision should be allocated (Becker et al., 2004). The border between the tactical and operational levels is vague (Laubacher et al., 1997), since the fulfillment of actual orders at operational level. The exact position of each decision-making element in the hierarchy therefore remains a question of relativity (Becker et al, 2004).

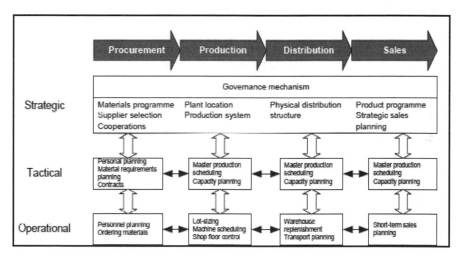

Fig. 2. The Supply Chain Planning Matrix (Rohde *et al.*, 2000; in: Fleischmann *et al.*, 2002; adapted)

4.3   E-Collaboration Technology Adopted in Decision-Making Process

Rapid changes in technology gives impact to the style of managing supply chain processes. Collaborations improve supply chain processes by increasing the intensity and scope of co-operative behavior between two or more independent decision-making units. Today, collaborative decision-making processes are supported by advanced ICT. It is argued that the value and importance of collaboration has changed, as we migrate from traditional supply chain management (SCM) approach to the e-SCM perspective (Williams, 2002). The evolution of supply chain collaboration technology can be seen from 1990's, from EDI to Web service enable. One of the most commonly implemented information technologies that aims to integrate the supply chain processes is Electronic Data Interchange (EDI). However, with the emergence of the Internet, EDI is slowly being replaced by other e-business standards. The main reasons why EDI implementation was seen as a challenge includes the availability of different standards in EDI, not being able to provide real time data transfer and the high implementation cost (Chong and Ooi, 2008). The 1990s saw organizations moving towards implementing business-to-business (B2B) technologies which allow them to integrate their supply chain processes better (Chou et al., 2004). However, researchers such as Chou et al. (2004), Chong et al. (2009) stated that from the year 2000 onwards, organizations have started to move towards using e-collaboration or collaborative commerce tools in their supply chain. E-collaboration tools do not focus on monetary transactions in B2B and instead cover the exchanges of information and ideas between the trading organizations and within organizations and allows them to collaboratively design, develop, build and manage products through their life cycle.

Figure 3 shows timeline of the evolution in supply chain collaboration from 1990 to 2005 (Pramatari, 2007) in retail and enabling technologies and this paper extends the evolution from 2005 to 2011 in Figure 4.

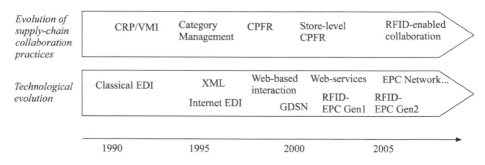

Fig. 3. Evolution of supply chain collaboration practices in retail and enabling technologies from 1990 to 2005 (Pramatari, 2007)

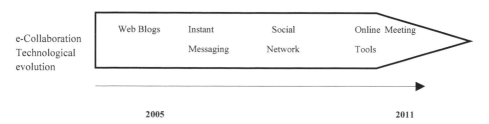

Fig. 4. Evolution of e-collaboration technology to facilitate decision-making in supply chain collaboration

T. McLaren *et al.* (2002) further clarified e-collaboration systems into three major types:

(1) Message-based systems that transmit information to partner applications using technologies such as fax, e-mail, EDI, or eXtensible Markup Language (XML) messages;
(2) Electronic procurement hubs, portals, or marketplaces that facilitate purchasing of goods or services from electronic catalogues, tenders, or auctions;
(3) Shared collaborative SCM systems that include collaborative planning, forecasting and replenishment capabilities in addition to electronic procurement functionality.

Rapid development in information communication technology has change the way people communicate. From 2007 until now, the boundary of e-collaboration extents it's capability to the new types of collaborative technology. Social networking and online meeting tools have been widely used by inter- and intra- organizations to facilitate decision-making processes. Of course they can reduce the process cost and time consumption. Besides that, it gives advantage to the organization to leverage the supply chain management network and transform existing business processes especially in the context of decision-making.

The synthesis of the literature leads to the development of evolution in e-collaboration (Figure 3 and 4). E-collaboration evolves from intra- to inter-organizational collaboration, from vertical to horizontal collaboration and from operational to strategic level of collaboration.

4.4   Factors Influencing Inter-organizational Trust Development

The adoption of e-collaboration technology as medium of communication and decision-making facilitation between collaborated parties arise trusting issues. Trust is a critical factor fostering commitment among supply chain partners. The presence of trust improves measurably the chance of successful supply chain performance (G.Kwon, 2004). Trust plays an important role in the adoption of e-collaboration tools as collaboration involves transparency and sharing of information among the supply chain members. When business partners want to adopt e-collaboration tools in their supply chain collaboration, an organization that trusts its partners is more likely to reach consensus in terms of achievable benefits by e-collaboration tools (Shang et al., 2005). In the case of e-collaboration adoption by inter-organizations, the trust is the firms' willingness to trust their supply chain partners in sharing important supply chain information, for example product design and research and development. Other scholars identifying trust as a significant factor in determining the adoption of inter-organizational systems include Ratnasingam (2001), Dubelaar et al. (2005), Barratt (2004), Ngai et al. (2008) and Hart and Saunders (1997).

From sociologist point of view, the role of the past in the creation of trust show that the history of previous interaction between organizations; including familiarity as well as relationship history leads to increased trust (Gulati, 1995). Although previous history clearly does not equate exactly to prospects for extended future collaboration, the question of how past ties and history serve as a signal of the "shadow of the future", and the associated trust or cooperation emanating from it, appears to be an unresolved issues (Zaheer and Harris, 2006). McEvily et al., 2003 suggest that vulnerability is an important aspect of trust creation. If vulnerability leads to trustworthiness, this may have indirect implications for organizational performance, because trustworthiness and performance have been shown to be linked (Dyer and Chu, 2003).

This study also indicates several other factors that influence inter-organizational trust development and the willingness of using e-collaboration technology as medium of communication as in Table 3.

Table 3. Factors influencing inter-organizational trust

Authors	Factors influencing trust
Fukuyama (1995), Husted (1994), Lane (1997), Lane and Bachmann (1996),	Location and national culture.
Dyer and Chu (2000)	National setting, length of time since the first interaction.
Sako (1998), Dyer and Chu (2003), Gulati (1995) and Singh (1998)	Regional and culture differences
Kramer (1999), Wicks and Berman (2004)	Social, institutional and psychological norms
Giddens (1984), Coleman (1990)	Coordination roles, role of third parties
Meyerson et al (1996)	Inter-personal trust

The argumentation in this section has shown that different aspect has justified the factors influencing inter-organizational trust. Some scholars agreed that the differences in culture and nationality have given impact in the development of trust. Norms and they way of thinking as well as capabilities in technology literacy influence the inter-organizational trust.

4.5   Collaborative Trust

From a research done by Fawcett et al. (2012), there are four stage of developing trust in supply chain. Stage 1 consists of limited trust, Stage 2 transactional trust, Stage 3 relational trust and Stage 4 collaborative trust. Relationships that reach Stage 4 entail a common belief leading parties to view supply chain partners' capacity and capabilities as an extension of their own business. When this occurs, companies share resources willingly to help partners improve their own processes and competitive positioning. This increased relationship commitment as not based on altruism but it arises out of a philosophy that competitive success depends on the strength of the supply chain team.

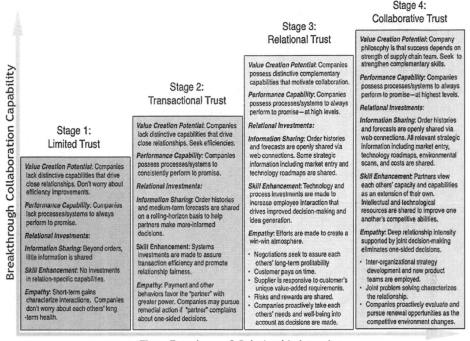

Fig. 5. Trust maturity framework (S.E. Fawcett et al. 2012)

5   Conclusions and Future Research

Using a literature review, this study described the relationship of e-collaboration adoption and factors influencing the development of inter-organizational trust, specifically in the context of collaboration decision-making in supply chain. Our analysis showed that types of decisions involve in supply chain are varies depending on the level of supply chain management. These decisions are made in various levels of supply chain management; strategic, tactical and operational level. Each level has its own activities and processes that need decision-making integration between collaborated supply chain organizations. The evolution in information communication technology has changed the way people communicate. This scenario able to assists collaborative companies to use the e-collaboration technology as a medium of communication and to make decision-making process more efficient. It gives advantage to the organization to leverage the supply chain management network and transform existing business processes especially in the context of decision-making. Trust plays an important role in the adoption of e-collaboration tools as collaboration involves transparency and sharing of information among the supply chain members. This study revealed several factors that influencing trust development between collaborated companies such as the company's past collaboration record, roles of inter-personal trust between people in the organization, culture differences and national setting.

There are significant amounts of literature discussing trust in organizational context as well as some other interesting fields such as interpersonal trust and social networks. However, there are lacks of scholarly work on relationship of e-collaboration technology and inter-organizational trust in supply chain area. Little empirical research has been carried out to assess the e-collaboration technology and it effectiveness in the context of decision-making process. This has been given opportunity for future research and to explore issues that are not studied in the literature.

References

1. Alain, Y.L.C., Keng-Boon, O., Amrik, S.: The Relationship Between Supply Chain Factors and Adoption of e-Collaboration Tools: An Empirical Examination. International Journal Production Economics (2009)
2. Anderson, J.C., Narus, J.A.: A Model of Distributor Firm and Manufacturing Firm Working Partnerships. Journal of Marketing (54), 42–58 (1990)
3. Arrow, K.: The Limits of Organization. W.W. Norton and Co., New York (1974)
4. Barber, B.: The Logic and Limits or Trust. Rutgers University Press, New Brunswick (1983)
5. Barratt, M.A.: Understanding the Meaning of Collaboration in Supply Chain. Supply Chain Management: An International Journal 9(1), 30–42 (2004)
6. Becker, J.F.F., Verduijn, T.M., Kumar, K.: Supply Chain Collaboration Across Strategic, Tactical and Operational Planning (2004),
   http://www.klict.org/docs/PPhr175.pdf
7. Bill, W., Irma Becerra, F.: Managing Trust and Commitment in Collaborative Supply Chain Relationships. Communication of the ACM 44(6), 67–73 (2001)
8. Bititci, U., Turner, T., Mackay, D., Keaney, D., Parung, J., Walters, D.: Managing Synergy in Collaborative Enterprises. Production, Planning and Control 18(6), 454–465 (2007)
9. Coleman, J.S.: Foundations of Social Theory. Belknap, Cambridge (1990)
10. Chong, A.Y.L., Ooi, K.B.: Adoption of Interorganizational System Standards in Supply Chains: An Empirical Analysis of RosettaNet Standards. Industrial Management & Data Systems 108(4), 529–547 (2008)
11. Chou, D.C., Tan, X., Yen, D.C.: Web Technology and Supply Chain Management. Information Management & Computer Security 12(4), 338–349 (2004)
12. Cropper, S.: Collaborative Working and the Issue Sustainablity. In: Huxam, C. (ed.) Creating Collaboratice Advantage. SAGE Publications Ltd., London (1996)
13. Dubelaar, C., Sohal, A.S., Savic, V.: Benefits, impediments and Critical Success Factors in B2C e-Business Adoption. Technovation 25(11), 1251–1252 (2005)
14. Dyer, J.H., Chu, W.: The Determinants of Trust in Supplier-Automaker Relationships in the U.S, Japan and Korea. Journal of International Business Studies 31(2), 259–285 (2000)
15. Dyer, J.H., Chu, W.: The Role of Trustworthiness in Reducing Transaction Costs and Improving Performance: Empirical Evidence From the U.S, Japan and Korea. Organization Science 14(1), 57–68 (2003)
16. Easterby-Smith, M., Thorpe, R., Jackson, P., Lowe, A.: Management Research, 3rd edn. Sage, London (2008)
17. Fukuyama, F.: Trust: The Social Virtues and The Creation of Prosperity. Free Press, New York (1995)
18. Frankel, R., Goldsby, T.J., Whipple, J.M.: Grocery Industry Collaboration in The Wake of ECR. International Journal of Logistics Management 13(1), 57–72 (2002)

19. Fleischmann, B., Meyr, H., Wagner, M.: Advanced Planning. In: Stadtler, H., Kilger, C. (eds.) Supply Chain Management and Advanced Planning: Concept, Model, Software and Case Study, 2nd edn., ch. 4, pp. 71–96. Springer (2002)

20. George, J.C., Swap, W.C.: Measurement of Specific Interpersonal Trust: Construction and Validation of a Scale to Access Trust in a Specific Other. Journal of Personality and Social Psychology 43(6), 1306–1317 (1982)

21. Stevens, G.C.: Successful Supply-Chain Management. Management Decision 28(8) (1993)

22. Giddens, A.: The Constitution of Society. Polity Press, Cambridge (1984)

23. Giddens, A.: The Consequences of Modernity. Polity Press, Cambridge (1990)

24. Gulati, R., Singh, H.: The Architecture of Cooperation: Managing Coordination Costs and Appropriation Concerns in Strategic Alliances. Administrative Science Quarterly 43(4), 781–814 (1998)

25. Hart, P., Saunders, C.: Power and Trust – Critical Factors in the Adoption and Use of Electronic Data Interchange. Organization Science 8(1), 23–42 (1997)

26. Harrison, E.F.: A Process Perspective on Strategic Decision Making. Management Decision 34(1), 46–53 (2000)

27. Husted, B.W.: Transaction Costs, Norms and Social Network: A Preliminary Study of Cooperation in Industrial Buyer-Seller Relationships in The U.S and Mexico. Business and Society 33(1), 30–57 (1994)

28. Huin, S.F., Luong, L.H.S., Abhary, K.: Internal Supply Chain Planning Determinants in Small and Medium-Sized Manufacturers. International Journal of Physical Distribution and Logistics Management 32(9), 771–782 (2002)

29. Huxam, C.: Collaboration and Collaborative Advantage. Creating Collaborative Advantage. SAGE Publications Ltd., London (1996)

30. Ireland, R., Bruce, R.: CPFR: Only the Beginning of Collaboration. Supply Chain Management Review, 80 (September/October 2000)

31. IBM, IBM Product Lifecycle Management (PLM) (June 2001)

32. Jarillo, J.C.: On Strategic Networks. Strategic Management Journal 9(1), 31–41 (1988)

33. Jones, S., Wilikens, M., Morris, P., Masera, M.: Trust Requirements in E-Business. Communications of the ACM 43(2), 81–87 (2000)

34. Johnson, M.E., Whang, S.: E-Business and Supply Chain Management: An Overview and Framework. Production and Operations Management 11(4), 413–422 (2002)

35. Jordan Jr., J.A., Michael, F.J.: Next Generation Manufacturing: Methods and Techniques. John Wiley and Sons Inc., New York (2000)

36. Kai, W., Kai, R.: Trust Building Potential of Coordination Roles in Virtual Organizations. The Electronic Journal for Virtual Organizations and Networks (2007)

37. Kim, P.H., Dirks, K.T., Cooper, Y.D.: The Repair of Trust: A Dynamic Bilateral Perspective and Multilevel Conceptualization. Academy of Management Review 34(3), 401–422 (2009)

38. Kock, N., Nosek, J.: Expanding the Boundaries of E-Collaboration. IEEE Transactions on Professional Communication 48(1), 1–9 (2005)

39. Kwon, G.: Factors Affecting the Level of Trust and Commitment in Supply Chain Relationships. The Journal of Supply Chain Management (2004)

40. Kramer, R.M.: Trust and Distrust in Organizations: Emerging Perspectives, Enduring Questions. Annual Review of Psychology 50, 569–598 (1999)

41. Kim, P.H., Dirks, K.T., Cooper, Y.D.: The Repair of Trust: A Dynamic Bilateral Perspective and Multilevel Conceptualization. Academy of Management Review 34(3), 401–402 (2009)

42. Kick, N., D'Arcy, J.: Resolving the e-collaboration Paradox: The Competing Influences of Media Naturalness and Compensatory Adaptation. Information Management and Consulting, Special Issue on Electronic Collaboration 17(4), 72–78 (2002)

43. Lane, C.: The Social Regulation of Inter-firm Relations in Britain and German: Market Rules, Legal Norms and Technical Standard. Cambridge Journal of Economics 21, 278–289 (1997)

44. Lane, C., Bachmann, R.: The Social Constitution of Trust: Supplier Relation in Britain and Germany. Organizations Studies 17(3), 365–395 (1996)

45. Laubacher, R.J., Malone, T.W.: MIT Scenario Working Group. Two Scenarios for 21st Century Organizations Shifting Networks of Small Firms or all Encompassing 'Virtual Countries'?, Working Paper, 21CWP (1) (1997)

46. Lippert, S.K.: An Exploratory Study into the Relevance of Trust in the Context of Information Systems Technology. Doctoral Dissertation, The George Washington University, Washington, DC (2001)

47. Mayer, R.C., Davis, J., Schoorman, F.D.: AN Integrative Model of Organization Trust. Academy of Management Review 20(3), 709–734 (1995)

48. McLaren, T., Head, M., Yuan, Y.: Supply Chain Collaboration Alternatives: Understanding the Expected Costs and Benefits. Internet Research 12(4), 348–364 (2002)

49. Meyerson, D., Weick, K.E., Kramer, R.M.: Swift Trust and Temporary Groups. In: Kramer, R.M., Tyler, T.R. (eds.) Trust in Organizations, pp. 166–195. Sage, Thousand Oaks (1996)

50. Muckstadt, J.A., Murray, D.H., Rappold, J.A., Collins, D.E.: Guideline for Collaborative Supply Chain System Design and Operation. Information System Frontiers 3(4), 427–453 (2001)

51. McDonnell, M.: E-Collaboration: Transforming Your Supply Chain Into A Dynamic Trading Community. Supply Chain Practice 3(2), 80–89 (2001)

52. Ngai, E.W.T., Lai, K.H., Cheng, T.C.E.: Logistics Information Systems: The Hong Kong Experience. International Journal of Production Economics 113(1), 223–224 (2008)

53. Nooteboom, B., Berger, H., Noorderhaven, N.G.: Effects of Trust and Governance on Relational Risk. Academy of Management Review 40(2), 308–338 (1997)

54. Ofstad, H.: An Inquiry into the Freedom of Decision. Norwegian Universities Press, Oslo (1961)

55. Pramatari, K.: Collaborative Supply Chain Practices and Evolving Technological Approaches. An International Journal of Supply Chain Management 12(3), 210–220 (2007)

56. Ratnasingam, P.: Inter-Organizational Trust in EDI Adoption. The Case of Ford Motor Company and PBR Limited in Australia. Internet Research: Electronic Networking Applications and Policy 11(3), 261–268 (2001)

57. Rohde, J., Meyr, H., Wagner, M.: Die Supply Chain Planning Matrix. PPS Management 5(1), 10–15 (2000)

58. Sako, M.: Does Trust Improve Business Performance? In: lane, C., Bachmann, R. (eds.) Trust Within and Between Organization. Oxford University Press, Oxford (1998)

59. Shang, R., Chen, C.C., Liu, Y.: Internet EDI Adoption Factors: Power, Trust and Vision. In: Proceeding of International Conference on E-Commerce (ICEC 2005) (2005), http://portal.acm.org

60. Fawcett, S.E., Jones, S.L., Fawcett, A.L.: Supply Chain Trust: The Catalyst for Collaborative Innovation. Business Horizons 55, 163–178 (2012)

61. Van Goor, A.R., Ploos van Amstel, M.J., Ploos van Amstel, W.: Fysieke Distributie, Denken in Toegevoegde Waarden. Stenfert Kroes, Houten (1996) (in Dutch)

62. Wehmeyer, K., Riemer, K.: Trust Building Potential of Coordination Roles in Virtual Organizations. The Electronic Journal for Virtual Organizations and Network 8 (2007)
63. Wicks, A.C., Berman, S.L.: The Effect of Context on Trust in Firm-Stakeholder Relationships: The Institutional Environment, Trust Creation and Firm Performance. Business Ethics Quarterly 14(1), 141–160 (2004)
64. Williams, L.R., Esper, T.L., Ozment, J.: The Electronic Supply Chain: Its Impact on the Current and Future Structure of Strategic Alliances, Partnerships and Logistics Leadership. International Journal of Physical Distribution and Logistics Management 32(8), 703–719
65. Zaheer, A., Harris, J.: Interorganizational Trust. In: Handbook of Strategic Alliances, pp. 169–197. Sage, Thousand Oaks (2006)
66. Zaheer, A., McEvily, B., Perrone, V.: Does Trust Matter? Exploring The Effects of Inter-organizational and Inter-Personal Trust on Performance. Organization Science 9(2), 141–159 (1998)
67. Zineldin, M., Bredenlow, T.: Strategic Alliances: Synergies and Challenges. International Journal Physical Distribution and Logistics Management 33(5), 449–464 (2003)

Quality Management to Support Single Companies to Overcome Organisational Challenges in Collaborative Enterprise Networks

Patrick Sitek and Klaus-Dieter Thoben

BIBA Bremer Institut für Produktion und Logistik GmbH,
Hochschulring 20, 28359 Bremen, Germany
{sit,tho}@biba.uni-bremen.de

Abstract. The paper discusses organisational challenges single companies face while joining collaborative enterprise networks (EN). Following an organisational design approach in organisational differentiation and integration in EN, organisational challenges are identified. Based on steps for designing and implementing quality management systems (QMS), an initial reference model is given as potential basis for future concepts to overcome those organisational challenges.

Keywords: Collaboration, enterprise networks, organisational challenges, quality management, SME.

1   Introduction

The development and production of complex products in EN is carried out along value chains composed of the contributions of different single companies [1]. In case that value chains are extended across organisational boundaries, the complexity of the chains heavily increases. In order to achieve e.g. the development of products in a satisfactory time-to-market, different EN members are required to develop components of this new product simultaneously. In such a case, each partner of an EN is embedded in organisational relationships with identifiable counterparts. Relationships can be e.g. the need for information and material sharing, the need for consensus or a common work on a specific design. The decentralized but simultaneous way of working in such environment results into new organisational challenges for single companies.

2   Problem to Be Solved

Modelling value chains by dividing required product and services development on different companies and modelling inter-organisational EN structures, results in work related interdependencies and interfaces between companies [2,3,4,5,6]. An increasing division of work like in collaborative EN lead to such interdependencies and interfaces. The existence of interdependencies und interfaces again leads to a higher need for coordination as single companies might not be able to overlook all structural interdependencies and process-related interfaces.

J. Frick and B. Laugen (Eds.): APMS 2011, IFIP AICT 384, pp. 342–349, 2012.

Following a single manufacturer scenario, it is possible to manage structural inter-dependencies and process-related interfaces efficiently. Customer requirements for good or service can be well defined in process descriptions and internally executed to achieve demanded characteristics of a required good or service (see Fig 1).

Fig. 1. Transferring customer requirements into process commands

Going one step further the same aspect can be discussed in the context of two and more manufacturers like in a supply chain cooperation. Cooperations in supply chains are characterised by a stable and fixed long-term relationship between companies based on a hierarchical buyer-seller relationship [1]. Due to a strong hierarchy it is possible for the original equipment manufacturer ("A" in Fig 2) to regulate and trans-fer requirements and corresponding information from customer (input) as downstream through the entire supply chain or at least to the first tier companies in the supply chain. The first tier companies ("B" and "C" in Fig 2) logically pass the requirements as significant information to the downstream tiers and receive the required goods or services back in the upstream. Divided in different supply tiers each company sup-plies its upstream tier with material based on strictly prior defined requirements (e.g. "D" supplies "B", "B" supplies "A" in Fig 2).

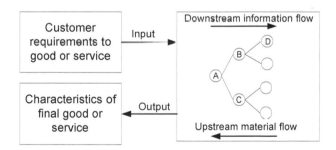

Fig. 2. Transferring requirements through a supply chain

This way customer requirements and process information can also be manageable in an inter-organisational supply chain scenario through a stricter handling of control, regulation and documentation by hierarchy. Compared to stable and long-term supply chains, EN can feature a more complex business environment, due to their dynamic behaviour. The dynamic behaviour can mainly be characterised by the organisational structure and operational processes in EN [7]. In regard of organisational structure an

abandonment of formal and hierarchical structures is possible which results in a multitude of degrees of freedom and retention of each EN partner's autonomy. In regard
of operational processes, temporary and in an extreme case uniqueness existence of
processes is possible. Organisational structures and operational processes in EN are
usually not determined by fixed and hierarchical partnerships of long duration. This is
what makes EN so dynamic and in turn it results in a higher complexity of the business environment [8] in form of EN life-cycle phases [9]. The advances of this dynamic behaviour that accrue on the one hand are a higher flexibility and response time
to the market but on the other hand they constrain stability and coordination of an
organisation. Compared to the hierarchical scenario in supply chains (see Fig 2), less
organisational stability and coordination in EN makes less manageable organisational
forms possible where tracing and coordinating of customer requirements in a down-
stream and material flows in a upstream become more challenging (see Fig 3). The
transformation of requirements (input) and the management of information flow between EN companies become more error-prone as less manageable.

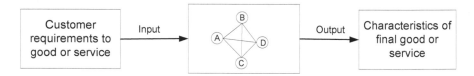

Fig. 3. Transferring requirements through an EN

3   Findings

To better understand the dynamic character of EN and the existence of relations and
interdependencies between single companies in EN, this chapter discusses EN from
the organisational design perspective. Organisational design is an instrument for an
efficient management of companies and overall business goal achievements.

The core function of organisational design is the organisational differentiation and
organisational integration [10]. The idea of organisational differentiation and integration as well as organisational structures and operational processes can be transferred
for EN as shown in Fig 4. Following this, the main business job in EN is the collaboration opportunity [11]. Within the task analysis and synthesis the right companies
need to be found based on their competences that matches in most promising way the
fulfilment of the business job requirements. Companies possessing the right competences are linked in a network that visualises the organisational structure of the EN.
Within the job analysis and synthesis the companies' individual operating value processes are identified, harmonised and integrated into an inter-organisational value or
process chain that visualises the process organisation of the EN.

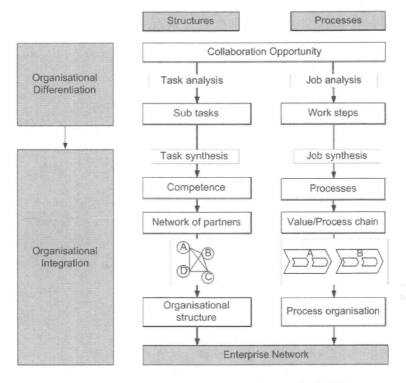

Fig. 4. Organisational differentiation and integration in EN

From operational process perspective there is the risk of not identified interfaces between companies within the inter-organisational value chain. Between two linked value adding company processes in a value chain there is an inter-organisational interface. The possibility of lack or loss of relevant information due to this interface becomes obvious (see Fig 5).

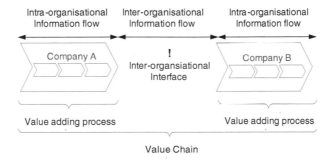

Fig. 5. Challenges on operational processes in collaborative EN

From organisational structure perspective there is the risk of not identified interdependencies between companies in an EN. Supply chains show stable, well-defined and by the time well-developed relations between companies. Temporarily, contract-specific and probably nonrecurring inter-organisational relations like in EN harbour a certain danger for companies not to identify all relations of a network constellation. Not identified relations lead to a wrong conclusion of the organisational structure of an EN. Fig 6 addresses a potential misinterpretation of an organisational structure for the company "A". In this case company "A" expect three relations with other companies in a network but de facto there are four relations and also four interdependencies to be taken into account.

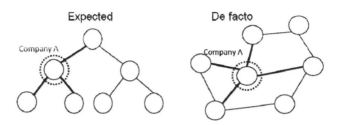

Fig. 6. Challenges on organisational structure in EN

Long-term and stable continuous production networks with a chain interdependency topology exhibit a clearer defined hierarchy with a defined relation mostly followed the material flow or a product structure logic (e.g. bill of material). Relevant information like customer requirements, product specifications and process instructions, can be easier communicated and controlled top (see Fig 2). Characterised by the absence of hierarchies keeping and respecting the autonomy of each network partner EN structures cannot be generalised and pre-defined as they are situation and case dependent. The duration of collaboration in an EN consisting of a variety of independent companies is limited, in extreme case, to one certain customer demand and the network has to be re-structured for the next demand. Summarising, while joining a collaborative EN a single company faces two main challenges:

1. Overcome of inter-organisational interfaces within the value chain of a collaborative enterprise network (operational process perspective).
2. Identification of interdependencies with other companies within the structure of a collaborative enterprise network (organisational structure perspective).

4   Results

To overcome these organisational challenges a quality management (QM) approach is proposed within this paper. This is due to the fact that usually companies organise their organisational objectives and management of process to realise these objectives in quality management systems (QMS). This is a new approach as mostly today's QM approaches still mostly focus on an intra-organisational perspective and or long-term oriented inter-organisational perspective [12].

In order to proceed towards an approach to support single companies in better managing organisational challenges in EN, it seems to be promising to bridge the two fields of EN and QM. For this purpose an initial reference model has been proposed that combines the two single and independent fields in a simplified way. Based on such a reference model the elements of future concepts to support building of organisational structure and process orientation in EN and the reduction of potential interorganisational information losses can be achieved. Following Fig 7 summarises the initial reference model combining EN and QM.

Fig. 7. Bridging EN life-cycle phases and steps for building QMS

The reference model bases on two pillars. It takes EN life-cycle phases (preparation, formation, operation and dissolution) [9] and usual steps in designing and implementing a QMS (planning, controlling, leading and improving quality) (see Table 1).

Table 1. Design and implement a QMS [13]

Quality Plan	• Determining customer needs, expectations and requirements. • Establishing quality objectives of the organisation. • Determining processes, resources and responsibilities to attain quality objectives.
Quality Control and Lead	• Establishing and applying methods to measure the effectiveness and efficiency of processes to attain quality objectives.
Quality Improvement	• Eliminating nonconformities within quality objectives. • Establishing and applying a process for continual improvement of processes to reach quality objectives.

The preparation phase of EN offers a proper timing for companies to determine and promote their competences that might be interesting for other business partners. Doing so it is also the timing to determine business expectations, the objectives for collaborative business and to determine and prepare or adapt needed processes, resources and actors to be able to properly offer the core competence within an EN. During the formation phase, after a business opportunity appeared and the customer needs and requirements are determined, contract specific activities for organisational linkage of selected partners and competences can be performed by synchronising and harmonising of the identified processes, resources and actors. Linkage of partners by their competences facilitates a proper EN structure and the identification of interdependencies. Process instructions for inter-organisational collaboration on the management of interfaces, can be implemented within a running quality planning in the QMS. The operation phase of EN offers the possibility to follow and monitor the created EN in terms of organisational structure/interdependencies and process orientation/interfaces. Therefore existing and applied methods implemented within existing QMS to measure the effectiveness and efficiency of processes can be used to attain network and quality objectives. The last phase of the life-cycle model of EN, the dissolution phase offers ideally the opportunity to take up gained knowledge during the operative monitoring and use it to improvement future collaboration preparation and operational activities. Potential suggestions for improvement can be retained and flow in quality planning issues in the preparation phase of an EN. This way a continuous improvement process can be realised even in temporarily business conditions like in EN.

5   Outlook

Companies are adopting new organisational forms that incorporate some level of 'virtuality' and 'modularity', that is, allowing certain processes to be performed outside the boundaries of the own company, and involving inter-organisational relationships at a deeper level than the traditional supplier-customer relationship. Such relationships might be characterised by short-term, temporary alignment of operations in EN where core competences of different actors are combined in a job-oriented fashion for a defined period. In this context, inter-organisational processes gain in importance when compared to the intra-organisational processes [14].

To transform customer requirements and to manage information in inter-organisational EN will require a shift in focus from the way the companies allocate and structure their internal processes and resources towards the way it relates own processes and structures to those of the other counterparts in a network. Therefore QM approaches can be useful but they need to take the inter-organisational trend into account. For single companies it is necessary to identify possible connections and interdependencies between network members. To allow this, the next step for approaches or adaptations of available QM approaches is to ask companies to question existing structures and processes and study potential room for open structures and processes for smart harmonisation and synchronisation. The better the level of harmonisation and synchronisation can be realised the more reliable exchange of relevant information between the network members can be achieved and guaranteed. Identifying interdependencies in networks and adapting own core competencies to the networked environment, is necessary for organisations to finally guarantee complex customer demands in EN.

At the end the main goal will be to provide smart guidelines to quickly identify relevant business requirements from an EN, these are mostly interdependencies between core competences as communication content, and to model them more easily as operational processes and organisational structures. Modelled and well understood inter-organisational structures, resulting in communication structures with understanding of relevant content to be exchanged, help to guarantee a successful distribution of customer requirements through the entire value chain of an EN. Further approaches based on the concept developed within this work could help to provide more transparency on information exchange on the inter-organisational level and thus contribute to process quality and value in EN. This will help in turn to reduce the lack of information that is a risk for quality in collaborative business and finally leads to higher satisfaction of customers by providing the demanded product/service with planned quality and to the planned price, and in the planned time.

References

1. Seifert, M.: Collaboration Formation in Virtual Organisations by applying prospective Performance Measurement. Dissertation at the University of Bremen (2009)
2. Albani, A., Dietz, J.L.G.: Current trends in modelling inter-organizational cooperation. Journal of Enterprise Information Management 22(3), 275–297 (2009)
3. Jones, G.R., Bouncken, R.B.: Organisation, Theorie, Design und Wandel, 5th edn. Pearson Studium Verlag (2008) (in German)
4. Vahs, D.: Organisation – Einführung in die Organisationstheorie und praxis, 6th edn. Schäffler-Poeschel Verlag, Stuttgart (2007) (in German)
5. Binder, M., Clegg, B.T.: Enterprise management: a new frontier for organizations. International Journal of Production Economics 106(2), 406–430 (2007)
6. Robinson, C.J., Malhotra, M.K.: Defining the concept of supply chain quality management and its relevance to academic and industrial practice. International Journal of Production Economics 96, 315–337 (2005)
7. Sitek, P., Seifert, M., Thoben, K.-D.: Qualitätsmanagement in dynamischen Unternehmensnetzwerken - Anforderungen an Qualitätsmanagementsysteme. Industrie Management 4, S.25–S.28 (2010) (in German)
8. Paetau, M.: Virtuelle Unternehmen zwischen Interaktion und Organisation. In: Boos, M., Jonas, K.J., Sassenberg, K. (Hrsg.) Computervermittelte Kommunikation in Organisationen, Göttingen, pp. 129–141 (2000) (in German)
9. Thoben, K.-D., Jagdev, H.S.: Typological Issues in Enterprise Networks. Journal of Production Planning and Control 12(5), 421–436 (2001)
10. Vahs, D.: Organisation: Einführung in die Organisationstheorie und –praxis. Schäffler-Poeschel Verlag, Aufl., Stuttgart (2007) (in German)
11. Sitek, P., Graser, F., Seifert, M.: Partner profiling to support the initiation of collaborative networks. In: Pawar, K.S., Thoben, K.-D., Pallot, M., Sophia-Antipolis (eds.) Proceedings of the 13th International Conference on Concurrent Enterprising, Concurrent Innovation: an Emerging Paradigm for Collaboration & Competitiveness in the Extended Enterprise, pp. 213–220 (2007)
12. Sitek, P., Seifert, M., Thoben, K.-D.: Towards inter-organisational perspective to manage quality in temporary enterprise networks. International Journal for Quality and Reliability Management 27(2), 231–246 (2010)
13. N.N.: ISO 9001:2008 – Quality Management Systems – Requirements (2008)
14. Petridis, K.D.: Qualität in der Informationsgesellschaft – Die Rolle der Qualität in virtuellen Unternehmen und E-Commerce-Strukturen. In: QZ – Qualität und Zuverlässigkeit (2001) (in German)

Toward Comprehensive Security Policy Governance in Collaborative Enterprise

Ziyi Su and Frédérique Biennier

Université de Lyon, CNRS
INSA-Lyon, LIRIS, UMR5205, F-69621, France
Villeurbanne, France
{ziyi.su, frederique.biennier}@insa-lyon.fr

Abstract. The lack of trust among software services spanning multiple organisations and the rather poor adaptability level of the current security policies are often seen as braking forces to collaborative-enterprise development. Removing this impediment involves re-thinking the security policy according to "due usage" requirements and setting security enforcement and regulations according to both the due usage and the runtime environment. This paper analyzes the nature of secured assets exchange management in collaborative enterprise, describing the assets sharing patterns and, accordingly, 'sub-context' partition method. Resource protection can be done by applying a 'collaborative usage control policy model' on each 'sub-context' to manage "due usage" control during service/information aggregation. In this way, a compendious but comprehensive security governance for collaborative enterprise is achieved.

Keywords: Security, Policy, Collaborative Enterprise, Negotiation, Aggregation.

1   Introduction

Information sharing is necessary for global optimization in collaborative enterprise. At the same time, new challenges come up for security governance and Information Control Technology. As information is shared beyond ownership boundary, there is always the risk of misuse of sensitive information, e.g. circumventing of trade secret, or even leakage to a competitor through partner. By now the information providers have partial control over sensitive information as it flows beyond organization borders, despite the persistence of protection requirements. Surveys [1, 2] show that risks as 'handling over sensitive data to a third party' are major barriers from moving to collaborative paradigm. Unfortunately, no much attention has been paid on this new requirement in existing security methods, architectures, toolsets or service security architectures: trust assessment [3] methods focus on the 'pre-decision' about selecting partners for business federation, based on historical comportment and the regulation of the partner behavior on the fly in the collaborative business process is traditionally out of the scope of concern. Security governance in collaborative enterprise needs not only a static trust assessment, but also a policy to express both participants' security requirements and regulations of the partner behavior, detailing "due usage" (namely information consumption actions) control to set

J. Frick and B. Laugen (Eds.): APMS 2011, IFIP AICT 384, pp. 350–358, 2012.

a continuous protection of resources even beyond organization boundary and to coordinate requirements to set a consistent protection policy in a (dynamic) business federation.

In former work [4], we brought to light one solution on continuously regulating (define, grant and deny) 'usage' policy upon corporate assets, giving these rights to a partner according to its 'Quality-of-protection'. This involves the expression of security factors ranging from the IT infrastructure to partner behaviour with a Collaboration Security Policy. This paper formalizes the policy model and presents a multidimensional resource protection framework for collaborative enterprise. The process of the collaborative-context security governance with the framework is discussed using a generalized business federation scenario.

2   Context

With the development of collaborative IS, security governance methodologies are developing toward open and collaborative paradigm, leading to the emerging of new security policy models adapting business federation scenarios.

2.1   Security Policies for Collaborative Contexts

Recent security researches are aware of the trends of Internet-based collaborative Network and shifting to such paradigm. At the infrastructure level, the requirement of supporting basic security services as Integrity, Confidentiality and authentication in Internet-based applications with key technologies as encryption, digital signature, etc. is being addressing by recent works [6, 7], aiming at promoting the security level of collaborative software solutions. At the same time, some discussions have emerged to introduce DRM technology to corporate IT management by implementing digital signature and data watermarking to corporate data [8]. These works shed lights on the service/information 'usage control' level governance for collaborative enterprise. However, as traditional risk evaluation methods, security architectures are designed according to a static vision of the information system organisation, they do not fit the dynamicity required by the collaborative and cloud-based XaaS economical model.

On the other hand, security policy models are developing to accommodate Internet-based, multi-services collaborative enterprise. A trend is evidenced as a paradigm changing toward more expressive policy models [9, 10, 11] beyond ACL and RBAC. Even though a comprehensive formal model is still expected, as well as a thorough security-property analysis as that has been done for RBAC, such thought has lead to a enriched policy language as XACML, which grants enriched access right, i.e. the 'usage' (consumption activity) of resource affiliated by obligations [12], that conditioned on multiple-attributes.

Our previous work (see [5] for more detail information) centers on a policy model that defines the access Rights upon the resource thanks to the refined attributes related to requester, resource and infrastructure, as well as obligations fulfilling on the granted rights. Policy is constructed through the logical combination of Assertion, which is a tuple:

$$Assertion = (O, SH, S, CN, R, RN, OB, L, T) \tag{1}$$

where the semantics of the factors are as follows. '**SH**' (Stakeholder) is the owner of the assertion, and is the owner or co-owner of the asset related to the assertion. '**S**' (Subject) is the party that can access the Right to the asset. '**O**' (Object) is the asset to be protected by the policy assertions. '**R**' (Right) is the Operation upon the asset defined by 'RH' that the Subject can be allowed to exercise. For example a restriction 'three times' may be used to refine the right 'rendering a piece of multi-media file'. '**CN**' (Condition) is the requirements that must be satisfied for the Subject to access Rights upon the Object. It is related to either *subject attributes (SAT)*, *object attributes (OAT)* or *context related attributes (CNAT)*. '**RN**' (Restriction) is the constraint upon the Right. '**OB**' (Obligation) is the obligation that must be exercised by the Subject when it accesses the Right. '**L**' (Logic Operator) is a set of logic operators as 'imply' ('←'), 'and' ('∧') and 'or' ('∨'). '**T**' (Time) is the temporal factor which defines the lifecycle of the rule.

The bidirectional property of trust implicates that a partners is a truster and a trustee at the same time. Thus it uses *'RoP'* assertions to express the 'Requirements of Protection' for its resource and *'QoP'* assertions to declare its security attributes and 'Quality of Protection' for resources it consumes. A temporal factor decorating policy assertions or attribute predicts defines their continuous lifecycles to the scope of beyond direct-requesters.

We can still see a gap between the security requirements of collaborative enterprise and IT management offering. By now, information security grounds mainly on an "instant" protection viewpoint, e.g. the decision to grant resource to customer access and the secured resource delivery channel. Collaborative Security Policy needs to describe not only the security factors from infrastructure level, or access control based on requestor attribute. It should have a "usage control" policy to take care of data even after grant it to partners, so to make continuous cooperating decision that reflecting partners conducts. It should also have a pellucid mechanism supporting coordination of policies from multiple partners, adapting to the complexity and dynamicity of collaborative context security governance.

2.2   Collaborative Context Management

A collaborative enterprise reveals its global scale 'quality-of-protection' as the aggregation of *QoPs* from the participants. It is also entitled with a consistent, accept-by-all security policy, which roots in the *RoPs* from individual partners, providing global scale protection to their assets. Due to the dynamicity of collaboration strategy, the global scale *QoP* and *RoP* set are updated on-the-fly as new partners join and quit, so to reflect security properties/requirements from current participants as well as global scale protection level and requirements. Collaboration context management involves a security policy update mechanism, which relies on the analysis of collaboration strategy. For example, the study of security policy interoperability in Virtual Organization [9] enables a subject to access privileges defined in another organization. The Federated Rights Expression Model [8] permits a content provider to trust external render rights. In IT infrastructure level, authors of [13] studied the reliable configuration of security policies from multiple components. A multi-organizational policy modeling mechanism is presented [10] that takes into consideration the business context characteristics, whereas the analysis of business components dependency [14, 15] sheds light on confinement to information access based on service composition, which greatly impacts the protection approach. In spite of such fruitful works, our 'usage control' view upon business federation involves a more in depth analysis of information assets consumption than those presented above.

3   Collaboration Context Management Based on Assets-Sharing Relation

The artifact of collaboration context (called 'C-Asset', i.e. 'C-Asset2' in fig. 1), can comprise information assets from multiple providers (called 'O-Asset', e.g. 'O-Asset1', 'O-Asset2' and 'C-Asset1' in fig. 1).

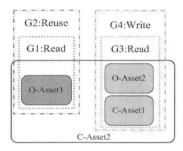

Fig. 1. Information Asset aggregation and Rights aggregation

Two traits can be observed regarding the aggregating process of *RoPs* from these providers. Firstly, if the asset from an individual provider can be separately identified in the collaboration artifact (e.g. inventory information from multiple up-stream providers, stock information from multiple brokers, financial-year report from different subsidiaries, etc.), the due *RoP* don't need to be aggregated. When a use of access a part of the artifact, it needs only to comply to the *RoP* relating to due part.

Secondly, if a provider defined different rights upon its assets, a consumer only needs to follow the part of the policy that concerns its rights upon the asset. An example is when a company defines a piece of data (e.g. price) available for anyone to access but only supply chain partner can modify it. Then a user only need to exhibit appropriate attributes in order to exercise different usages upon the data.

Thanks to this two observations, we can 'split' a collaboration context into several virtual 'sub-contexts' according to different resource aggregation and different consumption rights upon them:

- *Providers for the same C-Asset are deemed as the same 'sub-context'.*
- *All consumers having the same 'rights' upon the C-Asset(s) are deemed as in one 'group'.*
- *A participant can belong to more than one sub-context at the same time. it must follow the RoP of that sub-context.*

Four sub-context patterns can be identified according to these principles. We use a sample supply chain scenario with several information flows to describe each case:

- **EAOG** (Each Asset One Group) mode indicates the situation when each provider can differentiate its resource in the artifact of federated Business Process. In this model each provider attaches its policy to its due part (the O-Asset) in the resulting C-Asset. Future consumers just need to obey the due policy of the part it will request. A sample (see fig. 2) is when a down-stream provider (D) receives information 'Ia…In' (e.g. inventory) from upstream provider (UP) and combines them in one XML file 'I' as separate nodes, Manufactory (M) reads the nodes separately, and follows the due policy of UPs.

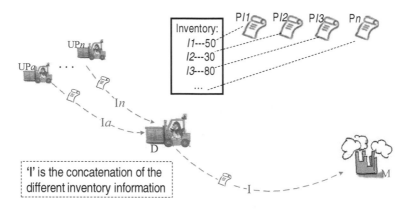

Fig. 2. Sample of **EAOG** mode

- **SASG** (Single Asset Single Group) mode is that all the consumers are given the same rights upon the artifact and thus is in one single group. The aggregation process should make sure there is no potential contradiction among *RoPs* of all the providers and *QoPs* of all the consumers. A sample of this mode (see fig. 3) occurs when (other information) 'C0a…C0n' (e.g. productivity) are blurred by 'D' to generate 'C4' (e.g. scheduling).

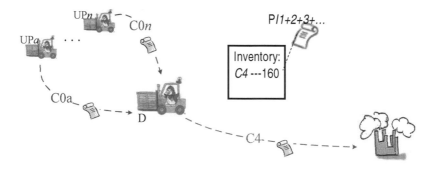

Fig. 3. Sample of **SASG** mode

- **SAMG** (Single Asset Multiple Group) mode means that there is only one single C-Asset, with different rights defined on it. Then consumers of different rights are deemed as in different groups. In other words, consumers accessing different rights need only to fulfill the due condition of that right. Fig. 4 shows such a sample case where D blurs information (C5), and aggregates UPs' policies to different CSPs, which are accessed by different down-stream partners 'Da…Dn'. By managing each 'right' and due 'condition' separately, the opportunity for finding adequate consumer increase, less privileged rights usually require less rigorous conditions.

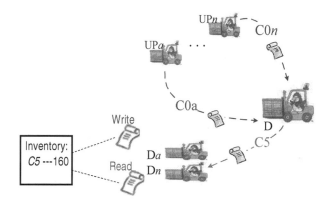

Fig. 4. Sample of **SAMG** mode

- **MAMG** (Multiple Asset Multiple Group) mode denotes when the artifact can be differentiated as sub-parts, e.g. when there are parallel branches in the business process and some branches will not merge with others till the end of process. A sample of this mode (see fig. 5) denotes if D splits a piece of information (e.g. to C1, C2 and C3) and some pieces (e.g. C3) do not merge with others in future steps.

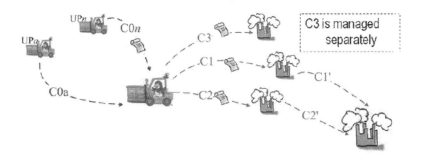

Fig. 5. Sample of **MAMG** mode

These 4 patterns generally exist in many collaborative contexts, as long as the issue of information asset protection and consumption exists. Imagining changing the sample case by switching the materials providers as Cloud providers or Service providers, the security management approaches still generally fall in our framework, with technical solution possibly variable.

4   Sub-context Participation

We can see now that the key issue is to identify the asset exchanging relations between partners. Analysis of the 'Initial example' in 'WS-BPEL 2.0 specification' sheds lights on how this is done.

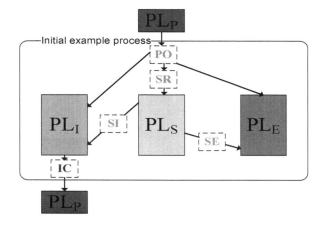

Fig. 6. Information exchanges in the 'Initial example'

This process receives an asset 'purchase order' (PO) from 'PartnerLink purchasing' (PL$_P$), then initiate three parallel processes (with temporal dependency defined by 'links'):

- Shipping: Assigning value from variable 'PO' to 'ShippingRequest' (SR), then calling 'PartnerLink shipping' (PL$_S$) with 'SR' and getting two feedbacks 'ShippingInfo' (SI) and 'ShippingSchedule' (SE).
- Calculating Price: Calling 'PartnerLink invoicing' (PL$_I$) with 'PO' and 'SI', getting a feedback 'Invoice' (IC).
- Scheduling: Calling 'PartnerLink scheduling' (PL$_E$) with 'PO' and 'SE'.

When these parallel processes terminate, the 'IC' is sent to 'PL$_P$' as response.

In these processes, security policy/profile negotiations take places between partners having asset exchange relation. Besides, when assets merge (e.g. in 'Calculating price' process, see fig. 7), security policies of providers should aggregation. The resulting policy reflects the security goals of both providers. In other words, if the resulting policy is fulfilled by a consumer, the original policies are also fulfilled.

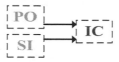

Fig. 7. Information aggregation in the 'Initial example'

5   Conclusion and Future Work

This paper describes a comprehensive security policy governance method in collaborative enterprise, based on asset sharing relations between partners. Therefore, only partners who are exchanging assets should have their security policies and profiles compatible, namely, the consumer's security profile fulfilling the provider's policy.

Deciding asset merging requires a more information about the business logic of partners ('PL_I' in above example). A natural thought would be adding annotations to partners descriptions, e.g. WSDL scripts.

Acknowledgements. This work is partly supported by the Process 2.0 process granted by the French Ministry of Economy and Industry – DGCIS.

References

[1] Linda, B.B., Richard, C., Kristin, L., Ric, T., Mark, E.: The evolving role of IT managers and CIOs–findings from the 2010 IBM global IT risk study. Technical report, IBM (2010)

[2] Jay, H., Mark, N.: Assessing the security risks of Cloud Computing. Technical report, Gartner (2008)

[3] Biennier, F., Aubry, R., Maranzana, M.: Integration of Business and Industrial Knowledge on Services to Set Trusted Business Communities of Organisations. In: Camarinha-Matos, L.M., Boucher, X., Afsarmanesh, H. (eds.) PRO-VE 2010. IFIP AICT, vol. 336, pp. 420–426. Springer, Heidelberg (2010)

[4] Su, Z., Biennier, F.: End-to-end Security Policy Description and Management for Collaborative System. In: Proc. IAS 2010, pp. 68–73 (2010)

[5] Su, Z., Biennier, F.: End-to-end security policy description and management for collaborative system. In: Proc. IAS 2010, pp. 137–142. MIR Lab. (August 2010)

[6] Paci, F., Bertino, E., Crampton, J.: An Access-Control Framework for WS-BPEL. Int. J. Web Service Res. 5, 20–43 (2008)

[7] Martino, L., Bertino, E.: Security for Web Services: Standards and Resarch Issues. Int. J. Web Service Res. 6, 48–74 (2009)

[8] Sans, T., Cuppens, F., Cuppens-Boulahia, N.: FORM: A Federated Rights Expression Model for Open DRM Frameworks. In: Okada, M., Satoh, I. (eds.) ASIAN 2006. LNCS, vol. 4435, pp. 45–59. Springer, Heidelberg (2008)

[9] Cuppens, F., Cuppens-Boulahia, N., Coma, C.: O2O: Virtual Private Organizations to Manage Security Policy Interoperability. In: Bagchi, A., Atluri, V. (eds.) ICISS 2006. LNCS, vol. 4332, pp. 101–115. Springer, Heidelberg (2006)

[10] Cuppens, F., Cuppens-Boulahis, N.: Modeling Contextual Security Policies. Int. J.Inf. Secur. 7, 285–305 (2008)

[11] Wang, L., Wijesekera, D., Jajodia, S.: A logic-based Framework for Attribute Based Access Control. In: Proc. FMSE 2004, pp. 45–55. ACM, New York (2004)

[12] Organization for the Advancement of Structured Information Standards (OASIS): eXtensible Access Control Markup Language (XACML) version 2.0. OASIS (2005)

[13] Alfaro, J.G., Cuppens-Boulahia, N., Cuppens, F.: Complete Analysis of Configuration Rules to Guarantee Reliable Network Security Policies. Int. J.Inf. Secur. 7, 103–122 (2008)

[14] Kheir, N., Debar, H., Cuppens, F., Cuppens-Boulahia, N., Viinikka, J.: A Service Dependency Modeling Framework for Policy-Based Response Enforcement. In: Flegel, U., Bruschi, D. (eds.) DIMVA 2009. LNCS, vol. 5587, pp. 176–195. Springer, Heidelberg (2009)

[15] Debar, H., Kheir, N., Cuppens-Boulahia, N., Cuppens, F.: Service Dependencies in Information Systems Security. In: Kotenko, I., Skormin, V. (eds.) MMM-ACNS 2010. LNCS, vol. 6258, pp. 1–20. Springer, Heidelberg (2010)

Framework for Improving the Design and Configuration Process of an International Manufacturing Network: An Empirical Study

Sandra Martínez and Ander Errasti

Engineering School, Tecnun, University of Navarra, San Sebastián, Spain
{smartinez,aerrasti}@tecnun.es

Abstract. As competition becomes global and the environment in which companies operate is becoming more complex, the design and managing of international manufacturing networks has become crucial. Therefore, it is important to do an analysis of the necessary decisions any company must make, such as facilities location, supply strategy, facility strategy role, etc., in order to accomplish the internationalization process with more reliability and success. The authors of this paper present the GlobOpe framework, which is a model to be used by managers to design and configure a new manufacturing network aided by various techniques. This paper also presents a case study in order to demonstrate the effectiveness of this model when reconfiguring an international manufacturing network for a wind generator manufacturer.

Keywords: Internationalization, framework, ramp up process, operations strategy.

1 Introduction

In the last decades, in addition to the multinational companies (MNEs) already in the market, more and more small and medium size companies (SMEs) are also engaging in international production. Specifically, both MNEs and SMEs are experiencing a trend toward multisite location and greater fragmentation of their productive and logistic processes. This fact highlights that the opening of borders in Eastern Europe and the eruption of countries such as China, Brazil and India into the global trade economy have forced companies to develop value added activities such as engineering, purchasing, manufacturing and assembly in different places, even in different countries. Due to the long-term impact on the competitiveness of companies, offshoring decisions are key aspects of strategic enterprise positioning [1-2], and they also play a crucial role in the competitiveness and the labour market of the regional and national economy [3].

According to Ferdows [1] and Farrell [4], there are four main reasons that explain the internationalization phenomenon: offshoring, entering new markets, disaggregating the value chain and reengineering the value chain and creating a new product and market.

J. Frick and B. Laugen (Eds.): APMS 2011, IFIP AICT 384, pp. 359–368, 2012.
© IFIP International Federation for Information Processing 2012

Thus, the internationalization of manufacturing networks means carrying out disaggregated value chain activities (i.e. engineering, purchasing, manufacturing and distribution) beyond a company's traditional market, which requires greater coordination in order to get acceptable levels of quality, flexibility and cost. Therefore, it is important to take into account that increased commitment abroad does not only promise opportunities, but it is also fraught with risk. For this reason, the relocation of production as well as auxiliary activities calls for a careful balancing of risks and benefits [5].

New manufacturing and supply configurations, which companies who are undergoing the internationalization process in order to enter new markets must face when installing new facilities abroad, is a topic which is becoming relevant in the science of operations management [1], [6]. Additionally, the coordination between agents involved the supply network chain and the supply strategy response to a highly dynamic and volatile environment when entering a new market could cause ramp up delays in time and volume, especially when new factors are introduced, which then leads to production losses [7].

Finding the best network for manufacturing and supply facilities adapted to new marketplaces is not a problem that is exclusive to MNEs, which operate in a worldwide context; it is now just as relevant for both SMEs or "late movers" who are undergoing an internationalization process and companies that are reconfiguring their multiple site networks [8].

Operations strategy has to gain more effectiveness and efficiency over operations resources through defining and implementing suitable Operations strategy decisions, managing tangible resources, and developing operations capabilities in order to reach the performance objectives of the market requirements.

The decisions that need to be made regarding a new manufacturing network configuration in the internationalization process are:

- Manufacturing facilities location decisions.
- Role of facilities strategy in the global network design.
- Integration or fragmentation of productive and logistic operations.
- Supply strategy.
- Suppliers and distribution network design.

Furthermore, the Global Operations trend gives rise to multiple configurations. Meixell and Gargeya [9] state that the raw materials, components, manufacturing and assembly stages could be locally or globally configured. As a result, internal functions such as engineering, purchasing, manufacturing, and external suppliers have to coordinate with the decision points and the action points to ensure the smooth functioning of the manufacturing system.

Practical experience has shown that strategy-specific checklists are needed, which might raise awareness of the real success factors of the pursued goal. Such checklists could serve managers as experience-based guidelines to identify the most important criteria and thus avoid unpleasant surprises [10]. Vereecke and Van Dierdonck [11] as well as Shi [12] state that Operations and Supply Chain management researchers should pay attention to providing understandable models or frameworks of international manufacturing systems that help managers to design and manage their networks.

Moreover, our examination of the literature revealed that simulation techniques could aid in configuring the supply strategy in an international manufacturing network design [13].

The Framework presented in this paper is intended to fill a gap left by Production systems (i.e. Toyota PS, Volvo PS, Bosch Siemens PS, etc.) and the lean manufacturing programs both of which lead the way to excellence when implemented in a facility in a stable environment but which are difficult to take advantage of in a dynamic market environment and in the new contexts of new offshore facilities implementation and the reconfiguration of an existing network [14].

Hence, this paper, after showing the literature of the relevant issues in Global Operations strategy, presents how a framework and associated techniques could aid when designing and configuring a new manufacturing network. To demonstrate the effectiveness of the proposed techniques, the researchers have been involved in a case study of a wind power sector company.

2   Literature Review

2.1   Business Strategy and the Ramp Up of Operations in an Internationalization Process

Some authors [15] state that Business strategy should be linked with Operations strategy. In this context, the production and logistic system strategy or Operations strategy conditions the decisions and reengineering projects to be carried out in a company in the medium and short term to improve the competitive advantage of the supply chain. Operations strategy has to gain more effectiveness and efficiency over operations resources through defining and implementing suitable operations strategy decisions, managing the tangible resources, and developing operations capabilities in order to reach the performance objectives of the market requirements.

When assessing production locations abroad, companies tend to underestimate the necessary ramp up times for securing process reliability, quality and productivity. The ramp up concept describes the period characterized by product and process experimentation and improvements [16], which strictly speaking starts with the first unit produced and ends when the planned production volume is reached [17]. Nevertheless, in order to manage such a ramp up with a high degree of precision, first a planning period phase is necessary, starting with the design of the product, the process and the supply chain network [18-19].

A study carried out in 39 internationally active German companies show that not only the small firms but also the larger companies tend to heavily underestimate ramp up times and coordination costs for foreign production sites. Specifically, on average, ramp up times are 2.5 times longer than originally planned. The absolute time required for the ramp up of foreign production sites until smoothly running production processes have been established ranges in almost all the cases from 2-3 years. Ramp up times do not only entail higher coordination costs, they can also considerably affect the calculated amortisation time, which for many companies is the decisive criterion tipping the scale for or against an offshoring engagement [10].

362 S. Martínez and A. Errasti

2.2 Supply Strategy in a Multisite and Fragmented Production System

Among relevant Operations strategies, the Quick Response Supply Chain strategy consists of reducing the lead time of the supply chain and allows a synchronized and demand driven production system, integrating manufacturers and suppliers. The production capacities of all echelons are balanced and there is a tangible takt time which tries to optimize the materials flow in terms of quantity, response time, stock, and equipment efficiency [20].

Nevertheless, in a multisite and fragmented production system, where the supplier network is composed of local or domestic suppliers and offshore suppliers and manufacturing facilities, these offshore suppliers and facilities need the coordination of quality control and the supply network with different delivery times and procurement reliability. The gap between customer delivery time and supply chain lead time needs forecast driven manufacturing, supplying and purchasing decisions. Here is the problem: due to the fact that Quick Response Supply Chain and Just in Time principles are not applicable in depth, and the gap between customer delivery time and supply chain lead time needs forecast driven manufacturing, supplying and purchasing decisions. In addition, multiple Decoupling Points and the Order Penetration Point have to be fixed to assure the supply strategy.

According to the strategy for responding to demand, two concepts should be differentiated: Order Decoupling Point (ODC) and Order Penetration Point (OPP). The lead time gap between the production lead time, i.e., how long it takes to plan, source, manufacture and deliver a product (P), and the delivery time, i.e., how long customers are willing to wait for the order to be completed (D), is key element of the supply chain [20]. Comparing P and D, a company has several basic strategic order fulfilment options: *Engineer to Order (ETO) – (D>>P), Make to Order (MTO) – (D>P), Assemble to Order (ATO) – (D<P) and Make to Stock (MTS) or Build to Forecast (BTF) – (D=0)* [21].

Given the inherent differences in these manufacturing strategies; MTO firms are characterized by low volume, customization, process flexibility, higher work-in-process inventory, lower finished goods inventories, and longer lead-times; and MTS firms are characterized by high volume, standardization, dedicated equipment, lower work-in process and higher finished goods inventories, and shorter lead-times [22].

Nevertheless, the implementation of the right supply strategy in global and fragmented production systems becomes more difficult because there is a need of settling down more than a decoupling point. Multiple Decoupling Points and the Order Penetration Point (OPP) have to be fixed to assure the supply strategy. The OPP divides the manufacturing stages that are forecast-driven (upstream of the OPP) from those that are customer-order-driven (the OPP and downstream). The OPP is defined as the point in the manufacturing Value Chain where a product is linked to a specific customer order. Sometimes the OPP is called the Customer Order Decoupling Point (CODP) to highlight the involvement of a customer order. Nevertheless, it is not the same because in a fragmented international material flow there could be various CODPs, but there is only one OPP. Thereby, the OPP is one of the strategic decisions because of its impact on the supply chain performance in terms of service and cost.

The Global Operations phenomenon proposes multiple designs for the different stages of the production system. These stages could be locally or globally configured [9].

Effective coordination between the agents of the supply chain and the supply strategy response in the Global network is really important for trying to avoid ramp up delays in time and volume.

2.3 Digital Factory and Simulation Techniques: DGRAI and Discrete Event Modelling Simulation

To carry out the production process and network development, the Digital Factory concept and the related tools like simulation techniques could be appropriate for planning and testing the different configurations in order to reduce the time to market [13].

Simulation techniques have been used in industry for many years, but the increase in the power of computers has expanded the scope of simulation tools, as well as facilitating their use in smaller companies. One definition of computer simulation is the following: "The practice of building models to represent existing systems, or hypothetical future systems, and of experimenting with these models to explain system behaviour, improve performance, or design new systems with desirable performances" [23]. Computer simulation is a technique that uses the computer to model a real-world system, especially when those systems are too complex to model with direct mathematical equations without disturbing or interfering with the real system [24]. The main advantages of simulation arise from the better understanding of interactions and the identification of potential difficulties, allowing the evaluation of different alternatives and therefore, reducing the number of changes in the final system. There are several simulation techniques; however, Discrete Event Simulation is the most commonly used [25].

Among simulation tools, the DGRAI tool is useful for planning and testing the decision centres of the operational planning and scheduling system. This system contains the plan, source, make and/or deliver decisions of different agents in the supply chain, as well as the impact on customer delivery and the coordination problems of the simulated supply strategy [26]. This simulation allows the coordination of the decision points and action points in order to ensure the adequate functionality of the manufacturing and supply system [6].

3 Research Methodology

The methodological framework used for this study was based on Constructive research theory. The Constructive research is an approach that aims to produce solutions to explicit problems and is closely related to the concept of innovative constructivism [27]. This approach produces an innovative solution, which is theoretically grounded, to a relevant practical problem. An essential component of constructive research is the generation of new learning and knowledge in the process of constructing the solution [28].

In order to test this proposition, a two phase research design based on the principles of Action Research (AR) was devised, i.e. a theory building and a theory testing phase.

The objective of the theory-building phase was to define a methodology/guide that could be used by practitioners in real organisations to design and configure a new manufacturing network, aided by different purpose-tailored techniques.

In the theory-testing phase, the approach used was tested and the results of the implementation process are shown. AR is a variation of the Case Study, where both researcher and client are actively engaged in solving a client-initiated project dealing with a certain business problem [29].

3.1   Theory Building: GlobOpe Framework

The GlobOpe (**Glob**al **Ope**rations) Model is a framework for the design of operations in facilities which are key nodes of the manufacturing networks but also the supply networks [6]. Thus, this Model aids facilities design or redesign process within a network.

The methodology/guide takes into account the position of the Business unit in the Value Chain and sets the stages which should help value creation. An analysis stage is used to analyze the factors and choose the content of the strategy. Moreover, the analysis contributes to a definition or formulation of the new facility and associated network ramp up process and then, a deployment stage of the formulated design is set. The deployment is a project-oriented task, where a process of monitoring and reviewing to facilitate the alignment of the organization to the Operation strategy is established [30].

This Framework consists of new facility decision drivers, Operations Management principles, Operations strategy key decisions and potential methods and techniques for aiding the decision process (see Fig.1).

Fig. 1. Schematic representation of the GlobOpe Framework

The principles of Operations Management are those paradigms to be taken into account in Global Operations. The scope of the Operations strategy key decisions are the strategic issues that managers have to decide on before starting with the physical and organisational design of operations involved in the plan, source, make and deliver process [31]. Moreover, the method also describes the implementation processes of the principles and the tools.

3.2   Case Research

The case company is a wind generator company that supplies generators for the wind energy sector. The company has a facility in the north of Spain, but due to the formulation of a Global Business strategy to enter new markets and give a quick response to strategic customers, especially the North American market, there is a need to implement a new facility in the USA.

To grow in sales and reduce business risk of investment in the new facility, the company proposes to fragment the current production process. The production processes header (stacking and winding) are held in Spain and the final processes (balancing and assembly) are implemented in the new location making a sequential industrialization in the generators range until the whole generators is manufactured in the American facility.

The researchers have responded to the five Operations strategy key decisions to engage in an internationalization process aided by the GlobOpe Framework and the associated principles and tools. The key decisions, the principles and tools will be briefly shown:

- **Location:** The facility location was decided considering the 13 factors identified by MacCarthy and Atthirawong [2]. Firstly, the area was chosen, which was North America; secondly, the country was chosen, in this case the USA, and finally the region was chosen, specifically, Wisconsin.
- **Role:** The strategy role of the plant was selected from among the different roles proposed by Ferdows [1]. The facility in the USA is a server, that is to say, the factory supplies specific national or regional markets. It typically provides a way to overcome tariff barriers and to reduce taxes, logistics costs, or exposure to foreign-exchange fluctuations.
- **Integration/Fragmentation of Productive and Logistic Operations:** The fragmentation of the ramp up process was selected from among four different alternatives [7] to achieve the maximum market impact in a short time at a minimal operations cost. The chosen strategy is to introduce the products and the manufacturing process sequentially in order to reduce the complexity of the individual steps. In addition, gaps in employee training can be filled successfully.
- **Supply Strategy:** Simulation techniques were used to decide from among different order fulfilment options and configurations (Engineer to Order, Build to Order, Assemble to Order and Make to Stock) and to choose strategic inventory positioning in the fragmented manufacturing system. It is decided that the American facility assembles the generators upon request, for that reason there must be a strategic inventory of subassemblies in the U.S.A, which are replenished based on forecasts by the Spanish facility. Then, the OPP of the system is the subassemblies inventory. Moreover, the Spanish plant also has to establish a strategic inventory previous to the manufacturing based on forecast; but in this case, this inventory is of critical parts (copper and sheet steal). On this occasion, there is an ODP in the critical parts storage to ensure the first phase of generator manufacturing whenever it is necessary. Thus, with the intention of cover the difference between the customer delivery time and the supply chain time is needed a MTO strategy, decision making

at purchase   and supply level, and the implementation of multiple ODP and OPP along of the supply chain. Therefore, in order to solve the previous problems, on the one hand, the Discrete Event simulation through the software AnyLogic 6.5.0 aids in defining the decoupling points positioning, the Inventory Policy (s, S) of subassemblies and critical parts, the security stocks, the reorder points and the replenishment quantities taking into account different demand patterns and supply uncertainty due to maritime transport of subassemblies. On the other hand, DGRAI allows the monitoring of the Decision system of production planning and scheduling to highlight the problems related to the decision coordination from a dynamic point of view.

- **Suppliers and Distribution Network Design:** Firstly, aided by Krajlic's [32] supply market matrix, the most appropriate purchase policies were mapped and defined. This approach takes into account the importance of purchasing and the complexity of supply market. The strategic importance of purchasing in terms of the value added by product line, the percentage of raw materials in total costs and their impact on profitability and the complexity of supply market in terms of supply scarcity, pace of technology and/or materials substitution, entry barriers, logistic costs, complexity, and monopoly or oligopoly conditions. By assessing the company´s situation in terms of these variables the supply strategy was determined trying to exploit purchasing potential and diminish risks. Secondly, aided by Meixall and Gargeya's [9] alternatives, the local and global supply chain configurations were designed.

4   Conclusions

The case study discussed in this paper provides several key conclusions:

- The researchers conclude from the learning process of the implementation that the initial Operations design should consider the following properties on a network level: adaptability to product demand changes, flexibility to product demand variety and contingency operability.
  - Firstly, adaptability lets companies handle a variety of requirements that could change, such as product volumes. Thus, the proposed design would have the ability to be scalable and adjustable to future needs at reasonable costs by coordinating the decisions of different agents in the supply chain.
  - Secondly, flexibility lets them handle the product mix, so the proposed design would have the capacity to accomplish constraints due to the increase in information and material flow complexity related to product mix increases.
  - Finally, the possible contingency plans need to cover supply uncertainty. They will allow companies to confront unforeseen events due to their high impact, even if the probability of occurrence of these events is not high.
- The analysis of the supply strategy to guarantee the service policy is becoming more complex due to longer lead times and the management of different stocks and order decoupling points (ODPs) in a multisite and fragmented international production system.

- Simulation techniques used with a structured approach could aid in increasing effectiveness when the design and the supply network of the manufacturing facilities are configured. Furthermore, these techniques help to increase the effectiveness of the supply chain configuration by increasing strategic customers' sales due to the reduction of ramp up time.
  - DGRAI technique allowed to highlight certain coordination problems between departments, check the staff saturation and distribute tasks.
  - AnyLogic simulation facilitated the visualization of the different scenarios proposed by the heads of the company and helped to ratify the decisions made.
- The multidisciplinary team involved in the research project considerer the GlobOpe Framework and simulation tools useful for decreasing ramp up delays and managing this process with a high degree of precision. Thus, it could be a management tool for a Steering Committee that is responsible for the effectiveness and efficiency of Global Operations.
- Until that moment, the researchers only thought to develop a framework in order to facilitate the ramp up process for the new facilities implementation abroad, but with this case is thought that it is necessary to expand the GlobOpe Model because there are also a lack of methods and techniques to accomplish the design and configuration process of a global production and logistic network.

References

1. Ferdows, K.: Making the Most of Foreign Factories. Harvard Business Review, 73–88 (March-April 1997)
2. MacCarthy, B.L., Atthirawong, W.: Factors affecting location decisions in international operations – a Delphi study. International Journal of Operations & Production Management 23(7), 794–818 (2003)
3. Porter, M.E.: Clusters and the new economies of competition. Harvard Business Review 6, 3–16 (1998)
4. Farrell, D.: Offshoring. Understanding the Emerging Global Labor Market. Mckinsey Global Institute. Harvard Business School Press (2006)
5. Lewin, A.Y., Peeters, C.: Offshoring work: business hype or the onset of fundamental transformation? Long Range Planning 39, 221–239 (2006)
6. Errasti, A.: International Manufacturing Networks: Global Operations Design and Management. Servicio Central de Publicaciones del Gobierno Vasco, San Sebastian (2011)
7. Abele, E., Meyer, T., Näher, U., Strube, G., Sykes, R.: Global production: a handbook for strategy and implementation. Springer, Heidelberg (2008)
8. Rudberg, M., Olhager, J.: Manufacturing networks and supply chains: an operating strategy perspective. Omega 31, 29–39 (2003)
9. Meixell, M., Gargeya, V.: Global Supply Chain Design: a literature Review and a Critique. Transportation Research Part E 41, 531 (2005)
10. Kinkel, S., Maloca, S.: Drivers and antecedents of manufacturing offshoring and backshoring. A German Perspective. Journal of Purchasing & Suppply Management 15, 154–165 (2009)
11. Vereecke, A., Van Dierdonck, R.: The strategic role of the plant: testing Ferdow's model. International Journal of Operations and Production Management 22, 492–514 (2002)

12. Shi, Y.: Internationalization and evolution of manufacturing systems: classic process models, new industrial issues, and academic challenges. Integrated, Manufacturing Systems 14, 385–396 (2003)
13. Spath, D., Potinecke, T.: Virtual product development – Digital Factory based methodology for SMEs. CIRP Journal of Manufacturing Systems 34(6), 539–548 (2005)
14. Mediavilla, M., Errasti, A.: Framework for assessing the current strategic plant role and deploying a roadmap for its upgrading. An empirical study within a global operations network. APMS, Cuomo (2010)
15. Monczka, R.M., Handfield, R.B., Guinipero, L.C., Patterson, J.L.: Purchasing and Supply Chain Management, 4th edn. South-Western Cengage Learning, USA (2009)
16. Terwisch, C., Bohn, R.: Learning and process improvement during production ramp up. International Journal of Production Economics 70 (2001)
17. T-Systems: White paper ramp up management. Accomplishing full production volume in-time, in-quality and in-cost (2010)
18. Kurtila, P., Shaw, M., Helo, P.: Model Factory concept-Enabler for quick manufacturing capacity ramp up (2010)
19. Sheffi, Y.: La empresa robusta, Lidl, Madrid (2006)
20. Simchi Levi, D., Kaminsky, P., Simchi Levi, E.: Designing and Managing the Supply Chain: Concepts, Strategies, and Cases. MacGraw Hill, USA (2000)
21. Khoshnevis, B.: Discrete Systems Simulation, p. 337. McGraw-Hill Inc., Singapore (1994)
22. Wikner, J., Rudberg, M.: Integrating production and engineering perspectives on the customer order decoupling point. International Journal of Operations and Production Management 25(7), 623–664 (2005)
23. Birou, L., Germain, R.N., Christensen, W.J.: Applied logistics knowledge impact on financial performance. International Journal of Operations & Production Management 31(8) (2011)
24. Khoshnevis, B.: Discrete Systems Simulation. McGraw-Hill Inc., Singapore (1994)
25. Banks, J., Carson, J.S., Nelson, B.L.: Discrete-Event System Simulation, 5th edn., p. 640. Prentice Hall, United States (2010)
26. Jahangirian, M., Eldabi, T., Naseer, A., et al.: Simulation in manufacturing and business: A review. European Journal of Operational Research, EJOP 203, 1–13 (2010)
27. Poler, R., Lario, F.C., Doumeingts, G.: DMDS Computers in Industry, vol. 49, pp. 175–193 (2002)
28. Meredith, J.: Theory building through conceptual methods. International Journal of Operations and Production Management 13(5), 3–11 (1993)
29. Mendibil, K., Macbryde, J.C.: Designing effective team-based performance measurement systems: an integrated approach. International Journal of Production Planning and Control 16(2), 208–225 (2005)
30. Schein, E.H.: Process Consultation Revisited, Building the Helping Relationship. Addison-Wesley, Reading (1999)
31. Feurer, R., Chaharbaghi, K., Wargin, J.: Analysis of strategy formulation and implementation at Hewlet Packard. Management Decision 33(10), 4–16 (1995)
32. Huan, S.M., Sheoran, S.H., Wang, G.A.: Review and analysis of supply chain operations reference (SCOR) model. Supply Chain Management: An International Journal 9(1), 23–29 (2004)
33. Krajlic, P.: Purchasing must become supply management. Harvard Business Review (1983)

Value Chain Based Framework for Assessing the Ferdows' Strategic Plant Role: An Empirical Study

M. Mediavilla[1], Ander Errasti[2], R. Domingo[3], and Sandra Martínez[2]

[1] BSH Home Appliances, Munich, Germany
Miguel.Mediavilla@BSHG.COM
[2] Engineering School, Tecnun, University of Navarra, San Sebastián, Spain
{smartinez,aerrasti}@tecnun.es
[3] Manufacturing Engineering Department, UNED University, Madrid, Spain
rdomingo@ind.uned.es

Abstract. In the current global economy, with an increased international presence of all type of organisations, the design and management of global operations networks (GON) plays a vital role in organisational competitiveness. Whilst all type of organisations are facing significant challenges for managing increasingly complex global operation, current literature on global operation networks is still limited in its scope. The aim of this paper is to discuss the development and evaluation of a construct for assessing the strategic plant role and developing of an improvement roadmap in GONs. This research makes a contribution to current knowledge on global operations by extending the model proposed by Ferdows and operationalizing it to enable its application for the design and optimisation of global operations networks.

Keywords: Global operations network, strategic factory role, case study.

1 Introduction

The internationalization trend among companies, both in sales and manufacturing has been mainly adopted by multinationals, but small-medium sized companies are also forced to go global [1]. Precisely as consequence of the economic globalization, the global operations network (GON) design will increasingly have to cover multiple regions and cope with higher network complexity [2-3], connecting markets to global supply and manufacturing sources beyond any geographical or shareholding border. Anyhow, the literature on global operations containing models to design and restructure GON is scarce and fragmented [1].

An interesting proposal was carried out by Ferdows [4-5], who stated that the management of GON could be executed based on the strategic plant role concept. However, there are few evidences of empirical testing of Ferdows' model and the deployment of the strategic plant role concept to an operational level [6],[22]. As a result, any attempt to design and/or restructure a GON is difficult to put into practice, as the plant role concept is complex to formulate, deploy and prioritize. This is paradoxical, as the higher the role the lower chance for a plant to disappear from the GON [23]. With the

J. Frick and B. Laugen (Eds.): APMS 2011, IFIP AICT 384, pp. 369–378, 2012.

current degree of globalization inefficient plants can no longer survive, even in distant local markets.

This paper will explore the application of Ferdows's model for the analysis of strategic plant roles in a GON and extend the scope of this model by discuss a framework for deploying an improvement roadmap, which facilitates a gradual upgrade of the strategic role of a plant within a GON.

2   Literature Review

In recent years the competitive environment has been characterized by a highly dynamic macro economical context and a global competitive landscape. In this environment, the internationalisation of operations has become a common trend for companies and this has further confirmed the necessity for strategies that continuously enable the renewal of organisational capabilities to adapt to this global competitive environment.

In this context, building and managing a GON is widely recognised as one of the most important challenges within international operations management [5],[37-38]. Evolving from an independently managed (or with lower interaction) plant network to a coordinated manufacturing network allows benefiting from the synergy among the plants [24],[39] by improving cost and delivery performance and enhancing the learning curve from the experiences of partners in the network [8]. However, the process and practice to optimise the overall performance of the operations network is still not well understood [40].

A common internationalisation approach, which looks for short-term cost reduction and competitiveness, is the establishment and management of foreign factories to benefit only from tariff and trade concessions, cheap labour, capital subsidies, and reduced logistics costs. Therefore, a limited range of work, responsibilities, network participation and resources are assigned to those factories [5]. Other companies demand much more from their foreign factories and, as a result, try to get much more out of them. This approach provides not only access to the already mentioned cost oriented incentives, but also a globally distributed manufacturing network with much higher proximity to potential regions, with close access to customers, suppliers, or specifically skilled, talented and motivated workforce. Those factories have a wider range of responsibilities and network interaction beyond a mere production work, as e.g. product or process engineering, purchasing decisions, after-sales service, etc. [4].

The questions that still remains unanswered is how to deploy the operations strategy in a multi-location GON and in particular how to balance the different competences and responsibilities of different plants within the network, taking into account that the each plant could assume different strategic responsibilities for themselves or for the whole GON.

The operations strategy is defined as the total standard of decisions that mould the long term capacities of any kind of operation and their contribution for the general business strategy through the reconciliation of the market requirements with the operations resources [7]. This operations strategy should in fact be reflected in the operations network design, which basically is about where to locate your supply sources and manufacturing and distribution operations, as well as the deployment of such operations, i.e. who should be supplying whom or the facility planning. It also arises when facing a rationalisation or restructuring an existing network [6].

Therefore, evolving from an independent managed (or with lower interaction) plant network to a coordinated manufacturing network allows to benefit from the synergy among the plants, to improve cost and delivery performance, and to enhance the learning curve from the experiences of network partners [8].

If managers do not consider manufacturing to be a source of competitive advantage, they are likely to establish foreign factories with a narrow strategic scope. In contrast, if managers regard manufacturing as a major source of competitive advantage, then the foreign plants will reward the company in the form of higher market share and greater profits [5].

The operations management literature has several models which cope with the supply chain analysis and performance (see a list of models e.g. in [1],[9]), but only few widen their scope from a supply chain perspective to an entire value chain approach – as defined by Porter [10]. Ferdows [4-5] implicitly covers the value chain and the international manufacturing network idea, especially when introducing the "lead plant" concept: it would be a plant contributing to the company's strategy by e.g. developing capabilities as new processes, products or technologies, or local skills, contact to end customers, suppliers, etc. These capabilities would be shared with other plants in the network.

However, despite of being reference model which is gaining academic recognition in the international operations field, as e.g. [1],[6],[11-15], there are still few evidences of empirical testing of Ferdows' model [6] - even when this model is easily recognisable in practice for executives.

The question that arises is how to deploy the operations strategy in a multi-location GON, i.e. how to balance the different competences and responsibilities along the different factories or facilities, taking into account that the different units of the GON could assume different strategic responsibilities for themselves or for the whole GON.

The intended strategy formulation and deployment is in fact a changing and adaptive exercise for the company: therefore the operations strategy and -by extension- the international manufacturing network design should integrate dynamic capabilities evaluation [16] as happens in any restructuring of a operations network.

These dynamic capabilities are defined by Teece et al [17] as "the ability to achieve new forms of competitive advantage to emphasise two key aspects that were not the main focus of attention in previous strategy perspectives. The term "dynamic" refers to the capacity to renew competences so as to achieve congruence with the changing business environment. The term "capabilities" emphasises the key role of strategic management in appropriately adapting, integrating and reconfiguring internal and external organisational skills, resources and functional competences to match the requirements of a changing environment".

Thus, the new paradigm in global operations strategy context is that if a company should adapt its operations to be as efficient and effective as possible, then there must be continuous reconfiguration of the manufacturing systems and the new proposal should consider the ability to be modified in the near future. The concept of Reconfigurable Manufacturing System (RMS) has posed salient inspiration for satisfying the aforementioned requirements: RMS was initially defined by [18] as "a machining system designed at the outset for rapid change in structure, as well as in hardware and software aspects, in order to quickly adjust production capacity and functionality within a part family in response to sudden changes in market or in regulatory requirements". The same principles can be easily applied to other system, as e.g. an operations network.

3   Research Questions and Methodology

The literature review confirms [3],[19] that in order to build and manage integrated GON could be the upcoming challenge for the operations management. Anyway the existing literature about how to design/restructure a GON is short and the study areas are dispersed [1],[20]. Furthermore the operations management literature has several models which cope with a supply chain analysis (SC) and performance (see [1] or [9]) but only few widen their scope from a SC perspective to an entire value chain approach –being the "Manufacturing Value Chain" [21] an interesting perspective that deserves attention.

Besides, the strategic factory role deployment to the operative level of sourcing, production and distribution has not been explicitly developed [6],[22]. Therefore any attempt to design/restructure a GON is difficult to put into practice, as the factory role concept is complex to formulate, deploy and prioritize. This is paradoxical, as the higher the role the lower chance for a plant to disappear from the GON [23].

Additionally two aspects related to GON need more research: 1) The understanding how to coordinate the operations of individual production units within a GON [22]: the network coordination itself can be a competitive advantage source [25]. 2) Diversified companies with different manufacturing networks (for different product typology) and their interdependence [19].

Therefore, this paper will cover the empirical application of the Ferdows model and extends its application to define how to systematically upgrade a plant strategic role acting within a GON by weakness-based identification, i.e. far beyond the solely analysis of the current strategic role.

At this point, the research question to be answered is the following: how could a facility improve its role – taking into account the systematic nature of the operations network? Which is the network strategy for balancing the different roles within the network? How could a facility role be operationalized in order to analyze the current and the target state respectively the drivers?

The methodological framework used for this study was based on Constructive research theory. The Constructive research is an approach that aims to produce solutions to explicit problems and is closely related to the concept of innovative constructivism [34]. This approach produces an innovative solution, which is theoretically grounded, to a relevant practical problem. An essential component of constructive research is the generation of new learning and knowledge in the process of constructing the solution [35].

In order to test this proposition, a two phase research design based on the principles of Action Research (AR) was devised, i.e. a theory building and a theory testing phase.

The objective of the theory-building phase was to define a methodology/guide that could be used by practitioners in real organisations to design and configure a new manufacturing network, aided by different purpose-tailored techniques.

In the theory-testing phase, the approach used was tested and the results of the implementation process are shown. AR is a variation of the Case Study, where both researcher and client are actively engaged in solving a client-initiated project dealing with a certain business problem [36].

4   Framework Proposal for Assessing/Upgrading Factory Roles

If the factory competences are not enforced in order to get an upgraded strategic role, usually the less successful plans may disappear from the map due to competitive pressure to reduce costs and concentrate the production volume in a smaller number of plants [26]. Therefore companies should redesign and reconfigure the supply chain multisite network – either from a global (top down or network approach) or partial (bottom-up or production unit approach) initiative.

The proposed framework related to the strategic factory role is called Akondia and is part of the GLOBOPE global framework. It aims to facilitate the practical usage of the Ferdows' model respectively extends the Ferdows's model application by defining how to upgrade a plant strategic role within the framework of a GON, i.e. far beyond the solely analysis of the current strategic role.

The framework bases on an evaluation of the current value chain status, utilizes this competitive position status for assigning a strategic role and finally can be applied for deploying an improvement roadmap to get other facility role. Depending on the analysis scope, the Akondia Framework is able to contribute to the sustainability of the network (by identifying the strengths of each network unit and prioritising the assignment/development of competences in the network perspective) or of the individual units (supporting the upgrade to a more attractive facility role).

The factory role, as originally defined by Ferdows, implicitly covers functions which are over a manufacturing facility, i.e. aspects within a GON which are not only part of a Supply Chain but of the Value Chain (especially in the "lead plant" concept).

The Akondia framework establishes its roots for the factory role assessment therefore in the Value Chain concept defined by Porter [10]. Based on this Value Chain definition, the framework has been initially created by defining 6 main analysis fields: 1) Markets and customers, 2) Suppliers, 3) Internal Operations, 4) HR Management, 5) Technology Management and 6) Socio-political and regulatory. The 6 fields are mentioned by Ferdows in the different generic factory roles.

The framework has been developed in two analysis levels: 1) The first level should go through a "macro" perspective along the 6 main analysis fields. 2) A second detailed and separated "micro" approach per field can be utilised (e.g. Benchmark models for the analysis field, as SCM SCOR Model or Lean Production applications).

The first analysis level aims to provide a strategic facility profile or competitive position as an output, which later could be compared to the generic roles defined by Ferdows. In order to systematize the analysis, a questionnaire for different competences has been developed: 38 questions related to the 6 analysis fields. Each question assesses a competence, which is evaluated in two dimensions: 1) level of influence of the factory to develop the competence (e.g. is the factory able to select its strategic suppliers or is a central decision? Has the factory any influence in the new product technologies or is it developed by other central functions or competence centres?); and 2) current competence level.

The Akondia framework has 3 main clear stages in its application. 1) A first analysis of the current competitive position of the facility (strategic profile), 2) a second step which finds out the affinity of the strategic profile to the generic strategic roles of Ferdows and 3) a final stage, where the improvement/upgrade efforts are identified and prioritized.

The first step is therefore based on the questionnaire. When fulfilling it, there is a competitive position evaluation as an output, which already provides a first overview of the competence level per analysis field. The main conclusion coming out from this competitive position is an overview of the strengths and weaknesses of each analysed facility, showing the evaluated level per competence. An interesting extension of this analysis is its usage to compare the internal assessment (management of the facility) and the external view of e.g. Business Unit or Headquarters.

The second step of the Akondia framework is an analytical phase to be able to convert the competitive position of a facility into a Ferdows strategic role. The key element of this step is to be able to model each of the 6 strategic roles of Ferdows in the questionnaire. The authors have developed generic competitive positions (strategic profiles) for each and all of the Ferdows roles and contrasted them extensively via Delphi-panels. Denote anyhow that this evaluation could vary depending on e.g. sector, size of the company, business unit or product range, or company strategy.

The comparison of the generic competitive positions with the results of the evaluated questionnaire gives plenty of different data treatment possibilities. In their analysis, the authors propose a model to quantitatively measure the affinity of a facility to the given roles. In order to finalise the second step, the most suitable graphical presentation is to summarise the whole analysis by utilizing the Ferdows's model and placing each of the analysed facilities. It can be easily done based on the quantitative affinity model already described.

The third step of the Akondia framework is focused on how to get another role for any analysed facility (usually it should mean a more valuable). In order to make it more systematically, it is recommended to prioritise the effort for achieving the new role status. It has two main working axes: 1) Strengthen the current facility role. 2) Develop improvement roadmap for achieving a new facility role. For strengthening the current facility role, it is necessary to know the weakest competences; anyhow, the reader should come back to the first step of the framework and remind that the utilised questionnaire was scored on two dimension: the competence level and the additionally the influence level of the facility in the competence.

It is logical to assume that the higher the influence level on a given competence, the easier to improve its level. The Akondia framework proposes a first strengthening of the current strategic role based on a periodization matrix. This matrix shows graphically each of the 38 assessed competences in the questionnaire: the Y-Axis shows the level of each competence, while the X-Axis provides the influence of a given facility for the assessed competence. Several graphical alternatives for a quick-scan of the fields can be developed by cross-matching influence/competence levels.

After strengthening the current competitive position by a focused improvement in competences where the influence is high, any facility could be suitable to develop a strategic role upgrade roadmap. Using the generic competitive positions (or strategic profile) for the strategic roles of Ferdows, a stepwise middle/long-term roadmap can be deployed. The authors recommend a deployment based on the 6 analysis field, balancing the current competence level, the influence level and the effort to achieve the required level (e.g. providing more influence to a facility by giving new responsibilities).These role changes could in fact imply organizational decisions or re-assignment of responsibilities.

Any detailed improvement roadmap per field should have a second-level analysis and detailed deployment in the operative level –.e.g. for manufacturing facilities/operations network the "Suppliers" or "Operations Management" fields are key elements that could be improved by Benchmark models.

5   Case Study: Data Collection and Theory Testing

The testing phase of the Akondia framework was developed under Action-Research (AR) principles. AR is a generic term, which covers many forms of action-oriented research that focuses on deriving knowledge through action as opposed to positivist methods that aim to create universal knowledge [30-31] that satisfy scientific precepts, e.g. repeatability and unbiased observation. AR is defined as "a participatory process concerned with developing practical knowing in the pursuit of worthwhile human purposes. It seeks to bring together action and reflection, theory and practical solutions to issues of pressing concern to people" [32].

The Akondia framework was applied to a GON (18 plants in 7 countries) of a worldwide operating white-goods corporation dedicated to the design, production and distribution., which posted above 8 billion Euros in 2009 and is one of the global leading companies in the sector. The company has over 40 factories operating in Europe, the USA, Latin America and Asia, with a workforce numbering with approx. 40,000 people. The final result and score has been extensively checked with a Delphi panel (Factory Management Team, Headquarters) to reinforce the validity of the results [27-28].

6   Conclusions

The framework goes beyond the supply chain perspective models [22] and arises the necessity to be more specific/extend topics from the value chain that also influence the strategic factory role (e.g. product/process innovation, strategic supplier management) and the absence of assessment regarding the original contribution of lead factories in the network -i.e. for new topics the rest of factories profit themselves from the experiences in lead factories, as e.g. new product platform launch.

Regarding the application of the Akondia framework, the main conclusions are:

1) It serves as analysis tool for assessing the strategic plant role; 2) It helps prioritising the improvement aspects for changing the factory role and 3) It covers the entire factory complexity, i.e. not only operations but also the value chain aspects

(e.g. product development, strategic purchasing). 4) The Akondia framework is an analysis and improvement tool for facilities which is able to cope with the 3 generic business strategies: operational excellence, product leadership and customer intimacy – as defined by Porter [8] and Kaplan and Norton [33]. Former attempts to model the Ferdows model were narrowed in their scope, due to the fact the unique generic business strategy that was properly assess was the "Operational Excellence" [22].

The case study provides: 1) New empirical application of the Ferdows' model; 2) Confirms that the framework can be broken down to model each factory role into operational aspects; 3) One of the first multi-product network assessment and possible interaction fields and 4) clear picture about how to utilise value-chain based models for analysing and improving any GON.

References

1. Corti, D., Egaña, M.M., Errasti, A.: Challenges for off-shored operations: findings from a comparative multi-case study analysis of Italian and Spanish companies. In: Proceedings 16th Annual EurOMA Conference, Gothenburg (2009)
2. Shi, Y., Gregory, M.J.: International Manufacturing Networks–to develop global competitive capabilities. Journal of Operations Management 16, 195–214 (1998)
3. Ernst, D., Kim, L.: Global production networks. Knowledge Diffusion and Local Capability Formation 31(8/9), 1417–1429 (2002)
4. Ferdows, K.: Mapping international factory networks. In: Ferdows, K. (ed.) Managing International Manufacturing, pp. 3–21. Elsevier Science Publishers, New York (1989)
5. Ferdows, K.: Making the most of foreign factories. Harvard Business Review, 73–88 (March-April 1997)
6. Vereecke, A., Van Dierdonck, R.: The Strategic Role of the Plant:Testing Ferdow's Model. International Journal of Operations & Production Management 22(5) (2002)
7. Slack, N., Lewis, M.: Operations Strategy, 2nd edn. Prentice Hall, Upper Saddle River (2002)
8. Flaherty, T.: Coordinating international manufacturing and technology. In: Porter, M. (ed.). Harvard Business School Press (1986)
9. Netland, T., Alfnes, E., Fauske, H.: How mature is your supply chain? - A supply chain maturity assessment test. In: Proceedings of the 14th EurOMA Conference 2007, Ankara (2007)
10. Porter, M.E.: Competitive Advantage. The Free Press, New York (1985)
11. Fusco, J.P., Spring, M.: Flexibility vs. robust networks: the case of the Brazilian automotive sector. Integrated Manufacturing Systems 14(1), 26–35 (2003)
12. Meijboom, B., Voordijk, H.: Internacional operations and location decisions: a firm level approach. Tijdschrift Voor Economische En Sociale Geografie 94(4), 463–476 (2003)
13. Maritan, C.A., Brush, T.H., Karnani, A.G.: Plant roles and decision autonomy in multinational plant networks. Journal of Operations Management 22(5), 489–503 (2004)
14. Vereecke, A., Van Dierdonck, R., De Meyer, A.: A typology of plants in global manufacturing networks. Management Science 52(11), 1737–1750 (2006)
15. Feldmann, A., Olhager, J.: Plant roles and decision-making in manufacturing networks. In: Proceedings 16th Annual EurOMA Conference, Gothenburg (2009)
16. Sweeney, M., Cousens, A., Szwejczewski, M.: International manufacturing networks design - A proposed methodology. In: Proceedings of the 14th EurOMA Conference 2007, Ankara (2007)

17. Teece, D.J., Pisano, G., Shuen, A.: Dynamic capabilities and strategic management. Strategic Management Journal 18(7), 509–533 (1997)
18. Koren, Y., Heisel, U., Jovane, F., Moriwaki, T., Pritschow, G., Ulsoy, H., Van Brussel, G.: Reconfigurable manufacturing systems. CIRP Annals-College International de Recherches Pour la Production 48(2), 527–540 (1999)
19. De Toni, A., Parussini, M.: International Manufacturing Networks: a literature review. In: 17th Conference EurOMA, Porto (2010)
20. Laiho, A., Blomqvist, M.: International Manufacturing Networks: a literature review. In: 17th Conference EurOMA, Porto (2010)
21. Singh Srai, J., Shi, Y.: Understanding China's Manufacturing Value Chain. University of Cambridge, Institute for Manufacturing Publishing, Cambridge (2008)
22. Mediavilla, M., Errasti, A.: Framework for assessing the current strategic plant role and deploying a roadmap for its upgrading. An empirical study within a global operations network. In: Proceedings of APMS 2010 Conference, Cuomo, Italy (2010)
23. Vereecke, A.: Network relations in multinational manufacturing companies. Flanders DC and Vlerick Leuven Gent Management School (2007)
24. Dubois, F.L., Toyne, B., Oliff, M.D.: International manufacturing strategies of U.S. multinationals: a conceptual framework based on a four-industry study. Journal of International Business Studies, Q2 24(2), 307–333 (1993)
25. Shi, Y., Gregory, M.: Emergence of global manufacturing virtual networks and establishment of new manufacturing infrastructure for faster innovation and firm growth. Production Planning & Control 16(6), 621–631 (2005)
26. De Meyer, A., Vereecke, A.: International operations. In: Werner, M. (ed.) International Encyclopedia of Business and Management. Routledge, London (1996)
27. Linstone, H.A., Turoff, M.: The Delphi Method: Techniques and Applications. Addison-Wesley, London (1975)
28. Turoff, M., Hiltz, S.: Computer based Delphi Processes,
http://eies.njit.edu/~turoff/Papers/delphi3.html
29. Westbrook, R.: Action Research: a new paradigm for research in production and operations management. Operations and Production Management 15(12), 6 20 (1995)
30. Coughlan, P., Coghlan, D.: Action research for operations management. International Journal of Operations and Production Management 22(2), 220–240 (2002)
31. Vignalli, C.: The marketing management process and heuristic devices: an action research investigation. Market Intelligence Plann. 21(4), 205–219 (2003)
32. Reason, P., Bradbury, H.: The Sage Handbook of Action Research: Participative Inquiry and Practice, 2nd edn. Sage Publications, Los Angeles (2008)
33. Kapland, R.S., Norton, D.P.: The Strategy-Focused Organization. Harvard Business School Press, Boston (2001)
34. Meredith, J.: Theory building through conceptual methods. International Journal of Operations and Production Management 13(5), 3–11 (1993)
35. Mendibil, K., Macbryde, J.C.: Designing effective team-based performance measurement systems: an integrated approach. International Journal of Production Planning and Control 16(2), 208–225 (2005)
36. Schein, E.H.: Process Consultation Revisited, Building the Helping Relationship. Addison-Wesley, Reading (1999)
37. De Toni, A., Parussini, M.: International Manufacturing Networks: a literature review. In: Proceedings of 17th Conference EurOMA, Porto (2010)

38. Netland, T.: Improvement programs in multinational manufacturing enterprises: a proposed theoretical framework and literature review. In: Proceedings of Euroma 2011 Conference, Cambridge, UK (2011)
39. Shi, Y., Gregory, M.: Emergence of global manufacturing virtual networks and establishment of new manufacturing infrastructure for faster innovation and firm growth. Production Planning & Control 16(6), 621–631 (2005)
40. Rudberg, M.: Linking Competitive Priorities and Manufacturing Networks: A Manufacturing Strategy Perspective. International Journal of Manufacturing Technology and Management 6(1/2), 55–80 (2004)

Part III

Strategy

Sustainability Risk for Global Production Networks in the Automobile Industry: A Case of Supplier Networks

Jakob E. Beer[*] and Jayantha P. Liyanage

University of Stavanger, Norway
{jakob.e.beer,j.p.liyanage}@uis.no

Abstract. Sustainability risk for global production networks can be considered more important than ever due to its distributed nature. The automobile industry relies heavily on its global supply networks. Nevertheless, little is being done to improve the sustainability of complex production environments. In practice, there is a number of factors that regulate the sustainability risk in any industry, and this paper pays special attention on how flexibility requirements can help mitigate sustainability risk by reducing the chance of unnecessary supply non-compliance performance.

Keywords: manufacturing networks, sustainability risk, automobile industry, production, capacity, flexibility.

1   Introduction

The emergence of low cost supply markets such as China, East Europe, and Mexico has made already globally spanning production networks even more complex, and amplified sensitivity towards reactions and overreactions [1]. In a permanent effort to reach economic efficiency and due to the visible increase of suppliers´ competencies, there have been some changes concerning the distribution of value-added throughout production networks. The reasons for this development are diverse, cf. [2–5]. Task division and outsourcing decisions do not only involve peripheral business activities but often times concern core competencies as well [6].

There is some consensus that production networks have become more vulnerable with rising complexity [7, 8]. The complexity of cars, however, requires that car producers rely on multiple partners to manage the development and production of cars in a timely and economic fashion. The consequence is that success is more about how well networks perform rather than about an individual OEM´s performance [9]. At the same time, globally distributed production bears some important implications regarding both ecological and social aspects. Transportation between different continents is quite energy intense; and efficiency improvements - from the OEM´s point of view - such as just-in-time or just-in-sequence delivery have increased traffic congestion with all the known related consequences for the natural and social environment.

---

[*] Corresponding author.

J. Frick and B. Laugen (Eds.): APMS 2011, IFIP AICT 384, pp. 381–389, 2012.

The consequence of all of the above is that globally acting production networks are necessary, yet problematic. For OEMs, they provide economic advantages - especially if operations run smoothly. For the public in supplier countries, they provide welfare. For the nature, though, they have inherent negative effects. And in case of unforeseen interruptions, the bottom line of some global sourcing decisions can easily turn red – and switching the transportation mode to air to speed up operations further worsens the ecological balance. The goal must therefore be to reduce the chance of non-compliance performance in global production networks to keep the risk of adverse effect on the economic outcome, the public, and the natural environment – i.e., to keep sustainability risks – as low as possible.

For several types of supply chain risks, flexibility represents an adequate approach to mitigate the negative impact in case of the occurrence of unfavorable incidents [10]. This paper is to contribute to this objective by highlighting flexibility agreements between OEMs and suppliers as one cause for sustainability risks in global automotive production networks and by introducing one approach to help mitigate sustainability risks.

2   Methodology

To understand the implications of flexibility agreements and to determine how flexibility agreements can be used to enhance the functionality of production networks, information from logistics and supply management experts from both car makers and suppliers have been collected through a round of 28 interviews, involving five European and American OEMs and six European suppliers.

The questions aimed at the link between OEMs and tier-1 suppliers, so for OEMs all questions were related to the supply side while for suppliers most questions were related to the demand site. The data covered the general capacity planning process, the importance of the capacity planning process in terms of management attention, transparency about capacity planning strategies of competitors, known weaknesses of the planning approach, and the effect of the global economic crisis and the subsequent boom on the capacity planning strategy. The interviews were conducted either face-to-face or on the phone, mostly by two interviewers, and took 40 to 150 minutes. Most interview partners were involved in supplier management and came from one OEM, but also several management positions of other OEMs and suppliers could be covered. 17 of the 28 interview partners were regular supplier management specialists while 11 interview partners were ranked manager, senior manager, director, or higher.

The purpose of the interviews was to get a better understanding of the general supply capacity planning process as well as to identify weaknesses of the common approaches. The data has not been used for statistical evaluation.

In addition to the interviews, information has been obtained from the day-to-day business in supplier management and from the review of some relevant literature and several automobile industry information services.

3   Status Quo Review

3.1   Supply Shortages

The 2008/2009 crisis left many suppliers behind with largely unused capacity and high inventories, particularly with those parts that have long production and delivery lead times. Several suppliers along the whole supply chain had to close production plants. When demand for automobiles started to recover in early 2010, the remaining inventories were used up quite fast, and supply shortages for several parts loomed ahead. Part shortages became a major concern in the industry on a global basis throughout 2010 and 2011. Several car and truck makers had to halt production for several days, sometimes for a week [11–14]. The situation has eased in 2012 with suppliers having been able to set up the required production capacities and strong demand downturn in several countries (e.g., due to the recurrence of the European debt crisis).

One reason for the severity of the supply situation can certainly be seen in the industry leaders´ effort to streamline their supply networks according to lean principles with low inventories, just-in-time or just-in-sequence deliveries, and mainly single-sourcing. In an interview, the director of supply chain management of the European division of an American car maker stated that his company does experience more shortages these days than it did in the 1990s before they started streamlining their networks.

The causes previously mentioned had led to the situation where OEMs competed for the scarce resource of supplier production capacity while many suppliers were running extra working shifts. The negative consequences were manifold: Frequent express deliveries by airplane, helicopter, and light trucks have been conducted - with obviously severe implications for the natural environment and for the financial results. Quality problems due to tool overutilization, skipped machine maintenance, and skipped quality control by suppliers have been experienced, which, of course, worsened the situation as capacity was wasted when parts were rejected. On the other hand, supplied parts with impaired quality that usually would have been rejected have been approved and accepted in some cases, which raises ethical questions with regard to the end customer. Some OEMs increased their pressure on suppliers to an extent that made suppliers use resources "reserved" for other OEMs to meet the demand of that OEM, which also raises ethical as well as legal questions. From some suppliers in East Europe, bribe of customs officials to speed up the border crossing process, which, again, is both an ethical and legal topic. When sustainability is one goal of responsibly acting organizations, then the points mentioned above represent sustainability risks deriving from situations of supply shortage.

3.2   Supply Networks and Supply Chains

The supply chain model has become quite popular during the course of the last two decades. Nevertheless, the model is rather incomplete [15] and the term 'supply chain' to some extent misleading. The automobile industry is characterized by a complex web of both vertical and lateral interrelations [16, 17]. Accordingly, lateral effects can affect organizational performance, which is not taken into account in a linear supply chain model [1]. Hence, a focus on supply chains might distract supply management professionals from lateral performance impact. The consequences can be manifold, and there is good reason to reconsider underlying assumptions in supply management, particularly when it comes to supplier capacity planning and thus to the question of standard production flexibility [18].

4   Results and Analysis

Research suggests that the problems outlined above do not simply happen to happen due to suppliers´ operational weaknesses but can rather be traced back to certain constellations on the OEM side that inherently bear the chance of unfavourable results. The items described below represent sources of supplier non-compliance performance that apply to the OEMs which were part of the study and may equally apply to other companies in this industry and other industries.

4.1   Capacity Planning

Supplier production capacity is determined around 24 to 36 months prior to start of production. This implies that capacity may be planned under very different economic circumstances than there will be once the production is going to get ramped up. For car models that are launched in late 2010 or in 2011, capacities may have been planned in the middle of the global economic crisis with generally lower sales expectations while demand for these models might be booming today.

4.2   Capacity Flexibility

When OEMs source production of certain assembly components to a supplier, they generally require the supplier to provide a certain amount of production capacity flexibility. It is obvious that supply networks often need to commit excess resources to production to ensure timely responses to the market since planned production quantities usually are based on forecasts instead of actual demand. Other arguments for paying particular attention to production capacity flexibility are, for example, a decreasing level of professionalism upstream the supply chains, the vulnerability of the automotive industry with respect to economic downturns, the threat of bullwhip effects, the decreasing level of transparency upstream the supply chain with respect to forecasted demand data, differences in data processing with different time horizons for forecasts and call-offs along the supply chain, and an increasing time lag between action and reaction with increasing length of the supply chain [18].

While there is broad consensus that some kind of flexibility agreement is necessary, there are different opinions on how much flexibility suppliers should be required to provide since flexibility – which basically is excess capacity – is expensive. Tang and Tomlin [10] point out that the benefit obtained by a certain flexibility level in most cases is represented by a concave function, which means that significant impact can be achieved with little adjustment in flexibility. It is therefore remarkable that capacity flexibility agreements between most OEMs and suppliers are not particularly sophisticated and do not take into account the different characteristics of parts. In fact, all interviewed OEMs require the same production capacity flexibility for all parts they source to suppliers, regardless of part characteristics, contracted volumes or whatsoever. Simply put: They employ a "one size fits all" approach. This approach has led to several problems in the past and yet seems to be widely accepted. The interviewed suppliers state that also other OEMs who have not been covered in this study employ the same approach. Those agreements usually include a required flexibility between 10 - 20% (depending on the OEM) and a timeframe within which the production output hike has to be reached, e.g. seven days.

5   Mitigating Measures

Generally, it is economically efficient for all partners when suppliers can reach high machine utilization while being performance compliant. Regarding forecast uncertainty, network effects, and volatile demand, this cannot always be the case, though. One way to reduce the chance of supplier non-compliance performance and thus to mitigate sustainability risks is to reconsider flexibility agreements with regard to the characteristics of the parts sourced. For this purpose, a set of criteria will be introduced that can be utilized to determine what assembly parts OEMs should require suppliers to provide higher capacity flexibility for.

5.1   Criteria for Higher Flexibility

One result of the research (among others that can be found in 18) was a set of criteria that can be used to identify those assembly parts for which OEMs should require suppliers to provide higher production capacity flexibility. The list can be divided into one group of factors that really points out the need to adjust flexibility and another group of factors that support the decision, i.e. how fast the supply network could react to unexpectedly high demand and how expensive it would be. Those factors could be considered "amplifiers" for the problem. Clearly, requiring higher flexibility would increase upfront costs of suppliers for setting up excess capacity, and thus leads to higher procurement costs; there is some reason to assume, however, that the benefits of lower sustainability risks would overcompensate for higher procurement prices and thus lead to increased production network sustainability. It is likely to be beneficial to require higher-than-usual capacity flexibility when the following criteria hold true:

The Uncertainty of the Forecasted Take Rate Is High. When parts are innovations, i.e. extra equipment that are new to the market, and there is no actual experience how well the extra equipment will be embraced by customers, it is harder to determine an accurate estimation of the take rate. Take rates for innovative extra equipments proved to be hard to predict. There are various cases of parts for which forecasted take rates were far away from actual sales, which eventually led to capacity shortages.

It should therefore be taken into consideration if the forecasted take rate can be expected to be rather accurate as it is based on past experience with the same or similar products or if it is more speculative as the extra equipment represents an innovation.

The Sales Forecast of the Car Model Is Uncertain. Of course, it may be the case that the sales forecast of a certain car model as such is highly uncertain. In particular, this applies to models that fill a niche or create a new market segment. When Mercedes-Benz, for example, introduced the R-Class, forecasted sales were much higher than they finally turned out to be. This may also apply to particularly expensive cars as their demand is more vulnerable to the global economic situation. Sales of the S-Class in 2011, for example, were much higher than it was expected, yet were severely affected by the global recession in 2008 and 2009. Parts that are used for only one car model may deviate faster from the predicted volumes than parts that are used in several models due to the risk pooling effect. This is particularly true when the one car model into which the component is built has very volatile demand itself.

The Part Is Sourced to a Single Supplier. If the assembly part is sourced to a single supplier, this supplier will need to provide higher capacity flexibility than it will need as only one of multiple supply sources. With dual or multiple sourcing, increases in demand can be balanced among suppliers while a single-source supplier would need to provide "full" flexibility to meet demand.

The Assembly Line Is Shared with Other OEMs. When the assembly line is shared with other OEMs, the available remaining capacity does not only depend on one´s own demand but also on other parties´ demand. In many market segments, there are products from different OEMs that aim at the same customers. Increasing and decreasing market volume thus potentially affects several customers that are supplied from the same assembly line. When demand for luxury cars booms - which has been the case since 2010 – then not only are more Mercedes-Benz E-Class cars sold but also more of Audi´s A6 and BMW´s 5 Series. On a shared assembly line, all customers affect each other in terms of available production capacity. Requiring the supplier to have additional production capacity available on short call can help avoiding capacity shortages for one´s own parts as otherwise the danger is evident that available excess capacity is used up by competing customers. In general, network effects should be taken into account when determining the required production capacity flexibility. Particularly strong network effects suggest a need for higher flexibility.

The Profit Margin of the Extra Equipment Is High. Especially in the luxury segment, profit margins of some extra equipment are particularly high - sometimes several hundred percent. Parts with particularly high profit margins may open the chance to secure supply with higher production capacity flexibility rather than those parts that hardly deliver profit. Additionally, in the luxury segment higher procurement costs due to higher flexibility may be compensated by higher prices that customers are charged - either directly through higher prices for the extra equipment or indirectly through bundling the extra equipment with additional extra equipment the customer has to pay for.

The Time Necessary to Set Up Additional Capacities Is High. When setting up additional capacity in case of tight production capacity takes particularly long, it is risky to plan very lean - especially when forecasted demands are uncertain (see above). Setting up additional production capacity can easily take several months in some industries. Requiring those suppliers to install excess production capacity to secure a certain amount of flexibility may justify higher upfront costs when part shortages can by avoiding long lead time for additional capacity.

Costs for Setting Up Additional Capacity within a Short Period of Time to Meet Higher Demand Are High. It may happen that the costs for higher flexibility are low when it is considered right from the beginning. In some situations, it may happen, though, that adding capacity in a later point in time during the series production process is accompanied by high cost as assembly lines or material flow has to be re-configured. Adding a second assembly line on a green field may be cheap, but moving equipment around to place additional machines may come along with the need to interrupt the production process for some time. Setting up additional machines during the series production process may require major changes in the factory layout. Sometimes, setting up additional machines may be less problematic, but having them set up within a short period of time can be expensive, for instance, when this needs to be achieved through express orders of tools and machines in order to avoid long lead time.

Air Traffic Is Necessary for Express Deliveries in Case of Supply Shortage. If supply shortages emerge, usually transportation time is to be reduced with express deliveries in order to avoid production interruptions. In case of suppliers being located in distant places, air traffic frequently replaces maritime or road traffic. This, however, adversely affects the environmental and economic sustainability of the production network.

5.2   Evaluation

Companies are reluctant to invest in flexibility as they are lacking a clear understanding of the benefits [10]. A simple simulation model might help to demonstrate the effect of lump sum standard flexibility

The model would need to incorporate two random input variables - the number of cars sold and the take rate - along with other parameters such as forecasted car sales and forecasted take rate. Also, "amplifying factors" can be defined as input variables based on whether or not costs for excess capacity are high, air traffic would be necessary, and so forth. The decision variable is the flexibility rate suppliers are required to provide. The output would be an analysis as to what extent actual demand for the assembly component exceeds production capacity including the reserved flexibility (cf. Fig. 1).

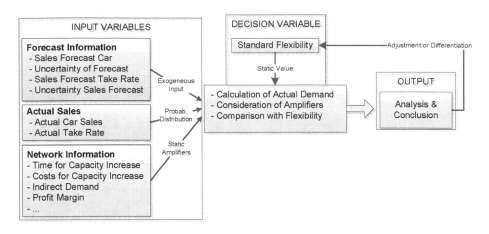

Fig. 1. Evaluation Framework

Such a model can easily be built as with any common discrete simulation tool and even with a spreadsheet and macros, e.g., as Monte Carlo simulation model. Network effects can be included and awareness for lateral performance impact can thereby be increased. This simple model cannot prove or predict any particular supply situation development (though the link with real life date can be created to make the model more realistic); its main purpose shall be the demonstration as to how fast a lump sum flexibility approach can result into supply shortage if assumptions sales forecasts are based on do not hold true.

6   Conclusion

This paper discusses the situation of frequent supply shortages in the automobile in-dustry in 2010 and 2011. Based on research in the automobile industry, including expert interviews, the paper suggests that certain structural weaknesses in the supplier production capacity planning process have contributed to the severity of the supply situation, involving different sustainability risks. It has been argued that in many cases supply shortages will eventually lead to significant adverse effects for society and environment.

Hence, to improve the supplier production capacity planning process and thus to mitigate sustainability risks a set of criteria has been defined and explained. These criteria are to support the identification of those assembly parts of an automobile that shall be produced with higher production capacity flexibility. Assembly parts for which one or more of these criteria hold true, it seems inadequate to use the tradi-tional lump sum standard production capacity flexibility approach.

The concept shows how diligent judgement of characteristics of sourcing relations can be used to improve on sustainability by helping to avoid unnecessary supply shortages.

References

1. Waldraff, A.: Dynamische Aspekte komplexer Logistiksysteme. In: Garcia Sanz, F.J. (ed.) Die Automobilindustrie auf dem Weg zur Globalen Netzwerkkompetenz. Effiziente und flexible Supply Chains erfolgreich gestalten, pp. 161–180. Springer, Heidelberg (2007)
2. Blanco, E.E.: Stay Ahead of the GHG Curve. Inside Supply Management 22(3), 32–33 (2011)
3. Holweg, M.: The Evolution of Competition in the Automobile Industry. In: Parry, G., Graves, A. (eds.) Build to Order. The Road to the 5-Day Car, pp. 13–34. Springer, London (2008)
4. Rennemann, T.: Logistische Lieferantenauswahl in globalen Produktionsnetzwerken, 1st edn. Rahmenbedingungen, Aufbau und Praxisanwendung eines kennzahlenbasierten Entscheidungsmodells am Beispiel der Automobilindustrie. Deutscher Universitäts-Verlag | GWV Fachverlage GmbH, Wiesbaden (2007)
5. Semmler, K., Mahler, D.: Von Beschaffung zum Wertschöpfungsmanagement - Gestaltungsdimensionen einer Funktion im Wandel. In: Garcia Sanz, F.J. (ed.) Die Automobilindustrie auf dem Weg zur Globalen Netzwerkkompetenz. Effiziente und flexible Supply Chains erfolgreich gestalten, pp. 25–48. Springer, Heidelberg (2007)
6. Roehrich, J.K.: Outsourcing: Management and Practice Within the Automotive Industry. In: Parry, G., Graves, A. (eds.) Build to Order. The Road to the 5-Day Car, pp. 75–97. Springer, London (2008)
7. Christopher, M., Peck, H.: Building the Resilient Supply Chain (2005)
8. Ritschie, B., Brindley, C.: Effective Management of Supply Chains: Risks and Performance. In: Wu, T. (ed.) Managing Supply Chain Risk and Vulnerability. Tools and Methods for Supply Chain Decision Makers, pp. 9–28. Springer, London (2009)
9. Urban, G.: Das ganze Zuliefernetzwerk im Griff – Innovations- und Effizienzpotenziale nutzen. Von der Zulieferkette zum Zuliefernetzwerk. In: Gehr, F., Hellingrath, B. (eds.) Logistik in der Automobilindustrie. Innovatives Supply Chain Management für wettbewerbsfähige Zulieferstrukturen; mit 6 Tabellen, pp. 1–4. Springer, Heidelberg (2007)
10. Hardin, G.J.: The Tragedy of the Commons (1968)
11. AutomotiveWorld.com: Audi CEO highlights supplier concerns, Germany (2011)
12. Lampinen, M.: Parts shortage halts Chrysler plant, Canada (2011)
13. Priddle, A.: Lack of engines idles 3,000 Ford workers at Dearborn plant. The Detroit News (January 25, 2011), http://detnews.com/article/20110125/AUTO01/101250325/1148/auto01/Lack-of-engines-idles-3-000-Ford-workers-at-Dearborn-plant (accessed January 25, 2011)
14. Supplier Business Ltd.: Volvo output affected by delayed component supply. Demand to further increase in European and North American market (2011)
15. Johnsen, T.E., Lamming, R.C., Harland, C.M.: Inter-Organizational Relationships, Chains, and Networks. A Supply Perspective. In: Cropper, S., Ebers, M., Huxham, C., Smith Ring, P. (eds.) The Oxford Handbook of Inter-Organizational Relations. Oxford handbooks, pp. 61–89. Oxford University Press, Oxford (2008)
16. Hensel, J.: Netzwerkmanagement in der Automobilindustrie. Erfolgsfaktoren und Gestaltungsfelder. Deutscher Universitäts-Verlag | GWV Fachverlage GmbH, Wiesbaden (2007)
17. Schonert, T.: Interorganisationale Wertschöpfungsnetzwerke in der deutschen Automobilindustrie. Die Ausgestaltung von Geschäftsbeziehungen am Beispiel internationaler Standortentscheidungen, 1st edn. Entscheidungs- und Organisationstheorie, Gabler, Wiesbaden (2008)
18. Beer, J.E., Schumacher, T., Liyanage, J.P.: Network Performance Impact on Supply Reliability in the Automobile Industry. Submitted to Portland International Conference on Management of Engineering & Technology (PICMET), Vancouver, CA, July 29-August 2 (2012)

Benchmarking Concept for Energy Efficiency in the Manufacturing Industry – A Holistic Energy Efficiency Model

Volker Stich, Ulrich Brandenburg, and Sebastian Kropp

Institute for Industrial Management at RWTH Aachen University,
Pontdriesch 14/16, 52062 Aachen, Germany
{Volker.Stich,Ulrich.Brandenburg,
Sebastian.Kropp}@fir.rwth-aachen.de

Abstract. Determination and comparison of the energy efficiency over all planning levels is one of the key challenges for small and mediums sized enterprises (SME). This is because there is a lack of transparency and information to identify the major energy consumers on plant level as well as on production and machine level. Therefore, there is a need to develop a holistic energy efficiency model which integrates all three planning levels supporting decision makers with the essential information. This paper presents first results from an ongoing benchmark study which is conducted with companies from Austria, Belgium and Germany. First results show, that there is a lack of information integration from the shop-floor to the planning levels which causes SMEs to fail their strategic energy efficiency targets.

Keywords: KPI, energy efficiency, ICT, energy management, benchmarking.

1 Introduction

Energy efficiency is becoming more and more important for producing industries. Research showed that close to 50% of the total energy consumed in a typical production plant is used up by producing machines [1]. In addition, due to growing awareness of customers for green products, stricter government regulations and, economically most important, growing prices for energy and resources [2] small and medium sized enterprises (SME) are forced to think about their energy management.

Energy management (EM) is defined as the proactive coordination of procurement, transformation, distribution, and consumption of energy within a company [3]. Within this paper, findings of the project *Eco2Cut* are presented, which focuses energy consumption and energy procurement of factories.

Today, initiatives for raising the energy efficiency are being conducted on machine and manufacturing process level [4]. Still, it is not possible to benchmark energy consumption as there is a lack of methods and criteria that allow a comparison between the production systems of different companies [5]. Since basic industrial processes

J. Frick and B. Laugen (Eds.): APMS 2011, IFIP AICT 384, pp. 390–395, 2012.

(e.g. milling, drilling, turning) and products are more or less the same across the world universal indicators need to be found. Industrial energy use indicators can serve as the basis for identifying promising areas to improve energy efficiency on the various planning levels of SMEs. These indicators complement benchmarking but should not act as a substitute [6].

2   Study Design

Benchmarking is a commonly used method to enable decision makers to decide based on key performance indicators (KPIs). Hence, benchmarking is a promising tool for monitoring energy efficiency and is therefore essential for an effective energy management.

Today, only few indicators for benchmarking exist especially on production and on the machine level [2].

Therefore, there is the need to develop a holistic energy management model including energy efficiency indicators on all planning levels of the company. This means that decision makers will be given the essential aggregated information to base their decisions on energy efficiency considerations.

Figure 1 illustrates the framework of the study framework. On top there is a strategic design element (EM strategy) where KPIs for the long-term orientation of the company are evaluated. The operative part of the study covers the major layers within a factory:

- **Heating, Ventilation and Air Conditioning (HVAC):**
  Within this layer a company's competence for reusing emitted heat, generating their own energy (photovoltaic, wind energy etc.) and building automation are checked.
- **(Energy) Purchase:**
  This layer evaluates a company's competence to interact with the energy supplier in an efficient manner. In the future concepts like Smart Grids will become more important for industry as well. Therefore, close horizontal information integration is needed.
- **Production:**
  Up to now, energy is not represented adequately as a criterion to plan and control the production. The main cause is that information of the flow of energy is not available due to a lack of vertical information integration from the shop floor to the planning levels. In addition, there is the need to improve energy efficiency on a technological and process level which is subsumed in the production layer. Companies need to replace or substitute technologies and processes that consume a high amount of energy for more efficient technologies and processes.

To ensure a holistic view on energy efficiency, these three layers are combined with three dimensions of a company namely Organization, Systems and Culture. Figure 1 illustrates nine operative design elements where companies need to gain excellence in order to be energy efficient.

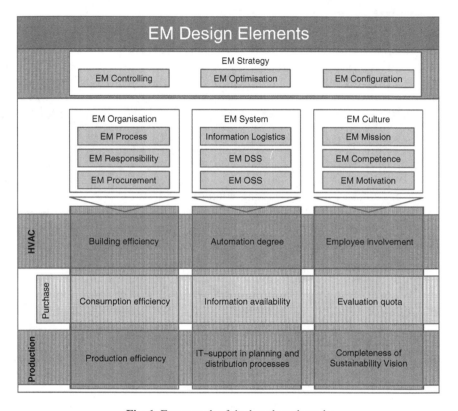

Fig. 1. Framework of the benchmark study

2.1   Scope of the Study

The focus of this benchmark study is on small and medium sized companies. Figure 2 gives an overview of the participants of the study[1].

---

[1] Within the production method multiple answers were possible.

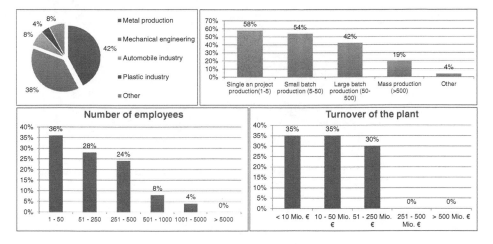

Fig. 2. Characteristics of the study participants

3 Findings and Practical Implications

EM-Strategy

The results of the study show that energy efficiency is a very relevant topic for SMEs. The study gave the following implications:

- More than 75% stated that energy efficiency is important to the management.
- 52% of the companies evaluate projects for improving the energy efficiency after their implementation.
- More than 50% agree to that the competence of measuring, controlling and analysing of energy data contributes towards a competitive advantage
- 55% stated that the changes of energy consumption are a strategic target figure.
- Only 44% stated that they obtained the planned energy reduction.

HVAC

The results of the study show that there is still a lot of work to do on the HVAC level:

- Only 4% of the companies use photovoltaic to generate energy. Where photovoltaic is used, it covers more than 60% of the total demand.
- 5% of the companies use waterpower. Where waterpower is used, it covers less than 30% of the total demand.
- Neither of the companies uses solar thermal energy, geothermal energy or wind energy.
- About 65% of the companies claim that the heating in the office buildings is still manually regulated.
- Automation of HVAC devices as well as lightning is not commonly used.

Purchase

- Less than 50% of the participating companies do an accurate energy consumption planning for the forthcoming year.
- 52% of the companies analyse their load profiles. Out of these 54% use computer-based assessments and 46% a manual analysis.
- On the other hand companies do not seem to measure KW-peaks (only 5%) and the load profile fluctuation (only 18%).
- 62% of the companies discussed possibilities to reduce peak loads with their supplier.
- 73% of the companies regularly invite offers from different energy suppliers.

Production

- Companies put quite a high effort into raising their energy efficiency in production from an EM-Organisation and EM-Culture point of view. For example, companies optimize their compressed-air systems or turn-off machines during idle times.
- From an EM-System point of view there is a big lack for a support of the production planning and controlling in terms of energy efficiency.
- More than 75% of the companies more or less agree that the integration of IT-systems would help them in their decision-making and operative planning.
- More than 75% more or less agree that only real-time processing of machine and operating data within the production planning and controlling leads to transparency and competence in the field of energy management.

4   Conclusions and Further Research

The benchmark study conducted within the project Eco2Cut reveals that energy efficiency and energy management are very much in the focus of SMEs within the manufacturing industry. The study clearly shows that SMEs try to integrate energy efficiency considerations into their corporate strategy. However, it became obvious that companies often lack the transparency, skill and technology to succeed with their strategic energy targets. With the results of the Eco2Cut benchmark study companies are provided with a holistic energy efficiency model that helps them identify the levers for increasing their energy efficiency. Key findings of the study were:

- SMEs strategically consider energy efficiency.
- SMEs conduct energy efficiency actions/projects on the shop floor level but without following a consistent strategy.
- SMEs lack the transparency of energy consumption due to a highly disintegrated ICT-infrastructure.
- SMEs neglect the possibilities of reducing energy costs on the supply side.

Therefore, future research should focus on integrating existing IT-systems with energy management systems to allow future calculations of energy consumed by products throughout the production process. Information and communication technologies (ICT) enable energy efficient manufacturing by integrating real-time data from the Manufacturing Execution Systems (MES) on the shop-floor into the Enterprise Resource Planning Systems (ERP) [2], [7]. Real-time data of the machines supports low-energy resource planning as, for example, idle times can be planned based on the order situation. By simulating alternative production processes within the ERP-System energy efficiency considerations can be included in machine procurement.

Consequently, this would add to the internet-of-things approach where products are given to ability to find their optimal (e.g. most energy-efficient) path through production. As a prerequisite companies need to conduct a thoroughly energy flow analysis to identify where information about energy consumption is need and where this information can be collected from shop floor to planning levels. Based on this vertical integration of the flow of energy and information companies can interact with their suppliers to negotiate tailor-made energy tariffs. Consequently, this would lead to the adaption of the Smart-Grids approach for the manufacturing industry.

References

[1] Klocke, F., Brühl, J., Döbbeler, B., Essig, C., Hein, C.: Nachhaltige Produktion. In: AWK Aachener Werkzeugmaschinen-Kolloquium (Hrsg.): Wettbewerbsfaktor Produktionstechnik. Aachener Perspektiven, Aachen (2011)
[2] Bunse, K.: Integrating energy efficiency performance in production management - gap analysis between industrial needs and scientific literature. Journal of Cleaner Production (2011)
[3] Grahl, A.: Handbuch für betriebliches Energiemanagement. Systematisch Energiekosten senken, Berlin (2009)
[4] Brecher, C., Bäumler, S., Bode, H.: Ressourceneffizienz im Werkzeugmaschinenbau. In: AWK Aachener Werkzeugmaschinen-Kolloquium (Hrsg.): Wettbewerbsfaktor Produktionstechnik. Aachener Perspektiven, Aachen (2011)
[5] Gesellschaft, F.: Energieeffizienz in der Produktion. Untersuchung zum Handlungs- und Forschungsbedarf (2008)
[6] International Energy Agency (IEA): Tracking Industrial Energy Efficiency and CO2 Emissions, Paris (2007)
[7] European Commission: ICT and e-Business for an Innovative and Sustainable Economy. 7th Synthesis Report of the Sectoral e-Business Watch (2010)

Developing Environmental Thinking
in Manufacturing Companies

Ana Maria Munoz-Marin and Astrid Heidemann Lassen

Aalborg University, Center for Industrial Production, Fibigerstræde 16
9220 Aalborg, Denmark
ahl@production.aau.dk

Abstract. This paper presents the development of a process for manufacturing companies to facilitate environmental thinking for the integration of environmental concerns into their business operations. The process takes its point of departure in Corporate Social Responsibility while maintaining focus on obtaining direct benefits for the business. By understanding the end-uses' perception, drivers, limitations and wants in regards to green products, as well as a general understanding of environmental impacts of the product, companies can detect environmental improvement options that are feasible to achieve and which consumers are interested in buying, therefore obtaining results that are good for the business and good for the environment.

Keywords: Corporate Social Responsibility, Design for Sustainability, User-Driven strategies, Environmental thinking, Life cycle thinking.

1   Introduction

The interest in social and environmental responsibility has been increasing at a high rate in both academia and in practice. Companies are gradually being encouraged to consider the ecological and social consequences of their business activities: Governments are creating stronger regulations but also educating consumers as part of the European 2020 strategy for smart, sustainable and inclusive growth (Europe 2020). As a consequence, social and environmental responsibility is moving from being order qualifying to being an order winning variable amongst consumers.

The EU Commission has defined Corporate Social Responsibility (CSR) as; "a concept whereby companies integrate social and environmental concerns in their business operations and in their interaction with their stakeholders on a voluntary basis. Being socially responsible means not only fulfilling legal expectations, but also going beyond compliance" (Commission of the european communities, 2006).

Different reasons lead companies to consider implementing CSR into their activities including ethical, legal, economic and competitive aspects. Such aspects are believed to include benefits such as e.g. 1) giving more options to the customers, 2) being prepared for stronger environmental regulations (legislative and disclosure requirements); 3) positioning the company as market leaders and innovators; 4) being competitive; and 5) developing brand differentiation.

J. Frick and B. Laugen (Eds.): APMS 2011, IFIP AICT 384, pp. 396–404, 2012.
© IFIP International Federation for Information Processing 2012

Research shows that "corporate reputation" is one of the most cited drivers, which includes the perception that consumers have on the company's products and services and the company itself. In the same way, the most common barriers to CSR have been identified as "cost/benefit ratio" and "risk" (Laudal, 2011). Companies and research alike seem to concentrate on the benefits and difficulties of adopting CSR and the importance of communicating and demonstrating their position and business actions towards social and environmental issues: considering internal actions towards the costumers.

In product design is well known the importance of considering the users as the main source of information, not surprisingly, innovation management literature also mention it as a considerable advantage (Chesbrough, 2003). This could also be used towards the integration of environmental issues into the business operation. Involving the users directly into the environmental thinking process will allow understanding the end-users' needs and wishes, which combined with the company strategies, processes and capabilities, will minimize the identified barriers on implementing CSR; resources can be used more effectively and the uncertainty risk can be reduced because the information comes directly from the potential costumers.

However, this inside-out approach leads to a gap in the understanding of CSR as a responsible action that can also bring tangible and intangible benefits to the business if its inputs come from the users unmet needs and desires. The research study reported in this paper targets this gap directly by answering the research question:

RQ1: How could a process for manufacturing companies be developed to facilitate environmental thinking by understanding the end users' perceptions, drivers and limitations, wants and preferences on green products?

This research allows for the development of a general understanding of the company environmental impacts during the product life cycle, involving employees and end-users to find possible solutions. Hereby, the company can detect environmental improvements options that are feasible to achieve and which consumers are interested in buying at the same time, and thereby be able to invest resources more effectively in CSR and work in-depth on the choices which prove valuable.

2   Methods

As outlined above, this research builds on the assumption that the premise of obtaining direct benefits for the business while "doing good" is the involvement of the users in the process. In order to research the correctness of such assumptions, the outlined research question is addressed through the following methodological approach.

2.1   Data Selection

In order to address the above stated lacks in knowledge, the research addressed in this article takes its point of departure in the research project InnoDoors. The InnoDoors project has the purpose of developing a systematic approach to engaging in user-driven innovation. Amongst others, one of the initiatives in InnoDoors is the aspect of CSR and environmental thinking based on user-integration. The InnoDoors project

was initiated with the focus on the Danish supply chain surrounding the design, production, sales and implementation of inner doors. InnoDoors has a unique possibility
to work with CSR activities and user-integration.

The selected data for the present paper is based on a work package with the purpose of developing a green product-line of doors. This is divided in two different
stages: User activities and Internal activities in order to identify the interplay between
inside-out and outside-in planned CSR activities.

2.2   Data Collection

The data collection was conducted over a period of 1 year, from the summer of 2010 to
the summer of 2011, and included a number of different approaches and types of interaction. The different processs of data collection were chosen based on their ability to take
the specificities of the industry into consideration, to capture different needs and competences of the users, and to develop the joint comprehension of the new approach to CSR
and environmental thinking. In Table 1 is an overview of data collected.

Table 1. Sources of evidence

Sources of evidence	
Interviews	Individual interviews with selected informants, experts on each topic. Informants represented product management, technology management, environmental specialist, production technical area, quality management and logistics (8 interviews with experts and 6 users)
Participant observation	Two "workshops" were executed for the User, Internal and Networking activities. Participants covered users, network partners and internal actors.
Questionnaires	One Physical (20 respondents) and one Web-based questionnaire (with 116 respondents) on user perceptions of green products

Each interaction was documented on video, photos and/or recorder. Conversations
were recorded and subsequently discussed with the interviewees, before synthesizing
into the frame of case scenarios. Furthermore, the interviews were conducted following the same protocol in order to ensure the reliability of the results as well as reflect
the validity of the differences emerging (Yin, 1994). Relevant documentation was
additionally provided by the respondents both prior to and after the interviews. This
included; strategic documentation, product development roadmaps, customer segmen-
tations and funding proposals. This data has been used to cross reference findings
from the interviews and to provide added historical background. The longitudinal
approach allowed for a gradual development of the understanding of the industry
specificities as well the needs for CSR.

2.3 Data Analysis

The data has been analyzed both in collaborative environments at workshops with project partners and more theoretically. Analytic induction was the main method in the workshops. These results were jointly discussed in order to create a joint understanding. The web based survey was analyzed based on descriptive statistics, as this provided the most meaningful presentation of the results.

3 Analysis and Discussion

Reduction of energy consumption along with reduction in other emissions (like CO_2 or NO_x gasses) (Mortensen, 2011) is a central aspects of the CSR activities in focus in this article. In the context of the construction industry Pohlmann (2002) finds that the Use stage is the most significant for energy consumption. This further underlines the importance of understanding the Use stage and how to impact users.

Approaching CSR from the environmental perspective it emphasizes the relevance of designing and manufacturing products taking into consideration their environmental impacts. Hence the Design for Sustainability (D4S) was considered. The D4S consists of three parts, the first explains the importance of design for sustainability and product innovation; the second presents how to do it in practice; and the third presents reference information like case studies and creativity techniques. Design for sustainability, as its name implies, attempts to go beyond of making "green" products to include the social and economic aspects embraced by the sustainable approach (Crul & Diehl, 2011). Using the D4S approach facilitates an environmental awareness of the selected product impacts during its life cycle and integrates the users into the innovation process to gain knowledge about their wishes and demands, giving the option to think in possible solutions for environmental impacts that at the same time fulfil the user wants.

In order to develop this environmental thinking and integrate it into the business operation, the data obtained from the workshops, questionnaires and interview were analyzed comparing the actual results with customer perception theory on environmentally friendly products and similar research findings on the field as well as the manufacturing company's strategies in order to obtain coherent results that were aligned with their plans in order to combine efforts and investment in the same direction.

Below, the data is analyzed following the initial conceptual argument; User driven innovation should be conducted in parallel to internal development activities in order to develop environmental CSR initiatives which create an actual impact in the market. We first report the findings of the user analysis conducted, next we report the internal development activities conducted, and thirdly we argue how such activities jointly amount into an agenda for relevant environmental CSR activities.

3.1 User Analysis

The web-based surveys show that the most important reason when buying environmentally friendly non-food products is "To save money during its use". It was further found that men are more sensitive to the savings during the purchase, while women tend to think more in the saving during use. The second highest prioritized reason was "Contributing to the environment".

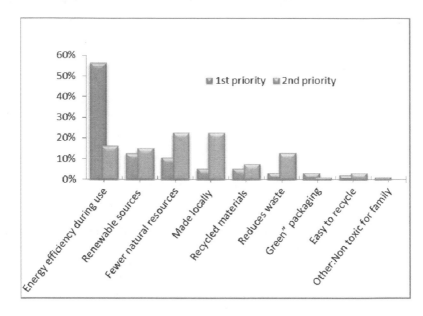

Fig. 1. Most important characteristics for green doors (1st and 2nd)

Price must be a careful decision according to the target group and should not interfere with the green door purchasing, offering variety in green alternatives, providing clear information about the product environmental performance and the product benefits, and last but not least: ensuring reliability. From the survey results there were identified "energy efficiency during use" as the characteristic with higher priority that consumers would like to find in a green door.

This result confirmed the findings from previous research by Muñoz (2010) on this topic where users prioritized: "The door increases energy efficiency" and "the process uses fewer natural resources". This is a positive finding taking into consideration the efforts governments have made on this matter to reduce, or cut, CO_2 emissions and fuel consumption and the tendency of consumers to show a clear preference for the characteristics from the Use stage in the Product life Cycle.

Without a doubt, energy efficiency is a characteristic which is very significant for electronic devises or products that have high consumption of energy during its use. For exterior doors this characteristic can be reflected, for instance, in insulation capabilities. However, when the product in consideration is an interior door, the reduction in energy consumption, although possible, is not significant; therefore other characteristics of the life cycle should be taken into consideration.

The second concept selected as first priority was *"The process uses renewable sources (controlled forest, wind energy)"*. In the case of controlled forest, the case company has already started with the FSC certification, and can continue emphasizing different programs that support it, such as planting new trees or considering the option of including "clean energy" into its process. These options have relation with the second priority selected by end-users: *"uses fewer natural resources"* and *"The door is made locally"* which is an alternative for reducing CO2 emissions during transportation.

Limitations are another way to identify what consumers value when buying green products, by analyzing why they do not. The term intention-behavior gap (Sustainability in action sports, 2011) is when consumers have an intention to purchase but find barriers (personal or external) to do it. For the general respondents, the five most important limits are:

Higher price,
Limited product range,
Lack of information about the product environmental characteristics,
Lack of information about the product benefits,
I don't trust that the products are really environmentally-friendly.

A very important result was found when the information was analyzed for the group that corresponds to the case company end-users target group (women between 31-50); although the five limitations are the same as the general respondents, the concept *"limited product range"* is considered less important than the other four, giving more importance to the concepts associated with lack of reliability: *"I don't trust that the products are really environmentally friendly"* and *lack of information on product benefits and environmental characteristics*. The case company, as a company that wants to be recognized for reliability should ensure that, especially its target group trusts the greenness of its doors by offering real environmentally friendly products.

Limitations to buy more green products

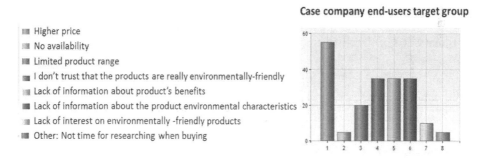

Fig. 2. Limitations to buy more green products. General respondents and the case company end-users actual target groups.

In total the user analysis of drivers and limitations provides us with the results outline in table 2. These results will be applied when evaluating the internal development efforts.

Table 2. Drivers and limitations to buy green products

	Reasons to buy green products		
End-user	Environmental characteristics	Save money during its use	Men are more sensitive to the savings during purchasing
			Women tend to think more in the saving during use
		Contribute to the environment	
	Limitations to buy green products		
	Limitations to buy green products	1.Higher price,	
		2.Limited product range,	
		3. Lack of information about the product environmental performance,	
		4. Lack of information about the product benefits,	
		5. I don't trust that the products are really environmentally-friendly (Number 2 for actual the case company target costumers - women between 31-50 years old)	

3.2   Internal Development Activities

The next part of the data analysis focuses on the internal development activities conducted in relation to environmental CSR activities in the case company.

Using different creativity processs during the workshop, the participants from the case company identified their Product environmental impacts during each of the product's life cycle stages: Material (Raw material and Component material), In-house manufacture, Distribution, Retail, Use and Disposal. After discussion in the internal team, supported by the environmental specialist, each environmental impact detected was addressed to its root causes: Material use, Energy use, Solid waste or Other emissions. This information was analysed using a qualitative method called Impact Matrix. (Crul & Diehl, 2011) which relates the environmental impacts in each stage of the product life cycle stages (what are the most relevant impacts and where are generated); and their Root cause (collecting them in main problems). See table 3

Table 3. Root causes

The door environmental impacts related with root causes							
	Raw material	Component material	In house manufacture	Transportation	Retail	Use	Disposal
Material Use	Not controlled sustainable wood		Formaldehyde, Glue, water-based paint, lacquering,	Plastic, packaging, transport material (pallets)			not separate materials,
Energy Use	Saw mill	Making MDF	Processes	Fuel consumption (oil, gas)	Exhibition (light), make to stock (heating)		
Solid waste	Saw mill	Packaging	production set-up (paint, wood), cuts		Packaging		Not information to the user
Other emissions		NH3 (ammonia)	VOC (Volatil Organic compounds)	CO2		VOC (Volatil Organic compounds)	NOx gasses, CO2

In order to find ideas to reduce the door environmental impacts detected, there were conducted two different Idea Generation workshops. The first one was performed in the focal company with representatives from Material, Manufacture, Product, Quality, Logistics, and Environmental specialist; and the second one, with one representative from the partners according with their capabilities to influence the product value.

Considering the environmental impacts detected, each participant of the internal team selected individually the areas where they consider the case company should focus its efforts. The three priority areas (that obtained the majority of answers) correspond to:

Material Use
Emissions
Energy consumption.

3.3   Added Value through Environmental Thinking

By understanding that "Saving money during use" and "Contributing with the environment" are the end-users' most important characteristics to buy green products, and their specific requirements for green doors are "Energy efficiency during use" and "Use of fewer and renewable Natural resources"; combined with the analysis of the Product life cycle workshop performed during the internal activities which defined "Material use",, "Emissions" and "Energy consumption" as their environmental priorities; and the concepts resulting from the Idea generation workshop; an environmental thinking was developed and expressed in terms of Green Values and Initial concepts.

In addition, using the information collected from the end-users about their limitations for buying green products and the communication of environmental characteristics, it was possible to reflect the environmental thinking in terms of concepts for communication and service.

4   Conclusion

Using the suggested approach to environmental CSR, it was possible to collect and analyse information from the end-users and align this with internal capabilities in order to facilitate an environmental thinking into the manufacturing company that led to the understanding of the "green door" meaning and guided to the identification of green values and initial concepts for products and services in order to integrate the environmental concerns into their business operations according to CSR guidelines.

Given the results of the research, we conclude that the suggested process when applied by manufacturing companies facilitates environmental thinking by understanding the end users' perceptions, drivers and limitations, wants and preferences on green products. As mention before, these Green values and initial concepts were inspired in the results obtained throughout the development of different activities during the carrying out of the designed process by combining the users' wishes and demands with the internal possibilities of reducing environmental impacts. With these results, the manufacturing company has an understanding of what green door means for the interested users and is aware of the relevant information that needs to be consider to develop green products. In this way, this process gives them the possibility to create the green values that are feasible for the company to contribute with their Corporate Social Responsibility and at the same time that are significant for the costumers.

References

1. Commission of the European Communities (2006), http://eur-lex.europa.eu/LexUriServ/LexUriServ.do?uri=COM:2006:0136:FIN:en:PDF (retrieved July 11, 2011)
2. Laudal, T.: Drivers and barriers of CSR and the size and internationalization of firms. Social Responsibility Journal 7(2), 234–256 (2011)
3. Chesbrough, H.: Open Innovation: The New Imperative for Creating and Profiting from Technology. Harvard Business School Press, Boston (2003)
4. Munoz-Marin, A.: Development of a Green product line in JELD-WEN Europe: Creating foundations for innovation through environmental products. Master Thesis, Aalborg University (2010)
5. Crul, D.M., Diehl, M.J.: D4S- Design for Sustainability, http://www.d4sde.org (retrieved March 2011)
6. Sustainability in action sports, Obstacles that prohibit green consumer behaviour in the context of eco-friendly sports outerwear, Sustainability in action sports (2011), http://sustainabilityinactionsports.wordpress.com/2011/02/26/surveyresults-% (retrieved March 23, 2011)
7. Yin, R.: Case Study Research. Design and Methods, 2nd edn. Sage, Thousand Oaks (1994)
8. Pohlmann: Energy use across the Lifecycle of a house. cited in Tackle Climate Change: Use wood (2002), http://www.wrcla.org/pdf/TackleClimateChange.pdf (retrieved March 23, 2011)

Social Responsibility, Sustainability
and Its Awareness in Brazil

Aline Rodrigues Sacomano and Pedro Luiz de Oliveira Costa Neto[*]

Paulista University-UNIP, Graduate Program in Production Engineering,
Rua Dr. Bacelar, 1212, 04026-002 – São Paulo, Brazil
{aline.sacomano,politeleia}@uol.com.br

Abstract. This paper discusses the importance of social responsibility as a base for sustainability and tries to provide an overview of this relationship in Brazil nowadays. It is recognized as necessary the existence of three classes of economical, ecological and social sustainability and the big challenge of reconciling these three elements. Are included the results and discussion of a research aiming to identify the different viewpoints on these subjects and its awareness in a group composed by lawyers and other professionals. It is expected that this research may contribute for the adoption of propositions able to improve this degree of awareness in Brazil, including a better commitment of the legal professionals.

Keywords: Sustainability, social responsibility, lawyers, awareness.

1   Introduction

The concept of environmental sustainability addresses the necessary arrangements for the environment we live in, circumscribed to the physical limits of the globe, so that it does not degrade itself to a point of becoming non-viable conditions for the exercise and preservation of the life of plant and animal species, human being included.

However, the concept of sustainability extends to the question of businesses economic survival, which generates jobs and produces goods and services necessary to society, as a social matter linked to the right that the people and the communities have to possess a worthy quality of life.

Thus, we must understand the sustainable development as the one who meets the needs of the present without compromising the ability of future generations to meet their own needs. The convergence between the economic, ecological and social objectives that prevails the conservation and sustainability of these elements is the basis of sustainable development. The big question that comes is the possibility of coexisting environmental, economic and social sustainability simultaneously. Are no they antagonistic? One does not exclude the resource from the other? Resolving this apparent incongruity is the formidable challenge that is presented to humanity and it must be accepted, otherwise the future will be tragic. This issue is extremely current,

---

[*] Corresponding author.

J. Frick and B. Laugen (Eds.): APMS 2011, IFIP AICT 384, pp. 405–411, 2012.

needs to be looked at a very short time, and is directly related to the issue of corporate social responsibility.

In fact, there is certainly much to do, because the major global issues, today recognized, are caused by massive existing of productive agglomerations not resolved and keeps affecting increasingly the environment, taking the less optimistic people to worry about a catastrophe in a near future. Global warming, the consequent melting of polar ice caps rising the sea levels, the limited resources of fossil fuels, increasing water shortages, air pollution, population growth incompatible with the resources necessary to survival with dignity, the rise of China with new demands of progress and well being, all of these and many other threats to humanity are demanding energetic and effective actions to ensure conditions so that the future generations may inhabit the planet decently.

In this frightening picture, it is up to industries to do its part, since, historically, many of them have been largely responsible for the degradation of nature in their surroundings, by the release of smoke polluting the air, toxic waste in rivers, garbage in nature, etc. From that comes the necessity to adapt to other obligations, to perform a cleaner production as a way to make a contribution to the salvation of the planet [1], [2].

2   Objectives

From the above assumptions, this paper seeks to situate the issue of social responsibility in Brazil as a part of major importance to economic, ecological and social sustainability. In this context, are raised conceptual, legislation and other issues related to this questions in the country. The results of a field research are also invoked to better know the awareness aspects related to the theoretical concepts.

3   Methodology

The research related with this paper consist of two parts, the first one based on selected references on the subjects of Social Responsibility, Sustainability and related topics, including also interviews with organs and persons linked with the topics of intents, two of which are presented in this paper. The second part of the research involves a questionnaire of interest to the subject, with 10 questions applied to 50 lawyers and 50 other professionals. These questions were selected among a total of 16 included in the original research, which can be seen in [3].

4   Social Responsibility in Brazil

As consequence of the implementation of the Brazilian Program of Quality and Productivity and the existence of the Brazilian Quality National Prize, now world-wide benchmark in some aspects, among others positive actions of the government and the society, the number of entrepreneurs conscious of the importance of the problem has grown significantly in Brazil. This constitutes certainly a good starting point, but clearly it is still not enough so that the global actions for sustainability be verified in practice.

It also fits to mention that the ABNT – Brazilian Association of Technical Standards anticipated itself to the proper ISO organization when launched the national standard ABNT NBR 16001: Social Responsibility – Management System – Requirements, showing the existing institutional concern with this question [4].

Such standard establishes the minimum requirements so that the organizations present a system of management of the social responsibility, such as: politics and objectives that take in account the legal requirements, the ethical commitments and its concern with the promotion of citizenship, sustainable development and transparency of its activities.

Moreover, as the ABNT NBR 16001 standard considers the sustainable development as being a minimum requirement to characterize a socially responsible organization, we can affirm that Social Responsibility without a Sustainability component does not exist. In a similar way, it is impossible to prosper in the Sustainability subject without considering the question of the preservation of the environment that is directly related to the Quality of Life of the citizens.

Brazil, even being still a developing country, is in an increasing process in the questions of Social Responsibility related with Sustainability. The specialized literature in the subject grows in number of national authors who reflect the Brazilian reality, showing cases of success pointing in the direction that the organizations are quickly understanding the competitive and comparative advantages with the adoption of measures of social responsibility, looking towards the sustainable development.

Brazilian authors as Alonso, López and Castrucci define Social Responsibility as being a taking of conscience of the company which leads it to freely assume activities and incumbencies in favor of the society where she is inserted.[5]

For [6], Social Responsibility is not a finite program in time and space, but a continuous process that grows in perfection with time. To have effective Social Responsibility, it is necessary the coherence between action and speech, promoting an attack to the causes of the problems.

Brazilian Federal Constitution says in its article 225: "Everyone has the right to the environment ecologically balanced, feasible for the common use by people and essential to the healthy quality of life, having the Public Power and the collectivity the responsibility of defend and preserve it for the present and future generations".

In [7] is added that the environment must be a central concern of the humanity, since all aggression to it can bring irreversible implications of impact for all the people. Due to this, and with the intention of protecting the environment against the annihilating and maleficent performance of man, it is why legal instruments of protection, also called ambient legislation, appear.

In addition, [8] argues that the Environmental Law is not worried only about the natural environment, the physical condition of earth, air, water. It also deals with the human environment – health and other social conditions produced by man that affect the living place of the human beings in the Land.

There are other Brazilian exceptional, specials and general standards applied to the current legal system that demonstrate the progress of laws in the country when it comes to environment and consumer. Among these standards are:

- Norms of the Customer Protection Code, that prioritize the civil liability of the manufacturer, producer, constructor or importer to protect consumers from damages;
- Norms integrated to environmental law, for example, specific rules on liability for nuclear damage, and general rules on liability for damage to the environment;
- Constitutional standards which reaffirm and consolidate the special and general legal rules on liability for environmental damage.

5   Results of Interviews

The two interviews given below were selected among others made in the original research [3], selected according to its interest to this article.

a) Ethos Institute

"The Ethos Institute is a nongovernmental organization with responsibility due to the Ministry of Justice. Our mission is to mobilize companies, to help them to manage its businesses on a socially responsible form and to make them partners for the construction of a more fair society."

"We think problematic to consider a company socially responsible or not. For example, the company may have a very advanced initiative in the relationship with the consumer and, on the other hand, have a devastating practice. Some indicators exist, as the Index of Enterprise Sustainability (ISE), but I do not consider that it is enough to certify or to guarantee that a company is socially responsible. Mainly, because ethics is very fluid. There exists the ISO 26000 standard, but it does not certify, exactly for this reason."

b) Dr. Paulo Hoffman, Lawyer and University Professor

"Law is common-sense! Had the people conscience of its obligations, as well as responsibility and honesty to carry out them, the Judiciary Power would become unnecessary. Anyway, it has a fundamental regulating and enlightening role, hindering doubts and divergences and thus providing improvement of the quality of life."

"It is not spread among the practitioners of the law activities the concern with sustainability and social responsibility. Excepting courses or specific disciplines on the subject, in general there is not more conscience or interest, and a complete lack of interdisciplinarity. Moreover, I would dare to affirm, even without scientific or academic sustentation, that the proper generic definition of sustainability and social responsibility would be of difficult delimitation for the scholars of the law science"

6   Results of the Questionnaires

To the 50 lawyers and 50 other professionals were formulated 16 questions in the original research [3]. Of these, 10 were selected, for being of better interest to the present article, whose enunciates are presented in Table 1, where

AC = I agree completely, A = I agree, I = I do not agree nor disagree, D = I disagree.

Table 1. Percentages of answers to the questions

N° (*)	Questions	Lawyers				Other professionals			
		AC	A	I	D	AC	A	I	D
2	Ethics is the base of social responsibility and sustainability.	22	60	12	6	50	40	10	0
4	The concern with sustainability and social responsibility is spread out among the practitioners of the law.	4	16	10	70	8	30	32	30
5	Social responsibility is a factor for the competitiveness of the companies.	12	30	24	34	22	48	12	18
6	Social responsibility of companies is evidenced by its philanthropic activities.	10	24	32	34	2	24	8	66
8	In buying, consumers take in account the factor social responsibility.	10	24	32	34	2	24	8	66
9	In the two last decades, the quality of life of society has increased significantly.	4	62	12	22	10	52	16	22
10	Environmental legislation is a tool for sustainability.	30	60	4	6	40	46	12	2
12	The quality of products and services is important for the sustainable development.	32	56	8	4	20	56	16	8
13	Companies implement total quality exclusively aiming the increase of profitability.	12	38	20	30	8	44	18	30
14	Organizations that respect the labor laws of the employees do it, not only to fulfill legislation, but, overall, looking for the improvement in quality of life of the society.	4	20	22	54	24	22	26	28

(*) Numeration as in the original research.
Source: [9]

Table 2. Results of tests where there are significant differences in the answers

Question	X_v^2	v	$X_{v,5\%}^2$	$X_{v,1\%}^2$
2	8,587*	2	5,991	9,210
4	16,505**	2	5,991	9,210
5	8,009*	3	7,815	11,345
6	12,853**	2	5,991	9,210
8	12,853**	2	5,991	9,210
14	11,479**	3	7,815	11,345

*: $\propto = 5\%$; **: $\propto = 1\%$
Source: [9]

To these answers it was applied the well know non parametric chi-square test of homogeneity as described in [10], through which is tested the hypothesis that the opinions are homogeneous between the lawyers and the other professionals.

This hypothesis was accepted, at the 5% of significance level, in questions 9, 10, 12 and 13. In the other questions, it was found significant difference between the two categories of respondents, as shown in Table 2.

It may be seen that the questions which present more significant differences, identified at the level of 1% of significance, are, in decreasing order of certainty, numbers 4, 6, 8 and 14, and with significant differences at the level of 5%, are questions 2 and 5.

Comments on Questions with Significant Difference

Question 2: There is strong agreement of the two groups in this question (82% x 90%), but the intensity of conviction is stronger among the non lawyers, perhaps because the lawyers think that law, more than ethics, supply this basement.

Question 4: The research demonstrates that the concern with sustainability is less spread among the lawyers than among the other professionals. This information is a too worrying one.

Question 5:   It is natural that the lawyers do not understand the social responsibility as a factor of competitiveness among companies, because this is not part of their world. No longer, in the other group, probably mainly for being included managers, entrepreneurs and engineers, the percentage is bigger on the affirmation that social responsibility is a factor of competitiveness of the companies.

Question 6: The result of the opinions demonstrates that among the lawyers was bigger the number of them who confuse social responsibility with philanthropy. This meets the results of questions 4 and 5, indicating that the subject is less spread out among the lawyers.

Question 8: The overall majority believes that the factor social responsibility is not taken in account by the consumers. Moreover, this belief is statistically stronger among the lawyers.

Question 14: Is big the number of interviewed professionals affirming that the labor legislation is only fulfilled due to law and inspection, mainly among the lawyers, since they know more closely this reality.

7   Conclusion

In the first part of this paper were made considerations, based in selected references and considerations by the authors, on the field of Social Responsibility and Sustainability, showing the close interconnection between these two very important and considered concepts in the XXI Century reality.

The research conducted with lawyers and other professionals brought some interesting comparisons, showing the first group less aware on sustainability issues. Something must be done towards their commitment, since they have in their hands the powerful tool of the law.

From these considerations, we reinforce the following ones due to its undeniable relevance:

a) The opinion of Dr. Paulo Hoffman about the little concern by the practitioners of the Law on sustainability and social responsibility. This consideration meets the result of question 4, suggesting the necessity of better to engage the legal class of professionals in the fight for sustainability.

b) The evidence given by some questions that lawyers are more attached to the cold text of the law, what often prevent them of having a deeper concern on aspects related to environmental sustainability.

c) The opinion, that was transparent in the research, that the companies are still more worried with attendance to the text of the laws, without any doubt important when related to the question of sustainability and social responsibility, than with the exercise of a conscious performance toward these problems.

References

1. Costa Neto, P.L.O., Canuto, S.A.: Management with Quality, pp. 150–151. Blucher, São Paulo (2010)
2. Sacomano, A.R., Costa Neto, P.L.O.: Corporate social responsibility in Brazil as an element to sustainability. In: APMS 2010 – International Conference on Advances in Production Management Systems, Como, Italy (2010)
3. Sacomano, A.R.: Social responsibility as an element for sustainability, quality of products and services and quality of life. M. S. dissertation, Paulista University, São Paulo (2011)
4. ABNT – Brazilian Association of Technical Standards: ABNT NBR 16001 – Social Responsibility – Management System – Requirements. Rio de Janeiro (2004)
5. Alonso, F.R., Lopez, F.G., Castrucci, P.L.: Course of ethics in administration. Atlas, São Paulo (2006)
6. Manzano, N.T.: A procedure that never runs out. Gazeta Mercantil. Social Responsibility report, São Paulo (2004)
7. Shigunov Neto, A., Campos, L.M.S., Shigunov, T.: Fundamentals of environmental management. Modern science, Rio de Janeiro (2009)
8. Antunes, P.B.: The Environmental Law. Lumen Juris, Rio de Janeiro (1998)
9. Sacomano, A.R., Costa Neto, P.L.O.: Some aspects on the awareness in Brazil toward sustainability. In: APMS 2010 – International Conference on Advances in Production Management Systems, Stavanger, Norway (2011)
10. Costa Neto, P.L.O.: Statistics, 2nd edn., pp. 137–142. Blucher, São Paulo (2002)

Ambiguity: A Useful Component
of "Fuzziness" in Innovation[*]

Eric Brun

University of Stavanger, 4036 Stavanger, Norway
Eric.brun@uis.no

Abstract. The early phases of new product development (NPD) processes are characterized by a high degree of uncertainty and ambiguity, a phenomenon commonly recognized as the *fuzzy front end* of NPD. A clear understanding of the term *fuzziness* is lacking in NPD literature. This paper suggests that its components can be understood through earlier scholars' use of concepts such as ambiguity, equivocality, lack-of-clarity and uncertainty. It is argued that resolving ambiguity is associated with knowledge creation, and hence that it is possible to separate useless from useful ambiguity and thus purposefully exploit ambiguity in a targeted manner to create new knowledge in innovation.

This theoretical paper provides an account of how ambiguity—as a component of fuzziness—has a useful role in the knowledge-building process in NPD.

Keywords: Fuzzy front end, innovation, new product development, ambiguity, learning.

1   Introduction

1.1   The Fuzzy Front End

The *front end* is the starting point that sets the initial direction of the NPD process. Many researchers have emphasized the importance of the activities occurring there [2-9]. Successful management of a new product development (NPD) project involves running the project in a cost- and time-efficient manner while at the same time providing optimal conditions for developing innovative products. To achieve these objectives, a substantial amount of information about relevant technology, market conditions, business potential etc, is required as a basis for making critical decisions at the onset of the NPD project. However, the earliest stage of NPD is especially prone to manifesting considerable uncertainty and ambiguity, or *fuzziness*: a characteristic that does not fit well with an approach that requires accurate and stable up-front information. This phenomenon is commonly termed the *fuzzy front end* of NPD [4, 8-11].   A common argument for the importance of early-phase activities is that the cost and time of corrective actions and engineering changes are then low

---

[*] This paper is based on, and develops further, work in Eric Brun's doctoral thesis [1].

J. Frick and B. Laugen (Eds.): APMS 2011, IFIP AICT 384, pp. 412–424, 2012.

while fuzziness is high, while they are high at the late phases of the NPD project when fuzziness is low [4, 5, 9]. Empirical studies have in fact confirmed the importance of early-phase activities in the successful launching of NPD projects [12, 13]. Reid and de Brentani [9] have therefore argued that research should be directed toward achieving a better understanding of the fuzzy front end and of ways in which to manage it. Various studies have been made to this end [e.g. 4, 8, 10, 11, 14, 15, 16] , but striking feature of almost all of them is their failure to define exactly what *fuzziness* is. All of the accounts of fuzziness described above imply that it somehow involves a lack of accurate knowledge or gaps in knowledge. This paper will first discuss how fuzziness can be described in terms of a few components that differ by their nature. Following this discussion, the paper will focus specifically on one such component—ambiguity—and address the question:

- Is ambiguity—as a component of fuzziness—entirely negative for the NPD process, or can ambiguity be useful?

2   Literature Review

2.1   Elements of Fuzziness

Fuzziness can mean many things. A precise, consensus definition of the term is lacking in NPD literature, but it is often used to describe the problems one experiences in NPD projects in defining critical elements such as product concepts, markets, and processes [e.g. 4, 8-10, 14]. Some terms that have been used to describe the characteristics of fuzziness are *uncertainty* [8, 9, 16], *ambiguity* [17], *chaos* [7], and *complexity* [6]. The term *fuzzy* is hence used in a non-specific sense to label situations where one experiences a lack of accurate information or accurate knowledge. As we shall see, there have been many contributions to define and distinguish between terms that characterize such situations.

2.2   Distinctions between Equivocality, Uncertainty and Ambiguity

A suitable starting point is perhaps the term *equivocality*, which is commonly used to denote the presence of two or more interpretations for the same piece of information [18, 19]. In *The Social Psychology of Organizing*, Weick asserts that the need for reducing equivocality is the basic reason for organizing. Organizing, as he defines it, is "a consenually validated grammar for reducing equivocality by means of interlocked behaviors" [19]. In their contributions on organizational information requirements, Daft and Lengel [18, 20] distinguish between *equivocality* and *uncertainty*. They draw on Galbraith's [21] definition of uncertainty, which is "the difference between the amount of information required to perform the task and the amount of information already possessed by the organization" [20]. This approach assumes that the organization operates in an environment where you can get clear answers to your various questions. When that is indeed the case, uncertainty can be reduced simply by acquiring new, well-defined data. But a far different situation exists when the organization is confronted with *equivocality*, which Daft and Lengel consider as synonymous with *ambiguity* and define it in the following way: "Equivocality means ambiguity, the existing of multiple and conflicting interpretations about an organizational situation" [20]. The approach they recommend to reduce equivocality is to reconcile these differences of perspective rather than to simply gather more information. Their notion of these two very different remedies for uncertainty and equivocality accords with Galbraith's conception from 1977 that uncertainty can be reduced by processing sufficient amounts of information and Weick's conception from 1979 that equivocality can be reduced by *consensually validated grammar* and *interlocked behaviors.*

In his landmark work *Sensemaking in Organizations* [22], Weick introduces the term *ambiguity*, which he accords two meanings. On the one hand, he says that ambiguity can be understood as *equivocality*—i.e., the presence of two or more interpretations. (He also uses the term *confusion* to designate this meaning of ambiguity.) On the other hand, he claims ambiguity can be understood as *lack of clarity*, which he equates with *ignorance*, the cause of which is insufficient information. This implies that the word *ambiguity* itself is ambiguous in Weick's [22] definition. Weick himself acknowledges the problem with this ambiguous definition, as the two forms of ambiguity require two quite different remedies. He agrees with Daft & Lengel [20] in believing that equivocality is reduced by face-to-face interaction, while reducing uncertainty requires collecting more information.

March has mainly discussed ambiguity as an aspect of decision-making. In March & Simon's [23] work on bounded rationality, the theme of ambiguity lies implicit in their discussion of how organizations consider available alternatives under limited access to information. In his more recent and comprehensive overview, March [24] sharply distinguishes between ambiguity and uncertainty. He claims that *uncertainty*, in most theories of decision-making, refers to imprecision in estimates of future consequences conditional on present actions. The basic assumption behind these theories, he contends, is that there exists an objective, real world that is imperfectly understood but that can in principle be discovered if enough information is made available. *Ambiguity*, meanwhile, refers to a state where the basic assumptions behind the view of uncertainty are challenged. Provision of more information may not in fact improve our understanding, and the world may actually be socially constructed rather than objectively real, meaning that it must be invented and negotiated rather than discovered. March's [24] conceptions of ambiguity and uncertainty therefore pertain to two very different epistemological views of the world. His understanding of ambiguity though, is twofold, although not as distinctly split as Weick's [22] dual definition. March [24] asserts that "Ambiguity refers to features of decision making in which alternative states are hazily defined or in which they have multiple meanings, simultaneously opposing interpretations" [24]. I believe that when alternative states are said to be *hazily defined* as March [24] puts it, this would mean that the decision makers lack the appropriate frames of reference they need to assign precise meanings to these states. Whereas when alternative states have *multiple meanings/opposing interpretations*, the meanings differ because they are interpreted from different perspectives; in other words, we have a situation of equivocality.

In this paper, the proposals and arguments presented rest on a definition of *ambiguity* as *the existence of two or more interpretations of a single cue*, in other words, equal to equivocality.

Despite the differences in definitions of ambiguity that we encounter in literature, a similarity between the authors reviewed so far is that they focus on reducing ambiguity, seeing it as an impediment—something that should be minimized so one can move forward. Eisenberg [25] has challenged this view. In his seminal article *Ambiguity as Strategy in Organizational Communication* [25] he questions the assumption of the central importance of clarity in organizational communication. Clarity, he claims, arises through a combination of the source of a message, the message itself and the receiver of the message. It exists when an individual (the source) encodes an idea into a language, and the receiver understands the message as it was intended by the source. Ambiguity will therefore arise when this condition is not met, i.e. when the source and receiver form their interpretations based on different "interpretive contexts" [25], i.e. different perspectives. He argues that clarity is a valid measure of effectiveness only when the organization aspires to be clear, and that individuals may, on occasion, purposefully deviate from clarity—i.e., strategically use ambiguity—to accomplish their goals.

2.3   Probability, Uncertainty and Ambiguity

Another view of uncertainty, commonly held in management literature, originated with Frank Knight [26]. When discussing it as it relates to probability judgment, Knight identified three types of uncertainty:

- When the outcome of an event is not known, but the probability distribution is known.
- When the outcome of an event is not known, and the probability distribution is unknown but can be estimated statistically.
- When the outcome of an event is not known, and the probability is unknown because a distribution is non-existent and cannot be estimated because we are dealing with situations that are unique, so statistical estimation based on a large number of homogeneous instances cannot be attained. In this situation probability cannot be estimated and is not susceptible to measurement.

Knight [26] used the term *risk* to denote the two first categories, which refer to measurable uncertainty, and used the term *true uncertainty* to denote the third, immeasurable type of uncertainty. Knight's account of true uncertainty focuses on the probabilities of the outcomes of events. Note however, that Knight assumes that the events themselves are known. This assumption is in my opinion questionable; I do not believe there is always agreement on what the events are. I argue that it is in the understanding of the event itself that ambiguity first emerges, as illustrated in Figure 1:

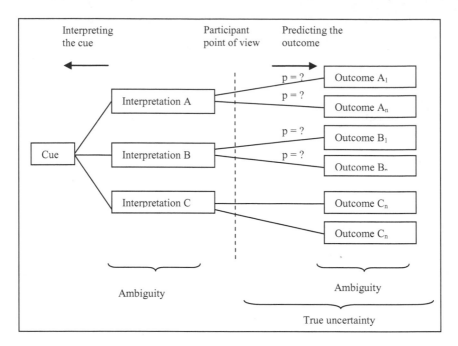

Fig. 1. Ambiguity and true uncertainty

I will illustrate with an example in the context of an NPD project. The process will typically be triggered by a cue, for example, a business opportunity that emerges. This cue will become subject to interpretation by the involved participants. Each interpretation will constitute an idea of what a sensible action may be to pursue the business opportunity. An idea may for example be an idea of a product concept to pursue. When multiple participants are involved, multiple interpretations (i.e. ambiguity) may occur. In our example, this may mean that the involved participants each have different interpretations of what they see as a sensible product concept.

The participants will however also assume alternative outcomes of each action, and each outcome will also be a participant's interpretation. For example, if a certain product concept is agreed upon, there may still be different interpretations of what the market's response to that particular product concept may be. Hence these outcomes, too, may be ambiguous. Furthermore, the probabilities of the outcomes cannot be determined, i.e. there is a situation of true uncertainty. So in this situation, there is first an occurrence of ambiguity about the events resulting from multiple interpretations of the cue, followed by another occurrence of ambiguity about the outcomes of these events. When the participants try to predict these outcomes, true uncertainty arises. Situations like this are typical of NPD processes. Ambiguity in NPD is thus related to Knightian true uncertainty, first as a precursor to true uncertainty, and then as a component of true uncertainty.

2.4   Thought Worlds – The Bases of Interpretations

Weick [22] contends that sensemaking depends on *paradigms*, or vocabularies of work, which in occupational communities are rules and conventions, standard operating procedures, shared definitions of the environment, and an agreed-upon system of power and authority. These paradigms help organizational members form their interpretations and make sense of the cues they perceive.

Dougherty [27] argues that different functional departments in an organization will have their own separate *thought worlds*. In her account, a thought world "is a community of persons engaged in a certain domain of activity who have a shared understanding about that activity" [27] and "evolves an internally shared system of meaning . . . . based on common procedures, judgments, and methods" [27]. Individuals tend to interpret an aspect of the innovation process according to the thought world of their own department. Thus development priorities and tasks will be interpreted differently by organizational members from different departments. Dougherty contends that cross-functional communication and collaboration help unify these thought worlds and so reduce the divergence of interpretations; in other words, they reduce ambiguity.   On a similar note, Daft and Lengel [20] argue that departments in organizations develop their own *frames of reference,* and that the differences in these departmental frames of reference give rise to ambiguity.

The terms we have just been encountering—*paradigms*, used by Weick [22], *thought worlds*, used by Dougherty [27], *frames of reference*, used by Daft and Lengel [20] and—as I will revert to—*horizon of understanding*, used in hermeneutics theory, all align as common terms for the bases from which interpretations develop. For the sake of simplicity I will mainly use Dougherty's term *thought world* in the further discussion.   This thought world will involve a number of "taken-for-granted" assumptions shared by the individuals in a social group. Therefore that group's common *tacit knowledge* is closely associated with the group's thought world. The concept of tacit knowledge was first launched by Polanyi [28], and Nonaka [29] later tied the term specifically to knowledge development in innovation. Leonard and Sensiper [30, 31] also discuss the role of tacit knowledge in innovation. They claim that when a group of individuals address a common challenge, each individual "frames both the problem and its solution by applying a mental schemata and patterns that he or she understands best" [31]. Leonard [30] uses the term *specialization* to denote this kind of mental schema and specifically describes it as similar to Dougherty's [27] concept of *thought world.*

3   Ambiguity and Learning

Although there is little research specifically addressing the theme of ambiguity in NPD, previous research has addressed uncertainty and uncertainty reduction in NPD. For example, Eisenhardt and Tabrizi [32] argue that NPD projects benefit from iterations and tests because frequent iterations build understanding of the product, and extensive testing gives frequent evaluations of the current design, provides multiple options and a wider set of ideas and thereby accelerates understanding and re-conceptualization of the product.   Their arguments for iteration and testing thus allude to a learning process involving new interpretations and new conceptualizations, which implies far more than the mere information gathering that would be required to reduce uncertainty. It is therefore relevant to explore the inner workings of such a learning process, where ambiguity reduction is associated with learning and development of thought worlds.

3.1   Ambiguity Reduction and Hypothesis Testing

Since ambiguity arises when a cue is assigned diverging interpretations, it is logical to direct our attention to theories of interpretation in order to enhance our understanding of ambiguity reduction. Hermeneutics constitutes one body of such theories. A central term in hermeneutics is the *hermeneutic circle*, and according to Føllesdal [33] and Føllesdal and Walløe [34], the hermeneutic method can be seen as a special case of the hypothetical-deductive method. They consider the hermeneutic circle to be a circle of continual hypotheses-testing.

They distinguish between *understanding* (as something we arrive at) and *interpreting* (as the process used to arrive at an understanding). When we say that we *understand*, we have a satisfactory hypothesis about the phenomenon we're confronting. The hypothesis is then more or less explicit; we are aware that we are working with one, that we are testing it and may have to reject or modify it. When we understand, our hypothesis has been tested and has withstood rejection, and it becomes more implicit. It has then become part of our *horizon of understanding*, a term commonly used in hermeneutics to express the amount of opinions, notions, attitudes, or beliefs we have at any given point, which we may or may not be aware of. Føllesdal and Walløe consider the horizon of understanding to be the set of hypotheses, auxiliary hypotheses, or underlying assumptions we employ when interpreting something. An interpretation can thus be considered a hypothesis, and each loop of the circle represents a test of that hypothesis, resulting in either its rejection or strengthening. Brun and Sætre [35] have accordingly shown that participants in NPD processes actively make use of a hypothetical-deductive approach to reduce ambiguity, by testing the competing interpretations, leading to their confirmation or rejection.

According to postmodernist critique, the hermeneutic circle cannot reach final closure—that is, it cannot reach agreement on the definitive meaning of a cue—so the hermeneutic circle is often described as an ever upward-moving spiral. The spiral does not end, which accords with Popper's [36, 37] argument that a hypothesis can never be fully verified; it can merely be refuted or corroborated as a result of withstanding refutation. The upwards move on the spiral represents a move towards reduced ambiguity through test, rejection, and refinement of competing interpretations—or, in other words, towards increased understanding with more refined and strengthened hypotheses. This also implies that our horizon of understanding develops with the upward movement on the spiral.

3.2   Ambiguity Reduction and Experiential Learning

I have argued earlier that ambiguity is one category of fuzziness, fuzziness being a lack of accurate knowledge. But if presence of ambiguity is a form of lack of knowledge, then I would argue that reducing ambiguity implies a move towards gaining knowledge, i.e. resolving ambiguity is associated with knowledge creation.

I believe this argument accords with the Hypothetical-deductive logic just described, which is essentially how knowledge is developed through scientific practice. That process is strikingly similar to the cycle by which knowledge develops through experiential learning as described by Kolb [38] and illustrated in Figure 2.

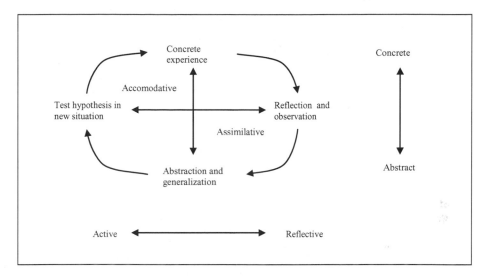

Fig. 2. Kolb's model of experiential learning

In the *observation* phase on the right-hand side of the model, an individual senses a cue. In the *abstraction and generalization* phase, he or she will interpret the cue and form an interpretation, i.e. generate a hypothesis. This *hypothesis* is then *tested* in phase on the left-hand side of the model, and then *experience* a result of the test. The individual will then *reflect* on the outcome of the test, i.e. decide whether the hypothesis is confirmed, or must be rejected. If the latter, then the individual forms a new hypothesis, i.e. re-interprets the cue, possibly in alignment with the interpretation of another individual, if this second individual's interpretation was confirmed by the same process. The amount of competing interpretations—i.e. ambiguity—has then been reduced through this learning process.

3.3   Ambiguity Development and Knowledge Creation in Innovation

Dougherty and her colleagues argue that sensemaking in innovative organizations leads to renewal of knowledge frames [39]. Their argument implies that thought worlds are not static entities, they develop over time. This argument accords with the logic of both the Hypothetical-deductive model and Kolb's model of experiential learning, wherein a community's total amount of hypotheses is continuously enhanced and refined, leading to development of new knowledge.

The notion of growing thought worlds is also demonstrated in Nonaka's [29] model of knowledge creation in innovation, illustrated in Figure 5. He describes four phases through which knowledge develops; Externalization, Combination, Internalization and Socialization.

1) In the Externalization phase, individuals turn their tacit knowledge into explicit knowledge.
2) In the Combination phase, individuals share and combine elements of their explicated knowledge and thereby create new explicit knowledge.
3) In the Internalization phase, the newly developed explicit knowledge is internalized in the team members and thus adds to their tacit knowledge.
4) In the Socialization phase, this added tacit knowledge is shared within the larger group as individuals share experiences "and thereby create a common tacit knowledge such as *shared mental models*" [40].

Through Socialization, tacit knowledge thus grows from an individual level to a larger pool of common tacit knowledge shared by a community. The same growth occurs for explicit knowledge through the process of Combination.

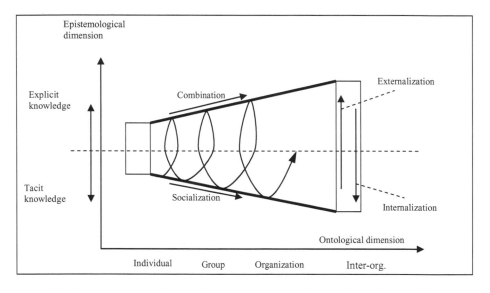

Fig. 3. Spiral of organizational knowledge creation. Adapted from Nonaka [29]

In Figure 3, the thick solid line going upwards towards the right as represents the growth of explicit knowledge as new product concepts are developed, refined and agreed upon throughout the organization and its immediate environment. The thick solid line going downwards towards the right represents the growth in common tacit knowledge and hence development of a common thought world throughout the organization and its immediate environment.

Whether such a pool of common understanding is denoted as a paradigm , thought world or frame of reference, or *shared mental model* as used by Nonaka and Takeuchi [40], it is clear that this pool is not static. As new tacit knowledge develops and is shared the pool of common understanding and shared assumptions changes as a result of innovation activity.

When the individuals in an NPD team sense a cue, such as a product idea, they will form different interpretations of this cue based on their differences in tacit knowledge, and ambiguity thus arises. When these different interpretations are explicated in the Externalization phase [29], the ambiguity is brought to awareness. These different and explicated interpretations represent ideas that are shared between the team members in the Combination phase [29] and act as raw material for innovation. When these ideas are combined ambiguity increases. Then, when ideas are selected ambiguity is reduced, and the selected ideas (i.e. selected interpretations) are further developed. According to Nonaka and Takeuchi [40] it is in the Combination phase that product concepts are developed as the individuals of an NPD team exchange and combine knowledge. Development of a product concept is thus associated with an initial increase and a following reduction of ambiguity and growth of knowledge. When the 4 phases in Nonaka's [29] knowledge development model are repeated in cycles, ambiguity thus oscillates between growth and reduction throughout the innovation process, in accordance with Brun and colleagues' [41] model of how ambiguity develops throughout the NPD process.

4   Distinguishing between Useful and Useless Ambiguity

From the preceding discussion we can see how reduction of ambiguity is related to learning and knowledge creation. Ambiguity in NPD is thus useful when it has potential to contribute to the knowledge-building that a company seeks with its innovation effort. In this respect, it is useful to consider Brun and colleagues' [42] model for classifying ambiguity in NPD, presented in Table 1.

Table 1. A Model for Classification of Ambiguity in NPD [42]

		Subjects of ambiguity.			
		Product	Market	Process	Organization resources
Sources of ambiguity:	**Multi-plicity**	Ambiguity arising from multiple interpretations of product issues.	Ambiguity arising from multiple interpretations of market issues.	Ambiguity arising from multiple interpretations of issues related to the work process.	Ambiguity arising from multiple interpretations of issues related to the organization's resources
	Novelty	Ambiguity arising from changing interpretations of the product	Ambiguity arising from changing interpretations of market issues.	Ambiguity arising from changing interpretations of the work process.	Ambiguity arising from changing interpretations of issues related to the organization's resources.
	Validity of info	Ambiguity arising from low validity of information about the product.	Ambiguity arising from low validity of information about the market.	Ambiguity arising from low validity of information about the work process	Ambiguity arising from low validity of information about the organization's resources.
	Relia-bility of info	Ambiguity arising from low reliability of information about the product.	Ambiguity arising from low reliability of information about the market.	Ambiguity arising from low reliability of information about the work process.	Ambiguity arising from low reliability of information about the organization's resources.

The columns in the table, i.e. the subjects of ambiguity, indicate what there is ambiguity *about*, i.e. issues about the Product, Market, Process and Organizational Resources. In any company, the purpose of an NPD project is to launch a new product in an appropriate market. One seeks to build knowledge about the product and the market and arrive at a description and understanding of what that product and what that market is. Ambiguity about the product and the market contributes to that knowledge-building process and should therefore be tolerated. For another subject of ambiguity—Process—the context of the NPD project will determine whether ambiguity related to that subject is useful. Companies in less regulated industries, as well as those developing service products, may well want to develop their NPD process along with the product. Ambiguity about the NPD process will then be a part of the innovation-related knowledge-building process and can therefore be useful. This will however not be so in a company in a highly regulated industry, requiring adherence to a well-defined NPD process. Here, the innovation-related knowledge-building is primarily associated with the subjects Product and Market. Ambiguity about the subject Process will not add to this knowledge-building and is therefore not useful.

In companies conducting NPD largely under their own control, ambiguity about Organizational Resources is unlikely to be a welcome ingredient in the knowledge-building process of their NPD projects. However, in contexts where companies are exploring and developing new collaboration patterns together as part of a common NPD project, ambiguity about Organizational Resources will indeed contribute to innovation-related knowledge-building and should hence be tolerated.

The rows in Table 1 also identify four sources of ambiguity (i.e. what gave rise to the ambiguity); Multiplicity, Novelty, Validity and Reliability. Ambiguity from the first two sources—Multiplicity and Novelty—is essential for innovation, so care should be taken throughout the project to not reduce ambiguity to the extent it jeopardizes innovation. Ambiguity can however also arise from two other sources, low validity or low reliability. As in scientific experiments, low validity and low reliability do not contribute to build knowledge; on the contrary, they contribute to error and low trustworthiness. Ambiguity caused by these sources in NPD projects should therefore consistently be reduced by using valid and reliable information sources.

As a second criterion to distinguish between useful ambiguity and useless ambiguity, I therefore contend that ambiguity is only useful when it has potential to contribute to the knowledge development that is related to the purpose of a company's innovation effort.

5   Conclusion

In this paper, I have addressed the question of what fuzziness is, and discussed the difference between the fuzziness components of uncertainty and ambiguity, and focused specifically on the concept of ambiguity. I have discussed how reduction of ambiguity is associated with learning, and how ambiguity—developing in a cyclical manner of increasing and decreasing— is an integral part of knowledge development in innovation. Ambiguity is thus a component of fuzziness that can be useful. However, ambiguity is only useful for NPD when it contributes to build the new knowledge one is seeking in the particular project. The subjects one seeks to build knowledge about depend on the context of the NPD project. Ambiguity related to these subjects is useful and should be tolerated whereas ambiguity not contributing to build this knowledge should not be tolerated.

This paper contributes to theory by providing a theoretical argument of how ambiguity, as a component of fuzziness, can be useful in innovation. This contribution can also be useful to practitioners. When confronted with situations that they experience as fuzzy in their innovation projects, they may be better able to identify what component is contributing to this fuzziness and thereby be better able to select the right means to reduce the fuzziness. If the component they are facing is ambiguity, then understanding it's role in the knowledge-building they are attempting to achieve can help them to purposefully exploit ambiguity to the benefit of their innovation projects.

References

1. Brun, E.: Understanding and Managing Ambiguity in New Product Development: Lessons from the Medical-Device Industry. Department of Industrial Economics and Technology Management 2010. Norwegian University of Science and Technology, Trondheim (2010)
2. Brown, S., Eisenhardt, K.: Product Development: Past Research, Present Findings, and Future Directions. Academy of Management Review 20(2), 343–378 (1995)
3. Cooper, R.G.: Predevelopment activities determine new product success. Industrial Marketing Management 17(3), 237–247 (1988)
4. Khurana, A., Rosenthal, S.R.: Integrating the Fuzzy Front End of New Product Development. Sloan Management Review 38(2), 103–120 (1997)
5. Verganti, R.: Leveraging on systematic learning to manage the early phases of product innovation projects. R&D Management 27, 377–392 (1997)
6. Khurana, A., Rosenthal, S.R.: Towards Holistic "Front Ends" In New Product Development. Journal of Product Innovation Management 15(1), 57–74 (1998)
7. Koen, P., et al.: Providing clarity and a common language to the 'Fuzzy Front End'. Research-Technology Management 44(2), 46–55 (2001)
8. Moenaert, R.K., et al.: R&D/Marketing Communication During the Fuzzy Front-End. IEEE Transactions on Engineering Management 42(3), 243–258 (1995)
9. Reid, S., de Brentani, U.: The Fuzzy Front End of New Product Development for Discontinuous Innovations: A Theoretical Model. Journal of Product Innovation Management 21(3), 170–184 (2004)
10. Montoya-Weiss, M.M., O'Driscoll, T.M.: From Experience: Applying Performance Support Technology in the Fuzzy Front End. Journal of Product Innovation Management 17(2), 143–161 (2000)
11. Reinertsen, D.G.: Taking the Fuzziness Out of the Fuzzy Front End. Research Technology Management 42(6), 25 (1999)
12. Cooper, R.G., Kleinschmidt, E.J.: Benchmarking the Firm's Critical Success Factors in New Product Development. Journal of Product Innovation Management 12(5), 374–391 (1995)
13. Urban, G.L., Hauser, J.R.: Design and Marketing of New Products, 2nd edn. Prentice Hall, Englewood Cliffs (1993)
14. Cooper, R.G.: Fixing the fuzzy front end of the new product process. CMA Magazine 71(8), 21 (1997)
15. Nobelius, D., Trygg, L.: Stop chasing the Front End process – management of the early phases in product development projects. International Journal of Project Management 20(5), 331–340 (2002)

16. Zhang, Q., Doll, W.: The fuzzy front end and success of new product development: a causal model. European Journal of Innovation Management 4(2), 95–112 (2001)
17. Kim, J., Wilemon, D.: Focusing the fuzzy front-end in new product development. R&D Management 32(4), 269–279 (2002)
18. Daft, R.L., Lengel, R.H.: Information richness: A new approach to managerial behavior and organizational design. In: Staw, B.M., Cummings, L.L. (eds.) Research in Organizational Behavior, pp. 191–233. Jai Press, Greenwich (1984)
19. Weick, K.E.: The Social Psychology of Organizing, 2nd edn. McGraw-Hill, New York (1979)
20. Daft, R.L., Lengel, R.H.: Organizational Information Requirements, Media Richness and Structural Design. Management Science 32(5), 554–571 (1986)
21. Galbraith, J.: Organization Design. Addison-Wesley, Reading (1977)
22. Weick, K.E.: Sensemaking in Organizations. Sage Publications, Thousand Oaks (1995)
23. March, J.G., Simon, H.A.: Organizations, 2nd edn. Wiley, New York (1958)
24. March, J.G.: A Primer on Decision Making: How Decisions Happen. The Free Press, New York (1994)
25. Eisenberg, E.: Ambiguity as Strategy in Organizational Communication. Communication Monographs 51, 227–242 (1984)
26. Knight, F.H.: Risk, Uncertainty and Profit. Houghton Mifflin Company, New York (1921)
27. Dougherty, D.: Interpretive Barriers to Successful Product Innovation in Large Firms. Organization Science 3(2), 179–202 (1992)
28. Polanyi, M.: The Tacit Dimension. Doubleday, New York (1967)
29. Nonaka, I.: A dynamic theory of organizational knowledge creation. Organization Science 5(1), 14–37 (1994)
30. Leonard, D.: Wellsprings of Knowledge: Building and Sustaining the Sources of Innovation. Harvard Business School Press, Boston (1995)
31. Leonard, D., Sensiper, S.: The Role of Tacit Knowledge in Group Innovation. California Management Review 40(3), 112–132 (1998)
32. Eisenhardt, K.M., Tabrizi, B.: Accelerating Adaptive Processes: Product Innovation in the Global Computer Industry. Administrative Science Quarterly 40(1), 84–110 (1995)
33. Føllesdal, D.: Hermeneutics and the Hypothetical-Deductive Method. In: Martin, M., McIntyre, L.C. (eds.) Readings in the Philosophy of Social Science, pp. 233–245. MIT Press, Cambridge (1994)
34. Føllesdal, D., Walløe, L.: Argumentasjonsteori, språk og vitenskapsfilosofi. Universitetsforlaget, Oslo (2000)
35. Brun, E., Sætre, A.S.: Ambiguity Reduction in New Product Development Projects. International Journal of Innovation Management 12(4), 573–596 (2008)
36. Popper, K.R.: The Logic of Scientific Discovery. Hutchinson, London (1959)
37. Popper, K.R.: Conjectures and Refutations: The Growth of Scientific Knowledge. Routledge and Kegan Paul, London (1963)
38. Kolb, D.A.: Experiential Learning. Prentice-Hall, Upper Saddle River (1984)
39. Dougherty, D., et al.: Systems of organizational sensemaking for sustained product innovation. Journal of Engineering and Technology Management 17(3-4), 321–355 (2000)
40. Nonaka, I., Takeuchi, H.: The Knowledge-Creating Company. How Japanese Companies Create the Dynamics of Innovation. Oxford University Press, New York (1995)
41. Brun, E., Sætre, A.S., Gjelsvik, M.: Benefits of Ambiguity in New Product Development. International Journal of Innovation and Technology Management 5(3), 303–319 (2008)
42. Brun, E., Sætre, A.S., Gjelsvik, M.: Classification of Ambiguity in New Product Development Projects. European Journal of Innovation Management 12(1), 62–85 (2009)

Dynamic Capabilities in New Product Development Process: The Case of Small Software Developing Companies

Tatiana Iakovleva[1] and Alexey Rudshin[2]

[1] University of Stavanger, UiS Business School, 4036 Stavanger, Norway
[2] StatoilHydro, 4036 Stavanger, Norway
`Tatiana.a.iakovleva@uis.no`

Abstract. This study investigates the product development process of two small firms in the Norwegian software industry. A firm's ability to mobilize its capabilities and align them dynamically with the changing environment is of vital importance as the firm constantly innovates to survive and create its own competitive advantage. While literature has addressed new product development process and challengers it cope with, a limited focus has been taken on what capabilities are necessary to successfully overcome them. In the present paper we discuss the challengers that SME's meet while introducing new product development process in software industry and dynamic capabilities they utilize to overcome these challengers. Our findings reveal two main challenges – the need to continuously competence improvement and the need to enhance the efficiency of product development process. We found that to cope with these challenge both firms extensively developed open innovation mode through knowledge generative capabilities as well as certain integrative capabilities.

Keywords: dynamic capabilities, new product development, software, case studies.

1   Introduction

The process of new product development of SME's in software industry has received scant attention in the literature. The empirical measures are often limited to the stages of which new product development consists, and even these findings are rarely depict the context in which small enterprise act. This approach is not very appropriate to explain *how* firms are developing new software products. Rather, one needs to look at the complex picture of knowledge creation and utilisation to get into insides and to access the cohesive whole of the problem (King, 2007). We will investigate deeply the ways of dealing with these challengers on the example of two Norwegian small firms operating in the software industry.

Developing new products is a difficult process in any industry, but the software industry is particularly demanding in regard to time and quality constraints (Blackburn, 1996; Sheremata, 2002). These conditions are especially critical for small and medium-sized

J. Frick and B. Laugen (Eds.): APMS 2011, IFIP AICT 384, pp. 425–436, 2012.

enterprises (SMEs) developing computer software (Ambrosini and Bowman, 2009). SMEs often are limited in their resource base, suffer from small scale disadvantages, have small strategic apex and risk being locked into the present strategy (Kuratko and Audretsch, 2009, Schindehutte and Morris, 2009). At the same time SMEs has initial advantage in the form of flexibility and capacity to adapt to a changing environment. To survive and successfully compete with larger companies, SMEs imply the entrepreneurial behavior that is characterized by innovation (technological development, new products, new services, and improved product lines), proactiveness and risk-taking (Miller, 1983; Zahra et al., 2006).

Because of resource limitation, small companies often apply open innovation approach to keep themselves competitive. Open innovation can be defined as the use of purposive inflows and outflows of knowledge to accelerate internal innovation, and to expand the markets for external use of innovation (Chesbrough et al., 2006). At the heart of the open innovation model is the recognition that today, competitive advantage often comes from inbound as well as from outbound connections. Inbound connections is the practice of leveraging the discoveries of others: companies need not and indeed should not rely exclusively on their own R&D. Outbound open innovation suggests that rather than relying entirely on internal paths to market, companies can look for external organizations with business models that are better suited to commercialize a given technology (Chesbrough, 2002). Open innovation has received increasingly attention in scientific research, but so far it has mainly been analyzed in larger enterprises drawn on in-depth interviews and case studies (Chesbrough, 2003; Kirschbaum, 2005; Vrande et al., 2009).

In the present study we will address the issues of *how* small firms do actually build capabilities to forester open innovation and entrepreneurial mindset of the firm with limited resources in hands.

We will approach this main research question by utilizing the dynamic capabilities approach. The dynamic capability approach elaborate on the characteristics of resources that increase the pace of change towards new, original, strategic adaptation patterns in future (Teece et al., 1997, Poulis et al. 2010). In order to employ open innovation model, SME's need to build some certain capabilities that might facilitate this process. So far dynamic capabilities to firm long-term competitive advantage is considered in the large organizations, including such DC as R&D (Helfat, 1997), acquisition process (Karim and Mitchell, 2000), product innovation process (Danneels, 2002), absorptive capacity (Zahra and George, 2002), organizational structure reconfiguration (Karim, 2006). However, recently these approach shown to be useful also for SMEs (Madsen et al, 2006; Foss et al., 2011). However, there is an absence of studies highlighting and specifying dynamic capabilities that constitute the core of open innovation in SME's during that new product development process. The present study is aimed to fill up this gap and to explore critical dynamic capabilities in the product development process of computer software developing in SMEs.

2   Dynamic Capabilities in Software Industry

2.1   Open Innovation as Roadmap

Due to labor mobility, abundant venture capital and widely dispersed knowledge across multiple public and private organizations, entrepreneurs can no longer afford to innovate on their own, but rather need to engage in alternative innovation practices (Vrande et al., 2009; Chesbrough, 2003; Gassmann, 2006). Recent finding confirms that innovation in SMEs is becoming more open, and many SMEs attempt to benefit from the initiatives and knowledge of their employees. In addition, most SMEs try to involve their customers in innovation process by tracing their modifications in products, proactively involving them in market research, etc. (Vrande et al., 2009; Von Hippel, 2005). One may claim that open innovation in SMEs is mainly motivated by market-related targets, since the main problem for small enterprises is not so much invention but commercialization (Gans and Stern, 2003).

Open innovation comprises both outside-in and inside-out movements of technological ideas (Lichtenthaler, 2008). We may expect SMEs to rely on both inbound and outbound open innovation simultaneously (van de Vrande et al, 2009). Examples are cross-licensing agreements, in which firms transfer some of their own technology to get access to external knowledge (Grindley and Teece, 1997). The adoption of open innovation may be sequential, starting with customer involvement, following with employee involvement and external networking, and ending with more "advances" practices like IP licensing, R&D outsourcing, venturing and external participations (Johannisson, 1997; Vrande et al., 2009). As SMEs may struggle with a limited strategic apex, the organizational features may be of vital importance.

One important challenge facing a going company is that the innovative processes of the firm have to run in parallel with implementation of the present strategies. The balancing of exploitation and exploration activities is a risk-provoking task and needs an adapted business configuration (Chesbrough, et al. 2006; Roaldsen & Borch, 2011).

How this balancing can be achieved is the main research we aim to address in this paper. As any company bases its activities on resources it disposes as well as on opportunities it sized, it seems that that is ability to recombine resources in order to achieve necessary level of innovativeness is the key capabilities SMEs needs.

2.2   Dynamic Capabilities for Open Innovation

As Teece (1998) writes, in an economy where the only certainty is uncertainty, the one sure source of the competitive advantage is knowledge. Continuous product development process requires the simultaneous presence of the fundamental knowledge-based dynamic capabilities at the organizational level: knowledge creation and absorption, knowledge integration and knowledge reconfiguration (Verona and Ravasi, 2003; Wang and Ahmed, 2007, Ambrosini and Bowman, 2009). According to Sheremata (2002), software development projects of SMEs need the dynamic capability to access a large quantity of creative ideas, in-depth knowledge, and accurate information and these projects need to build integrative dynamic capability providing the project managers with structural sources of influence. Sheremata (2002) pointed out knowledge generating and integrative dynamic capabilities in new software development process.

Firms developing new software act in uncertain and dynamic environments and to succeed they tend to use an iterative process, which emphasizes learning and adaptation (MacCormack and Verganti, 2003). Studies of software development stress the importance of information about customer needs and new technologies. These studies indicate that increasing the quantity and quality of ideas, knowledge, and information a software development project can access both improves product quality and speeds development (Blackburn, 1996; Iansiti and MacCormac, 1997).

The team factors such as personnel capability and experience, personnel motivation, coordination and communication among team members are critical for project success in software development (Sheremata, 2002; Krishnan, 1998; Carmel and Sawyer, 1998). Integration can also improve product quality (Cusumano and Selby, 1997). According to Sheremata (2002), new product development is a task that consists of interdependent components. Software development is characterized by a need to coordinate the work of individuals on a day-to-day basis.

Summarizing, the following research model is suggested for the present study:

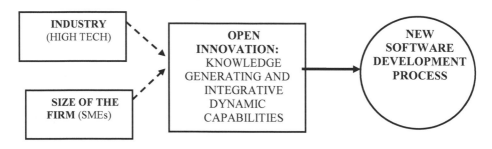

Fig. 1. The research model

3   Methods Used

3.1   Research Methodology

In order to grasp the embedded, processual and contextual nature of the dynamic capabilities, a case study design was chosen. Following the theoretical sampling of cases, we build on the suggestive arguments that multiple cases create more robust theory grounded in varied empirical evidence (Eisenhardt and Graebner, 2007).

Similar with other studies (Heaton 1998, Tuunanen and Vainio, 2005), our case selection was based on the theoretical sampling to obtain information from comparable cases (Glasser and Strauss, 1967, Orlikowski, 1993). A list of relevant firms was obtained from Confederation of Norwegian Enterprise (NHO) which satisfied following selection criteria : (1) Companies working within software development industry , 2) Small companies, less than 100 employees 3) Companies that showed good financial results over the last few years 4) Companies operating on roughly similar business-to-business markets 5) Companies that constantly introduce new products into the market. Those firms were further scanned with the help of information available thought their web-pages. Because of money and time constraint we choose those firms from the ones that satisfied initial criteria that were physically situated close to us. We ended up with two firms operating in software development industry, operating on the business-to-business market. Data were collected through a series of interviews organized between October 2003 and May 2004. We conducted in-depth individual, semi-structured interviews with the CEOs, development managers, and other managers of two small Norwegian firms developing computer software. Each interview lasted about 1 hour and was tape-recorded and transcribed. Overall, we conducted 9 interviews.

After having identified dynamic capabilities influencing the software development process in both firms, we applied to them Sheremata (2002) classification and divided them into two groups – knowledge generating and integrative dynamic capabilities.

3.2   Description of Cases

Company Alpha is one of the leading suppliers of ticket system in Nordic cinema industry, and is represented in five countries. Company Betta is a dominant player in the Norwegian health-care sector, selling patient software systems for hospitals in Norway and represented in five regions in Norway. It accounts for 35% of the total Norwegian market of somatic hospitals. Betta experiences almost 80% increase in turnover during one year period prior to research was carried on. Both firms have less than 100 employees, with firm Alpha having 19 employees and firm Betta having 40 employees. Both firms were constantly introducing new products or services to the market and exhibiting growth in turnover and marked share. At the same time, firms differs somewhat in size, services they provide and market niche, leaving opportunities to explore a verity of new product development challenges and ways to overcome these challenges in software industry

4   Findings

4.1   Product Development Process in High-Tech Sme's – Contextual Influence

Interviewees from both firms agree that high tech industry and small size of their firms dramatically affect the product development process. Different industries are characterized by different extent of dynamism. In this study we elaborate on the software industry. Firms acting in this industry find themselves in a situation of rapid and unpredictable change that craves from dynamic capabilities, according to Eisenhardt and Martin (2000), to be simple, experiential, and unstable processes relying on quickly created new knowledge. At the same time SME's often have limited resources, both financial, human capital and other types of resources. We have identified several challengers firms meet during the product development process.

Technology in the software industry changes very fast. Due to small size, it is impossible for SMEs in software industry to achieve comprehensive competence within software. The development manager of Alpha said that in the software industry it is impossible to have comprehensive knowledge. It leads to lacking competence in the development department. "The field of programming is enormously large. With seven developers it is impossible to cope with the whole field. However we cope with it. In general, we have the competence we need, but I am sure that we could have more competence". Developers of company Alpha are in continuous learning process. According to the development manager "new versions of programming tools are coming very often. Our developers must learn all the time." Because of complexity of software systems that company Alpha develops, it takes, according to the managing director, 1-2 years before a developer understands what the firm is really doing. The professional development of software developers goes on during the work.

The same problem was outlined by company Betta.   Due to its size, it is impossible for company Betta to have comprehensive competence within software. The firm collaborates with other companies within the industry that have experience in areas Betta lacks competence. For example another firm creates mobile solutions for Betta. According to the development manager, "this firm has competence not only about the mobile solutions, but about how to create it, about the concept". There is very much dialoging with partners about how the best possible system is going to be realized. Summarizing, there is a need for continues competence improvement.

Because the firm has limited human resources each employee have to deal with lots of different task, which results in low efficiency. The development manager of company Alpha said: "Due we are a little firm each developer should have wide knowledge in the programming field to perform very different tasks. It affects negatively efficiency, because each developer has too much tasks simultaneously." In the same time the development manager of company Betta noted that "when the firm was smaller, – eight persons, it was easier to react in time to market changes. Now it goes more slowly. We have more people and we are doing more, but I am not satisfied with the level we have today." The company needs more teams of developers to cope with increased demand on its product. The development manager said: "we have few teams of developers now." We can conclude that companies experience a need to enhance the efficiency of product development process.

4.2   Knowlegde Generating Capabilities of New Product Development Process: Case Illustrations

Both companies considered in the study developed and successfully implement knowledge generating dynamic capabilities. Following capabilities were identified: decentralization, reaching for information from customers, reaching information about technologies and free flow of information as well as monitoring of competitor competences. We describe below these capabilities, illustrated by the case examples.

The first capability identified was *decentralization*. Because knowledge is often tacit, software development projects must cross organizational boundaries to gain access to it (Dougherty, 1996). Developers in company Alpha often have informal meetings, they self decides whom they want to meet. "We go away from PCs. We go to the meeting room and discuss projects and tasks we are working with. Everybody can go there, independently of groups". In company Betta developers work with formally delegated nurse from customer service department, which allows to create cross-discipline teams. While both companies have developed decentralization routines, they perform it in different ways. Developers in Alpha discuss the development work with everybody they want, while developers in B work with formally delegated nurse from customer service department that can reduce positive influence of decentralization on new software development.

The second capability was named *reaching for information from customers*. Reaching for information from customers and about technologies and markets increases the probability of successful development (Ancona and Caldwell, 1992) Both, Alpha and Betta, involve customers in process of new software development. Customers actively participate in all stages of development that dramatically increases reaching for information from them and allows immediately react on market changes.

In company Alpha customers often work together with developers and participate in technology tests: "Customers may say: we have a need for something new. Also, we collaborate with customers during testing of the ready product." In Betta, customers are also active and advise on the product. "A lot of demand and ideas are coming from customers".

Next, a capability that we called *Reaching for information about technologies* was found. Alpha extended its knowledge base by acquiring new highly competent human resources: "We had usual experience of database programming and we worked with usual internet information server. We employed one DOT Net specialist and one Java specialist. Thanks to these persons we have improved our knowledge dramatically". Company Betta shares technological competence with partners through common projects and courses. The firm collaborates with many firms in the industry.

Further, companies performed *free flow of information*. Removing obstacles such as differences in social status, and physical distances between individuals increases the quantity and quality of knowledge available for problem solving, which then helps organizations innovate successfully (Jelinek and Schoonhoven, 1990). In company Alpha all de-velopers are sitting together in the common room. Company tends to remove such obstacle as physical distance between software developers "There is a group that is responsible for the product. And their knowledge is divided to everybody in the group." Company Betta had changed its organizational culture to increase the free flow of information: "We change culture from the situation when each developer develops his own system to the situation when it will be just a part of the whole system."

Last, but not least, we observed *monitoring of competitors' competence*. The company's Betta leadership has regular meetings with competitors. It helps the organization to innovate successfully. "We monitor competitors' competence, we meet them and discuss with them." Betta considers competitors as a source of expertise. Ancona and Caldwell (1992) point out that effective product development processes have extensive external communication as dynamic capability that is applicable for regular meetings of Betta's leadership with its competitors.

4.3   Integrative Capabilities of New Product Development Process: Case Illustrations

Both companies developed several integrative dynamic capabilities to improve their product development process, including direct contact, project management influence, cross-functional team influence and temporal pacing, as well as inter-team collaboration and prioritizing.

First integrative capability executed by companies was *direct contact*. Increasing interaction among individuals in the project through direct contact appears to speed development, by increasing feedback, error correction, and the synthesis of different points of view (Clark and Fujimoto, 1990). In company Alpha, developers who work logically with the same theme are sitting around one table. According to the development manager the firm faced higher dynamism of the product development process when the development work was organized as a team work around one table. "We experienced very high rise of job satisfaction between employees when they moved to one room. Developers are talking together and we noted that the system became more coordinated".

Thus, eliminating a physical distance is one way of enhancing direct contact between the team members. In Betta, team leaders collect their teams in once a week. During these meetings team leaders make priority of task fulfillment and discuss different tasks with employees. Therefore, this established order of team meetings also enhances the direct contact between the team members. Team work in Alpha and Betta differs in high extent, and although direct contact is present in both cases, it is performed in slightly lower degree in Betta.

Next capability was *project manager influence*. A project manager needs power – the ability to change another's attitudes, beliefs, or behaviors in an independent direction – to be an effective integration mechanism. Sources of this power include formal position authority, control over critical scarce resources, expertise, and a central position in the flow of information (Sheremata, 2002; Haefliger and von Krogh, 2004). Formal and informal authority of team leaders are of high importance in Betta. As it comes from interviews, powerful project leader influences positively on new software development process. The personal characteristics of team leaders are of high importance in Betta, because, according to the managing director, they influence dramatically on product development process. The team leader should be in stand to place him in the work situation of hospital specialists that will work with the product. It is important to understand the customer's weekday. He should lead a group of people in work and simultaneously run the process in the systematic way. In the same time, there are no leaders in development teams in company Alpha. The development manager points out that there are only informal leaders because they worked longer in the firm. The development manager doesn't point out a person that will be a team leader. In one project it is one person that is natural leader, while in another project it will be another person. Therefore, project management influence cannot be named an important antecedent of the product development process in Alpha. This fact can be partly explained by the smaller size and less formal structure of the company Alpha in relation to Betta, and partly by the differences in the product characteristics between two companies.

Further, an important integrative capability is *cross-functional team influence* and *temporal pacing*. A cross functional team usually includes representatives from functions who provide function-level leadership to the project, and a project manager who supervises the work of functions through these representatives (Clark and Wheelwright, 1992). Representatives must actively and regularly participate in cross-functional teams for them to wield any influence and therefore any integrative capability (Dougherty and Hardy, 1996). There is organized the product board in company Alpha to improve the product development process. This product board acts as a cross-functional team with active participation of representatives from all departments. The product board consists of development manager, project manager, sales manager, support manager, and director. At the same time the product development process is built as team work in Alpha. That means that employees actively and regularly participate in cross-functional teams. Betta is under the organizational changes today. The firm is growing very fast and the organizational structure does not manage to adapt these changes. Interviewees noticed that the firm lacks knowledge in project management. That is why such useful structures as cross-functional teams are under construction in B at the moment

Next, *inter-team collaboration* is an important capability. In company Alpha two team of developers were moved to one room. According to the development manager of Alpha, "these teams began to collaborate. As a result the firm improves quality of new software." According to Eisenhardt and Martin (2000), effective product development processes involve routines that ensure that concrete and joint experiences among team members, such as working together to fix specific problems or participating in brainstorming sessions occur. This definition clearly reflects the capability developed by Alpha that united two teams in one room to increase inter-team collaboration.

Finally, last capability we observed was labeled *prioritizing*. Thanks to priorities in better quality and better quality control Betta dramatically improved the product development process. "Our priorities are better quality and better quality control. We use more time to create even better product. That dramatically improved product development process of the company." The need to coordinate tasks (Helfat and Peteraf, 2003) implies that a capability involves coordinated effort by individuals. The Betta's leadership performs tasks coordination prioritizing better quality and better quality control that dramatically improved product development process. Danneels (2002) names quality assurance tools as dynamic capability affecting product development process.

5   Discussion

The empirical findings of this study show that that knowledge generating and integrative dynamic capabilities are critical for new product development process of new software producing SMEs. In addition to the dynamic capabilities previously identified in the software development process, we found several new dynamic capabilities – one knowledge generating dynamic capability that we named "monitoring competitors", and two integrative dynamic capabilities that we named "prioritizing" and "inter-team collaboration".

The firms also underlined the importance of all capabilities to achieve competitive advantage. Generation of knowledge is crucial to the process of new product development. Small firms do not possess all necessary resources, and opening up for collaboration with customers, sometimes even with potential competitors can turn weaknesses into strengthens. Our cases stress that there is a conflict of archiving efficiency and implementing new ideas, and through decentralization, free flows of information, reaching information from customers and new technologies, monitoring competitors firms can overcome the challenge of newlines.

However, it is also important integrate new knowledge in effective way. This task is achieved in our cases by practicing direct contact, cross-functional teams, inter-team collaboration, prioritizing, in some cases project management influence.

6   Conclusion

6.1   Contribution

Finding of critical dynamic capabilities in software development process gives guidance as to the best suited management approaches in software industry. Managers can increase their probability of meeting their product quality goals. They can encourage groups and individuals to find problems through search, or they can design their organizations so they can both access and integrate knowledge as they solve problems.

Software development projects that combine all of these dynamic capabilities have the highest probability of attaining their schedule and product quality goals. Unfortunately, reaching outward for ideas, knowledge, and information while turning inward to integrate them is inherently difficult, and searching for problems is not intuitive or comfortable for many. However, projects that rise to this challenge and successfully develop these dynamic capabilities may be far more likely to realize their goals – to see their visions embodied as products in market.

6.2   Limitations and Future Research

This study's findings might not generalize beyond the computer software industry. Future research should determine whether these findings apply to other industries. The fast pace of competition in the computer software industry may change the dynamics of schedule attainment in a way that precludes generalization. Moreover, the abstract character of the product may change the dynamics of attaining schedule and product quality goals – by putting more of a premium on access to ideas, knowledge, and information, for example.

The difficulty of obtaining data from firms developing software products limited this study in other way. It quickly became obvious that trying to gather data from software developers was a difficult task. Pervasive time pressure in this industry works as a barrier in conducting the research. A larger sample as well as a longitudinal study might reveal more findings on the topic. A more in-depth study of problem identification might provide even greater insights.

Nevertheless, we believe that present study has added to the growing body of knowledge by exploring important processes leading to the successful new product development through application of a open innovation approach when we studied those processes as embedded into the small firm context and to the environmental industrial context.

References

Ambrosini, V., Bowman, C.: What are dynamic capabilities and are they a useful construct in strategic management? International Journal of Management Reviews 11(1), 29–49 (2009)

Ancona, D.G., Caldwell, D.F.: Bridging the boundary: External process and performance in organizational teams. Administrative Science Quarterly 37(4), 634–665 (1992)

Blackburn, J.D.: Improving the speed and productivity of software development: A global survey of software developers. IEEE Transactions of Software Engineering 22(12), 875–885 (1996)

Carmel, E., Sawyer, S.: Packaged software development teams: What makes them different? Information Technology and People 11(1), 7–19 (1998)

Chesbrough, H.: Open innovation: The new imperative for creating and profiting from technology. Harvard Business School Press, Boston (2003)

Chesbrough, H.: Business model innovation: Opportunities and barriers. Long Range Planning 43, 354–363 (2010)

Chesbrough, H., Growther, K.: Beyond high tech: early adopters of open innovation in other industries. R&D Management 36(3), 229–236 (2006)

Chesbrough, H., Vanhaverbeke, W., West, J.: Open Innovation: Researching a New Paradigm. Oxford University Press (2006)

Chesbrough, H.: Graceful exits and foregone opportunities: Xerox's management of its technology spinoff organizations. Business History Review 76(4), 803–834 (2002)

Clark, K.B., Fujimoto, T.: The power of product integrity. Harvard Business Review 68(6), 107–118 (1990)

Clark, K.B., Fujimoto, T.: Product Development Performance: Strategy, Organization, and Management in the World Auto Industry. Harvard Business School Press, Boston (1991)

Clark, K.B., Wheelwright, S.C.: Organizing and leading "heavyweight" development teams. California Management Review 34(3), 9–28 (1992)

Cusumano, M.A., Selby, R.W.: How Microsoft builds software. Communications of the ACM 40(6), 53–61 (1997)

Danneels, E.: The dynamics of product innovation and competencies. Strategic Management Journal 23, 1095–1121 (2002)

Dougherty, D., Hardy, C.: Sustained product innovation in large mature organizations: Overcoming innovation-to-organization problems. Academy of Management Journal 39, 1120–1153 (1996)

Eisenhardt, K.M., Martin, J.A.: Dynamic capabilities: What are they? Strategic Management Journal 21, 1105–1121 (2000)

Eisenhardt, K.M., Graebner, M.E.: Theory Building From Cases: Opportunities and Challenges. Academy of Management Journal 50(1), 25–32 (2007)

Foss, L., Iakovleva, T., Kickul, J., Oftedal, E., Solheim, A.: Taking Innovations to Market: The Role of the Firm's Strategic Choice on the Process, Creation, and Evolution of its Dynamic Capabilities During the Early Commercialization Process. International Journal of Entrepreneurship and Innovation 12(2), 105–116 (2011), doi:10.5367/ijei.2011.0029

Gassmann, O.: Opening up the innovation process: towards an agenda. R&D Management 36(3), 223–228 (2006)

Grindley, P., Teece, D.: Managing intellectual capital: Licensing and cross-licensing in semiconductors and electronics. California Management Review 39(2), 8–41 (1997)

Haefliger, S., von Krogh, G.: Knowledge creation in open source software development. In: Tsoukas, H., Mylonopoulos, N. (eds.) Organizations as Knowledge Systems, pp. 109–129. Palgrave Macmillan, Houndmills (2004)

Heaton, L.: Talking heads av. Virtual workplaces: a comparison of design across cultures. Journal of Information Technology 13, 259–272 (1998)

Helfat, C.E.: Know-How and Asset Complementarity and Dynamic Capability Accumulation: The Case of R&D. Strategic Management Journal 18(5), 339–360 (1997)

Iansiti, M., MacCormac, A.: Developing products on Internet time. Harvard Business Review 75(5), 108–117 (1997)

Jelinek, M., Schoonhoven, C.B.: The innovation marathon. Lessons from high technolandy firms. Basil Blackwell, Oxford (1990); Karim, S.: Modularity in organizational structure: the reconfiguration of internally developed and acquired business units. Strategic Management Journal 21, 1061–1081 (2006)

Johannisson, B.: The dynamic of entrepreneurial networks. In: Frontiers of Entrepreneurship Research. Babson Colledge (1997)

Karim, S., Mitchell, W.: Path dependent and path-breaking change: reconfiguring business resources following acquisitions in the U.S. medical sector, 1978-1995. Strategic Management Journal 21, 1061–1081 (2000)

King, W.: A research agenda for the relationships between culture and knowledge management. Knowledge and Process Management 14(3), 226–236 (2007)

Kirschbaum, R.: Open innovation in practice. Research on Technology Management 48, 24–28 (2005)

Krishnan, M.S.: The role of team factors in software cost and quality: An empirical analysis. Information Technology and People 11(1), 20–35 (1998)

Kuratko, D.F., Audretsch, D.B.: Strategic Entrepreneurship: Exploring Different Perspectives of an Emerging Concept. Entrepreneurship Theory and Practice 33, 1–17 (2009)

Madsen, E.L., Borch, O.-J., Wiklund, J.: Developing dynamic capabilities in small firms: The role of entrepreneurial orientation, entrepreneurial activities, and firm performance. In: 26th Babson College Entrepreneurship Conference. Indiana University, Kelly School of Business, Bloomington (2006)

MacCormack, A., Verganti, R.: Managing the sources of uncertainty: Matching process and context in software development. The Journal of Product Innovation Management 20, 217–232 (2003)

Orlikowski, W.: Case tools as organizational change: Investigating incremental and radical changes in system development. MIS Quarterly 17(3), 309–340 (1993)

Poulis, E., Poulis, K., Jackson, P.: Dynamic capabilities: Theoretical approaches and practical applications. In: EURAM Conference Proceedings (2010), http://www.euram2010.org/userfiles/EDLEILH_KIIME_UU2YE8XY.pdf

Schindehutte, M., Morris, M.H.: Advancing strategic entrepreneurship research: The role of complexity science in shifting the paradigm. Entrepreneurship Theory and Practice 33, 241–276 (2009)

Sheremata, W.A.: Finding and solving problems in software new product development. The Journal of Product Innovation Management 19, 144–158 (2002)

Teece, D.J., Pisano, G., Shuen, A.: Dynamic capabilities and strategic management. Strategic Management Journal 18(7), 509–533 (1997)

Tuunanen, T., Vainio, M.: Communication flows in software product development: A case study of two mobile software firms. Journal of Information Technology and Application (JITTA) 7(3), 27–48 (2005)

Von Hippel, E.: Democratizing Innovation. MIT Press, Cambridge (2005)

Vrande, V., de Jong, J., Vanhaverbeke, W., de Rochemont, M.: Open innovation in SMEs: Trends, motives and management challenges. Technovation 29, 423–437 (2009)

Zahra, S.A., George, G.: Absorptive capacity: a review, reconceptualization and extension. Academy of Management Review 27, 185–203 (2002)

Zahra, S.A., Sapienza, H.J., Davidsson, P.: Entrepreneurship and Dynamic Capabilities: A Review, Model and Research Agenda. Journal of Management Studies 43(4), 917–955 (2006)

Assessment of Sustainable Practices
in New Product Development

Gökan May, Marco Taisch, and Endris Kerga

Politecnico di Milano, Department of Management,
Economics and Industrial Engineering, Piazza L. da Vinci, 32 - 20133 Milano, Italy
{goekan.may,endris.kerga}@mail.polimi.it,
marco.taisch@polimi.it

Abstract. Decisions during NPD process have impact on 80-90% of a product's life cycle sustainability performance. The objective of this study is to investigate the integration of sustainability into product design, mainly focusing on the environmental aspects. The investigation has been carried out by means of a questionnaire developed based on a 3-pillar framework outlining the essential elements for successful integration of sustainability and Life Cycle thinking in NPD process. 10 manufacturing companies with high innovation cycles, operating in Italy in mechanical, electrical and automotive sectors was assessed, supporting the questionnaire with 2 complementary case studies. The results revealed that companies fail to implement sustainability in product development process and gap exists in all the enablers since companies just try to tackle the legislations, considering sustainability as a constraint rather than exploiting the opportunities for eco-innovation.

Keywords: Sustainability, Eco-efficiency, New Product Development (NPD), Eco-design tools.

1 Introduction

In the last couple of decades, significant research work has been carried out in order to investigate different ways of supporting engineers in the development of more sustainable products. However, most of the efforts and studies are mainly directed towards the environmental aspect of sustainability as the industrial world has changed its approach to the environment. The importance of the environmental sustainability of industrial products and processes derives not only from the ever stricter-becoming environmental legislations issued in most of the developed countries, but also from the higher awareness of customers concerning environmental problems. In particular, the competitiveness of putting on the market more sustainable products is becoming a key factor in recent years [1].

Product development is one of the most critical aspects for companies in reaching their sustainability objectives as almost all the products are outputs of the product development process. In particular, early design decisions can have a very significant

J. Frick and B. Laugen (Eds.): APMS 2011, IFIP AICT 384, pp. 437–447, 2012.
© IFIP International Federation for Information Processing 2012

impact on sustainability. These decisions not only concern choices of material and manufacturing but also have a strong impact on the product's entire lifecycle [2].

Based on the estimation from the EU report, 80-90% of all product-related environmental impacts are determined during the design phase of a product. Hence, eco-design is a way to improve products' life-cycle environmental performances by systematically integrating environmental aspects at a very early stage in product design [4]. As a matter of fact, key challenges have to be overcome to enable eco-design methods to be applicable in early design stages.

With this study, we aim to understand the main motivations, limitations, and effectiveness of integrating sustainability in new product design and to understand how and what companies are doing currently to integrate sustainability in their products and product development processes. In doing this, the focus is mainly on company characteristics, sustainable strategies and applications of the company, ecodesign tools and relevant product development processes. In this context, we identify the main research objectives as below:

- Understand how and what companies are doing currently to integrate sustainability into their products and product design processes

- Determine the priorities of companies during product design and stimuli for sustainable product design
- Understand the level of consideration given to integration of sustainability into product design on the industry side
- Develop insight into the use of eco-design tools in companies' product design practices
- Identify the gap between the literature and the practice.

This paper is structured as following: State of the art for relevant concepts and the framework used for designing the survey is provided in part 2. The methodology followed is explained in detail in part 3. Next, the results of the analysis is shown and discussed in part 4. The main insights from the paper and conclusions are presented in part 5 and finally part 6 mentions the limitations of the study together with some ideas for future research.

2   State of the Art

2.1   Framework of Enablers for Integrating Sustainability in NPD

The study and the survey are constructed based on a framework from a previous study of the authors. The framework has 3 main components: Drivers/barriers, the enablers which foster efficient and effective integration of sustainability in NPD (i.e. strategic paradigms, supporting tools and manufacturing process paradigms) and impact of integrating sustainability in NPD on NPD performance measures, as shown in Figure 1 below [5]:

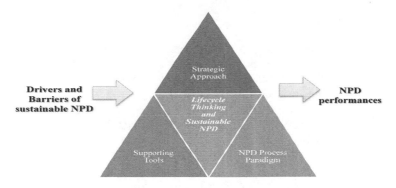

Fig. 1. Framework of enablers for successful integration of sustainability in NPD [5]

2.2   NPD Process Paradigms

Analyzing NPD process paradigms concerns assessing how companies organize their NPD processes in such a way that sustainability is effectively integrated into product design. To design any product, some set of processes should be followed and types of processes depend on the type of products as well as companies' considerations of different aspects and related decisions in product development. Hence, the structure of a design and development process affects the sustainability performance of a product to be designed [3, 7].

Conventional NPD process is generally structured in a sequential manner called serial engineering [8]. Sequential design process models are characterized by freezing design specifications early in a design process so that designers have a single design option to discern till it reaches a control gate. At design gates, the design concept will be tested if it meets design requirements, and at that point if the design doesn't meet the requirements either design iterations or sub-optimal product will be the result [7, 8, 9]. Thus, companies first decide the fate of the product early in the process and problem will be revealed later at the design gates in such process models. If sustainable products need to be designed following such process paradigm, two problems will happen [6]; the first one is that, if the designers found that the product does not meet some environmental requirements at latter design gates they need to redesign again, which in turn affect time to market and incur additional cost for the company. Second, since environmental considerations are taken secondary in industries, once environmental problems have been found at the gates, designers overlook the problem and prefer to launch sub-optimal products from sustainability perspectives.

Concurrent engineering (CE) was born to improve the problem of serial engineering approach of NPD process [10]. In CE, manufacturing engineers intervene in a design process to consider and improve the manufacturability of the design. Such NPD paradigm is more effective in addressing sustainability issue than sequential paradigm [3]. Therefore, successful integration of sustainability in NPD depends on how NPD process is structured in a company. This phenomenon has been a focus of investigation for the companies surveyed in this paper.

2.3   Ecodesign Concept and Tools

Ecodesign is a practice by which environmental considerations are integrated into product and process engineering design procedures. Ecodesign practices are meant to develop environmentally compatible products and processes while maintaining product, price, performance and quality standards [11].

Many efforts have been made to develop tools that support integration of sustainability in NPD. The most powerful and prevalent tools used in sustainable product design are those which consider environmental aspect of sustainability, so called "eco-design tools". Many the so called eco-design tools and methods exist [12]: some are extremely simple and qualitative (such as checklists), while some are complex and quantitative (Such as LCA), and others based on QFD (such as Green QFD). The selection of the best tool for a given application depends on the individual situation of the context of the design and development process [13].

The simplest classification of tools is into those which perform data analysis, and those, which are aimed at improvement. Analysis tools provide a measurement of the potential environmental impact of a product. They are mostly used before design starts, by analyzing a previous product or that of a competitor. Alternatively, they may be used at the end of a design project to verify the result. Improvement tools, on the other hand, are used during the design process to direct activity and provide information on the process.

Mistakes in selecting the most suitable tool depending on the specific situation may limit the effectiveness, usability and applicability of the tools. Criteria that should be taken into account during the selection of the adequate tools could be: the aim of conducting the study, the type of business or product considered, level of information available, the time available, the nature of data input, the quality of the expected results, the intended user and the design stage a tool is intended to be used (i.e. concept stages, system design level, embodiment design, and detail design) [14].

In this study we have considered around 30 eco-design tools that have been found in the literature. In the survey, we investigated companies if they adopt these kind of tools in their practices and how efficient and effective they are in applying such tools.

3   Research Methodology

In this study, literature published in the last 15 years (1995-2010) have been studied, including academic journals, books and conference proceedings, to understand what have been written and practices in literature and industries till now to integrate sustainability in new product design. This literature review formed the basis to identify the research objectives and the structure of the survey questions. The investigation has been carried out by means of a questionnaire developed in alignment with the research objectives based on a framework to assess manufacturing companies operating in Italy in mechanical, electrical and automotive sectors. The analysis was carried out on 10 companies with high innovation cycles, which are subject to many product based EU legislations (i.e. WEEE, ELV, EuP, REACH, RoHS, and others). The questionnaire was supported by 2 complementary case studies including face to face interviews and analyzing the internal documents, to increase the relevance of the work.

3.1   Survey Design and Procedures

Based on the research objectives and framework described in section 2.1 that identifies essential elements to successfully integrate sustainability and life-cycle thinking in NPD process, a questionnaire of 25 questions has been developed to assess the companies. This survey was composed of questions about company characteristics, sustainable strategies and applications of the company, ecodesign tools and relevant product development processes. The questionnaire has been approved after some revision phases in which some of the questions have been modified in order to simplify their understanding, and other questions have been added, in order to gain all the possible information aligned with our objectives. The expected recipients of the questionnaire were product development department responsible.

On-line version of the questionnaire has been created using Survey Monkey and was sent to companies via the following link: http://www.surveymonkey.com/s/ZD5ZLPR

The on-line questionnaire has been proposed to over 200 contacts, of which 10 companies replied directly via the link provided by e-mail.

3.2   Survey Questions

Questionnaire was based on the framework to implement sustainability in new product development (NPD): So, questions have been identified considering the main components of the framework as listed below:

1. Drivers/Barriers:

- The stimuli factors considering sustainability in NPD
- Barriers of incorporating sustainability in NPD
- Causes of Eco-design projects failures and successes, etc.

2. Enablers

A. Strategic approach

- Mandatory and voluntary sustainability policies and legislations company adopts
- Commitment of top management
- Environmental parameters used in product design
- Sustainable product strategy
- Expected benefits of applying ecodesign
- Trade-off between traditional design performances (e.g. cost, quality, time to market) and environmental and social issues, etc.

B. Supporting tools

- Types of sustainability design tools used
- Criteria to choose specific tools
- The impact of using sustainability design tools on the NPD performances, etc.

C. NPD Process Paradigms

- Systematic integration of sustainability issues throughout a design process
- Coordination between product's lifecycle partners
- Product's lifecycle consideration
- Exploration and utilization of past project's knowledge
- Level of innovation adopted (e.g. product improvement, product redesign, new product concept, new product system, etc.)

3. NPD Performances

- Financial and non-financial benefits gained
- Impact of integrating sustainability on the traditional NPD performances such as time to market and project costs
- Internal changes due to sustainability consideration in NPD.

3.3   Sample Firms and Response Collection

Questionnaire was sent to a combination of large companies and SMEs that might have already been integrating sustainability into their product design processes for several years. Sample firms were selected from manufacturing companies operating in Italy in mechanical, electric and automotive sectors. Although the questionnaire was proposed to over 200 companies, we got the responds from and analyzed 10 companies with high innovation cycles, which are subject to many product based EU legislations (i.e. REACH, RoHS, WEEE, EuP, ELV and others). The respondents were all relatively large companies. Some of the SMEs responded to mails to inform whether they don't consider this kind of approaches during product design or they are not interested in such activities. Thus, this information might be considered as a clue for a low-level adoption of sustainable practices and especially ecodesign tools among SMEs.

3.4   Complementary Case Studies

We carried out two complementary case studies to support the results achieved by the survey analysis. The aim was to collect relevant information about sustainability practices and sustainable product design processes of the companies via face to face interviews, analysis of their internal documents and going deeper in their responds to survey, as complementary to survey analysis. The two companies selected for case studies were globally known large enterprises; one automotive manufacturer and one tire manufacturer. Face to face interviews have been made with technical responsible in both cases. The other dimension of the analysis was to analyze the documents such as annual sustainability reports, sustainable strategy reports, etc. for supporting the results gained by the prior survey study.

4   Research Results and Discussion

First of all, almost 90% of the companies responded that they consider sustainability in NPD. However, the definitions of sustainability differ from company to company and most of them take sustainability and environmental consciousness as same without a comprehensive approach of sustainability as the balance between Economic-Environment-Social dimensions.

However, the results demonstrate that companies still consider sustainability as a constraint rather than opportunity for eco-innovation. Furthermore, companies are trying to meet only the minimum requirements asked by legislations despite the efforts from academia side to drive strategic push, effective tools, and suitable NPD process paradigms to foster sustainable product innovations. In fact, companies won't be spending time and money in implementing sustainability unless government legislations forced them. Indeed, quality and cost seem to be the most important factors considered during product design. Environmental aspects and legal requirements are not the priority ones for the companies. Indeed, companies showed mostly used environmental parameters in product design as raw material consumption, energy consumption and energy efficiency, all of which can be directly related to costs.

Companies implementing sustainability in NPD could have many reasons or drivers to do so. Among them; long-term benefits (i.e. image improvement, new market opportunities) and innovation potential, genuine environmental impact reduction, improved resource and process efficiency, customer demand due to increasing environmental consciousness, reduction of costs and risk are the reasons given by companies interviewed. In reality, most of the decisions and interest depend on either costs or long term plans as image improvement and entering to new markets. On the other hand, there are many barriers on the way of companies for implementing sustainability. Companies mentioned that the lack of time and budget to discern sustainability (in terms of investment in new or modified technologies, materials, etc.) in NPD are the most important barriers.

Most of the companies interviewed have high level sustainability initiatives such as CSR (corporate social responsibility) strategic scheme, ISO14001 EMS (Environmental management system), and EH & S (Environment, health and safety) polices. This shows that top managements are also committed for overall sustainability of the industries. However, when it comes to the ground level, as of NPD, there is no evidence that sustainability is properly integrated in top-down approach. Almost all interviewed companies adopt only mandatory EPR (extended product responsibility) EU policies (i.e. REACH, RoHS, ELV, WEEE and EuP, etc.) which ask only minimum requirements to be fulfilled. Hence, the main focus is on the current legislation with little effort to impact future EU policies that might give further competitive advantage.

Investigating how tradeoffs are handled between Economic considerations (cost, performance, and functionality), environmental and social considerations gave us the possibility to check strategic alliances of sustainability in NPD. Therefore, companies seem to consider sustainability in a balanced way although high priority is given for economic considerations (about 50-60% importance comparing to environmental (30%) and social ones (20%)).

The level of investment for sustainable innovations shows that only 5-10% of total R&D budget is invested in average. This figure cannot be taken as absolute measure since 5-10 % might be huge for one industry and small for another. However, sustainable innovation level is limited to product upgrading or modification instead of investing in new and more sustainable materials and technologies.

The reason why companies mostly talk about or direct to environmental commitment appears to be mostly a matter of marketing and advertisement. Even though top managements seem to focus on green marketing on strategic level, there is no evidence that sustainability is properly integrated in top-down approach when it comes to ground level, as of NPD.

Companies interviewed emphasized the fact that fully integrating sustainability in NPD projects cost them more than the gain they could have achieved. Moreover, time to market could be extended if sustainability issues are addressed effectively. As mentioned above, the reasons are mainly internal problems (lack of designers' knowledge, eco-design tools are time consuming, new innovations in terms of material and technology take time and huge investments). On the other hand, they also stress that non-financial gains have been achieved such as; new skill and competencies, company image, customer acceptances, and overall sensitivity towards environmental impacts have been raised inside the company. However, the performance benefits come with penalty in development cost and time to market. Therefore, the main issue here is how to structure NPD strategy, tools, and process in such a way those traditional NPD performances are either unaffected or even improved.

Although the selected companies have claimed that they adopted sustainability for so long (5-10 years), only six out of the ten companies adopted 'proper' eco design tools ranging from simple checklists (e.g. Banned material and chemical lists, disassembly lists and so on) to full or simplified LCA tools. LCA based, QFD based and checklist based tools are the most prevalent tools used in companies' practices. Most of the other tools present in the literature are not used and even sometimes not recognized by companies. This is probably due to the fact that current ecodesign tools are too much expert tools that are little adapted to designers' current needs, tools and practices. Indeed, the methods available in the literature are not good enough to support designers and there are few to help designers find solutions in Design for Environment (DFE) for variety of processes. That is to say, most of the current methodologies and tools serve in a fragmented way which limits designers in finding effective solutions to sustainability problems in product design. There is a huge gap here between literature and the applications of companies. In all likelihood, ecodesign has not been routinely practiced in design teams.

In real, companies have multiple criteria to choose among tools, and the important ones are: easy to implement and easy to learn, delivering accurate results, less amount of required information and less resources for the assessment. This shows that sophisticated ecodesign tools have little importance to bring sustainability to the mainstream NPD practices. Hence, there is a need to modify effective but sophisticated tools such as LCA (Life Cycle Assessment) so that they could be adopted more in new product design. Disseminating and introducing such tools to industry is a viable way to foster sustainability in product design.

Certainly, most eco-design projects fail for two main reasons according to the industries interviewed. The first one is due to insufficient information available and knowledge about the impact of complex product systems on the environment and society. The other one is the existence of many uncertainties in developing sustainable products such as: Suppliers' compliance issues, integrating manufacturing capabilities, and uncertainty about the market acceptance of the product by the customer. Although these reasons are obvious, proper attention should be given to deal with supply chain and lifecycle uncertainties for the success of ecodesign projects.

Many companies reported that they have life cycle view of the product they are designing and they consider all except logistic phase of a product life cycle (material extraction, manufacturing, use, and end of life phases). In particular, manufacturing is given high priority to be considered in design. This could be from the fact that CE is almost applied in all companies nowadays, and it is easy to coordinate and evaluate the manufacturing phase compared to other parts of the life cycle phase.

Crucially, companies responded that they consider sustainability issues mostly at embodiment design phase (60% of the time) and detail or prototyping phase (30% of the time) and never at concept development stage. This gives an intriguing insight as designers have a lot of potential for sustainable innovation at concept design but they don't consider it at this phase. Moreover, design arrives at embodiment stage or prototyping stages after committing a lot of resources (time, cost). If sustainability targets are not met at these phases, designers tend to ignore them and prefer to launch inferior products, since sustainability requirements are considered as something additional comparing to time to market or cost. Even if designers want to improve the sustainability performance of the design, they need to re-iterate the process, which in fact is additional waste of time and cost.

Last, in general companies have no means of using past product's knowledge to be used for future product development. This might hinder the continuous knowledge development inside the company about products' sustainability performances.

5   Conclusion

In this study, we assessed the companies in terms of their level of sustainability practices and found out that companies fail to implement sustainability in product design due to below reasons:

- Decisions depend mostly on cost factors.
- Existent tools are not adapted to designers' needs (especially relevant tools not available for product design phase). Most of the tools present in the literature are not used and even sometimes not recognized by companies.
- Companies especially SMEs consider it as a time consuming and costly activity.
- Companies are mostly focused on improving processes instead of improving products by means of implementation in product design.
- Companies are just trying to meet the minimum requirements asked by legislations despite the efforts from academia side to foster sustainable product innovation.

- Sustainability is not integrated during early design in most of the cases but in the later phases.
- There is not enough coordination and cooperation between academia and industry, which might foster the use of applicable theoretical solutions in practice.

To sum up, cases in this study revealed that the consideration of sustainability is not matured enough to attain the general sustainability goal expected by multiple stakeholders. Thus, academia should not only focus on developing sophisticated tools but also on the need to investigate new way of NPD process structures and to better align strategy objectives with sustainability goals.

6   Limitations and Further Research

First of all, as most of the companies are not interested in such activities or do not apply such practices effectively, it is hard to make a detailed analysis on companies, especially on SMEs. So, it is hard to get respond to requests from the industry side. It is not so hard to see that there is a huge difference between what is in the literature and what is applied in companies' current practices. Another limitation lies in the companies' responds to the questionnaire. For many of the questions, intentional or unintentional bias would occur in the answers as some companies would be willing to see/show themselves more sustainable than what they really are. A potential weakness of the study is the impossibility to use a number of tools and techniques to compare the data obtained by our on-line survey. For example, because of the nature of the data (mostly qualitative) it is difficult to use a correlation analysis or other BI analysis techniques.

From this research, we realize that this topic is still at its earliest stage and the extensions of this research filed are unlimited. Here we recommend the following topics by worthy of further study:

- Further researches should be done taking more cases and samples to better understand the maturity level of integrating sustainability in new product design and development.
- A modified or new method of integrating sustainability criterions into the product development processes that fill the existing gap would be developed for a better application in the industry.
- Sustainable product design in a SBCE (Set Based Concurrent Engineering) environment would be studied.

Acknowledgement. This work was partly funded by the European Commission through the LeanPPD Project (NMP-2007-214090, www.leanppd.eu). The authors wish to acknowledge their gratitude and appreciation to the rest of the project partners for their contributions during the development of various ideas and concepts presented in this paper.

References

1. Gupta, S.M., Lambert, A.J.D.: Environmental Conscious Manufacturing. CRC Press (2008)
2. Ramani, K., et al.: Integrated Sustainable Lifecycle Design: A Review. Journal of Mechanical Design 132 (2010)
3. Hallstedt, S.: A Foundation for Sustainable Product Development. Doctoral Dissertation Series No. 2008:06, P.16, Blekinge Institute of Technology (2006)
4. EU commission (EC).: Eco-design of Energy using Products (2010), http://ec.europa.eu/energy/efficiency/ecodesign/eco_design.en.htm
5. Kerga, E., Taisch, M., May, G., Terzi, S.: Integration of Sustainability in NPD Process: Italian Experiences. In: The IFIP WG5.18th International Conference on Product Lifecycle Management, Eindhoven, Netherlands (July 2011)
6. Melnyk, S.A., Handfield, R.B., Calantone, R.J., Curkovic, S.: Integrating Environmental Concerns into the Design Process: The Gap between Theory and Practice. IEEE Transactions on Engineering Management 48(2) (2001)
7. Cooper, R.G., Kleinschmidt, E.J.: New Product Processes at Leading Industrial Firms. Industrial Marketing Management 20(2), 137–147 (1991)
8. Cooper, R.G., Kleinschmidt, E.J.: Benchmarking the Firm's Critical Success Factors in New Product Development. Journal of Production Innovation and Management 12, 374–391 (1995)
9. Cooper, R.G., Edgett, S.J.: Maximizing Productivity in Product Innovation. Research Technology Management (March 2008)
10. Winner, R.I., Pennell, J.P., Bertrend, H.E., Slusarczuk, M.M.G.: The role of Concurrent Engineering in Weapons System Acquisition. IDA Report R-338. Boston, Massachusetts, USA. Institute for Defense Analyses (1988)
11. Graedel, T.E., Allenby, B.R.: Industrial Ecology. Prentice Hall, New Jersey (1995)
12. Devanathan, S.: Integration of Sustainability into Early Design through the Function Impact Matrix. Journal of Mechanical Design 132 / 081004-1 (2010)
13. Taisch, M., Kerga, E., Helvaci, E., May, G.: Integration of Sustainability in Product Development Process: Supporting Tools. In: Quaderni della XV Summer School "Francesco Turco", September 14-18. Impianti Industriali Meccanici. Porto Giardino (2010)
14. Sakao, T., Fargnoli, M.: Coordinating Ecodesign Methods in Early Stages of Industrial Product Design. International Journal of Environmentally Conscious Design & Manufacturing 14(2) (2008)

Bringing about Sustainable Change
in Product Development: Theory versus Practice

Elli Verhulst[1,2] and Casper Boks[2]

[1] Department of Design Sciences, Artesis University College Antwerp,
Ambtmanstraat 1, 2000 Antwerp, Belgium
elli.verhulst@artesis.be
[2] Department of Product Design, Faculty of Engineering Science and Technology,
Norwegian University of Science and Technology,
Kolbjørn Hejes Vei 2B, 7491 Trondheim, Norway

Abstract. Using a change management perspective, this paper studies the implementation process of life cycle thinking and sustainable design in practice, based on empirical data from eight firms involved in product development. The data indicate that different firms take different trajectories and approaches towards implementation, which in turn depends on a number of human factors, including participation of employees, training, resistance to change etc. As a result of this study, a model for the implementation of sustainable design is presented. Firms can use the model and the insights for the improvement and adaptation of existing methodologies and for choosing a fitting approach for integrating life cycle thinking.

Keywords: sustainable design, life cycle thinking, implementation process, implementation approach, case study.

1   Introduction

The translation and implementation of academic theories, concepts and innovations into successful business applications is a well-known challenge. In the field of sustainable design such challenges exist as well [1]. This field has, since the early nineties, passed through a series of transitions, making this implementation process gradually more complex, as these transitions have for example demanded a shift from a product to a systems perspective, from an environmental to a sustainability context, and from concept development to technology transfer and commercialization [2]. Academic improvements in addressing sustainability criteria in product development have been proposed by many scholars, often in the form of methods and tools [3]. Other scholars propose methodologies for sustainable product development –also referred to as life cycle thinking- that suggest when and how sustainability criteria should be taken account of and which tools may (or even should) be used [4]. Most of these tools focus merely on methodological aspects. Moreover, many of these existing roadmaps offer support for pilot initiatives only, and/or are based on pilot studies only, whilst the main challenge lies with moving from successful pilot initiatives to recurring initiatives that lead to long-term

J. Frick and B. Laugen (Eds.): APMS 2011, IFIP AICT 384, pp. 448–457, 2012.
© IFIP International Federation for Information Processing 2012

sustainability [5]. Literature on sustainability in business offers some approaches that cover a long-term implementation process on a general level within the firm [6]. However in the field of sustainable design, such a holistic view on the complete implementation process is lacking, both from a theoretical and from an empirical perspective.

The field of change management profoundly studies change processes with the aim to support and streamline this complex and lengthy process. A holistic view is thereby taken, whereby methodologies, as well as different approaches and variable influencing factors consider the aim to successfully reach the change. Lewin for example proposed that a process of change can be divided into three stages: unfreezing, changing and refreezing [7]. There is considerable consensus on this three stages model of organisational change [8]. Literature on change management also indicates different approaches that can guide an organisation through these subsequent stages of a change process [9], [10]. These approaches emphasize e.g. a directive, educative or participative approach of the process to reach the goals of the change. Factors that influence a change process can be related to practical and organisational issues, which in turn may have a substantial relationship to personal or emotional factors. This latter group of factors, the human dimension of the implementation process, is so far insufficiently studied in sustainable design research [1,11-13]. This human dimension forms the subject of a broader study that focuses on human factors and how they influence the implementation process of sustainability criteria in product development [14], [15]. This paper forms a part of that study, but limits its focus to the implementation approach that is followed and the process steps that are taken during this specific implementation process.

The aim of this paper is to provide insights - based on an empirical study - on the overall implementation process of integrating life cycle thinking in product development and on approaches that can be taken to reach the sustainability targets. Knowledge on change management is thereby used to broaden insights on the followed trajectories in business. Two research questions are formulated:

I. Which steps are taken in the implementation process of sustainability criteria in product development that support the transformation of academic knowledge into practical applications?
II. Which approaches are used for the implementation process of sustainability criteria in product development?

2   Research Approach

A qualitative case study research approach is used to provide answers to the two research questions and to offer insights on similarities and distinctions between different firms on the implementation process. The empirical data are also used to shed light on the specificity of sustainability as the subject of the incorporation process. Apart from a geographical location in the Benelux for practical reasons, two criteria have been used to select eight case study firms, making it possible to obtain a good understanding of the phenomenon under study [16]: firms were selected that incorporate an own product development department, and have taken at least the first steps towards the integration of sustainability criteria in the firm and in product development. Interviews with company representatives related to both product development and the process of implementing sustainability criteria in product development or in the firm are the main source of data, which is supplemented by archive data, company documentation and observations [17]. The analysis of the empirical data has been done in two main stages, of which the first has a descriptive nature, whereas the latter is explanatory. In a first step, different topics that have been touched upon in the data set were coded and subsequently clustered. A second part of this step contained the description of the phenomenon under study, i.e. the implementation process of sustainability in product development, subsequently followed with an analysis of each case. This step provides insights in the approach, activities a firm has gone through in the implementation of sustainability criteria in the firm. In a last step, a cross-case analysis between the different cases was made, subsequently followed by the development of a model for the sustainable design implementation process.

3 Study Findings

The empirical data for this study is based on almost 20 hours of interview data from eight different medium and large sized Belgian and Dutch firms, from various sectors (including the furniture, electronics, chemical and construction industry). These interview data have been supplemented with observations during meetings with the informants, and several documents such as year reports, sustainability reports and folders, and internal documents. From the respondents that cooperated, eight had clearly defined responsibility in implementing sustainability within the firm and the product development process. The functions of these people vary within the different firms: as a coordinator of CSR, coordinator of quality, health and environment, communication manager, or R&D manager.

3.1 Process Steps

The first research question addressed in this paper concerns the process steps of the implementation process that firms pass in practice. A first stage is indicated in literature to *unfreeze* or prepare for the change, which in this case is the implementation of sustainable design. Table 1 gives an overview of the activities that the case firms dealt with in this preparatory stage in the eight cases. The table indicates that in only one of the cases, all aspects of the preparatory stage are fulfilled. Knowledge on change management was indicated as a basis for any change to occur in this firm. In the other firms however, one or more aspects of this preparatory stage are not prepared or carried out. In three of the cases, less than two elements have been achieved. The empirical data however indicate that independent initiatives are performed to initiate the integration of sustainability criteria, without the preparatory stage being (fully) achieved. The development of a vision, mission, strategy and planning were thereby indicated in several cases to take place after the completion of these independent initiatives. This indicates that the succession of activities during the first stages of the implementation process differs from the activities of this preparatory stage suggested by literature as conditions for success.

Table 1. Overview of activities in preparatory stage

Case	Establish need for sustainability	Build change team	Vision and mission	Strategy general level	Strategy for product development	Planning
Case 1	x	x	x	x	x	-
Case 2	x	x	-	-	x	x
Case 3	x	x	-	x	x	x
Case 4	-	-	-	-	-	-
Case 5	x	x	x	x	x	x
Case 6	x	-	x	x	x	x
Case 7	-	-	-	-	x	x
Case 8	-	-	-	-	x	x

The data thus demonstrates that the development of a vision, mission and general strategy are not necessarily needed as a first step, and more importantly, this implies that a product development department can take the role of initiating the integration of sustainability criteria in product development. However, in order to bring the incorporation of sustainability to a higher, broader and permanent level within the firm, the different elements of the preparatory stage need to be further developed and supported by the management, as illustrated by the following quote:

'We first did some independent, smaller projects with external partners, more because we didn't really know what we wanted to do, so more isolated initiatives. But now there has been decided to take a look at sustainability more profoundly, especially towards the end of the lifecycle of our products. This direction comes from the top management, but the projects are proposed by the R&D managers.' (product developer of case 7)

A second stage in a change process -described as the *change stage* in literature on change management- includes several interventions. In all cases, different activities, projects and actions that are considered to support changes towards sustainability in the firms, were found to take place in the eight case firms. Different interventions were indicated to take place simultaneously as well as consecutively. This suggests that completing a pilot project functions rather as a startup of the implementation of sustainability criteria in product development, but also that multiple product development processes need to be performed before full integration of sustainability criteria in design can be reached. Five types of interventions are identified to occur in practice: *product development projects with specific sustainability goals* (in cases 1, 2 and 7) are projects that focus specifically on certain aspects of sustainability, e.g. on the recyclability of the product's materials. Such projects are considered to run parallel with other, generic product development projects within the firm. *Product development projects with sustainability criteria incorporated in the firm's product development process.* In four of the cases, an adapted methodology was developed and spread throughout the employees within or connected with the product development department. In case 3 for example, sustainability criteria that fit the priorities of the firm, i.e. recyclability of materials, have been included in the different product development process steps starting from the product specifications. In this firm, small but continuous improvements lead to further integration of sustainability criteria in the product development process. In several of the cases, *specific sustainability projects occur on a general level* within the firm. This type of project is directed to raise awareness with the employees on sustainability issues, e.g. a yearly social day (case 7), to improve the overall sustainable profile of the firm, such as efforts on energy-efficiency (case 7), or to improve the overall sustainable image of the firm, such as brochures on sustainability in the firm (cases 3 and 5) or a (renewed) website with sustainability information (case 3). *Research projects on the subject of sustainability* occurred in all cases. In cases 2 and 7, this occurs in the own research department of the firm, as well as in cooperation with external experts and partners. All firms indicated to cooperate with research institutes and universities, either by collaborating in research projects or by outsourcing research to those institutes that are aimed at improving sustainability efforts in the firm. This sort of intervention broadens the knowledge on certain sustainability aspects and strengthens the external network. *Interventions that aim at supporting the overall implementation process of sustainability criteria in product development* are interventions that are not necessarily related to product development projects or to the subject of sustainability, but that are considered to support the implementation process. Training and communication are two examples of such interventions (cases 1, 2, 3 and 5).

3.2   Implementation Approach

The second research question in this paper concerns the implementation approach that is applied in practice for incorporating sustainability criteria in product development. Table 2 offers an overview of the implementation approaches used in the eight cases in this study.

Table 2. Implementation approach used in eight cases, criteria based on [9]

Cases	Implementation approach
Case 1	People are central Change is seen as change in human behaviour Return is respect and appreciation Empowerment of people is important Involvement of all employees is the goal
Case 2	Changing is learning: change people with own motivation and learning capacity Only people that come in contact with product development (PD) and sustainability issues are involved and trained Many procedures are used and followed 'Learning from mistakes'
Case 3	People are central Change is seen as change in human behaviour Return is respect and appreciation Empowerment of product development department is high Product development and sales are strongly involved, production less

Table 2. (*continued*)

Case 4	Opportunities lead towards sustainability
	Opportunities are facilitated and supported
	Implementation is not clearly planned
	Only employees involved in the PD process are involved in sustainability issues
Case 5	Change is very well prepared – rational process
	Goals, measures and results are important
	Many procedures are used and followed
	Results are used as examples of best practices
	Involvement of all employees is the goal
Case 6	Strong focus on combined advantages of sustainability perspective
	Opportunities are facilitated and supported
	Change people with own motivation and learning capacity
	Procedures are developed and applied in practice
	Goals and measures are important
	From voluntary towards obligatory implementation in the PD process
Case 7	Change people with own motivation and learning capacity
	Project-based
	Involvement of all employees is the goal, apart from production
Case 8	Methods and tools are developed to support the design process
	Change people with own motivation and learning capacity
	Voluntary basis of implementation in the product development process
	Project-based
	Involvement of all employees is the goal

The empirical data indicate that few of the firms use a generic approach for incorporating sustainability criteria as 'a change as many others', whereby an approach is consciously used that supports all changes that occur within that specific firm (cases 2 and 5):

> 'We identify the issue -like the green stuff- we find an approach, we run a pilot, we map it on the process, we update procedures and then we identify the training needs. That is done for all changes here. We always go through that same cycle.' (case 2)

All firms however adapted the implementation approach to the firm's culture. An adaptation to the firm's culture is mentioned in literature as an important point of attention to raise the chance of successful implementation [10]. In practice, this adaptation seems to occur naturally, but not always consciously. The data indicate that this leads to interesting differences in approaches that emphasize other elements of the implementation process. In case 4, the creation of new challenges formed the main element of sustainable innovations. In some cases, control, structure and organization form the dominant characteristic in the applied approach (cases 2 and 5), whilst in other cases, the employees are considered as a central element in the process, whereby change is seen as a shift in human behaviour (cases 1 and 3). In half of the cases, change is considered mostly as a learning process, whereby the motivation and learning capacity of the employees is seen as an important element that can provide the changes needed (cases 2, 6, 7 and 8). The empirical data thus indicate that different approaches can lead towards sustainability in product development, depending on the culture of a firm. On the other hand, the subject of change - sustainability criteria in product development - also implies specific points of interest that need attention during the implementation process, such as the complexity of the subject, a lack of clarity on the concept of sustainability and a lack of clear and uniform measurement systems. This adaptation to the subject of sustainability seems to occur less in the firms studied.

4   Discussion

The empirical data in this study indicate a different order of activities during the implementation process of life cycle thinking in design in practice, than the order of activities as suggested in literature, especially in the unfreeze stage. In practice, this stage consists of independent projects that include sustainability aspects, whereas in literature, this unfreeze stage entails the development of a vision, mission, strategy, etc. These activities are indicated to take place in the cases, but often after completion of several of the individual projects. Several interventions are mentioned in the data set to take place both in the unfreezing as in the change stage, whereby different types of projects occur that support the translation of academic knowledge into practical applications. Some of these projects aim at passing theory and knowledge on sustainable design towards employees and partners, whilst other projects aim at supporting the implementation process and its approach. In all cases, external partnerships, amongst others with universities, are created to strengthen the link between theory on sustainable design and its application in the firm. This type of projects is thus recognized in all cases, but might need further exploration to support the implementation process more profoundly.

The insights on the implementation process steps and approaches, together with the results of a broader study on the implementation of sustainable design, have been used as input for the development of a descriptive model. This model shows the main process stages of the implementation sustainable design, as well as it includes human factors that came forward in the broader study. The model combines theoretical insights that have been gathered in a review of sustainable design and change management literature- with the understandings that were gained in practice. This combination of theoretical and empirical insights offers valuable indications on the process steps and human factors for scholars and practitioners to raise their understanding on the implementation process of sustainable design and the human factors within (Fig. 1).

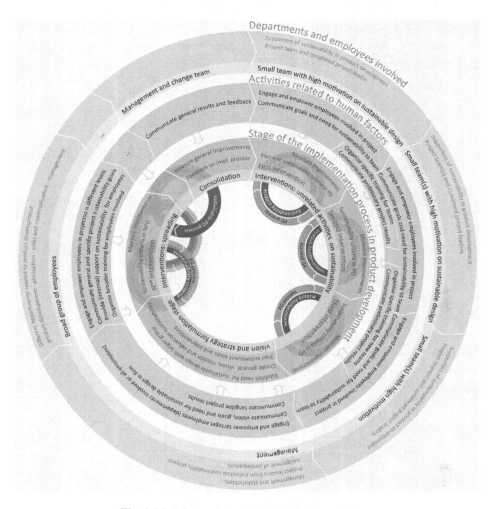

Fig. 1. Model on sustainable design implementation

The model consists of three circles that represent I) the implementation process steps in the inner circle, II) human factors that have been indicated as significant to take account of in each process step, represented in the middle circle, and III) employees or departments that come forward in the study to be involved in the corresponding step of the implementation process, represented in the outer circle. The inner circle offers an overview of the implementation process on a long term. It indicates how firms evolve from one or more pilot projects on sustainable design towards an integrated sustainable design process. The model thereby places the product development process in the broader perspective of the implementation process.

Apart from the process stages in the inner circle, the model presents which human factors are indicated in the study as significant to be incorporated or taken account of in the different implementation stages, such as engaging employees. Several of these human factors appeared to be recurrent in the different stages, e.g. in the subsequent interventions, but directed to another –and growing- group of employees. This expansion of the group of employees involved explains the importance of the third circle in the model, which shows the (new) employees or departments on which the human factors are indicated to apply to, as for those people, that moment forms the start of the implementation of sustainable design. The outer circle also indicates a small number of employees that is indicated to be involved in the beginning of the implementation process. This group of employees is found to grow slowly at first, but suddenly this growth was indicated to be much faster after the development of a general vision and strategy on sustainability in product development and in the firm.

Further research could focus on a validation of the descriptive model by applying it in practice from the start of the implementation process of sustainable design and measuring the success of the process. Another direction for future research is suggested to focus on the implementation process of sustainable design in firms that are active in the same sector and that have a similar organisational culture, with a focus on the choice and application of a specific implementation approach in comparable situations.

5   Conclusion

This paper studies the implementation process of life cycle thinking in practice, starting from empirical data. Knowledge on change management is thereby used to shed light on the processes that occur and the approaches that are taken by the participating firms. The knowledge from change management and the empirical data together provide a holistic view on the complete implementation process in practice, which is currently lacking in the field of sustainable design, both from a theoretical point of view as from an empirical perspective. This study indicates that different trajectories are followed that depend on the context of the firm. Moreover, variable approaches are indicated to occur in practice in which differences in emphasis are put on methodology, participation of employees, training, etc. A descriptive model is presented in the paper that shows the relationships between three levels in the implementation process of sustainable design: process, human factors and employees and departments involved. It offers a visual overview on how the process can be approached on these three levels. To both firms and scholars, this model and the insights from this study for the improvement and adaptation of existing methodologies may be useful for both scholars and firms, and guide them in choosing a fitting approach for integrating life cycle thinking in product development.

References

1. Baumann, H., Boons, F., Bragd, A.: Mapping the green product development field: engineering, policy and business perspectives. Journal of Cleaner Production 10, 409–425 (2002)
2. Boks, C., McAloone, T.: Transitions in Sustainable Product Design Research. International Journal of Product Development 9(4), 429–449 (2009)

3. O'Hare, J.A.: Eco-innovation tools for the early stages: an industry-based investigation of tool customization and introduction. PhD thesis at University of Bath, Department of Mechanical Engineering, UK (2010)
4. Brezet, Van Hemel: Ecodesign: a promising approach to sustainable production and consumption. Rathenau Institute. TU Delft and UNEP, Paris (1997)
5. Wilson, E., MacGregor, G., MacQueen, D., Vermeulen, S., Vorley, B., Zarsky, L.: Innovating for environment and society: an overview. IIED Briefing Business models for sustainable development (2009)
6. Dunphy, D., Griffiths, A., Benn, S.: Organizational change for corporate sustainability, 2nd edn. A guide for leaders and change agents of the future. Routledge, New York (2007)
7. Lewin, K.: Field Theory in social science. Greenwood, NY (1951)
8. Kanter, et al.: Managing change in organisations. Simon and Schuster, NY (1992)
9. de Caluwé, L., Vermaak, H.: Leren veranderen. Een handboek voor de veranderkundige. Kluwer, Deventer (2006)
10. Kotter, J.P., Schlesinger, L.A.: Choosing strategies for change. Harvard Business Review, 130–139 (July-August 2008) (reprint of original article from 1973)
11. Verhulst, E., Boks, C., Stranger, M., Masson, H.: The human side of Ecodesign from the Perspective of Change Management. In: Advances in Life Cycle Engineering for Sustainable Manufacturing Businesses – Proceedings of the 14th CIRP Conference on Life Cycle Engineering, pp. 107–112 (2007)
12. Boks, C.: New academic research topics to further ecodesign implementation: an overview. International Journal of Product Development 6(3/4) (2008)
13. Boks, C.: The Soft Side of Ecodesign. Journal of Cleaner Production 14(15-16), 1346–1356 (2006)
14. Verhulst, E., Boks, C., Masson, H.: Colour-print thinking to measure and support human factors in the implementation process of sustainability criteria in design. In: Proceedings of EcoDesign 2009, Sixth International Symposium on Environmentally Conscious Design and Inverse Manufacturing, Sapporo, Japan, December 7-9 (2009)
15. Verhulst, E., Boks, C.: The role of human aspects in design for sustainability strategies and approaches. In: Electronic Pre Proceedings of APMS 2010 International Conference, Cernobbio, Italy, October 11-13 (2010)
16. Patton, M.Q.: Qualitative Evaluation and Research Methods. Sage, US (1990)
17. Yin, R.K.: Case Study Research, 3rd edn. Applied Social Research Methods Series, vol. 5. Sage Publications, USA (2003)

Collaborative Innovation: Internal and External Involvement in New Product Development

Bjørge Timenes Laugen[1] and Astrid Heidemann Lassen[2]

[1] University of Stavanger, UiS Business School, 4036 Stavanger, Norway
[2] Aalborg University, Center for Industrial Production,
Fibigerstræde 10, 9220 Aalborg, Denmark
bjorge.laugen@uis.no, ahl@production.aau.dk

Abstract. Industry and academia alike are increasingly becoming aware of the fact that innovation does not take place in isolated cells or functions within the firm. During the last the years the term open innovation has emphasized the importance of internal and external collaboration in order to increase the competitiveness of companies. Although the idea of involving internal and external actors in the new product development (NPD) process is not new, the knowledge about the benefits and pitfalls is still limited. This paper aims to contribute to refining the concept of open innovation, by investigating how strategic priorities influence the degree of external and internal involvement in the NPD process, moderated by contextual factors.

Results based on analyses of 584 companies from the International Manufacturing Strategy Survey (IMSS) 2005 indicate that suppliers are heavily involved in the NPD process in firms in B2C markets aiming at increasing the innovation volume. For B2B companies the reverse picture emerges. However, when the aim is to increase the radicality of new products, suppliers and customers are heavily involved for firms in B2B markets. Further, market uncertainty, and to some extent company size, seems to moderate the relationships between strategy and involvement considerably.

Keywords: Strategic priorities, NPD collaboration, survey.

1 Background

The term 'open innovation' was introduced by Chesbrough (2003), suggesting that innovation does not and should not take place on isolated islands within a company, but rather involve actors broadly both internally and externally to the company. Chesbrough (2003) argues that a shift from closed to open innovation principles is necessary for business survival.

However, the idea of involving internal and external actors in the innovation processes of companies is hardly new. Rothwell (1994) argued that '[t]hese practices include internal organizational features, strong inter-firm vertical linkages, external horizontal linkages' (Rothwell 1994). Internally, collaboration between production and R&D to avoid the 'throw over the wall' problem has been on the agenda for a

J. Frick and B. Laugen (Eds.): APMS 2011, IFIP AICT 384, pp. 458–469, 2012.
© IFIP International Federation for Information Processing 2012

long time, through concepts such as integrated problem solving (Wheelwright and Clark 1994), design-for-manufacturing (DFM) (Susman 1992), computer aided design/manufacturing (CAD/CAM) systems, and concurrent engineering. Externally, market-pull and customer involvement in NPD, including lead user involvement (von Hippel 1998), have been proposed to counteract the dominant technology-push paradigm and to ensure that the NPD process develops products the market actually requests.

Several researchers have focused on cooperation between different business functions, such as R&D, marketing, manufacturing and engineering, in product development projects within an organization (i.e. Griffin and Hauser 1996; Adler, 1995), or investigated a broad spectrum of cooperative relationships with such diverse partners as customers, suppliers, research institutes, competitors, co-suppliers, and distributors (Anderson et al. 1994; Gemunden et al. 1996; Hagedoorn 1993), to enhance success in product development.

Some of the benefits with external collaboration are that close linkages with suppliers can reduce development cost and increase development speed (Rothwell 1994, p. 18). Further, accessing external know-how can also speed up new product development, as can buying or licensing-in existing technology. In cases of technology fusion, external alliances should, on the face of it, help to reduce both the time and the cost of developing radical new products (Rothwell 1994, p. 20).

Powell et al. (1996) argue for networks as the locus of innovation, through access to complementary competence and resources. 'Rather than using external relations as a temporary mechanism to compensate for capabilities a firm has not yet mastered, firms use collaborations to expand all their competencies' (Powell et al. 1994, p. 143). This study was performed based on a sample of more than 200 biotech firms, primarily from the US.

Other authors argue that inter-organizational collaboration might imply access to complementary assets, foster knowledge transfer and spreading R&D costs (Faems et al. 2005). Studying 221 Belgian manufacturing firms Faems and colleagues (2005) find that the more firms engage in a variety of different inter-organizational collaborations, the more likely they are to create new or improved products that are commercially successful. Moreover, this study shows that collaboration with different types of partners coincides with different types of innovation outcomes.

Investigating eight in-depth case studies O'Connor (1998) finds that customers play an important role in providing input for incremental product development, but do not usually know the requirements for radically new products. She claims that conventional market research techniques focusing on product level problems, rather than application market level, may discourage major innovations. This is also in line with Christensen (1997), who argues that existing customers in general contribute with knowledge related to the existing product paradigm, but do not contribute with knowledge related to disruptive innovations.

Connor (1999) argues that information from the market and customer is important for various types of innovations to take place. Slater and Narver (1998, 1999) also recognize the importance of customer and market input, but emphasize the importance to distinguish between the two by stating that innovative firms need to be market-led rather than being customer-led. Being customer-led is, according to Slater and Narver (1999), to satisfy the buyers' expressed needs. Being market-led is to develop products with superior benefits, by trying to discover the customers' latent needs beyond what the customers are able to express and specify. Market-led companies, however, do not ignore the expressed needs of the existing customer base, but dedicate a considerable proportion of their activities on understanding the latent needs of the customers (Slater and Narver 1999).

All of the above show that rather than depicting open innovation as a radically new idea, it is more appropriate to consider it as a phenomenon that has organically developed and matured over a considerable period of time. The concept of open innovation condenses, to the extent that it has recently started to generate quite some attention in both industry and academia, mostly triggered by Chesbrough's (2003) work. However, despite its popularity, the concept of open innovation is not coherently well-developed and operationalized in scientific terms, and the benefits have hardly been rigorously documented and tested empirically.

Considering the statement that open innovation is necessary for business survival, Chesbrough (2003) implicitly suggests that internal and external involvement in innovation processes affects a firm's strategic outcomes. There is evidence, as outlined above, that internal and external collaboration may lead to improved performance or innovation outcome. However, there are weaknesses related to some of these studies considering sample size, industry representativeness, geographical selection, and so on. Further, we are not aware of studies that empirically investigate how the pattern of external and internal collaboration in NPD relates to the strategic priorities of firms. Insight into the link between strategic priorities, and external and internal collaboration would help researchers and managers to develop an understanding and knowledge about how to effectively manage and organize NPD efforts and innovation processes by designing effective internal and external relationships. The main purpose of this paper is to explore the relationships between opening up the NPD process to actors internal and external to the firm and their competitive strategy. We therefore investigate the following research questions:

RQ 1: How does firms' competitive strategy relate to collaboration with internal and external partners in the NPD process?

RQ 2: How do contingencies influence these relationships?

2   Methods Used

2.1   Data

To analyze the research question we use data from the International Manufacturing Strategy Survey (IMSS IV) database. The database consists of 711 companies in 23 countries representing a wide range of manufacturing and assembly industries (ISIC 28-35). We removed outliers based on company size, which reduced the sample to 628 companies.

2.2   Operationalisation of Variables

Strategic Priorities

The responding companies' competitive strategy is operationalized in the questionnaire through the companies' order-winners, measured on five-point Likert-scales. We ask the respondents to indicate the current importance of 11 strategic priorities, ranging from 'Not important' (1) to 'Very important' (5). From these we focus on four priorities closely linked with innovation activity and strategy. These are 'superior product design and quality', 'wider product range', 'offer new products more frequently', and 'offer more innovative products'.

Involvement

Furthermore, the questionnaire contains questions prompting the respondents to indicate to what extent the marketing and manufacturing departments, suppliers and customers are involved in the NPD process. The degree of involvement is measured on five-point Likert-scales, from 'no collaboration' to 'high collaboration'.

Position in the Supply Chain

To investigate possible effects from the companies' position in the supply chain, we split the sample into two groups indicating whether the companies operate in business to business (B2B) or business to consumer (B2C) markets. Companies with a proportion of sales larger than 60 % to system integrators and finished products manufacturers are categorized as B2B (N = 234). Companies with a proportion of sales larger than 60 % to wholesalers/distributors and end users are categorized as B2C (N = 350). 44 companies could not be classified based on these criteria and were left out of the analyses.

Contextual Contingencies

Company size was measured as number of employees in the plant.

Market uncertainty was measured as the average value of one variable measuring market span and one variable measuring market dynamics, both by using five-point Likert-scales. Market span ranging from 'few segments' to 'many segments', market dynamics ranging from 'declining rapidly' to 'growing rapidly'. Before the merging of the variables these were transformed into three-point scales. For market span values 1 and 2 were set to 1, the value 3 to 2, and the values 4 and 5 to 3. For market dynamics the values 1 and 5 were set to 3, the values 2 and 4 to 2, and the value 3 to 1, in order to capture the degree of change irrespective if this is decline or growth.

2.3   Analyses

We analyze the relationships between the variables using regression analyses, where the order-winners (representing a company's competitive strategy) are used as independent variables, and the degree of internal and external involvement is used as dependent variables. We also control for the direct and moderating influence of the two contextual factors, company size and market uncertainty. We did the analyses separate for B2B and B2C environments in order to capture the possible effects of this contingency.

Table 1. Results of the regression analyses. The standardized coefficients (beta) are reported. Sig. level: $* = p < 0,1$, $** = p < 0,05$, $*** = p < 0,01$

	B2B (N = 234)				B2C (N = 350)			
	Suppliers	Manufacturing	Marketing	Customer	Suppliers	Manufacturing	Marketing	Customers
				**	**	***	***	***
(Constant)	-,060	,127	,211	,104	-,004	-,325	,081	-,163
Product design	,293	,084	,424	-,221	-,568**	-,461*	-,246	-,006
Product range	-,741*	-,368	-,186	-,626	,504*	,877***	,560*	,118
New products more frequently	,723**	,452	,389	,586*	,016	,170	,417*	,007
More innovative products	,643	,364	,285	-,132	-,400	,001	,417	,091
Company size	,017	,312	,751*	,210	-,063	,008	,408	-,360
Market uncertainty	-,630	-,166	,324	,321	,209	,182	,304	,206
Product design *Size	,584	-,031	-,412	-,274	,049	,499	-,096	,408
Product design *Uncertainty	,230	,006	-,236	,084	,490*	-,012	-,135	-,456
Product range * Size	-,511	-,004	-,378	,103	,640*	,652*	,392	,246
Product range * Uncertainty	,541	,211	-,181	-,289	-,399	,075	-,314	-,100
New products more frequently *Size	,943*	,386	,394	,961*	-,660*	-1,166***	-,496	-,290
New products more frequently * Uncertainty	-,696*	-,381	-,192	-,023	,232	-,256	-,275	,168
More innovative products * Size	-,954*	-,560	-,384	-,609	,108	-,173	-,369	,049
More innovative products * Uncertainty								
r^2	0,099	0,058	0,121	0,126	0,067	0,044	0,108	0,036
Sig.	0,106	0,603	0,030	0,020	0,078	0,427	0,001	0,630

3   Results

3.1   B2B

For companies in B2B markets we find mixed and insignificant relationships between pursuing product design or wider product range as strategic priorities and the involvement of internal or external parties. Companies competing on launching new products frequently have a negative relationship with the involvement of suppliers (beta=-0,741, p<0,1), and negative and insignificant relationships with the other actors. For companies competing on launching more innovative products the reverse picture emerges. The relationships with involvement of suppliers and customers are positive (beta=0,723, p<0,05, and beta=0,586, p<0,1, respectively). The relationships with manufacturing and marketing involvement are positive but insignificant.

Considering the influence of contingencies we do not find company size or the degree of market uncertainty to have a significant direct influence on any of the collaboration parties, except for marketing involvement in highly uncertain markets (beta=0,751, p<0,1).

These contingencies do not moderate the relationships between the strategic priorities product design and wider product range, and the involvement of internal and external parties in NPD, either. However, the relationship between frequent launch of new products and involvement of suppliers and customers are moderated positively by market uncertainty (beta=0,943, p<0,1, and beta=0,961, p<0,1, respectively). These findings indicate that companies with a strategic focus on launching new products frequently actively involve external parties in the NPD process when market uncertainty is high. Further, the relationship between launching more innovative products and involving suppliers is moderated negatively by company size (beta=-0,696, p<0,1), indicating that large companies involve their suppliers less in the NPD process when pursuing this strategic priority. The moderating effects from size on involving the other actors are negative but insignificant. The same pattern holds for the moderating effects of market uncertainty. Firms pursuing a strategy of more innovative products are less likely to involve suppliers in the NPD process in highly uncertain markets (beta=-0,954, p<0,1).

3.2   B2C

For B2C companies we do not find any significant relationships between product design strategy and the involvement of internal or external parties in the NPD process. Offering a wider product range has negative relationships with the involvement of suppliers and manufacturing (beta=-0,568, p<0,05, and beta=-0,461, p<0,1, respectively). Launching new products frequently has positive relationships with the involvement of suppliers, manufacturing and marketing in the NPD process (beta=0,504, p<0,1, beta=0,877, p<0,01 and beta=0,560, p<0,1,respectively). Launching more innovative products has a positive relationship with the involvement of marketing (beta=0,417, p<0,1).

Size and market uncertainty do not have significant direct relationships with the involvement of internal or external parties in NPD. Further, the relationships between product design strategy and involvement in NPD are not moderated significantly by size or market uncertainty. The relationship between wider product range and involvement of suppliers in NPD is moderated positively by company size (beta=0,490, p<0,1). Market uncertainty moderates the relationships between wider product range and the involvement of suppliers and manufacturing (beta=0,640, p<0,1, and beta=652, p<0,1, respectively). Market uncertainty negatively moderates the relationships between a strategy aimed at launching new products frequently and the involvement of suppliers and manufacturing (beta=-0,660, p<0,1, and beta=-1,166, p<0,01, respectively). The relationships between launching more innovative products and involvement of internal or external actors are not moderated by size or market uncertainty.

4   Discussion

Companies competing on superior product design do not seem to have any particular degree of involvement of internal or external parties in the NPD process. This finding indicates that internal and external parties are involved to some extent in the NPD process, but to a varying degree and without a consistent pattern among the respondents. An explanation could be that some companies involve other actors actively, while others leave the responsibility to the NPD function to maintain the issue of product design.

In B2B markets we do not find any significant degree of involvement of external or internal actors in the NPD process for companies focusing on developing a wider product range, indicating that internal and external actors are to some extent involved in NPD but without any clear pattern. In B2C markets however, we find low involvement of suppliers and manufacturing. This finding indicates that the NPD function for broadening the product range takes place without involving these actors. An explanation for this could be that developing a wider product range is based on further exploitation of existing product platforms, and this is a task which primarily requires technical modifications of the existing portfolio. For such products, incoming parts and materials are most likely similar to the existing product portfolio, so close collaboration with suppliers should not be necessary. Similarly, manufacturing should be aware of the challenges of the manufacturability of the existing products, so there should be no strong needs to involve manufacturing actively.

Suppliers are to a very low degree involved in NPD by companies in B2B markets aiming at launching new products more frequently. The involvement of the other actors is also low, but these relationships are insignificant. These findings seem to suggest that the NPD function is responsible for increasing the volume of innovation and does not seek advice or competence in other internal functions or external actors, in particular so for suppliers. The reverse picture emerges for companies in B2C markets. Here we find a high involvement of all actors, except for customers. An explanation for this could be that companies search more broadly for new ideas to be able to develop new products on a regular basis. The marketing function could provide market information and market needs that NPD can transform into new products. Instead of involving the customers directly in the NPD process, which could be difficult in B2C markets if there are many customers, the marketing function may aggregate customers input to information useful for NPD. This could explain low direct customers involvement. Manufacturing could on the one hand suggest modifications on the existing product portfolio and through that contribute in the innovation process. On the other hand, manufacturing may have to be more involved when the volume of innovations increases, in order to ensure the manufacturability of the new products. Earlier research (Laugen and Boer, 2007) suggests that the importance of involving manufacturing in the NPD process increases with the volume of new products launched, and that it becomes affordable to establish processes and organizational arrangements for this when higher volumes. Why we do not find a similar finding of manufacturing involvement for B2B markets is not clear.

In B2B markets suppliers and customers are heavily involved in NPD for companies focusing on launching more innovative products. This finding suggests that B2B companies search the expertise among external actors in order to develop more radically innovative products. This is at odds with some literature arguing that customers and suppliers generally are unable to provide input and knowledge about radical and disruptive new products (Christensen 1997, O'Connor 1998). This issue will be discussed more thoroughly in section 4.2 below. In B2C markets, however, we only find a strong involvement of the marketing function. These findings seem to confirm the arguments of (Christensen 1997, O'Connor 1998), on the lack of contribution from suppliers and customers in radical innovations. The high involvement of the marketing function could indicate that market information is important for development of radical new products, but not the type coming from existing customers. The difficulties in sharing information between the two functions have been widely acknowledged in the NPD literature (Brown and Eisenhardt, 1995; Griffin and Hauser, 1992; Li and Calantone, 1998; Song and Dyer, 1995). Marketing and NPD usually have different objectives, and may thus value different forms of information (technological vs. market) in developing new products differently. Innovativeness, though, should enhance the firm's internal alignment between NPD and marketing. Innovativeness is based on a shared vision, support for new ideas, and risk taking behavior. Thus, innovativeness eliminates the cross-functional communication barriers and coordinates the activities of NPD and marketing (Brown and Eisenhardt, 1995). Our findings seem to confirm Brown and Eisenhardt (1995), namely that marketing is actively involved in the NPD process when the aim is to develop more radically new products.

4.1   Interaction Effects from Contingencies

The relationships between product design strategy and involvement do not seem to be moderated by company size or market uncertainty.

The same is the case for developing a wider product range strategy for companies in B2B markets. In B2C markets though, we find that larger companies involve suppliers to a higher extent in NPD than smaller firms. Companies pursuing a strategy for a wider product range also involve suppliers and manufacturing function actively when the market uncertainty is high. Growing markets and exposing the business to many segments could imply the need to producing higher volumes of both existing and new products. An explanation for involving suppliers more could be that the companies need stable deliveries of materials and components, and involving the suppliers in the NPD process could reduce the risk of unstable deliveries. Manufacturing would need to be involved to handle different products in manufacturing and maybe also because the production vo- lume needs to be scaled up due to growing markets and larger market span.

In B2B markets, companies focusing on new products more frequently tend to in- volve suppliers and customers in the product development if there is high market uncertainty. For companies in B2C markets, however, the reverse picture emerges. Pursuing a strategy of launching new products more frequently is significantly nega- tively related to the involvement of suppliers in the NPD process, if high market un- certainty. The same is the case for involvement of manufacturing. These findings seem to suggest that there are considerable differences among B2B and B2C compa- nies, in terms of how they involve internal and external parties in the NPD process.

In B2B markets, supplier involvement seems to have a negative relationship with more frequent launch of new products, while supplier involvement seems to be more important in uncertain markets. First mover advantage or short time-to-market be- comes more important in uncertain markets and requires companies to increasingly involve their supply chain and suppliers in the launch of new products.

4.2   Involvement in NPD in B2B vs. B2C Markets

According to literature, customer and supplier involvement is regarded more impor- tant in B2B than B2C markets (Campbell and Cooper, 1999; Hartley et al. 1997; Ragatz et al. 2002). Our findings seem partly to confirm existing theory. It seems to be the case for companies aiming at developing more innovative products, which could suggest that suppliers and customers could provide ideas for more radical prod- ucts. Regarding suppliers this could be through providing new technological solutions which could lead to the development of radically new products. Customers could contribute to radically new ideas by providing information about new needs. Our finding is also in line with Rothwell (1994), who argues that external alliances can reduce time and cost of radical product innovation projects. B2B market can be re- garded as more professional markets than B2C, some customers can probably be re- garded as lead users (von Hippel 1988). Tessarolo (2007) argues that firms in a B2B context, its suppliers, and its customers usually share a mainly cognitive and technical approach to the product - as opposed to the mainly perceptive perspective of the cus- tomer in a business-to-consumer context. Furthermore, each supply chain actor is technically qualified since it has its own development processes and can easily share what it knows and wants with the other entities (i.e., customers and suppliers) in- volved in the process. In other words, the type of information exchanged, which usually entails the exchange of e.g. CAD drawings or well-defined product metrics (e.g., technical specifications for the product or process, performance requirements), is easily understood by all three players, and the media used for the exchange (e.g., e- mail, network-enabled electronic data interchange (EDI) systems, face-to-face meet- ings) are well established and familiar to all three players. (Tessarolo 2007). In B2C markets, on the contrary, our findings suggest that external actors do not seem to be heavily involved in the NPD process when the companies aiming at developing radi- cally new products. This is in line with much literature stating that suppliers and customers do not provide input suitable for developing radical type innovations (Christensen 1997, O'Connor 1998).

However, customer and supplier involvement does not seem to be important for B2B companies aiming at developing new products more frequently. This finding, thus, is at odds with the existing literature (Campbell and Cooper, 1999; Hartley et al. 1997; Ragatz et al. 2002). Although, when companies in B2B markets aiming at developing new products more frequently in markets with high market uncertainty they tend to rely on the involvement of suppliers and customers. So, our findings refine the literature regarding involvement of external actors in the NPD process for companies in B2B and B2C markets, by adding the element of strategy as a determining factor, as well as market uncertainty and size as a moderating variable.

5   Conclusion

5.1   Contribution

The paper contributes to refining current contributions on open innovation by providing empirical evidence of how collaboration in the NPD process relates to the strategic order-winners of firms. Supplier involvement appears to be negatively related to the frequency of launch of new products as an order winner in B2B markets, while involving suppliers is positive in B2C markets. However, in markets with high uncertainty the reverse picture emerges for both B2B and B2C companies. Firms aiming at developing more innovative products involve external actors actively in the NPD process in B2B markets. These relationships are moderated negatively in markets with high uncertainty.

In B2C markets the marketing function is heavily involved for companies aiming at developing new products more frequently or more innovative products. Manufacturing involvement is considered negative to develop a wider product range, while positive for developing more new products. In B2B markets, we find no clear pattern on the internal involvement in NPD.

The findings raise interesting questions as to when and where the use of open innovation is appropriate; a discussion of these questions which will facilitate a much needed detailing of the open innovation proposition.

5.2   Managerial Lessons

The findings in this paper lead to a set of suggestions for managers. First, the degree of internal and external involvement in NPD depends largely on the firms' strategic priorities. If the aim is to increase the volume of development of new products, or if the aim is to increase the innovativeness of the products, companies should choose two different paths in selecting what actors to involve in NPD. Further, depending on the position in the supply chain, B2B or B2C, the degree of involvement differs considerably between the strategic priorities. Finally, market uncertainty is an important moderating factor for the relationships between strategies and involvement and must be taken into consideration by managers when dealing with these issues.

5.3   Limitations and Further Research

In this paper we investigate a set of innovation-related strategic priorities, and investigate the relationships with involvement of internal and external actors in the NPD process. Although the innovation-related strategy measures are relevant, there are of course several other strategic priorities that might influence the choice of involvement in NPD. There are reasons to believe that both external and internal actors can be involved in order to reduce cost and development time, and to increase the firms' quality and flexibility. Further investigation into how a broader set of strategic priorities relate to involvement in NPD could reveal this.

Further, we investigated the involvement of manufacturing and marketing, and suppliers and customers. These actors are in the literature considered to be highly important to involve in the NPD process, but there are other both internal and external actors that could be taken into account.

We investigated the direct and indirect influence of size and market uncertainty on the relationships between strategic priorities and involvement, in addition to the separate analyses for B2B and B2C markets. Other contingencies, such as innovativeness, industry type and production process, could contribute to an increased understanding of the relationships.

References

Adler, P.S.: Interdepartmental interdependence and coordination: The case of the design/manufacturing interface. Organization Science 6(2), 147–167 (1995)

Anderson, J.C., Hakansson, H., Johanson, J.: Dyadic business relationships within a business network context. Journal of Marketing 58, 1–15 (1994)

Brown, S.L., Eisenhardt, K.M.: Product development: Past research, present findings, and future directions. Academy of Management Review 20(2), 343–378 (1995)

Campbell, A.J., Cooper, R.G.: Do customer partnerships improve new product success rates? Industrial Marketing Management 28(5), 507–519 (1999)

Chesbrough, H.W.: The logic of open innovation: managing intellectual property. California Management Review 45(3), 33–58 (2003)

Christensen, C.M.: The Innovator's Dilemma. Harvard Business School Press, Boston (1997)

Connor, T.: Customer-led and market-oriented: A matter of balance. Strategic Management Journal 20, 1157–1163 (1999)

Faems, D., Van Looy, B., Debackere, K.: Interorganizational collaboration and innovation: Toward a portfolio approach. Journal of Product Innovation Management 22, 238–250 (2005)

Gemunden, H.G., Ritter, T., Heydebreck, P.: Network configuration and innovation success: An empirical analysis in German high-tech industries. International Journal of Research in Marketing 13(5), 449–462 (1996)

Griffin, A., Hauser, J.R.: Patterns of communication among marketing, engineering and manufacturing - a comparison between two new product teams. Management Science 38, 360–373 (1992)

Griffin, A., Hauser, J.R.: Integrating R&D and marketing: A review and analysis of the literature. Journal of Product Innovation Management 13(3), 191–215 (1996)

Hagedoorn, J.: Understanding the rationale of strategic technology partnering: Interorganizational modes of cooperation and sectoral differences. Strategic Management Journal 14(5), 371–385 (1993)

Hartley, J.L., Zirger, B.J., Kamath, R.R.: Managing the Buyer–Supplier Interface for On-Time Performance in Product Development. Journal of Operations Management 15(1), 57–70 (1997)

Laugen, B.T., Boer, H.: New product development and manufacturing integration – a contingency approach. In: Proceedings of the 14th Annual International EurOMA Conference, Ankara, Turkey (2007)

Li, T., Calantone, R.: The impact of market knowledge competence on new product advantage: conceptualization and empirical examination. Journal of Marketing 62(4), 13–29 (1998)

O'Connor, G.C.: Market learning and radical innovation: a cross case comparison of eight radical innovation projects. Journal of Product Innovation Management 15, 151–166 (1998)

Powell, W.W., Koput, K.W., Smith-Doerr, L.: Interorganizational collaboration and the locus of innovation: Networks of learning in biotechnology. Administrative Science Quarterly 41(1), 116–145 (1996)

Ragatz, G.L., Handfield, R.B., Petersen, K.J.: Benefits Associated with Supplier Integration into New Product Development under Conditions of Technology Uncertainty. Journal of Business Research 55(5), 389–400 (2002)

Rothwell, R.: Towards the fifth-generation innovation process. International Marketing Review 11(1), 7–31 (1994)

Slater, S.F., Narver, J.C.: Customer-led and market-oriented: Let's not confuse the two. Strategic Management Journal 19(10), 1001–1006 (1998)

Slater, S.F., Narver, J.C.: Market-oriented is more than being customer-led. Strategic Management Journal 20, 1165–1168 (1999)

Song, X.M., Dyer, B.: Innovation strategy and the R&D–marketing interface in japanese firms: A contingency perspective. IEEE Transactions on Engineering Management 42(4), 360–371 (1995)

Susman, G.I. (ed.): Integrating design and manufacturing for competitive advantage. Oxford University Press, New York (1992)

Tessarolo, P.: Is integration enough for fast product development? An empirical investigation of the contextual effects of product vision. Journal of Production Innovation Management 24, 69–82 (2007)

von Hippel, E.: The Sources of Innovation. Oxford University Press, New York (1988)

Wheelwright, S.C., Clark, K.B.: Accelerating the design-build-test cycle for effective product development. International Marketing Review 11(1), 32–46 (1994)

3D Printing for Rapid Manufacturing: Study of Dimensional and Geometrical Accuracy

Hirpa G. Lemu and Safet Kurtovic

Department of Mechanical Engineering and Materials Technology
University of Stavanger, N-4036 Stavanger, Norway
Hirpa.g.lemu@uis.no

Abstract. 3D printing (3DP) is one of the innovative developments in rapid prototyping (RP) technology. The goal of the initial inception and progress of the technology was to assist the product development phase of product design and manufacturing. The technology has played an important role in educating product design and 3D modeling because it helps students/designer to visualize their design idea, to enhance their creative design process and enables them to touch and feel the result of their innovative work. This paper presents the results of the study done on the in-built potentials and limitations of 3DP technology when used for rapid manufacturing purposes.

Keywords: 3D printing, rapid prototyping & manufacturing, printing accuracy.

1   Introduction

Rapid prototyping (RP) technologies are nowadays widely applied for production of parts that are based on additive fabrication principles. The technology integrates key disciplines and sets a different approach to the traditional procedure from design to manufacturing where 3D physical model of any shape directly from a Computer aided design (CAD) model is built layer by layer. As one of the leading RP technologies, the inception and development of 3DP technology has highly contributed in the product development phase of a product. Among others, the technology provides a unique opportunity to control the material composition [1-3] of the product by jetting different powder-based materials from different nozzles. The technology is playing an important role in educating product design and 3D modeling because it helps students/designers to visualize their design idea and to enhance their creative design process. It stimulates innovative work because it enables designers to touch and feel the result of their idea. It simplifies communication between different actors of a product, even with nontechnical ones.

Further, it enables to develop prototypes at a comparatively high speed and low cost. The development of many other capabilities and techniques such as selective use of different materials, suitable post treatment (PT) techniques and color printing capabilities have opened many and diverse fields of applications.

J. Frick and B. Laugen (Eds.): APMS 2011, IFIP AICT 384, pp. 470–479, 2012.
© IFIP International Federation for Information Processing 2012

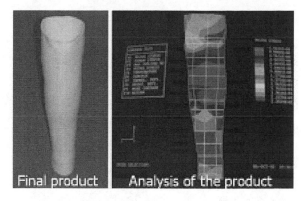

Fig. 1. Example of integrating 3DP with finite element analysis, adapted from [4]

These include pattern making, design aids for tooling equipment, anatomical modeling and prototyping of human organs and implants, reconstructive surgery aids and others. Emerging new applications are also enabling 3DP machines to satisfy further scientific and engineering needs such as molecular modeling and the presentation of the results of finite element analysis (FEA). The biomedical area represents a typical example where integration of 3D modeling, 3D printing and FEA play a significant role in the future (Fig. 1). As physical testing of prostheses is demanding, full FEA in this area can open opportunities to apply the gained knowledge on new designs. In recent years, the application of RP technology in medical area has grown and a new discipline, known as medical rapid prototyping (MRP) is in the making [5]. The advance in this direction will involve manufacture of accurate 3D physical models of human anatomy derived from medical image data.

Another potential area is integration of advanced 3D modeling technologies with thermal and flow analysis through computational fluid dynamics (CFD) simulation. This enables application of advanced solid modeling techniques such as NURBS to improve the shape for aerodynamic performance. The prototype can easily be built in 3DP, without tooling, and digital or physical testing enables integration of advanced 3D modeling, 3D printing as well as digital and physical testing. Some researchers indicate, however, that this technology as a rapid manufacturing tool remains at present more of a goal than reality for the industry [6].

Based on the huge potential that 3DP technology can play in the future to realize true RP&M, many 3DP products with varying capabilities are now available on the market. One of the most future oriented 3DP technologies is marketed by Z-Corporation (Z-corp.) that is based on MIT's ((Massachusetts Institute of Technology) ink jet technology. This 3DP variant is classified as a typical "concept modeler", a low-end system, and represents the fastest RP process. It is rapidly spreading worldwide and it has become the third most widely used layered manufacturing equipment within three years of its early market life [7].

On the other hand, the availability of diverse technologies in 3D printing has created certain level of challenge for the user because of varying capabilities and limitations to a particular need. Literatures published within the last decade indicate that complexity of part geometry, material used in the prototyping model, compatibility with 3D CAD models and other technical aspects still need in-depth study. The major problems focused in those recent researches include: accuracy and limited availability of materials [8], porosity [9], and surface finish [10]. These limitations can result in limited range of mechanical properties. Additional research issues of 3DP at current stage involve part size and profile (including thickness), compatibility with 3D CAD models and other computer aided tools, application ranges and customer satisfaction.

Our in-house experience with the use of Z510, one of the latest machines from Z-corp., also indicates the need for further research to clearly identify the potentials and limitations of this technology. The study partially presented in this paper is aimed to build a full capability profile of 3DP technology including dimensional and geometrical accuracy, data transfer compatibility, surface roughness, build time and strength (in terms of wall thickness) of this technology. In the end, the accumulated knowledge from such studies will contribute in classification of the 3D printing qualities in accordance with international standards.

2   Brief Description of the Z510 3DP and the Printing Process

The study reported in this article is based on the capabilities and limitations of Z510 3D printer (3DP). This machine was selected because the CAE laboratory of the University of Stavanger owns the machine.

The part building method using RP technologies has a series of important features or procedures (Fig. 2) that are in general almost identical for all RP machines. All of the technologies require input of a solid model from a 3D CAD system, usually as slices. The designed model from a CAD system is then tessellated and exported to a suitable file format. With its development roots in the 1960s, STL-format is the current industry standard for facetted models. The STL file represents the model using information about the coordinates and outward surface normal of triangles. At this phase, the technology integrates CAD and CAM (computer-aided manufacturing) avoiding elaborate process planning and machine set up activities.

When the part model is ready in the printing machine, two important processes take place upon pressing the start button: (1) the software calculates how the layers look like for the model and (2) printing starts when five layers are calculated. This is one of the features of 3DP that makes it best in terms of the building speed. The manufacturers claim that 3DP from Z-corp is 5 – 10 times faster than other RP technologies. The machine uses a default layer thickness of 0.1016 mm; if not a particular layer thickness is selected by the operator.

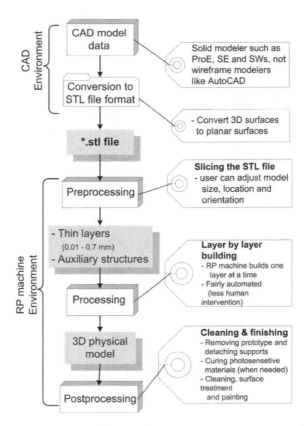

Fig. 2. Common features or procedures of RP technologies

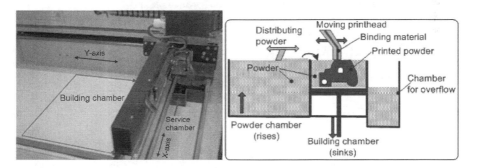

Fig. 3. Coordinate system definitions and components of the part building area in 3DP

Figure 3 shows the definition of the coordinate systems and the important components in the part building area. By convention, the data slicing takes place in the X–Y plane and the part is built in the Z direction. The movement along the X-axis is designated as the slow speed axis and its task is to lay the binding materials. The Y-axis, on the contrary is a high speed axis. These two movements cover the 2D geometry of the development area of the model. The volume is then defined by the vertical movement of the building chamber corresponding to the layer thickness.

As illustrated in Figure 3 (right), the printer performs 5 different operations in the process of printing (adding a layer of powder).

1. Lowering the powder chamber
2. Moving the printhead back the powder chamber
3. Lifting the powder chamber
4. Lowering the building chamber   and
5. Distributing the powder from the powder chamber to the building chamber.

Some 3DP machines need warming up to 38^0 C so that the binding material sets quickly. Latest machines, such as Z510 – the one available in our laboratory, however, do not need this. It warms up after the model is developed so that it can cure.

3   Tests and Materials

There are many possible sources of surface inaccuracy of products produced by 3D printing process. For instance, error in data exchange process at preprocessing, part positioning and layer thickness at processing, and finishing works or post print operations at postprocessing phase can be mentioned. Closer observations show that achieving accuracy as specified by manufacturers is not always an easy task. Based on the experience of the existing limitations and supported by indications from the literature study, some test cases were identified. This paper presents the tests done on the following selected cases:

- influence of file transfer formats on part accuracy,
- achievable accuracies such as flatness and surface finish and
- minimum wall thickness.

Z510 uses mainly four powder materials. The main powder material used in the tests conducted as part of this study is ZP 131, high performance composite powder that is material of choice for color printing. The other three materials, i.e., elastomeric material, ZP14 Investment casting material and ZCast 501 Direct metal casting material, are considered as special material types for prototyping parts with specific need.

4   Discussion of Test Results

4.1   Influence of File Transfer Formats on Part Accuracy

All RP machines by default use STL (standard template library or streriolitography file format). Observing inaccuracies compared with manufacturer specifications, a comparative study between the data transfer formats was proposed. The rationale to make this test is also that STL file format is an old file transfer format from 1970's that has been used to describe straight lines and planar surfaces. The format cannot represent curved surfaces exactly. Z510 supports four file formats: STL (standard), VRML, PLY and 3DS. The CAD system used for 3D modeling of the part (Solid Edge) on the other hand supports, among other neutral file formats, the STL and VRML file formats that are compatible with 3DP. For this test, a 3D model was developed (Fig. 4(a)) with intentionally introduced features such as cylindrical and prismatic holes with different size and curved external edges. The same 3D model was transferred to 3DP software using the two file formats. The printed prototypes are shown in Fig. 4(b) and (c).

Geometrical Deviation: The difference in geometrical deviation between the two printed models is clearly visible with a naked eye. The inaccuracy in the cylindrical (hole) surface, i.e. roundness and the curved edge indicates that the models built using STL file transfer are less accurate than those built from VRML files. The VRML file format without exception produces circular features with better accuracy because it approximates curved edges with finer chords resulting in better circularity or profile form accuracy. The accuracy improves when the radius of the curve/circle decreases.

Dimensional Deviation: Dimension of models built from each file format were measured and compared with the original dimensions in the CAD model. The results of selected dimensions are shown in Fig. 5 together with tabulated dimensions. Apart from a couple of exceptions, the results show that interior dimensions shrink, while exterior dimensions expand in all directions. This indicates that the material volume increases in both cases. The ZPrint software has a function known as anisotropic scaling with a scaling factor between 0.8 and 1.2 that is intended to compensate for this material volume deviation particularly in experience based generalized scaling. Otherwise, the final product should undergo post print operations such as grinding, cutting or drilling

Though STL file format is the default file transfer format for 3DP and many other data exchange processes, this study reveals that it is not as good as the VRML format in terms of dimensional and geometrical accuracy. This obvious drawback puts a question mark on the possible use of this technology for rapid manufacturing purposes.

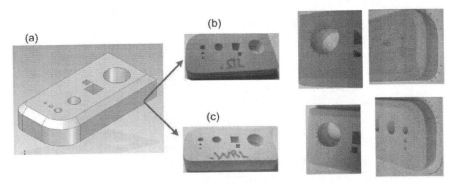

Fig. 4. Test samples: (a) original CAD model (b) part built from STL file as input (c) part built from VRML as input

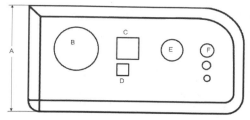

Dimension	CAD model	STL model	VRML model
A	50.00	50.15	50.10
B	Ø20.00	Ø19.55	Ø19.60
C	10.00	9.95	9.80
D	5.00	5.05	5.00
E	Ø10.00	Ø9.70	Ø9.90
F	Ø6.00	Ø5.65	Ø5.70

Fig. 5. Comparison of dimensional deviations

Flatness deviations

X-direction:
Maximum = 0.95 mm
Average = 0.54 mm

Y-direction:
Maximum = 0.45 mm
Average = 0.36 mm

Fig. 6. Test setup and measured and measured values for flatness deviations

4.2   Test for Achievable Surface Flatness

As mentioned earlier, printing in 3DP is done without support structures, i.e. the under laying powder supports the built model. This, on the other hand, influences the accuracy on surface flatness. Though the printing temperature is not so high to create significant thermal deformations, moderately good flatness requirement for relatively thin features may not be expected.

For this test, a simple thin plate of size 100 x 120 x 8 mm was printed and the flatness accuracy was measured using a dial indicator (Fig. 6). The measured deviations show that the flatness error is highest in the X-direction, max. 0.95 and average 0.54 mm, while the deviation in Y-direction is max. 0.45 and average 0.36 mm. According to ISO 2768-2 the general geometrical tolerance for flatness recommended for this size is: H-class (fine) = 0.2 mm, K-class (medium) = 0.4 mm and L-class (rough) = 0.8 mm. This indicates that the 3DP process achieves a flatness accuracy that is almost equivalent to that of machining parts from steel materials.

4.3   Test for Achievable Surface Finish

Though Z-corp [11] claims that their 3DP machines are known to have ultra-smooth surface quality compared with other RP technologies, reports from some published data [12, 13] indicate as this is not the case. Thus, in addition to developing better understanding of the achievable surface quality in 3DP in general and using Z510 in particular, this test was intended to study the influence of post treatment such as hardening and polishing on the surface quality. Further, a surface quality comparison between a surface normal to the building direction (the XY plane) and the surface parallel with the part building direction (XZ plane) was done.

Two parts – untreated part and a post-treated (hardened) part were tested. One face of each sample was polished while the rest were not. Among others, the following materials and equipment were used: polishing machine (Knuth-Rotor 2), epoxy (XD4360), hardener (XD4361) and Mitotoyo surfacetest-20.1.

The Mitotoyo surface test apparatus gives surface roughness qualities in three parameter values: R_A, R_Z and R_T. In order to study the influence of the building orientation and the post treatment on the surface roughness, measurements were done on both as printed and post treated surfaces. The measurements were taken on the surface parallel to the building direction (on XZ-plane) and on one of the surfaces normal to the building direction (on XY- plane).

The test results for these samples are given in Table 1. Apart from few exceptions, the XZ-plane has the highest roughness level as expected. This is due to the stair-steps formed by the layer thickness while building. This roughness is expected to increase for curved edges and surfaces. The results also show that post treatment operations like hardening reduce the possibility to improve the surface quality by polishing.

Table 1. Measured surface roughness values (Ra) in [μm]

	As printed				Hardened			
	Unpolished		Polished		Unpolished		Polished	
Plane	XY	XZ	XY	XZ	XY	XZ	XY	XZ
Sample	A1	B1	C1	D1	E1	F1	G1	H1
Single measurement	7.76	17.74	13.99	9.73	9.84	21.63	0.34	8.7
Average roughness	7.82	16.05	13.40	11.25	9.73	20.95	2.22	6.15

4.4   Minimum Printable Wall Thickness

This test represents the most important part of this project where understanding the lowest possible part thickness that can be safely built is sought. This is especially important in cases of down scaling a prototype. The study was intended to reveal the possible risks of damaging the prototype under the following steps:

1. Processing (part building)
6. Withdrawal from the building chamber
7. Depowdering and
8. Post treatment of the prototype.

Two test models were drawn with features of different thickness (down to 1 mm) and located in the building chamber with different orientations as shown in Fig. 7 (L). The orientations were intended to study the significance of having the part against the XY-YZ walls and XY-XZ walls.

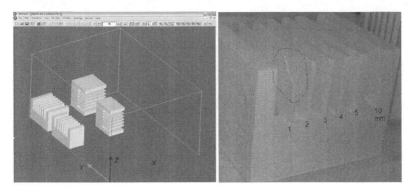

Fig. 7. Part orientation in building chamber (L) and an example of a broken part (R) under test

All of the samples survived the first test (processing stage) while removal from the building chamber was not error free, at least needs extreme care for thin-walled parts. One example of a broken part under this postprocessing stage is shown in Fig. 7 (R). The general conclusion drawn from this test is that orientation of thin-walled parts is very important. With no doubt, resting the face of a thin-walled feature against the XZ-plane increases the risk of damaging the prototype while withdrawing from the building chamber. The study also shows that orienting the weakest geometry against the XY-plane avoids this problem, for instance buckling including due to the part's own weight. This consideration, however, contradicts with the orientation of a part in the building chamber with respect to an optimum printing time. In other word, the orientation that secures good part strength is not always the optimum orientation.

A Case Study: a typical wall thickness problem is of high concern when parts are downscaled to the size that can be printed by the 3DP (maximum 350 mm). Several cases were studied including a bobsled that was modeled in the CAD tool and printed. The model with maximum length of 3200 mm was downscaled to 10% size and this represents an obvious challenge for the wall thickness. As illustrated in Fig. 8, several weak points were observed that needed extreme care during postprocessing. Repeated trials indicate that experience in handling and positioning avoids some of the observed failures.

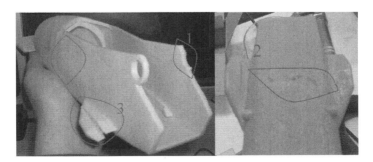

Fig. 8. Examples of inaccuracies and failures on printed bobsled

5   Conclusion

Initiated by in-house experience with the use of 3DP, the study on dimensional and geometrical accuracy of Z510 from Z-corp. has been reported in this article. The investigated limitations are of course not limited to this specific 3DP machine. Experimental tests on the influence of file transfer formats on part accuracy, dimensional and geometrical deviations and minimum wall thickness were studied. The research findings indicate that both dimensional and geometrical deviations take place on printed parts and the size of the deviations depends on the type of file transfer format. This study reveals also that STL format in general is not as good as VRML format. While the achievable flatness accuracy of 3DP in general is comparably as good as machining operations, the achievable surface roughness depends on the layer thickness and geometric form. The wall thickness is an important factor to be considered particularly when the part is to be downscaled. The study results indicate that manageable minimum wall thickness depends on several factors including the positioning of the part in the chamber.

Acknowledgement. The technical support provided by Y. A. Amith is appreciated.

References

1. Hopkinson, N., Hague, R., Dickens, P.: Rapid Manufacturing: An Industrial Revolution for the Digital Age. Wiley, Chichester (2006)
2. Jackson, T.R., Liu, H., Patrikalakis, N.M., Sachs, E.M., Kima, M.J.: Modeling and Designing Functionally Graded Material Components for Fabrication with Local Composition Control. Mater. Design 20(2-3), 63–75 (1999)
3. Cho, W., Sachs, E.M., Patrikalakis, N.M., Troxel, D.E.: A Dithering Algorithm for Local Composition Control with Three-dimensional Printing. Comput.-Aided Des. 355(9), 851–867 (2003)
4. http://rehabtech.eng.monash.edu.au/cadcam/INFO/present.htm (last access: April 18, 2012)
5. Hieu, L.C., Zlatov, N., Vander Sloten, J., Bohez, E., Khanh, L., Binh, P.H., Oris, P., Toshev, Y.: Medical Rapid Prototyping Applications and Methods. Assembly Automation 25(4), 284–292 (2005)
6. Dimitrov, D., Schreve, K., De Beer, N.: Advances in Three Dimensional Printing – State of the Art and Future Perspectives. Rapid Proto J. 12(3), 136–147 (2006)
7. Bak, D.: Rapid Prototyping or Rapid Production? 3D Printing Processes move Industry Towards the Latter. Assembly Automation 23(4), 340–345 (2003)
8. Levy, G.N., Schindel, R., Kruth, J.P.: Rapid Manufacturing and Rapid tooling with Layer Manufacturing (lm) Technologies, State of the Art and Future Perspectives. Annals of the CIRP 52(2) (2003)
9. Dimitrov, D., Van Wijck, W., Schreve, K., De Beer, N.: Investigating the Achievable Accuracy of Three Dimensional Printing. Rapid Proto J. 12(1), 42–52 (2006)
10. Karapatis, N.P., Van Griethuysen, J.-P.S., Glardon, R.: Direct Rapid Tooling: A Review of Current Research. Rapid Proto J. 4(2), 77–89 (1998)
11. (March 07, 2011), http://www.zcorp.com/en/Products/Rapid-Prototyping-Machines/spage.aspx
12. Stankiewicz, M., et al.: The Scope of Application of Incremental Rapid Prototyping Methods in Foundry Engineering. Arch. Foundry Eng. 10, 405–410 (2010)
13. Frank, W.L.: Rapid Prototyping and Engineering Applications, A Toolbox for Prototype Development. Taylor & Francis Group, Boca Raton (2008)

Securing Collaborative Business Processes:
A Methodology for Security Management
in Service-Based Infrastructure

Pascal Bou Nassar[1,2], Youakim Badr[1,2], Frédérique Biennier[1,2], and Kablan Barbar[3]

[1] Université de Lyon, CNRS
[2] INSA-Lyon, LIRIS, UMR5205, F-69621, France
{pascal.bou-nassar,youakim.badr,
frederique.biennier}@insa-lyon.fr
[3] Faculty of Sciences, Lebanese University, Fanar, Lebanon
kbarbar@ul.edu.lb

Abstract. In order to secure collaborative business processes, we present a methodological approach that early integrates security and risk management throughout the design process of service-oriented architectures. We develop our methodology based on two complementary axes: the first being the business needs while the second, is ensuring a consistent security between partners at the runtime. The information security is globally applied to business needs, service specifications and infrastructure deployment. Finally, we annotate services with security parameters that could be used to improve the selection of secure services in run-time.

Keywords: Business Processes, Service Oriented-Architecture, Methodology, Risk Management, Business Process Modeling.

1   Introduction

The frequent changes in the organization nowadays, need an alignment of business processes on business strategies, which, at the same time, require a set of methods, tools, management practices and the adaptation of information and communication technologies. Besides, the development of technology led enterprises to go beyond their own boundaries and establish collaborative business processes. This trend increases the need for interoperability not only at the organizational level (i.e. the partners should share common business objectives and management rules) but also at the technological level (i.e. the informational flows should be understood by the different partners). [1]

Recently, the Service-Oriented Architectural style (SOA) proves to be an efficient design method of business processes from independently developed and deployed services. A service consists of a logical representation of a repeatable business activity that has a specified outcome, such as "check customer credit", "provide weather data", or "consolidate drilling reports". A service is also self-contained, may be

J. Frick and B. Laugen (Eds.): APMS 2011, IFIP AICT 384, pp. 480–487, 2012.
© IFIP International Federation for Information Processing 2012

composed of other services, and appears to be a "black box" to its consumers [2]. By such SOA guarantees flexibility and adaptability, which are fundamental characteristics of modern business requirements by enabling services to be dynamically selected and composed [3].

As an attractive solution in implementing business processes and ensuring technical interoperability, SOA seems to be a convenient architecture for inter-enterprises collaboration since it is based on semantic information modeling, which describes the information of the business domain and permits the design of business documents to be used in service interactions between partners. Despite these advantages, SOA raises new challenges related to the information security level between partners. Information security is determining what needs to be protected and why, what it needs to be protected from, and how to protect it. Establishing security involves securing data communications, data in rest, managing access rights, etc. In SOA, a coherent security view must be shared, a trust network should be established, and global security policies' enforcement should be accomplished. For these reasons, managing security is crucial aspect of online business collaboration and should support an end-to-end security strategy at the organizational and technical levels and consider the entire services' life cycle. Services Life cycle is characterized by two main time intervals: Design-time and Run-time, during which, services are transformed from concepts into deployed entities. Services, which are established at design time, should be analyzed, designed, constructed and tested. At the run-time, they are managed, monitored and controlled to ensure their execution as expected.

In our work, we shed the light on both the design and the run-time of secure service-oriented architecture for business collaboration and base our approach on two complementary axes: the first is the business needs for evolving the architecture and optimizing the return on investment; while the second, is ensuring an end-to-end consistent security.

The rest of the paper is organized as follows: Section 2 examines previous methodologies in securing service oriented architectures and discusses the need for improvements. Section 3 presents our proposed methodology covering the design of a secure SOA. Section 4 introduces our proposed architecture for dynamic selection of secure services. Section 5 presents future work and our conclusion.

2   Related Work

Due to the success of service-oriented architectures, many design methodologies have been developed and lead to the maturity in service design [4] [5] [6] [7] [8]. Some of these methodologies focused on business aspects of SOA, while others were more technical. Particularly, the 'Service-oriented design and development methodology' proposed by M. Papazoglou covers both the design and the run-time phases of the service's life cycle. However, we have found that none of the above listed methodologies meets our needs in developing a secure service-oriented architecture.

In [9], the author has integrated a risk managing process in designing SOA applications; however, the work appears to target web services' technology, without emphasizing on the business aspects, which is very important since SOA is an architecture style and not a technology. In our work we will try to fill the above mentioned gaps and we emphasize on the fact that security does not only concern internal actors of the enterprise but also the partners. Therefore, will provide a mean for the partners to express the security capabilities of their services and guarantee the security requirements needed for the provision of a secure collaborative business process.

3   Methodology for Designing Secure SOA

By integrating security and risk management in the SOA design process, we have developed a new methodology (Fig. 1) and this to achieve two complementary objectives: on one hand, it will ensure business alignment, flexibility and reuse of services while on the other hand; it will leverage secure SOA applications by treating the identified security risks.

A successful application of the methodology is based on creating a common dialogue between business and technical managers; stages of the methodology should be well prepared to acquire all available information in order to take the best decisions. The methodology consists in integrating a risk management process into the process of services' design. As illustrated in Fig. 1, we have separated between the 'identification and specification', 'risk management' and 'annotation' phases in order to cover separation of concerns between services, risk management and services' annotations.

In the following subsections, we will emphasize the above mentioned phases.

3.1   Phase 1: Services Identification and Specification

We start in step 1 by identifying the elements of the business domain which are the business objectives, the list of actors and partners, the business strategies and finally, the list of global interactions in between the domain actors. Step 2 is dedicated for the business process and the business document modeling. These tasks are accomplished in two parallel steps because they share a common element: the business document. In step 2A, we focus on modeling the business processes in order to meet business objectives; this is an important step that leads to the identification of business services. In step 2B, we establish a data structured model, which allows us to determine the documents to be exchanged within processes and ensures business interoperability among partners. Subsequently, we identify in step 3, security objectives that cover the business level such as the identification of legal and organizational constraints, the definition of a Protection Level Agreement (PLA) for managing secure interactions between partners. Step 3 must be conducted by the business managers supported by security analysts, brainstorming sessions are also required to determine the appropriate security objectives based on business needs.

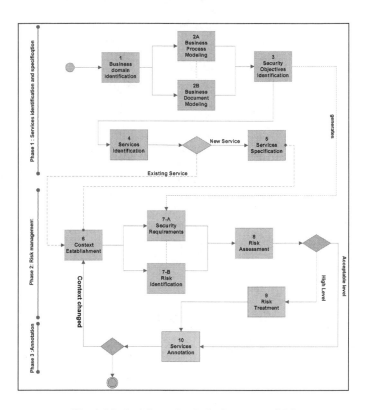

Fig. 1. Methodology for designing secure SOA

In a collaborative business process, activities are realized through local services in addition to the partners' services. Step 4 is dedicated to the identification of these services. We rely on the business process model, established in step 2A, to identify the existing services, the partners' services and the services to create. Step 5 is dedicated to the specification of new services in which we approach the business and technical specifications excluding security aspects, they will be determined following the risk management process. The specification of a service must provide information about the service capabilities and its requirements while hiding the implementation details.

3.2   Phase 2: Risk Management

Implementing a service-oriented architecture never starts from scratch; we always rely on existing resources and services. The integration of a risk management cycle (steps 6 to 9) allows us to study the design context by identifying the existing security measures on relevant elements, improving these measures or creating new ones:

We begin this cycle by establishing the context in step 6; this is done by gathering the business and technical elements forming the design context. Subsequently, we identify in steps 7A and 7B the security requirements and the risks. These steps are accomplished in parallel because they share a common entry: the context establishment. Security requirements are the specification of security objectives; we rely on the security objectives determined in step 3 to derive the security requirements at each of the elements forming the design context.

In our previous work [10], we showed that, in a service environment, managing security and handling threats requires advanced methodologies for risk management. In order to accomplish the risk identification in step 7B, we relied on a threat modeling approach, particularly the Coras approach [11] due to its flexibility to be used in service environments. We also hinge on the context's essential elements and the relevant security requirements to identify the risks, which consist of threat scenarios, threats, vulnerabilities and unwanted incidents. In step 8, we assess identified risks based on their impact and the probability of their occurrence. We recall that the risk is the probability of occurrence of an unwanted event and its impact on resources. We establish the impact's scale in terms of value reduction of the assets (e.g., insignificant, minor, moderate, major) and a probability scale for a fixed period of time. (e.g., rare, unlikely, possible, certain), finally we elaborate a risk evaluation matrix.

In step 9, we take the necessary measures to reduce, transfer, avoid or accept the risks. Security protocols, security mechanisms, security policies, security services are different types of measures that could be implemented or improved. In the next section; we will discuss the security annotation phase.

3.3   Phase 3: Service Annotation

In the service design process, we have decided to annotate the services for multiple reasons:

- Enrich the services' description: Security annotations describe security capabilities.
- Improve the dynamic selection of services: Security annotation could be used in run-time to improve services' selection based on security requirements in addition to functional requirements. This would allow the interconnection of collaborative business processes on the fly.

The main challenge with security annotations is that they must not disclose the service weaknesses' and this by providing private information about essential elements while guaranteeing the security on both service and infrastructure levels. To solve this issue:

1. We set the following security concepts to be included in the annotation:

- Availability: specifying service availability based on mechanisms of redundancy or automatic restoration, for example.
- Privacy: This element must ensure that private data, exchanged or stored by the service is protected against unauthorized access.
- Monitoring: specifying the services of auditing and logging. For example: Policies must be clear, enforced by the partners' systems, service operations must work as expected, etc…

2. We generate a calculated value for each of the above security concepts based on the implemented security measures. The calculated value results from an overall security assessment. Table 1 illustrates a conceptual example in calculating the availability of service "check customer credit". For simplicity purposes, we have chosen three technical elements that constitute the hosting environment of the service.

Table 1. Example calculating the service availability

	Essential element	**Security measure**	**Value**
check customer credit service	Application server	None	0
	Web server	Periodic security updates	1
	Internet Connection	Redundancy	1

The availability value will be 2/3 = 66, 6 % and will represent a level of an overall availability of the technical elements relevant to the service's security. This value in addition to the values of other concepts will form the service's security annotation.

4   Architecture for Secure Services' Selection

Service oriented architectures improve application and business alignment by adapting or creating business processes from distributed services. In a closed environment, invocation and interaction with services are static and service registry is accessible to the enterprise and to its partners. However, in a distributed environment, static interaction with services becomes obsolete and their invocation must be accomplished dynamically. A dynamic SOA provides means to dynamically adapt the architecture on runtime. It allows services to communicate even if they aren't recognized in advance [12].

Service oriented architectures are commonly built using web services standards that have gained broad industry acceptance. Web services architecture is composed of three phases where, in the first phase, service description is published to a registry. The second phase consists in inquiring a service based on its functional parameters. Finally, the binding phase consists in invoking a service from the list of candidate services populated in the registry. In this section, we propose extending the Web services architecture by adding an intermediate service 'Security Broker'. This service allows:

- Publishing secure services' description in the registry.
- Checking and validating of security annotations.
- Selecting web services based on their functional parameters and their security annotations.

The Security Broker is composed of the following modules:

- The publishing module manages publishing functional and security parameters into the registry. It adds the security annotation into the 'security annotation registry' as well.
- The selection module searches for the best service candidate in the registry.
- The 'Security Annotation registry' stores for each service its annotations for further validation.

Fig. 2 illustrates the interactions in services' publishing and selection.

Step 1: The provider publishes the service's description via the publishing module.
Step 2: The security broker publishes the service's description into the registry.
Step 3: The security broker saves a copy of the security annotation into the security annotation registry.
Step 4: The client sends a request to the security broker to select a service based on functional requirements.
Step 5: The security broker searches the registry for services that meet with the functional requirements
Step 6: The security broker validates the security annotations with the security annotation registry and searches for the best secure service.
Step 7: The client binds to the chosen service.

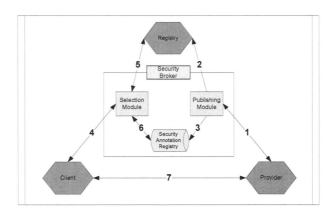

Fig. 2. Architecture for secure service selection

5 Conclusion

Securing collaborative business processes from the early design phases is a must. Security parameters must be taken into account as any other functional parameter. In this work, we have presented a methodology for designing secure service-oriented architectures. Our methodology is based on integrating risk management cycle into the service design process. Besides, we use the security measures to annotate the services with security parameters. Annotations will be used to design new secure business processes or improve the security of business processes created on the fly.

We would like to note that the methodology presented in this work is an overview of the developed methodology which consists of models and best practices to guide the analysts in their work. The details were omitted due to the paper limit space.

Besides, we have presented an extended web services architecture which allows selecting services based on their functional and their security parameters as well.

In our future work, we will enrich the methodology by developing: (1) a secure service model which will be used to improve the security awareness in service's design. (2) a security annotation ontology representing the annotation elements (3) a process defining the security assessment for calculating the security annotation elements' values.

References

[1] Badr, Y., Biennier, F., Tata, S.: The Integration of Corporate Security Strategies in Collaborative Business Processes. Transactions on Services Computing (2010)

[2] The Open Group, SOA white paper, https://www2.opengroup.org

[3] Chaari, S., Badr, Y., Biennier, F.: Enhancing web service selection by QoS-based ontology and WS-policy. In: Proceedings of the 2008 ACM Symposium on Applied Computing, pp. 2426–2431 (2008)

[4] Papazoglou, M.P., Van Den Heuvel, W.J.: Service-oriented design and development methodology. International Journal of Web Engineering and Technology 2(4), 412–442 (2006)

[5] Arsanjani, A., Ghosh, S., Allam, A., Abdollah, T., Gariapathy, S., Holley, K.: SOMA: a method for developing service-oriented solutions. IBM Syst. J. 47(3), 377–396 (2008)

[6] Emig, C., Krutz, K., Link, S., Momm, C., Abeck, S.: Model-driven development of SOA services. Cooperation & Management, Universität Karlsruhe (TH), Internal Research Report (2008)

[7] Bate, C., Mulholland, A., Capgemini, U.K.: A methodology for service architectures (2005)

[8] Zimmermann, O., Schlimm, N., Waller, G., Pestel, M.: Analysis and design tech-niques for Service-Oriented Development and Integration. IBM Deutschland (2005)

[9] Kokash, N.: Risk Management for Service-Oriented Systems. In: Baresi, L., Fraternali, P., Houben, G.-J. (eds.) ICWE 2007. LNCS, vol. 4607, pp. 563–568. Springer, Heidelberg (2007)

[10] Nassar, P.B., Badr, Y., Barbar, K., Biennier, F.: Risk management and security in service-based architectures. In: International Conference on Advances in Computational Tools for Engineering Applications, ACTEA 2009, pp. 214–218 (2009)

[11] Lund, M.: Model-driven risk analysis: the CORAS approach. Springer, Berlin (2010)

[12] Parigot, D., Boussemart, B., et al.: Architecture Orienté Service Dynamique: D-SOA (2008)

Information Management for Manufacturing SMEs

Thorsten Wuest and Klaus-Dieter Thoben

Bremer Institut für Produktion und Logistik GmbH (BIBA),
Hochschulring 20,28359 Bremen, Germany
{wue,tho}@biba.uni-bremen.de

Abstract. Manufacturing SMEs are the backbone of the prosperous German engineering sector. Known for advanced technology and premium quality, they face a constant need to improve their processes. This is especially true for SMEs involved in collaborative production networks. Within these networks, each partner is required to constantly improve their process and product quality. One possible method to accomplish this, is by improving the information management based on the product state. An elementary requirement for such a system is to understand the SME specific challenges. This paper will provide an overview of special conditions of manufacturing SMEs, derive requirements on product state based information management and provide insights and recommendations of implementing such a system by using practical examples.

Keywords: information management, SME, manufacturing, product state, collaboration, in-process, quality.

1   Introduction

The prosperous German economy, seen as an engine of growth within the European Union [1], depends heavily on the strong industrial sector, in particular, the division of mechanical engineering due to its reputation for advanced technology and premium quality [2, 3]. The backbone of this German engineering success are at large the specialized manufacturing Small and Medium Sized Enterprises (SMEs). However, being successful does not necessarily mean that there is no potential for further improvements [4]. On the contrary, as manufacturing SMEs develop over time, they face new challenges brought forth by global competition, which focuses heavily on quality and price. Partly, the manufacturing processes of certain SMEs are not competitive compared to Multinational Enterprises (MNEs) which actively manage their value adding processes [4]. Manufacturing processes are constantly becoming more complex and are increasingly carried out at multiple locations [5]. This developments add to the need to strategically engage in process improvement in order to stay competitive on a global scale. As SMEs are part of collaborative production networks that are actively involved in complex product creation with other companies of different size and organization (e.g. MNEs, SMEs), they have to fulfill certain requirements on both process and product quality or even have use certain technologies for the sake and as a basis of collaborative success (see Fig.1) [6, 7]. Therefore, end product quality does

J. Frick and B. Laugen (Eds.): APMS 2011, IFIP AICT 384, pp. 488–495, 2012.
© IFIP International Federation for Information Processing 2012

not only depend on internal quality of each stakeholder but also on interdependencies amongst these stakeholders. A vivid understanding of these interdependencies can be seen as a basic requirement for improving quality in collaborative networks [8].

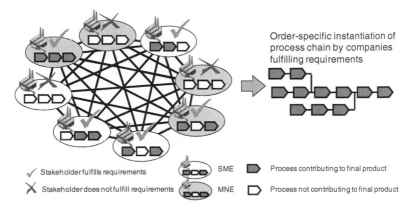

Fig. 1. Necessity for stakeholders to fulfill requirements (e.g. on quality like ISO 9001) in order to participate in collaborative production (compare [5])

Manufacturing SMEs today, even with their highly specialized operations and complex products, often have out-dated solutions for their information management. Another frequently found options is that the companies have up-to-date information management systems but either no trained or responsible personnel or no transparency over the own manufacturing processes and information/data needs.

One important aspect within this area is the ability to continuously derive detailed information of a product throughout the whole manufacturing process, e.g. supported by tracking and tracing. This creates the basis for practical information management systems as well as quality improvement and assurance [9]. On the one side, such a system helps to improve internal quality of stakeholders and thus provides the basis for enhanced quality of the whole network and the final product. On the other side, it provides customers with a continuous proof of the product state [10] along the manufacturing process. In some high-tech industries such as the aerospace industry, there are already specifications in place which enforce a continuous tracing of products and permanent access to connected information throughout the whole supply chain [11]. All companies trying to conduct business within this industry need to prove their capability to comply with these requirements. Other industries, like the food or pharmaceutical industry have to follow rigid legislations as well [12].

In the following section, general characteristics of manufacturing SMEs will be presented incl. two practical example of manufacturing SMEs mainly active in the automotive sector, one producing gear wheels and the other impellers. Section three will shortly introduce information management in the manufacturing industry. Whereas section four will derive requirements and recommendations for manufacturing SMEs which are planning to implement information management. Section five will conclude the paper and will also provide an outlook for further areas of research.

2   Characteristics of Manufacturing SMEs

SMEs represent the majority of companies in Germany and are crucial for the economy [4, 7]. In this section, major characteristics of manufacturing SMEs in Germany with information management will be presented (see table 1).

As the name already implies, SMEs are smaller, both in sales volume and number of employees (less than 250 employees according to EU definition [13]) than for example MNEs. Thereby, the organizational structure of SMEs is less complex and informal [14]. This allows SMEs to be more flexible and react quickly to changing market conditions. They also have strong ties to their customers and have to fulfill the quality requirements that are demanded [15]. At the same time, SMEs have not enough spare personnel to run specialized departments for supporting processes like knowledge management, quality management or Information Technology (IT) [13, 16, 17]. These very important supporting activities [18] often have to be outsourced or must be carried out by employees in addition to their tasks within the primary activities. Similar to human resources, available financial resources are also a limiting factor for most SMEs. The organizational structure can be characterized as less bureaucratic than larger companies [15]. At the same time, the leadership can often be described as being conservative and more patriarchic. Compared to MNEs the company's strategy is not derived of intensive and methodical accurate analyses and market research but dictated by a strong leader, often the owner of the SME. All these factors do affect the IT strategy of SMEs [17]. Often SMEs do not have an in-house IT department to develop own solutions, at the most, they have a few IT administers to keep the infrastructure running. All other IT related needs like software development are often outsourced [17, 3]. SMEs tend to buy tailored solutions for particular problems and try to avoid standardized, companywide and expensive solutions (like SAP). One of the reasons in which SMEs opt out of such a commitment is due to substantial financial and time investment in software licenses and training of employees [19, 13] as well as dependency on regular updates [17].

Table 1. Advantages and Disadvantages of SMEs compared to larger companies [7, 14, 15, 20]

Advantage	Disadvantage
High flexibility	Less financial resources
Less bureaucratic (informal)	Less human resources (e.g. for supporting activities)
Strong ties to customers and suppliers	Often conservative and patriarchic structures
Often low fluctuation	Strategy often dictated by strong patriarch
Strong focus on customer needs	Dependent on few knowledge carriers
Often inimitable knowledge and experience in special area (hard to replace)	Often no strong links to external partners for knowledge transfer (e.g. universities, research institutes)
	No systematic human resource development

In the following paragraphs two practical examples of German manufacturing SMEs with a background in mechanical engineering will be presented. The first company produces a wide variety of products, e.g. gear wheels, for a large and diversified customer base with roughly 220 employees most of them blue collars working in manufacturing. The batch size varies from over 1000 to just a single product. A small number of white collars, mostly engineers, are responsible for production planning and control, product development and quality management etc. They have very limited capacity for anything other than direct value adding processes. The company's IT infrastructure has grown over time and was adapted by new IT solutions of external sources whenever new functionalities were needed.

Lately, the customer requirements on product quality and documentation increased, for example some customers requested a complete product resume for the whole production process. Currently, the company is not able to fulfill this request yet, as, first, the existing information system is not prepared for handling such information and second, there is no comprehensive physical tracking and tracing of individual products from raw material to final product in place yet. Concrete actions tackling the challenge are not planned in the near future as the personnel in charge consider the needed resources, both time and money, as too high. At the moment, the SMEs' strong standing in the market with special product knowledge and one-of-a-kind products allows the company to negotiate these customer demands.

The second company, a 1st Tier automotive supplier, is merely ten years old and just recently reached the mark of 100 employees. The company grows significantly over the last years, doubling their production facilities since 2007. Their main products are impellers for turbo chargers for the automotive industry which they produce in large numbers. The company has up-to-date machinery, high level of automation and prides itself with the high quality of their products. The focus on quality leads to a 100% control of the products at the end of the manufacturing process and additional checks after specific process steps. As the company grows and the output increases, the company experiences that their processes become more complex and are not transparent any more. The company generates a big load of data during the manufacturing process but is as of today not able to fully utilize this potential. The executives slowly acknowledged the problem, especially thinking about the future under the promise of further growth and even higher quality requirements from the customers' side and see the need to improve their information management system. The challenge is, with company and all white collar personnel running at full capacity, to find a way and the time to assess the needs and current condition as well as the future dimensions of the information management system and create an implementation plan.

The experiences of projects with these companies confirmed the observation derived from literature presented at the beginning of the section. In the following sections, an insight on information management in a manufacturing environment is given, also supported by findings of the practical projects with the SMEs.

3   Information Management in Manufacturing SMEs

There are numerous benefits that result from implementing a functional information management system. For a manufacturing company being able to do that, it first has to be capable to track and trace individual products, or at least products on batch level throughout their manufacturing processes. This already implies a major challenge for some manufacturing SMEs. At the companies introduced in section two, it is not possible to track an individual product over the whole chain and attach measuring data at different steps to it. Interestingly, the second company was at the beginning convinced that they are capable of at least tracking batches throughout their manufacturing process but a closer analysis resulted in various pitfalls changing the original order along the process. One of these pitfalls was just the automated loading of machining robot where always three parts stayed in the cell when the batch was changed.

A general benefit of tracking individual products is that companies can combine relevant product and process information and put it to use later. In the manufacturing of small batches or even single products this offers the advantage of always being able to check what process steps the product already passed and what parameters have been used. This can be the basis for an in-process adjustment of parameters based on the product state before each process step to increase quality in terms of reducing scrap and rework. Other benefits include, for example, proof for demanding customers, efficient product life cycle management and feedback in case of product failure.

When thinking of information management in manufacturing SMEs, one of the major points is that the information processes and the information management infrastructure have to be able to handle the increased information flow and put it to use. Or at least the existing IT infrastructure must offer interfaces to add additional solutions providing the information and interpret it in a valuable way. Engineering specific is the sheer amount and variety of possible information based on process parameters and changes of product state along the production chain. This is crucial as without a capable information infrastructure, the additional amount of information and data can cause more problems than doing well by overwhelming users and systems.

Another aspect to be considered thinking of information management is that manufacturing is a very physical and rough environment. Today, information is often still distributed on paper as screens and computers are considered too fragile by some workers. So it is not only the technical challenge but also a question of rising awareness and creating an open mindedness with the critical stakeholders.

4   Requirements and Recommendations for Implementation

Based on the two previous sections, general organizational and operational requirements and recommendations for successful implementation and utilization of a practical information management for manufacturing SMEs will be derived. The focus is on the technical perspective, especially processes and products, to support the SMEs.

In this paper, organizational requirements also include strategic and financial aspects. It is a strategic decision of a company to enforce the implementation of an information management system which involves all hierarchical levels. The management of the SME must not only carefully consider if the company's organizational capability in terms of change management is sufficient but also consider partners and key customers, their demands, interfaces and interdependencies. Furthermore, such a complex project needs qualified personnel with a very specific skill set who can invest the needed time for the project. It is key that there is a commitment from corporate level towards the successful implementation. However, blue collar workers have to be involved as well. Especially in SMEs without highly bureaucratic structures and operation instructions, the blue collar personnel working in manufacturing often have their own unique knowledge and experience and finally will be the stakeholders actively using the newly implemented system on a daily basis. If they are not convinced of the benefits of the change, the success of the project is at risk.

The financial aspect cannot be valued high enough. SMEs with a tighter financial basis need to carefully consider the possible costs of the entire project including hardware, software, testing, training, maintenance etc before starting the implementation considering the Total Cost of Ownership (TCO) over the whole life-cycle. A hands on blind start without a realistic estimation of the total costs can lead to chaos and leave the processes in worse conditions than before the implementation effort if the costs get out of hand and the project has to be abandoned half way.

The operational requirements mainly involve technical requirements and requirements concerning the existing information management including IT infrastructure. On the operational level, a basic and very important requirement is to have transparent processes. This requirement is crucial as without knowledge of the own processes, no serious plan can be developed and a successful implementation is off to a bad start. Furthermore, the own products and the information involved to describe these products during the manufacturing process have to be assessed carefully. The product state based view can offer a valuable concept to structure and quantify the information needs on a process and product level [10, 21].

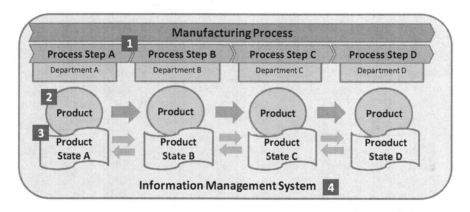

Fig. 2. Main Aspects of the Product State Based View

Fig. 2. provides an overview how the information can be structured through the product state based view. Number one in the figure indicates that the whole manufacturing process has to be considered even so not all process steps take place in one location. In that case it is necessary to think about physical and virtual interfaces between department or company boarders. The physical product (number two) is in the center of the concept. The flow of the physical product is one directional and at each process step value is added to the product and such the product state (number three) changes. The product state compromises all information of the product needed for a successful operation of manufacturing, and thus value adding, processes to reach the desired quality. The product states have descriptive characters and are interdependent to each other. The surrounding information management system (number four), integrates the process (number one) and product (number two/three) information, processes the information if needed [21] and distributes it to the right addressee.

Additionally, stakeholders have to be aware of existing capabilities and the available IT infrastructure. It is important to carefully assess and plan the integration of the new system in the available infrastructure. This is challenging for SMEs with their diversified IT solutions and small IT departments as they might need to add additional functionalities to existing systems and at the same time consult different software providers. To assess the dimension of the planed system, the content, the data and information attached to the product at different stages have to be clear. In this case, a consistent application of the product state based view and thus assessment of the relevant information of the product and process in combination with logistics key performance indicators can help to estimate the dimensions realistically. This part is essential, since it is the basis for developing and dimensioning a possible IT solution.

5   Conclusion and Outlook

This paper gave an insight on the characteristics of manufacturing SMEs. Therefore, an example of two manufacturing SME from the automotive industry were presented. Following the examples, information management in general was elaborated on. Finally, requirements and recommendations for manufacturing SMEs implementing an information management system were offered.

The manufacturing industry is without a doubt a very challenging environment for implementing information management. But there are without doubt numerous benefits of having an integrated information management system for manufacturing SMEs. If a company has a clear vision of its goal and takes the right precautionary measures, the implementation of information management can increase the competitiveness and strengthen the ties to collaboration partners.

But these benefits do not come free of charge. The most significant requirement is transparency of the own processes and products. Also the available IT infrastructure and IT competence within the company have to be considered carefully. The SME has to be able to judge its own capabilities (human, knowledge and finance) unbiased.

In a next step the product state based concept will be developed further. Within this approach, a special focus will be laid on illustration of manufacturing process chain wide interdependencies on the product state characteristic level and derive information needs from customer specifications.

Acknowledgement. This work has been partly funded by the European Commission through ICT Project COIN: Collaboration and Interoperability for networked enterprises (No. ICT-2008-216256). The authors wish to acknowledge the Commission for their support.

References

1. Thesing, G., Randow, J., Kirchfeld, A., Berberich, S., Webb, A.: New Rules And Old Companies. Bloomberg Businessweek 4198, 72–75 (2010)
2. N.N.: The problem with solid engineering. Economist 8478, 71–73 (2006)

3. Fink, D., Disterer, G.: International case studies: To what extent is ICT infused into the operations of SMEs? Journal of Enterprise Information Management 6, 608–624 (2006)
4. Schiersch, A.: Inefficiency in the German Mechanical Engineering Sector. DIW Berlin Discussion Paper 949, 1–27 (2009)
5. Seifert, M.: Collaboration Formation in Virtual Organisations by applying prospective Performance Measurement. Dissertation at the University of Bremen, Bremer Schriften zur Integrierten Produkt- und Prozessentwicklung (2009)
6. Sitek, P., Seifert, M., Thoben, K.-D.: Towards inter-organisational perspective for managing quality in virtual organizations. International Journal for Quality and Reliability Management 27(2), 231–246 (2010)
7. Donath, S.: Methode zur Einführung der RFID-Technologie in KMU. In: Ruhland, J., Kirchner, K. (eds.) Jena Research Papers in Business and Economics 10. Interuniversitäres Doktorandenseminar Wirtschaftsinformatik, pp. 49–56 (2009)
8. Wuest, T., Sitek, P., Seifert, M., Thoben, K.-D.: Organisational and technical interdependencies in collaborative production. In: Proceedings of the 17th International Conference on Concurrent Enterprising (ICE 2011), Aachen, Germany, pp. 343–349 (2011)
9. Van Dorp, K.-J.: Tracking and tracing: a structure for development and contemporary practices. Logistics Information Management 15, 24–33 (2002)
10. Wuest, T., Klein, D., Thoben, K.-D.: State of steel product in industrial production processes. Procedia Engineering 10, 2227–2232 (2011)
11. N.N.: Qualitätsmanagementsysteme, Anforderungen. DIN EN ISO 9100 ff:2000 (2000)
12. N.N.: Regulation (EC) No 178/2002 of the European Parliament and of the Council of January 28, 2002 (2002)
13. Ritchie, B., Brindley, C.: CT adoption by SMEs: implications for relationships and management. New Technology, Work and Employment 3, 205–217 (2005)
14. Wagner, K.W., Zacharnik, M.: Qualitätsmanagement für KMU: Qualität sensibilisieren, realisieren, leben. Hanser Verlag, München (2006)
15. Allan, C., Annear, J., Beck, E., Van Beveren, J.: A Framework for the Adoption of ICT and Security Technologies By SME'S. In: 16th Annual Conference of Small Enterprise Association of Australia and New Zealand, pp. 1–10 (2003)
16. Caldeira, M.M., Ward, J.M.: Understanding the successful adaption and use of IS/IT in SMEs: an explanation from Portuguese manufacturing industries. Information Systems Journal 12, 121–152 (2002)
17. Harindranath, G., Dyerson, R., Barnes, D.: ICT Adoption and Use in UK SMEs: a Failure of Initiatives? The Electronic Journal Information Systems Evaluation 2, 91–96 (2008)
18. Porter, M.E.: On Competition. Harvard Business School Publishing, Boston (2008)
19. Wymer, S.A., Reagan, E.A.: Factors influencing e-commerce adaption and use by small and medium businesses. Electronic Markets 4, 438–453 (2005)
20. Forschungsinstitut Betriebliche Bildung (2011), http://www.qualifizieren-im-betrieb.de/wissensmanagement/warum/besonderheiten/besonderheiten.rsys
21. Irgens, C., Wuest, T., Thoben, K.-D.: Product state based view and machine learning: A suitable approach to increase quality? In: Borangiu, T., Dolgui, A., Dumitrache, I., Pereira, C.E., Vrba, P. (eds.) Information Control for Smarter Manufacturing. Proceedings of the 14th IFAC Symposium on Information Control Problems in Manufacturing, Bucharest, Romania, May 23-25, pp. 190–195 (2012)

Enterprise Information Systems as a Service: Re-engineering Enterprise Software as Product-Service System

J.C. ("Hans") Wortmann[1], Hans Don[2], Jan Hasselman[2], and Alex Wilbrink[2]

[1] Groningen University, The Netherlands
[2] Vanenburg Software, The Netherlands

Abstract. This paper draws an analogy between developments in enterprise software and in capital goods manufacturing industry. Many branches of manufacturing industry, especially automotive industry, have grown in maturity by moving from craftsmanship to mass production. These industries subsequently move from mass production towards mass customization, introducing lean practices. Finally, full maturity is reached by increased servitization resulting in product-service systems (PSS).

This paper analyzes the developments of enterprise information systems in the same terms. The paper shows that the enterprise software follows a similar pattern as capital goods manufacturing industries, with a few interesting differences.

However, lean delivery of enterprise applications is still at the threshold of being practised. Lean delivery requires single versions of applications and delivery in multi-tenant mode. Combining lean delivery with large variety requires automated configuration of application systems components. This is enabled by software-as-a-service from the cloud. Enterprise software "from the cloud" is comparable to servitization in other branches of industry. It goes together with re-engineering enterprise software according to the SaaS paradigm.

Keywords: Enterprise information systems, SaaS, ERP, Cloud computing, servitization.

1 Introduction

Innovation in manufacturing companies has always gone hand-in-hand with investments in plant equipment and capital goods. However, over the last decades a substantial part of the investments has been spent in enterprise information systems (EIS), such ERP, CRM and SCM. This paper studies the question, if production and distribution EIS is comparable to the production and distribution of capital goods and other physical products.

There is a striking analogy between the developments in many physical supply chains and the developments in the supply of enterprise software. In particular, the

J. Frick and B. Laugen (Eds.): APMS 2011, IFIP AICT 384, pp. 496–505, 2012.

industry trends towards mass production, increasing variety, multi tier component supply, lean production and servitization can all be recognized in enterprise software supply networks. Cloud computing allows lean supply to be combined with servitization. However, the combination of large variety, lean supply, and servitization is not yet attained in enterprise software. Such a combination will require configurators of standard software components.

This paper provides a short overview of major trends in supply of physical goods in section 2. The analogy with enterprise software is discussed in section 3. Section 4 concludes the paper.

2   Manufacturing Industry Developments

2.1   From Craft Production to Mass Production

From the beginning of the industrial revolution till the start of the 20th century most production was "craft production" (or one-of-a-kind production). Craft production executes the process of manufacturing by hand with or with the aid of general tools, but not dedicated tools or machinery. A side effect of the craft manufacturing process is that the final product is unique. The product volume for each model was low, while the quality of the product could vary from low to extremely high quality.

2.2   From Mass Production to Mass Customization (Lean)

Lean manufacturing aims to bring back or exceed the quality of craft production and remedy the inefficiency of mass production through the elimination of waste. In order to align the variation of demand towards the supply 'mass customization' principles were applied.

Most manufacturers realized though that craft production practices, as well as mass production and lean techniques were still needed to fulfil customer demand. Each of these practices had their own characteristics and logistical principles. Key distinction was the decoupling between demand and supply: the so called 'customer order decoupling point - CODP' (see e.g. Hoekstra and Romme [1992], and Ollhager [2010]).

In order to manage the variability of products, a new product modelling approach was introduced, allowing to represent product platforms or product families (see e.g. Forze and Salvador, 2002, and Wortmann and Alblas [2009]). Generic Bills of Material, generic process sheets (routings), generic pricelists were containing of all optional engineered products. Based on customer preferences the final product variants were *configured:* created, assembled using existing subassemblies or new produced components (see Figure 1).

As illustrated in the left part of figure 1, the Bill-of-Material structure for a platform takes the form of a diabolo (see Erens [1996]).

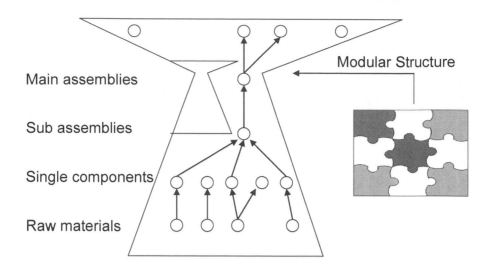

Fig. 1. Product families and platforms

Finally, is should be noticed that the main components of a product family may again be a product family. For example, an engine or gearbox in a vehicle may be a generic product, just like a vehicle. This is illustrated in figure 1 (left) by the small diabolo inside the large diabolo. See Hegge [1992] and Alblas et al.[2010] for elaboration of the generic Bill-of-Material.

In should be noted that there are many configuration solutions which have more domain-specific knowledge than generic bills of material. For example in construction industry, a CAD system for piping solutions can be seen as a configurator, because it allows to create a huge variety of solutions from a limited number of standardized elements (such a pipes with varying lengths and diameters

2.3   From Mass Customization to Multi-tier Components

In order to fulfil the increasing market demand, manufacturers moved to pre-engineered products and services. Subassemblies and modules were standardized. This standardization made the production repeatable at lower costs, due to economies of scale. Tailoring was originally limited to final assembly processes and flexibility was limited to the options provided by the engineers of manufacturers. This results in short lead times: lead times were reduced since subassemblies were made on stock. Interfaces between the standard components were predefined and also standardized.

However, for many sub-assemblies the same principles apply, viz. that their markets enforce the CODP upstream. Accordingly, a world market appears for many products, with an increasing number of tiers and highly specialised manufacturers of materials, components, and subassemblies. The more mature the branch, the more the CODP moves upward. Accordingly, more sophisticated supply chain co-ordination is needed.

Moreover, the number of tiers in the supply network tends to increase, while the number of different suppliers per product tends to decrease. In other words, the manufacturing Bill of Material gets more levels and less components per level. This is also reflected in the Generic Bill of Material.

2.4   From Manufacturing towards Outsourcing and Servitization

In order to survive for manufacturing companies in developed economies, OEM manufacturing firms cannot comprise all value-adding manufacturing activities and at the same time they cannot restrict their activities to manufacturing.

On the one hand, the supply of components had to be outsourced to specialized firms who could apply economies of scale. Outsourcing of non-core activities up or down the supply chain created dynamic business networks to provide value in the most efficient way. Many of the components can be made at lower cost at outside the OEM.

On the other hand, OEM firms have to move beyond manufacturing and offer services and solutions, delivered through their products. Recent technological developments – especially in data capture and information processing – are enabling manufacturing firms to develop new business models, exploiting the potential of their products over the life cycles.

Servitization of capital goods was introduced a few decades ago. An example is the photo copying industry, who started to lease (rather than sell) their machines. In automotive industry, the fleet owners pushed servitization of passenger cars by requesting lease contracts with full service. Life cycle costing became popular in many markets where customers invest in capital goods, and vendors accordingly started to offer service contracts.

In academic literature, the trend towards servitization of physical products is also reflected. Of ten the term *product service system (PSS)* is used (see e.g. Mont [2002], Tukker and Tischner [2006], Aurich et al. [2009], and Shimomura and Hara [2010]). Key elements are:

- a life cycle costing orientation with suppliers and customers
- focus on service level agreements
- ownership of the physical assets stays with the supplier (often an OEM)
- a network of service suppliers has to be organized for delivery.

3   Software Industry Developments

3.1   From Bespoke Software Engineering to Standard Software

Several decades ago, in the 1970s and 1980s, application software was largely bespoke, and bespoke software engineering can be characterized as *craftsmanship.*

Over the years, *complete standard enterprise solutions* (Enterprise Resource Planning) were built, implemented and deployed. The shift from bespoke enterprise information systems to standard software which took place in the 1990-ties is completely in line with the move from craftsmanship to mass production in other branches of industry (see Figure 2 – derived from Womack et al. [1991]).

The client/server based ERP solution was also adopted by the midmarket. The implementation costs were lower and competitive pressure –and therefore the need for automation- also increased for midmarket companies. This is again completely in line with the developments in other markets where the introduction of standard products leads to lower prices and therefore wide-spread adoption in lower market segments.

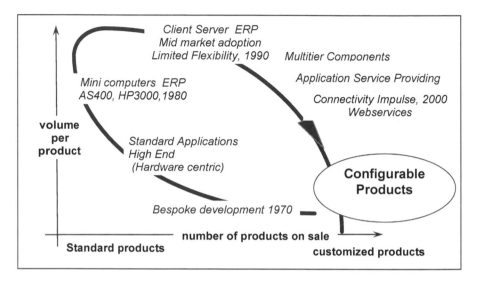

Fig. 2. Development of enterprise applications market

3.2   From Standard Packages to Multi-tier Software Components

Vendors of enterprise applications have always adopted mature standard software components, e.g. the database management system. However, other components, such as the license manager, the UI handler, the development toolkits (based on fourth generation languages), and the runtime environment were all developed and maintained by the ERP vendor.

The need for lower prices and more flexibility makes 'bespoke vendor specific development' replaced by solutions assembled from standard components. Large standard software component suppliers such as MicroSoft, Oracle and Google enter the market with software components and tools which are used by vendors of enterprise applications. This development is completely mirroring the development in physical goods manufacturing.

3.3   Application Service Providing (ASP) by Hosting: A First Step to Servitization

The idea of hosting is not new. *Application Service Providing* (ASP) for long represented the idea of servitization of standard software products. It consists of the following elements:

- The ASP offers the hardware/communication infrastructure to the customer as a service. Therefore, customers do not own this infrastructure and have no operational responsibility. Later this has become known as *infrastructure-as-a-service (IaaS)*
- The ASP offers the systems software, server management, firewalls, database management system and other support software to the customer as a service. Again, the customer does not "own" this software: *platform-as-a-service (PaaS)*
- The ASP offers the application suite to the customer as a service. Therefore, the customer does not "own" the application but relies on the application service provider to make the application available: this offering is called *software-as-a-service (SaaS)*.
- Payment by the customer to the ASP occurs on a periodic basis, based on actual use by the customer of the services provided by the ASP.

It is generally acknowledged that IaaS and PaaS may lead to substantial savings, due to economies of scale, due to virtualization and due to the law of Moore (continued increase of price-performance ration in ICT infrastructural assets). Therefore, pure ASP offerings have been in competition with more general outsourcing value propositions form ICT service providers to customers. Accordingly, the ASP market has grown over the last decade, but Application Service Providing per sé it is not a disruptive technology.

3.4   From Standard Software to Limited Configured Packaged Applications

Standard ERP provides limited flexibility. The flexibility of these applications is determined by parameters. However, parameters increase complexity and costs. The same holds for customization tools. Moreover, customization tools shift the decoupling point back from MTS to ETO and returns to craftsmanship. Altogether, the dominant delivery model of ERP is MTS.

Moreover, the delivery model of standard software packages as ERP is not *lean*. The effort to implement these packages is dramatically high as compared to the mere software costs. After initial implementation, the dynamics of the customer cannot be easily captured to keep the system synchronized with the company progress. Last but not least, the dynamics of the vendor (new upgrades) cannot be properly managed.

These upgrading problems have motivated vendors of monolithic standard enterprise applications to strive for *componentization* of these monolithic applications. Many vendors announced that they split their ERP application to provide more flexibility for upgrading. Accordingly, vendors move towards an *assemble-to-order* mode of delivering configured enterprise applications.

There are three other forces which drive vendors towards this componentization and the accompanying standardizations of interfaces between their components. These are new technologies, integration issues, and business process management.

3.5   Servitization Using Single-Code Based Software Products

Maintaining multiple different versions of a software component implies multiple investments in knowledge, multiple integration problems, multiple functionality issues and technology issues to be solved. This continues to hamper efficiency of service delivery. Multiple versions can never become *lean* delivery. To solve these issues, a variety of customers should be served from a single code base: a service provider has only one version of running code of an application suite, from which all customers are served   *software as-a-service* (SaaS).

Together, IaaS, PaaS and SaaS constitute *cloud computing*. The advantage for the service supplieris, that the single code base dramatically reduces the effort in knowledge management and integration. Companies such as Force (see www.Force.com) claim to offer such a solution. However, this form of software delivery is not easy. For example, the data of all customers have to be kept separated, which is called *multi-tennant* database management.

3.6   Servitization Using Single-Code Based *Configurable* Software Products

The final step to a SaaS offering consists of *configurable* single-code based software components. In addition, a vast variety of vendors can offer other components for which there is a market, much like the *apps stores* in smart phones. Unlike these consumer apps, EIS components have considerable complexity due to at least the following three features:

- Components of EIS manage (structured) data
- Components of EIS collaborate via data integration or business process integration
- They use many devices, requiring adaptable user interfaces and interaction models.

An important question related to *what* is being configured. When thinking in analogies, then classical product configurators use *parameters* for configuration (see Section 2.2.).

If a configurator of enterprise information systems can work with a single code base for every component, it may lead to a very efficient delivery *(lean)* delivery model, which may cover a huge variety of requirements regarding functionality, deployment an ease of use. Such a development would complete the analogy of trends in physical goods and in enterprise information systems towards servitization, agility and variety.

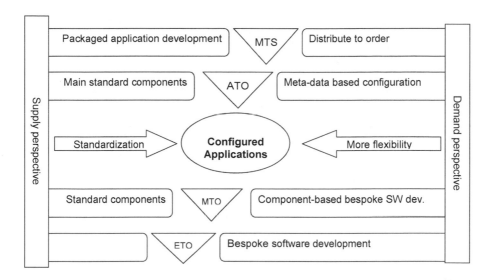

Fig. 3. Customer order decoupling point in enterprise information systems

3.7   Re-engineering the Services Offered by Enterprise Apps

In the realm of physical components, there is a tendency to increase the number of tiers in the bill-of-material. In the lower level components, vendors work for a world market, with a very few competitors. In automotive industry supply, there is only one supplier on earth for all gears inside the movable external mirror of a car. There are only a few suppliers of tires, mufflers, car radios, and so on. The economies of scale drive towards world dominance.

Exactly the same happens in the world of services. Services re-engineering creates a world of very elementary services which are shared across all kinds of applications (including enterprise applications). Some of the basis services which will be needed in a SaaS landscape are already visible.

The services available under a SaaS architecture (see figure 3) are all based on a set of ICT services such as storage (including backup and recovery), communication (including security), etc. On top of these ICT services, *content* related services will be offered.

One service which is needed often is an authentication ("Log-in") service: it constitutes a basic requirement for further user management SaaS applications to build on. A second service is related to open data such as related to the public space (postal addresses, traffic-related data and objects, measurements of noise, radiation, temperature, moist, substance etc.), events (health incidents, fires, calls for police services), statistics, utilities, etc. A third service which will anyway be needed is probably a (micro) payment infrastructure for other electronic services: after all, in business-to-business it is not tenable that all services are for free (as some consumers still believe).

A fourth service which will be needed are services which allow granting authorization to third parties to use functionality or data. On top of such an authorization service, there will emerge the need for more sophisticated services to share documents and allow reuse of content in a way which is traceable, so that it can be licensed and that usage can be controlled. More sophisticated services related to geographic information is also likely to be needed.

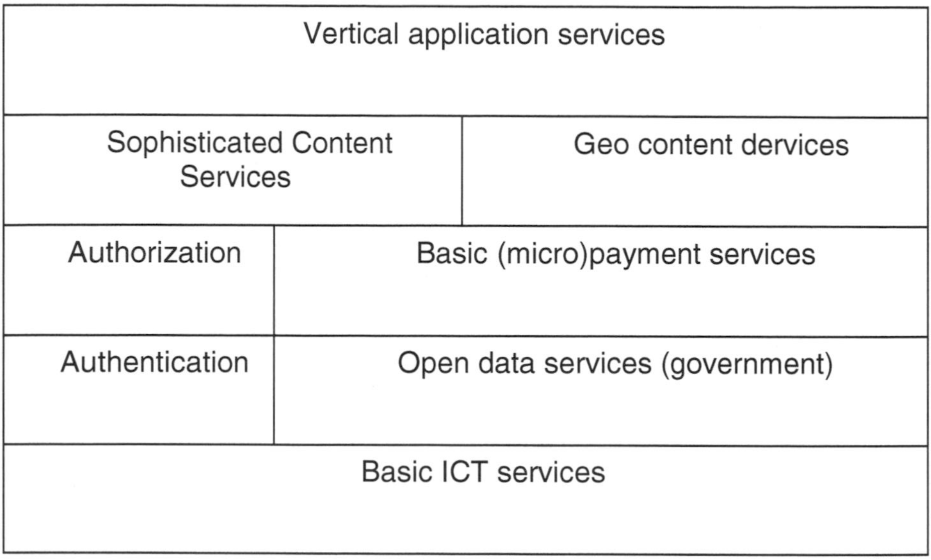

Vertical application services	
Sophisticated Content Services	Geo content dervices
Authorization	Basic (micro)payment services
Authentication	Open data services (government)
Basic ICT services	

Fig. 4. Basic set of services available under SaaS

4   Conclusion

In this paper, we explored the analogy between major trends in delivery of physical products as compared with the delivery of enterprise information systems. The similarities are striking.

Both in capital goods manufacturing and in enterprise information systems the earliest stage of maturity is characterized by craftsmanship. In capital goods, this is encountered as *engineer-to-order* manufacturing and delivery, whereas craftsmanship in enterprise information systems takes the form of *bespoke software development.*

The second stage of development is characterized by standard products. In enterprise information systems, it takes the form of *standard packages of application software,* such as ERP and CRM. Despite parameterization, these products remain standard products. Alternatively, when customization of these products is practised, the route back towards craftsmanship is paved.

Accordingly this paper conjectures that the next step in enterprise information systems is going to be an assemble-to-order delivery model based on configuration of standard main components. It will be a cloud service which has three distinct characteristics that differentiate it from traditional hosting. It is sold on demand, it is elastic -- a user can have as much or as little of a service as they want at any given time; and the service is fully managed by the provider (the consumer needs nothing but a personal computer and Internet access).

References

[1] Alblas, A.A., Zhang, L., Wortmann, J.C.: Representing Function-Technology Platform based on Unified Modelling Language. International Journal of Production Research (2011) (accepted for publication)

[2] Aurich, J.C., Wolf, N., Siener, M., Schweitzer, E.: Configuration of product-service systems. Journal of Manufacturing Technology Management 20(5), 591–605 (2009)

[3] Erens, F.J.: The synthesis of variety- developing product families. PhD dissertation, Eindhoven University of Technology (1996)

[4] Forza, C., Salvador, F.: Managing for variety in the order acquisition and fulfilment process: the contribution of product configuration systems. International Journal of Production Economics 76(1), 87–98 (2002)

[5] Hegge, H.M.H.: Intelligent product family descriptions for business applications. PhD dissertation, Eindhoven University of Technology (1992)

[6] Hoekstra, S., Romme, J.A.C.: Integral logistic structures. McGraw-Hill (1992) ISBN 0 7707552 8

[7] Meijler, T.-D., Pettersen Nytun, J., Prinz, A., Wortmann, J.C.: Supporting Fine-Grained Generative Model-Driven Evolution. Journal of Software and Systems Modelling (SOSYM) 9(3), 403–424 (2010)

[8] Mont, O.: Clarifying the concept of product-service system. Journal of Cleaner Production 10, 237–245 (2002)

[9] Olhager, J.: The role of the customer order decoupling point in production and supply chain management. Computers in Industry 61(9), 863–868 (2010)

[10] Shimomura, Y., Hara, T.: Method for supporting conflict resolution for efficient PSS Development. CIRP Annals – Manufacturing Technology 59(1), 191–194 (2010)

[11] Tukker, A., Tischner, U.: Product-Services as a Research Field: Past, Present and Future. Reflections from a Decade of Research. J. of Cleaner Prod. 14, 1552–1556 (2006)

[12] Womack, J.P., Jones, D.T., Roos, D., Sammons Carpenter, D.: The machine that changed the world: the story of lean production. HarperPerennial (1991) ISBN 0 0609417 9

[13] Wortmann, J.C., Alblas, A.A.: Product platform life cycles: a multiple case study. International Journal of Technology Management 48(2), 188–201 (2009)

An Agile Governance Method
for Multi-tier Industrial Architecture

Juan Li[1,2], Frédérique Biennier[1,2], and Chirine Ghedira[1,3]

[1] Université de Lyon, CNRS
[2] INSA Lyon LIRIS, UMR5205, F-69621, France
[3] Université Lyon 1, LIRIS, UMR5205, F-69621, France
{juan.li,frederique.biennier}@insa-lyon.fr,
cghedira@liris.cnrs.fr

Abstract. To fit the ever-changing business context, developing large scale net-worked and collaborative strategies involve increasing both enterprise and information system agility and interoperability. At the same time, lean and six sigma theories have also been used in industries to improve the industrial process itself so that profitability, quality and reputation are increased. In order to achieve these goals, an efficient and comprehensive governance method is necessary. However, mostly existing governance methods are isolated, they do not allow a dynamic composition of monitoring services, and they lack of a converging Business Process Management and Service Oriented Architecture as a holistic ecosystem. To overcome these limits, this paper propose an agile governance method for multi-tier industrial architecture, this architecture can couple the IT service principles with the Lean-6 sigma theories. This comprehensive governance architecture could eliminate monitoring blind spot lead to eliminate waste and defects.

Keywords: Service-Oriented Industrial Governance, SOA, Lean Six Sigma.

1 Introduction

To fit the renewed globalised economical environment, enterprises have to develop new large scale networked and collaborative strategies, involve increasing both enterprise and information system agility and interoperability. This trend has been favored by the development of interoperable and rather agile IT technologies based on services leading to SOA-based information systems reorganization. At the same time, lean and six sigma theories have also been used in industries to improve the industrial process itself so that profitability, quality and reputation are increased. One of the key points of lean six sigma consists in monitoring each step of manufacturing process and business service information as well as avoiding blind spots for governance.

However, most of the existing industrial services architecture governance methods are rather "fixed" and lack agility, overall perspective governance as they have unilateral perspective, just focused on the service level or IT vision. They do not support efficiently dynamic collaborative organization. As these isolated governance systems

J. Frick and B. Laugen (Eds.): APMS 2011, IFIP AICT 384, pp. 506–513, 2012.

do not allow a dynamic composition of monitoring services and these service strategies lacks (by now) of an efficient governance system coupling the different layers of this complex ecosystem (including business strategies, business/industrial/IT services, execution platforms and infrastructure means).

To overcome this limit, we propose a multi-layer industrial service governance method, introducing the motivation and background (section 2). After, section 3 presents our multi-tier governance architecture's. Lastly, section 4 presents discussion and further works.

2   Background

In order to manage the increasing complexity of information technology systems and to deliver maximum real business value, Enterprise Architectures (EA) have been developed more than 20 years [1]. An EA explains how all the information technology elements in an organization – systems, processes, organizations, and people – work together as a whole [2]. Enterprise Architecture Framework (EAF) defines how to organize the structure and views associated with an EA [3].

A well functioning EA Governance is necessary to achieve a successful IT organization. Appropriate governance methods enable IT to become a key differentiator in creating an agile, adoptable enterprise [4].

Weill, P. and Ross, J. have presented that even some organizations have noticed the importance of EA Governance, most of the EA Governance methods separate the IT governance from business-performance metrics. There is still a big gap between business requirement and IT technology capacity, and it is difficult to make them understand each other [5].

Consequently, with the evolution of technology and management, industrial organization commonly has three layers: business layer, service layer, IT infrastructure layer. Service layer is an abstract layer connects business layer and IT infrastructure layer. Service-Oriented Architecture (SOA) is becoming the architectural style of choice in many enterprises.   One of SOA's greatest strengths is its enhanced flexibility of services. It enables agile business processes and loose couple with specific technology [6]. Figure 1 gives a high-level view of the various SOA layers [7].

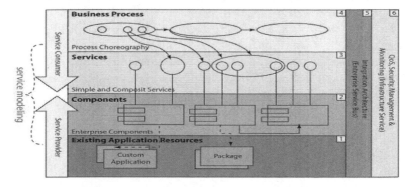

Fig. 1. High-level view of SOA layers (from Business-driven development IBM: http://www.ibm.com/developerworks/webservices/library/ws-bdd/)

Due to the nature of SOA: demand for better business and IT alignment, the discipline of SOA governance has evolved. SOA governance defines the organizational structures and processes that are required to successfully adopt SOA, it helps minimize complications. SOA governance increases the connection among business processes, functional capabilities, organizational entities, end users, applications, and data. So SOA governance is a must if a company is to maintain and grow market share in a marketplace where customers expect and demand speed of delivery.

Numerous models for SOA Governance have been proposed so far. Michael N. and Julian E. et al. presented an approach for a generalized SOA Governance model. They identified six main components which form a mechanism for the optimal support of governance activities for an SOA system in a company. Nevertheless their SOA governance model, (as the most of SOA Governances) lack of ability to govern the IT infrastructure and ignore the infrastructure performance could impact the service performance [8]. Jan B. and Detlef S. outline a reference model for SOA governance that is based on the standardized SOA-RM [9] and motivated from aspects relevant to methodologies for SOA [10]. However, their model is conceptual and they did not propose approach to connect their model to common frameworks for IT governance and Enterprise Architecture. SOA Governance methods, cannot give a comprehensive perspective of industrial governance to combine the IT infrastructure ability with the business benefits. To face the challenge of improving competitiveness we need increase both enterprise and IT system agility and interoperability.

At a business layer, governance aims at managing business process, leading to BPM approaches. There is widespread usage of the terms Business Process Management (BPM) and SOA interchangeably. According to Gartner [11], Business Process Management "organizes people for greater agility," while SOA "organizes technology for greater agility." Business processes need to adapt to changes in the operating conditions and to meet the service-level agreements (SLAs) with a minimum of resources. According to Toyota case study, business processes hide inefficiencies. One has to follow the flow of information as the design evolves into the finished product [12]. Another good example of the benefits of BPM is the classic Ford case, from Hammer and Champy's seminal work [13].

With the recent economic turmoil, there is a trend of practically applying Lean 6 six sigma principles into industrial organization. This trend of combining six sigma quality with lean speed, which needs comprehensive governance methods to govern business, services and infrastructure performance, and clear interdependence of different layers' non-functional properties.

To overcome existing technological and organizational limits and lead the trend of utilizing Lean Six Sigma theory into collaborative industrial, we propose a multi-layer industrial service governance method to meet the ever-changing business requirements. It gives a global perspective of industrial governance, includes business level governance, service level governance and IT infrastructure governance. This comprehensive governance architecture could eliminate monitoring blind spot lead to eliminate waste and defects. With this governance method, industrial organization could achieve goals of Lean six sigma and their ultimate business requirements.

3   Contributions

3.1   Overview of Our Multi-tier Governance Architecture

Our multi-tier governance architecture is designed to set a global governance environment to avoid any monitoring blind spot and could increase both enterprise and information system agility and interoperability, narrow the gap between business, service and infrastructure, reducing wastes and errors, enhancing the robustness of industrial multi-layer architecture and contribute to some commercial value.

We organize a global multi-tier governance architecture used to support both functional and non-functional management. Functional management deploys management engines to achieve functional requirements. Non-functional management cooperates with functional management and deploys performance indicators to evaluate performance of business processes.

To combine and orchestrate all the elements, we organize our multi-tier governance architecture as this way:

- A presentation Interface Layer (IL) to connect with users and to display governance results by customized dashboard.
- Platform Layers (PL) to achieve governance requirements. All management engines and performance indicators are orchestrated by customized agreements and governance rules. In this Platform Layers, we have 3 sub-levels to achieve business and governance requirements: (See figure 2) Business Level (BL) contains all of business context (business actors: deciders, clients and workers); Service Level (SL) is an abstraction level set between the BL and IT infrastructure. It includes all the components which are related to the services (service providers, service customers, service registry and middleware); and Application Level (AL) includes the entire infrastructures which should meet the needs of services (hardware, software, databases, firewalls, Intrusion prevention sys-tem, ctc...). Management engines and indicators are deployed in

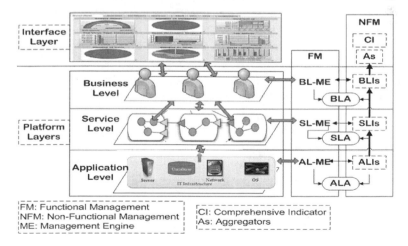

Fig. 2. Overview of Multi-tier Governance Architecture

each level, Comprehensive Indicator (CI) and Aggregators combine scattered governance results from level indicators into comprehensive results for performance of business requirements.

Non-functional management transversal layer governs performance of functional management abide by agreements. Agreements are set at each level (BLA, SLA, ALA) to standardize non-functional constraints and to constrain the business value flow through entire enterprises.

- BLA as a guide to comply with the Business Quality Standards which could assist companies control quality (include manufacture quality and service quality) and maintain a high standard of customer satisfaction. BLA keeps the two key principles for company: "fit for purpose—the product and service should be suitable for the intended purpose; and right first time—mistakes should be eliminated."
- SLA in our multi-tier governance architecture is beyond the normal SLA in SOA. Our SLA is not only a negotiated agreement between service customers and extern service providers, but also it is the evaluation criteria for quality of service within our multi-tier governance architecture.
- ALA lists the expected functional and non-functional properties in application level. It set out the policies, strategies, specifications and criterion of application level. ALA defines all acceptable performances of infrastructure. It plays an important role for Application level indicators to measure performance of applications in this layer.

3.2   Non-functional Governance Working Principles

In order to make use of Lean 6 sigma theory to increase business efficiency, we should make sure every operation can add value to end customers, and we should eliminate any extra steps which cannot create profit to enterprise, the value flow and working operation steps of enterprise (from input raw material to distribute outputs through manufacture factor, must be taken into account).

Attributes of Functional Requirements and Non-functional Requirements: Functional Requirements (FRs) satisfy clients' business requirements; each 'business requirement' is completed by series Tasks; each 'task' is completed by some 'actions' at each level. Non-Functional Requirements (NFRs) constrain FRs. NFRs are divided into different NFRs-Families and NFRs-classes, according to the feature of NFRs. "FR", "action" and "NFR" could be defined and identified by their attributes. "Taskstamp" is synchronized with current task. "Level mark" labels a certain level. "Family mark" identifies NFPs belong to specific NFRs-Family and "class mark" identifies NFPs belong to specific classes. Therefore "family mark" and "class mark" are flags to automatically link relevant NFPs cross this multi-tier architecture. (Fig. 3)

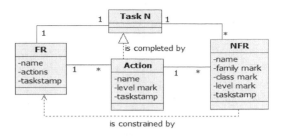

Fig. 3. Relation and Attributes of FRs, NFRs, Tasks and Actions

In order to make non-functional governance strategy convenient to retrospect governance situation and expediential to locate and correct mistakes, we take each "task" as a unit to govern and to give report. For each task, each level indicator provides the real-time level governance report. Aggregators according to NFRs' feature to combine relevant scattered of level governance results to aggregate comprehensive governance results. After that the CI integrates and analyzes aggregators' reports, provides a comprehensive report to users by dashboard. Users can modify the way dashboard shows the governance results, such as users can choose charts or data to display timely governance results. As well as, dashboard can be customized to display level governance results or comprehensive business performance. All governance reports are business readable and non-programming.

Figure 4 gives us the horizontal and vertical view of this non-functional governance architecture's working principles. We can see that this non-functional governance architecture monitor completion performance of each task horizontally, and it monitor the completion performance of entire business requirement vertically.

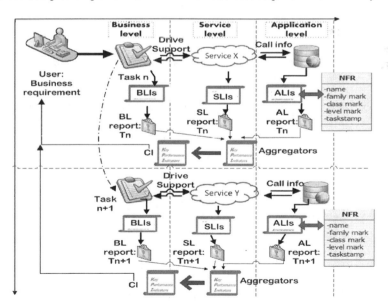

Fig. 4. Details of Horizontal and Vertical view of Governance

The combination strategy of BLI, SLI and ALI plays an important role in this multi-tier architecture. According to the classification of NFRs, all of relevant NFRs cooperatively constrain FRs. Following picture gives us an example of NFRs' connection: NFRs in NFR-family (T) and NFR-class (RT and ET), these related NFRs could comprehensively constrain FRs cross three levels. (See figure 5)

This multi-tier governance architecture has ability of position precise governance point, and it has ability to evaluate any operation step could or not bring value to end users. It will improve agility of business and technologies. If there is any problem impedes value flow smoothly through entire enterprise, this architecture could find it out and fix it without impact other normal value flow steps.

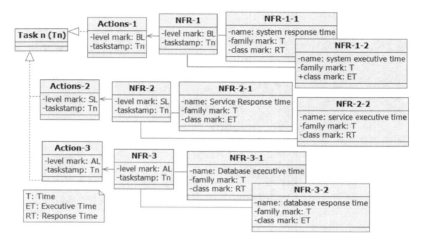

Fig. 5. Connection of Related NFRs

4   Conclusion

In this ever-changing economic environment, an ideal governance method could be significant for enterprises to achieve their business goals, to realize business and IT agility, to maximize their profits, to close the gap between business and IT, to eliminate wastes, to improve customer satisfaction, to enhance enterprises' comprehensive competitiveness, to win the future. According to the importance of governance architecture, we propose a multi-tier industrial governance architecture, which relies on the ability of linking dynamically industrial services in a customized industrial organization to fit the client requirements. This approach partly inspired by the Lean Six Sigma vision, extends the horizon of SOA to reveal a global vision, the enterprise business organization, abstract service network and its information infrastructure could be more agile.

Acknowledgments. This work extends the service showing strategy of the project process 2.0 granted by the DGCIS.

References

1. Lankhorst, M., et al.: Enterprise Architecture at Work –Modeling, Communication, and Analysis. Springer, Heidelberg (2005)
2. Morganwalp, J.M., Sage, A.P.: Enterprise Architecture Measures of Effectiveness. International Journal of Technology, Policy and Management 4(1), 81–94 (2004)
3. Enterprise Architecture Framework, http://en.wikipedia.org/wiki/Enterprise_Architecture_framework
4. Infosys Technologies Limited whitepaper: EA: A Governance Framework (2005)
5. Weill, P., Ross, J.: A matrixed approach to designing IT governance. MIT Sloan Management Review 46(2) (2005)
6. Hitachi Consulting a knowledge-driven consulting whitepaper: SOA Governance: revolutionizing business to meet customer demands (2007)
7. Mitra, T.: Business-driven development, IBM, Software Group, http://www.ibm.com/developerworks/webservices/library/ws-bdd/
8. Michael, N., Julian, E., Nicolas, R., Ralf, S.: Towards a Generic Governance Model for Service Oriented Architectures. In: Proceedings of AMCIS 2008 (2008), http://aisel.aisnet.org/amcis2008/361
9. MacKenzie, C.M., Laskey, K., McCabe, F., Brown, P.F., Metz, R.: OASIS Reference Model for Service Oriented Architecture 1.0 (October 2006)
10. Bernhardt, J., Seese, D.: A Conceptual Framework for the Governance of Service-Oriented Architectures. In: Feuerlicht, G., Lamersdorf, W. (eds.) ICSOC 2008. LNCS, vol. 5472, pp. 327–338. Springer, Heidelberg (2009)
11. Hill, J.B., Jim, S., David, F., Michael, J.M.: Gartner's position on business process management. In: Business Issues. Gartner, Inc. (2006)
12. Ryan, K.L.K.: A computer scientist's introductiory guide to business process management (BPM). In: Crossroads, vol. 15(4), ACM, NY (2009)
13. Michael, H.: Re-engineering work: Don't automate, obliterate. Harvard Business Review, 104–112 (1990)

Influence of AHP Methodology
and Human Behaviour on e-Scouting Process

Lucio Compagno, Diego D'Urso, Antonio G. Latora, and Natalia Trapani

Department of Industrial Engineering
University of Catania
{lcompagn,ddurso,latora,ntrapani}@diim.unict.it

Abstract. The e-scouting process, to search for and select products whose characteristics are known in catalogues, is often inefficient and ineffective: the overload of information available on the Web and the human limitations in processing information, are the main cause. Experiments, in order to simulate the e-scouting process of a leverage [1] product by a set of student buyers, were performed and results on effectiveness and efficiency of e-scouting process strategies and methods are collected and analyzed. Referring to the strategic evaluation of the e-scouting process, results show that a Decision Support System (DSS) based on Analytic Hierarchy Process (AHP) methodology [2], supports the buyer- Human Decision Maker (HDM) to interpret in a coherent way the strategic guidelines previously set by the high level management. Regarding to method's evaluation of e-scouting process, was appreciated that if quantitative product features are known and limited in a range of variation, the Human Decision Maker's evaluation substantially coincide with the evaluation of a Virtual Decision Maker (VDM) based on Analytic Hierarchy Process. On the contrary, the difference among HDM and VDM is considerable when quantitative product characteristics are unknown or unlimited. The work carried out has shown that using a DSS based on AHP is always useful to improve efficiency and effectiveness on e-scouting process' strategies however efficiency and effectiveness on e-scouting process' method can be improved by DSS based on AHP only if the human evaluation about product features is limited.

Keywords: AHP, e-procurement, supplier selection, managerial human behaviour.

1   Purpose of the Paper

The contribution of I&CT as enabled the establishment of a global market characterized by:

1. proliferation of products, services and suppliers;
2. competition among products, services and suppliers;
3. high number of information shared about products, services and suppliers.

In this scenario, the e-scouting process to search for and select products whose characteristics are known in catalogues, presents at the same time strength and weakness due to the great number of information available on the Web and the human limitations in processing this great number of information.

J. Frick and B. Laugen (Eds.): APMS 2011, IFIP AICT 384, pp. 514–525, 2012.
© IFIP International Federation for Information Processing 2012

Kraljic, who has transformed the primary purchasing in supply management, suggested strategies related to the supply market complexity and the purchasing importance. A direct consequence of the Kraljic matrix is the attention to products with high market complexity and high importance of supply at the expense of other products, consumer or business, easy to find on the market and/or not important in terms of value .

In order to buying decisions on non-strategic items, in B2C environment can affect personal issues while in B2B is expected by the buyer a rational decision, result obtained by optimization of a multi-objective function can summarize all the features listed in the web catalogues. However, encoding and optimization of a multi-objective function with qualitative and quantitative variables are hard for a buyer - Human Decision Maker, also even in B2B may affect personal aspects, so the procurement process can be inefficient and ineffective.

The present study tries to obtain assessments of efficiency and effectiveness for the e-scouting, and more particularly:

1. strategic evaluation to e-scouting process using a AHP based Decision Support System;
2. method evaluation to e-scouting process comparing Human Decision Maker and AHP based Virtual Decision Maker evaluation.

2   Methodology

The e-scouting process of a product or service requires the analysis of an information content detected by product or service features; in table 1 we propose a product features breakdown by type and mode of perception.

Table 1. Classification of the nature of information

Feature		Type	
		Quantitative	Qualitative
Mode of Perception (MOP)	Objective	Measurement	-
	Subjective	-	Judgment

In order to evaluate how the human behaviour can influence the e-scouting process a campaign of experiments was designed, in particular the results of the research and selection process of a given item, which were performed by a number of   buyers - Human Decision Makers equal to 51, were compared with those obtained by a Virtual Decision Maker.

The selection of a car, in order to renew the fleet of a car rental company, is the object of the e-scouting process; the item was identified taking into account the following aspects:

1. is a finished good with a catalogue of known features;
2. is designed for mass consumption and has features referred in an universal meaning;

3. has significant quantitative and qualitative features;

4. belongs to the scenario of B2B supply, so the contribution of qualitative features is limited and does not exceed that of the quantitative ones.

Criteria and sub-criteria which have to be taken in to account to solve the e-scouting problem can be set according to the main features of the desired item (Table 2); we assume that strategic guidelines were previously set by the high level management. We assume also that the preliminary high level analysis performs the problem recognition, defines the minimum requirements description and finds the product specification [3], [4], [5]. The importance assigned by a buyer - decision maker to each criteria and sub-criteria can be defined as the e-scouting strategy.

Table 2. Criteria, sub-criteria, types, the mode of perception, measurement e judgement

Criteria	Sub-Criteria	Type	MOP	Measurement	Judgment
Safety	Strength	quantitative	objective	EU NCAP code	-
	Accessibility	quantitative	objective	Number of doors	-
Environment	Air pollution	quantitative	objective	Gas specific emission [g CO2/km]	-
Economy	Overall cost	quantitative	objective	Specific cost [€/km]	-
Performance	Dynamic	quantitative	objective	Acceleration 0 to 100 km/h [s]	-
	Utility	quantitative	objective	Luggage capacity [l]	-
Aesthetic	Design	qualitative	subjective	-	Semantic scale
	Image	qualitative	subjective	-	Semantic scale

Table 3. Qualitative assessment of criteria

Criteria	Sub criteria	Weights
Safety	Strength, Accessibility	Absolute important
Environment	Air pollution	Very important
Economy	Overall cost	Important
Performance	Dynamic, utility	Almost important
Aesthetic	Design, image	Less important

3   Design of Experiments

Referring to the strategic evaluation of the e-scouting process, a Decision Support System based on Analytic Hierarchy Process methodology, was created to supports the buyer- Human Decision Maker to interpret in a coherent way the strategic guidelines previously set by the high level management (Table 3). Regarding to method's evaluation of e-scouting process, the Human Decision Maker's was compared with the evaluation of a Virtual Decision Maker based on Analytic Hierarchy Process.

Two type of experiments were designed and given after buyers were involved in a short course (2 hours) concerning the introduction of basic concepts of AHP:

- E1. The objective of the e-scouting process was submitted to the valuations of a first group of 26 buyers; the strategy that leads e-scouting process, in terms of criteria's weights, were set out in a qualitative manner (Table 4); limits which refer to the variation of the product features were defined in a qualitative manner even if they can be measured quantitatively (Table 5); alternatives that can be assessed belong to the whole those are trade (about 6,000 models and variants of each model); each buyer was provided of an Excel® spread sheet application that contains an empty schema for pairwise comparison among focused criteria and sub-criteria (Table 6) and a routine that enables the general product ranking once the buyer, surfing web, has defined and collected the specifications of all alternatives using only a semantic scale whose intensity belongs to [1, 2..9].
- E2. The same objective of the e-scouting process was submitted to the valuations of a second group of 25 buyers; criteria's weights were set out in a qualitative manner still according to Table 4; limits which refer to the variation of the product features were defined in a strictly quantitative manner if they can be measured (Table 5); each buyer was provided of an Excel® spread sheet application that

Table 4. Qualitative assessment of product features limits

Product features	Assessment phrase for limit
Dimensions	"...compact"
Environment	"low emission"
Economy	"low consumption"
Performance	"enjoyable to drive" & "comfortable for people and things"

Table 5. Quantitative assessment of product features limits

Product features	Limit
Length	<= 400 cm
Acceleration 0 to 100 km/h	$\in$ [8..11] s
Number of doors	5
Number of seats	5
Luggage capacity	$\in$ [200..400] dm^3
Average annual mileage[1]	20.000 km

---

[1] An equation enables the buyer to evaluate the overall annual cost which takes in to account: property tax, which depends on car power, price of fuel to 20.000 km per year, environment emission class, price of car and interest rate.

contains an empty schema for pairwise comparison among focused criteria (Table 6); during the experiment, on the basis of information acquired via web, the buyer can give an opinion relating to the sub criterion of choice (safety, performance, economy of operations, aesthetics perception) by using the semantic scale whose intensity belongs to [1, 2..9], supplied with the software application; thus the assessment of a product is based on the method of comparison with an indefinite and non-limited number of alternatives; with reference to the experiment E1, now buyers know more specifically the sub-criteria and the edges of their variation.

Table 6. Pairwise criteria comparisons

Criteria	Aesthetics	Technique	Economy	Environment	Safety	Weights
Aesthetics	1	1/3	1/5	1/7	1/9	0,033
Performance	3	1	1/3	1/5	1/7	0,063
Economy	5	3	1	1/3	1/5	0,129
Environment	7	5	3	1	1/3	0,262
Safety	9	7	5	3	1	0,513

Table 7. Quantitative car features, ranges of variation and semantic attribute

Criteria	Safety		Performance		Environment	Economy	Aesthetic	
Sub-criteria	Strength	Accessibility	Dynamic	Utility	Air pollution	Overall cost	Design	Image
Semantic attribute	EUNCAP	Number of doors	Acceleration 0 to 100 km/h	Luggage capacity	Gas specific emission	Specific cost	Design	Image
[ ]	[-]	[-]	[s]	[dm^3]	[g CO2/km]	[€/km]	[-]	[-]
HH	5	5	<8	> 900	<90	<1	9	9
HM	4,5		[8, 8,5[	[900, 800[	[90, 100[	[1, 1,2[	8	8
HB	4		[8,5, 9[	[800, 700[	[100, 110[	[1,2, 1,4[	7	7
MH	3,5		[9, 9,5[	[700, 600[	[110, 120[	[1,4, 1,6[	6	6
MM	3		[9,5, 10[	[600, 500[	[120, 130[	[1,6, 1,8[	5	5
MB	2,5		[10, 10,5[	[500, 400[	[130, 140[	[1,8, 2,0[	4	4
BH	2		[10,5, 11[	[400,300[	[140, 150[	[2,0, 2,2[	3	3
BM	1,5		[11, 11,5[	[300, 200[	[150, 160[	[2,2, 2,4[	2	2
BB	1	3	>11,5	<200	>160	>2,4	1	1

The buyers used for the experiments are students of the Master Degree in Engineering Management. To motivate the students-buyers, it was declared that a premium in terms of didactic credits would been assigned to the solution that best interprets the strategic vision, performed in the shortest time [6],[7].

During each experiment, the research environment was represented by the web database and by a search engine provided by an important Italian car magazine; the database contains all the features of all products that market offers; the search engine was used during all experiments with the same potential; it allows buyers to operate query on the database using defined product features as a reading key. To each buyer was given a maximum time of one hour to perform the task.

The virtual decision maker

The virtual decision maker is based on the AHP methodology; it allows to translate the strategy that inspires the selection criteria and weights of criteria in a holistic manner; the virtual model of e-scouting process includes the following basic steps:

(a) modelling strategy that inspires the supply by semantic scale; definition of criteria and relevant weights; definition of s sub-criteria and relevant weights according to AHP equation $A*W = \lambda max*W$ where: A is the pairwise criteria or sub-criteria comparisons matrix; W is the normalized eigenvector of matrix A with the local criteria o sub-criteria weights, λ_{max} is the maximum eigen value of the matrix A;

(b) recording of conditions in which the product will work (in some cases this allows to calculate the value of a variable that depends from some product features and can be used during the selection process, such as the annual overall cost);

(c) registration of supply product feature limits;

(d) e-scouting for alternatives and collection of their information content;

(e) recording the value of each quantitative feature; the qualitative ones have been evaluated with equal weight in the pairwise comparisons;

(f) definition of direct features comparisons for each chosen alternative under each sub-criteria;

(g) calculation of general ranking according to Ri=Ii*Wi were Ri is the i-alternative general rating, Ii is the chosen intensity value, Wi is the respective sub-criteria weight [8].

4   Findings

Figure 1 shows the criteria's average weight derived from the interpretation of the supply strategy of Table 3, by the virtual decision maker (VDM) and by the human decision makers (HDM).

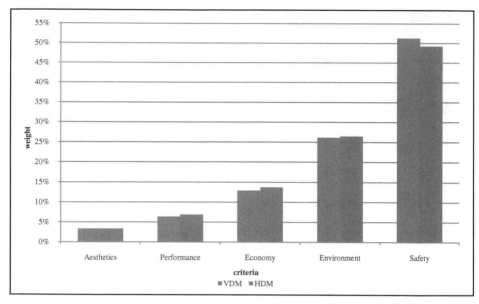

Fig. 1. VDM e HDM criteria's weights comparison

As regards to tests E1 and E2 , chosen by each buyer alternative, was submitted to the Virtual Decision Maker based on Analytic Hierarchy Process; the pairwise comparisons among different alternatives, along each defined sub-criterion, were performed by using direct ratio of quantitative measures derived by technical information resident on web; so it was possible to create, for each k-scenario played by each k-buyer, a ranking $R_{i,k}$ with i ∈ [1..nk] and k ∈ [1..N] (where n_k is the number of alternatives chosen by each buyer and N is the number of buyers).

Finally it was possible to verify the quality of collected alternatives and if each buyer was able to choose the best alternative from ones she/he evaluated.

In order to assess efficiency and effectiveness of the buyer's e-scouting process, the following performance indicators were defined:

- Absolute Frequency of Matching
  $AFM = \frac{N\prime}{N}$; where N' is the number of buyers who chose, among the scouted alternatives, the same of the VDM and N the overall number of buyers;

- Weighted Frequency of Matching
  $WFM = \frac{\sum_{k=1}^{N} n_k M_k}{n_t}$;   where: $n_t = \sum_{k=1}^{N} n_k$; $M_k = \begin{cases} 1 & \text{if matching VDM} - \text{HDM} \\ 0 & \text{otherwise} \end{cases}$

- Efficiency as average number of scouted alternatives per buyer
  $E = \frac{n_k}{n_t}$, where: $n_t = \sum_{k=1}^{N} n_k$.

Figures 2 and 3 show the efficiency and effectiveness of each buyer in order to choose the best alternative of each k-scenario.

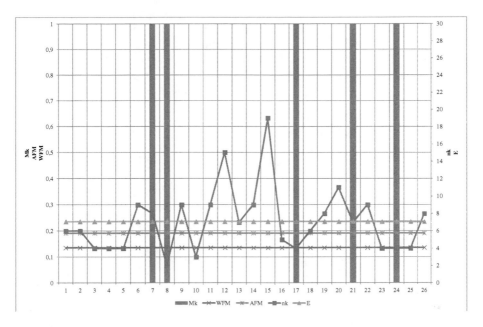

Fig. 2. Absolute Frequency of Matching (AFM), Weighted Frequency of Matching (WFM), Efficiency (E) (Test E1)

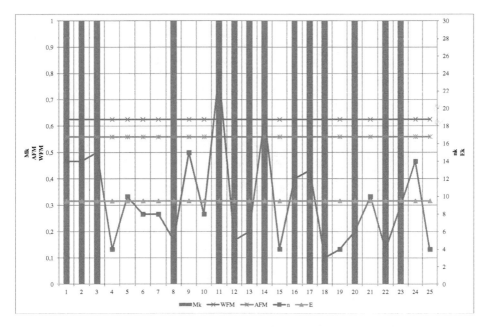

Fig. 3. Absolute Frequency of Matching (AFM), Weighted Frequency of Matching (WFM), Efficiency (E) (Test E2)

Figure 4 shows the comparison between the i-alternative rating, R_i (see page 4), which is evaluated by the VDM AHP based, and the judgments declared by human buyers by means of the semantic scale of table 6-7; this behaviour shows how the evaluation of the collected alternatives can be distorted either by human perception and by the limited human capacity to perform consistent pairwise comparisons among alternatives under each sub-criterion.

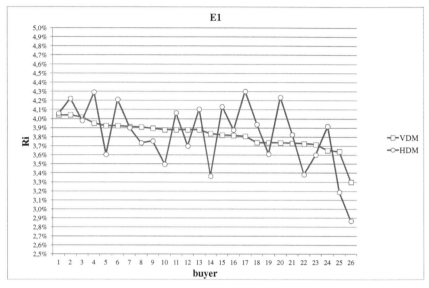

Fig. 4. The general ranking of all alternatives, R_i, performed by HDM and by VDM (test E1)

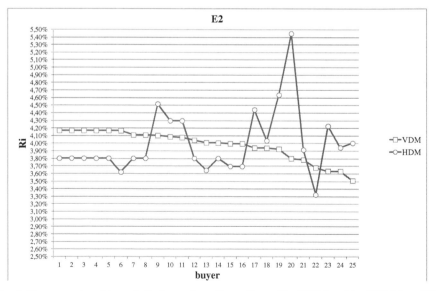

Fig. 5. The general ranking of all alternatives, R_i, performed by HDM and by VDM (test E2)

Figure 6 shows the rating performed by each buyer according to the test which was played, table 8 summarizes some statistics data of performed tests.

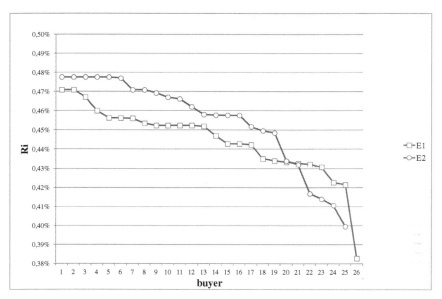

Fig. 6. Performance of buyers along the tests E1 and E2

5   Discussion

The results of tests E1, E2 provide the opportunity for the following considerations:

1. Test E1: the number of buyers is N=26, the overall scouted alternatives   is n_t=184; when product features are declared qualitatively the efficiency or average number of scouted alternatives per buyer is E=7,08 alternatives/buyer; the absolute frequency of matching is AFM=   19,23% and the weighted frequency of matching is WFM=13,59 %;
2. Test E2: the number of buyers is N=25, the overall scouted alternatives   is n_t =238; when product features are declared quantitatively the efficiency or average number of scouted alternatives per buyer is E= 9,52 alternatives/buyer; the absolute frequency of matching is AFM=   56,00% and the weighted frequency of matching is WFM=62,61 %;
3. when product features are expressed quantitatively by a measure (Test E2), effectiveness of e-scouting process grows (ΔWFM=+361% ΔAFM=226%) ; the average number of analysed alternatives, per buyer, is significantly higher (+22%) than the one is obtained when product features and sub criteria are expressed only qualitatively (test E1);
4. an unbound research process leads to find, generally, alternatives with a worse rating (see Figure 6);

5. buyers follow the strategic mission assigned in a consistent way for both the experiment (see Figure 1);
6. generally, each buyer expresses a personal aesthetic judgement also if the aesthetic master criteria is evaluated as negligible.

As part of purchasing a consumer product, with many features that must be evaluated (sub-criteria), it can be concluded that the human contribution, although assisted by decision support tools based on the type AHP methodology, does not produce significant benefits because of the difficulty of evaluating a product taking into account all of those analyzed and because of the limited number of alternatives that are taken into account.

In this context, at the same time the growth of alternatives to be evaluated increases the difficulty of analysis and potential effectiveness of the choice; it is therefore concluded that for this class of supplying the electronic contribution and the semantic web are absolutely remarkable.

Further experiments are being carried out in order to verify the methodological contribution of AHP to the evolution of process of product selection; in particular further experiments have to be designed in order to repeat the supply experience involving skilled buyers. The aim is to determine the contribution of learning by doing in this area.

The research path can also be extended to the configuration of system which characteristics are known by catalogue, for example in the design of industrial plant and civil facilities.

The validity of the study is limited to research products with well-known features.

6   Conclusions

When supply strategy is shared and the limits on quantitative product features are defined effectively, once a consolidated know-how on the item e-scouting process is collected, human behaviour coincides with that of a virtual decision maker that incorporates the steps of the AHP only if supply strategy and selection criteria and sub-criteria are strictly defined. When it doesn't occur, human scouting can be inefficient and misleading.

The result of the study confirms the necessity of automating the process of scouting and selection of products whose technical features are known by catalogue and expressed according to a common semantic.

The overall performance improvement of the procurement process is therefore achievable through:

(a) the validation of information;
(b) the semantic homologation of the product features;
(c) the strengthening of informatics tools by the integration of holistic decision making methodologies (AHP).

The deepening of the analysis of product scouting and selection can lead the development of management supply systems to obtain the following benefits:

(a) the informative flow transferred by artificial intelligence (e.g. improvement the potential of the Semantic Web);
(b) the automated implementation of the basic steps of the methodology of AHP where, due to limited resources, this is not allowed (Small and Medium Enterprises);
(c) decreasing of subjective judgments, devoting the human contribution to cases where this latter option represents an opportunity rather than a limit.

References

[1] Kraljic, P.: Purchasing must become supply management. Harvard Business Review 61(5), 109–117 (1983)
[2] Saaty, T.L.: How to make a decision: The analytic hierarchy process. European Journal of Operational Research 48(1), 9–26 (1990) ISSN 0377-2217
[3] Robinson, P.J., Faris, C.W., Wind, Y.: Buying Behaviour and Creative marketing. Allyn & Bacon, Boston (1967)
[4] De Boer, L., Van der Wegen, L., Telgen, J.: Outranking methods in support of supplier selection. Eur. J. Pur. Supp. Manag. 4, 109–118 (1998)
[5] Weber, C.A., John, R., Current, J.R., Benton, W.C.: Vendor selection criteria and methods. European Journal of Operational Research 50(1, 7), 2–18 (1991) ISSN 0377-2217
[6] De Boer, L., Labro, E., Morlacchi, P.: A review of methods supporting supplier selection. Eur. J. Pur. Supp. Manag. 7, 75–89 (2001)
[7] Johnston, W.J., Lewin, J.E.: Organizational buying behavior: toward an integrative framework. J. Busi. Res. 35, 1–15 (1996)
[8] Saaty, T.L., Vargas, L.G.: Models, methods, concepts & applications of the analytic hierarchy process. Kluwer, Boston (2001)

The Evaluation of Mobile Sector in Turkey in Terms of Mobile Supply Chain Management Practices

Zumrut Ecevit Sati[1] and Burak Oclu[2]

[1] Istanbul University, Faculty of Political Sciences
zsati@istanbul.edu.tr
[2] Istanbul University, Institute of Social Sciences
burak.oclu@gmail.com

Abstract. Today companies face enormous pressure to reduce costs while increasing innovation and improving customer service and responsiveness. Supply Chain Management enables collaboration, planning, execution and coordination of the entire supply network, empowering companies to adapt their supply chain processes to an ever-changing competitive environment. Obviously, companies should replace traditional linear supply chains with adaptive supply chain networks in which partners are given simultaneous, accurate information about purchase, production, demand, supply, sale and other operational activities. In order to compete in the market place, mobile supply chains remedy their products and services in order to meet the needs of the increasing flow of information in small-scale companies to large-sized companies. This means that advances in mobile technology are critical for mobile supply chains. In this sense, this paper examines mobile sector in Turkey and analyze how the value of information technology in mobile supply chains presents a growing opportunity in Turkish markets.

Keywords: Mobile Supply Chain Management, Mobile Commerce, Mobile Sector in Turkey.

1 Introduction

In today's global, competitive and dynamic business environment, the competitions among enterprises have transformed from company versus company to supply chain management versus supply chain management [1]. These days implementing techniques that reduce project time and cost, and improve productivity and performance is very important. The need for new ways to face these challenges has long been recognized. Recent years have also seen a movement towards using methods that influence and effect on the internet platform [2]. In today's economic globalization era, customers' expectations are very different to those of a few years ago. They demand the exact products they want, when they want them, at the right price. Each of the five major supply chain steps (Plan, Source, Make, Store and Deliver) need to be integrated and harmonized into a single application in order to derive maximum value from the supply chain and meet customer expectations [3]. Nowadays, more and more enterprises have paid or are paying attention to replace

J. Frick and B. Laugen (Eds.): APMS 2011, IFIP AICT 384, pp. 526–533, 2012.

traditional linear supply chains with mobile and adaptive supply chain management, helping firms to reduce management cost and gain supply chain responsiveness or other competitive advantage [4]. With the development of communication technologies and mobile networks, the supply chain management in the mobile environment has become more and more prevalent and necessary [5]. The Internet has many impacts on the supply chain. One of the most covered topics in the literature is the impact of *e-business*, which refers to the ability of a firm to electronically connect, in multiple ways, many organizations, both internally and externally, for many different purposes [6]. Another impact refers to *information sharing*, how the Internet can be used as a medium to access and transmit information among supply chain partners [7].

2   Mobile Commerce

Today, the e-commerce is increasing prevalence, internet technology is more secure and well-developed, the computer hardware and software equipment are more advanced, advanced mobile communication technology is widely used in the field of logistics, all of these directly spawn the mobile supply chain management [8].

In the literature, all mobile commerce definitions are very similar. In principle, any transaction with a monetary value conducted via mobile communication networks can be considered mobile commerce [9]. Dependent on this definition, [10] define mobile commerce as a new type of e-commerce transaction conducted through mobile devices using wireless telecommunication networks and other wired e-commerce technologies; [11] defines mobile commerce as the application of wireless communications networks and devices to the execution of transactions with monetary value; [12] define mobile commerce as any form of mobile communication between a business and its customer; [13] define mobile commerce for electronic commerce transactions carried out via mobile phones [14].

Mobile commerce is generally defined as conducting information inquires and/or any transaction with monetary value by using mobile devices wireless communications [15;16] Wireless and mobile networking have presented an entire new way for companies to further extend their supply chain–mobile commerce. Mobile commerce has extended the functions of e-commerce and thus the e-supply chain system to previously unimagined dimensions [17]. With mobile applications, the supply chain system will be accessible anywhere anytime by various devices, such as PCs, TVs, PDAs, and cellular phones. A number of m-commerce applications have been developed and are already use, covering a wide range of business functions from advertising, banking, ticketing, booking, games, to payment on the Internet, and payments of goods and services in shops, restaurants and corner stores [18;16]. With the advancement of this technology, mobile commerce is undergoing a rapid growth and exerting significant impacts on the business. Developments in mobile technology and use of mobile phones by consumers have made the mobile commerce market more consumer-oriented, more global in scope and more device-dependent [19;14]. The forces underpinning the emergence of mobile commerce can be summarized as (1) proliferation of mobile devices, (2) convergence of mobile telecommunication networks and Internet, (3) transition 3G, and (4) the emergence of broad set of highly personalized location applications and services [20;14]

3   The Basis of the Mobile Supply Chain Management (mSCM)

The essence of the supply chain is the network of communication through each link within the "chain" [21]. In order to make the most informed, intelligent decisions for their business, managers needed the ability to obtain information in real time from each stage in the process [21]. The objective of a favorable supply chain management should ensure to deliver the right product, at the appropriate time, at the competitive cost, and with customer satisfaction for keeping the competitive advantages [22]. The supply chain is involved in the information flow, materials flow and funds flow from suppliers to customers [3]. The mSCM causes timesaving and highly accurate means of capturing data on movements of goods and other events [2]. Mobile SCM is based on the traditional supply chain management platform to integrate existing mobile communication technology, computer hardware and software technology and Internet technology, which implements the Real-time management of a specific logistics part in order to achieve: internally reducing business costs, externally improving customer response time, enhancing the competitiveness of the whole supply chain [8].

Mobile SCM is to use the most advanced mobile communication technology and facilities to promote the rapid flow of capital, information, business logistics, enhancing operational efficiency and effectiveness of the supply chain participants [8]. Managing and sailing the Web content to mobile users, based on their preferences and locations and controlling the products during producing, distributing, logistics and delivering are becoming now a leading point in a mobile electronic commerce (m-commerce) and mobile supply chain management [2]. Mobile SCM also refers to the use of mobile applications and devices to aid the conduct of supply chain activities, and ultimately help firms to gain cost reductions, supply chain responsiveness and competitive advantage [23].

3.1   The Features of Mobile Supply Chain

The mobile supply chain management is not to replace the original supply chain management platform. Mobile supply chain management is a part of supply chain management, the relationship between them is the overall and local [8]. Mobile supply chain system supports the interface of a mobile client device with a networked computer system [24]. Simply speaking, mobile supply chain management is only through the mobile communication technology and equipment to achieve some of the traditional supply chain management functions, to a certain extent, mSCM extends and expands these features [25]. Mobile SCM is highly targeted, especially for information processing. The mSCM solution takes supply chain visibility to new levels. It facilitates a convenient, time-saving, and highly accurate means of capturing data on movements of goods and other events. These capabilities simplify checking and monitoring tasks and provide up-to-date information on process status, which can be shown in mobile production management, mobile inventory management, mobile shipment planning, mobile sales management and Event Management [24].

Mobile SCM expands the traditional supply chain functions; information sharing and real-time delivery can improve the interactivity and integration capabilities of the members, and then can improve the whole supply chain competitive advantage [8].

From the perspective of supply management, mSCM has a high degree of flexibility, intelligence and accuracy [8].

3.2   The Applications of Mobile Supply Chain Management

Mobile supply chain applications introduce new challenges particularly for implementation. Mobile technology extends SCM capabilities through new virtual and remote ways of conducting supply chain activities [23]. With the characteristics of mobile commerce and its enabling technologies described above, mobile commerce has the potential to make information flows more efficient, coordinate the operations within the extended enterprise, and thus improve SCM [26]. Discussed below are methods detailing how mobile commerce can prepare organizations to meet the challenges imposed upon SCM.

Mobile email and Internet for corporate users: Mobile email is the key application for wireless data usage. It serves as the primary communication link for corporate users to stay in touch with their organizations while on the move [26].

Mobile customer care: Mobile commerce can provide customers automated, unassisted operations directly from mobile terminals [26].

Mobile enterprise implementations: Mobile commerce can be used to manage logistics and work flow and streamline inventory and distribution control. For example, Bluetooth devices are ideal for inventory control [26].

Mobile Logistics Management: MSCM enables more efficient circulation of the cargos or assets in supply chain [3].

Mobile Supply and Marketing Management: Through mobile supply and marketing management, second tier suppliers or second-tier distributors can make real-time information interaction with core enterprises, strengthen the channel controlling capability of core enterprises, shorten the distances among numerous second-tier distributors which locate in wide area and core enterprises or first-tier suppliers and distributors, so that they are more closely connected [3].

Mobile Manufacturing Management: Basically, mSCM realizes the real-time interaction between managers and workers in a factory [3].

Mobile Inventory Management: By utilizing mobile equipments or wireless devices, the inventory and management capability for raw materials of enterprises is greatly increased [3].

4   The Evaluation Mobile Sector of Turkey for Potential MSCM Applications

There have been significant changes in telecommunications market in last few decades. During this time period, innovative new technologies changed people's lifestyles and the way people communicate. Demand and interest of consumers to new telecommunication services are growing up rapidly which in turn makes the competition among operators more intense.

There are several factors that caused this significant growth in mobile market. First, the privatization and regulation of telecommunications market in most countries allowed new players to enter the market and provide innovative mobile services with lower rates. Second, mobile phone manufactures have been able to offer more capable phones at more economical prices by utilizing economics of scale. As a consequence, demand for mobile phone increased which resulted even smarter and more user friendly mobile phones.

Turkey is the country which is connecting Europe and Asia. Geopolitical position is one of the most important factors in increasing mobile sector. It promotes ICT sector especially supply side. Turkish companies can reach the source which is they need easily. On the demand side, especially young people are highly interested in technological improvements. The median age of Turkey, which has a young population structure, is 28.8 [27]. During the past decade, mobile phone has surged to the forefront of the Turkish telecommunications industry [14]. Mobile communication market is rapidly growing. By the end of 2010, 90% of population had adopted mobile phones. The number of mobile phone subscribers in Turkey had exceeded 73 million (73 722 988) by 2010 [28].

Mobile internet subscribers are rapidly growing after 3G service introduced in 2009. According to these improvements, mobile internet demand is increasing in Turkish mobile sector. Mobile internet prices also affected the usage of the technology. The gap between fixed line and mobile internet prices are closing. As a result the annual growth rate for the last quarter between 2010-2011 reached % 345, 8 (Table 1). In the meantime, broadband subscribers' rate is increasing according to connecting availability [29].

Table 1. Internet Subscribers in Turkey [29]

	2010-4	2011-3	2011-4	Quarter growth rate (2011-3 – 2011-4)	Annual growth rate (2010-4 – 2011-4)
xDSL	6.640.911	6.792.013	6.776.036	-0,2%	2,0%
Mobile Internet	1.448.020	5.655.444	6.454.801	14,1%	345,8%
Cable Internet	273.908	407.502	460.451	13,0%	68,1%
Fiber	154.059	220.777	267.144	21,0%	73,4%
Other	155.478	129.858	159.383	22,7%	2,5%
Total	**8.672.376**	**13.205.594**	**14.117.815**	**6,9%**	**62,8%**

Table 2. 3G Subscribers Data in Turkey 2010-2011 [29]

	2010-4	**2011-3**	**2011-4**
3G subscribers	19.407.264	28.608.069	31.375.507
Mobile internet subscribers	1.448.020	5.655.444	6.454.954
Mobile internet usage, Gbytes	4.387.315	8.766.845	10.708.533

While the ratios of computer usage and Internet access in enterprises were 87.8% and 80.4%, respectively, in January 2005, these levels increased to 92.3% and 90.9% in January 2010 [27] .Even though these two ratios increased by years, a downward trend is seen in web page ownership. The web page ownership rate of enterprises with Internet access dropped from 63.1% in January 2007 to 57.8% in January 2010 [27]. To give an example, while computer usage, Internet access, and web page ownership rates were around 91.3%, 89.7%, and 53.5%, respectively in enterprises with 10 – 49 employees in 2010, these rates were around 98.5%, 98.4%, and 88.8% for enterprises with 250+ employees. [27].

The type of connection most frequently used by enterprises for Internet access in January 2010 was DSL (ADSL, etc.) represented by 87.3%. With the spreading of the 3G technology as of 2010, a serious increase was observed in the rate 12.9 % of enterprises using mobile broadband connection with the help of portable computers [27].

When we compare connection types with europe avarage, mostly xDSL connection type is prefered with 93,5% in Turkey. However, it is only 79% in Europe avarage [28]. The year 2009 is a milestone for mobile internet users. Introducing 3G techology caused fast mobile internet experiences. At the begining, 3G subscribers were %7,1 of total mobile internet subscribers. At the end of the 2010, this rate increased to 19,4%.

When the mobile internet penetration rates are compared with those of the EU, Europe average is %126 however Turkey has only % 89 penetration rates after Norway and France. In addition to this ratio, we can examine mobile broadband connection penetration according to population. Finland is in the first place with %21,5. European average is 6,1% between Poland and Holland. Following Ireland, Portugal and Sweden, Turkey is in the seventh place with 8,8% [29].

We aimed to increase the ICT usage throughout our country and to close the gap with developed countries. However, even though a progress was made during the 2007 – 2009 period, the difference in terms of ICT usage still continues between the EU and our country (The values for the EU were obtained from EUROSTAT (as of June 2010) and those for Turkey were obtained from TURKSTAT. The value for Turkey concerning 2006 is an estimate of the SPO [27].

Another matter that needs to be evaluated is the Internet access and broadband Internet ownership in households. Even though a significant increase was achieved during the 2007-2009 period, as in the Internet usage, there is a major difference between our country and the EU in terms of the ratios of Internet access and broadband Internet ownership in households [30: 31]. When the Internet access ownership rates of the enterprises of Turkey are compared with those of the EU, a significant tendency of convergence is observed by years until 2008; however, this convergence is seen to have receded in 2009. While the ratio of Internet access by the enterprises in our country increased from 80.4% in 2005 to 89.2% in 2008 by displaying a major progress in three years, this rate receded back to 88.8% in 2009. In the EU this ratio reached the levels of 93 - 95 % in 2008 and 94 - 96 % in 2009 from 91 - 92 % in 2005 [30: 31]. In addition to this, the enterprises in Turkey showed a higher convergence to the EU in terms of broadband Internet access in 2007 and 2008 and reached a ratio higher than the average values of the EU 25 and EU 27. However, this ratio showed a slight drop in 2009 and took place between the average values for the EU 25 and EU 27.

In addition to this, the enterprises in Turkey showed a higher convergence to the EU in terms of broadband Internet access in 2007 and 2008 and reached a ratio higher than the average values of the EU 25 and EU 27. However, this ratio showed a slight drop in 2009 and took place between the average values for the EU 25 and EU 27 (The values for the EU were obtained from EUROSTAT (as of June 2010) and those for Turkey was obtained from TURKSTAT).

5   Conclusions

Supply chain transformation is proceeding at the same speed as technological developments. The two most important factors driving this transformation in supply chains are: an increasingly competitive environment and customer awareness. In order to compete in the market place, mobile supply chains remedy their products and services in order to meet the needs of the increasing flow of information in small-scale companies to large-sized companies. This means that advances in mobile technology are critical for mobile supply chains to ensure swift and accurate data transmission for their customers

In the meantime, analysis of the potential of mobile supply chains with an information technology perspective is an important issue in Turkey. The concept of mobile characteristics meets the needs of Turkish firms. Along with globalization, Turkish firms should continuously upgrade their supply chains with the latest in information technology.

This situation represents a growing opportunity for mobile supply chains in Turkey. However, one of the biggest obstacles facing the mobile supply chain transition process appears to be the lack of information technology within the infrastructure of Turkish firms. In addition, corporate culture along with revision of business processes also present formidable problems that threaten to delay this transition. Ubiquitous business efficiency and customization are some of the major advantages in mobile supply chains.

References

1. Barbuceanu, M., Fox, M.: Coordinating multiple agents in the supply chain. In: Proceedings of the Fifth Workshops on Enabling Technology for Collaborative, pp. 134–141 (1996)
2. Zarei, S.: RFID In Mobile Supply Chain Management Usage. International Journal of Computer Science and Technology 1(1), 11–20 (2010)
3. Zha, M., Lui, X., Zhang, Z.: Research on Mobile Supply Chain Management Based Ubiquitous Network, pp. 1–4 (2008)
4. Öztemel, E., Kurt Tekez, E.: Interactions of agents in performance based supply chain management. Journal of Intelligent Manufacturing 20, 159–167 (2009)
5. Zhao, W., Wu, H., Dai, W., Xuan, L.: Integration Middleware for Mobile Supply Chain Management. In: Proceedings of the Second Symposium International Computer Science and Computational Technology, ISCSCT 2009, pp. 521–524 (December 2009)
6. Fahey, L., Srivastava, R., Sharon, J., Smith, D.: Linking e-business and operating processes: The role of knowledge management. IBM Systems Journal 40(4), 889–907 (2001)
7. Giménez, C., Lourenço, H.R.: Supply Chain Management: review implications and directions for future research. Document de Treball / Working Paper, 17 (October 2004)
8. Li, L., Guo, W., Wang, Y.: Mobile Supply Chain Management:Theory and Method. In: 2010 International Conference on E-Product E-Service and E-Entertainment (ICEEE), pp. 1–8 (November 2010)
9. E-Business Report, Mobile E-Business- Mobile Commerce, European Commission Enterprise Directorate General, No. 3 (2000)
10. Siau, K., Lim, E.P., Shen, Z.: Mobile commerce: promises, challenges, and research agenda. Journal of Database Management 12(3), 4–13 (2001)

11. Clarke, I.: Emerging value propositions for mobile commerce. Journal of Business Strategies 18(2), 133–148 (2001)
12. Frolick, M.N., Chen, L.D.: Assessing mobile commerce opportunities. Information Systems Management 21(2), 53–61 (2004)
13. Dholakia, R.R., Dholakia, N.: Mobility and markets: emerging outlines of mobile commerce. Journal of Business Research 57(12), 1391–1396 (2004)
14. Barutçu, S.: Customers' Attitudes Towards Mobile Commerce and Mobile Marketing in Consumer Markets. Review of Social, Economic & Business Studies 9/10, 29–56 (2010)
15. Barnes, S.J.: The mobile commerce value chain: analysis and future developments. International Journal of Information Management 22(2), 91–108 (2002)
16. Wei, W., Shen, J., Ji, S.: Introducing Mobile Channel into Electronic Supply Chain. In: The 3rd International Conference on Grid and Pervasive Computing - Workshops, pp. 121–127 (2008)
17. Siau, K., Shen, Z.: Mobile Commerce Applications in Supply Chain Management. Journal of Internet Commerce 1(3), 3–16 (2002)
18. Kreyer, N., Pousttchi, K., Turowski, K.: Mobile payment procedures. e-Service Journal 2(3), 7–22 (2003)
19. DSTI/CP (Final Directorate for Science, Technology and Industry Committee on Consumer Policy), Mobile Commerce, OECD/OCDE (2006)
20. Sadeh, N.: Mobile commerce: Technologies, Services, and Business Models. Wiley Computer Publishing, New York (2002)
21. Airclick. the mobile supply chain of the future (July 20, 2011), http://www.airclic.com/download/ac.whitepaper.mobility_100929.pdf
22. Yonghui, F., Rajesh, P.: Multi-agent enabled modeling and simulation towards collaborative inventory management supply chains. In: Proceedings of the 2000 Winter Simulation Conference, pp. 1763–1771 (2000)
23. Eng, T.-Y.: Mobile supply chain management: Challenges for implementation. Technovation (26), 682–686 (2006)
24. Qi, Y., Zhao, X., Zhang, Q.: Key Technology and System Design in Mobile Supply Chain Management. In: International Symposium on Electronic Commerce and Security, pp. 258–263 (2008)
25. Wang, M.: Supply chain management development under E-commerce environment - mobile supply chain management. Public Automation Magazine 9 (2006)
26. Siau, K., Shen, Z.: Mobile Commerce Applications in Supply Chain Management. Journal of Internet Commerce 1(3), 3–16 (2002)
27. Republic of Turkey Prime Ministry, Undersecretariat for State Planning. Information Society Statistics. Ankara, Turkey: Republic of Turkey Prime Ministry, pp. 1–202 (2011)
28. Turkish Statistical Institute (2011), Turkey in Statistics 2010, TÜİK (June 08, 2012), http://www.tuik.gov.tr/IcerikGetir.do?istab_id=5
29. Organization of Information Technologies and Communication (May 2011). The Sector of Turkey Electronic Communication, Three Months Market Data Report (April 29, 2012), http://www.btk.gov.tr/kutuphane_ve_veribankasi/pazar_verileri/ucaylik11_4.pdf
30. EUROSTAT (2010), http://epp.eurostat.ec.europa.eu/cache/ITY_OFFPUB/KS-QA-10-049/EN/KS-QA-10-049-EN.PDF, http://epp.eurostat.ec.europa.eu/cache/ITY_OFFPUB/KS-QA-10-049/EN/KS-QA-10-049-EN.PDF (July 24, 2011)
31. TURKSTAT (2010), http://www.tuik.gov.tr/VeriBilgi.do?tb_id=60&ust_id=2 (July 24, 2011)

A Framework for the Transfer of Knowledge between Universities and Industry

Allen T. Alexander[1] and Stephen J. Childe[2]

[1] University of Exeter Business School,
Streatham Court, Exeter, UK
[2] University of Exeter, College of Engineering, Mathematics & Physical Sciences,
Harrison Building, North Park Road, Exeter, UK
{A.T.Alexander,S.J.Childe}@ex.ac.uk

Abstract. This paper describes research to examine the process of knowledge transfer between universities and industry, where the transfer of knowledge can be a valuable source of innovation for a company, in terms of new product development (radical innovation) but also as a source of knowledge for process or product improvement (incremental innovation). The view is adopted that the most useful knowledge for industry is knowledge that leads to action, known as tacit knowledge. However, tacit knowledge is seen as the most difficult type of knowledge to transfer. The paper builds on the research in this area of strategic knowledge management and uses case-study style research to review a framework that shows how knowledge can be codified for transfer, transferred and then assimilated. The paper concludes with comments about the use of the framework and directions for future research.

Keywords: Knowledge transfer, universities, industry, tacit knowledge.

1 Purpose

Companies in business and commerce need innovation to develop and compete. One source of innovation is by adopting ideas and techniques that are developed or simply better understood in institutions such a universities, other research bodies or higher education institutions (HEI). This exhibited itself in the first part of this century with 'collaborative manufacturing enterprises' joining other organisations, in networks where continuous improvement and incremental innovation practices could be developed and shared[1]. In this decade the focus has broadened to Open Innovation, which dispenses with the "old" linear model of innovation and promotes *"the use of purposive inflows and outflows of knowledge to accelerate internal innovation, and to expand the markets for external use of innovation, respectively"*[2]. Based in a university that works closely with industrial partners, the researchers were keen to understand the process of knowledge transfer so that it could be improved, but found little substantiated theory on managing knowledge flows.

This paper presents a practical framework that focuses on the act of transferring knowledge from one party to another and is set in the context of knowledge transfer activity between higher education and industry. The framework is structured around

J. Frick and B. Laugen (Eds.): APMS 2011, IFIP AICT 384, pp. 534–548, 2012.

the well-known categories of tacit and explicit knowledge [3] where implicit knowledge exists between tacit and explicit forms[4]. The framework has practical relevance to managers and participants in knowledge transfer projects and can be used in the planning stages of a knowledge transfer; can be used to analyse actions during the activity of transferring knowledge and can be used to review a completed knowledge transfer.

To explore if this framework worked in practice semi-structured, face-to-face interviews with expert respondents from recently completed knowledge transfer projects (25 interviews representing 19 completed projects) were undertaken. This work builds on a definitive list of the channels of knowledge transfer, developed by Alexander & Childe [5].

2   Context

The drive to gain competitive advantage fuels businesses development worldwide. According to Grant [6] knowledge has become the most important of a firm's resources and authors such as Teece, Drucker, Cohen all talk of the importance of achieving a knowledge society. Competitive Advantage is seen to come from the transfer of external or new knowledge into a company as an important source of Innovation [7]. Universities are important sources of knowledge and a number have shifted their strategy from only pursuing research and teaching students to position research and knowledge transfer activities as their first priority. If companies are able to gain competitive advantage from working with universities then effective ways of transferring knowledge are required [8]. Chilton & Bloodgood [9 p.76] state "*a stream of research needs to investigate moving tacit knowledge directly into outcomes*". Further Meier states there is a "*lack of research on which knowledge management practices are most useful in order to transfer different types of knowledge*" [10 p.17] . By understanding the performance of the different channels of knowledge transfer using the framework, the flows of knowledge between the two organisations can be considered and actions can be undertaken to improve the likelihood of the success of any particular knowledge transfer.

For industry to be able to exploit knowledge, our previous work has shown that that knowledge is needed to support action. We therefore take the view in this study that for useful exploitation, a successful transfer of knowledge would be one that resulted in the transfer of tacit knowledge [5].

2.1   Typologies of Knowledge

Beckman [11 p.23] defines knowledge as "*reasoning about information and data to actively enable performance, problem solving, decision making, learning and teaching*". Polanyi's definition of knowledge [3] distinguishes between tacit or theoretical knowledge and explicit, recognised or scientific knowledge. Grant [6] states that tacit knowledge is "knowing-how" and explicit knowledge "knowing-about".

Companies are collectives of humans and to some extent they learn accordingly. If we consider Piaget's theory of child learning [12], as a child gains new experiences or learns new things they reflect these back to existing experiences in order to be able to comprehend and understand them. This is not only a reflection of how children learn, adults use the same method of reflection and assimilation, using like experiences to process new information and to turn it into tacit knowledge. This was identified by Scribner [13] whilst studying the collective learning of workers employed within a dairy. It is this cognitive absorption that occurs within the transfer of explicit knowledge to tacit knowledge (according to Polanyi in 1966 and later Scribner in 1985 amongst others) and at this point of cognition that the knowledge takes on the "ability to act".

An argument can be made that explicit knowledge, in the form of instruction manuals, is an explicit representation of tacit knowledge and as long as the instructions are clear enough to follow, explicit knowledge should provide an ability to act. From that point of view, the ability to act is not solely dependent upon tacit knowledge. However Scibner etc argue that the instructions replicated in a manual (or articulated in process and procedures for dairy workers) are explicit and still require the cognitive absorption, assimilation with like experiences and reflection in order for them to be used at create an ability to act – which is the development of tacit knowledge. Scribner offers that, in developing the tacit knowledge, employees often then abandon explicit instructions and explicit knowledge, in favour of improved routines and personalised actions.

The literature suggests a spectrum of views, ranging from those that believe that knowledge is seated in the knower and therefore cannot be transferred at all, and those that believe that knowledge can be externalised and therefore transferred. We take the view that tacit knowledge can be transferred but that this is hard to achieve. It subscribes to the view of Chilton & Bloodgood who suggest a continuum in which fully tacit knowledge is completely embedded and fully explicit knowledge is entirely codified and that the remainder of the knowledge in the world lies somewhere upon this continuum. This realises that tacit knowledge can be transferred, but this transferrable knowledge is not located at the extreme, "tacit pole". It also recognises that explicit knowledge can include aspects of know-how (or tacit knowledge) in relationship to an instructional manual and this perspective is not located at the extent of the "explicit pole" bounding the continuum.

This representation of a tacit-explicit knowledge continuum is criticised by Tsoukas [14] and Gourlay [15]. They argue that the interpretation of the tacit to explicit continuum or at least the one presented in the 'SECI' process developed by Nonaka & Takeuchi [16] is incorrect and does not respect the original explanations of tacit and explicit knowledge presented by Polanyi [3]. They explain that instead of tacit knowledge existing and then being converted, through the process of socialisation, into explicit knowledge, the two types of knowledge exist simultaneously and represent "two sides of a coin" instead of two ends of a continuum. To illustrate this they suggest that there are two sort of awareness and that each state of awareness relates to a type of knowledge. They use an example of driving a nail. The person holding the hammer focuses on the head of the hammer and the head of the nail – this is their focal awareness. The person hammering is not consciously aware of how the hammer feels within their hand or how their muscles feel as they bring down the head of the hammer – this is their subsidiary awareness. Tsoukas [14] likens focal awareness to explicit knowledge and tacit knowledge to subsidiary awareness. He argues that as tacit knowledge is within one's subsidiary awareness it cannot be separated from the person and is therefore intangible. This perspective can only promote the transfer of knowledge via personnel movement.

Tsoukas [14] and Gourlay [15] however are arguing that the conversion between tacit and explicit knowledge, explained in the SECI process of knowledge creation, does not actually create new knowledge and they do not mention the transfer of knowledge. The second example provided by Tsoukas [14] may help to understanding how tacit knowledge can be transferred in this context. When examining a cavity, a dentist's primary focus is on the pointed probe in their hand and the view they can obtain using the mirror – the subsidiary awareness is the feel of the probe in their hand and the feedback they get as they move the probe into the cavity etc. If the dentist becomes unable to see the end of the probe, nor view the inside of the cavity, their focus shifts to their subsidiary awareness - to the feel of the probe in their hand and the physical resistance presented by the cavity. This is built through reference to experience and suggests that differing levels of tacit and explicit knowledge can exist, depending on the situation. The continuum explained above recognises the polarised position of transfer of pure tacit and this would reflect a sole focus on subsidiary awareness. Likewise it recognises the transfer of purely explicit knowledge, which would represent the transfer of only focal awareness. The continuum suggests that there are a range of intermediate states where tacit knowledge can transfer to some extent, and this would represent a blend of focal awareness and subsidiary awareness.

A revised continuum is therefore presented in Figure 1.

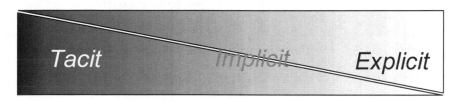

Fig. 1. The Tacit to Explicit Continuum

At the left-hand end the knowledge is tacit and cannot be transferred as it is entirely within the knower. This represents a predominance of subsidiary awareness – like the dentist who is operating 'blind'. The right-hand end is explicit, fully codified knowledge and with a dominance of focal awareness, with little realisation of tacit knowledge and subsidiary awareness.

Liebowitz & Beckman [17] introduce a third property of knowledge that they suggest lies between tacit and explicit, that of 'implicit' knowledge.

According to Beckman (17 p.p. 1-4):

- Tacit (residing in human mind, or organisations) is accessible indirectly with difficulty (through knowledge elicitation and observation of behaviour);
- Implicit (residing in human mind or organisation) is accessible through querying and discussion (but informal knowledge must be first located and then communicated);
- Explicit (residing in document or computer) is readily accessible, as well as documented into formal knowledge sources that are often well organised.

The inclusion of implicit knowledge may help to understand the stages of a knowledge transfer.   In considering actual knowledge transfers and therefore exploring if this model works in practice, the inclusion of the term implicit knowledge may make it easier to recognise the transition between tacit and explicit.

In this paper, Tacit Knowledge is defined as "knowledge that is resultant from both the cognition of information and the interaction with experience and encompasses the ability to act" [18] while "explicit knowledge can be expressed in words and numbers and shared in the form of data, scientific formulae, specifications and manuals" [19]. Implicit knowledge exists between these categories (that represent the poles on a continuum) and refers to the start of codification of tacit knowledge or the refocus toward subsidiary focus, where the knowledge starts to become structured or organised [4]. The framework proposed within this paper draws on these definitions.

2.2   A Framework for Knowledge Transfer

Whilst it is possible in some cases to transfer knowledge at the tacit level, from one person's deep understanding and ability direct to another's, this is likely to take considerable time (for example apprenticeships) and is rather limited as a source of innovation.   Alternative channels facilitate transfer at different levels on the continuum between tacit and explicit.   For example, as a member of staff from a university prepares to transfer knowledge, they use their intellectual ability organise their knowledge on a subject (making it implicit) and then they codify their knowledge into an explicit state - language, information, data or text that can be used for the transfer.   The transfer occurs with the participation of the recipient, a member of the commercial organisation, who must then learn and understand the new knowledge in the context of the organisation and develop the experience to apply the knowledge in action. This processing is shown in Fig. 1. (As knowledge transfer is a two directional activity, there is also a transfer occurring in the reverse direction, although for simplicity this reciprocity is not shown in Fig.2.)

One route to enable knowledge transfer, for which there is extensive agreement, involves codification of tacit knowledge prior to transfer. For example, as an instructor prepares to teach a class they begin to assemble the knowledge they possess on the teaching subject. This is the translation or codification stage where tacit knowledge retained within the instructor is first made implicit (organised, structured and ready to transfer) and then fully codified (in words, language, demonstration, images etc) as it is transferred [16 p. 9] This is an example of teaching or education and not knowledge transfer, but is relevant, to explain how knowledge is codified in a simplistic way.

Explicit knowledge could manifest in the form of data or text.   The working definition of explicit knowledge above refers to "words and numbers and shared in the form of data, scientific formulae, specifications and manuals".

The Information Systems research of Checkland & Howell [20] develops a routine or set of steps to translate data into knowledge.   Whilst this has 'knowledge-based management' origins, as opposed to 'strategic knowledge management', the theory may still be relevant. Each step (or process) relates to the capture of data, being pure figures or text and the subsequent undertaking of capta, the act of placing relevance to the data to make it information.   The theory suggests data with capta becomes information and that with the addition of cognitive structures and some form of longevity this becomes

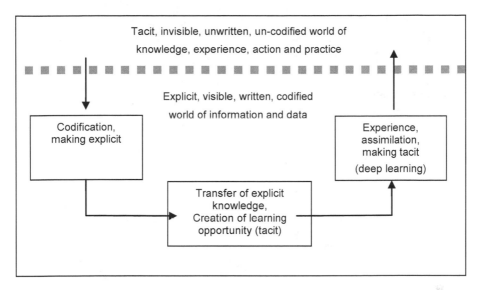

Fig. 2. Pre-transfer and post-transfer processing of knowledge

knowledge. This progression from data through to knowledge could be considered to be similar, in as much as there is linearity in the process of conversion, to the progression from explicit to tacit as explained by Sveiby [21]. The key step in Sveiby's suggested process that converts explicit into tacit knowledge is, for one thing, the addition of the "ability to act" or to "apply it". He goes on to argue that each time a codification or translation occurs, and the parties begin to transfer explicit information, a potential exists to lose a component of that knowledge through the interpretation stage. The act of codification between tacit and explicit can be represented on a linear scale (similar to the progression between data and knowledge referred to in 'knowledge-based management') as can the cognition (or interpretation) that occurs as the knowledge is re-codified by the recipient, to add the ability to act / application. There is a significant amount of research that considers the intellectual processes that occur to embed this ability to act. These include the referencing of new knowledge to other personally embedded experiences that are similar that allow the cognition and embedding of this knowledge [22]. Another process referred to is the repetition of 'like actions' that lead to individuals being able to digest and therefore vary their work patterns to accommodate local efficiencies in cognitive processes [13].

All of the perspectives considered above suggest that the transfer of knowledge is complex. A way to reflect the perspectives of the authors above, who are trying to create explanation around the act of transferring knowledge, whilst trying to define the properties of knowledge, is to create a way to visualise the subject. Epp & Price [23] suggest that a "sensitising framework" could be one way to enable people to visualise and comprehend an intangible. Wacker [24] also suggests that some form of a framework or mental model is a good way of visualising theory.

A framework for review has therefore been developed to aid practitioners and people who will become involved in knowledge transfer to understand how the properties of knowledge can change during and transfer of knowledge. This is shown in Figure 3.

For simplicity the framework takes only two stakeholders into account; the University and the Company and does not consider the additional stakeholders promoted by Etzkowitz [25] and Stevens & Bagby [26]. This is because normally the third stakeholder (the government) and the fourth stakeholder (society) do not directly become engaged in the actual process of transferring knowledge.

The framework portrays the transfer of knowledge between Universities and Industry or commercial organisations, firstly in the form of tacit-to-tacit knowledge shown at the top of the framework and toward the lower half in the form of explicit exchange of knowledge, importantly in two directions from the university to the company and reciprocally between the company and the university. According to Polanyi [3] the transfer of tacit knowledge is hard to achieve; this is represented by the size of the transfer arrows in the model, but no scalable relationship is inferred by the relative size of the arrows.

The lateral arrows represent the properties of knowledge and show a shift in the types of knowledge progressing from tacit (at the top), through implicit to explicit (at the bottom). The left hand arrow relates to codification and cognition as does the right hand arrow. The top of each arrow represents high levels of tacit knowledge, resulting from experiences and education and laden with the ability to act. The bottom represents a dominance of explicit knowledge. This continuum exists between the poles of "entirely tacit" knowledge and "entirely explicit" knowledge, however there is never a state where either no explicit knowledge exists, and vice versa. This corresponds to the view of Tsoukas [14] and Gourlay [15].

Real examples, where knowledge was transferred at the tacit level, and also those where the route from tacit-to-tacit is via codification, explicit transfer and understanding or assimilation were used to validate this framework. The purpose of this research is to create a guideline that identifies which channel is likely to transfer tacit knowledge most effectively. This is achieved by referencing the work of authors such as Schmoch et al [27], and Schartinger et al [8] and then triangulating their findings against real examples of typical knowledge transfer projects (to understand the transfer of knowledge within each type of channel) and reflecting on the framework. The results can be used to influence the choice of knowledge channel for both industrial managers and academic institutions.

3   Methodology

A detailed research protocol was established as part of this strategic knowledge management research – a research field that unlike its sibling "Knowledge-based Management (an evolution of information systems), is still in it infancy and lacks robust, empirically tested theory. In relation to operations research, and the three dominant systems perspectives (hard, soft and critical), in general terms a "hard systems perspective" employs only a positivist approach to study "objective data" (which can be likened to seeking only explicit knowledge) whereas, a "soft" systems perspective however treats knowledge in a more phenomenological way as being *"tacit, generated and consumed in social action... and it is assumed that this knowledge is Innovation"* ([28] p. 388). By combining methodologies into a dualist, social constructivist approach and seeking mode 2 knowledge creation [29], a robust three-step data collection protocol was established around participant enquiry and participant interaction.

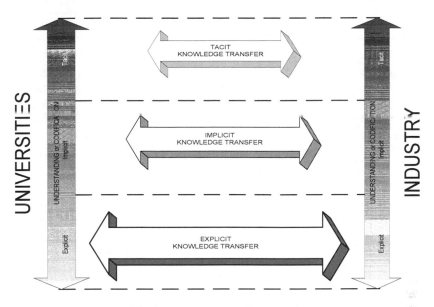

Fig. 3. The Assessment Framework

The research instrument was derived (within step 1) by reference to a Delphi-style expert panel, made up of 10 'innovation-focussed' policy executives and subsequently posing a broad-range question to a community of practice. Step 2 involved data collection using semi-structured interviews lasting 90 minutes, in certain cases followed by a second 60 minute interview, undertaken after a period of interviewer reflection. Each interview was transcribed and returned to the subject for approval before being summarized in a partially-coded in-case tabulated summary. To ensure that the data collected was representative a sample size and selection criteria were develop for the second and third parts of the study. In total 19 completed projects were chosen for review in 25 interviews, not all with an operational management focus, but taken pan-sector and across a range of innovation disciplines. Reliability, validity and generalisability were expressly considered as was the role of experimental control for this study, which looks to build theory, before subjecting it to deductive-style testing within further research.

4   Findings

The knowledge transfer projects that were studied included the development of a spin-out company exploiting engineering-based research in software analysis and three patents involving a range of research, from novel techniques in spectroscopy to a bio-science application.

In the 19 interviews undertaken in step 2, all respondents acknowledged that the framework did reflect the way that knowledge transfer occurred within their projects. The 6 interviews taken in two further case studies (step 3) representing triangulated stakeholder opinions agreed that the framework typically represented how knowledge transferred as well. A summary of the interviews and results is shown in Table 1.

A good example of a response that affirmed the framework in detail is a "joint supervision" case study (TRMU) focussed on the development of materials for a museum of local culture. The respondent stated that the transfer took place over a long period and they felt that tacit knowledge transferred at the outset as face-to-face interviews and subsequent transcripts were developed. This led to the development of explicit material that could then be displayed in the form of teaching materials in local schools. Further explicit material were developed in the form of a booklet that was circulated within the local community and also uploaded to the internet.

Analysing the content of the response and referring it back to the framework it could be suggested that the transfer of tacit-to-tacit knowledge via face-to-face communication was one act of knowledge transfer, between interviewer and interviewee. In relation to the preparation of the media and dissemination in the form of a booklet etc, this could be considered as a second act of knowledge transfer and be identified as tacit-to-explicit prior to transfer, however this is not true knowledge transfer as this element of the project is only one-directional. This project does relate back to the framework and the responses have confirmed the aim of the framework, which is to enable the subject to consider the implications of transferring different types of knowledge.

In multiple interviews from a case in contract research and consultancy (RDEP) the second interviewer states the "flows reflect the model but there was a mix of tacit and explicit in varying proportions during the project. There was an exchange of tacit at the beginning. As the project became more defined, with more knowledge then the University could provide more focussed knowledge into the products, so it started off with having mostly tacit knowledge, with some explicit and as the project moved on the knowledge became more explicit". This reflected a deeper response than some of the interview candidates had made, when reviewing the framework.

The other respondent from the same project stated "the framework is OK – I have never thought of it like that I guess, we mostly transfer [knowledge] across the big arrow at the bottom as companies can't wait or can't afford the tacit bit". The third respondent from this case stated the "first process is the transfer of tacit knowledge to explicit knowledge from industry to university, second is the transfer of the tacit knowledge from the university staff into explicit knowledge in the product and the third is the transfer of our explicit knowledge to explicit knowledge for the industrial partner. Also each transferred tacit knowledge to tacit knowledge at the beginning, then tacit knowledge was transferred to explicit in the form of the product design specification and then we transferred explicit to explicit knowledge in the prototype".

During the interview response above the design engineer traces their finger across the framework picture to correspond with the flows that they are verbalising.

Table 1. Summary of results

Interview Number	Interview Code	Knowledge Transfer Channel (number)	Acknowledgement	Affirmed in detail	Affirmed with suggestions
KEY RESPONDERS					
N/A	N/A	Graduate Employment	N/A		
1	UEME	Joint Conference		X	
2	ATT1	Spin Out (1)		X	
3	ICO3	Spin Out (2)		X	
4	SIMP	Spin out (3)		X	
5	AEBS	Professional Journal			X
6	EDSN	Network 1			X
7	3DAC	Joint Supervision 1	X		
8	TRMU	Joint Supervision 2		X	
N/A	N/A	Training & CPD	N/A		
9	PATC	Collaborative Research		X	
10	KELL	Contract Research & Consultancy (1)		X	
N/A	N/A	Shared Facilities	N/A		
11	SYNG	Patent 1		X	
12	MALA	Patent 2	X		
13	ATT3	Patent 3		X	
14	ARGA	Joint Venture 1	X		
MULTIPLE RESPONDERS					
15	QINE	Joint Venture 2		X	
16	QINE (2)		X		
17	RDEP (1)	Contract Research & Consultancy (2)			X
18	RDEP (2)			X	
19	RDEP (3)			X	

In the third patent project (ATT3) the respondent indicates that "there was definitely a flow of information from tacit to explicit, but the whole model was definitely skewed to the left-hand side; any release of knowledge to industry was done in a stage managed way". In patent 2 (MALA) the respondent felt that "the whole model [framework] was going on, but there was probably more explicit knowledge" and in patent 1 (SYNG) the respondent agreed "it is basically what happened, we have tacit knowledge about fungi and fungicides that we used to test the patent from [name] and it proved to work and we then presented the work in explicit form to the company, the company has taken up the knowledge and it will become tacit with them".

Contract research & consultancy 1 (KELL) suggested the framework "reflects the study. At the beginning the children had tacit knowledge which was shared with the university staff; the university staff also have some tacit knowledge. The children's knowledge in terms of diaries, measurements etc was codified, understood and then the data was collected and written down in the form of a report. This knowledge is then passed to the company".

Three of the respondents also suggested improvements to the framework. The respondent that had been interviewed because of their experience of networks to transfer knowledge (EDSN) felt that the framework reflected knowledge transfer in networks but to differing extents and this related to each particular network. The respondent went on to suggest a modification to the framework, so that instead of pure transfer of knowledge occurring on the x-axis (horizontally) a time line could be superimposed to show how the transfer of tacit knowledge changed over the duration of the knowledge transfer.

The academic responding from their experiences of consultancy (RDEP) affirmed the model represented their particular knowledge transfer "almost". They then described key stages of their particular transfer with reference to steps within their project. The first step was explained as being the translation of tacit knowledge into explicit knowledge as the industrial partner defined the problems and sent documents relating to context and needs – a brief or scope of works. The second step was explained as the University translating the explicit knowledge within the brief into tacit knowledge (to develop a proposal of what they intended to undertake). The next step was the codification of the tacit knowledge into a material artefact (where drawings were prepared, further codified into the software and printed on an additive layer rapid prototyping machine to create the end product) in the form of a prototype and finally, the transfer of explicit information between the parties as the prototype and report are exchanged to complete the project.

The professor and co-author responding in respect to the joint academic publications (AEBS) stated "on a simplistic level I can understand how this model applies to the project but I see knowledge transfer as more circular and fluid. I think the transfer was not as linear as the model implies; knowledge can happen on various different levels with more or less tacit and explicit knowledge being exchanged at one time, which is why I think the model has to be put into context. It needs to take into consideration time. I can see how a circular model of knowledge transfer can happen in an hour and can also take several months. Also I think that generally the model has to be put into context in the problem situation and that it is important to define outcomes". The comment relating to the simplistic level is important as this framework can only really work at a high level where management guidelines and review instruments are often most effective - they operate best at a simplistic level and taken too literally can be misleading.

It is important to understand that the framework has a broad range of applications – it can be used to take a "snapshot" of how knowledge is being transferred at a particular point in time, but it can also be used in planning, to create an ambition of transferring mostly tacit knowledge or it can be used in reflection to consider how knowledge flowed in a project, perhaps as part of a post project review process or lessons-realised exercise.

In summary the responses received from the interviews taken from completed knowledge transfer projects suggest that the framework is a helpful map to enable interviewees to reflect on their particular the study has knowledge transfer projects. We have demonstrated that the framework stimulates the thoughts of professionals focussed around what types of knowledge flow between a company and a higher education. All of the respondents were able to relate this framework to their real life examples of completed knowledge transfer projects that were promoted by their respective companies, universities or government organisations as successful examples. Each respondent either acknowledged the pertinence of, or affirmed in detail or with suggestions how the framework could be related to their particular project. The only exception to this arose during the interview with the company respondent representing a project to develop a 3-dimensional CAD facility within a traditional boat building firm. When asked if the framework reflected the flow of knowledge in the project the respondent replied "No, the knowledge transfer was the reverse of this model" however there were two interesting notes made by the interviewer relating to this statement. These were that the subject was unable to articulate how flows could act in reverse and that the subject could not elaborate around the framework and became dismissive". The most likely answer to this, is that the respondent had failed to grasp the two-directional nature of the framework (and was referring to the reverse flow as right to left and not left to right) or that the term reverse relates to there being only explicit knowledge in the heads of the project participants, which then became tacit as the project progressed. It would seem that without reference to this respondent further a clear explanation cannot be offered, however it does seem that the framework has still achieved what it set out to do, which was to make the respondent consider the way in which knowledge transferred in their project.

In obtaining more than 12 responses this research proposes that the framework could form the basis of a useful construct, which when applied to a phenomenon (where company and academic personnel promote the success of a knowledge transfer without reference to objective measures or detailed comparative analysis), improves the understanding of what is occurring within the projects.

The responses (including some that looked to try to improve the way the framework represented knowledge transfer) demonstrated to the researchers that the framework has achieved what it set out to do. A summary of the results can be seen in Table 1. It stimulates professionals' thought into what types of knowledge flow between a company and a higher education and allows people to visualise knowledge (which is often overlooked due to the difficulty in visualising it). All of the respondents were able to relate this framework to their real life experience of knowledge transfer projects undertaken by their respective companies, universities or government organisations. Each respondent either acknowledged the pertinence of the framework, or affirmed its usefulness in detail, or affirmed while adding suggestions how the framework could be related to their particular project.

5   Practical Application of the Framework

The framework and the understanding gained from the knowledge transfer cases will lead to a tool that can be applied to stimulate innovation by allowing managers to select the most appropriate channels for transferring knowledge into companies from universities, using such channels as staff secondment, jointly supervised projects, consultancy, contract research etc. The research also allows universities to configure their offerings to industry in order to tailor their activities to offer the maximum benefit according to the situation and the type of knowledge to be transferred.

As a particular example studied, a process-based outsourcing service company undertook a two year joint-supervision project (within a UK-specific grant funded scheme entitled Knowledge Transfer Partnership – KTP). The aim of the project was two fold: to review the contract and order fulfilment capability within the company (which at the outset turned-over around £500k per annum and employed 12 staff working across shop-floor and IT-based service provision) and undertake an Activity Based Costing appraisal to highlight the contracts with the greatest yield and to redesign the order fulfilment processes to greater increase the contract yield, whilst downscaling the sales and marketing activity for poorly performing contracts.

As a result of the project the company reported an increase in net profits of more than £300k which they attributed to improved operational efficiency (28%), targeting only profitable contracts (27%), longer duration contracts (33%) and increased production capacity (27%).

When questioned the company respondents stated *"The people who fund the project* [in reference to the grant body] *want explicit knowledge because they want to be able to measure it. Some explicit knowledge is needed, but the essence of the project, and its greatest benefit, is the transfer of tacit knowledge"*. Whilst reflecting on the framework the university respondent stated that *"most of* [the knowledge transferred] *is in the implicit stage and it happens on a continuum"*. The company respondent, in this case the Managing Director, stated "[the knowledge flows] *were definitely happening but at different rates and in numerous forms, some of which is still going on* [the interview took place 6 months after project completion] *and I would say that we are at the implicit stage for embedding (on right-hand axis of the framework)"*.

6   Conclusions and Future Research

The conclusion for this research is that by referencing experts in this area and by studying the outcomes of participation in collaborative projects, transferring knowledge back and forth between industry and higher education, we have developed a useful and practical visualisation framework. Within an immature research landscape, where main contributors in this area relate to the barriers to; benefits from and motivations for knowledge transfer, we have contributed to theory. By focussing on certain attributes or properties of knowledge the framework can be used to aid in planning a knowledge transfer activity and visualising how knowledge might flow during the project. This will in-turn affect decisions on governance (where a partnering style of governance can lead to more tacit knowledge being transferred[30]), geographic location of the knowledge partner (in relation to the ability to hold face to face meetings [5]) amongst a number of other factors.

Future research in the this area will focus on balancing the extensive qualitative data collected within this study with more objective measurements of performance, again taken across completed knowledge transfer project as the second, more deductive phase of theory development (according to [31]).

In terms of further application of this research, a study developing this framework into a set of management guidelines for policy makers, managers and participants within knowledge transfer projects has already been undertaken and the results are awaiting publication. It is planned to extend these guidelines further by incorporating them into a policy decision-making tool based on innovation management capability and innovation channel suitability.

References

1. Chapman, R.L., Corso, M.: From continuous improvement to collaborative innovation: the next challenge in supply chain management. Production Planning & Control: The Management of Operations 16(4), 339–344 (2005)
2. Chesbrough, H.: Open Business Models: How to thrive in the new innovation landcape. Harvard Business School Press, Boston (2006)
3. Polanyi, M.: The Tacit Dimension. Routledge, London (1966)
4. Liebowitz, J.: Key ingredients to the success of an organization's knowledge management strategy. Knowledge and Process Management 6(1), 37–40 (1999)
5. Alexander, A.T., Childe, S.J.: Innovation: A Knowledge Transfer Perspective. In: Garetti, M., et al. (eds.) Advances in Production Management Systems. Poliscript, Como (2010)
6. Grant, R.M.: Toward a knowledge based theory of the firm. Strategic Management Journal 17, 109–122 (1996)
7. Bessant, J., Phelps, R., Adams, R.: External Knowledge: A review of the literature addressing the role of external knowledge and expertise at key stages of business growth and development. Advanced Institute for Management Research London, pp. 1–78 (2005)
8. Schartinger, D., et al.: Knowledge interactions between universities and and industry in Austria: Sectoral patterns and determinants. Research Policy 31, 303–328 (2002)
9. Chilton, M.A., Bloodgood, J.M.: The dimension of tacit and explicit knowledge: A descriptive and measure. International Journal of Knowledge Management 4(2), 75–91 (2008)
10. Meier, M.: Knowledge Management in Strategic Alliances: A Review of Empirical Evidence. International Journal of Management Reviews 13(1), 1–23 (2011)
11. Beckman, T.J.: A Methodology for Knowledge Management. In: IASTED AI & Soft Computing Conference (1997)
12. Piaget, J.: The language and thought of the child (1997), http://search.ebscohost.com/login.aspx?direct=true&scope=site&db=nlebk&db=nlabk&AN=145960
13. Scribner, S.: Knowledge at Work. Anthropology & Education Quarterly 16(3), 199–206 (1985)
14. Tsoukas, H.: Do we really understand tacit knowledge? In: Easterby-Smith, M., Lyles, M. (eds.) Handbook of Organisational Learning and Knowledge. Blackwell, Oxford (2005)
15. Gourlay, S.: Conceptualizing Knowledge Creation: A Critique of Nonaka's Theory. Journal of Management Studies 43(7), 1415–1436 (2006)
16. Nonaka, I., Takeuchi, H.: The Knowledge Creating Company. University Press, Oxford (1995)
17. Liebowitz, J., Beckman, T.: Knowledge Organisations: What every manager should know. CRC Press, Danvers (1998)
18. Clinton, M.S., Merritt, K.L., Murray, S.R.: Using Corporate Universities to facilitate Knowledge Transfer and Achieve Competitive Advantage: An exploratory model based on media richness and type of knowledge to be transferred. International Journal of Knowledge Management 5(4), 43–59 (2009)
19. Civi, E.: Knowledge Management as Competitive Advantage. Marketing, Intelligence and Planning 18(4), 166–174 (2000)
20. Checkland, P., Holwell, S.: Information, systems and information systems. Wiley, Chichester (1998)
21. Sveiby, K.E.: The New Organisational Wealth. Berrett-Koehler Pub. Inc., San Francisco (1997)

22. Argyris, C., Schon, D.: Organizational Learning: A theory of action perspective. Addison-Wesley, Reading (1978)
23. Epp, A.M., Price, L.L.: Family Identity: A Framework of Identity Interplay in Consumption Practices. Journal of Consumer Research 35 (2008)
24. Wacker, J.G.: A definition of theory: research guidelines for different theory-building research methods in operations management. Journal of Operations Management 16(4), 361–385 (1998)
25. Etzkowitz, H.: The triple helix of university-industry-government: Implications for policy and evaluation in Report 2002:11. SISTER Swedish Institute for Studies in Educations: Stockholm (2002)
26. Stevens, J.M., Bagby, J.W.: Knowledge transfer from universities to business: returns for all stakeholders. Organisation 8(2), 259–268 (2001)
27. Schmoch, U., Licht, G., Reinhard, M.: Wissens und Technologietransfer in Deutschland. Fraunhofer IRB Verlag, Stuttgart (2000)
28. Sheffield, J.: Pluralism in Knowledge Management: a review. Electronic Journal of Knowledge Management 7(3), 387–396 (2009)
29. Gibbons, M., et al.: The New Production of Knowledge: The dynamics of science and research in contemporary societies. Sage Publishers Ltd., London (1994)
30. Perkmann, M., Walsh, K.: How firms source knowledge from universities: Partnerships versus contracting. In: Bessant, J., Venables, T. (eds.) Creating Wealth from Knowledge: Meeting the Innovation Challenge. Edward Elgar, Cheltenham (2008)
31. Carlile, P., Christensen, L.: The Cycles of Theory Building in Management Research. Innosight Innovation Resources, 1–25 (2005)

Leadership Redundancy in a Multiteam System[*]

Idar A. Johannessen[1], Philip W. McArthur [2], and Jan R. Jonassen[1]

[1] Stord/Haugesund University College, Norway
[2] Action Design, Cambridge, MA, USA

Abstract. Inspection, maintenance, and repair (IMR) operations of the subsea infrastructure off Norway's coast are performed from specialized vessels by multiteam systems. A case study shows how leadership is organized and practiced to coordinate interdependencies, and to cope with the risks inherent in this type of complex and tightly coupled operation. *Leadership redundancy* is proposed as a mechanism that can contribute to the smooth and safe functioning of a multiteam system operating in a volatile environment.

Keywords: HRO, reliability, multiteam systems, offshore operations, leadership, redundancy.

1 Introduction

Since complex and flexible organizational designs are used to conduct high-risk work in potentially extreme environments [5], we need to understand the leadership dynamics that enable them to be effective. There is a growing body of research and theory on multiteam systems (MTS)[6], [7] as well as on organizations that operate successfully in high-risk environments (HROs) [2][11]. Both of these bodies of literature contribute to our understanding of how to manage complexity. However, to our knowledge, these perspectives have not been integrated. We find no studies, for example, on commercial multiteam systems engaged in high-risk operations. Our research study provides an opportunity to fill that gap.

In this paper we examine how leadership is organized and executed in a multiteam system that performs inspection, maintenance, and repair on oil and gas installations on the Norwegian Continental Shelf – complex operations that entail substantial risks given the nature of the work and the extremity of the environment. We explain how both MTS Theory and High Reliability Theory deepen our understanding of the leadership of this particular organization, and how our findings contribute to both theories. We describe how leadership in this MTS is organized and exercised both to coordinate a highly interdependent operation and to cope with unexpected events that can compromise the effectiveness and safety of the operation. We propose that a

---

[*] The Research Council of Norway and companies in the petromaritime industries in the Haugesund region have funded the project Managing Complexity in Petromaritime Operations at Stord/Haugesund University College. The authors are grateful for advice from Silvia Jordan, Preben H. Lindøe, Amy Edmondson, Nils M. Sortland, Lene Jørgensen, Amy Meltzer and Paul Wilson Glenn.

J. Frick and B. Laugen (Eds.): APMS 2011, IFIP AICT 384, pp. 549–556, 2012.

previously unidentified mechanism, which we call *leadership redundancy*, can contribute to the reliability of this multiteam system. Finally, we discuss the implication of our findings for research and practice.

2   Multiteam Systems and High-Reliability Organizations

In their seminal paper on multiteam systems, Mathieu et al. [7] define the features of this unique organizational structure, and the factors that determine its effectiveness. A multiteam system (MTS) is a "team of teams" that works together to achieve a unifying purpose. The component teams in an MTS may come from the same company or from different companies. For example, an emergency response MTS is comprised of fire fighters, emergency medical technicians, a surgery team, and a recovery team. Each team has its own purpose, capabilities, and tasks, but they are united by the common goal of saving lives. To be considered part of an MTS, each component team must be interdependent with at least one other team on three dimensions: inputs (e.g. people, equipment, information), processes (e.g. the interaction required between teams to complete their respective tasks), and outputs (e.g. rewards, benefits, costs, task goals). The component teams may operate sequentially (where one team must complete its task before the next team can begin), in parallel, or in some combination of the two. Given that the component teams of an MTS are highly interdependent, the fundamental challenge they face is how to effectively coordinate their activities. For the purpose of this paper we focus on two critical factors that have been identified by MTS theory: leadership and shared mental models.[1]

Leadership in an MTS is complex. Leaders of the component teams must focus on what is happening both within their teams and between teams. They must ensure that their team's activities are aligned with the larger goal of the MTS. Leaders of the MTS as a whole must provide strategy and direction for the system, and coordinate the interdependent activities of all the component teams. In dynamic and volatile environments, MTS leaders must be mindful of changing and competing demands and be able to switch quickly from the routine to the non-routine. Consequently, MTS leaders face a dilemma. To ensure coordination within and between teams, procedures, roles, and tasks must be standardized so they can be implemented consistently. Standardization can, however, limit the teams' ability to adapt quickly to change. In comparison to leaders of single teams "the MTS leadership team will typically need to devote more of their work time ensuring system flexibility" [7].

Shared mental models help MTS members know what to expect from each other, communicate effectively, and coordinate their activities efficiently. MTS theory proposes four critical mental models for members of the multiteam system. They need a shared understanding of the purpose and task of their own team, and how it integrates with the goal of the MTS (task model). They must understand the capabilities and resources of each team in the system (team model), and how to coordinate their activities with those of the other teams (team interaction model). In addition, they must agree on how to adapt and adjust their actions to the demands of their dynamic environment (strategic mental model).

---

[1] See Mathieu et al. for a discussion of the role of IT and reward systems.

Finally, MTS researchers have proposed that the process of multiteam systems, like individual teams, has two phases: a transition phase in which planning takes place, and an action phase during which work is executed [7]. Experimental studies have found that the ability of team leaders to coordinate their interdependent activities in the action phase of an MTS operation is influenced by the quality of their planning in the transition phase [6].

When operations are complex^2 and tightly coupled^3 small errors can escalate quickly and create catastrophic consequences^4 [8]. Yet, some organizations that engage in high-risk work (such as nuclear power plants, submarines and aircraft carriers, and power grids), while not immune to accidents, do not experience the failure rates that one might expect [11].

Research on high reliability organizations (HROs) has identified factors that account for their success. These factors include: 1) exercising centralized control through core values, leaving decision making to the operational level [11]; 2) developing shared ways of thinking and acting that enable the organization to anticipate and respond to error, risk, and surprise [10]; 3) adopting hierarchical decision-making structures that encourage authority to migrate to those with the most expertise, regardless of their formal position [1]; and 4) designing multiple forms of redundancy (of workers, equipment, or capacity) into the system to increase the margin for error [9][11].

Since reliability is produced mainly through culture, it is "not bankable" [11] and must be continually regenerated. Leaders must take responsibility both for shaping, cultivating, and maintaining desired mindsets and behaviors with a long time perspective [9].

Both multiteam systems theory and high reliability theory address how organizations can succeed in turbulent, dynamic environments. Both emphasize the need for organizations to balance structure and flexibility, and both see culture (shared mental models) playing a key role to this end. MTS theory emphasizes the role that shared mental models play in coordinating interdependencies in a multiteam system, while HRT emphasizes the role that shared values and "cognitive mechanisms" (i.e., specific ways of thinking and acting) [10] play in managing surprise and error. While MTS theory identifies the leadership challenges and leadership functions in an MTS [7], HRT is more specific about how leaders and operators can think and act to ensure organizational flexibility (such as paying close attention to weak signals of impending failure, not being lulled by past success, testing assumptions publicly, and being open to diverging perspectives).

Both theories inform the interpretation of our data, and both have gaps that our research can help to address. Many studies of HROs concern organizations with multiple teams; however, the theory has not addressed the dynamics of multiteam systems as such, and the leadership challenges of this particular structure. In addition, multiteam system researchers have not conducted field studies of commercial multiteam systems comprised of teams from multiple companies that are engaged in high-risk work. MTS theory emphasizes that coordination of the MTS as a whole is a

---

^{2} Many parts whose interactions are not fully predictable or even visible.

^{3} Highly interdependent with little room for improvisation.

^{4} This brief discussion cannot do full justice to these concepts, that are in themselves complex.

critical leadership function, but it has not addressed how this coordinating role is exercised. Research on individual team leadership has proposed that effective leaders must pay attention to both task accomplishment and group maintenance [4]. MTS theory has argued that these two needs must be taken care of by the leaders of an MTS as well; however, it has not addressed how these two needs are met in practice.

3   Design and Methodology

Starting with the broad question about how complexity is managed in petromaritime operations, we chose to study IMR operations for three reasons: 1) they are highly complex in terms of technology, leadership, and organization; 2) they have consistently performed potentially dangerous work without major accidents; 3) they are configured similarly across the industry, which makes comparisons possible between our initial research and future research.

Our present study is based primarily on a two-week field trip following an IMR operation on one vessel. 14 semi-structured and 16 unstructured interviews were combined with some 160 hours of observation. In addition, documents were studied, and 12 interviews were conducted on shore, before and after the field trip. All interviews were transcribed and included in an NVivo database, together with the field log.

Descriptions of the formal and informal organization on the vessel were created and tested for accuracy with insiders. To explore mechanisms for coping with complexity, instances where leaders faced non-trivial choices were selected from the most demanding phase of an IMR trip, the actual execution of the subsea operation.

Guided by principles of theoretical sampling [3] we sought to explore the mechanisms that permitted these operations to proceed successfully and safely. We identified non-trivial choice situations, and tracked how they were addressed and by whom. We distinguished between situations where procedures, rules, and codified knowledge seemed to provide sufficient guidance and situations in which leaders found themselves in dilemmas. We grouped and analyzed the examples of leadership dilemmas, and examined how the informants chose to deal with them. This gave us an insight into the culture and organization of leadership in the IMR context.

4   The Research Context

The IMR business is organized as a supply chain. The oil companies have operators on call, in our example on long-term frame contracts. Operations are performed from specialized vessels that the operators, in turn, hire from shipping companies. The IMR vessel in this research is a 110 meters long, high-tech environment with approximately 70 crewmembers.

The IMR trip is a collaboration between five companies and requires the tightly coordinated interaction of seven key individual and team roles: 1) the subsea operations team, which flies the two remotely-operated vehicles (ROVs) that perform work on the installation, 2) the tower crane operator, 3) the rigging team, 4) the main crane operator,

5) the professional support teams, 6) the Dynamic Positioning (DP) team (which holds the vessel stationary while the subsea operation takes place), and 7) the pumping team that helps inject cleaning chemicals into the wells. The company that commissions the operation has two representatives on board; the Client Representative who is the liaison for this vessel over many trips, and the Licensee Representative, who represents the specific oil field requiring an IMR operation on this trip.

In a complex IMR operation teams must interact in mutually dependent ways. Priorities frequently change, weather conditions are unstable and most projects involve surprises. The environmental context is potentially extreme. Hannah et al. [5] define an extreme context as one "where one or more extreme events are occurring or are likely to occur that may exceed the organization's capacity to prevent and result in an extensive and intolerable magnitude of physical, psychological, or material consequences to—or in close physical or psycho-social proximity to—organization members." An IMR trip involves many potential risks for the crew, vessel (e.g. a big gas leak can sink the vessel), and the environment (e.g. pollution). The vessel is isolated at sea, often in rough weather. The different teams that carry out the operations are exposed to different levels of physical risk. The deck (where heavy objects and containers with chemicals are stored) is the most dangerous location on the vessel, especially during the mobilization and operational phases. Several activities often occur in parallel, including lifting or moving dangerous objects.

The Sub-Sea Team that flies the ROVs, and the tower crane operator who must lift and lower tools and equipment with great accuracy, operate within the closed environments of their respective control rooms. While these groups are more protected from the elements than the crews on deck, mistakes on their part can lead to catastrophic consequences.

5   Findings

A multiteam system can be an effective structure to harness the diverse resources necessary to carry out a complex operation, provided that the component teams are coordinated effectively [7]. Our research objective was to understand the factors that facilitate this coordination in a commercial MTS conducting high-risk work in a potentially extreme environment. Our findings in this case study are consistent with existing research and theory on multiteam systems and high-reliability organizations, and also add to those theories.

Consistent with MTS theory, an IMR operation is comprised of two distinct phases: a transition phase and an action phase. In the transition phase a series of planning and preparation processes help members of the MTS develop shared mental models about how individuals and teams are supposed to think and interact during the course of an operation. Such processes (e.g., Safe Job Analyses, Tool Box Meetings, and Task Plans) help members of the MTS to see the big picture of the operation, reinforce standard operating procedures, anticipate problems, and minimize their occurrence[5]. However, given the complex nature of the work and the dynamic environment in which

---

[5] These processes are described in detail in the "Descriptive Review of IMR Operations" (forthcoming).

it takes place unexpected events will occur and the system must be able to respond quickly. This has implications for the leadership structure of the operation.

While the Offshore Manager has overall responsibility for an IMR operation, once the vessel arrives over the seabed installation and the action phase starts, a transformation of the organization and leadership takes place. A hierarchical and centrally controlled multiteam system is mobilized to perform the actual work. Authority migrates from the Offshore Manager to the Shift Supervisor who is in charge of coordinating the operational MTS. He controls all operational resources, assembles all available information and decides what and how much information to distribute to the relevant parties. The leaders of the component teams, regardless of their company affiliation and their role in the hierarchy, defer to the direction of the Shift Supervisor. We also observed that the Shift Supervisor, during certain phases of the operation, would hand over control to third-party specialists. The mobilization of a latent hierarchy, and the migration of authority (with regard to sense-making and decision-making) that we observed in this MTS have been identified in previous research on high reliability organizations as factors that promote organizational reliability and effectiveness [1] [11]. Our research suggests that authority also can move upwards and laterally in the system, and that it may include several other leadership functions, such as coaching and boundary management.

During the execution of an IMR operation, the component teams of the MTS are tightly coupled. They operate within narrow timeframes, must interact in a specific sequence, and follow established procedures. Given the limited slack in the system, small errors can escalate quickly. Putting the operation on hold is a fallback option, which does get used, but which can be costly. While some component teams may experience idle time (e.g., ROV pilots waiting for equipment to be ready), the Shift Supervisor is seldom able to leave his post. He must process a continuous flow of information, and focus almost solely on coordinating the tasks of the interdependent teams, with little time left to attend to other leadership functions, such as "group maintenance" [4] of the MTS as a whole. When problems arise in the MTS (either within or between the component teams), which the team leaders are not able to manage, the Shift Supervisor is in a difficult bind.

For example, in one situation an inexperienced Deck Foreman had difficulty with a new crewmember (a rigger). The rigger was behaving erratically, seemed unaware of the potential hazards on deck, and was unresponsive to feedback. The Deck Foreman approached the Shift Supervisor for help and asked him to intervene directly. The Shift Supervisor faced a dilemma: If he intervened, he would take his attention away from coordinating the highly complex and interdependent flow of the operation. If he did not intervene, there was a risk that the rigger's behavior could cause serious problems that would jeopardize the operation and the safety of the vessel. We observed several situations in which disturbances in the MTS could create this type of dilemma for the Shift Supervisor. In some cases, as the following three examples illustrate, tensions within the MTS were managed not by the Shift Supervisor or by component team leaders, but by leaders on the vessel who were not directly engaged in executing the IMR operation.

1. In one situation there was an oil leak in one of the ROV manipulators, and the vehicle was brought to the surface for repairs. While the recovery was underway,

several people gathered in the ROV control room, including the Client Representative. The Client Representative initiated a discussion about why the accident happened and how it could have been prevented. The Offshore Manager, who had just arrived on the scene, saw the Client Representative's intervention as inappropriate and potentially distracting for the team and for the Shift Supervisor, who was in his control room nearby. He intervened to move the discussion away from the ROV control room. The Offshore Manager in this case fills a leadership function of guarding the boundary of a team, strictly speaking under the command of the senior ROV supervisor and ultimately the Shift Supervisor. Tensions are relieved and the team can focus back on immediate damage control, while the learning discussion is moved to a space where it is more likely to succeed.

2. While informal cooperation and communication takes place regularly between all the stakeholders, difficulties arise when the Client Representative (or the License Representative) asks the Shift Supervisor to perform duties that may go beyond contractual obligations or to engage in tasks that prevent the Shift Supervisor from devoting full attention to the operation. For example, a License Representative requested that the Shift Supervisor take over responsibility for a pumping operation. The Offshore Manager, whose expertise includes knowledge of contractual matters, overheard the conversation and pointed out to the License that this was the duty of the Third Party, hired directly by the License on a different contract. Again, the Offshore Manager handles boundary management and prevents the Shift Supervisor from going beyond his competencies and potentially harming the operation.

3. In a third example, the Medic noticed that the Deck Foreman was having difficulty with his team and not delegating tasks effectively. The Deck Foreman lost oversight over activities on deck, which could jeopardize effectiveness and safety. In his role, the Medic has both the mandate and the time to address health, safety, and environment (HSE) matters on-board and make ad hoc interventions. When the Deck Foreman was off-duty, the Medic asked to speak with him and offered his feedback. In this example, a non-leader performs coaching, which would enable the Deck Foreman to be more effective in the future.

Our research findings suggest that the demands of a multiteam system performing high-risk work in a potentially extreme environment require that authority be centralized in the role of a coordinator. Under stress the coordinator will feel compelled to prioritize task coordination over other leadership functions (e.g., coaching, conflict management, and boundary management) [4]. When frictions occur in the MTS, which need immediate attention, the coordinator is in a bind. For the MTS to function effectively, other leaders who are not directly engaged in the execution of the operation step in to help. We refer to this availability of additional leadership resources as *leadership redundancy*.

6   Implications

Our findings contribute to an understanding of the challenges of an MTS in two critical areas: 1) the role that redundancies play in the effectiveness of complex operations; and 2) how leadership roles in an MTS can be implemented to enable effective coordination of the operation, while also attending to the inter-group maintenance of the MTS as a whole. Both findings contribute to our understanding of a core paradox identified by both MTS theory and HRT: the need for complex organizations to be both structured and flexible.

A limit of our study is that our findings are based on data from one case study. More research is underway to test our hypothesis about leadership redundancy. We need to understand the factors, other than capacity, that influence the effective utilization of leadership redundancy. We need to know how shared understandings of the appropriate use of leadership redundancy (how, when, who) are shaped. For example, not all deck foremen might welcome being coached by a medic on leadership issues. Leadership redundancy may add complexity and stress as well as relieve it, particularly if members of the multi-team system do not have a shared mental model about its execution.

References

1. Bigley, G.A., Roberts, K.H.: The Incident Command System: High-Reliability Organizing for Complex and Volatile Task Environments. Academy of Management Journal 44, 1281–1299 (2001)
2. Bourrier, M.: Das Vermächtnis der High Reliability Theory. In: Weyer, J., Schulz-Schaeffer, I. (eds.) Management komplexer Systeme - Konzepte für die Bewältigung von Intransparenz, Unsicherheit und Chaos, Oldeburg, München (2009)
3. Corbin, J.M., Strauss, A.L.: Basics of qualitative research: Techniques and procedures for developing grounded theory, 3rd edn. Sage, Thousand Oaks (2008)
4. Hackman, J.R., Walton, R.E.: Leading groups in organizations. In: Goodman, P.S.A. (ed.) Designing Effective Work Groups. Jossey-Bass, San Fransisco (1986)
5. Hannah, S.T., Uhl-Bien, M., Avolio, B.J., et al.: A Framework for Examining Leadership in Extreme Contexts. Leadership Quarterly 20, 897–919 (2009)
6. Marks, M.A., DeChurch, L.A., Mathieu, J.E., et al.: Teamwork in Multiteam Systems. J. Appl. Psychol. 90, 964–971 (2005)
7. Mathieu, J.E., Marks, M.A., Zaccaro, S.J.: Multi-team systems. In: Anderson, N., Ones, D., Sinangil, H.K., et al. (eds.) Handbook of Industrial, Work and Organizational Psychology, vol. 2. Sage, London (2001)
8. Perrow, C.: Normal accidents: Living with high-risk technologies. Basic Books, New York (1984)
9. Roberts, K.H.: Some Characteristics of One Type of High Reliability Organization. Organization Science 1, 160–176 (1990)
10. Weick, K.E., Sutcliffe, K.M., Obstfeld, D.: Organizing for high reliability: processes of collective mindfulness. In: Staw, B.M., Sutton, R.I. (eds.) Research in Organizational Behavior, vol. 21, pp. 81–123. Elsevier Science/JAI Press (1999)
11. Weick, K.E., Sutcliffe, K.M.: Managing the unexpected, 2nd edn. Jossey-Bass, San Francisco (2007)

Study on Need Assessment of Mechatronics Education in Norway and Poland

Hirpa G. Lemu[1,*], Jan Frick[1], Tadeusz Uhl[2],
Wojciech Lisowski[2], and Piotr Piwowarczyk[2]

[1] University of Stavanger, Stavanger, Norway
[2] AGH University of Science and Technology,
Department of Robotics and Mechatronics, Kraków, Poland
Hirpa.g.lemu@uis.no

Abstract. This article presents a summary result of the survey on the need for mechatronics education. The study was conducted as a cooperation project between two teams established at two universities: AGH-UST from Poland and University of Stavanger (UiS) from Norway. Both companies and High School Pupils are surveyed in this project, but only feedbacks from the former are analyzed in this article. As a result of the declining interest for engineering and science education in general and mechatronics education in particular, the project is intended to work out an International Curriculum for mechatronics education that can stimulate pupils for science and technology fields as well as to encourage students in engineering education. The field of mechantronics has been focused because this field, as a new and multidisciplinary area, has a high potential to integrate topics that are necessary for modern engineering industries and can provide graduates in a multi-skill and knowledge.

Keywords: Mechatronics, mechatronics curriculum, multidisciplinary field.

1 Introduction

Complex mechanical systems of today like airplanes, cars, industrial process machines and spaceships have many embedded mechanical and electronic systems that monitor and control the behavior to avoid catastrophic failure and improve the performance. With its origin in Japan in late 1960s [1] the term mechatronics was in principle coined to define such control and operation systems. The concept has since spread all over the world and a significant international growth has been observed within the last three decades. According to technology review of MIT press [2], mechatronics is identified as one of the top 10 technologies that will change the future world. The field is in general viewed as the vehicle by which students are introduced to and made to comprehend the diverse disciplines (Fig. 1) such as computer science, electrical and mechanical engineering areas concurrently. By combining diverse fields, mechatronics curriculum provides sufficient background, knowledge, depth and breadth enabling the graduates to tackle complex engineering problems.

---

[*] Corresponding author.

J. Frick and B. Laugen (Eds.): APMS 2011, IFIP AICT 384, pp. 557–566, 2012.

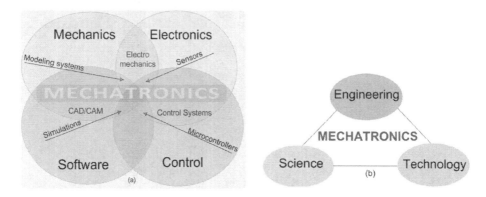

Fig. 1. Illustration of the diverse fields and concepts making up mechatronics

Understanding the fact that mechatronics is a newly emerging branch of study, that can interlink engineering, science and technology (Fig. 1(b)), many universities [3-5] have examined the curriculum in order to, among others, improve the structure and content of the program, increase the recruitment of students and improve effectiveness of teaching.

A number of these recent studies have attempted to investigate the organization of universities and how teaching of this discipline can be conducted. Some of the previous studies focused on the issue from the view of education philosophy of engineering [6] while others worked on the programs of curriculum [7] as well as the evolutionary development of the field as an engineering branch and the possible standardization of the education on nearly universal base [8]. The reported surveys, mainly in universities, have both national and regional characteristics[9].

Other studies [10] have attempted to define the identity and legitimacy of mechatronics as well as the implications on the selectivity and communication of the subject. This identity definition considers mechatronics as the "synergistic combination of precision mechanical engineering, electronic control and systems thinking in the design of products and manufacturing processes" rather than the descriptions of the discipline solely as an interdisciplinary subject, as the union between mechanical and electrical engineering, control theory and computer science or other combinations of traditional disciplines within an engineering sphere. It is also important to recognize that mechatronics is not only a combination of engineering subjects, but it, as a multidisciplinary field of study, integrates science and technology with engineering (Fig. 1(b)).

The focus on formulation of mechatronics curriculum and defining its identity is, in a way, well motivated because comprehending a multidisciplinary field is challenging unless a suitable curriculum that motivates the students is outlined. At the same time it is essential that the formulated curriculum fulfils the expectations of the job market. A recent review by Alvarez Cabrera, et. al. [11] highlights the list of some of the existing challenges in design of mechatronics curriculum and systems for both the academia and industrial sector.

Based on the declining trend of interest for mechatronics study at well established universities like AGH-UST of Kraków, Poland, assessment of the need for this study has been initiated. The purpose of this study partially reported in this article is primarily to formulate a fundamentally new curriculum that enables a greater degree of self-direction in designing and developing mechatronics systems. To make the survey more comprehensive the expectations of students concerning the mechatronics study were also taken into account during the assessment. This article attempts to present a brief summary of the results of this cooperative research.

The rest of the article is organized as follows: Some highlight of the assessment approach used in the study and analysis of the company feedbacks are given Section 2 and 3 respectively. Section 4 discusses the practical implications of the feedbacks and Section 5 presents briefly students' expectations to mechatronics study. Finally, conclusion is given in Section 6.

2   Assessment Approach

This study is a result of a collaboration project between two teams: one team from AGH-UST of Kraków, Poland, and the second team from University of Stavanger (UiS), Norway. During formulation of the project objectives the team understood the mission of universities in formulating the curriculum as twofold:

1. Supporting professional success of their graduates on the labor market, and
2. Providing the candidates that suit the needs of the job market.

To achieve both objectives, questionnaires were prepared and concurrently distributed among companies and high schools in Norway and Poland. The study in this article presents the analysis results of company feedbacks in which 25 companies from Krakow area, and 12 companies from Stavanger area, are involved. In line with the stated project objectives, the questionnaires focus on two main parts.

1) *Collecting information on the companies:* this involves, among others, company size, profile, business life and the legal form of the company, and the role of mechatronics as a multidisciplinary area of knowledge as well as the extent of research oriented activity in the company and cooperation with universities.

2) *Assessing the companies' expectations:* this focuses on what the companies expect from a university graduate (possible recruit) related to the knowledge and predispositions. This includes what guides the company's recruitment policy and the basic knowledge, competence and skill the company expects from a graduate. In order to collect sufficient information for this part of the questionnaire, the survey has attempted to address the following three issues:

   i. personal traits of the graduates,
  ii. the theoretical knowledge base of the graduates and
 iii. the necessary practical engineering skills.

3   Analysis of Company Feedbacks

3.1   Characteristics of the Surveyed Companies

Company Size, Profile and Legal Form: As depicted in Fig. 2(a), some specific features are observed regarding the results of the survey. The survey from Stavanger area covers mostly SME companies that were founded recently. This has a clear historical reason related with the recent development of oil industries in the region. Quite a large number of these companies have operated as individual business companies. The survey indicates also that about a half of them are involved in R&D activity and knowledge-based products and/or services do not constitute the critical part of their output.

The Polish partners, on the other hand, conducted the survey mainly at large companies, where a considerable amount of them have been operated quite long and currently most of them are international firms (with partial ownership). Majority of the companies conduct their own research at their R&D units. Most of the products and/or services offered by these companies are knowledge-based ones. The majority of the companies in both areas are involved in production and services (Fig. 2(b)). Further, the legal form of the companies involved in this study, in both areas, is limited liability ones that are usually the most innovative part of the technical service as well as manufacturing market.

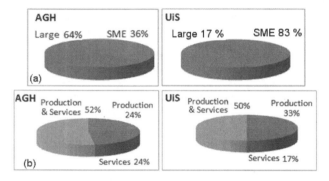

Fig. 2. (a) Size and (b) profile of surveyed companies

A good communication between industries and the academia can be considered as a key to correlate the needs of the job market and the content and depth of teaching as well as the conducted research at universities. The diagrams in Fig. 3 show the results of two of the questions forwarded to the companies in order to get some indication on the level of R&D activities in the companies and the degree of cooperation with universities. The survey shows that many of the companies in both areas have their own R&D department and they do cooperate with universities. The usual forms of the cooperation are R&D projects and support of teaching by arranging visits and internships for students. The companies in Stavanger area do have high level of cooperation with universities, particularly in research consulting. On the contrary, the important area of cooperation between companies and universities in Kraków area is support of testing by universities.

Role of Mechatronics in the Companies: One possible reason for the declining interest in mechatronics can be the fact that this discipline is multidisciplinary. It demands, among others, to device or to develop new methods and engineering tools for the teaching process and the demonstration of mechatronics solutions in terms of modeling, simulation, evaluation and optimization. The developed methods and tools should have an advanced character targeting the non-homogeniety of the knowledge among the involved disciplines.

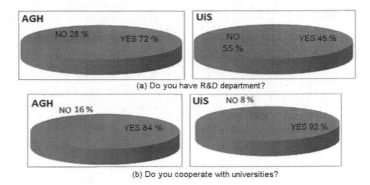

(a) Do you have R&D department?

(b) Do you cooperate with universities?

Fig. 3. (a) Availability of R&D department at the company and   (b) degree of cooperation with universities

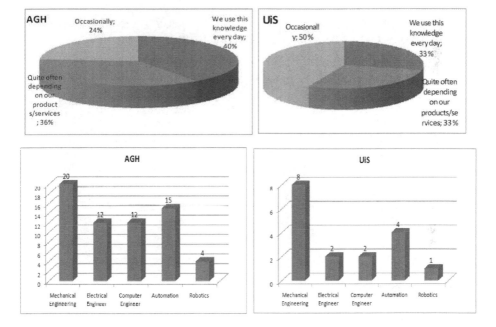

Fig. 4. Role of mechatronics in industry (top) and areas of mechatronics used in industry

Further, the role of mechatronics field of study will depend on how the identity of the field is defined and recognized both at universities and on the job market. A challenge to universities in stimulating interest in this discipline is to find the right identity in terms of coining courses from computer, electrical and mechanical engineering fields and clear professional definition of the graduates so that the job market understands the skill and knowledge gained by a graduate. Clear definition of the identity will have high implications on, for example, the design methodology, the modeling approach, the manufacturing processes and the material selection of mechanical products, components and systems.

Contrary to the suspicion of the project team, the feedbacks in general show that the companies use mechatronics as the methodology of solving problems in their everyday activity (Fig. 4 (top)). Among the areas listed in the questionnaire, the feedbacks indicate that mechanical engineering and automation are mostly used (Fig. 4 (bottom)). Quite strikingly, the distribution profile of the used technology in both surveyed regions is similar.

Most preferred plan of teaching for mechantronics:

3.2   Expectation of Companies from Mechatronics Education

Apart from few exceptions, the feedbacks from both regions have similar characteristics in terms of expectations and preference to mechatronics education and its curriculum. Most of the companies consider professional knowledge to be the most important skill of a candidate to be recruited. In order to contribute to this expectation, they stressed that practical application of knowledge through internships or trainings should be focused as part of education in engineering, compared with laboratory works and lectures (Fig. 5). Though the general preference tendency is similar in both regions, companies in Poland indicate a significant interest in lectures and laboratory work based teaching.

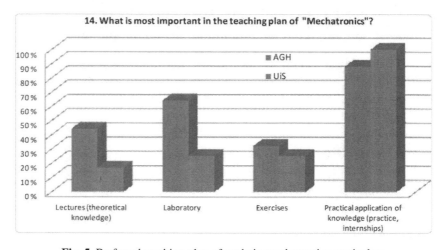

Fig. 5. Preferred teaching plan of study in mechatronics curriculum

With respect to preference of personalities of a graduate, the feedbacks (Fig. 6) indicate that the following are most appreciated by the employers: ability to work in team, creativity, independence, responsibility and loyalty with integrity.

In addition, companies in Poland stressed ability to seek self-knowledge through patents and standards, while Norwegian companies indicated importance of the communication skills and ability to cope with stress as their best preference. One main objective of the project is to formulate a new mechatronics curriculum that reflects the needs and expectations of the modern industry. The assessment (as depicted in Fig. 7) indicates that companies from both countries have high preference for

- ability to integrate knowledge from different fields,
- ability to analyze structural behavior and functionality of products in their environment,
- knowledge of computer-aided engineering systems,
- knowledge of mechanical systems and
- knowledge of construction and operation of machines.

The companies from Poland highly prefer practical knowledge of a foreign language as a language of professional communication, while the response of companies from Norway indicates very low preference for this skill.

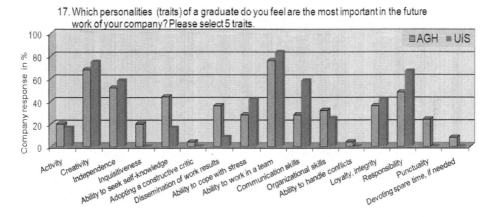

Fig. 6. Feedbacks on required personalities of a graduate in engineering

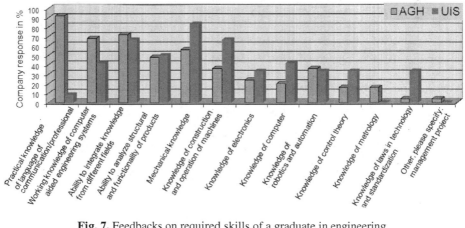

Fig. 7. Feedbacks on required skills of a graduate in engineering

The last question in the questionnaire focuses on assessment of expectations with respect to specific skills that are important for the company in the future. The preference of the companies in those specific skills (Fig. 8) is no exceptional. Most preferred skills include knowledge of use of computer-aided design (CAD) systems, knowledge of manufacturing technologies and selection of the engineering materials.

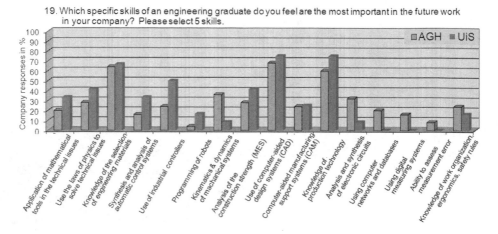

Fig. 8. Feedbacks on important specific skills required for a future graduate in engineering

4   Some Practical Implications of the Feedbacks

Though only few companies are assessed in this study, the feedback gives some indications to be taken care of in formulating a new curriculum for mechatronics education. The majority of the companies are willing to cooperate with universities in order to improve teaching methodology in the filed. Unless this is materialized, it is difficult to include practical trainings and internships in the study program. This study has also brought some obstacles to our attention. Introducing internships in both countries bears difficulties and risk of making the study program longer. Though a successful internship may require only 2 - 3 months, it is impractical to be completed parallel with the studies in accordance with the current academic plan.

The companies, in general, seem to underestimate theoretical knowledge and give less emphasis on skills in application of mathematical tools and laws of physics, while concurrently they demand the innovative approach and skills that need training. To train these skills a project based teaching and problem solving in a team with clear distribution of tasks and responsibility is suggested by the project team.

5   Students' Expectations

The goal of any student to attend a given field of study is gaining knowledge and skills that provides him/her with well earned job. In addition, there are certain other factors that drive to enroll into a study program and strive to complete it. This involves primarily the correlation between interest and capability. One important challenge for mechatronics curriculum is thus its multidisciplinary character. The curriculum can be viewed as the means of introducing the subject matter in those diverse areas such as mathematics, electronics, mechanical and computer engineering fields. Lack of interest or fundamental understanding in one or several of these elements possibly leads to lack of interest in mechatronics study.

The other issue is making the teaching process interesting. This can be enhanced by introducing a practical oriented teaching process as discussed in the previous section. Experience shows that students, particularly engineering students, prefer hands-on learning than theory based ones. This demands resources in terms of cooperation with industries and qualified teaching staff.

The field of mechatronics is relatively new and not well known in the ordinary people's life. In a survey carried out as part of this project in Stavanger area, about 44% of the responded High School pupils do not know/understand what the word "mechatronics" means. Some work is needed to make the field well known to the potential candidates of the university enrollment.

6   Conclusions

The survey reported in this article was initiated due to an existing problem in recruiting students to mechatronics study program. As stated earlier in this article, few articles have appeared in the literature addressing this issue with a target of formulating an effective curriculum for mechatronics education. As it stands now, the solution to the problem has more of regional or local characteristic than universal. Among others, the knowledge and skill needed by the locally operating companies influence the content, depth and method of teaching. The feedbacks from this assessment have provided key indications in the extent to which mechatronics is known and implemented in companies and enabled us to identify their preferences. This will for sure help us to formulate an effective and attractive curriculum of the future. Further, it is highly expected that the obtained responses in the assessment will provide a good basis for discussions among members of the project team on the study curriculum, methodology of education, and contents of the didactic materials.

Acknowledgement. The authors gratefully acknowledge the financial support provided by Island, Liechtenstein and Norway by means of co-financing by European Economic Area and Norwegian Financial Mechanism under the Scholarship and Training Fund, project number FSS/2008/X/D5/W/0045.

References

1. Buur, J.: Mechatronics Design in Japan. Institute for Engineering Design, Technical University of Denmark (1989)
2. Technology review. MIT Press (2003)
3. Lyshevski, S.E.: Mechatronic curriculum – restrospect and prospect. Mechatronics 12, 195–205 (2002)

4. Meek, S., Field, S., Devasia, S.: Mechatronics education in the Department of Mechanical Engineering at University of Utah. Mechatronics 13, 1–11 (2003)
5. Akpinar, B.: Mechatronics education in Turkey. Mechatronics 16, 185–192 (2006)
6. Parasuraman, S., Ganapaty, V.: Philosophy and objectives of mechatronics education. In: Industrial Technology, IEEE ICIT 2002, December 11-14, vol. 2, pp. 1199–1202 (February 2002)
7. Kayis, B.: Trends in undergraduate mechanical, manufacturing, aerospace and mechatronics programs Wordwide: In-depth Study of 55 Universities Programs. In: Proc. of IEEE Int. Engineering Management Conference, vol. 1, pp. 178–182 (2004)
8. Grimheden, M., Hanson, M.: Mechatronics - the evolution of an academic discipline in engineering education. Mechatronics 15, 179–192 (2005)
9. Acar, M.: Mechatronics Engineering Education in the UK. In: Mechatronics: the basis for new industrial development, pp. 763–770. Computational Mechanics Publications (1994)
10. Grimheden, M., Hanson, M.: What is Mechatronics? Proposing a Didactical Approach to Mechatronics. In: Proc. of 1st Baltic Sea Workshop on Education in Mechatronics, Kiel, Germany (2001)
11. Alvarez Cabrera, A.A., Foeken, M.J., Tekin, O.A., Woestenenk, K., Erden, M.S., De Schutter, B., van Tooren, M.J.L., Babuška, R., van Houten, F.J.A.M., Tomiyama, T.: Towards automation of control software: A review of challenges in mechatronic design. Mechatronics 20, 876–886 (2010)

Innovation Processes – Reference Model, Collaboration via Innovative Zone and Integration into Enterprise Environment

Iveta Zolotová[1], Peter Kubičko[1], Lenka Landryová[2], and Rastislav Hošák[1]

[1] Department of Cybernetics and Artificial Intelligence, Technical University Kosice,
Letná 9/A, Kosice, the Slovak Republic
[2] Department of Control Systems and Instrumentation, VSB Technical University Ostrava,
17.listopadu 15, Ostrava, the Czech Republic
{iveta.zolotova,rastislav.hosak}@tuke.sk,
peter.kubicko@student.tuke.sk, lenka.landryova@vsb.cz

Abstract. The purpose of the paper is to describe existing possibilities and to propose new possibilities for a permanent improvement of an innovation process as an integral part of the core business processes. This article focuses on the definition and design of the draft reference model of the innovation process as a base for developing a methodology for implementation of an innovation reference process in terms of BPM (Business Process Management) and its related standards. The paper also analyzes the methodology and proposes its implementation in business using a common collaboration area and also an innovation zone. Practical verification of implementing the reference innovation process will be demonstrated by its implementation in a particular organization.

Keywords: innovation process, innovation zone, innovation idea, innovation project, innovation information system, process measuring, reference model, model.

1   Introduction

Innovation has become an integral element of survival and adaptation to the market situations of each company. It is made possible to focus the company activities, affect the actions, control its core processes in accordance with business processes, and minimize the risk of transactions only with a system approach, which allows the company to constantly work out new and innovative topics and process them to obtain a competitive advantage. Submission and processing of innovative topics into implementable forms shall not be understood as an occasional or exceptional activity of individuals, but presented as a system model adaptable to any business whose future depends on the ability of adaptation. In our article we would like to present a process of innovation with measurable changes of resulting values.

The resulting value of an innovative idea can also be considered a new work experience and verification ideas, which are going to be captured in the form of information arising from the implementation of innovative projects. The systematic processing of ideas and creating an environment for innovation and a process

J. Frick and B. Laugen (Eds.): APMS 2011, IFIP AICT 384, pp. 567–577, 2012.
© IFIP International Federation for Information Processing 2012

innovation in the innovative zone require the selection of an appropriate methodology for processing. After consideration of what is suitable for the company and its environment, since it does not deal with industrial production, but with the supply of IT services, and because of its BPM (Business Process Management) orientation and its project management confirmed by the certificate ISO 9000, it was proposed to design an innovation zone based on business processes, although companies worldwide use other methods to support a systematic approach to innovation process, for example, CREAX, TRIZ, WOIS.

Analyses of the IPA [1]. in European companies showed the following barriers to innovative projects:

- Lack of a systematic methodology - Innovation is often confused with methods for new product development, marketing or simple creative techniques (brainstorming)
- Lack of innovation culture in business
- Not suitable model for managing the innovation process
- Inappropriate methods for generating new solutions - using the method of trial and error
- Lack of knowledge management - up to 70-80% of the knowledge generated in innovative projects is forgotten or lost.

Neglect of the measurement and evaluation of the benefits of innovation.

2   Reference Model of an Innovation Process

The essence of an innovation process reference model is to describe the process with its essential attributes (input, output, resources, rules). This process, however, has a

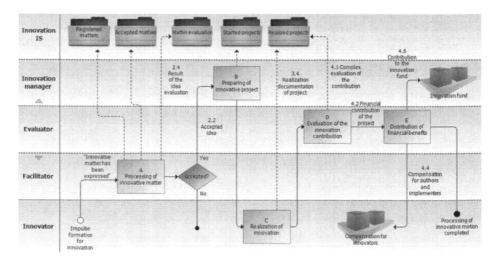

Fig. 1. Innovation process

special status in a company that is being "protected" by a so called innovative zone, which is supposed to maintain an environment that creates a breeding ground for innovative ideas without prejudging the final outcome.

In a classic business environment mainly profit is monitored at every business activity and in every project, where the loss is unacceptable.

An innovation zone deflects the primary goal of business in the form of making a profit from the innovation process. An innovation process can primarily generate an economic loss, but secondarily creates a potential for future values and the creation of profit.

2.1   Innovative Zone

Under the innovation zone it is necessary to understand the limited space of companies in which the innovative zone is implemented (either enterprise, enterprise group or regional or cluster of networking enterprises) with specific management, performance, evaluation and incentive policies. It serves to accelerate innovation in the company. Its role is also in filtering out the impact of the organization, which is under normal conditions resistant to changes that affects adversely especially in the early stages of an innovative project. The innovation zone must be able to meet increased demands for changes in the environment that must be modeled separately, but without compromising the company's standard processes. The innovation zone should have a separate system of financing, planning, monitoring, evaluating the benefits and communication of results of innovative projects. This article presents the idea of implementation the innovation process that is integrated to other business processes using the innovative zone. By introducing an innovation process in the innovation zone the generation of innovative ideas and acceleration of innovative projects can be achieved in a way that does not to interfere with the normal operation of the company, but its results are positively affecting innovative projects. Projects and activities of an innovation zone must improve the company's standard business processes. Results coming from an innovation zone are implemented in standard processes, supported by the top management of a company. Operating costs of innovative zones are minimized by the fact that resources (human, technical, financial) of processes can be shared. The results of an innovation zone are also shared and provided throughout the company. It is important to apply the principle of openness within the company. An innovation zone cooperates with the organizational units of the organization.

The innovative zone thus provides a space where ideas can take root and where they are protected from the effects of organizational inertia as long as they are able to prove their value. The innovative zone also provides an opportunity to implement the ideas of people who are unable to independently transfer their ideas into reality. The innovative zone contains the building blocks necessary for the existence and survival of the zone within which ideas get through the entire process.

The building blocks of an innovative zone are as follow:

- Ownership of ideas
- Evaluation of ideas
- Support of ideas
- Storage of ideas
- Measurement of ideas

Ownership of Ideas. Ownership of ideas is difficult to accept and maintain if the organization supports an environment and culture where ideas are freely provided, not registered or carefully protected, in considering theft (unauthorized ownership). In organizations, where an innovative zone is successfully used, the owners of the ideas are well respected and rewarded.

Evaluation of Ideas. Ideas that are generated and expressed need to be thoroughly assessed so the owners trust the processes through which ideas will be implemented. Organizations need a set of published values together with examples of successful ideas.

Support of Ideas. It defines the way in which the innovative zone will bring together a team who gives the best opportunity for an idea to evolve and be successful. Supporters of the idea are respected members who facilitate the proper parties to bring an idea to success. For this purpose registration and collaboration tools may be helpful, for example templates and clear rules to protect property rights in the future use of the results of the idea.

Storage of Ideas. It's a place where the ideas, which currently are not required, are stored but can be used in the future. Storage should include all of the historical data from their beginning through their evaluation to reasonable storage to ensure that the selected attributes are available for a possible case use idea.

Measurement of Ideas. It is the process of measuring the value of an idea. It is often regarded as too difficult a task, since many ideas can only be a part of an innovation, or can be directly converted to the currency value. The measurement must be approached in a way so that it will take into account the specific conditions of a business (the needs of relevant ideas and their results), but also the social value and market value. Not every business can have for the same result the same rating scale. Therefore an innovative zone must have available the range of values of the organization in which it is implemented.

The innovative zone ensures that the building blocks exist in the organization and that they are combined into a single process that continuously generates new ideas and filters them.

The creation of the innovative zone in organizations is based on management decisions to build and promote sustainability of the innovative zone in the company. Without the creation of conditions in the form of rules of operation and financing, it can be assumed that it is impossible to build and positively operate the innovative zone in any business. Under positive operation it can be understood that the innovative zone serves the purpose of promoting the capture and evaluation of new ideas in the business of the organization. So decision-making and supporting the innovative zone by management should be embedded in the company's strategy, which is the main framework for the control of all business processes, but the innovative zone must have sufficient competence for processing new ideas so that its operation was not impeded by the effects of other processes. Otherwise, there will be a slowdown and the owners will lose their interest.

An innovation zone is an area that can be compared to a catalyst for new ideas. To effectively fulfill this role, it must be accepted by the surroundings, but it needs to consist of all the necessary instructions, templates, adequate budgets and skills of participating managers accelerating its own submission, evaluation and verification, as well as collaboration of its participants.

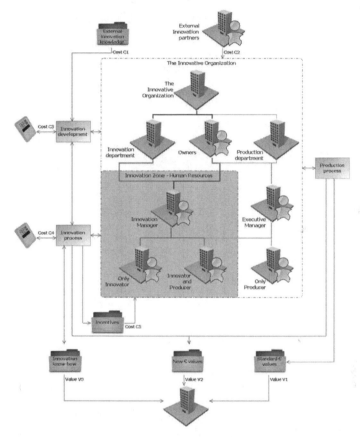

Fig. 2. The model of an innovation organization with innovative zone. C – Cost, the total cost of innovation is a sum of C1, C2, C3, C4, C5 costs, C=C1+C2+C3+C4+C5, where C1 – cost of access to external sources of innovation know-how, C2 - cost of including external partners into collaboration, C3 – cost of innovation development, C4 - cost of innovation process operation, C5 – cost of ideas, V – Value, added value to innovation is a sum of V1, V2, V3, where V=V1+V2+V3, V1- a standard value expressed in currency which is produced by manufacturing with or without implemented innovations, V2- new values are a combination of a value coming from production and from the innovation process, also expressed in currency, V3 – the value of knowledge newly emerged during the innovation process (innovation know-how), but not measured in currency.

External innovation knowledge is an external source of innovative knowledge, the necessary to link the internal sources of knowledge and their confrontation, the maximum utilization of knowledge for the innovation process, respectively.

External innovation partners are engaged in the innovation process, they have access to the innovative zone and they may be a part of the innovation process in different roles, whether as evaluators or as submitters of ideas.

Innovation development includes all activities related to a promotion of the innovation development of an organization, ensuring resources and training and the acquisition of interests of employees for innovative activities.

The innovation process is owned by an innovative manager who is also in the position to control the innovative zone. An idea is the input of the innovation process and an implementation project with a proven idea is the output.

The production process of the organization provides the main output of the organization. Workers involved in production processes can be participating in the innovation process during their working hours in order to not disrupt the operation of production processes.

2.2   Attributes, Roles and Policies of an Innovation Process

Input into the innovation process is a new idea that is supported by motivational tools in the form of rewards for owners of successfully implemented ideas. Selection and evaluation of new ideas is made by independent evaluators (at least three reviewers) to minimize subjective views on the continuation of the presented idea. After reaching a certain number of points the innovative idea is developed and the manager of innovation administration asks for an approval of a budget required to implement an innovative project. The total budget for innovative projects is set out at the beginning of a financial year so that it can finance innovative projects. Each already implemented project contributes to this budget with their agreed percentage of profits, which can also fully use the results of innovative projects. It is necessary to distinguish the implementation project and an innovative project. The innovative project usually does not strictly keep the rules of project management, as confirmed by Sergey Filipov and Herman Mooi in [3], which indicates that "to specify the idiosyncratic nature of innovative projects as opposed to conventional projects."

The innovation process can distinguish the following roles:

Innovation manager is the main coordinator of all innovation activities from the submission of an innovative idea through the selection of evaluators to assess the inclusion of an innovative project and its outcomes in the innovation fund. He provides communication with employees on the course of innovation, nominates the members of the commissions, submits proposals for project managers, supervises the running of an innovative information system and prepares quarterly evaluation of the course of innovation activities. It is a role that is constantly busy and for the whole process indispensable.

An innovator submits innovative ideas, formalizes the idea of them in writing into an understandable form for further processing. It is the author of the idea, problem solutions or also the author of implementing regulations (e.g. a project), or he may actively contribute to implementation. The role of an innovator can be received by any employee who actively participates in the presentation of innovative ideas formalized through an innovative portal to which employees are encouraged to submit innovative ideas.

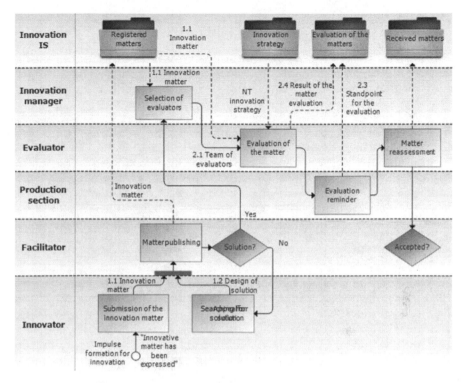

Fig. 3. A process for administrating an innovation idea

A facilitator identifies ideas and supports the authors, to whom he helps to formulate problems or ways of implementing ideas. He may be authorized to represent the innovators (idea authors') in the evaluation process. He informs members of an innovative zone about new innovative ideas, the solutions of the implemented projects and their benefits. He recruits members into the project teams.

An evaluator participates directly in evaluating the innovative proposals. The outcome of an evaluation decides the future of an innovative idea. The evaluator is actively involved in the innovation process and can re-review the idea (after re-submitting, or after specifying details of some parts), or assess the benefits of innovation.

A project leader is the manager of the innovative project after headquarters has authorised the project proposal.

The Production Department is an organizational unit of the company, which uses the result of an innovative project for its commercialization.

An innovative information system is the information system supporting the innovation process. Its main function is to collect ideas and record them during the innovation process to the implementation themselves, creating new business value for future use. It allows you to register ideas, helps to tune these ideas with a company's business strategy, supports the evaluation of ideas, creates a business environment and collaboration systems for both authors and evaluators of ideas, but also for implementation and project teams and communicates information directly to a company's management.

2.3   Measuring an Innovation Process

An open question remains for further research and that is the correct setting for innovation process metrics. If we use only the traditional metrics, such as a number of submitted ideas (inputs into the innovation process) and the number of ideas implemented (as a continuous indicator), so we could get a difficult to read benefit which to the short term point of view brings higher overhead costs without generating an immediate sales value for the company. The ratio of the number of ideas and implemented ideas is also misleading, because there is a question: what's better? If the ratio is close to zero or to one? This ratio cannot be evaluated in this way because the main value is in the quality it brings and then in the future usefulness of the results of the innovative project. Our aim is to clarify the indicators of the innovation process especially in terms of future benefits. However, the current metrics (measurable indicators), which were set only in terms of estimated future value creation are: the number of outputs of the innovative project, the usefulness of the implementation project (using the repeatability of output), the number of identified outcomes as a business opportunity, the number of contracts (signed contracts) transformed from the business opportunities created by innovative outputs, etc. Considering the short term history of operating the innovative zone in the company it is not possible to use values of these metrics and indicators, the results will be published in terms of these indicators later in the future work of our team.

2.4   Implementation

Organizational arrangements and the creation of an innovative environment for an innovative zone is the role of top management. To create an environment for innovation and flexible collaboration space the portal solution can be used. Suitable for implementation of the innovation process can be company's portal using Microsoft SharePoint in a particular company's environment. The portal includes features in addition to a normal company's site, which are especially dedicated to the presentation of innovative ideas. The innovator completes his ideas in an innovative corporate portal environment, which is used daily in his work, this is very important in order to minimize barriers when he needs to express innovative ideas.

The following figures bring closer the options for collecting ideas, which are accessible also to unregistered users, or just random visitors to the portal.

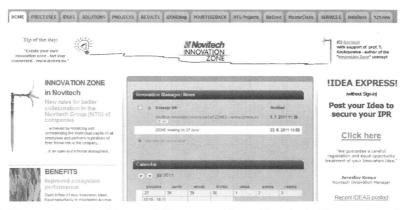

Fig. 4. Company's portal with a possibility to enter ideas without login (for unregistered users)

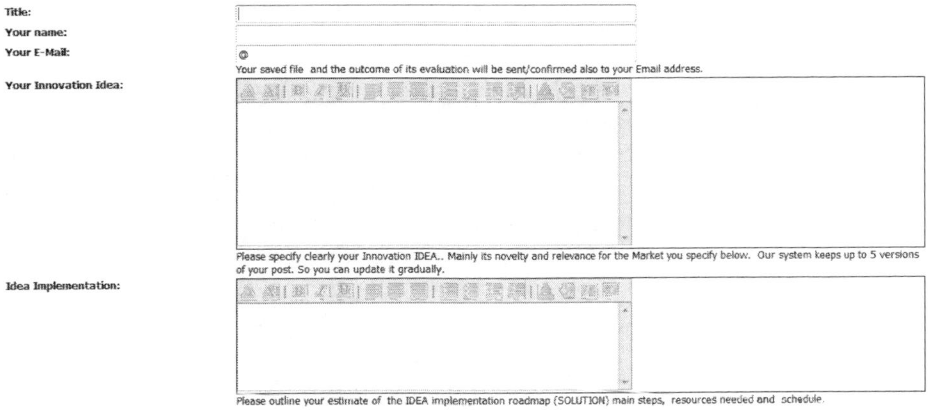

Title:

Your name:

Your E-Mail:

Your saved file and the outcome of its evaluation will be sent/confirmed also to your Email address.

Your Innovation Idea:

Please specify clearly your Innovation IDEA.. Mainly its novelty and relevance for the Market you specify below. Our system keeps up to 5 versions of your post. So you can update it gradually.

Idea Implementation:

Please outline your estimate of the IDEA implementation roadmap (SOLUTION) main steps, resources needed and schedule.

Fig. 5. A screen used by authors of submitted innovative ideas

The company, which actually operates the portal, maintains the principle of openness and creates a competitive hub provoking to share ideas with their own innovative topic for outsiders. For the internal staff it may create a feeling of uncertainty and fear by ideas coming from outside, but on the other hand, it encourages and leaves no one asleep, because it is in the interest of each employee that he thinks of actions in terms of enhancing the effect of "your" business through his own ideas.

Fig. 6. Overview of all innovative ideas and the webpart Idea evaluation report from the idea evaluators

3   Conclusion

The presented attempt to create an innovative zone and implement innovation in a business environment has the ambition to eliminate the above mentioned obstacles and to verify the viability of a reference model for an innovative zone in a company. For the first quarter of year of the operation of the innovative zone over 70 new ideas were recorded of which 4 have been implemented and another 10 were approved for implementation. Compared with the previous period of time when new ideas were very rarely introduced, or perhaps even in greater numbers, but with not enough determination and self motivation, and implementation was doomed to failure, because neither the environment and culture in a company was ready for developing the innovative ideas. It was not necessary because the company's operation was secured by long-term contracts, which are now being converted to the short-term. The aim of creating the innovative zone is to enhance the creative potential of employees involved in creating new ideas in line with a company's strategy and thus increase the chances of the company to compete on the market, due to the higher number of transformed ideas into real verification and outputs, respectively. A company will form a reservoir of knowledge and experience of practical verifications, which can be a benefit for the company either by direct trade with the results or their application in specific projects in different forms of benefits (reducing the development cycle of a new product, a cheaper product development, fewer resources required to implement a project or product delivery). With this verification of the reference model the innovation process can be applied in other companies, where this is in line with the company's strategy and the willingness of management of companies to accelerate their capital in favor of the mental agility of the company's future.

Acknowledgments. This work was supported by grant KEGA No. 021TUKE-4/2012 (65%), the project Development of Centre of Information and Communication Technologies for Knowledge Systems (26220120030) supported by research and development operational program financed by the ERDF (25%) and the CP-IP 214657-2 FutureSME, (Future Industrial Model for SMEs), EU project of the 7FP in the NMP area (10%). The team also thanks Novitech Company for a willingness, which allowed us to examine conditions for implementation of innovation zones in the real business environment, especially thank the President and Chairman of the Board (Chairman of the Board of Directors), Dr. Attila Toth, for his inspiring advice and transfer of experience to us.

References

1. IPA Independent Project Analysis Ltd., http://www.ipaglobal.com
2. Mann, D.: Hands-on Systematic Innovation. CREAX Press, Belgium (2002)
3. CREAX Innovation Suite, http://www.creax.com
4. Filipov, S., Mooi, H.: Innovation Project Management. Journal on Innovation and Sustainability 1(1) (2010) ISSN 2179-3565

5. Koulopoulos, T.M.: The Innovation Zone. Published by davies-Black Publishing, a division of CPP, Inc., Mountain View (2009) ISBN 978-0-89106-234-9
6. Révészová, L., Paľová, D.: Basics of modeling business processes, 1st edn. Technical University of Košice (2009) (in Slovak) ISBN 978-80-553-0174-7
7. Hrnčiar, M.: Analyze of processes, services with the use of approaches of ISO/IEC 15504. In: International Scientific Conference on Diagnostics of the Company, Controlling and Logistics III, pp. 81–84. University of Žilina (2006) (in Slovak) ISBN 80-8070-527-5
8. Řepa, V.: Business processes, Process control and modeling, 2nd edn. Grada Publishing, Praha (2007) (in Czech) ISBN 978-80-247-2252-8
9. Zolotová, I., Kubičko, P., Landryová, L., Hošák, R.: A design of a reference model of an innovation process and its implementation in business using an innovation zone. In: APMS 2011 International Conference on Advances in Production Management Systems, September 26-28, pp. 1–9. Stavanger, Norway (2011) ISBN 978-82-7644-461-2
10. Innovation zone in Novitech, http://izone.novitech.sk/default.aspx

Boundaries Matter – The Pros and Cons of Vertical Integration in BIM Implementation

Teemu Lehtinen

Enterprise Simulation Laboratory SimLab,
Department of Industrial Engineering and Management,
Aalto University School of Science, Espoo, Finland
teemu.lehtinen@aalto.fi

Abstract. Boundary spanning systemic innovations such as building information modeling (BIM) are difficult to implement. Literature suggests that vertical integration facilitates the implementation of systemic innovations. This study examines the role of vertical integration in the implementation of BIM as an example of a systemic innovation. It analyzes and compares two opposite case studies from the Finnish construction industry including a vertically integrated and a vertically disintegrated project networks. The findings propose that there are seven structurally relevant factors in BIM implementation; (1) management support, (2) coordination and control, (3) learning and experience, (4) technology management, (5) communication, (6) motivation, and (7) defining roles. Moreover, there are not only advantages but also disadvantages from vertical integration related to each of these implementation factors. Thus, in order to achieve as smooth and successful implementation as possible, managers should understand the impact of the network structure and plan the BIM implementation projects accordingly.

Keywords: Vertical integration, technology implementation, systemic innovation, building information modeling (BIM), the construction industry.

1 Introduction

Systemic innovations, such as *building information modeling* (BIM), that span over several organizational boundaries are extremely difficult to implement. As opposed to autonomous innovations that can be introduced as such without any major changes to the rest of the business system, systemic innovations require significant adjustments in other parts of the business system in order to be implemented successfully [1-3]. Many researchers have suggested that *vertical integration* (VI) facilitates the implementation of systemic innovations [1,4-7]. VI refers to a combination of several or all functions in the value chain under a single firm [8].

BIM is broadly a set of interacting policies, processes, and technologies generating a methodology to manage the essential building design and project data in digital format throughout the life cycle of a building between different stakeholders [9,10]. The acronym BIM can be used to refer to a product (*building information model*, a structured dataset describing a building), an activity (*building information modeling*,

J. Frick and B. Laugen (Eds.): APMS 2011, IFIP AICT 384, pp. 578–585, 2012.

the act of creating a building information model), or a system (*building information management*, the business structures of work and communication that increase quality and efficiency) [11]. Over the years, other terms for BIM have also been used, such as *building product modeling*, *product data modeling* or *virtual design and construction* (VDC) [9,12]. In this study, BIM is defined broadly as a process and technology and the acronym refers to the term building information modeling as it seems to be gaining popularity in both industrial and academic circles [10].

BIM has been expected to bring significant improvements in the productivity of the construction industry since the 1980's but the implementation has been slower and more difficult than expected, largely due to its interorganizational and systemic nature [7,13-15]. At the same time, there has been an emerging trend of VI in the construction industry globally [16]. This paper aims to shed more light on the connection between BIM implementation and the organizational structure. The research question of this study is: what are the advantages and possible disadvantages of vertical integration in the implementation of BIM as an example of a systemic process innovation?

The empirical research of this study is based on a qualitative comparison of two opposite case studies from the Finnish construction industry; a vertically disintegrated project network and a vertically integrated project network. Both case studies included a single construction project in which BIM was being implemented. The qualitative data consists of project documentation, interviews, and observations. A theoretical model of the advantages and disadvantages of VI was first constructed based on the literature review. The model was later tested with the empirical data and refined into an improved model based on the analysis. Based on the findings, there are seven structurally relevant factors in BIM implementation with not only advantages but also disadvantages from VI. Thus, in order to achieve as smooth and successful implementation as possible, managers should understand the impact of the network structure and plan the BIM implementation projects accordingly.

2   Advantages and Disadvantages of Vertical Integration in the Implementation of Systemic Innovations

The literature on the advantages and disadvantages of VI was found on the general level and in the contexts of systemic innovations and the construction industry. Similarly, the literature related to the implementation of systemic innovations was found from three perspectives; the general implementation of organizational change, the implementation of collaborative technologies as an example of systemic process innovations, and the implementation of systemic innovations in the construction industry. A theoretical model was constructed as a synthesis of the literature review including these both perspectives. The constructed model consisted of six structurally relevant implementation factors which were (1) *management support*, (2) *coordination and control*, (3) *learning and experience*, (4) *technology management*, (5) *communication*, and (6) *motivation*. Each of these implementation factors included both advantages and disadvantages from VI.

First factor, *management support*, emerged from the frameworks of Salminen [17] and Munkvold [18] which highlighted the importance of the management support for providing legitimacy for the implementation and gaining access to critical resources. The management support as such did not directly occur in the advantages and disadvantages of VI, however, as VI enables better control and coordination over several integrated units [19-21], top management support over all these units is easier. Mahoney [21] also brings up the benefit of audit and resource allocation in vertically integrated firms which relates to the more effective allocation of necessary resources between integrated units [17,18]. As a disadvantage, the extension of the management team and differing managerial requirements could lead to diverse management support over different integrated units and hinder the implementation [8,19].

Second factor, *coordination and control*, occurred often in the literature on the advantages and disadvantages of VI. Similarly, coordination and control activities are focal factors in implementation and change management. The advantages of VI are easier management of changing liability and contractual issues as there is no need to negotiate contracts [15,20,22], the ability to make adaptations, adjustments, and redistribution of work timely and efficiently [1,4,15,23,24], and more stable relationships of different units which reduces uncertainty, boundary strength and enable the utilization of efficient processes [7,15,19,23-25]. The disadvantages are the inflexibility to change partners or processes when needed [8,19,20,23,24], broad management with differing managerial requirements which may be difficult to coordinate and control [8,19,21], and the fact that systemic innovations may be too complex and large to manage under a single integrated firm [2,3].

Third factor, *learning and experience*, emerged from the literature of systemic innovations and the project-based construction industry. As a systemic process innovation is a collection of interconnected innovations related to the boundary spanning working practices of the whole business system, it cannot be implemented at once. Thus, in a project-based context the implementation occurs over several projects. Therefore, cumulative learning and experience is pivotal in the successful implementation of systemic process innovations. The advantages of VI are faster proceeding of learning and experience between integrated units [6,26], the cumulative learning through the possibility to transfer the same organization and expertise from one project to another which reduces the organizational variety [7,23,24], and the facilitation of feedback loops and cross-pollination of ideas between different units [15,23,24]. The disadvantage is that VI may prevent access to external research, know-how, and relevant capabilities related to the systemic process innovation [1,8,20,22].

Fourth factor, *technology management*, is derived from the frameworks of Munkvold [18] and Taylor [15]. Others have also mentioned the improved technological intelligence being related to VI [1,8,20,22]. The advantages of VI are the ability to ensure the interoperability of technology between integrated units and compatibility with existing technologies by selecting specific systems and software platforms [15,18], the possibility to experiment with technology between integrated units [15], and the possibility to establish shared supportive infrastructure, guidelines, and feedback mechanisms for all integrated units [18,27]. The disadvantages are that VI may prevent the firm from perceiving technological advances related to the systemic process innovation in the market [1] or some relevant technological capabilities needed in the systemic process innovation may exist outside of the integrated firm [22].

Fifth factor, *communication*, emerged from the frameworks of Salminen [17] and Munkvold [18] in which the information sharing between all participants was emphasized. At the same time, communication was highly emphasized in the context of systemic innovations where a complete open exchange of information between different participants is essential. The advantages of VI are faster and more accurate information flow between integrated units [1,8], the easier and safer exchange of information between integrated units [28], and more efficient communication through an internal coding system that can develop in integrated environment [21]. The disadvantage is the possible communication distortion which may be accidental or deliberate and arises from the increased hierarchical levels and spans of control [21].

Finally sixth factor, *motivation*, occurred in several implementation frameworks. To achieve successful implementation, different participants need to be motivated to implement and use the systemic innovation at hand. Salminen [17] also specified the need for change and goal setting as separate success factors which are closely related to motivation. The advantages of VI are the development of trust, solidarity, and communal spirit between integrated units [21], and the ability to understand shared interests and holistic goals which can motivate units that do not directly benefit from the systemic innovation [15]. The disadvantage is that the absence of internal competition decreases the overall motivation to change and implement new technologies [8].

3   Methodology and Data

The empirical research of this study is based on a comparison of two opposite case studies from the Finnish construction industry. The first case study was a unique university building project designed and constructed by a vertically disintegrated project network between 2003 and 2006. The second case study was a typical residential building project designed and constructed between 2007 and 2010 by a vertically integrated project network in which the owner, all the designers, and the main contractor were from the same organization.

The qualitative data consisted of project documentation, interviews, and observations. The project documentation was used as a basis for preparing for the interviews. The interviews included both single and group interviews. Overall, 46 individuals from 13 different organizations participated in the interviews. After the interviews, three full-day process simulation events were held to further validate the results. Altogether 66 individuals from 14 different organizations participated in the process simulation events. In addition to the empirical data from the project documentation and the interviews, these simulation events provided a rich source of observation data.

The empirical data were analyzed by using the constructed theoretical model. The model provided the categories for data coding and classification. The data reduction and analysis consisted of three phases. In the first phase, the transcribed data were gone through line by line by highlighting all the organizational structure related quotes concerning the BIM implementation. This resulted in total 148 quotes from the both case studies. At this phase, these quotes were also given a descriptive label. In the second phase, the collected quotes were classified with the six implementation factors in the constructed theoretical model. After the classification, there was a group of 12 quotes that did not fit into any of the six implementation factors. This group formed an additional implementation factor to the refined model. In the final phase of the analysis, the quotes under each implementation factors were compared with the pros and cons of VI in the constructed theoretical model. The conclusions were drawn based on the comparison.

4   Findings

The findings of this study propose that there are seven structurally relevant factors in BIM implementation; (1) *management support*, (2) *coordination and control*, (3) *learning and experience*, (4) *technology management*, (5) *communication*, (6) *motivation*, and (7) *defining roles*. There are also both advantages and disadvantages of VI related to each of these implementation factors.

The few findings related to the *management support* did not support the two advantages in the model, and thus further research is needed. These were the top management support over several integrated units at once, and the effective allocation of resources between integrated units. The findings supported the disadvantage whereby the broad management with differing managerial requirements may lead to diverse support over different units. But instead of differing managerial requirements, the different types of people as managers and varying economic situations of different integrated units emerged to be the sources of diverse management support which may have negative implications for the overall implementation of BIM.

The findings regarding the *coordination and control* supported the advantages related to the easier management of changing liability and contractual issues, and the ability to make adaptations, adjustments, and redistribution of work in a timely and efficient fashion which is facilitated especially by the shared location. The findings, however, did not support the advantage of stable relationships. Regarding the disadvantages, the findings supported all three disadvantages in the model except the inflexibility to change processes. Regarding the broad management, the findings highlighted the diverse geographical locations as a source of coordination and control difficulties. Finally, as BIM spans more broadly than just within the vertically integrated firm, both internal and external implementation need to be taken into account which makes the implementation more complex for vertically integrated firms.

In *learning and experience*, the findings supported all the advantages and the disadvantage in the model. Especially the advantage of cumulative learning and the disadvantage of not accessing relevant capabilities were highlighted. The findings did not provide any new perspective to the model regarding the learning and experience.

The findings related to the *technology management* supported all the advantages of VI in the original model. These were ensuring the interoperability through joint selection of software, experimenting with technology, and establishing shared supportive infrastructure. The findings, however, did not support the two disadvantages which stated that technological capabilities may exist outside, or that VI may prevent from perceiving technological advances in the market. These would require further research. In addition, the findings introduced an additional disadvantage of VI which was stiffness and slowness of a centralized IT department and bureaucracy. The inability to make quick adjustments in the IT environment of a vertically integrated firm may hinder the implementation of BIM.

In *communication*, the findings supported the advantages related to the faster and easier exchange of information between the integrated units but highlighted the shared location as a source. The findings, however, did not support the more efficient communication through a developed internal coding system. The findings also supported the disadvantage of increased hierarchical levels and spans of control which may lead to accidental or even deliberate communication distortion. Here, accidental communication distortion may arise because communication is taken for granted in a vertically integrated firm. Similarly, deliberate communication distortion may arise from "*sibling envy*" caused by the independence of different integrated units.

The findings regarding the *motivation* supported only the advantage of understanding the shared interests and holistic goals. The advantage of developing trust and solidarity, and the disadvantage of absent internal competition were not supported by the empirical data. The emergence of new work and the need to redistribute work in BIM implementation may cause conflicts of interests between different participants, and thus, decrease motivation. This issue seems to be easier to handle in a vertically integrated firm as understanding the shared interests and holistic goals can motivate those integrated units that do not directly benefit from BIM.

The findings also introduced the seventh additional structurally relevant factor that was not in the original model; *defining roles*. As an advantage, it is easier to define and fulfill the new roles needed in BIM implementation from the holistic perspective in a vertically integrated project network. The disadvantage is, however, that "*buck passing*" may emerge in vertically integrated firm which means that everything related to the implementation may be pushed to the new role, and thus, hindering the implementation.

5   Conclusions

The findings of this study introduced seven structurally relevant implementation factors with related advantages and disadvantages of vertical integration. These factors are (1) *management support*, (2) *coordination and control*, (3) *learning and experience*, (4) *technology management*, (5) *communication*, (6) *motivation*, and (7) *defining roles*. The findings related to the advantages and disadvantages in these factors both reinforced the previous knowledge and provided new knowledge to the field. Mainly, this study confirms that in addition to the expected benefits from VI in BIM implementation there are also many disadvantages from VI that may greatly hinder the implementation efforts. Some of the advantages and disadvantages in the original theoretical model could not be confirmed in the study but these could not, however, be challenged by the empirical data either, and therefore, they were kept in the improved theoretical model. In order to determine the significance of these unconfirmed issues, further research is needed.

According to the findings, the organizational structure of the project network does affect the implementation of BIM in both positive and negative ways. More specifically, vertically integrated project network has its advantages and disadvantages during the BIM implementation. Both advantages and disadvantages need to be taken into account in order to be able to implement BIM more smoothly and successfully at least in a vertically integrated project network. Thus, managers should understand how the network structure of their company and project network could influence the implementation efforts and embrace the advantages and try to overcome the disadvantages when implementing BIM and possibly other systemic process innovations.

There are some limitations to this study. First of all, the study investigated only two project networks and two separate implementation projects in the construction industry. The two opposite project networks, however, provided good insights into the focus of this study. However, more case studies targeting on different project networks and even other kinds of systemic innovations is needed. Second, some of the elements in the theoretical model could not be confirmed in the cases as they would have required more longitudinal research. As the overall BIM implementation requires several successive implementation projects, a further examination of successive projects within these same project networks might introduce interesting new insights to the model. Finally, the case studies were from the Finnish construction industry, and thus, the findings may not be generalizable to other countries. For example, the different industrial structures or cultural differences could affect the findings. Addressing these limitations would improve the generalizability of the findings.

References

1. Teece, D.J.: Firm Organization, Industrial Structure, and Technological Innovation. Journal of Economic Behavior & Organization 31, 193–224 (1996)
2. De Laat, P.B.: Systemic Innovation and the Virtues of Going Virtual: The Case of the Digital Video Disc. Technology Analysis & Strategic Management 11, 159–180 (1999)
3. Maula, M.V.J., Keil, T., Salmenkaita, J.-P.: Open Innovation in Systemic Innovation Contexts. In: Chesbrough, H., Vanhaverbeke, W., West, J. (eds.) Open Innovation: Researching a New Paradigm, pp. 241–257. Oxford University Press, New York (2006)
4. Armour, H.O., Teece, D.J.: Vertical Integration and Technological Innovation. The Review of Economics and Statistics 62, 470–474 (1980)
5. Chesbrough, H.W., Teece, D.J.: Organizing for Innovation: When Is Virtual Virtuous? Harvard Business Review 80, 127–135 (2002)
6. Langlois, R.N.: Transaction-Cost Economics in Real Time. Industrial and Corporate Change 1, 99–127 (1992)
7. Taylor, J.E., Levitt, R.: Understanding and Managing Systemic Innovation in Project-Based Industries. In: Slevin, D., Cleland, D., Pinto, J. (eds.) Innovations: Project Research 2004. Project Management Institute, Newtown Square, pp. 1–17 (2004), http://crgp.stanford.edu/publications/bookchapters/TaylorLevitt.pdf (accessed July 15, 2011)

8. Porter, M.E.: Competitive Strategy - Techniques for Analyzing Industries and Competitors. The Free Press, New York (1980)
9. Penttilä, H.: Describing the Changes in Architectural Information Technology to Understand Design Complexity and Free-Form Architectural Expression. Electronic Journal of Information Technology in Construction 11, 395–408 (2006)
10. Succar, B.: Building Information Modelling Framework: A Research and Delivery Foundation for Industry Stakeholders. Automation in Construction 18, 357–375 (2009)
11. National Institute of Building Sciences: United States National Building Information Modeling Standard, Version 1 – Part 1: Overview, Principles, and Methodologies, http://www.wbdg.org/pdfs/NBIMSv1_p1.pdf (accessed August 5, 2011)
12. Kunz, J., Fischer, M.: Virtual Design and Construction: Themes, Case Studies and Implementation Suggestions. CIFE Working Paper Number 97. Stanford University (2009)
13. Fischer, M., Kam, C.: PM4D Final Report: Case Study HUT-600. CIFE Technical Report Number 143, Stanford University (2002)
14. Taylor, J.E., Levitt, R.: Innovation Alignment and Project Network Dynamics: An Integrative Model for Change. Project Management Journal 38, 22–35 (2007)
15. Taylor, J.E.: Antecedents of Successful Three-Dimensional Computer-Aided Design Implementation in Design and Construction Networks. Journal of Construction Engineering and Management 133, 993–1002 (2007)
16. Cacciatori, E., Jacobides, M.G.: The Dynamic Limits of Specialization: Vertical Integration Reconsidered. Organization Studies 26, 1851–1883 (2005)
17. Salminen, A.: Implementing Organizational and Operational Change - Critical Success Factors of Change Management. Industrial Management and Business Administration Series 7 (2000)
18. Munkvold, B.E.: Implementing Collaboration Technologies in Industry: Case Examples and Lessons Learned. Springer, London (2003)
19. Blois, K.J.: Vertical Quasi-Integration. The Journal of Industrial Economics 20, 253–272 (1972)
20. Harrigan, K.R.: Formulating Vertical Integration Strategies. Academy of Management Review 9, 638–652 (1984)
21. Mahoney, J.T.: The Choice of Organizational Form: Vertical Financial Ownership Versus Other Methods of Vertical Integration. Strategic Management Journal 13, 559–584 (1992)
22. Krippaehne, R.C., McCullouch, B.G., Vanegas, J.A.: Vertical Business Integration Strategies for Construction. Journal of Management in Engineering 8, 153–166 (1992)
23. Winch, G.: The Construction Firm and the Construction Process: The Allocation of Resources to the Construction Project. In: Lansley, P., Harlow, P. (eds.) Managing Construction Worldwide: Productivity and Human Factors in Construction, vol. 2, pp. 967–975 (1987)
24. Winch, G.: The Construction Firm and the Construction Project: A Transaction Cost Approach. Construction Management and Economics 7, 331–345 (1989)
25. Williamson, O.E.: The Vertical Integration of Production: Market Failure Considerations. The American Economic Review 61, 112–123 (1971)
26. Langlois, R.N., Robertson, P.L.: Explaining Vertical Integration: Lessons from the American Automobile Industry. Journal of Economic History 49, 361–375 (1989)
27. Nadler, D.A.: Managing Organizational Change: An Integrative Perspective. Journal of Applied Behavioral Science 17, 191–211 (1981)
28. Gopalakrishnan, S., Bierly, P.: Analyzing Innovation Adoption Using a Knowledge-Based Approach. Journal of Engineering and Technology Management 18, 107–130 (2001)

How Innovation and Improvement Ideas Are Created for a Production System by a Kaizen Team: A Protocol Analysis

Hajime Mizuyama

Dept. of Industrial and Systems Engineering, Aoyama Gakuin University,
Sagamihara Kanagawa 252-5258, Japan
mizuyama@ise.aoyama.ac.jp

Abstract. This paper presents a process model describing how a Kaizen team collectively creates innovation and improvement ideas for a production system and a protocol analysis approach based on the model. The process model captures the team-based creative problem solving practice as a process of updating a shared mental space comprising production system mental models (PSMMs) through exchanging utterances among the team members, where each utterance element characterizes an existing PSMM and/or creates a new PSMM. The paper also applies the proposed protocol analysis approach to an actual case, confirms its applicability and draws some insights into the process.

Keywords: Collective intelligence, continuous improvements, creative problem solving, innovation, mental models, mental space, protocol analysis.

1   Introduction

The competitiveness of a production system has a dynamic nature and hence should be maintained through innovations and continuous improvements. How to accomplish them effectively is not simply a matter of choosing an optimal one from a given set of solutions, but is rather the matter of creating the solutions themselves as well as finding the concrete problems to solve. This means that introducing innovations and improvements to a production system should be regarded as another ill-defined creative problem solving process carried out somewhat tacitly by a cross-functional Kaizen team. Consequently, it is not clear how the process should be operated and managed, what kind of supports are possible and effective, etc. to enhance its productivity. Thus, a deeper understanding of the process is strongly demanded.

One may understand the creative problem solving process carried out by a Kaizen team as an idea generation process similar to a well-studied brainstorming session [1][2][3]. However, this view captures only a partial aspect of the process: The members of the Kaizen team not only generate and enumerate innovation and improvement ideas suitable for the target production system but also deepen and share the understanding on the production system as well as evaluate and elaborate the ideas. Further, the three aspects of the process seem to be mutually coupled tightly

J. Frick and B. Laugen (Eds.): APMS 2011, IFIP AICT 384, pp. 586–597, 2012.

together in a synergetic way. Hence, the possible synergy among the aspects should also be well understood to be capable of managing and supporting the process effectively, and it requires a process model suitable for studying the synergy. Thus, this paper proposes a new process model for describing how innovation and improvement ideas for a production system are being created through creative discussion among the members of a Kaizen team from all the three aspects.

Although it is usually not formally externalized during the discussion, the understanding (shared among the team members) on the target production system should form a certain mental model. Thus, the second aspect of the creative discussion can be captured as a kind of group model building [4][5]. However, the structure of the mental models created here seems to be more qualitative and vague than the system dynamics model, which is widely used in ordinal group model building sessions. Hence, an original model structure is developed for the proposed process model. Further, each innovation or improvement idea can be considered as corresponding to how the mental model representing the current status of the production system should be changed. Thus, the process model captures the first and the third aspects of the creative discussion as actions of introducing new mental models and evaluating and refining existing mental models.

Accordingly, the proposed process model treats the team-based creative problem solving process as a sequence of updating a set of mental models of the target production system shared by the team members through exchanging utterances among them. Further, it utilizes a protocol analysis technique [6][7][8] in order to follow the process based on the utterances. In addition, the applicability and utility of the proposed process model and accompanying protocol analysis approach are also confirmed by actually capturing an example practice of discussing how to improve a two-stage assembly cell by them. The analysis reveals some interesting characteristics of the team-based creative problem solving process.

In the remainder of the paper, section 2 presents the proposed process model of the team-based creative problem solving process, and section 3 applies the proposed model to a case and draws some relevant insights into the process. Finally, section 4 concludes the paper.

2   Process Model of Team-Based Creative Problem Solving

2.1   Mental Space and Mental Models

In the situation considered here, a Kaizen team is in charge of conducting innovations and continuous improvements for a production system. The Kaizen team is assumed to be properly motivated and cross-functional having different background knowledge. At least some of the members are familiar with the current status of the target production system.

The process model to be proposed below formally conceptualizes the creative discussion among the team members for collectively creating innovation and improvement ideas for the production system. It outlines the discussion as a process of producing some output, like a manufacturing process. However, what the discussion process produces is not visible unfortunately. In the case of a manufacturing process, the subject is a visible raw material, part or subassembly, and what transform it are some operations like machining, assembling, etc. Analogically, in the case of the discussion process, an invisible concept on the target production system can be regarded as the subject, and interactions, such as exchanging utterances, among the team members can be deemed as transforming operations. Hence, the key is how to envision the invisible subject and how they are transformed through the discussion process.

Fauconnier [9][10] introduced a schema called *mental space* for visualizing the subject of verbal communication. In order to utilize the aforementioned analogy, the process model proposed here applies this schema and captures the team-based creative problem solving process as a sequence of updating a shared mental space through utterances. The contents of the mental space considered here are limited to those related to the production practice conducted in the target production system, and are called production system mental models (PSMMs). PSMMs can be stated as inter-subjective concepts on the target production system. The PSMMs that appear in the team-based creative problem solving process can be classified into the following two classes:

Real PSMMs: Each of them is a concept regarding the production practice actually conducted or experienced in the target production system.

Imaginary PSMMs: Each of them is a concept made by changing a part of another PSMM. It is a candidate concept of how the target production system should be innovated or improved.

2.2   Characteristics of Production System Mental Models

The mental space shared by the team members contains several PSMMs as described later and each of them is characterized by a number of attributes and the relationships among them. The attributes and relationships can be qualitative and abstract. For enabling a posteriori analysis on the scope of discussion, the attributes of a PSMM are classified into the following three layers:

Objective Layer (OL): This layer includes observable facts in the PSMM.

Subjective Layer (SL): This layer contains unobservable feelings, thoughts and mental tasks of the operators in the PSMM.

Judgmental Layer (JL): This layer gathers interpretations or evaluations on the PSMM of the Kaizen team members.

Further, since the practice of creative problem solving is composed of problem finding and solving activities, the attributes are also distinguished into the following two categories:

Problem-Related (PR): An attribute in this category is related to a problematic situation in the target production system.

Solution-Related (SR): An attribute in this category is concerned with a solution to a problematic situation in the system.

Most attributes of a PSMM are not stand-alone but are related to one another. During the creative discussion process, the team members can elaborate a PSMM not only by adding a new attribute to it but also introducing a new relationship among its attributes. Here, the possible relationships among the attributes of a PSMM are first classified into directional, hierarchical and non-directional: Directional relationships include those from a cause to its effect, from a premise to its consequence, from a reason to its evaluation or interpretation, from a problem to its solution, etc. Hierarchical relationships appear between an abstract characteristic and its detailed features. Whereas, a pair of analogically mapped characteristics or alternative solutions are connected by a non-directional relationship. Then, the relationships can be deemed as corresponding to the following knowledge handling actions:

Ordinal inference: This action is represented in the proposed model by adding a new directional relationship.

Generalization/Specialization: A new hierarchical relationship appears when this action is taken.

Analogical-mapping/Alternative-seeking: Taking this action corresponds to introducing a non-directional relationship.

2.3   State Transitions through Utterances

In the proposed process model, the process of creating innovation and improvement ideas for the target production system through creative discussion among the team

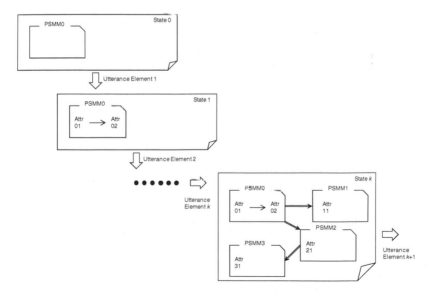

Fig. 1. Overview of proposed state transition model

members is captured as follows: First, it starts with the initial mental space, called State 0, where there is only an empty real PSMM. Then, as shown in Figure 1, the state is being updated step by step by utterances exchanged among the members. For example, a new attribute is added to an existing PSMM; a pair of attributes are connected by a relationship; a new PSMM is introduced, etc. The PSMMs are numbered in the order of appearance to the mental space.

Since the shared mental space itself is not visible, it must be *reverse-engineered* from the recorded utterances exchanged during the creative discussion. The proposed approach applies a protocol analysis technique for this purpose: After irrelevant parts are screened out from the utterances, they are sorted out into meaningful elements. Then, each utterance element is encoded in terms of on which PSMM it is talking about and what attribute and relationships it adds to the PSMM, as described in the next section.

3   Case Study

3.1   Case Overview

A two-stage assembly cell for a product (a lego block car) is used as an example production system, and four university students are engaged in the experiment. The experiment is composed of some production sessions and discussion sessions. In a production session, two of the participants actually experience operating the cell and produce 16 products, and the other two members observe the operation as analysts. The assignment of the roles to the participants is determined by the participants themselves. In the following discussion session, which is about one hour long, they discuss how to enhance the production rate of the assembly cell. The innovation and improvement ideas created in the discussion session are actually introduced into the cell, and then the next production session is started. The fee paid to the participants is set proportional to the highest production rate of the production sessions performed in the experiment, and which is announced to them before starting the first production session. It is left up to the participants how to organize the discussion session. However, the number of ideas introduced to the cell after each discussion session is limited up to three, so that they would concentrate on refining ideas rather than simply enumerating simple ones. The discussion sessions are video and voice recorded.

3.2   Encoding Discussion Sessions

The transcript of the utterances exchanged in the first and the second discussion sessions is analyzed according to the proposed state transition model. All the utterances are first extracted from the recorded data and those which are judged not directly related to the creative problem solving practice are screened out. If a certain statement is repeated, only the original one appearing first is included in the analysis and the rests are omitted. The remaining utterances are then divided into elements so that each of them should have a separate meaning. Finally, each utterance element is encoded in terms of the attribute, relation and PSMM introduced in the previous section, respectively.

Table 1 shows a part of the result. For example, the attribute added by utterance element 1 is classified as a problem-related one of PSMM0 in the judgmental layer, and that added by utterance element 2 is encoded as a problem-related one of the same PSMM but in the objective layer. Further, it is considered that the second element introduced a directional relationship from the second to the first attribute and thus functioned as an ordinal inference.

Table 1. Example utterance elements and their codes (translated from Japanese)

ID	Utterance element	Attribute	Relation	PSMM
1	The assembly operation in cell 1 is more difficult than that in cell 2.	JL-PR		0
2	The idle time of operator 2 is almost as long as his working time in each cycle.	OL-PR	Directional (2, 1)	0
3	Inserting operation of operator 1 is sometimes imperfect.	OL-PR		0
4	There are moments when an operator changes the holding angle of a part.	OL-PR		0
5	What about making it possible to insert the part without changing its holding angle?	OL-SR	Directional (4, 5)	1
6	There are more parts to be inserted in cell 1 than cell 2.	OL-PR	Directional (6, 1)	0

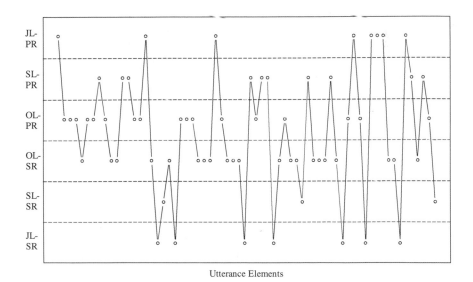

Utterance Elements

Fig. 2. Sequence of added attributes in discussion session 1

It is observed during the analysis that the participants themselves sometimes become confused on which PSMM they are currently talking about. Because of this, encoding is most difficult in terms of PSMM. If this analysis can be made online, visualizing the result and feeding it back to the participants will help them prevent themselves from getting lost and stay aware of where they are.

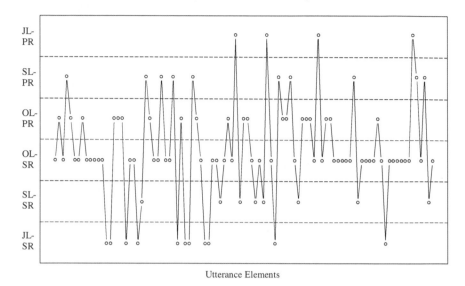

Utterance Elements

Fig. 3. Sequence of added attributes in discussion session 2

3.3   Outline of Discussion Sessions

Figures 2 and 3 represent the sequence of added attributes in the first and second discussion sessions, respectively. Although repeated attributes are omitted, an overview of how the scope of discussion changes along time can be obtained from the figures. What is interesting in the figures is that the scope does not always move from abstract (JL) to concrete (OL) and from problem (PR) to solution (SR) but it moves in the opposite direction almost equally frequently. Further, the distribution of attributes across the scopes does not seem to be stable over the whole discussion process. This implies that the discussion process is composed of several distinguishable phases.

Table 2. Number of attributes added in each scope

	JL-PR	SL-PR	OL-PR	OL-SR	SL-SR	JL-SR
Session 1	8	10	17	21	3	7
Session 2	4	10	20	44	8	11
Total	12	20	37	65	11	18

Table 2 shows the number of attributes added to each scope during the sessions. It is noticed that the distribution is quite similar between sessions 1 and 2. For example, many attributes are located in the objective layer (OL) in both sessions. It suggests that this layer is used as the main field of elaborating problems and solutions. Further, there are more solution-related attributes than problem-related ones in the objective layer (OL), but the opposite is true in the subjective layer (SL). This interesting feature suggests that objective solutions tends to bring about subjective side effects in one's mind and vice versa.

Table 3. Frequencies of scope changes in discussion session 1

	JL-PR	SL-PR	OL-PR	OL-SR	SL-SR	JL-SR
JL-PR	2	1	3	2		
SL-PR		2	4	3		1
OL-PR	2	2	6	5	1	1
OL-SR	1	3	2	9	1	5
SL-SR		1		1		
JL-SR	2	1	2	1	1	

Table 4. Frequencies of scope changes in discussion session 2

	JL-PR	SL-PR	OL-PR	OL-SR	SL-SR	JL-SR
JL-PR		1		2	1	
SL-PR			4	3	2	1
OL-PR		1	7	10		2
OL-SR	3	5	5	21	4	5
SL-SR	1	1	2	4		
JL-SR		2	2	3	1	3

Tables 3 and 4 show the frequencies of scope changes in sessions 1 and 2, respectively. The focus of discussion moved from a scope corresponding to the row to the next one corresponding to the column. The distributions shown in the tables are also similar to each other. Further, as conjectured above, the focus moved frequently within the objective layer (OL) as well as from/to the problem-related scope in the subjective layer (SL-PR). It is also noticed that the focus sometimes moved from the solution-related scope in the objective layer (OL-SR) to the solution-related one in the judgmental layer (JL-SR) and then to various ones. This suggests that a judgment of a member given to a concrete solution functions as a watershed of the discussion flow.

Figures 4 and 5 visualize the upper triangular matrices showing between which attributes relationships are given in sessions 1 and 2, respectively. Each blacked out box represents that one of the relationships defined earlier is introduced between the attributes corresponding to the row and the column. The distributions of the black boxes in the figures are even surprisingly similar to each other. That is, there are many local clusters along the diagonal line as well as some plots away from the line, which represent occasional relationships between attributes far away from each other. Those attributes to which relationships are introduced even from far downstream may be regarded as functioning as the main topics of discussion.

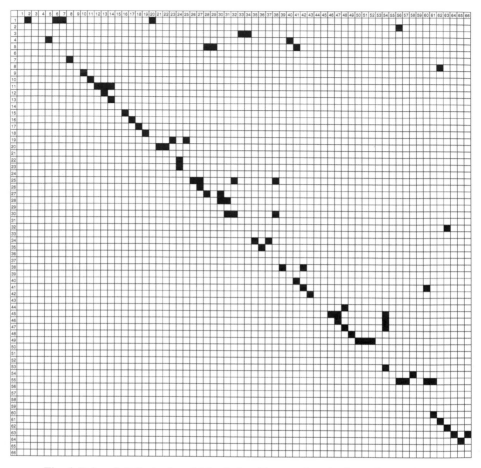

Fig. 4. Pairs of attributes for which relationships are given in discussion session 1

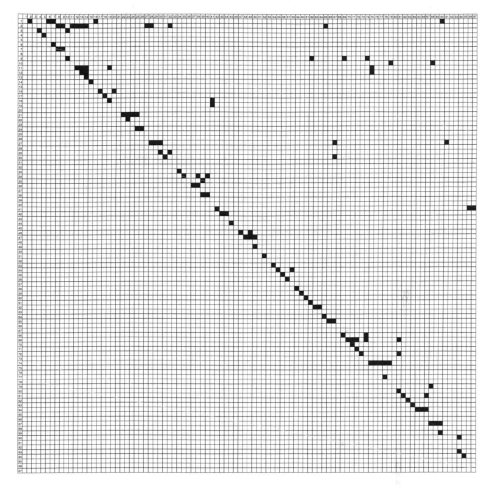

Fig. 5. Pairs of attributes for which relationships are given in discussion session 2

3.4   Knowledge Handling Actions

This subsection studies the knowledge handling actions taken in the discussion sessions. Table 5 sorts out the frequencies of the ordinal inference actions, that is, the directional relationships introduced in the sessions. Each of them derives an attribute in the scope corresponding to the column from another in the scope corresponding to the row. The table shows that this action is quite frequently taken between various scopes, which are not only from problem to solution but also within problem, within solution and even from solution to problem.

Table 5. Frequencies of ordinal inference actions

	JL-PR	SL-PR	OL-PR	OL-SR	SL-SR	JL-SR
JL-PR				7		1
SL-PR	1	2	2	8		
OL-PR	8	9	7	12	1	4
OL-SR	3	9	13	4	8	7
SL-SR				1		1
JL-SR			1	1		2

Table 6 summarizes the frequencies of the generalization/specialization actions, that is, the hierarchical relationships defined in the sessions. Each of them connects an abstract characteristic in the scope corresponding to the row and its detailed feature in the scope corresponding to the column. It is observed in the table that this action is also frequently taken and, in most cases, the detailed feature lies in the objective layer (OL). This action is usually used within problem or within solution but between problem and solution.

Table 6. Frequencies of generalization/specialization actions

	JL-PR	SL-PR	OL-PR	OL-SR	SL-SR	JL-SR
JL-PR	3				1	
SL-PR		1				
OL-PR			3			1
OL-SR				33		
SL-SR						
JL-SR				14	1	1

Table 7 shows the frequencies of the analogical-mapping/alternative-seeking actions, that is, the non-directional relationships mentioned in the sessions. Each of them bridges between a pair of attributes in the scopes corresponding to the row and column. Since the relationship is non-directional, the table is a lower triangular matrix. The table shows that this action is frequently taken and it is mostly within solution. It implies that this action is an effective vehicle for exploring the solution space. It is further observed that this action can be used not very often but also within problem and even between problem and solution.

Table 7. Frequencies of analogical-mapping/alternative-seeking actions

	JL-PR	SL-PR	OL-PR	OL-SR	SL-SR	JL-SR
JL-PR						
SL-PR		1				
OL-PR		1	3			
OL-SR			1	22		
SL-SR	1	2		1		
JL-SR	1			2		1

4   Conclusions

This paper proposed a state transition model for analyzing how a Kaizen team collectively creates innovation and improvement ideas for a production system, and captured actual sessions of creative discussion according to the process model. The analysis shows that the team-based creative problem solving practice is not a simple unidirectional process from abstract to concrete and from problem to solution. It is also observed that knowledge handling actions, such as ordinal inference, generalization, specialization, analogical-mapping, alternative-seeking, are frequently used in the process.

A future research direction is to reveal standard features of the team-based creative problem solving process by conducting more case studies. Further, it is also an interesting challenge to develop the proposed process model into a systematic tool for supporting the discussion process of creating innovation and improvement ideas for a production system. Possible directions of this include cognitive support by using the model as a computerized minute, automatic proposition of potentially effective knowledge handling actions, creativity support by combining the process model with TRIZ [11], etc.

Acknowledgments. This research was partially supported by the Japan Society for the Promotion of Science, Grant-in-Aid for Creative Scientific Research 19GS0208 and Grant-in-Aid for Scientific Research (B) 20310087.

References

1. Strobe, W., Diehl, M.: Why Groups Are Less Effective than Their Members: On Productivity Losses in Idea-Generating Groups. European Review of Social Psychology 5, 271–303 (1994)
2. Paulus, P.B., Yang, H.C.: Idea Generation in Groups: A Basis for Creativity in Organizations. Organizational Behavior and Human Decision Processes 82, 76–87 (2000)
3. Taggar, S.: Group Composition, Creative Synergy, and Group Performance. Journal of Creative Behavior 35, 261–286 (2001)
4. Vennix, J.A.M., Akkermans, H.A., Rouwette, E.A.J.A.: Group Model-Building to Facilitate Organizational Change: An Exploratory Study. System Dynamics Review 12, 39–58 (1995)
5. Vennix, J.A.M.: Group Model Building: Facilitating Team Learning Using System Dynamics. John Willey & Sons (1996)
6. Gero, J.S., Mc Neill, T.: An Approach to the Analysis of Design Protocol. Design Studies 19, 21–61 (1998)
7. Trauth, E.M., Jessup, L.M.: Understanding Computer-Mediated Discussions: Positivist and Interpretive Analysis of Group Support System Use. MIS Quarterly 24, 43–79 (2000)
8. Sakao, T., Paulsson, S., Mizuyama, H.: Inside a PSS Design Process: Insights through Protocol Analysis. In: 18th International Conference on Engineering Design (2011)
9. Fauconnier, G.: Mental Spaces. Cambridge University Press (1994)
10. Fauconnier, G.: Mappings in Thought and Language. Cambridge University Press (1997)
11. Savransky, S.D.: Engineering of Creativity: Introduction to TRIZ Methodology of Inventive Problem Solving. CRC Press (2000)

How to Implement Product Requirements
for Market Niches with Innovative Business Processes

Rosanna Fornasiero and Andrea Zangiacomi

Institute of Industrial Technologies and Automation
National Research Council, Via Bassini 15,
20133 Milano, Italy
{Rosanna.Fornasiero,Andrea.Zangiacomi}@itia.cnr.it

Abstract. In order to stay competitive, European manufacturing companies need to enter new markets implementing innovative business processes based on networking economy. Through business processes and requirements analysis hold on some European SMEs, this work proposes a supply chain mapping of the most relevant processes, procedures and techniques comparing European fashion supply networks through multiple case studies. The innovative production model will be based on the integration of fashion companies towards both suppliers and customers to support sustainable production of small series addressed products for target groups like obese, disabled, elderly people.

Keywords: Fashion sector, supply collaborative networks, target groups, business and customer requirements.

1 Introduction

This work is part of a research framework held at European level aiming at implementing innovative tools and methods for supply chain management to support European Textile, Clothing and Footwear Industry (TCFI) to produce small series of functional and fashionable footwear and clothing of high quality, affordable price and eco-compatible. The model of networked small series production will be tested specifically for target groups like disable, diabetic, obese and elderly people.

As the manufacturing sector in general, the combined effects of labour intensity, low entry and exit barriers, and changes in international trade regulations have made TCFI a global industry, where competition is planetary and key players are both in Europe and North America as well as in emerging low labour cost countries [1]. Small firms have struggled to survive, often unsuccessfully, and have been progressively weeded out [2]. Moreover, the overall performance of TCFI is deeply affected by unpredictable and seasonal demand as well as emerging consumers' needs in terms of comfort, health and environmental attention [3].

This context forces European TCFI companies to rethink their market as well as their operations strategies. To stay competitive, EU manufacturing companies need to enter markets which are not reachable yet by competitors from low cost countries providing customers with innovative products where healthy and functional

J. Frick and B. Laugen (Eds.): APMS 2011, IFIP AICT 384, pp. 598–610, 2012.

requirements related, for example, for what concerns shoes, to prevention of foot pain and injuries, should be complaint with fashion and aesthetic needs.

This work specifies in detail relevant as-is business processes and the to-be business requirements of each of the TCFI analysed company and of their networks to define a new collaborative supply chain reference model. Analysed companies represent both the perspective of traditional producers (from shoe and garment sectors) and of innovative players like online shirt sellers and shoe producers based on advanced technologies. Also technology providers like digital printing providers and service providers like foot monitoring devices producers are analyzed to understand how to implement the customer functional requirements with their support. This view on different type of TCFI networks will allow to have an holistic approach to the solutions to be proposed, which should fit with the need of producers, suppliers and customers.

2   Literature Review

Competition within TCFI is nowadays among global networks and key issues are how to develop and implement innovative managerial models and methods to support collaborative practices [4] [5]. The new paradigm of demand-driven supply networks [6], [7] emerges as a collaborative scheme to better respond to consumers' direct signals and needs. Moreover, as Adler [8] effectively discussed, the new enlarged/extended structures, characterized by high cognitive content exchanges, can no longer be coordinated by traditional hierarchy/market instruments as they require trust in order to share knowledge and leverage on external, updated and complementary competencies (i.e. Open Innovation model).

Along this vein Camarinha-Matos [9] investigate collaborative networks as new research field, analysing the different types, forms, characteristics and pre-conditions need for their development. Cooperative networks are formed to combine their core competences to be able to react to the requirements of their turbulent environments.

Companies need to improve their competences significantly through new business models, up-to-date strategies, technological capabilities and processes. Companies are increasingly restructuring their internal operations, information systems, production processes as well as collaboration strategies with other firms in complex value chains, business ecosystems, which extend globally [10]. These collaborative business networks are complex entities, where proper understanding for designing, implementing and managing is needed, for business success based on collaborative decision making [11]. Virtual Organization Breeding Environment (VBE) or Virtual Organization (VO), are models for long term and short term strategic alliances respectively [12, 13]. In particular in Romero and Molina [13] a complete framework of the business processes for VBE and VO is proposed and can be partially useful also for this work when specific business opportunities are encountered by a network of companies.

3   The TCFI Context: Industries Facing New Market Needs

The TCFI in Europe consists of more than 267.000 enterprises (about 90% SMEs), approximately 3 million employees and a turnover of around €235 billion [14], [15] for a total impact on the European GDP for 4% [16]. Total value added produced by the sector is around €65 billion. After China, the EU is the world's second largest exporter of textile products with 31% including intra-EU trade. In 2010 the EU exported €33.8 billion worth of textiles and clothing products and continues to dominate global markets for up-market and high quality textiles and clothing. The EU is also a major producer and exporter of footwear, especially high quality, high value fashion shoes. In 2010 the EU was the second global exporter of footwear exporting €4.9 billion worth of shoes globally. However, contrary to the overall trend in the EU-27's manufacturing industry, in the past decade the sector's added value has fallen by over 40% (50% in the case of clothing and even 60% in the case of footwear). Employment in the sector followed a similar downward trend [17].

Trade liberalisation does not seem to have had a decisive impact on this trend in the sector. It was indeed affected by other key factors including, in particular, changes in distribution and supply due to new environmental standards and health protection, rising energy and transport costs, which are making salaries less of a key factor in setting the end prices for goods, and changes in exchange rates [16].

Companies must turn these challenges into opportunities by improving their efficiency and by increasing innovation and excellence.

Small and medium-sized enterprises (SMEs) dominate the TCFI and each of them produces at one process stage. As for all TCFI companies, manufacturers are tightly integrated in European-wide networks covering the whole production chain starting from (chemical) fibre production up to the finished garments (representing roughly the 40% of the market for textiles) and technical textiles applications (60%) in aerospace industry, construction, automotive, and - of course - also in footwear.

The TCFI networks do not only consist of companies along the production chain but also of suppliers (e.g. trimmings for garment or chemicals for treatment and components as soles, insoles and lasts for shoes) and service providers (from design centers, to development services, to production services for garment cut-make-trim, to quality checker, to maintenance service providers, to third party logistics providers, to distribution centers). The improvement of productivity, flexibility and quality of one company in the network will directly influence the competitiveness of the whole network.

At European level SMEs are most of the time grouped in regional clusters with an high level of industrial homogeneity. This structure can be considered as both a strength and a weakness, as SMEs are generally more flexible, and yet at the same time more likely to lack investment capability.

As above mentioned, today, the European TCFI is strongly pulled by a highly unstable and rapidly changing demand, due to fashion-related and seasonal fluctuations, as well as emerging consumers needs in terms of well being, health and sustainability. For this reason measures to diversify and to help and support SME to develop niche markets are key elements: the future of the TCF sector depends on the manufacturing of high-tech, innovative or fashionable products with high added value, which meet consumer needs. [16].

There is in fact a share of market willing to buy products not only for low price but also for their performance in terms of comfort, health care, and environmental attention [18]. The increasing demands for socially and environmentally accountable industrial production represent a challenge for European companies. The need for environmental protection could in fact provide the sector with new opportunities, in terms of both the adoption of new production processes and the development of new products and materials [16].

More and more, firms need to pursue innovation strategies based on creativity, quality and differentiation to realize more complex products focused on different kind of customers and their specific needs. Small and specialized companies can face this challenge only working in demand-driven and customer oriented networks. Small series and specialized high value added products are a key opportunity for knowledge base European SMEs in the consumers goods sector [16][18]. In particular here the specific consumer target group addressed are elderly, obese, diabetics, and disables.

3.1   New Market Niches

The target groups addressed represent a large share of European citizens, according to present figures hereafter described. As underlined in the last resolution of the European Parliament the diabetes epidemic is a pressing issue. There are now more than 32 million EU citizens living with diabetes, which amounts to 8.1% of the adult population. This figure is set to rise to 50 million – 10% of the EU population – by 2025. Besides, Europe has the highest numbers of children with Type 1 diabetes. Each year, diabetes and related complications claim the lives of 325,000 EU citizens [19]. For what concerns elder people, in 2010 the population aged 65 years or over accounted for 17.4%. By 2050, the number of people in the EU aged 65 and above is expected to grow by 70% and the number of people aged over 80 by 170% [20]. Obesity is one the major health challenges worldwide and has become an epidemic over the last decades. Europe has the highest number of overweight and obese people in the world. The number of obese people has in fact tripled over the last 20 years in the Europe, according to the WHO [21]. Today, over 130 million people are obese in Europe and 400 million people are overweight. Moreover there are 80 million Europeans with disabilities. This is over 15% of the whole population. One in four Europeans has a family member with a disability [22]. In conclusion, it has also to be underlined that the four target groups are not completely separated both in terms of physical diseases and functional needs. As underlined by the EU commission, these data raises important challenges for the 21st century: meet the higher demand for healthcare and also for specific requirements.

The above mentioned categories in fact need products to fulfil their requirements in terms of improved comfort and functionalities of wearables, which is to protect the body from regular environmental impact (e.g. heat, cold, water, humidity) in a high comfort and high quality. High comfort means perfect fit, easy to dress/undress or low effort for washing and ironing. High quality means long-lasting appearance in terms of colour and shape, perfect assembly (durable seams) and high quality of material. Particularly, comfort in shoes is very important for elderly, obese, diabetics and disabled people due to changes in the foot morphological shape and bone disease which may cause problems during walking and standing. The business opportunity here described is to provide mainly products for preventive reasons and first level of disease. The focus is set on fashion companies willing to enlarge their business, covering a market niche that otherwise is not considered since the only specific products offered to these consumers are orthopaedic ones and generally products with medical prescription. Anyway it is important for companies to be supported by experts in the field to design and produce these kind of new added value products.

4   Customer and Business Requirements

4.1   Product Requirements from Target Groups

Main requirements from the TGs collected for the scope of the work are based both on interviews with people belonging to the categories and to experts like doctors and companies already producing for the TGs. Approximately 10-25% of all diabetics develop some foot problems during the course of their illness from simple calluses to major abscesses and osteomyelitis. Moreover nerve damage from diabetes can cause lose feeling in feet which makes difficult to be aware of pain and injuries caused by incorrect shoes or walking behaviours [23]. Foot injuries in diabetics can cause ulcers and infections and for this reason it is important to wear correct shoes and monitor the status of foot pressure on the insole using special customized shoes, with sensors [24]. In case of fashion companies willing to produce goods for preventive reasons the focus should be limited to diabetic people of category 0 (high foot risk and no ulceration) and I (superficial ulcer), according to the Wagner's classification of the diabetic foot [25]. This represent an important preventive approach aiming to provide diabetic people, which have not already incurred in heavy consequences of their condition, with not specifically medical products able to support them in avoiding possible foot problems. The impact in terms of future benefits is relevant if we consider not simply the percentage of diabetics covered but the fact that this approach is addressed to all diabetics at the beginning of their illness and will help them in maintaining the initial health condition of their feet, improving their future quality of life. Moreover it is an approach allowing also fashion companies to approach a new market without the need to enter into the system of the National service support for medical products.

Table 1. Target groups requirements

	REQUIREMENT	CATEGORY
Product structure, components and materials		
Specific features required for product components	Control the shape of the components, rigidity, dimensions.	Diabetics, Elderly, Obese
Specific properties required for materials	Possibility to choose materials according to functional specifications like transparency, anti-sweating, anti-allergic, softness.	Diabetics, Elderly, Obese, Disable
Specific properties required for the whole	Control stability, shock absorbtion, skin/bone protection, easy to dress	Diabetics, Elderly, Obese, Disable
Size & fit		
Need to redistribute feet pressure and pressure points	Insole realized according to measured walking pressure	Diabetics, Obese, Elderly
Need to adapt product design to body shape	Morphotype	Obese
Need to adapt product design to foot shape	Last realized according to feet geometry	Diabetics, Elderly, Disable

Obesity is a medical condition in which excess body fat has accumulated to the extent that it may have an adverse effect on health. It is defined by Body Mass Index (BMI) and further evaluated in terms of fat distribution via the waist–hip ratio and total cardiovascular risk factors. In this category focus is on people from obesity class I, which includes, referring to obesity classification established by the World Health Organization (WHO) in 1997 and published in 2000 according to BMI, values in the range 30-35. Associated needs are for special reinforced shoes and oversize shirts and garments. All products should also be realized with materials able to guarantee the best comfort and to respond to specific requirements of the group as, for example, anti-sweating features. Regarding dimensions, these products don't have the same proportions as the normal size products and so it is not only a matter of expanding the number of sizes in catalogue but specific rules have to be used during the design phase. Each person needs personalized shoes and garment according to a series of parameters which have to be defined and measured by companies.

In case of disability it is more difficult to categorize and define features and specifications which are valid for the category, In fact it is a very heterogeneous field and include many different kinds of pathologies. For this work the focus is on people with mobility limitation, in particular those using wheelchairs, and people with difficulties in dressing up and undressing. People with mobility limitation need to use customized shoes and garments very easy to dress up like for example with Velcro opening and elastic bands, to avoid tiny buttons and laces. Moreover measurements and size can be different from normal size due to permanent sitting position.

Elderly is a wide category and for the purpose of this work have been considered in particular elderly with mobility problems due to deformity of feet. Elders feet have often decreased plantar sensory, fragile skin and reduced healing abilities and need to be protected from possible hazard in environment. For these reason elderly people need special customized comfort shoes [26]. Moreover falls, particularly injurious ones, are a significant problem for the elderly. Although falls have multifactorial causes, foot problems and inappropriate footwear have been established as major falls risk factors for this population [27]. For very old people with mobility problems requests are similar to the ones of disabled.

In table 1 requirements for all the different categories are summarized according to different aspects in order to underline how the needs of the four target groups are often common and overlaps.

4.2   New Business Processes from TCFI Companies

As previously underlined TCFI Supply chain is characterized by many small companies collaborating each other along the value chain. Beside big brands like Zara, H&M, Benetton there are many own brand producers which cover a reasonable market share producing mainly high quality products sold all over the world. While most business networks have been formed along the value chain and were formed for long-time purpose, the current market asks for more flexible organizational structures which can quickly adapt to new customer needs and challenges. Therefore these networks have much shorter life-time and capitalize a lot on the concept of virtualization. Distributed information and knowledge are seen as main assets within such networks. Fashion is one of the industries more exposed to direct market evaluation, and focal companies are responsible for their products both in terms of economic performance and environmental and social problems caused not only by themselves directly, but also by their suppliers.

An innovative group of companies from TCFI have been chosen and includes SMEs aiming to radically change their business model and supply chain structure, leveraging on environmental sustainability to compete in new market niches like disable, diabetic and obese people to provide healthy and fashionable products.

Research methodology has been based on business case analysis, interviews with managers, brainstorming with operations managers. BPMN formalization has clearly revealed which are the processes where fashion companies should implement changes to address the needs of the target groups and improve their supply network operations and identifying the potential benefits of methods and supporting tools. The summary of the requirements collected for process improvement for a new supply chain approach have been summarized in table 2. Here the main actors of the different process are highlighted. It has to be underlined that customers for small series can be both retailers interested in the realization of a small collection for a target group or end customers belonging to one (or more) target group that want to purchase a product according to their specific needs. Also for what concerns experts, different typology are considered. In CD1, where needs of TGs and functionalities for new product have to be defined, actors include medical experts whereas in CD2 it is foreseen the support of technical experts in the implementation of the selected functionalities like insole medical suppliers in the case of footwear.

Table 2. New business Processes and related Requirements

Id	Process Requirement description	Main Actors	Process
IM1	**Traditional shopping support for specific customer groups:** Direct customer acquisition of footwear, textiles or clothing products should be supported by the possibility to manage special features for the consumer target groups (elderly, obese, diabetics and disabled people) with the possibility of product configuration both aesthetically and functionally. Full visualization of products characteristics with advanced rendering systems.	End-Customer, shop assistant, producer	Sales, product configuration
IM2	**Online visualization, configuration and acquisition of garment/leather/footwear product:** customer acquisition of product special features, configuration and full visualization of products characteristics through online systems for collaboration during sales process	End-Customer, retailer, producer	Sales, product configuration

Table 2. (*Continued*)

CD1	**Co-design with support of Knowledge Management Tools:** Through data mining approaches, consumer-oriented market analysis should be useful to define needs of customer segments. Subsequent knowledge management tools can support designers in the identification of market needs and consumer preferences for new products and functionalities in the footwear and accessories, textile and garments sectors.	Marketing managers, Trendsetter, Medical experts	Market analysis
CD2	**Definition of Collection for specific target groups:** this implies to have a collaborative environment where different type of users (internal and external to the company) with different roles (and IT skills) can contribute to define a collection of suitable products for the target consumers.	Managers, Stylists, main suppliers, Designers, Technical experts	Design phase
CD3	**Product Design with CAD modelling support:** This activity is carried out by the (internal and external) designers and produces the CAD technical models of the product. Also includes selection of materials for both clothing and footwear.	Customers (retailers), Designers, modelists	Design phase
CD4	**Process planning support:** Process planning is related to product engineering and has the aim to decide how to manufacture the product and to produce all related information. In this phase suppliers and outsourcers are identified and defined and the costs for the different manufacturing phases are fixed. Also the BOM, the working cycles and the production times of the new product model are also defined.	Producers, Suppliers, outsourcers	Process planning
CM1	**Partner Search support:** partner search is a process embedded in other processes like Process planning in CD4 and CP2 as well as CP3. Companies need support for the identification of the correct performance indicators to be used for the search and selection. Suppliers and outsourcers can be involved in the collaborative definition of the indicators and in the monitoring activities.	Production managers, designers, suppliers, outsourcers	Design phase, process planning, production planning
CP1	**Customer order processing support:** Automatic pre-processing of customer orders for administrative and pre-production checks and issues. The final output is the list of customer orders ready to be processed for production.	Production manager	Order management

Table 2. (*Continued*)

CP2	**Support for collaborative process planning:** after order collection process planning done in CD4 needs to be specified for creation of set of Production Orders; external activities (to be outsourced) require the identification of potential partners to be assigned. The output is the set of production orders ready to be scheduled.	Production manager, Supplier, Outsourcer	Process planning
CP3	**Collaborative production planning and control:** Production Orders related to the same customer's orders can be scheduled using a collaborative tool where Manufacturer and Partners can share a view of the production order schedules and close a "negotiation" for the definitive launch of manufacturing activities. The result is a set of production orders scheduled and ready to be launched.	Manufacturer	Production planning and control
CP4	**Partner monitoring and trace support:** Production Orders launched can be monitored and KPI related to Quality and Sustainability can be evaluated for that specific set of production orders. The outcome includes overall status, alerts/warnings and KPIs.	Manufacturer, Supplier, Outsourcer	Production planning and control
TP1	**Technologies to support aesthetical personalization:** This process includes sustainable and flexible Digital (Textile) Printing using textured markers and the application of a decoration design (as included in the CAD design) through a laser engraving machine, on leather components of a possibly customized product in leather, like shoes or leather clothes.	Manufacturer, Outsourcer	Production
TP2	**Technologies to support functional characterization: (insole and last – make to measure)** this process is referred to footwear scenario and includes the outsourced realization of a customized insole according to results from foot pressure measurements by sensors and of a customized last in case of made to measure shoes.	Manufacturer, Supplier, Outsourcer	Production

In table 3 are indicated important relationships between the functional requirements and analyzed companies and it shows how, according to the type of company, different process improvement are necessary.

The process change requirements cover the major coordinated intra- and inter-sector networking of producers/service providers using innovative production technologies as well as innovative organizational models based on cross-supply network integration and collaboration. New actors and new interaction mechanisms are part of the networks and new level of information should be exchanged both in terms of product and process improvement.

Table 3. Process Requirements-Company matrix

Requirements Vs Companies	Sector	IM1	IM2	CD1	CD2	CD3	CD4	CP1	CP2	CP3	CP4	TP1	TP2
Make-to measure producer	Clothing		✓	✓		✓	✓	✓	✓	✓	✓	✓	
Technology provider	Clothing					✓	✓					✓	
Traditional producer	Footwear	✓	✓	✓	✓	✓	✓	✓	✓	✓	✓	✓	
Mass customization producer	Footwear		✓	✓		✓	✓	✓	✓	✓	✓	✓	✓
Traditional producer	Clothing	✓	✓	✓	✓		✓	✓	✓	✓	✓		
Service provider	Footwear		✓			✓		✓					✓

5 Conclusions and Ongoing Developements

The approach proposed in this paper allows to cover many different issues along the supply network. From the customer interaction point of view, what emerges is that companies need to change the way customers are involved in the design and production process to be able to interact with them. This happens to collect first information on market trends for understanding new target groups, and second information about product functional characteristics via web-based configurators. This means to support fashion companies to reach customer satisfaction not only through aesthetic details but also and mainly with application of new materials (e.g. transpirant, waterproof, flexible materials..), customized production processes (e.g. no internal stitching for diabetics..) or new components (e.g. personalized insole..) to make shoes and garment more comfortable to prevent injuries and pain.

Consumer requirements emphasize the need to apply different level of customization and product personalization and this can be taken into consideration according to the type of company willing to implement this production model: while traditional companies are interested to small series production, innovative companies are more oriented to a make-to-measure approach or to a configure-to-order approach.

From the supply chain management point of view, to increase capabilities of companies to produce small series means to formalize partner search and selection to ease the quick reconfiguration of networks. In fact in the fashion sector there is the need to define framework agreements at the beginning of the season so that suppliers and outsourcers allocate capability to a certain production and during the season they are ready to answer to production needs according to specific requests.

Comparing some European fashion supply networks through multiple case studies, this work proposes innovative business processes that support the implementation of fashion products based on functional requirements of niche markets represented by elderly, diabetic, obese and disabled people.

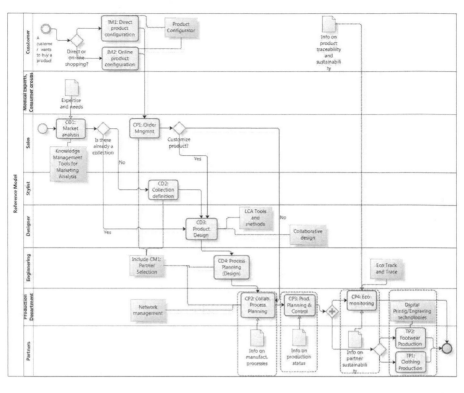

Fig. 1. The high level of the Reference Model

The functional requirements analysed and previously presented call for new approaches to TCFI business process management and have been then also used to develop a specific reference model based on the definition of three important dimensions in the networked companies (as from the model proposed in [29]): ICT, knowledge and organization . For each of the process the three dimensions have been developed both in terms of innovative practices and of related tools. The high-level of the reference model is shown in figure 1 and represents an outlook on the business processes summarizing the whole flow which is then developed in details at tactical level. This detailed level of the Reference Model is undergoing a further refinement based on best practices collected from literature and case analysis.

Acknowledgments. This work has been partly funded by the European Commission through the FP7-2010-NMP-ICT-FoF Project *CoReNet:* 'Customer-Oriented and Eco-Friendly Networks for Healthy Fashionable Goods' (Grant Agreement 260169). The authors wish to acknowledge the Commission for their support. We also wish to acknowledge our gratitude and appreciation to all the CoReNet project partners for their contribution during the development of ideas and concepts presented in this paper.

References

1. Gereffi, G., Humphrey, J., Sturgeon, T.: The governance of global value chains. Review of International Political Economy 12(1), 78–104 (2005)
2. Leonidou, L.C.: An analysis of the barriers hindering small business export development. Journal of Small Business Management 42(3), 279–302 (2004)
3. TCFI ETPs: European Technology Platform for the Future of Textiles and Clothing (ETP FTC), http://www.textile-platform.eu
4. Dyer, J.H., Singh, H.: The Relational View: Cooperative Strategy and Source of Interorganizational Competitive Advantage. Academy of Management Review 23(4), 660–679 (1998)
5. Camarinha-Matos, L.M., et al.: Towards a framework for Creation of dynamic virtual Organizations. IFIP International Federation for Information Processing, vol. 186, pp. 69–80 (2005)
6. Childerhouse, P., Aitken, J., Towill, D.R.: Analysis and design of focused demand chains. Journal of Operations Management 20(6), 675–689 (2002)
7. De Treville, S., Shapiro, R.D., Hameri, A.: From supply chain to demand chain: the role of lead time reduction in improving demand chain performance. Journal of Operations Management 21(6), 613–627 (2004)
8. Adler, P.S.: Market, Hierarchy and Trust: the Knowledge Economy and the Future of Capitalism. Organization Science 12(2), 215–234 (2001)
9. Camarinha-Matos, L.M., Boucher, X., Afsarmanesh, H. (eds.): PRO-VE 2010. IFIP AICT, vol. 336. Springer, Heidelberg (2010)
10. Myers, J.: Future Value Systems: Next Generation Economic Growth Engines & Manufacturing. In: Proceedings of the IMS Vision Forum 2006, Seoul, Korea, pp. 30–47 (2006)
11. Camarinha-Matos, L.M., Afsarmanesh, H.: A Comprehensive Modeling Framework for Collaborative Networked Organizations. J. Intell. Manuf. 18, 529–542 (2007)
12. Romeo, D., Galeano, N., Molina, A.: Virtual Organization Breeding Environments Value System and Its Elements. J. Intell. Manuf. 21, 267–286 (2010)
13. Romeo, D., Molina, A.: VO Breeding Environments & Virtual Organizations Integral Business Process Management Framework. Information System Frontiers (ISF) 11, 569–597 (2009)
14. (2007), http://ec.europa.eu/enterprise/textile/statistics.htm
15. (2008), http://ec.europa.eu/enterprise/sectors/footwear/statistics/index_en.htm
16. The future of the textile,clothing and footwear sectors in Europe, EU Commission (2008)
17. (2010), http://ec.europa.eu/trade/creating-opportunities/economic-sectors/industrial-goods/textiles-and-footwear.htm
18. Fornasiero, R., Chiodi, A., Carpanzano, E., Carneiro, L.: Research Issues on Customer-Oriented and Eco-friendly Networks for Healthy Fashionable Goods. In: Ortiz, Á., Franco, R.D., Gasquet, P.G. (eds.) BASYS 2010. IFIP AICT, vol. 322, pp. 36–44. Springer, Heidelberg (2010)
19. http://www.idf.org/epresolution.htm
20. http://ec.europa.eu/health-eu/my_health/elderly/index_en.htm
21. http://www.who.int
22. http://www.edf-feph.org/

23. Frykberg, R.G., Lavery, L.A., Pham, H., Harvey, C., Harkless, L., Veves, A.: Role of neuropathy and high foot pressures in diabetic foot ulceration. Diabetes Care 21, 1714–1719 (1998)
24. Cavanagh, P.R.: Therapeutic footwear for people with diabetes. Diabetes Metab. Res. Rev. 20, 51–55 (2004)
25. Wagner Jr., F.W.: The diabetic foot. Orthopedics 10(1), 163–172 (1987)
26. Mickle, K.M., Munro, B.J., Lord, S.R., Menz, H.B., Steele, J.R.: Foot shape of older people: Implications for shoe design. Footwear Science 2(3), 131–139 (2010)
27. Mickle, K.M., Munro, B.J., Lord, S.R., Menz, H.B., Steele, J.R.: Foot pain, plantar pressures and falls in older people: A prospective study. Journal of the American Geriatrics Society 58, 1936–1940 (2010)
28. Fornasiero, R., Zangiacomi, A., Stellmach, D.: A Reference Model for Customer-Oriented and Eco-Friendly Networks for Healthy Fashionable Goods. In: Frick, J. (ed.) Proceedings of the APMS 2011 Conference - Advances in Production Management Systems, September 26-28, Published at the University of Stavanger, Norway (2011)
29. Filos, E., Banahan, E.: Towards the smart organization: An emerging organizational paradigm and the contribution of the European RTD programs. Journal of Intelligent Manufacturing 12(2), S.101–S.111 (2001)

Innovations through the Supply Chain and Increased Production: The Case of Aquaculture

Frank Asche[1], Kristin H. Roll[1], and Ragnar Tveteras[2]

[1] Department of Industrial Economics, University of Stavanger, N-4036 Stavanger, Norway
[2] Stavanger Centre for Innovation Research,
University of Stavanger, N-4036 Stavanger, Norway
{Frank.Asche,Kristin.H.Roll,Ragnar.Tveteras}@uis.no

Abstract. During the last decades, aquaculture has been the world's fastest growing food production technology. This is primarily due to the fact that control with the production process has allowed innovations thorough the supply chain, leading to increased demand and thereby increased production. We investigate this process for three leading species; salmon, sea bass and shrimp. The process has been very different for the three species. Sea bass show that despite impressive performance on the cost side, production growth in an industry that is not able to create demand growth will be limited. Shrimp show that as soon as innovation and productivity growth upstream is hindered, production growth will also be limited. Salmon has achieved a better balance between upstream and downstream innovations, and has had a smoother increase in production.

Keywords: Aquaculture, innovation, increased production.

1 Introduction

During recent decades, aquaculture has been the world's fastest growing food production technology, creating a blue revolution [1,2]. Salmon and sea bass are leading species in Europe, and salmon and shrimp as the globally leading species [3,4]. Innovations leading to productivity growth and demand growth are the main forces driving this process. The effect of technological and market innovations as well as productivity growth is well understood, as control with the production process enables innovations that increase productivity, reduce production cost and increase competitiveness [4]. This makes it profitable to increase production despite of declining prices, and transfer a significant share of the productivity growth to the consumers in the form of lower prices [3].

While we have a good understanding of the effect of productivity growth, less is known about product development and demand growth in product as well as geographical space. [5] note that species where the price development indicates a substantial productivity growth will have limited production growth if there is no demand growth. Sea bass in the Mediterranean is an example of a species where the price decline has been as rapid as for salmon, but where production growth is less

J. Frick and B. Laugen (Eds.): APMS 2011, IFIP AICT 384, pp. 611–619, 2012.

than a tenth of the growth for salmon. [4] highlights the importance of demand side innovations as more efficient logistics, and use salmon and shrimp as examples of species where these have been important driving factors.

In this paper we will study the interaction between demand growth and production growth for different aquaculture species; salmon, shrimp and sea bass. These species are characterized by a substantial productivity growth leading to a significant reduction in production cost. However, the production expands much more rapidly for salmon and shrimp than for sea bass and sea bream. This difference is primarily caused by the different demand growth. We will use salmon as our base case, as this is the species which most data is available for, and the insights will then be applied to the other species.

2   Aquaculture

While aquaculture is an old production technology, it was not very important in terms of quantity produced until the 1970s. Then, a significant change took place as better control of the production process enabled a number of new technologies and production practices to be developed and implemented. This improved the competitiveness of aquaculture products both as a source of basic food and as a cash crop. The competitiveness of aquaculture has further been increased by the product development and marketing that was possible with a more predictable supply. The combined effect of productivity and demand growth has made aquaculture the world's fastest growing animal-based food sector in recent decades [2].

Since 1970, aquaculture production has grown from being an insignificant source of seafood to an important provider of protein for human consumption. In 1970, aquaculture production was still rather miniscule with a produced quantity of about 3.5 million metric tons, representing 5.1 percent of total seafood supply. In 2008, aquaculture accounted for about 40 percent of total seafood supply with a production of 58 million metric tons. Fisheries production, on the other hand, has fluctuated between 90 and 100 million metric tons in annual landings, with no particular trend. The increased production in aquaculture is accordingly the only reason why global seafood supply has continued to increase since 1990. Moreover, the increased production has been sufficient to not only maintain but also to slightly increase global per capita consumption of seafood.

3   Salmon

We will start by looking more closely at salmon, because this is one of the species with the most data available. Most of the data used her will be taken from or be extensions of [3]. For any product, the production volume over time is determined by the producers' profitability, with production tending to increase if it is very profitable. On the other hand, production will decrease if other uses of capital and labor are more profitable and if producers are losing money. A decline in the price of salmon (and other aquaculture species) has been necessary to induce greater consumption of the product. For this to be profitable, production costs must also have been substantially reduced. This has indeed been the case [6-9], as production cost has followed the price. The main factors behind reduced production costs are productivity growth and technological change.

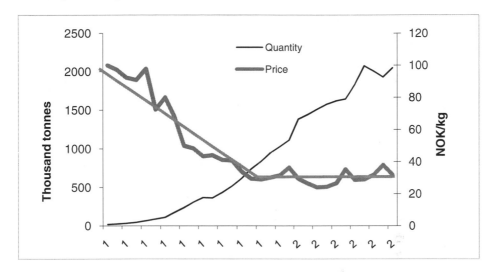

Fig. 1. Real export price and production cost for farmed Atlantic salmon, 1985-2011

Figure 1 shows real production cost and export price for salmon in Norway. Both variables have a clear downward trend, and the gap between them is consistently small. The average price in 2011 was about a quarter of the price in 1985, and the reduction in production cost was of the same magnitude. The important message here is that there is a close relationship between the development of productivity and falling export prices. Productivity gains are therefore able to explain a great deal of the decline in farmed salmon prices, as the price has been moving down with the production cost, keeping the profit margin relatively constant. This is also to be expected in a competitive industry, since high profitability is the market's signal to increase production. As the cost reduction has been translated into lower prices, it is also clear that the productivity gains have been passed on to consumers. The main effect for the producers is that they become larger and hence earn a higher profit due to the larger quantities produced.

The reduction in production costs is due to two main factors. First, fish farmers have become more efficient, so they produce more salmon with the same input. This is normally referred to as the fish farmers' productivity growth. Second, improved input factors (e.g., better feed and feeding technology and improved genetic attributes due to salmon breeding) make the production process less costly. This is due to technological change for fish farmers and productivity growth for the fish farm suppliers. This distinction is often missed, and the productivity growth for the farmers, as well as for their suppliers, is somewhat imprecisely referred to as productivity growth for the whole industry. In addition, while the focus is on the production process, productivity gains in the distribution chain to the retail outlet are equally important.

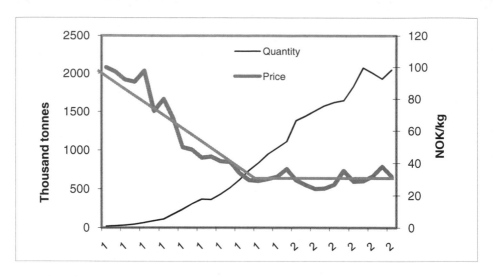

Fig. 2. Real Norwegian export price global production of farmed Atlantic salmon

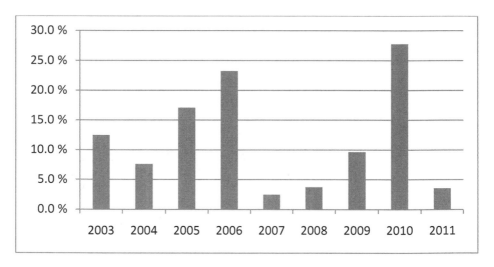

Fig. 3. Global demand growth for farmed Atlantic salmon, 2002-2011

As productivity and demand growth both constitute important factors in this market, it is an excellent market to study the impact of demand growth. To support this argument, Figure 2 shows aggregate production of Atlantic salmon together with the real Norwegian export price. The trend line shows that up to the mid-1990s, productivity growth clearly outpaced demand growth resulting in a significant downward shift in the real price. However, from the mid-1990s onward, the real price has been relatively stable indicating that demand growth has kept pace with productivity growth. With the continued increase in salmon production, this suggests substantial demand growth. [10] shows that the demand growth for salmon in France is 4.7% and for the EU it is 7.6% for the period 1996 to 2009. As production has been growing at a higher rate, this suggests that demand growth has been faster outside of Europe. Using the same approach [11] and a demand elasticity of -1.1 for data covering the world for the period 2003-2011 we find that this is the case as the average annual demand growth is 11.9%. However, as shown in figure 3, and as found by [10] for Europe, it is highly variable. This match the production growth for the period well, although the cyclicality in the prices (figure 2) and the demand growth (figure 3) indicates that the process is anything but smooth and leads to substantial volatility in profitability. This indicates that supply side explanations are not the only cause for price volatility [12], and that the demand side can have contributed to the increased price volatility observed by [13].

The market has expanded in two dimensions; geographical space and product space. Early on, the geographical space was most important, as the two main product forms, whole fresh salmon and smoked sides of salmon was introduced in new markets. This process was facilitated by a number of innovations in logistics, distribution and transports. Of particular importance was the use of truck-lines in Europe that allowed fresh salmon to be in the fish counter anywhere in Western Europe less than three days after it was out of the sea. This turned local fresh fish markets into a regional European markets. In the mid 1980s one also created the infrastructure to allow large scale air transport of salmon, linking first the USA and then Japan to the European salmon market, and then enabling Chile to become a major producer. From the mid 1990s the salmon market has been global, as Chile and Norway, ship salmon to more than 160 countries. However, the real revolution has taken place in product space, as salmon is now sold in hundreds of product forms, and the food processing allows salmon to reach new consumers by introducing new product forms every year. This development has occurred because food processors has found that salmon is a competitive input that can be sold not only in new types of cuts that develops the traditional product, but also in ready-to-eat packages and other product forms away from the fish counter.

4   Sea Bass

After salmon, sea bass is the most successful farmed fish in Europe. Farmed production started to grow in the late 1980s, and passed 1,000 tonnes in 1987. In 2008 about 116,000 tonnes sea bream was produced, and a quantity of a similar magnitude was also produced of sea bream under similar conditions. As shown in Figure 4, superficially the development looks very similar to salmon and shrimp with a strong production growth and a rapidly declining price. The price has declined at a similar magnitude as for salmon, but even more rapidly. The production has increased, but production in 2008 is at 116,000, which compares to almost two million tonnes of salmon. The difference is primarily demand growth. Sea bass is primarily marketed as portion-sized fish at 300-500 grams. This is small relative to salmon, but has the advantage that turnover in production becomes much higher. As the most valuable of the wild sea bream landed are substantially larger, this has also separated the markets for wild and farmed fish. The producers have not succeeded to any extent in expanding the geographical size of the market, as most of the fish is being sold in the EU-countries bordering the Mediterranean. The portion size of the fish is also a limitation on the number of product forms that are marketable. Product development is very limited relative to salmon, despite the fact that sea bass are as accessible to French processors as salmon. The fact that production in recent years (from 2002) has increased without a strong negative price effect is a sign that finally the market is being expanded. In particular, the industry has started producing larger fish, so that it is not restricted to the portion size fish market.

Fig. 4. Real price and global production of sea bass, 1989-2008

5   Shrimp

Shrimp is the most valuable farmed species and the seafood species with the highest trade value. Several species are farmed, with white shrimp and black tiger prawns being the most important. Aquaculture production started increasing in the 1970s, and in 2008 was about 3.4 million tonnes. Production growth has, with the exception of the last few years, been slower than for salmon. There have also been more challenges. In particular, there have been several serious diseases, the most serious being the white spot disease. There have also been substantial environmental challenges. These challenges have led to substantial shifts in what have been the most important producer countries [14], and have also led to periods of slower growth as production has been substantially reduced in some regions.

There are several reasons why shrimp aquaculture has faced these challenges. Production technology in shrimp farming is much more diversified than for salmon. It ranges from relatively simple operations where wild caught larvae are placed in crudely dug ponds to sophisticated closed production systems comparable to salmon aquaculture. Moreover, production in many cases takes place on land with little economic value (such as mangroves) and poorly defined property rights in countries with no environmental regulations. This has led to environmentally unsound practices in several cases. With high stocking densities, there is high exposure to disease. Moreover, in countries with poor environmental regulations, it may be more profitable to produce with high density for a few years and leave a devastated piece of land than to operate on a sustainable basis. However, technology is steadily improving and best practice producers with closed production systems operate with little risk of disease and in an environmentally sound manner. These sounder practices will most likely win market share, as the scope for technological innovation and productivity growth is highest under such conditions. There are also efforts to promote them in the market place. For instance, the Global Aquaculture Alliance (GAA) is providing certification of good shrimp farming practices.

Farmed shrimp production for 1980 through 2008, along with the price to producers in real US$ per kilogram, is shown in Figure 5. The average price in 2008 of 4.2 US$/kg is less than half of the price in 1984. Prices stabilised in the mid 1990s when production growth was flat, then declined rapidly after 2000 while production essentially trebled over the next five years. As with salmon, increased production has led to reduced prices. However, the price reduction for shrimp seems to be less than for salmon, up to quite significant volumes. One likely explanation for this is that the supply of wild shrimp is relatively higher, and therefore, there was a large market to win market share from.

As for salmon, shrimp producers have also done well in expanding market size in geographical as well as product space. The market has become global, and the number of product forms has vastly expanded. This has to some extent also been fuelled by trade issues with the USA taking the lead, as anti-dumping tariffs have been imposed on some unprocessed product forms from some countries.

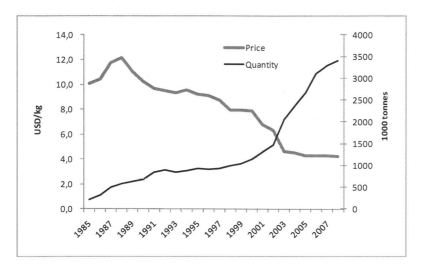

Fig. 5. Real US import price and global production of farmed shrimp, 1985-2008

6   Conclusions

Aquaculture has during the previous two decades been the world's fastest growing production technology. This blue revolution has been possible because increased control with the production technology created condition allowing productivity growth not only in the production, but also through the whole supply chain due to improved logistics, distribution, processing and product development [15]. This has created the demand growth necessary to allow a rapidly increased production to be sold at profitable prices.

We have in this paper reviewed three cases. Salmon has the smoothest productivity growth, but since the mid 1990s, demand growth has been equally important in explaining the growth of the quantity produced. Production increase for shrimp halted in the 1990s when disease problems prevented productivity growth, but has again picked up as these were solved. Sea bass operates at much lower quantities than salmon and shrimp because there have been no marketing innovations creating demand growth, and the whole productivity growth is taken out as lower prices by pumping more fish into the same markets. The price development is similar for all aquaculture species [16], and the quantity development therefore is largely determined by the factors discussed for these three species.

Acknowledgments. The authors would like to thank the Norwegian Seafood Council and the Norwegian Seafood Research Fund for financial support.

References

1. Smith, M.D., Roheim, C.A., Crowder, L.B., Halpern, B.S., Turnipseed, M., Anderson, J.L., Asche, F., Bourillón, L., Guttormsen, A.G., Kahn, A., Liguori, L.A., McNevin, A., O'Connor, M., Squires, D., Tyedemers, P., Brownstein, C., Carden, K., Klinger, D., Sagarin, R., Selkoe, K.A.: Sustainability and Global Seafood. Science 327, 784–786 (2010)
2. FAO, The state of world fisheries and aquaculture 2010. FAO, Rome (2010)
3. Asche, F., Bjørndal, T.: The Economics of Salmon Aquaculture. Blackwell, Oxford (2011)
4. Asche, F.: Farming the Sea. Marine Resource Economics 23, 507–527 (2008)
5. Asche, F., Roll, K.H., Trollvik, T.: New Aquaculture Species – The Whitefish Market. Aquaculture Economics and Management 13, 76–93 (2009)
6. Asche, F.: Trade Disputes and Productivity Gains: The Curse of Farmed Salmon Production? Marine Resource Economics 12, 67–73 (1997)
7. Tveterås, R.: Flexible panel data models for risky production technologies with an application to salmon aquaculture. Econometric Reviews 19, 367–389 (2000)
8. Guttormsen, A.G.: Input Factor Substitutability in Salmon Aquaculture. Marine Resource Economics 17, 91–102 (2002)
9. Asche, F., Roll, K.H., Tveteras, R.: Economic Inefficiency and Environmental impact: An application to Aquaculture Production. Journal of Environmental Economics and Management 58, 93–105 (2009)
10. Asche, F., Dahl, R.E., Gordon, D.V., Trollvik, T., Aandal, P.: Demand growth for salmon in the European market. Marine Resource Economics 26(4), 255–265 (2011)

11. Marsh, J.M.: Impacts of Declining U.S. Retail Beef Demand on Farm-Level Beef Prices and Production. American Journal of Agricultural Economics 85, 902–913 (2003)
12. Aasheim, L.J., Dahl, R.E., Kumbhakar, S.C., Oglend, A., Tveteras, R.: Are Prices or Biology Driving the Short-Term Supply of Farmed Salmon? Marine Resource Economics 26, 343–357 (2011)
13. Oglend, A., Sikveland, M.: The Behaviour of Salmon Price Volatility. Marine Resource Economics 23(4), 507–526
14. Anderson: The International Seafood Trade. Woodhcad Publishing, Cambridge (2003)
15. Asche, F., Roll, K.H., Tveteras, R.: Productivity Growth in the Supply Chain – Another Source of Competitiveness for Aquaculture. Marine Resource Economics 22, 329–334 (2007)
16. Tveterås, S., Asche, F., Bellemare, M.F., Smith, M.D., Guttormsen, A.G., Lem, A., Lien, K., Vannuccini, S.: Fish Is Food - The FAO's Fish Price Index. PLoS One 7(5), e36731 (2012), doi:10.1371/journal.pone.0036731

Innovations and Productivity Performance in Salmon Aquaculture

Frank Asche[1], Kristin H. Roll[1], and Ragnar Tveteras[2]

[1] Department of Industrial Economics, University of Stavanger, N-4036 Stavanger, Norway
[2] Stavanger Centre for Innovation Research,
University of Stavanger, N-4036 Stavanger, Norway
{Frank.Asche,Kristin.H.Roll,Ragnar.Tveteras}@uis.no

Abstract. Since the 1980s a large number of innovations have radically transformed the production process in salmon aquaculture. Increased degree of control with the production process, increased scale of plants, and more intensive use of farm locations are some of the consequences. Until the mid 1990s the industry also experienced rapid productivity growth leading to production costs to be reduced to 1/3 of their initial levels in Norwegian salmon aquaculture. But thereafter productivity has been stagnant. This paper analyses the innovation process and productivity growth in the Norwegian salmon industry, and discusses the challenges for the future.

Keywords: Innovation, productivity growth, salmon aquaculture, translog cost function.

1   Introduction

A growing global population requires increased production of marine proteins, and this can only come from aquaculture since global wild fish stocks are generally fully exploited or over-exploited [1]. Consumers will not only demand more seafood but also increased product quality and diversity as they become wealthier [2]. Aquaculture is better positioned than fisheries to provide the product quality and diversity that future consumers will demand. But with scarce farming areas, high local environmental impacts and limited marine feed raw material sources global aquaculture cannot continue to expand with current technologies. Aquaculture sectors need to innovate in several key areas to be able to satisfy the increasing global demand for seafood [3]. This is also the case for salmon aquaculture, one of the technologically leading sectors.

Our study focuses on salmon aquaculture, which has increased its degree of control with the production process through many innovations in key technologies such as fish feed, feeding equipment, IT based monitoring of live fish, vaccines and genetics [4], [5], [6]. Salmon production has moved from a technological regime with poor degree of control of many processes to one that can be described as approaching 'biological manufacturing'. Many of the tasks that before was manual, such as fish monitoring, fish feeding, fish harvesting and equipment maintenance, have now been

J. Frick and B. Laugen (Eds.): APMS 2011, IFIP AICT 384, pp. 620–627, 2012.
© IFIP International Federation for Information Processing 2012

automated to a large extent. This has contributed to significantly increasing productivity and improving the quality of farmed salmon since the 1980s.

This paper discusses the past innovations and accompanying productivity effects (section 2), estimates how the rate of technological progress changes over time in salmon aquaculture using an econometric cost model specification on a large data set of salmon firms, and links the estimated rates of technological change over time to innovations in key technology areas (section 3). Finally, the paper discusses the future innovation challenges for the salmon industry, several which it share with other aquaculture sectors (section 4).

2   Innovations and the Innovation System in Salmon Aquaculture

Innovations in salmon aquaculture include technology areas such as feed, fish health and equipment, but also regulatory innovations. Examples of innovations are presented in Figure 1.

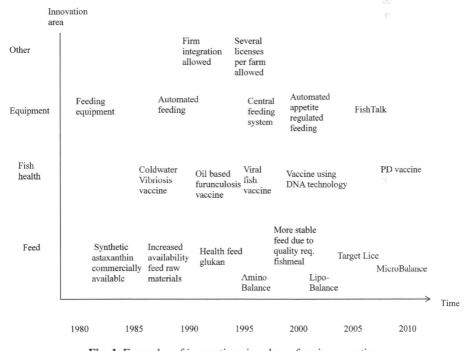

Fig. 1. Examples of innovations in salmon farming over time

As a consequence of these innovations, salmon aquaculture has evolved from a technological regime with poor degree of control of many processes to one that can be described as approaching 'biological manufacturing' [4], [5], [6]. The industry has moved from a labor-intensive production where workers had few formal skills, to a production which is more capital-intensive and where computer hardware and software based technologies have replaced several of the manual tasks of labor. At the farms the monitoring of the salmon, feeding, and environmental variables are based on sophisticated information technologies. Labor input has become more specialized; workers now tend to have certificates, and there is a much higher proportion of labor with a variety of specialized university educations.

Salmon feeds, which represent over 50% of farms' production costs, have experienced radical innovations partly due to large investments in R&D. Formulation of salmon feeds are now based on extensive knowledge of how different ingredients influence salmon growth and health and interact with each other. R&D has also played a significant role in disease management, where a number of targeted vaccines have been developed to combat various diseases. To some extent these have replaced curative medication such as antibiotics. Salmon farming now uses much less antibiotics per kilo of meat produced than is the case in terrestrial meat production such as pork and poultry.

Innovations in key technologies have contributed to a significant productivity growth in salmon farming. The cost of producing farmed salmon has declined to less than 30% of production costs in the late 1980s, as shown later in Figure 3. However, productivity growth in the salmon industry as measured by the cost of production per kilo of live salmon has stagnated in the recent decade.

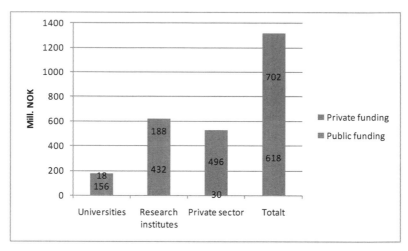

Fig. 2. R&D by performing sector and funding source in million Norwegian kroner (Source: NIFU-Step)

In the innovation system [7], [8] related to salmon aquaculture technology the Norwegian government, particularly the Ministry of Fisheries, has been a central actor through legislation, policies and funding. A technological innovation system can be defined as 'a dynamic network of agents interacting in a specific economic/industrial area under a particular institutional infrastructure and involved in the generation, diffusion, and utilisation of technology' [9]. The private actors in the innovation system include the salmon farming companies and their suppliers, feed companies, equipment and software suppliers, pharmaceutical companies, etc. Universities have also been important actors both as suppliers of trained labor and researchers, but also through the R&D they have undertaken. Independent research institutions that are predominantly funded by the public sector is another group of actors that have played a pivotal role through their R&D activities.

Many innovations in salmon aquaculture that have contributed to productivity growth have been made possible by R&D that has been at least partly funded by the Norwegian government. The public sector has played an active role both in financing and in carrying out R&D through public research institutions and universities. In the private sector fish feed companies and pharmaceutical companies have also played important roles in financing and carrying out R&D related to salmon feed, fish health, vaccines etc. According to Figure 3 the private sector funded 53% of R&D in aquaculture in 2009, and did around 40% of the R&D activities, while the remaining 60% was undertaken by universities and research institutions.

Salmon farming companies have historically played a smaller direct role in undertaking and financing R&D themselves. Initially, the industry was dominated by small companies with limited financial and human resources. Their role in innovation processes was often to adopt innovations made by suppliers to the industry, such as feed companies, equipment suppliers and pharmaceutical companies. However, the industry has since the early 1990s developed an industrial structure which also includes large scale multinational companies. Salmon companies should be expected to have a more prominent role in future innovation processes due to industry consolidation that should increase their ability to both finance and manage R&D.

3   Estimation of Productivity Growth

In this study we estimate the rate of technological change in salmon farming. This is done by econometric estimation of a translog cost function on a data set of 4904 observations on individual salmon firms from 1985 to 2008. We are able to separate the effects of input prices, scale economies and technical change on real costs.

The long-run translog cost function is specified as:

$$\ln C = \alpha_0 + \Sigma_i \alpha_i \ln w_i + 0.5 \Sigma_i \Sigma_j \alpha_{ij} \ln w_i \ln w_j + \alpha_y \ln y + 0.5 \alpha_{yy} (\ln y)^2 \qquad (1)$$
$$+ \Sigma_i \alpha_{iy} \ln w_i \ln y + \Sigma_t \alpha_t D_t + \Sigma_t \Sigma_i \alpha_{it} \ln w_i \cdot D_t + \Sigma_t \alpha_{yt} \ln y \cdot D_t + u.$$

In this model C is inflation-adjusted cost of production, y is output level, w_i is the inflation-adjusted price of input i (i = Feed, Labor, Capital), D_t is a vector of time (year) dummy variables (t = 1986, ..., 2008) for the years after the base year 1985, u is a stochastic error term, and α are parameters to be estimated. To improve the efficiency of the parameter estimates, the cost function is estimated together with the cost share equations $S_i = \partial \ln C / \partial \ln w_i$, using Zellner's [10] seemingly unrelated regression technique. The above econometric model specification allow us to decompose technological progress into three components: (1) neutral ($\Sigma_t \alpha_t D_t$),

(2) input biased ($\Sigma_t\Sigma_i\alpha_{it}\text{ln}w_i\cdot D_t$), and (3) scale biased ($\Sigma_t\alpha_{yt}\text{ln}y\cdot D_t$) components. The rate of technical change (TC) with these three components is specified as:

$$TC = (\alpha_t - \alpha_{t-1}) + \Sigma_i((\alpha_{it}\text{-}\ \alpha_{it-1})\text{ln}w_i) + ((\alpha_{yt}\text{-}\ \alpha_{yt-1})\text{ln}y). \qquad (2)$$

If there is technical "progress" this cost based measure is negative. The rate of technical change is our measure of how innovations and other factors influence productivity growth. It is not possible to obtain a "pure" measure of the effects of innovations as it is hard to identify variables that measure innovations and the adoption of these. Moreover, in a biological production sector such as salmon farming the TC measure will also be influenced by biophysical shocks such as diseases. It is therefore possible to obtain negative rates of technical change.

From the cost function one can also derive returns to scale, which are defined as $RTS = 1/(\partial\text{ln}C/\partial\text{ln}y)$. The conditional own price elasticity of demand for input i is defined as $E_i = (\alpha_{ii} + S_i^2 - S_i)/S_i$ (i = Feed, Labor, Capital) [11].

Table 1 presents sample mean elasticity estimates from the estimated translog cost function. The full set of parameter estimates can be obtained from the authors. Sample mean returns to scale (RTS) is increasing with a value of 1.152. The conditional own-price elasticities (E_i) all have the expected negative sign, with feed input having the lowest elasticity. They are within the range of estimates from previous econometric studies of Norwegian salmon farming [6], [12], [13], [14].

Table 1. Sample Mean Elasticity Estimates from Estimated Translog Cost Function*

Variable	Mean	St.Dev.	Min	Max
RTS	1.152	0.076	0.924	1.527
E_{Feed}	-0.155	0.045	-0.329	0.018
E_{Labor}	-0.387	0.210	-0.435	12.124
E_{Capital}	-1.062	0.052	-1.256	-0.913
TC	-0.034	0.060	-0.257	0.247

*No. of observations is 4904, except for TC (N=4723) due to omission of observations in 1985.

Our main variable of interest is the rate of technical change. According to Table 1 the overall sample average rate of technical change is -0.034, i.e. an annual average 3.4% rate of technical progress.

However, this technical progress varies considerably over time, as shown in Figure 3, where we have plotted the development in the annual average rate of technical change (the negative of TC) together with the development in real production costs including feed, labor and capital. We see that the highest rates of technical progress were experienced from 1987 to 1995. After that technical progress, as measured by our econometric model, has been low. This is mirrored in the development in real production costs per kg produced fish, which declined rapidly until the middle of the 1990s, but has since experienced a much smaller decline, and been more or less stable around 12-13 NOK/kg since 2000.

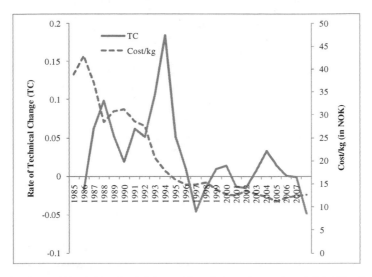

Fig. 3. Production cost including feed, labor and capital per kg produced fish (Cost/kg) and the estimated rate of technical change (TC).

An important explanatory factor behind the decline in technical progress is the inability to reduce salmon mortality rates, which have fluctuated around 20-30% of the stock of live salmon since the 1990s. The growth in salmon production has lead to an increase in disease pressure among the fish, as fish population densities have increased both at the regional and farm site level. The salmon industry has not been able to innovate sufficiently fast to reduce disease losses. Innovations in automation, such as automated feeding and fish monitoring, and other areas have contributed to increasing production per employee by several times the levels in the 1990s. But this has not been sufficient to compensate for the lack of innovations in fish health and disease management.

4 Future Innovation Challenges

The future technological bottlenecks that need to be resolved in global aquaculture in general and salmon aquaculture in particular will be more complex than those faced historically. One can argue that each of the bottlenecks on average will require higher investments in R&D, reflecting more input of researcher man-hours and higher expenditures on equipment and materials. Furthermore, the R&D projects will have a higher level of technical and organizational complexity, and thus increased risk of failure or low returns to R&D investments. The implications of these assertions is that in order to produce innovations at a sufficient rate, the industry needs higher D&D funding and increased quality of human capital involved in the R&D projects, and the organization of the projects.

In order to understand important aspects of the innovation challenges salmon aquaculture faces it is necessary to understand the nature of innovation processes in the industry. The innovation literature distinguishes between two modes of innovation. One, the 'Science, Technology and Innovation' (STI) mode, is based on the production and use of codified scientific and technical knowledge. The other, the 'Doing, Using and Interacting' (DUI) mode, relies on informal processes of learning and experience-based know-how [9]. One can find many examples of both modes of innovation in salmon aquaculture. But it can be argued that STI based innovation processes generally have led to more radical innovations than DUI processes in salmon aquaculture. This is the case for several innovations related to e.g. feed and vaccines. Also in the future should we see both modes of innovation. However, the more radical innovations that the industry needs to increase its productivity and grow have to be based on STI processes. But it should be pointed out that STI processes can have different characteristics, including what types of agents fund R&D and what types of agents perform the R&D activities. For Norwegian salmon aquaculture a major actor in selection and funding of research projects has been the government's Norwegian Research Council (NRC), a body dominated by scientists from academia, where projects have been largely selected on the basis of the academic credentials of the applicants. Publication of results in international peer-reviewed scientific journals have generally been regarded as an important indicator of success for NRC funded projects, and innovation outcomes have received less attention. Innovations in salmon aquaculture have often been based on results from NRC funded projects, but have been made in separate, later projects with commercialization objectives.

There may to some degree be complementarities between the research focused on creating new knowledge and publication in peer-reviewed journals funded by the government through the NRC and R&D funded by the private companies with more direct commercial objectives. However, one important question for the future is who should decide on the allocation of NRC funding – how much influence should the academic sector have and how much influence should private sector have in the formulation of NRC research program objectives and selection of projects? Until recently the dominance of academia can be explained by the lack of sufficiently trained candidates from the private sector. But the private sector is increasingly recruiting employees with scientific training, and this should facilitate a change in the balance between the academic and private sector in the future.

In the future innovations are required in all key technology areas. For salmon feed, which represents over 60% of total costs, it is necessary to continue the replacement of scarce marine ingredients with vegetable ingredients to reduce ingredient costs. The industry faces several salmon diseases which require improved vaccines and other strategies to reduce mortality. There are also other more environmental challenges which may not affect productivity directly, but will have consequences for the industry's ability to expand, as future expansion is dependent on its environmental impacts. Salmon farm cages and other structures need to be further improved to reduce the likelihood of salmon escaping. Innovations are also required to reduce the presence of salmon lice in the surroundings of salmon farms.

It is necessary to increase the productivity of salmon aquaculture R&D in the sense that it should lead to more innovations per million Norwegian kroner invested in R&D. R&D financed by the government and undertaken by government institutions have been highly necessary in the past to develop key technologies. But in the future it may be essential to have greater proximity between those who finance and undertake R&D and the industry to increase the innovation rate. This is to an increasing the degree possible as the industry itself has much greater financial and human resources today than in the past to finance, manage and undertake R&D.

References

1. Asche, F.: Farming the Sea. Marine Resource Economics 23, 527–547 (2008)
2. Jensen, H.H.: Changes in seafood consumer preference patterns and associated changes in risk exposure. Marine Pollution Bulletin 53, 591–598 (2006)
3. Guttormsen, A., Myrland, Ø., Tveterås, R.: Innovations and Structural Change in Seafood Markets and Production. Marine Resource Economics 26, 247–253 (2011)
4. Asche, F., Guttormsen, A.G., Tveteras, R.: Environmental Problems, Productivity and Innovations in Norwegian Salmon Aquaculture. Aquaculture Economics and Management 3, 1–29 (1999)
5. Tveteras, R.: Industrial Agglomeration and Production Costs in Norwegian Salmon Aquaculture. Marine Resource Economics 17, 1–22 (2002)
6. Tveteras, R., Battese, G.E.: Agglomeration Externalities, Productivity and Technical Inefficiency. Journal of Regional Science 46, 605–625 (2006)
7. Carlsson, B., Stankiewicz, R.: On the Nature, Function, and Composition of Technological systems. Journal of Evolutionary Economics 1, 93–118 (1991)
8. Freeman, C.: The 'National System of Innovation' in historical perspective. Cambridge Journal of Economics 19, 5–24 (1995)
9. Jensen, M., Johnson, B., Lorenz, E., Lundvall, B.-A.: Forms of knowledge, modes of innovation and innovation systems. Research Policy 36, 680–693 (2007)
10. Zellner, A.: An Efficient Method for Estimating Seemingly Unrelated Regressions and Tests for Aggregation Bias. American Statistical Association Journal 58, 348–368 (1962)
11. Binswanger, H.P.: A Cost Function Approach to the Measurement of Elasticities of Factor Demand and Elasticities of Substitution. American Journal of Agricultural Economics 56, 377–386 (1974)
12. Guttormsen, A.G.: Input Factor Substitutability in Salmon Aquaculture. Marine Resource Economics 17, 91–102 (2002)
13. Andersen, T.B., Roll, K.H., Tveteras, S.: The Price Responsiveness of Salmon Supply in the Short and Long Run. Marine Resource Economics 23, 425–437 (2008)
14. Asche, F., Roll, K.H., Tveteras, R.: Economic Inefficiency and Environmental impact: An application to Aquaculture Production. Journal of Environmental Economics and Management 58, 93–105 (2009)

Author Index

Printed by Publishers' Graphics LLC